William Ambrose Rucker
Annie Chappelear Rucker

THE RUCKER FAMILY GENEALOGY

WITH THEIR

ANCESTORS, DESCENDANTS AND CONNECTIONS

• • •

COMPILED BY
SUDIE RUCKER WOOD

From original records, letters and other material collected over a period of thirty years.

• • •

RICHMOND, VIRGINIA
OLD DOMINION PRESS, INC.
MCMXXXII

FIRST REPRINTING
1973
OSCAR RUCKER, II
BEREA, KENTUCKY

SECOND REPRINTING
1991
HERITAGE BOOKS, INC.
BOWIE, MD.
for
THE RUCKER SOCIETY
304 CHARMIAN ROAD
RICHMOND, VA. 23226

Dedicated

in affectionate remembrance

to my parents

William Ambrose Rucker

and

Annie Chappelear Rucker

CONTENTS

CONTENTS—Continued

PART THREE

ILLUSTRATIONS

ERRATA

Page 24—Augustus Caesar, not Ceasar.

Page 29—James Barnett Rucker, of Gallaway, not Galladay.

Page 39—Kathryn Rucker m. Rene de Qulin, a native of Britany, France, a lecturer, artist and orator. They live in New York.

Page 56—Col. John S. Mosby, not Mosley.

Page 61—Alfred^6 Douglas (Nancy^5, Wm.^{4}, John^3, not George^3 Rucker).

Page 93—7. Georgia^7 Parks Rucker, of the 7th generation, not the 6th.

Page 93—8. Margaret McDaniel Rucker has been placed after her two children instead of before.

Page 182—Martha Snyder, not Sydner, daughter of Michael.

Page 187—Simeon, not Simson.

Page 195—John Steel, not Stell.

Page 202—William Herndon, in right of his wife Mary.

Page 220—James M. Hull, not Hall.

Page 221—Tinsley^8 W. Rucker, not Tucker.

Page 323—Eleazer Le Master, not Lancaster.

Page 248—Mordicai Rucker married Susanna Rayder, not Susanna Rucker.

Page 265—Leroy Frake, not Fraker.

Page 281—Fountaintown, not Mountaintown.

Page 394—Eliza Chappelear, not Elizabeth.

Page 419—Sarah Porter Cheatwood did not marry 2nd Robert Berry.

Page 438—Francis Kirtly, not Kirthy.

Page 477—Nicholas Spencer, not Spercer.

Page 483—Thornhill Carter, not Thornbhill.

Page 488—Mary B. Shields, not Shieds.

Page 530—Brother Benjamin Hobson's children, not brothers.

PREFACE

FOR many years, as a labor of love and of family interest, the writer has from time to time made genealogical notes. Finally as these grew in number and opportunity permitted and inclination urged, these notes took form and the present volume is the result. Much information has been compiled from family Bibles and other family records, but for the most part, from long and painstaking research into state and county records. Correspondence with representatives of the family who have moved from Virginia has made it possible to complete their lines.

The descendants of Peter Rucker, first of his name in America, are scattered throughout the United States. No doubt in the hearts of many of them is a desire for accurate knowledge of their lineage and of their forbears, which this volume attempts to supply.

Grateful acknowledgment is made to all who have contributed items of family history and extracts from court records. Special acknowledgment is made of the invaluable assistance rendered by the late Mrs. James G. Tanner for her untiring efforts in creating among the scattered Ruckers, interest in collecting family history. Finally, acknowledgment is made to Mrs. Ellen Theisz for years so graciously expended in compiling some of the records used in this book.

If those members of the family into whose hands this volume may come, shall find in it something of interest and of value, the writer will feel amply repaid for the time and labor expended.

SUDIE RUCKER WOOD.

PART I

THE RUCKER FAMILY

CHAPTER ONE
Peter Rucker

Peter Rucker, first of the name, settled in Virginia about 1690. The tradition is that he was a French Huguenot, shipwrecked near the mouth of the James River, and that he swam ashore, living there for a time.

A search in the land office does not show that he patented land there nor in Essex, where he was living in 1704, and paying tythes on 500 acres of land (Quit Rent). If he patented this tract of 500 acres of land, it was never recorded in the land office. Since no deeds appear in Essex County, he may have divided this land between his children before his death, for he does not divide it in his will. In 1743, his son, William, sold 193 acres, "land received by inheritance."

Peter Rucker may have been a French Huguenot, for he was naturalized with a number of Frenchmen. We know, too, that his children were protestants. His son, John, in 1732, assisted in locating an Episcopal Church.

There is in *The Legislative Journal of the Council of Colonial Virginia,* Vol. 1, page 390, Monday, April 24, 1704, "The petitions of Peter Rucker, Cypian Prou, John James Veillon, Teliffe Alverton, Peter Fouyeilles, Francis Colonis, Jacqueline Jaque, Bartholomew Depucy, Isaac ffiguier, and John Rossett, praying for naturalization, were read and ordered to be recorded; the same to be referred to the confederation of The House of Burgess."

Also, in *The Journals of the House of Burgess,* 1702-12, page 74, Monday, May 8, 1704, "Upon consideration of the report of the said committee, upon the petition of Peter Rucker, Cypian Prou, and others—praying to be naturalized, the House agrees to the naturalization."

From Brook's *Emigrants,* "Many emigrants from France and Holland went to London first, where the expense of the transportation to America was borne by the Relief Committee of London. They settled along the Potomac, Rappahannock, and James Rivers. The French Huguenots were exempt from taxes for fourteen years." Peter was paying tythes in 1704, therefore if he were from France or Holland, he must certainly have been here by 1690.

Taken from *The German Element in America* by Herrmann Schuricht, Vol. 1, p. 43, in reference to the French and German migration, "Numerous migrations of French Huguenots and Calvanists from Alsace and Lorraine came to America, settling in tidewater Virginia."

A careful search in London does not show that Peter Rucker lived in London before coming to America c. 1690. Mr. C. E. Lart, of London, an authority on the French Huguenot emigration, says the name is certainly German or Dutch. He tried to locate Peter Rucker through the Walloon Church Records in Leyden, without success.

A superficial search has been made in Berlin among the "Deutschen Hugenottenvereins" with no result.

Dr. F. C. Wieder of the Biblintheek der Rijks Universitiit, of Leyden, Holland, says there is a very full list of the Walloons, who passed through that port, but the Rucker name does not appear until 1725, too late for our family.

Frederick[2] Coghill (James[1]) and wife Sara leased to Peter Rucker 56 acres of land on Cockleshell Creek on the Rappahannock River in 1707. Later, Frederick deeds this 56 acres to John, son of Peter Rucker, for "love and affection" (see John[2] Rucker).

Richard Booker, of Essex County, for "love and affection for John Pemberton" deeded 50 acres of land near "Peter Rucker's line" (D. B. 17, p. 140), Feb. 19, 1723, Essex.

Elizabeth, wife of Peter Rucker, may have died in 1752, the year when his slaves were divided. "Thomas Rucker, William Rucker, William Offell, and Shem Cook, agree to legacies" paid by James and Ephraim Rucker, executors of Peter Rucker, dec'd, "out of his estate to each a slave" and also, to Isaac Tinsley and Ephraim Rucker (D. B. 1, p. 400), Feb. 21, 1752, Orange.

Will of Peter Rucker, dated, June 18, 1743; probated, Feb. 23, 1743 (W. B. 1, p. 299), Orange:

In the name of God amen I Peter Rucker of Saint Marks Parish in the County of Orange planter being weak in body but of pursued mind and memory knowing that it is appointed for all men once to die do make and ordain this my Last will and Testament in manner following: Imprimis I do order that all my Just Debts and funeral charges be paid and satisfied. Item I lend unto my beloved wife Elizabeth Rucker all my Estate both real and Personal During her natural life and after her Decease to be Devided in the following manner. Item I give and bequeath unto my beloved Daughter Margaret Tinsley and my Son In-law Isaac Tinsley a negro boy named yerkshire to them and their heirs forever. Item I give and bequeath to my beloved Son Ephraim Rucker a negro Girl named Phillis to him and his heirs forever. Item I give and bequeath to my beloved Daughter Ann Cook and my son in law Shem Cook a negro girl named Jeney to her and her increase to them and their heirs forever. Item I do Desire that all the Remainder of my Estate both real and personal after my wifes Decease as aforesaid to be sold by my Exr. hereafter named at public auction to the highest bidder on six months credit for Current Money the Buyer giving Good Security and the money arising by Sale to be Equally Devided amongst my beloved Children by name as followeth Thomas Rucker, Elizabeth Pierce, William Rucker, Mary Offell, James Rucker, Ephraim Rucker, and ann Cook and to their heirs forever, and lastly I do Constitute and appoint my beloved Sons James Rucker and Ephraim Rucker to be my Whole and sole Executors of this my last will and Testament hereby revoking and Disannuling all other Testaments and wills by me made Confirming this and no other to be my Last will and Testament in witness whereof I have hereunto set my hand and Seal this 18 day of January 1743.

Signed sealed. Published in the presence of

Wm. Jackson	his
Wm. Offell,	Peter x Rucker
Mich. Holt.	mark

At a Court held for Orange County on Thursday ye 23 Day of Febry. 1743. The Last Will and Testament of Peter Rucker Dec'd. being presented into Court by James Rucker and Ephraim Rucker Exrs. Therein named and proved by the oaths of Wm. Jackson and Mich. Holt two of the Witnesses Thereto who also made Oath that they saw William Offell sign the same as an Evidence and the sd Exrs. having severally Taken the Oath of an Exr. and having Entered into bond with Mic. Holt, George Holt and Richard Mauldin Junr., Their Securities, before their due Execution thereof, Probate is Granted them and the said will together with the Bond was admitted to record.

Test:

Jonath Gibson.

Issue:

1. John^2 Rucker,
2. Peter^2,
3. Thomas^2,
4. Elizabeth^2 Pearce,
5. Margaret^2 Tinsley,
6. William^2,
7. Mary^2 Offall,
8. James^2,
9. Ephraim^2,
10. Ann^2 Cook.

CHAPTER TWO

John Rucker

1. John[2] Rucker (Peter[1]) appears first in Essex County. Later he moved to Orange, now Madison, and died there in 1742, still a young man. His wife, Susanna, may have been the daughter of Frederick and Sarah Coghill, of Essex County, who "leased to Peter Rucker and wife Elizabeth, 56 acres of land on a branch of Cockleshell Creek, adjoining Wm. Scott's, Frederick and James Coghill's, and is part of 1000 acres granted to said Coghill's father, James" (D. B. 13, p. 90), Jan. 28, 1707, Essex.

The same day (p. 91), "Frederick Coghill and wife Sarah of Essex Co. for 2000 lbs. of tobacco paid by Peter Rucker, and for the 'kind love and affection I owe unto John, Peter, and Thomas Rucker, sons of said Peter Rucker,' convey unto John Rucker the land leased to Peter Rucker, and in default of heirs to John, to go to Peter, and if Peter dies without heir, to go to Thomas.

Witness: Richard Cook.

his
Thomas x Jack
mark

Same book, day, and page. Sarah Coghill appointed Robert Marshall "my lawful attorney to convey by 'a deed of gift' 56 acres of land which my husband, Frederick Coghill, gave to John Rutter of Essex."

Signed: Sarah Coghill.

Witness: Samuel Poe,

his
Thomas x Jackson.
mark

Power of attorney from Susanna Rucker of St. Mark's Parish, Spotsylvania County, to William Beverly, to relinquish her dower rights in 56 acres of land (D. B. 19, p. 228), July 15, 1731, Essex Co.

John Rucker was appointed constable from the Rappahannock River to the Parish line, including the South Mountains (O. B. 1730-38, p. 35), May 4, 1731, Spotsylvania.

Peter, John, and Thomas Rucker of Spotsylvania Co. sold to Edw. Murrough of Essex, for 25 lbs. sterling, 56 acres of land in St. Anne's Parish, Essex, on the south side of the Rappahannock River on a branch of Cockleshell Creek, adjoining Wm. Scott's line, and James Coghill's patent, and was a part of said patent.

his
Peter P. Rucker
Witness: Daniel Gaines mark
Isaac Tinsley. Thomas Rucker
John Rucker

Elizabeth, wife of Peter Rucker, and Susanna, wife ot John Rucker, by William Beverly, attorney for said Susanna, signed the deed (D. B. 19, p. 229), March 13, 1731, Essex.

John Rucker began buying land in 1725. From that we assume that he had just come of age. On May 29, 1725, James Taylor, of St. Stephen's Parish, King and Queen Co., sold to John Rucker of the same, 100 acres part of a patent, dated 1722, on a branch of North Anna River, adjoining Edward Tinsley's land.

John Rucker of St. George Parish patented 977 acres of land in the same parish on the lower side of a run of the Rappahannock River, adjoining that of Michael Holt (L. Gr., Vol. 13, p. 161), Aug. 17, 1727.

He was a witness to a deed, July 6, 1731, when William and Ann Phillips sold land to John Davis (Spotsylvania). He was one of the witnesses on May 4, 1731, when John and Mary Rowse sold land to William Edding of St. George Parish in Spotsylvania Co.

John Rucker of Spotsylvania Co. sold to Philip Stockdale of St. Anne's Parish, Essex, 703 acres. 150 acres of this was part of a patent granted to said Rucker in August, 1729, out of 977 acres, and 533 acres was part of a patent granted Thomas Rucker on June 19, 1730, and sold to John Rucker by deed, Feb. 5, 1732, in Spotsylvania Co. Susanna, wife of John, relinquished her dower right, May 5, 1733 (Spotsylvania).

Thomas Rucker of Caroline Co. sold to John Rucker of Spotsylvania, for £20, 476 a. of land in St. Mark's Parish, part of a patent granted to said Thomas. Elizabeth, wife of Thomas, signed the deed.

Witness: Thomas Chew, Joseph Hawkins, Robert Turner.

Meade's *Old Churches,* page 94, mentions some of the members of the church in Orange, St. Mark's Parish, including the Vawters, Whites, Burtons, Ruckers, ————. This church was built at "The two springs on the Germanna Road." In Slaughter's

St. Mark's Parish Notes, the author mentions this church near Ruckersville. "A church was built convenient to the South West Mountain road, on the first run below the chapel. John Lightfoot and John Rucker were to pitch on a place near to some good spring." John Rucker may have been one of the church wardens, being chosen to select the location of this church, which was built in 1732.

John Rucker, of St. Mark's Parish, Spotsylvania, deeded 420 acres of land to Peter Rucker and wife, Elizabeth, for their natural lives; afterwards to be divided between Peter Jr. and Ephraim Rucker by a line drawn from William Rucker's line running south to William Hall's, then to Philip Stogdale's, land now in the actual possession of said Rucker out of 977 acres patented by John in the forks of the Robinson River, adjoining Isaac Tinsley's, William Hall's, William Rucker's, and Peter Rucker Jr's. (D. B. B, p. 493), Feb. 5, 1734, Spotsylvania. John deeded this land to his parents and his two younger brothers.

John sold to William Rucker, both of Spotsylvania Co., for £20, 200 acres of land in St. Mark's Parish, adjoining that of Michael Holt.

Witness: Thomas Chew, Wm. Crosthwait, Wm. Bartlett. June 4, 1734.

John of Spotsylvania Co. in behalf of himself and others, exhibited a proposition for the division of this county, which was admitted and ordered to be certified, 1734.

This same year he was paid 700 lbs. of tobacco for 7 wolve's heads.

In 1734, he deeded to his sister, Mary, wife of Wm. Offall, 100 acres of land in St. Mark's Parish, Spotsylvania, beginning at Anne Rucker's ——— to Michael Holt's and to John Rucker's line (D. B. B, p. 496), Spotsylvania.

John Foster of Spotsylvania Co. sold to John Rucker of Orange 599 acres for £75, land on the north side of the Rapidan River, on Maple Run, in the first forks of Rappahannock River. Isabell signed the deed (D. B. 1, p. 54), June 16, 1735, Orange.

Witness: Thomas Chew, Richard Winslow, Wm. Philips.

John Rucker of Orange deeded to Isaac Tinsley and wife, Margaret, 100 acres adjoining that of said John Rucker.

Witness: G. Holmes, William Philips, Robert Martin (D. B. 1, p. 290), May 17, 1736, Orange.

The trustees of Fredericksburg sold to John Rucker of Orange, Gent., for £5, 5 shillings, "½ acre, or a lot of land No.

5, in the town of Fredericksburg, situated on the Rappahannock River, being one of the river side lots." Others were "on one of the Great Streets of the town, called Sophia, and on two of the lesser streets, called William, and George." Signed: Hen. Willis, John Waller. Aug. 2, 1737.

He was appointed surveyor of the road in Orange Co., in June, 1735, in the "room of John Lightfoot dec'd."

In 1736, Henry Downs, John Rucker, and James Cowherd viewed the road that Joseph Philips cleared.

John Rucker was paid 50 lbs. of tobacco for the county stamp (O. B. 1734-39), Oct., 1734, Spotsylvania.

Zachary Taylor, Gent., of St. Mark's, sold to John Rucker, for £5, 27 acres adjoining the latter's land, Orange (D. B. 3), Aug. 21, 1738.

John of Orange sold to Thomas Rucker, 599 acres for £50, on the north side of the Rapidan River, on Maple Run, land bought of Foster (D. B. 3, p. 171), May 23, 1739, Orange.

John applied for a grant of land, in 1739, containing 5850 acres of land in Goochland Co. on the north side of the James River, on Harris Creek and the Tobacco Row Mountains. However, he died, in 1742, three years before this grant was recorded in the name of his son and executor, Peter Rucker, who divided it, in 1751, among his six brothers "according to the will of his father" (Va. L. Gr., Vol. 22, p. 596).

John Rucker, Gent., was sworn as Commissioner of the Peace of Orange Co. on Nov. 23, 1741 (O. B. 1741-43, p. 51).

John Rucker, Gent., having "taken ye Oath as appointed by act of Parliament, and subscribed ye test, was sworn to his military commission of Captain for Orange Co.", May 22, 1740 (O. B. 1738-41, p. 163).

"Peter Rucker, executor of John Rucker, dec'd," claimed, on Aug. 23, 1744, 2000 lbs. of tobacco for carting arms, Wm. Lucas guarding them (Orange Co.). John evidently was in active service.

He was certainly interested in politics, judging from the scrap that took place at an election in Orange Co. The following is copied from the *Journals of the House of Burgess of Virginia*, 1742-47, p. 50-69: "On Saturday, June 5, 1742, Mr. Richard Winslow, Sheriff of Orange Co., John Rucker, John Burk, John MacCoy, Honorious Powell, John Snow, and Timothy Terrell, are found guilty of Great Misdemeanours. The said John Rucker, during the time of the election, gave several large bowls of Punch among the people, crying out for those persons who intend to vote for Mr. Slaughter, to come and drink his punch.

The sheriff stayed the Poll and said he would not have any Punch drank on the Bench, but would have a fair election, to which Mr. Chew replied that he would have Punch and drink it, and that the sheriff should not hinder him.

As soon as the tumult ceased, the candidate and sheriff returned to the Court House. Proceeding to take the Poll, Mr. Jonathan Gibson and John Newport stood at the doors with drawn swords. After the undersheriff, John Newport, was placed at the door, one, Mr. John Rucker, came to the door, and demanded entrance, which he had, and then the said Rucker threw the undersheriff and another person, headlong out of the door. The said Rucker insisted to clear the doors, that every one might have free entrance. He seized the undersheriff's sword with both hands, endeavoring to break it, which the undersheriff prevented by drawing it through his (Rucker's) hands. One, John Burks, came to the said Rucker's assistance and laid violent hands on the undersheriff, who was rescued by the bystanders. There was so much disturbance that the sheriff closed the poll til eight of the clock the next morning, Saturday, June 19, 1742."

A petition of John Rucker, John McCoy, Honorious Powell, and Timothy Terrell, setting forth that "they had surrendered themselves being truly sensible of their offences," was presented to the House and read. After being reprimanded from the Chair and paying fees, they were discharged.

Six months after this occurrence in the court house, John Rucker died, a young man.

A final settlement of his estate occurs in 1797, £94 being left to each of the children of his son, John. "To each of John Rucker's grandchildren, children of John Rucker of Amherst, to receive their share of their grandfather's estate, each of the nine legatees to receive £94. Jan., 1797. (W. B. 3, p. 436), Amherst.

The following is the will of John Rucker, dated, Jan. 11, 1742, and recorded, Jan. 28, 1742 (W. B. 3, p. 436), Orange:

"In the name of God Amen, I, John Rucker of Saint Marks Parish in the county of Orange, Planter, being weak in Body, but of perfect mind and Memory and knowing that it is appointed for all men once to Dye Do make and ordain this my last will and Testament in manner and form as following. Imprimis I do order that all my Just Debts & funeral Charges be paid and satisfied. *Item,* I give to my well beloved wife Susanna Rucker, four negroes, namely Bristol, Tony, Doll & Sue and one third part of my household Furniture & Stock, Horses excepted, one horse I give to my wife named Roger, the menticned negroes to remain my wife's no longer than her widowhood after to be sold and divided as the rest of my Estate hereafter mentioned. *Item,* I give to my son Peter Rucker one black horse called Jockey and his choice of my guns. *Item,* I give to my son John Rucker one Gray horse Called Oglesby and a gun the next choice after his brother. *Item,* I give to Thomas Wright Belfield one lot in Fredericksburg No. 5 to him and his heirs forever. My desire is that one half my land on the Branches of James River may be sold by my Ex'rs for six months Credit to the highest bidder, likewise my Wagon and five horses & horse kinds in the same manner in order to pay my debts, I likewise leave My dwelling house and Land thereunto Adjoining to be sold at the direction of my Ex'rs, if my debts can't be complied with; if they can be the dwelling house and land to remain my wife's during her widowhood. If she marry to be sold by way of Auction. *Item,* I give to my well beloved sons Peter Rucker, John Rucker, Ambrose Rucker, Benjamin Rucker, Rueben Rucker, Isaac Rucker, Anthony Rucker, and to their heirs forever half the land I hold on the Branches of James River to be equally divided between the seven brothers, the rest of my estate I desire equally divided among my beloved children as follows. Peter Rucker, John Rucker, Sarah Rucker, Winifred Rucker, Ambrose Rucker, Benjamin Rucker, Rueben Rucker, Isaac Rucker, Anthony Rucker, Mildred Rucker, Phebė Rucker to them and their heirs forever. *Item,* I give to my Daughter Margaret Smith one Shilling Sterling and lastly I do constitute and appoint my beloved wife Susanna Rucker my Ex'r and my beloved son Peter Rucker and my beloved friend George Taylor my whole and sole Ex'rs of this my last will and Testament, hereby revoking, Disannuling all other Testaments and wills by me made. Confirming this and no other to be my last will and Testament. In Witness whereof I have hereunto set my hand and seal this XI day of January 1742.

John Rucker (Seal)

Signed, Sealed, and Published in presence of: Robert Seayre, Joseph Hawkins, Richard Cross."

At a Court continued and held for Orange County on Friday the 28th Day of Jan. 1742:

"This the last will and Testament of John Rucker Gent. Dec'd being presented into Court by Susanna Rucker his widow and Relict, & Peter Rucker his son, two of the Ex's therein named who made oath thereto according to Law and being proved by the Oaths of Robert Seayre and Richard Cross two of the evidences thereto who also made oath that they saw Joseph Hawkins sign the same as an evidence the said will is admitted to Record on motion of the said Ex'rs, and their performing what is usual in such cases Certificate is granted them for obtaining a Probate thereof in due form and the said Susannah and Peter Rucker together with Anthony Head, Michael Holt and James Picket their securities acknowledged their bond for the said Susannah and Peter Rucker—faithful and true Ad'mon. of the Estate of John Rucker Dec'd which bond is admitted to Record.

Jonath Gibson. Cl. Cur.

C. W. Woolfolk, Clerk

Issue:

1. Peter[3] Rucker,
2. John[3],
3. Ambrose[3],
4. Benjamin[3],
5. Rueben[3],
6. Isaac[3],
7. Anthony[3],
8. Sarah[3],
9. Winifred[3],
10. Mildred[3],
11. Phoebe[3],
12. Margaret[3].

The male laboring tithables belonging to Susanna Rucker and Henry Rucker to be added to Benjamin Rucker's gang on Stovall's Road (O. B. 1769, p. 451), Amherst.

1. Peter[3] Rucker (John[2], Peter[1]) lived and died in 1794, in what is now known as Greene County, married 1st Elizabeth Terrell, 2nd Jemima Crawford, of Orange, Jan. 3, 1773.

He was the executor of his father's will, and divided the land in Albemarle (now Amherst) among his six brothers "according to the will of his father" on Nov. 11, 1751 (D. B. 1, p. 357), Albemarle.

Peter sold 204 acres of the above 5,850 acres of land patented by his father in 1739 in Albemarle, to David Rosser, adjoining the land of Bernard Gaines, dec'd, and Ambrose Rucker, in 1751.

Witness: John and Ambrose Rucker, Geo. McDaniel and William Miller.

Elizabeth signed the deed (D. B. 1, p. 356), Albemarle.

Peter and wife, Elizabeth, of Orange, sold 460 acres of land in Albemarle Co. to John Goff, for £200. All of this tract, known as "Rucker's Lot", was sold except 10 acres adjoining Robert Rose's line.

Witness: John Rucker, William Miller, Geo. McDaniel, David Rosser. X[th] of Nov. 1751 (D. B. 1, p. 382), Albemarle.

He and his mother, Susanna Rucker, executors of John Rucker, dec'd, figure in a suit against Thomas Chew. The case was referred to George Wythe and Zachary Lewis, Mch. 28, 1747 (D. B. 9, p. 140), Orange.

For £40, Peter bought 60 acres of land in Orange from William Doneaugh, who had bought it from Zachary Taylor. Mch. 22, 1749 (D. B. 11, p. 179), Orange.

Signed Peter Rucker.

He bought 115 acres from John Gough of St. Mark's Parish, Orange, at the South Mountains, adjoining the land of Susanna Rucker, John Baylor, William Golding, and Tinsley Crosswaite. Nov. 21, 1750 (D. B. 11, p. 217), Orange.

He was paid 416 lbs. of tobacco in 1746, for viewing the tobacco fields of Orange.

Peter Rucker of Orange sold to Ambrose Booten of Culpeper (1st cousin), 210 acres of land in Culpeper, on a branch of Elk Run, in the forks of the Rapidan and Robinson Rivers, all buildings, stock, etc., the land adjoining John Stockdale's.

Signed: Peter Rucker.

Witness: Wm. Vawter, Robert Gaines, Lewis Booten. Aug. 14, 1767 (D. B. E, p. 395), Orange.

He sold to Andrew Shepherd for £85, 115 acres of land, "land he now lives on," bounding Susanna Rucker's, Col. John Baylor's, William Bell's, and Erasmus Taylor's. Jan. 26, 1769 (D. B. 15, p. 23), Orange.

Susanna Rucker, late of Orange County, and Peter Rucker of the same, executors of the "Last will and testament of John Rucker, dec'd, for £70, sold 130 acres of land that Susanna had formerly lived on, adjoining that of Col. John Baylor, Thomas Bell, and Wm. Moore. Signed: Susanna Rucker, Peter Rucker. May 27, 1769 (D. B. 15, p. 94), Orange.

Peter Rucker of Orange Co. deeded to Benjamin Rucker 526 acres of land beginning at Benjamin Rucker's line, and adjoining Robert Rose's (D. B. C, p. 24), October 6, 1769, Amherst Co. Witness: Anthony, John, and Ambrose Rucker.

In 1770, he bought 372 acres of land in Orange from Christopher Singleton and wife, Sara, of Caroline, for £100, adjoining the land Peter "now lives upon, on the main road" (D. B. 15, p. 206), Orange.

The following year he sold the above 372 acres of land to Thomas Burbage of Culpeper, for £100 (D. B. 15, p. 430), Orange.

His wife, Elizabeth, may be deceased; she signs no deeds after 1751. In the will of her father, Robert Terrell, dated 1786, she is mentioned as deceased.

Peter and his second wife, Jemima, sold land on the Mountain Road in 1789, for £160. He and his wife, Elizabeth, had bought these tracts at the South West Mountain and on the Main Road (Mountain). (D. B. 19, p. 452), Orange.

On Aug. 27, 1783, in Orange, Peter bought 400 acres from Joseph Wood and his wife, Elizabeth, of Brumfield Parish, for £40.

They sold 245 acres of this tract in 1787, to Thomas Herring for £100. Witness: Wm. Ballard, Elijah Ballard, George Berry (D. B. 19, p. 119), Orange.

On April 4, 1786, Peter and wife, Jemima, sold 302 acres for £120, to James Doughany. This land Peter had purchased from the executors of Littlepage's Estate. Witness: Jeremiah White, May Burton, Joseph Chapman, Oliver Crawford (D. B. 17, p. 404), Orange.

Peter died in 1794, leaving a will in which he only mentions two children. Jemima was still living in 1807, for she was paying a personal tax on two slaves until then.

Peter Rucker's 1st wife, Elizabeth, was dec'd before 1786. Her children are mentioned in her father's will.

Will of Robert Terrell dated Feb. 13, 1786, Orange Co.:

To sons Robert, John and William Terrell; to dau. Mary Hudson, and grandson, Rush Hudson; to dau. Sarah, widow of Joseph Towles; to heirs of dau. Ann Moore, dec'd; to children of my son, Edmund, dec'd; to children of my dau. Elizabeth Rucker, dec'd; Ephraim Rucker; Rueben Rucker; Mary Creed; Elizabeth Herring.

Will of Edmund Terrell (1740-1785), dated 1785, Culpeper Co.:

To wife Margaret (Willis), (born 1741); dau. Mary Foster [m. Rueben[4] Rucker (Peter[3])]; dau. Elizabeth (m. Wm. Cornelius); dau. Jane (m. Joseph Bishop); dau. Nancy (m. Rev. Thomas Henderson); dau. Frances Washington (m. Charles Christian Lacy); dau. Lucy (m. Robin Botts); son John (m. Rebecca Cornelius); son Rueben (m. Mildred, dau. of John and Mary Wood).

Will of Peter Rucker, dated May 4, 1794, recorded June 23, 1794: "To my wife, Jemima, my whole estate; to my two children, son, Claiborne, and daughter, Phoebe ———."

Peter Rucker.

Executors: May Burton Jr., Wm. Crawford.

Witness: May Burton Jr., Joseph Chapman, Wm. Ballard, John Miller (W. B. 3, p. 306), Orange.

Each time Peter signs a deed, either with his wife, Elizabeth, or Jemima, it is signed as above.

Issue (by 1st wife):

1. Ephraim[4] Rucker,
2. Rueben[4],
3. Elizabeth[4] Herring,
4. Mary[4] Creed.

Issue (by 2nd mar.):

5. Phoebe[4], m. Henry Allen of Madison Co., Jan. 28, 1798.
6. Claiborne[4], m. Frances Ballard in Botetourt Co., Mch. 24, 1796, Rev. Edward Mitchell, officiating.

Claiborne[4] Rucker with Elizabeth Ballard patented 970 acres of land in Greenbrier Co. (Land Grants).

In 1799, and until 1806, Claiborne paid a personal tax in Monroe County, W. Va. In 1801, he paid taxes on 118 acres as his own land, and on 970 acres jointly owned with the Ballard Estate. This 970 acres was divided up in 1810, Claiborne receiving 225 acres on Turkey Creek, adjoining Samuel Ewing's land.

1. Ephraim[4] Rucker (Peter[3], John[2], Peter[1]) moved to Henry County before 1782. The personal tax books in that county show that he was paying a tax on one slave, from 1783 until 1791.

On Oct. 2, 1788, he gave the power of attorney to his brother, Rueben, of Orange, to sell 170 acres of land bought in 1786, from John Hawkins and wife Ann, for £170. This land, called "Black Level", was adjoining that of John Scott and James Madison. Witness: John Scott and Jonathan Cowherd (D. B. 19, p. 185), Orange.

2. Rueben[4] Rucker (Peter[3], John[2], Peter[1]) m. Dec. 28, 1785, Mary[3] Foster Terrell (Edmund[2], Robert[1]) in Orange. It is recorded there in the land tax books of 1786, that he was paying taxes on 170 acres of land which he had bought from John and

Ann Hawkins in Orange and Albemarle, for £170, Sept., 1786 (D. B. 17, p. 15), Orange. This same land he sold in 1791, to Colby Cowherd, for £160 (D. B. 20, p. 47), Orange.

In 1787, he was paying a personal tax in Orange, on 2 horses and 3 head of cattle. It was continued until 1797.

Rueben and his wife, Mary Foster, in 1795, sold to John Daniel, for £350, 185 acres of land in Albemarle and Orange Counties, adjoining that of Waddle, Walker, and Terrell.

In 1793, he paid his first tax on 189½ acres of land in Albemarle Co. He continued it for 2 years only. 180 acres of this was acquired from Oliver Towles.

Oliver Towles of Spotsylvania Co. sold to Rueben Rucker and John Terrell Jr. of Albemarle County, 370 acres. (This land was conveyed to Oliver Towles by John Whittaker Willis and wife, Ann, of Spotsylvania Co., Feb. 25, 1791 (D. B. 20, p. 481), Orange.

In 1829, Rueben acquired 20 acres of land in Madison Co. on the Rapidan River. He paid a tax on this land for only one year. There are no personal taxes recorded. He shortly moved to Boone County, Ky.

Issue:

1. Nancy[5] Rucker,
2. Ambrose[5].
3. Reuben[5].
4. Edmund[5] Terrell.

1. Nancy[5] Rucker (Reuben[4], Peter[3], John[2], Peter[1]), m. John Henderson, of Brown Co., Ky., Sept., 1810.

- 1. William[6] Henderson, b. Oct. 20, 1820, in Ala., d. May 3, 1892, Indianapolis, Ind., m. Martha Ann Paul Henderson. He was an attorney-at-law.
  - 1. Sarah[7] Henderson, b. at Newcastle, d. June 20, 1931, moved with parents to Indianapolis in 1851. She was a great student and writer of short stories, m. July 24, 1867, Joseph Pyle Wiggins, d. 1882.
    - 1. Dudley[8] Howard Wiggins.
  - 2. Ambrose[7] Rucker Henderson, of Dallas, Tex.

4. Edmond[5] Terrell Rucker (Reuben[4], Peter[3], John[2], ——), m. Jane Brown.

- 1. Richmond[6] Harvey Carroll Rucker, d. in infancy.
- 2. Reuben[6] Terrell.

3. Samuel[6] Brown, b. Jan. 2, 1825; m. Martha McGaughy, of Lawrence Co., Ala.

1. Edmund[7] Rucker.
2. Samuel[7].
3. Oscar[7].
4. Mary[7].
5. Ellen[7].
6. Emma[7].
7. Laura[7].
8. Ida[7].
9. Augusta[7].

2. John[3] Rucker (John[2], Peter[1]) (c. 1720-1780), d. in Revolutionary service, lived in Amherst Co., and m. Eleanor Warren, d. 1797 (dau. of James, who was living in Goochland, later Amherst, as early as 1735). John may have gone there when his father patented land in 1739. However, no record of it is found there. Yet, from a deed made by Eleanor's brother, John Warren, of Amherst, in 1749 (see Warren line, Part III), we know that they were already married. They lived in Lexington Parish, on the east side of Tobacco Row Mountain, on land extending to Paul's Mountain. His eldest son was born in 1746. John was born in Orange and was grown in 1742. The following court order proves he was of age:

Ordered that John Rucker, Gent., with his own people clear the road, and make "bridges and cawseys" from the road half a mile from his race grounds, into the road called the Court House Road, and that he be exempt from all other roads. March, 1742 (O. B. 1741-43, p. 122).

In the division of the 5,850 acres of land patented by his father, in 1739, John received on Nov. 10, 1751, 318 acres on Harris Creek, adjoining the land of John Gough, Ambrose Rucker, William Miller and John Harris (D. & W. B. 1, p. 355), Albemarle.

This 318 acres was devised by John[3] to his son, Dr. Isaac[4] Rucker, in his will, after the death of his wife, Eleanor. John patented 124 acres of land in Bedford on Apr. 6, 1769, on West Branch of Elk Run, adjoining David Crew's and Woodrow's land. At the same time he patented 97 acres on the east point of Elk Run, on the spur of "No Business Mountains".

John bought 285 acres in Bedford Co. in 1768, from Martin King on Elk Run, at Penn's Corner in Hardy's line, to the end of Fleming's Mountain (D. B. 3, p. 182), Bedford Co., Va.

On July 25, 1772, he bought 51 acres on Elk Run, adjoining his own land, from John Crew for £17 (D. B. 4, p. 329), Bedford.

On July 4, 1772, John Rucker and wife, Eleanor, of Amherst, deeded to James Rucker, their son, for "love and affection",

196 acres in Bedford Co., adjoining Thomas Thorpe, Daniel Crew and said Rucker (D. B. 4, p. 330), Bedford.

This same month, John had sold to Thomas Thorpe of Bedford, for £60, 12½ acres, a part of Rucker's tract (D. B. 4, p. 327), Bedford.

Sept. 6, 1762, David Rosser of Bedford Co., sold to John Rucker of Amherst, for £40, 204 acres adjoining Bernard Gaines' and Ambrose Rucker's land. Witness: John Goff and Ambrose Rucker (D. B. A, p. 64), Amherst. Eleven years later, John and Eleanor Rucker deeded 202 acres of this land, adjoining Gaines' in Amherst, to their son, John. This land was bought by Rosser in 1751 from Peter Rucker out of the 5,850 acre tract, patented by his father, John.

John and Eleanor, in 1772, sold to Ambrose Rucker 9 acres of land. The same day, Ambrose Rucker and wife, Mary, sold to John and Eleanor 9 acres of land.

John and Eleanor Rucker, for love and affection to son, John, 202 acres of land in Amherst, adjoining Gaines' line, May 3, 1773 (D. B. C, p. 524), Amherst.

From the *Colonial Records of North Carolina,* Vol. 4, p. 196, we learn that John Rucker was a dispatch bearer during the Revolutionary War.

The following is taken from a letter written by Captain Richard Henderson to Gov. Caswell, in reference to the Virginia troops:

"Greenville, N. C.,
Aug. 15, 1779.

——— I shall set off tomorrow in order to keep the gentlemen from Virginia from returning. The expense on our state will be great, without the least benefit, and Virginia will be complaining with just cause. The bearer, Mr. John Rucker, will wait your excellency's leisure, and bring such dispatches as may be delivered."

Cabells and Their Kin, p. 103, "The General Assembly passed an act to embody militia for the relief of South Carolina. The proportion from Amherst was 135 men. The militia for South Carolina, and the continentals for General Washington were furnished by Amherst, without being drafted."

Hening's, Vol. 7, p. 204, mentions John Rucker as "furnishing provisions to the continental army, in 1755, from Albemarle County."

Hardesty's *Historical and Genealogical Encyclopaedia of Amherst County* mentions John as a Revolutionary soldier, "died in service."

The will of John Rucker of Lexington Parish, Amherst Co., dated Dec. 1, 1779, probated Sept. 4, 1780 (W. B. I, p. 529):

To wife, Eleanor, 4 negroes, one-half the bedding, and all the rest of the household furniture plantation tools, and one-half of the land.

To my son, William, one horse, new saddle, feather bed, and furniture, rifle gun, one half my tract of land on Elk Creek, Bedford County.

To son, George, the other half of land on Elk Creek.

To daughter, Nelly, one slave, etc.

To daughter, Betty, one slave, etc.

To daughter, Suckey Coward, a tolerable cow.

Son, Isaac, one-half the tract I live on, and all at his mother's death; James and John each have had a horse; also George, William, and Isaac, one each.

Each of the children: James, Sarah Pendleton, John, Sucky Coward, George, William, Nelly, Betta, and Isaac nine slaves and residue of estate to be divided among them. Executrix: wife, Eleanor; sons: James and John; Brother, Isaac. Witness: Ambrose Rucker, Rueben Rucker, William Whitten.

Isaac, James, John, Ambrose, and Anthony Rucker, and John Penn went security for the executors of the will of John Rucker, dec'd, to the extent of £100,000, Sept. 4, 1780 (W. B. 1, p. 532), Amherst.

George McDaniel, David Tinsley, and John McDaniel appraised the estate of John Rucker, dec'd, on Nov. 6, 1780. The valuation of personal property in Amherst was £78,407 (W. B. 2, p. 1) and in Bedford, £414. In this inventory was mentioned one gold sword.

In the settlement of the estate of John Rucker, dec'd, after the death of Eleanor, his wife, by sons James, John and Isaac Rucker, executors, this John Rucker, executor, signs himself "the elder". John Rucker's estate was not fully divided until June 19, 1797, when each of his nine children received £94, their share of their grandfather's, John Rucker's, estate (W. B. 3, p. 436), Amherst.

Issue:

1. James[4] Rucker.
2. Sally[4] Pendleton.
3. John[4].
4. Susan[4] Coward.
5. George[4].
6. William[4].
7. Elizabeth[4] North.
8. Isaac[4].
9. Nellie[4].

1. James[4] Rucker (John[3], John[2], Peter[1]), b. before 1746, in Amherst Co., d. 1828 in Caldwell Co., Ky., m. 1st, Ann (Nancy) Morton (dau. of John H., and sister of Jeremiah); 2nd, Susanna.

In 1772, John and Eleanor Warren Rucker deeded to their son, James[4], 196 acres of land in Bedford Co., on Elk Run (D. B. 4, p. 330), Bedford. On August 28, 1780, James sold this land to Thomas Thorpe, and wife, Ann, joined in the deed (D. B. 7, p. 16), Bedford. They then moved to Kentucky.

In 1794, Joshua Early of Bedford Co. appointed James Rucker of Woodford County, Ky., his attorney to divide into two parts, 400 acres of land in that county (D. B. 9, p. 354), Bedford.

The will of James Rucker of Caldwell Co., Ky. (W. B. A, p. 422) dated July 14, 1818, recorded, Oct. 20, 1828, mentions his wife, Susanna. The Executors are his sons: John, Jeremiah, and Morton Rucker. His children mentioned in his will are as follows:

1. John[5] Rucker.
2. James[5], m. Sept. 12, 1792, Mildred Rucker, 1st cousin.
3. Sally[5] Thomas.
4. Nellie[5], m. Ahmed Rucker, 1st cousin.
5. Morton[5].
6. Joshua[5] (dec'd).
7. George[5], m. Oct. 24, 1804, Lucy[2] Estes, dau. of Benjamin.
8. Sookey[5] Tanner.
9. Jeremiah[5].

1. John[5] Rucker (James[4], John[3], John[2], Peter[1]) (Sept. 17, 1768-March 27, 1856), of Amherst Co., Va., was mentioned in the personal tax books as "John, son of James", paying two tythes in 1788, but upon no land. He married his 1st cousin, Rachel Rucker (1772-1803), on August 12, 1791. The marriage bond was signed by: John, Isaac, and Moses Rucker, in Amherst, Va. He married, 2nd, Mary Young. (The following is con-

tributed by Mr. W. C. Rucker, of Princeton, Ky., and Mr. John G. Drinnan, of Chicago.)

Issue (by 1st mar.):

1. James^{6} Willis Rucker.
2. Isaac^{6}.
3. Nelson^{6} Dawson, d. unmar.
4. Sally^{6} Plunkett Rucker.

Issue (by 2nd mar.):

5. Thomas^{6}, m. Deadema^{6} Rucker (Ahmed^{5}, John^{4}, John^{3}). See Ahmed^{5}.
6. Young^{6}, b. 1809; m. Maria Webb.
7. Joshua^{6}.
8. John^{6} A.
9. Gideon^{6}, m. Addie Catlett.
10. William^{6} Morton.
11. Washington^{6}.
12. Emily^{6}.
13. Jane^{6}, m. Richard Harris.
14. Laura^{6}, m. Enic Young.
15. Henry^{6}.
16. Julia^{6}.

1. James^{6} Willis Rucker (John^{5}, James^{4}, John^{3}, John^{2}, Peter^{1}) (Oct. 13, 1793-1872), m. Elizabeth Elrod Jones, of Ky. (1805-July 2, 1884), dau. of Major Jones, who served in the War of 1812. James Willis and his wife lived at Baxter Springs, Kansas.

1. David^{7} Rucker (July 22, 1832-Mch. 15, 1857), m. C. Hopkins.
2. Matilda^{7} Ann (Sept. 5, 1834-Jan. 6, 1857), m. Mch., 1851, Jeremiah Dorris of Missouri.
3. Rachel^{7} S. J. (Feb. 11, 1837-Feb. 17, 1859), m. John S. Boswell.
4. Laura^{7} E. E., b. June 5, 1839, m. Martin Warren, of Phoenix, Arizona, 1859.
5. John^{7} Willis, b. Jan. 3, 1842; a Confederate soldier; m. Susan F. Lillington, of Denver, Col.
    1. Kyle^{8} Rucker, Colonel in U. S. Army.
    2. Eva^{8} Bassett, Berkley, Calif.
6. Thomas^{7} Allen, b. May 1, 1844, m. Miriam Pemberton, of Asher, Calif.; was a Confederate soldier.
7. Atterson^{7} Walden Rucker, b. Apr. 3, 1847, Harrodsburg, Mercer Co., Ky., m. Mch. 5, 1873, Celeste E.

Caruth (Apr. 13, 1854-Nov. 1, 1906), dau. of Hon. S. B. and Jane Brown Caruth, of Ill. They lived at Mount Morrison, Col.

He served in the Confederate War; enlisted in 1862 in Shelby's Brigade, was attached to Gen. Price's Army during the campaign through Missouri; was in the engagement of Carthage, Lexington, etc. He was taken prisoner in August, 1862, and imprisoned at Springfield, Mo., for 6 months, then paroled.

After the war, at the age of 20, he studied law at Lexington, Ky., and was admitted to practice in 1868. With his brother, Thomas, he opened a law office at Baxter Springs, Mo. He later moved to Kansas City, and was appointed Judge of the Criminal Court of Lake County.

In 1885, he moved to Denver, Col., where, in 1908, he was elected a member of Congress as a democrat. While in Congress, he served as a member of the Insular Committee, and as such went to Porto Rico, Honolulu, Japan, China, and the Philippines.

2. Isaac^{6} Rucker (John^{5}, James^{4}, John ^{3}, John^{2}, Peter^{1}), m. 1st, Edna K.; 2nd, Frances W. Lived in Ky.

Issue (by 1st marriage):

1. Mary^{7} Katherine (Aug. 8, 1830-Jan. 10, 1857), m. Jan. 1, 1852, W. T. Scott.
2. Emily^{7} Wilson, b. Feb. 28, 1838.
3. Rachel^{7} Ann, m. Aug. 2, 1842, Needham C. Nichols.

Issue (by 2nd marriage):

4. Isaac^{7} Pearce, b. Nov. 7, 1852.
5. Laura^{7} Gray, b. Nov. 20, 1856.

7. Joshua^{6} Rucker (John^{5}, James^{4}, John^{3}), b. 1815, m. Surella Crow, of Princeton, Ky.

1. William^{7} Rucker, Judge of Cook Co., Ill.; portrait in the Court House of Chicago.

8. John^{6} Rucker (John^{5}, James^{4}, John^{3}), m. Nancy Bembrey.

1. Charles^{7} Webb Rucker.
2. Mary^{7} C.
3. Nancy^{7} Jane.

10. Wiliam^{6} Morton Rucker (John^{5}, James^{4}), d. in service during Civil War; m. Martha Roscoe.

1. Julia^{7} Rucker, m. C. Webb Rucker, 1st cousin.
2. W. C.^{7}
3. Thomas^{7} M.

11. Washington^{6} Rucker (John^{5}, James^{4}), m. Adela Lester, b. 1834, Princeton, Ky.

1. Dora^{7} Martin Rucker.
2. Dixie^{7} Vivian.
3. Sidney^{7} J.

12. Emily^{6} Rucker (John^{5}, James^{4}), m. Moore Wimberly.

1. Henrietta^{7} Wimberly.
2. Francis^{7}.

1. Henrietta^{7} Wimberly (Emily^{6}, John^{5}, James^{4}, John^{3}) (Sept. 1, 1831-Nov. 3, 1911), m. Mch. 13, 1850, John L. Drennan, b. Nov. 14, 1827 son of Eli and Margaret McDowell Drennan.

1. Alfred^{8} M. Drennan, b. 1855, unmar.
2. Franklin^{8} P., b. 1853, m. Mary Moore.
3. John^{8} G.
4. Adilade^{8} J., b. June 17, 1856, m. John Cole.
5. Laura^{8} A. E., b. 1858, m. James George.
6. Margaret^{8} E., b. 1859, m. Clayton Clements.
7. Henry^{8} E., b. 1861, m. Mollie Maxwell.
8. George^{8} R., b. 1863, m. Lucinda H.
9. Henrietta^{8} A., b. 1865, m. Lewis Wilson.
10. Cora^{8} H., b. 1867, m. Miles Scott.
11. James^{8} L., b. 1869, m. 1st, May Jones.
12. Thomas^{8} M., b. 1870, m. Blanch Sale.
13. Charlotte^{8} O., b. 1874.

3. John^{8} G. Drennan (Henrietta^{7}, Emily^{6}, John^{5}), b. Dec. 3, 1843, m. Margaret Slater of Taylorsville, Ill., May 26, 1881. He is an attorney, representing the I. C. Railroad, office in Chicago.

1. Major Leonard^{9} H. Drennan b. 1889; graduate of West Point 1908, served in Philippines in Spanish-American War. As Lieut. Col., he served in the World War. He was a flyer, commanding the Handley-Page expedition. In 1926, he resigned from the army, now lives with his family near Baltimore, Maryland.
2. Walter^{9} R. Drennan, b. 1888; graduate of State University at Champaign 1909, was 1st Lieut., Air Corps, in World War; now lives in Chicago.
3. Helen^{9} Louise, b. Dec. 3, 1895, at Springfield, Ill., m. Major W. R. Gruber, located at Fort Leavenworth, Kansas.

2. Francis[7] Wimberly (Emily[6], John[5], James[4]), b. Mch., 1833, m. Leak Sacket, and moved from Kentucky to Mount Auburn, Ill. He joined the Union Army in 1861 and served 3 years.

1. Thomas[8] Wimberly, lawyer living at University Place, Omaha, Neb.

5. Morton[5] A. Rucker (James[4], John[3]) (1785-Aug. 8, 1856), of Caldwell Co., Ky., m. Salina D. Boyd, Jan. 7, 1834.

1. James[6] Rucker, b. 1838.
2. Eliza M.[6], m. ——— Collins.
    1. Annie[7] Collins, m. ——— O'Hara.
    2. Stuart[7].
3. Andrew Jackson[6] Rucker.
4. Lynn Boyd[6].
5. Milton[6].

2. Sally[4] Rucker (John[3], John[2], Peter[1]) (July 25, 1750-Oct. 16, 1825), m. 1769, James[4] Pendleton, son of Wm.[3] and Wife, Elizabeth Tinsley, John[2], of Orange, Philip[1] Pendleton.

1. Elizabeth[5] Pendleton (1787-1835), m. Wm. McDaniel 1774-1851).
    1. James[6] Pendleton McDaniel (1815-1877), m. 1832, Mary Robinson Glenn.

The will of Wm.[3] Pendleton was filed in Amherst on Nov. 1, 1779, bequeathing possessions "to my wife, Elizabeth; sons: James, Edward, Richard, John, Rueben, Wm., Isaac; and daughters: Mary Sarah, Franklin, and Bella."

3. John[4] Rucker (John[3], John[2], Peter[1]) (c. 1748-April 24, 1814), m. 1st, Sarah Plunkett, dau. of John and Mildred Plunkett, of Orange (1754-Dec. 14, 1796), d. in Ky. (see Plunkett line); m. 2nd, Patsy.

In 1773 his father deeded 202 acres of land in Amherst to him, land John[3] had bought from David Rosser on Sept. 6, 1762, who had bought it from Peter[3] Rucker (D. B. A, p. 64), Amherst.

John Rucker and wife, Sarah, of Amherst, sold to Ambrose Rucker of same, 202 acres for £280, land on Harris Creek (north branch), down Harvey's Road, adjoining David Woodroof's, and to Ambrose Rucker's line near the old store. Sept. 16, 1795 (D. B. G, p. 207).

John was in Revolutionary service (*Hardesty's H. and G. Encyclopaedia of Amherst County* and *State Historical Register of Kentucky,* p. 62). The application for pension of John Rucker of Woodford County, Kentucky, is found in the Virginia list of Revolutionary soldiers compiled by the State Auditor, 1910-11, p. 363, and also in Mr. Alexander Brown's list of Amherst Revolutionary soldiers and Adjustment Rev. Claims of Amherst, 1781.

John^{4} Rucker died in Fayette County, will dated June 18, 1812, and probated in May, 1814 (W. B. C, p. 136). He left to his wife, Patsy, 50 acres during her widowhood.

Issue (from will):

1. Rachel^{5} Rucker.
2. Ahmed^{5}.
3. Mildred^{5}.
4. Barnett^{5}.
5. William^{5}.
6. John^{5}.
7. James^{5} Plunkett.
8. Joshua^{5} Plunkett.
9. Isaac^{5}.
10. Benjamin^{5} Asbury.
11. Lewis^{5} Dawson.

A tract of land in Campbell County on Dry Creek, patented by Theodorick Noel, 575 acres to be divided between wife and sons. Executors: Ahmed, Barnett, and William Rucker. Witness: Robert L. Chambers, Thomas B. Young, Joseph Chambers.

The Amherst court settled the Revolutionary claims in 1781. Sums were paid to John Rucker for driving public beeves on July 30, 1780, Nov. 3, 1780, and July 1, 1781.

1. Rachel^{5} Rucker (John^{4}, John^{3}) (Oct. 18, 1772-Mch. 4, 1865), m. 1791, John^{5} Rucker, 1st cousin (James^{4}, John^{3}). See p. 18.

2. Ahmed^{5} Rucker (John^{4}, John^{3} ———) (Nov. 17, 1775-June 2, 1840), m. Nov., 1798, his 1st cousin, Nellie Rucker (James^{4}, John^{3} ———), of Jessemin County, Ky. Ahmed was a minister and lived in Illinois.

From knowledge of his own family he wrote his "Memoirs" in 1873, when he was sixty-two years of age. This paper is now in the possession of Dr. William Colby Rucker of New Orleans. He wrote that he was raised in the midst of the children of John and Eleanor Rucker, his grandparents, who had settled on the south side of Paul's Mountain. This land John had given to his five sons, and the equivalent to his daughters in slaves. John was born in 1720, and died in 1780, in his sixtieth year, "much beloved". He married Eleanor Warren (1728-1798), who died in her seventieth year. Ahmed wrote that he knew her very well and corresponded with her after he had moved to Kentucky. His own mother was Sally Plunkett, daughter of John and Mildred (Hawkins) Plunkett of Orange. Mildred later married Capt. Isaac Rucker, and moved to Amherst. The Hawkins family, Rachel Garrett, Sarah Morton, Lucy Moore, Benjamin Williams, and James Hawkins moved to Kentucky with the Ruckers. Ahmed tells that he was born on Tate Creek, Campbell County, two miles from Lynchburg. At that time his father, John, was overseer for his uncle, Benjamin Rucker of Amherst.

1. Lucy[6] Clampit.
2. Nancy[6] Smith.
3. Deadema[6] Rucker.
4. Patsy[6] Wickersham.
5. Rebecca[6] Knox.
6. Pamelia[6] Burford.
7. James[6] C. Rucker, a minister of Clinton, Illinois.
8. Harris[6] A. Rucker.
9. Zerilda[6] Haynes.

1. Lucy[6] Rucker (Ahmed[5], John[4] ———), m. Moses Clampit.

1. Susan[7] E. Clampit, married ——— Akers.
   1. Eliza[8] Ellen Aker.
   2. James[8] William.
2. William[7] Clampit.
3. John[7] J. F.
4. Mary[7] Ann.
5. Martha[7] Ellen.

2. Nancy[6] Rucker (Ahmed[5], John[4] ———) (May 9, 1800-Jan. 9, 1829), buried near Mortonville, Woodford Co., Ky., m. in Woodford Co., James Smith (1792-1858, b. in Maryland.

1. Franklin[7] Smith, d. age 17.
2. Samuel[7] Parker.
3. Augustus[7] Ceasar, b. 1826.

2. Samuel[7] Parker Smith (Nancy[6], Ahmed[5], John [4] ———), b. Woodford Co., Ky., Feb., 1822, d. in Shelby Co., Ky., Oct. 12, 1873, m. Sarah Margaret Yost on Oct. 12, 1845, b. Jan. 2, 1823, in Frankfort, Ky., and d. Aug. 14, 1905, in Shelby Co.

1. James[8] Howard Smith, b. Jan. 18, 1848, in Richmond, Ky.
2. Nancy[8] Reed, b. June 16, 1850, d. 1853, Versailles, Ky.

3. Franklin^{8} Evans.
4. William^{8} Rucker, b. Aug. 5, 1855, at Kaskasia, Ill.
5. Augustus^{8} Yost, b. June 19, 1858, at Kaskasia, Ill.
6. Holly^{8} Reed.

3. Franklin^{8} Evans Smith (Samuel^{7}, Nancy^{6}, Ahmed^{5}), b. Mch. 31, 1853, at Liberty, Ill., d. Mch. 17, 1926, m. Anne Clemons on June 3, 1891.

1. Abigail^{9} Lee Smith, b. Feb. 6, 1892, m. Cornell Douglas Chale, July 20, 1916.
    1. Thomas^{10} Holbrook Chale, b. Feb. 20, 1921, Louisville, Ky.
2. Paul^{9} Clemons Smith, b. Aug. 6, 1895.
3. Franklin^{9} Redford, b. Sept. 15, 1898.
4. Anson^{9} Neil, b. July 7, 1906.

6. Holly^{8} Reed Smith (Samuel^{7}, Nancy^{6}, Ahmed^{5}), b. Sept. 27, 1861, at Prairie Le Rocke, Ill., d. Mch. 27, 1901, in Orlando, Fla., m. Martha Jane Lee, of Leesburg, Lake County, Fla., b. July 30, 1862.

1. Margaret^{9} Lee Smith, b. May 10, 1888, Leesburg, Fla., m. John Pendleton Holbrook of Orlando, Fla., Apr. 29, 1909.
2. Frank^{9} Augustus Smith, b. Apr. 9, 1890, m. Hallie Loretta Lee, May 24, 1916.
    1. F. Augustus^{10} Smith, Jr., b. Oct. 28, 1917.
    2. Jane^{10} Lee, b. Mch. 3, 1920.
    3. Margaret^{10} Estelle, b. Oct. 8, 1922.
    4. Lucy^{10} Holly, b. Jan. 26, 1926.
3. Marian^{9} Holly Smith, b. Mch. 14, 1896.
4. Helen^{9} E., b. Nov. 10, 1899, m. Lyman Ange, Sept. 11, 1926, Orlando, Fla.

3. Deadema^{6} Rucker (Ahmed^{5}, John^{4}, ———) (Dec. 12, 1806-1863), m. in Woodford County, Ky., Apr. 15, 1831, Thomas Rucker (John^{5}, James^{4}, John^{3} ———), b. in Caldwell County, Ky., on Oct. 29, 1807, and moved to Sangamon County in 1832. Lived in Springfield, Ill.

Thomas Rucker later m. Mrs. Julia A. Leonard, formerly Mrs. Boatwright, nee Russel, b. Apr. 7, 1813, in Murry, Tenn.

Issue (1st marriage):

1. James^{7} H. Rucker, b. June 16, 1832, d. young.

2. Bishop^7 Emory (Dec. 12, 1834-Oct. 9, 1897), d. Christian Co., Ill., m. Lucinda Shafer.
3. Permelia^7 Jane, b. Dec. 12, 1836, m. George W. Forden, of Col.
4. Martha^7 Ellen, b. June 2, 1838, d. Sangamon Co., m. Andrew L. Crowls.
5. Mary^7 Catherine (May 1, 1840-1840).
6. Joshua^7 Young (Nov. 11, 1842-1861).
7. Lucy^7 Armenda (July 3, 1843-Sept. 8, 1916), m. Thomas Upton Butler, of Nebraska.

4. Patsy^6 Rucker (Ahmed^5, John^4, ———), b. Oct. 17, 1805, m. Josiah Wickersham.

1. Wesley^7 Wickersham.
2. James^7.

5. Rebecca^6 Rucker (Ahmed^5, John^4, ———), b. Dec. 12, 1809, m. Dr. Elijah Knox, July 7, 1833, of Mason Co., Ill.

1. Elijah^7 Wesley Knox, b. April 21, 1834, m. Sarah Lowe, Oct. 25, 1857.
2. Naomie^7 Ellen, b. Oct. 10, 1835.
3. James^7 O. (Dec. 22, 1837-1838).
4. John^7 A. Morris, b. June 16, 1839.
5. Zerilda^7 Pamelia, b. Mch. 22, 1843.
6. Richard^7 W., b. Jan. 27, 1850.

6. Pamelia^6 Rucker (Ahmed^5, John^4 ———) (Dec. 12, 1812-May 16, 1837), d. in Kentucky, m. Miles W. Burford, Sept. 25, 1829.

1. Ann^7 Jane Burford, b. Nov. 9, 1830, m. Wm. Forgman, Aug. 5, 1847.
2. Martha^7 Ellen (June 4, 1835-Sept. 12, 1858), m. Braden.
3. Elisha^7 Spruill, b. May 14, 1837.

8. Harris^6 Ahmed Rucker (Ahmed^5, John^4 ———) (Oct. 20, 1824-1877), lived at Clinton Ill., m. 1st cousin, Sarah Fletcher Rucker, dau. of John and Elizabeth Burton Rucker.

1. Hamilton^7 Presby Rucker, b. Feb. 19, 1848, in Dakota, m. 1st Lydia Maria Colby, dau. of Jonathan and Lydia Ingalls Colby; m. 2nd Catherine, of Oakland, Calif.
    1. Dr. Wm.^{8} Colby Rucker, formerly Assistant Surgeon General, U. S. A., now located in New Orleans.

2. Ellen^{7} Sowers Rucker, b. Aug. 26, 1849.
3. Lewis^{7} Howard, b. Jan. 12, 1852, Jacksonville, Ill., moved with his parents to Clinton, Ill.; m. 1878 Alice Trowbridge of Kennerdy, moved to Ashland, Ky. He organized a number of schools. Lived in Minneapolis, being president of the University of Commerce and Finance.
4. Mary^{7} Perces, b. Aug. 26, 1855, m. ——— Houser, of Jacksonville, Ill.
5. Mattie^{7} Burton Rucker (Jan. 3, 1861-July 23, 1920), lived in Clinton, Ill., d. in Chicago.

9. Zerilda^{6} Rucker (Ahmed^{5}, John^{4} ———) (Aug. 15, 1818-Dec. 19, 1857), d. in Illinois, m. Oinsber Hayne.

1. Richard^{7} Ahmed Hayne, b. Oct. 20, 1838.
2. James^{7} Henry, b. July 19, 1840, consul to France for 20 yrs.
   yrs.
3. Nancy^{7} Ellen, b. April 29, 1844.
4. Mebsilla^{7}, b. April 23, 1846.
5. William^{7} Summerfield, b. April 14, 1849.
6. Lucy^{7} Naomie, b. Aug. 15, 1852.
7. Oinsber^{7} Wilson, b. July 13, 1856.

3. Mildred^{5} Rucker (John^{4}, John^{3}, John^{2}, ———) (Feb. 13, 1777-Mch. 13, 1855), m. James^{5} Rucker (James^{4}, John^{3}, ———), Sept. 12, 1792. The marriage bond is signed by John Rucker, John Rucker, Jr., Isaac Rucker, Jr., and Elizabeth Rucker, witnesses. They moved to Kentucky.

Issue:

1. Ambrose^{6} Rucker.
2. Betsy^{6}.
3. Lucinda^{6}, b. June 30, 1800, d. Caldwell County, Ky., m. John P. Sasseen.
4. Wyatt^{6} (Mch. 1804-Jan. 7, 1830).
   1. James^{7} W. H. Rucker.
5. Sarah^{6} Plunkett, b. Dec. 5, 1807.
6. Jonathan^{6} M., b. 1810.
   1. Susan^{7} Mildred Rucker, b. 1751.
7. Ann^{6} Eliza.

1. Ambrose^{6} Rucker (Mildred^{5}, John^{4}, John^{3}, ———) (Oct. 29, 1794-Sept. 12, 1843), m. ——— Rucker.

1. Gelneston^{7} Winston Rucker, b. Mch. 9, 1838.
2. Daniel^{7}, b. Jan. 4, 1841.

2. Betsy[6] Rucker (Mildred[5], John[4], John[3], ———) (Aug. 6, 1798-1843), d. in Pettis Co., Mo.; m. Judge Jesse Pemberton.

1. Melissa[7] Mildred Pemberton.
2. Warren[7] Wyatt (June 6, 1821-Aug. 18, 1840).
3. Lucinda[7] Ann, b. Nov. 13, 1823, m. Dr. Thomas B. Pemberton.
4. George[7] Allen (Jan. 13, 1826-July 23, 1830).
5. Sarah[7] Ellen, b. Jan. 24, 1828.
6. Eliza[7] Brooks, b. Apr. 26, 1830, m. David Cooper of Mo.
7. Jesse[7] Middleton, b. Nov. 3, 1832, m. Polly Lenox.
8. Judith[7] E., b. Jan. 11, 1834, m. Watts A. Ewin.
9. Matilda[7] E., b. May 24, 1836.

1. Melissa[7] Mildred Pemberton (Betsy[6], Mildred[5], John[4], ———), b. June 26, 1818, m. George W. Pemberton.

1. Thomas[8] Fitzhugh Pemberton, b. May 9, 1840.
2. Jesse[8] Brooks, June 11, 1842.
3. Warren[8] Goodlow, b. Aug. 25, 1845.
4. Marian[8] B., b. May 28, 1849, m. Thomas A. Rucker.
5. Lucinda[8] B., b. July 27, 1851, m. Monroe H. Garton.
6. Elizabeth[8], b. Oct. 17, 1853.
7. George[8] Middleton, b. Oct. 14, 1856, m. Grace B. waters.

5. Sarah[6] Plunkett Rucker (Mildred[5], John[4], John[3], ———), b. Dec. 5, 1856, married ——— Boyd. They and their children died in Caldwell Co., Ky.

1. Lucinda[7] M. Boyd, } twins, b. 1837.
2. Wyatt[7] P., }
3. Charles[7] C., b. 1840.
4. Elmira[7] Frances, b. 1842.
5. Finis[7] Robert.

7. Ann[6] Eliza Rucker (Mildred[5], John[4], ———) (May 13, 1814-March 15, 1857), d. in Texas, m. Charles Hodge.

1. Mary[7] Mildred Mosley, b. Aug. 27, 1838.
2. Lucinda[7] Arema, b. Oct. 8, 1840.
3. Eliza[7] Jane, b. Oct. 29, 1842.

4. Barnett[5] Rucker (John[4], John[3], ———) (May 25, 1778-June 4, 1833), may have married twice. In the list of marriage bonds of Kentucky compiled by Mrs. Johnson is to be found the marriage of Barnett Rucker to Elizabeth Holloway, June 5, 1803. From the will of James Holloway of Jessamine Co., Ky., dated

Apr. 20, 1828, probated Oct., 1829, we find him mentioning his dau., Mary, wife of Hugh Cruchter, and Judy Rucker; sons, George, Spencer and Samuel; wife, Martha Owen Holloway. These heirs already mentioned had petitioned for Bounty Land for the services rendered by James Holloway while serving as a lieutenant in the Revolution, of Fayette Co., Ky. The Bounty Land was granted to them in Louisiana. Both Barnett and Julia died of Asiatic cholera, and were buried in the North City Cemetery. Julia was b. 1784.

1. Thomas^{6} Holloway Rucker.
2. James^{6} Spenser.
3. Martha^{6}, unmar.
4. Garrett^{6} Flournoy, of Lexington, Ky., unmar.

1. Dr. Thomas^{6} Holloway Rucker (Barnett^{5}, John^{4}, ———), b. Feb. 24, 1815, m. Aug. 4, 1836, Sarah McCracken Jesse, of Woodford Co., Ky., Oct. 9, 1857, lived in Evansville, Ill. In January, 1858, he married Marion T. Liley.

Issue (1st marriage):

1. Julia^{7} Elizabeth Rucker, b. July 30, 1837.
2. Mary^{7} Thomas, b. Mch. 25, 1839.
3. James^{7} Barnett Rucker, a lawyer, of Evansville, Ill., b. Feb. 1, 1844.
   1. Jean^{8} Holloway Rucker Galladay, now of Lebanon, Wilson Co., Tenn.
4. Thomas^{7} Somerville (Nov. 10, 1845-Sept. 10, 1854).

2. James^{6} Spencer Rucker (Barnett^{5}, John^{4}, John^{3}, ———), m. Elizabeth Bartlett in 1836.

1. Sarah^{7} Julia Rucker (Aug. 7, 1837-1839).
2. Thomas^{7} Holloway, b. May 5, 1839.
3. James^{7} Addison, b. Jan. 26, 1841.
4. Henry^{7} Lenoidas, b. May 13, 1843.
5. Zlexonia^{7} Vedan (May 17, 1845-Sept. 17, 1846).
6. Samuel^{7} Albert, b. Jan. 13, 1850.

5. William^{5} Rucker (John^{4}, John^{3}, ———) (Nov. 5, 1780-Jan. 23, 1854), m. Sally Morton, lived in Ill.

1. Melissa^{6} Lear Rucker, b. April 20, 1807.
2. Lucinda^{6}.
3. Alitha^{6}, b. Sept. 1, 1813, m. Robert Mosby.
   1. William^{7} Mosby, b. May 30, 1838; m. ——— Markee.

4. Hester^{6} Ann.
5. William^{6}, b. July 20, 1818.
6. Melinda^{6}, b. July 28, 1820; m. 1st Smith, 2nd Simpkins.
7. Benjamin^{6} R., b. Nov. 1, 1822.
8. Dr. John^{6} M., b. Feb. 1, 1830, Jacksonville, Ill.
9. Sophronia^{6} Ellen, b. Dec. 17, 1833; m. M. W. Fry, Jan. 14, 1859.

2. Lucinda^{6} Rucker (William^{5}, John^{4}, John^{3}, ———), b. Jan. 16, 1811, m. Ansel Wilhoit, whose family came from Culpeper.

1. Melinda^{7} S. Wilhoit, b. April 29, 1837, m. Jackson.
2. Mary^{7} F., b. May 18, 1838, m. G. U. Grans, Apr. 20, 1858.
   1. Edwin^{8} Grans, b. Feb. 2, 1859.
   2. Vassie^{8}.
   3. Dora^{8}.
   4. Frank^{8}.
   5. George^{8}.

4. Hester^{6} Ann Rucker (William^{5}, John^{4}, ———), b. June 4, 1816, m. ——— Willard.

1. Vassalonia^{7} M. Willard, b. Feb. 7, 1839.
2. Dr. James^{7} Polk Willard, b. May, 1844, Denver, Col.

6. John^{5} Rucker (John^{4}, John^{3}, ———), b. Sept. 22, 1782, m. Elizabeth Burton, Nov. 7, 1805, in Fayette County, Ky. Lived in Ill.

1. Presley^{6} William Rucker.
2. Eliza^{6} Ann Browning (Sept. 8, 1807-Sept., 1841).
3. Greenberry^{6} Rucker.
4. Sedonia^{6} Crum, b. Nov. 27, 1810.
5. John^{6} Fletcher Rucker (Dec. 16, 1812-Sept., 1813).
6. Mira^{6} Ann Rucker, b. June 17, 1815, m. 1st ——— Williams, 2nd ——— Sinclair.
7. Elizabeth^{6} Rucker, b. Nov. 16, 1817, m. William Hindle.
8. Polly^{6} Elvina Rucker (Mch. 23, 1820-1831).
9. Sarah^{6} F., b. June 21, 1822, m. Harris Ahmed Rucker.
10. Nancy^{6} Jane Redmond, b. Dec. 3, 1825.

1. Presley^{6} W. Rucker (John^{5}, John^{4}, ———), b. Aug. 29, 1806, m. Rucker.

Issue:

1. Catherine[7] E. Rucker, b. March 19, 1849.
2. John[7] R., b. May 29, 1850.
3. Greenberry[7], b. Nov. 5, 1852.
   1. Frank[8] W. Rucker, Independence, Mo., b. Jacksonville, Ill.
4. Presby[7] H., b. Apr. 6, 1854.

3. Greenberry[6] Rucker (John[5], John[4], ———) (Feb. 2, 1809-Feb. 3, 1845), m. Rucker.

1. Mary[7] Elizabeth Rucker, b. July 3, 1836.
2. Nancy[7] Eliza Rucker (Oct. 1, 1840-1856).
3. Mira[7] Annie Rucker, b. Aug. 17, 1853.

7. James[5] Plunkett Rucker (John[4], John[3], ———) (Feb. 9, 1784-Jan. 24, 1858)), m. 1st, Sally McDaniel, and 2nd, Polly McDaniel. Lived in Ind.

Issue (by 1st mar.):

1. Polly[6] Mitchel, b. March 31, 1804.
2. America[6], m. George Crutcher.
3. Valentine[6].
4. Orson[6].

by 2nd mar.:

5. Eliza[6] Ann Rucker, m. ——— Dabney.
   1. James D. Dabney, b. Oct. 2, 1837.
6. Amilda[6] Torbett.
7. Martha[6] Jane Magruder.
8. Vassalonia[6], b. Sept. 19, 1830, m. 1st Dale, 2nd Benj. Spouse.

Step-sons:

1. Sanford[6] McDaniel, b. 1810.
2. Cornelius[6] McDaniel, b. 1812.

3. Amilda[6] Rucker (James[5] Plunkett, John[4], John[3], ———), m. ——— Torbett.

1. Mary[7] Ann Torbett.
2. Henry[7] Torbett.
3. Alicia[7] Torbett.

7. Martha[6] Jane Rucker (James[5] P., John[4], ———), b. Apr. 22, 1818, m. Thomas G. Magruder.

1. James[7] D. Magruder, b. Jan. 4, 1838.
2. Thomas[7] Edgar Magruder, b. Dec. 26, 1840.
3. Robert[7] Danport Magruder, b. Mch. 22, 1843.
4. Mary[7] Susan Magruder, b. July 16, 1847.
5. Francis[7] W. Magruder, b. June 26, 1849.

6. Vassie[7] E. J. Magruder, b. Nov. 9, 1851.
7. Warren[7] E. Magruder, b. June 19, 1856.
8. Martha[7] A. Magruder, b. Dec. 30, 1858.

8. Joshua[5] Rucker (John[4], John[3], ——) (May 23, 1786-Jan. 24, 1858), m. 1st Elizabeth B. Chambers in 1809, and 2nd Mrs. Yost, widow of James Yost. She died in Shelby County, Ky., July 29, 1872. Joshua was living in Chicago and moved to Louisiana on account of health. The following is a letter from him to Isaac Rucker; the letter is now in the possession of Mrs. Summers, of Nashville, Tenn.

Madison Parish, La.
New Carthage Feb. 1, 1858.

Dear Nephew Isaac:

You may be somewhat surprised at receiving a letter from me and more especially so when I inform you that I am now in the State of Louisiana, where I have come to spend the winter with my two daughters Mary E. Noulen and Josephine W. Smith. One object of ths communication is this; when I started out on a visit to my relations in the year 1856 (the time myself and brother, William, were at your house) my youngest daughter, Josephine, wishing to have a record of all the children and grand children of all my brothers and sisters, and as I forgot at the time I was at your house to get the record of your family we wish now to get it in order if we can to complete the record up to the first of Jan. 1856. You will, therefore, please to send me the full names with the date of the birth of all of your children and grand children, also the names of the husbands of your married daughters. I also wish you to give me the date of your own birth. The object of this record is that when she, my daughter Josephine or any others of my family hears of the name of Rucker they may know what kin or relation they are to our family; we have already on the records upwards of two hundred names and there are quite a number more yet we wish to get and amongst them your brother, James Willis's family and I should like to know his post office address, so I can write to him. It may not be of much interest to you, but I will give you the names of all my children who are living beginning with the eldest, Henry Louis, born Dec. 6, 1809; Susan Martha, born Aug. 1, 1817; Mary Elizabeth Noulen, b. Aug. 23, 1819; Edward Augustus, b. Jan. 24, 1822; Sophronia Louisa Root, b. Jan. 29, 1824; Joseph Wm., b. Feb. 1827; Henrietta Louise Aiken, b. June 1, 1829; Josephine W. Smith, b. Mar. 3, 1834; which is the youngest of my children. I was born May 23, 1786; so you see that I was 71 years old last May. All my children, except eldest daughter and two youngest are married and all are doing well so far as the goods of this world is concerned, I mean as to property. My daughter, Mary, by the death of her husband, Dr. Elias P. Noulen last June is a widow with two children, the eldest of which a daughter about 16 is now in Chicago, getting her education, her principal studies now are the French language and music. I will inform you why I am here to spend the winter. In the last three or four years I found that the cold winters of the north in Chicago and my health has been seriously affected, and I am troubled with what is called dry asthma, sometimes a wheezing and difficult of breathing. Myself and wife and dau. Susan and grand daughter, Marie Louise Rucker, came down here and spent the last winter, and I found my health so much improved that I concluded to try it again this winter and think it necessary for my health for me to spend the future winters, I may be permitted to live in this or some other climate. I could say much more I shall be pleased to receive a letter from you either here before the middle of April or after that at Chicago, Ill., where I expect to be by first of May.

Please present my love to all your family.

Your affectionate Uncle

Joshua Rucker.

Issue:

1. Henry[6] Louis Rucker.
2. Edwin[6], July 4, 1812.
3. Susan[6] Ann, b. Nov. 8, 1813.
4. Benjamin[6] Franklin, b. June 21, 1815.
5. Susan[6] Martha, b. Aug. 1, 1817.
6. Mary[6] Elizabeth Noulen.
7. Edward[6] Augustus, b. Jan. 24, 1822.
8. Sophronia[6] Louisa Root.
9. Joseph[6] William, b. Feb. 6, 1827.
10. Henrietta[6] Louise Aiken.
11. Josephine[6] W. Smith.

1. Henry[6] Louis Rucker (Joshua[5], John[4], ———), b. Dec. 6, 1809, m. 1st M. G. Heckenuder, 2nd Mary Burnap, 3rd Mary P. Fitch, and 4th Mary Kellogg.

Issue (by 1st mar.):

1. Thomas[7] H. Rucker (Dec. 25, 1835-1837).
2. Helen[7] Victoria (Sept. 28, 1837-1838).
3. Anna[7] Maria, b. Feb. 10, 1840.
4. Louis[7] Henry.
5. Susan[7] George (Dec. 22, 1838-1842).
6. Ellen[7] Augusta, b. Aug. 4, 1843.

7. Thomas^{7} Heckenuder, } twins, b. and d. 1849.
8. Joseph^{7} Joshua, }

Issue (2nd mar.):

9. Maria^{7}, m. 1st M. W. Love, 2nd J. M. Stanbrough.
10. Camilla^{7} Burnap (Nov. 25, 1852-1853).
11. George^{7} Hite, b. and d. 1854.

Issue (3rd mar.):

12. Eunice^{7} E. (Feb. 3, 1857-1863).
13. Francis^{7} (1859-1865).

4. Gen. Louis^{7} Henry Rucker (Henry^{6}, Joshua^{5}, John^{4}, ———), m. 1st Gertee L. Briggs of California, and 2nd Cinderella Rusette.

1. Shelby^{8} Rucker.
2. John^{8} Rucker.
    1. Lewis^{9} Henry Rucker.
3. Col. William^{8} Rucker.

6. Mary^{6} Elizabeth Rucker (Joshua^{5}, John^{4}, ———) (Aug. 23, 1819-1857), m. Dr. Elias T. Noulen Dec. 11, 1838.

1. Susan^{7} E. Noulen (Aug. 1, 1841-1891), m. D. L. Beck, 1857.
2. Madura^{7} Alice (Nov. 13, 1843-Sept., 1846).
3. James^{7} (Feb. 2, 1845-Nov. 30, 1848).
4. Mary^{7} Josephine (Dec. 19, 1846-July, 1851).
5. Robert^{7} (June 8, 1849-1849).
6. Ida^{7} S., b. Nov. 24, 1863.

8. Sophronia^{6} Louisa Rucker (Joshua^{5}, John^{4}, ———), b. Jan. 29, 1824, m. Nathan T. Root, Oct. 11, 1849, of California.

1. Elizabeth^{7} Sabre, b. Aug. 18, 1850.
2. Nathan^{7} Henry, b. Nov., 1855, m. Mary Donahue.
3. Edward^{7} Rucker, b. Oct., 1857.

10. Henrietta^{6} Louise Rucker (Joshua^{5}, John^{4}, ———), b. June 1, 1829, m. 1st, Oct. 11, 1849, Charles M. Aiken, and 2nd W. B. Trest. Lived in Chicago.

Issue (by 1st mar.):

1. Charles^{7} Rucker Aiken, b. Sept. 1, 1852, m. Susan Chase.

2. William^7 Edward, b. Aug. 25, 1854, m. Ida L. E. Noulen, cousin.
3. Fannie^7 E., b. Dec. 28, 1856.
4. Robert^7 Henry, b. April 17, 1859.

11. Josephine^6 Rucker (Joshua^5, John^4, ———), b. Mch. 3, 1834, m. Ebenezer Smith, Dec. 10, 1855. Lived in La.

1. Margaret^7 Elizabeth Smith, b. Dec. 15, 1857.
2. Pliny^7 E., b. Jan. 28, 1859.
3. Maud^7 A., b. Aug. 5, 1861.
4. Ira^7 Gertrude, b. 1863, d. in infancy.

9. Isaac^5 Rucker (John^4, John^3, ———), Dec. 6, 1788-July 26, 1856), m. Agatha^5 Rucker (Abner^4, Anthony^3, John^2, ———), of Woodford County, Ky., who "died, Nov. 25, 1845, not having reached her fortieth year" (Family Bible).

1. Edward^6 Rucker, b. 1820, m. ——— Daniels; moved to Ill.
2. Nancy^6 Jane (1820-1852), unmar.
3. Susan^6 Margaret Rucker.
4. Martha^6 (1827-1908), m. Charles Ware, no children.

3. Susan^6 Rucker (Isaac^5, John^4, ———) (1825-1903), m. Dec. 24, 1861, James Hudson (Oct. 15, 1825-1883), b. near Athens, Fayette County, Ky.

1. William^7 Henry Hudson, b. 1864, m. 1895 Emma Bond, b. 1865.
    1. Leva^8 Ware Hudson, m. 1922 Wade Hampton George.
    2. James^8 Bond Hudson, m. 1924 Caroline Vincent Noel.
        1. Cecil^9 Noel Hudson, b. 1926.
    3. Susan^8 Belinda, m. 1918 Fred Ward.
        1. Nannie^9 Louise Ward, b. 1920.

10. Benjamin^5 Asbury Rucker (John^4, John^3, ———((June 9, 1790-Feb. 9, 1859), d. in Williamson County, Tenn., m. 1st Matilda^5 Rucker (William^4, John^3, ———) and 2nd, Elizabeth Waller. Lived in Nelson Co., Tenn.

Issue (by 1st mar.):

1. Virginia^6 Tennessee Rucker.
2. John^6 William Fletcher Rucker.
3. Benj.^{6} Lewis, b. Sept. 29, 1823, m. Mrs. Jane Smith Akerson, Dec. 13, 1858.
4. Robert^6 Henry (Feb. 19, 1825-Sept. 4, 1857).
5. Sarah^6 Ann (May 20, 1826-1830).
6. Melinda^6 Susan, b. Nov. 24, 1828, m. John Hart.
7. America^6, b. Oct. 20, 1831.

Issue (by 2nd mar.):

8. Thomas^6 W. Asbury, b. Feb. 4, 1834.
9. James^6 Price, b. Mch. 13, 1835.
10. Sterling^6 Brown, b. July 24, 1836.
11. Martha^6 E., b. May 9, 1838, m. Jonathan M. Rucker, of Ky.
12. Latimer^6 Blackman.
13. Jonathan^6 Harrison, b. Dec. 9, 1841.
14. David^6 O., b. Jan. 22, 1844.
15. Mary^6 S. A., b. Mch. 29, 1845.
16. Henriet^6 McKinley, b. Oct. 14, 1846.

1. Virginia^6 Tennessee Rucker (Benjamin^5 A., John^4, John^3, ———), b. Jan. 28, 1820, m. Wiley Saunders, Feb. 15, 1842.

1. Sarah^7 Melinda Saunders, b. May 25, 1850.
2. Asbury^7 Jerome, b. Nov. 16, 1852.
3. Lucy^7 Ewer, b. July 15, 1856.

2. John^6 William Fletcher Rucker (Benj.^{5} A., John^4, ——) (Jan. 1, 1822-Feb. 20, 1899), b. near Brentwood, ten miles from Nashville, Tenn., m. Tennessee Bumpus, Jan. 17, 1849.

1. Benjamin^7 F. Rucker (Dec. 3, 1849-Aug. 24, 1877).
2. John^7 William B. (June 18, 1852-Aug. 7, 1853).
3. Malinda^7 Elizabeth Rucker.
4. Harding^7 Billings Rucker.
5. John^7 Fletcher, b. May, 1859, m. Linnie F. Rucker.
6. Robert^7 Hatton, b. Nov. 29, 1861, m. Nannie Harding.
7. Susanna^7 Eugenia (Mch. 20, 1864-1878).
8. Abraham^7 Spottswood, b. Nov., 1866.
9. William^7 Edwards (Apr., 1869-1888).

3. Malinda^{7} Elizabeth Rucker (John^{6} W., Benj.^{5} A., John^{4}, ———), b. July 20, 1854, m. Howard Vaughan.

1. William^{8} Henry Vaughan, b. July 7, 1880.
    1. Nannie^{9} M. E. Vaughan.
    2. William^{9} Tracy Vaughan.
    3. Edna^{9} Earl.
    4. Ella^{9} Claire.
2. Benjamin^{8} A. Vaughan (June 13, 1883-1910), m. Hattie Horn.
    1. Edward^{9} Vaughan.
    2. Thelma^{9} Vaughan.
3. Martha^{8} Tennessee Vaughan, b. Apr. 2, 1888, m. T. A. Peach, June 9, 1907.
    1. Lula^{9} Belle Peach, b. June 21, 1911, Nashville, Tenn.
4. Nannie^{8} Belle Vaughan, b. June 4, 1889, m. C. A. Daniels, Dec. 25, 1909.
    1. Martha^{9} Elizabeth Daniels.
    2. Mary^{9} Rose Daniels.
5. Wm.^{8} Henry Rucker Vaughan, m. June, 1904, Jennie McCarthy.

4. Harding^{7} Billings Rucker (John^{6}, Benj.^{5}, John^{4}, ———), b. Nov. 2, 1856, m. Mary Elizabeth Boone, b. May 6, 1863, dau. of George Boone, of Sumner County, Tenn.

1. Horace^{8} Billings Rucker, b. July 15, 1883, Davidson Co., Tenn., m. Frances Theo. Hicks, Apr. 26, 1906.
    1. Frances^{9} Louise Rucker, b. Feb. 17, 1908.
2. Elizabeth^{8} Tennessee Rucker, b. Dec. 17, 1885, unmar.
3. William^{8} Edward Rucker, b. June 2, 1889, in Sumner Co., Tenn., m. Louise Petty, of Fort Worth, Tex., Sept. 18, 1922.
    1. Mary^{9} Belle Rucker, b. Sept. 27, 1924, Fort Worth, Tex.
4. Virginia^{8} Gertrude Rucker, b. Nov. 9, 1894, Sumner Co., Tenn., m. Mch. 14, 1920, Hubard Saunders, in Davidson Co., Tenn.
    1. Edward^{9} Saunders, b. Mch. 23, 1921, Davidson Co., Tenn.
    2. Betty^{9} Jane Saunders, b. Dec. 12, 1922.

5. Marvin^{8} Irvin Rucker, b. July 3, 1897, Sumner Co., m. Hazel Marie Brunnell, July 3, 1917, in Hamilton, Ohio.
    1. Katheryn^{9} Marie Rucker, b. Mch. 10, 1919.
    2. Mary^{9} Evelyn Rucker, b. Apr. 25, 1921.

11. Lewis^{5} Dawson Rucker (John^{4}, John^{3}, ———) (Sept. 13, 1794-July 1, 1869), m. 1st Margaret Goddard, 2nd Amelia Brancamp, and 3rd Hannah Krouse, Georgetown, Ky.

Issue (by 1st mar.):

1. Henry^{6} McDaniel Rucker, of Paris, Ky.
2. Margaret^{6} Ann Rucker, b. Apr. 24, 1839.
3. Mary^{6} Catherine Rucker.
4. John^{6} Alphus Rucker.
5. Joseph^{6} Barnett Rucker.

1. Henry^{6} McDaniel Rucker (Lewis^{5}, John^{4}, John^{3}, ———), b. Sept. 22, 1820, m. Fannie S. Scott, of Jassamine Co., Ky., Nov. 1, 1849.

1. Henry^{7} Rucker, b. Dec. 4, 1850, m. Julia A. Allen, of Mo., Dec. 3, 1874. He is a lawyer of Georgetown, Ky.
2. William^{7} Richardson, b. July, 1855.

3. Mary^{6} Catherine Rucker (Lewis^{5}, John^{4}, John^{3}, ———), b. May 23, 1833, m. William J. Rusk. Lived in La.

1. Martha^{7} Leonora Rusk, b. Feb. 15, 1853.
2. Mary^{7} Urzilla Rusk.
3. William^{7} Lewis Rusk.

2. Mary^{7} Urzilla Rusk (Mary^{6}, Lewis^{5}, John^{4}, ———), b. Nov. 25, 1855, m. Clarence Hetherwick, of Cheneyville, La.

1. Mary^{8} Catherine Tanner.
2. Clarence^{8} Hetherwick.
3. Hettie^{8} Campbell.
4. Clara^{8} Hetherwick.
5. Jefferson^{8} Hetherwick.
6. Elba^{8} Tanner.
7. Minnie^{8} Hetherwick.
8. Septimus^{8} Hetherwick.
9. Sidney^{8} Hetherwick.
10. Edwin^{8} Hetherwick.

3. William^{7} Lewis Rusk (Mary^{6}, Lewis^{5}, John^{4}, ———), b. Dec. 25, 1857, m. Lilly Rucker, of New York. They lived in Kentucky.

1. Mary^{8} Urzilla Rusk.

4. John^{6} Alphus Rucker (Lewis^{5}, John^{4}, ———), b. Nov. 4, 1838, m. Rachel ———, of La.

  1. Edwin^{7} Augustus Rucker, m. Emma ———, of New Orleans.
     1. Emma^{8} Rucker.
     2. Edwin^{8} A. Rucker, Jr.

5. Joseph^{6} Barrett Rucker (Lewis^{5}, John^{4}, ———) (Nov. 16, 1842-Sept. 19, 1892), m. Anne Hamilton, of Ky.

  1. Robert^{7} Hamilton Rucker, of New York.
  2. Lilly^{7} Rucker, of New York.
  3. Kathryn^{7} Rucker de Quélin, of New York.

4. Susan^{4} Rucker (John^{3}, John^{2}, Peter^{1}), m. Reuben Cowherd (son of James and Elizabeth Cowherd, of Orange Co., who died in 1756, leaving a will in which he mentioned son Jonathan, m. Sarah Kirtly, son James and son Reuben), Reuben moved to Shelby Co., Ky.

5. George^{4} Rucker (John^{3}, John^{2}, ———), b. in Amherst, 1754, d. 1818 in Bedford, m. Martha Tucker, dau. of Drury and Susanna (Douglass) Tucker. George's father willed him half his land in Bedford Co., on Elk Creek. See Tucker line.

In 1780, he bought 100 acres of land in Bedford, on Elk Creek from Abraham North. Again, in 1804, he bought from John North and wife, Lucy, and Susanna North, 285 acres of land on Elk Creek, and 96 acres in 1813.

George also owned land in Bourbon and Woodford Counties, Ky. In 1806, he appointed his brother, John Rucker, of Woodford Co., and Thomas Camady, of Bourbon Co., his attorney to collect rents from Benjamin Penn of the above counties (D. B. 11, p. 253, Bedford Co.).

He built his house on an elevation at the foot of No Business Mountain, extending to the west overlooking a beautiful valley called Pleasant Vale through which flows Elk Creek, at the foot of Rocky and Buck Mts. toward the east. Further down this valley is to be seen the place where his brother, William, lived. This was inherited by his son, Bernard. The family burying ground is near the old place of George Rucker's, now owned by his great-grandson, Waller Rucker.

George Rucker and wife, Martha, of Bedford, sold his part in the estate of Drury Tucker, Feb. 5, 1807 (D. B. K). See Tucker.

He was ordained a Baptist minister in 1803. On Dec. 25, 1803, he officiated as minister at the marriage of his niece, Nancy Rucker, and John Douglas.

There was a George Rusher, son of Andrew, of Bedford Co., that is sometime confused with George Rucker of the same County, the following court record is the service of Rusher and not of Rucker (O. B. 1774-82), Sept. 28, 1774, Bedford Co. George Rusher proved to the satisfaction of the court that he had served in Col. Byrd's campaign in 1760 and that he had never transferred his claim to any land he was entitled to for that service, which was ordered to be certified in the Register Land Office.

He was a private in the Battle of Point Pleasants in 1774. See Campbell's *History of Virginia,* p. 582; Wayland's *History of Rockingham,* p. 450; *Dunmore's Wars,* p. 405, and Atkinson's *History of Kanawha County,* p. 34, state that the Bedford troops at the battle of Point Pleasants were under Capt. Buford.

W. B. 5, p. 229, Bedford County, October Court 1818. Estate of George Rucker appraised: 16 slaves, 6 horses, 15 head sheep, 28 hogs, 15 head cattle, 12 dishes, 40 plates, 3 bowls, 1 set white ware, 6 silver table spoons and 12 tea spoons, 7 Windsor chairs, 2 looking glasses, 8 beds and furniture, 3 spinning wheels, etc. His estate was divided in November, 1818. The legatees were: William Ballenger, Susan, Daniel, and Mrs. Rucker. Jonathan and William B. were administrators.

George Rucker and Martha, his wife, were mentioned in the settlement of the estate of his father-in-law, Drury Tucker, in Amherst (W. B. 4, p. 25; 1798-1801). See Tucker.

Martha d. Nov. 26, 1840. The appraisement of her estate was recorded Dec. 12, her son, Wm. B. Rucker being one of the administrators. Legatees in the appraisement were: Capt. Nelson Thompson; heirs of Elizabeth Hatcher, dec'd; heirs of Daniel Rucker, dec'd; and James and William Ballenger Rucker.

In 1840 a division of slaves was made among the children of George and Martha Rucker.

Issue:

1. Susan[5] Rucker.
2. Elizabeth[5] Rucker.
3. Daniel[5] Rucker.
4. Sarah[5] Rucker.
5. Jonathan[5] Rucker.
6. James[5] Rucker.
7. William Ballenger[5] Rucker.

1. Susan^{5} Rucker (George^{4}, John^{3}, John^{2}, ———), m. Capt. Nelson A. Thompson Oct. 13, 1830; no children; her will Dec., 1840 (W. B. 10, p. 364, Bedford).

2. Elizabeth^{5} Rucker (George^{4}, John^{3}, ———), m. Jeremiah Hatcher Dec. 24, 1800, in Bedford Co.; witness George Rucker.

3. Daniel^{5} Rucker (George^{4}, John^{3}, ———), d. 1833, m. Elizabeth Bourne, of Amherst, Oct. 25, 1813, dau. of Henry Bourne, dec'd. The marriage bond was signed by John Brown. Daniel was paying taxes in Bedford in 1819, later he moved to Bourbon Co., Ky. A deed signed by Daniel Rucker and his wife, Elizabeth, of Bourbon Co., Oct. 13, 1825, to a sale of 47 acres on Rocky Mts. for $100 to Lee Milner of Bedford Co., is on record. This land was bought by Daniel on Nov. 1, 1813, from Tammerlane Davis and wife, Jane, for $75.

His health was failing so he decided to visit his old home and family in Bedford Co., Va. Below is a part of a letter written to his wife, Elizabeth, but addressed to Stokley Rion in Ky.

Bedford Co. Va. October 16th, 1832.

My Dear Wife: Iv'e set down to write you and family a few lines to let you know my situation and health every since I left home till the present. I traveled by myself till the fourth day before I got with any company and then overtook two gentlemen that were traveling to Virginia from the Mo. County and found them very agreeable companions. I overtook them at the mouth of the Big Sandy River on the state line and we continued together till we got to Charlestown on the Kanawha River and there we overtook General Andrew Jackson and Young Mr. Brethert, his company keeper. Brethert is a brother of our present Governor of Ky. We all traveled together for several days until we got to the White Sulphur Springs and there we parted from each other. I found the old gentleman to be very much a gentleman indeed, and so was Mr. Brethert, so that we spent the time with a great deal of satisfaction together. I am much better pleased with the general than I was before, if possible. He is a plain old gentleman and smokes his pipe and converses freely on different subjects, not on polytics, but other subjects.

Tell Mr. Mitchell and his friends to still persevere in the good cause of Liberty and for to be sure and attend at the election and the victory is ours without a doubt. No more on that subject. I arrived at mothers on Saturday the 13th, which made me eleven days on the road, and have enjoyed better health than

I could have expected, but am not well as yet, but think that I am still mending and have gained in flesh some since I left home but still retain some misery in the brest and shoulders at times, but I hope nothing very serious. My appetite has remained very good every since I started. I expect to start to Mr. Carter's to-morrow morning and Brother William will go with me. I am told that your Brother William has bought land in Nelson County near New Glasgow and is living there, but not married as yet. My horses performed very well, Ned took the Destemper on the road and has reduced some and so had Kit reduced some, but not very much. Jose is about the same, but have done nothing with them as yet but intend to bring Jose back with me if he lives. I found my friends all on Elk Creek tolerable well except my old mother, which is very poorly indeed at the present, but she tells me that she is much better than she has been, she, by the help of her cain, can get to the front porch to look out but with much difficulty. She is low in flesh and very weak and has lost the use of one of her hands entirely and shows old age but I think she bears up under her difficulties more than could be expected of a person in her situation.

Sally appears to enjoy a moderate portion of health and has not broke much. William and Family are tolerable well, I have not as yet seen Jonathan nor James. Captain Thomas and Family are all well. Have not been to Jermiah Hatchers as yet. Monroe's and James' two eldest children are going to school from Mothers at this time.

I am at a loss to say when I shall be at home. As yet, I have done none of my business but shall be there as soon as the nature of the case will admit. I want you to tell Will to attend to business and let nothing be neglected on his part while I am absent. Also tell all the rest of the blacks the same, especially Isaac and Stuban. Tell John Row that I want him to use all the care that he possible can with my horses and wagons as I don't mean that he shall loose anything by me. Be careful of fire in the houses, particularly in the hitching and tobacco houses. I hasten to a close, hoping that these lines find you and all my family well. Tell my children all houdy, Robert included with the rest. Give my love to S. Rion and Marthann and N. Rion and Mr. Joseph Mitchell and Mrs. Mitchell, Mr. Wheat and family and all of my beloved neighbors that inquire after me. Mother and Sally send their love to you and all of my children, Mr. Rion and Marthann. Tell Stokely that I want him to attend to my business as much as he can conveniently. I begin to want to see you all, so fairwell. I remain your friend and husband till death.

Daniel Rucker.

The following letter is written by Phebe Bourne, the wife of Joseph R. Carter, of Amherst, to her sister, Elizabeth B. Rucker, of Ky.

Amherst County, Va. April 24th 1841.

Dear Sister,

It has been a long time since we have received a letter from you or heard anything particularly about you until two days past we were visited by Wm. Estill, your son-in-law. We were highly pleased at his visit (though it was very short) and to hear from you, your children, etc. We were not informed whether you received a letter from us by Brother Creed, on his return to Mo. some four years ago, or not, in which we gave you the number of children and other particulars, and presuming that that letter was not received, we will state that we have nine children their names are as follows commencing at the eldest: Robert Abram Henry, Susan Mary, Amanda, Elizabeth Ann, Sarah Agnes and Malinda Frances twins, William Bourne, Leanna Jane and Joseph Creed the youngest nearly five years old. Susan Mary has been married about four years, she married William M. Davis son to Francis S. K. Davis Decd. She has two children, a daughter whom they call Mary Elizabeth and a son named Joseph Francis, they and our eldest son went to Missouri last fall, we have received several letters from them since their arrival there from which we learn that they are pleased with the country and seem to be satisfied. Brother Wm. Bourne is still living a widower, he was well on Monday last. He lives about twenty miles from us in Nelson County. He has four children living one son and three daughters all grown, his eldest daughter married a man by name, Nathaniel Mantiply she is dead left one child a son, who is living with his Grand Pa. Bourne, his name is Wm. Henry. It has been something like fifteen years since we received a letter from Brother Henry until about two months ago, he is living in Elbert County, Ga. and should you write to him direct to Cooks Law Office, He writes that in 1833 he married the Widow Mary Hearce, since which time they have had four children two are living viz Henry William and Pawhatan Barnard, Henry is six years old and Pawhatan going on three. He owns some 5 or 6 thousand acres of land about 18 slaves, and stands unrivaled in his profession, some years ago he fought a duel with broad swords with a man of superior strength and got worsted. Step Mother Bourne is living within about six miles of us with her Brother Peter Cashwell, I have not seen her for something near two years. She does not enjoy good health. Hannah the black woman and her son left her by Father, are both dead. Milly Cashwell is also dead. The Widow Hansard is living near Step-Mother. Sister

Nancy Bourne's children are all married except John Benjamin the youngest son. Wm. Henry married Mary Drummond and has several children. Mary Ann married John Cruse, they have two children, both daughters. They live near Lynchburg. He follows a very profitable Business. Father and Mother Carter are both living, his age is 78 years, she is seven years younger, they enjoy tolerable health for persons of their age. Brother Robert has never married, he lives with them. We omited to mention in a proper place that Jane Bourne, the youngest daughter of Bro. John married a man by the name of John Bailor, they, we believe live in Augusta County in this state, and have one child a son. Brother John Davis lives within a mile of us, is the Pastor of the Baptist Church to which we belong, his family is well. Sister Davis desired to be remembered in love to you, she has three daughters and 5 sons. Two of her daughters are married, one of them a Dr. Gibson who is practicing medicine in this neighborhood with success. Dr. C. B. Gilbert is also a near neighbor of ours. He married his cousin Martha Dibell. They have four children 2 sons and 2 daughters. Wm. Estill only staid with us some two or three hours, but he has promised to bring you and his wife on a visit to see us next fall come year, and should the Lord spare us until that time, I will anticipate a happy meeting, and should it not be in his good pleasure to permit us to see each other in this world we have a hope through faith in the Lord Jesus Christ that we shall be permitted to enjoy his presence and praise his name forever and ever, for which let us pray continualy. Our children unite with us in love to you, to your husband, to Wm. Rion and cousin Martha and her children and to cousin Cordelia. Farewell.

Phebe Carter.

After Daniel Rucker's death in Ky. and that of his mother, Martha, in 1840 in Bedford, the heirs in Ky., in 1841 demanded a quick settlement judging from the following record found in Bedford.

"1841 Stokeley T. Rion and William Estell, the heirs-at-law of Daniel Rucker, deceased, late of the County of Bourbon, State of Kentucky, who was a son and heir-at-law of George Rucker of the State of Virginia, gave Power of Attorney to Benjamin Estell of said County of Bourbon to demand, sue for and receive from Jonathan Rucker of Bedford Co., Va., personal representative of George Rucker, deceased, and from all others such sums of money, slaves and other property including land as was due to said Daniel Rucker in his life time, in order to obtain for us the whole proceeds of the said George and Daniel Rucker and also to execute a Deed for land already sold."

Daniel certainly had two daughters, the wives of Stokeley T. Rion and William Estell, and possibly more children.

1. dau.^{6}, m. William Estell.
   1. William^7 Estell, m. Cordelia Rucker.
2. Martha^6 Ann Rucker (Mch. 2, 1815-Sept. 20, 1864), m. Stokeley Towles Rion.
   1. Stokeley^7 Towles Rion.
   2. William^7 Rion.
   3. Daniel^7 Rion.
   4. Susan^7 Rion, m. Robert Pollock Dow.
   5. Pauline^7 Rion, m. John Brown, no issue.
   6. George^7 Rion m. Annie Oldson.
      1. Stokely^8 T. Rion.
   7. Martha^7 Ann Rion m. Frank Oldson.
   8. James^7 Berryman Rion.

8. James^7 Berryman Rion (Martha^6, Daniel^5, George^4, ———) (Mch. 9, 1847-Nov. 4, 1903), m. Martha Jane Current.

1. Martha^8 Jane Rion m. Thomas J. Current.
2. Annie^8 Lee Rion m. G. Y. Reynolds.
3. Myrtle^8 Rion.
4. George^8 Rion (dec'd).
5. James^8 Berryman Rion.

4. Sarah^5 Rucker (George^4, John^3, John^2, ———), invalid, unmar., lived with parents.

5. Jonathan^5 Rucker (George^4, John^3, ———) (Feb. 25, 1782-1850), m. Oct. 20, 1808, Margaret Hatcher, "of full age", dau. of Rev. Jeremiah Hatcher, a Baptist Minister of Bedford. They lived at the home place of Jonathan's father, George, after his younger brother, William B., moved to Amherst.

Beside owning his share of his father's land, he bought 260 acres on Nobusiness Mts. from Edward G. Watkin, adjoining George and William Rucker, Feb., 1818 (D. B. 13, p. 828). On May 10, 1817, he bought 197½ acres on Goose Creek from William Haynes and his wife, Agnes, adjoining Dawson (D. B. 15, p. 198). In 1825 he bought 118 acres more on Goose Creek.

1. James^6 Monroe Rucker (Feb. 9, 1814-June 4, 1878), m. Dec. 9, 1837, Marinda^5 McDaniel (Lodowick^4, George^3, George^2, John^1) (Mch. 27, 1818-July 2, 1889).

Issue:

1. Marianna^{7} Rucker.
2. Sarah^{7} Margaret Rucker.
3. Albon^{7} McDaniel Rucker.
4. Eliza^{7} Rucker.
5. Lodowick^{7} Rucker (1846-July 19, 1875), unmar.
6. Virginia^{7} Catherine Rucker.
7. Warren^{7} Dulaney Rucker.
8. Waller^{7} Jonathan Rucker.
9. Marinda^{7} Rucker.
10. Lelia^{7} Vixella Rucker (July 10, 1858-June 6, 1878), unmar.

1. Marianna^{7} Rucker (James^{6}, Jonathan^{5}, George^{4}, ———) (July 29, 1838-June 8, 1888), m. July 1855 Daniel^{6} H. Rucker (William^{5}, George^{4}, ———) (see page ——).

2. Sarah^{7} Margaret Rucker (James^{6}, Jonathan^{5}, ———) (Dec. 2, 1839-Mch. 24, 1922), m. Dec. 13, 1859, William A. Almond, of Lynchburg, who d. Mch. 9, 1914.

1. Olive^{8} Almond (1863-1927), m. Fuller Kinnear.
2. Lucy^{8} Almond, b. May 17, 1867; m. Oct. 12, 1897, W. C. Harrell, d. Sept., 1923, Newport News, Va.
    1. William^{9} Almond Harrell, b. 1898.
    2. Olive^{9} Harrell, b. 1900.
    3. Charles^{9} McDaniel Harrell, b. 1902, Bluefield, W. Va.
    4. Ernest^{9} Ashby Harrell, b. 1904.

3. Albon^{7} McDaniel Rucker (James^{6}, Jonathan^{5}, ———) (1842-Mch. 1863), d. from wounds received in Battle of Gettysburg.

4. Eliza^{7} Rucker (James^{6}, Jonathan^{5}, ———) (June 23, 1844-July 15, 1909), m. Nov. 22, 1865, Charles H. Almond, of Lynchburg.

6. Virginia^{7} Catherine Rucker (James^{6}, Jonathan^{5}, ———) (Apr. 24, 1849-Feb. 13, 1883), m. June 2, 1869, Albert^{2} S. Burks (Martin), (see Burks line).

7. Warren^{7} Dulaney Rucker (James^{6}, Jonathan^{5}, ———) (Jan. 20, 1851-Jan. 31, 1919), m. May 5, 1874, Lucy Jane Turpin, of Bedford Co.

Issue:

1. Hugh^{8} Rucker, d. young.
2. Edward^{8} Rucker, d. young.
3. Mabel^{8} Virginia Rucker, m. Robert Carey Nickols, Roanoke, Va.
   1. Robert^{9} Carey Nickols, Jr.
4. Lelia^{8} Ashby Rucker, m. Harry Hale Derrick, Civil Engineer, W. Va.

8. Waller^{7} Jonathan Rucker (James^{6}, Jonathan^{5}, George^{4}, ———), b. Dec. 27, 1852, m. Russelle^{7} McDaniel (John^{6}, James^{5}, William^{4}, John^{3}, George^{2}, John^{1} McDaniel), Jan. 15, 1879. They lived at the homestead of his ancestors, George and Martha Tucker Rucker, on Elk Creek, Bedford Co.

1. Claude^{8} Nelson Rucker, M. D.
2. Vernon^{8} Ashby Rucker.
3. Waller^{8} Rucker.
4. Marianna^{8} Blanche Rucker.
5. Aline^{8} Rucker.
6. Marion^{8} Glenn Rucker, b. 9 Sept. 1895.
7. Lelia^{8} Vixella Rucker.
8. Reginold^{8} Rochester Rucker.

1. Claude^{8} Nelson Rucker (Waller^{7}, James^{6}, ———), b. 21 Mch. 1880; m. 14 May 1904, Emma M. Hooper, b. 8 July 1882, Charleston, W. Va.

1. Marinda^{9} Catherine Rucker, b. 21 Jan. 1906; m. 4 Sept. 1926, Frank Nathaniel Eklund, Lieut. in U. S. Navy.
2. Erle^{9} Taliaferro Rucker, b. 21 Apr. 1907.
3. Claude^{9} Nelson Rucker, Jr., b. 14 Oct. 1911.
4. Eleanor^{9} Warren Rucker, b. 24 Dec. 1915.
5. Rhodes^{9} Stockton Rucker, b. 24 Apr. 1921.

2. Vernon^{8} Ashby Rucker (Waller^{7}, James^{6}, ———), b. 8 July 1882; m. 20 Dec. 1925 Lorraine Roadcap, Roanoke.

1. Henry^{9} Rex Mann Rucker, b. 8 Dec. 1926.

3. Waller^{8} Rucker (Waller^{7}, James^{6}, ———), b. May 15, 1885; m. Feb., 1914, Katherine Nelson Elliott (Dec. 9, 1894-1919).

Issue:

1. Gerald^{9} Rucker (Nov. 16, 1914-1915).
2. Margaret^{9} Virginia Rucker, b. 10 Mch. 1916.

4. Marianna^{8} Blanche Rucker (Waller^{7}, James^{6}, ———), b. Sept. 5, 1888; m. May 3, 1924, Cecil Dubois Rainey, at Leesburg, Va.

1. Samuel^{9} Charles Rainey, b. 12 July, 1927, in Manilla.
2. Robert Cecil Rainey, b. Sept. 15, 1928, in Lynchburg, Va.
3. David Miller, b. Sept. 25, 1930.

5. Aline^{8} Mallard Rucker (Walter^{7}, James^{6}, ———), b. May 19, 1893, m. Nov. 8, 1912, Robert Allen Conard.

1. Robert^{9} Allen Conard, Jr., b. July 29, 1913.
2. Aline^{9} Russell Conard, b. Oct. 3, 1914.
3. Joan^{9} Conard, b. May 26, 1916.
4. Joy^{9} Conard, b. Nov. 20, 1927.

7. Lelia^{8} Vixella Rucker (Waller^{7}, James^{6}, ———), b. July 30, 1898, m. John Lewis White, June 11, 1920.

1. Lewis^{9} Marion (Jack) White, b. Aug. 22, 1921.
2. Philip^{9} Ashby White, b. June 14, 1923.
3. Barbara^{9} Jeanne White, b. Aug. 30, 1925.
4. Polly^{9} Pendleton White, b. Aug. 26, 1928.

8. Reginald^{8} Rochester Rucker (Waller^{7}, James^{6}, ———), b. June 27, 1901, m. July 15, 1925, Thelma Kavanaugh.

1. Bettie^{9} Lou Rucker, b. May 31, 1927.

9. Marinda^{7} Rucker (James^{6}, Jonathan^{5}, ———) (1854-Dec. 26, 1885), m. Jan. 13, 1876, John^{6} Celphas Rucker (John^{5}, Rueben^{4}, Isaac^{3}, John^{2}, Peter^{1}).

7. William^{5} Ballenger Rucker (George^{4}, John^{3}, John^{2}, Peter^{1}), b. Dec. 11, 1791, in Bedford and d. Dec. 18, 1861, in Amherst, m. Dec. 25, 1822, Mary Ann Dawson Rucker (Jan. 11, 1809-Mch. 11, 1863), the dau. of his second cousin, Ambrose Rucker, of Amherst. He took his bride to his father's home in Pleasant Vale, Bedford Co.; later he built a log house near his father's home, where several children were born. These children died and were buried in his father's grave yard near the house.

William B. sold his land in Bedford, buying at Pleasant View in Amherst Co. on Horsley's Creek, and building his home facing the valley on three sides (with the Tobacco Row Mt. to the south east) at the foot of Turkey Run Mts. to the north west. They attended New Prospect church about a mile distant.

Now, the farm has been sold, and fifteen farmers own it. The house tract is owned by the great niece of Mr. Barnes, who was the overseer for William Ballenger Rucker. The grave yard is back of the house in the usual state of old burying grounds. There may be as many as one hundred sunken graves with unmarked stone markers. Only three have marble stones, Wm. B. Rucker, his wife, Mary Ann Dawson Rucker, and a child of their only dau., Susan Smith, named Mary Willie Smith. William[5] B. died of typhoid fever contracted from nursing his son, William Ambrose, in Aug., 1861, who had taken it in the army.

William B. Rucker was a very successful business man, owning about nine hundred acres of land in Amherst, 654 acres home tract and two others containing 114½ and 136½ acres. The writer has a tax receipt from Amherst County, dated May 21, 1866, for $28.42 paid on 905 acres of land for the estate of William B. Rucker; signed Jas. P. Barlouey, Collector.

William B. was very deaf, always carrying a slate and pencil with him. He was a private under Capt. James Leftwich, of Bedford Co. militia in the war of 1812 (Archives, Richmond, Va.), was paid for services, allotted to the command of Maj. Woodford, of Bedford, 3 Sept. 1814, served with John Rucker.

Will of William Ballenger Rucker, Amherst Co., Va., dated Dec. 27, 1860, probated Feb. 17, 1862. I give to my wife, Mary Ann Dawson, 12 negroes during her natural life, also my manor house tract of land. To sons Addison C., Daniel A., and William A. Rucker, and dau. Susan M. Smith. Executors: "My Friend", A. B. Rucker and my son, D. H. Rucker. Witness: Joseph R. Carter, William H. Barnes, and James M. Watts (W. B. 16, p. 121).

Issue:

1. Daniel[6] H. Rucker.
2. Susan[6] Margaret Rucker.
3. William[6] Ambrose Rucker.
4. Addison[6] Clay Rucker.

1. Daniel[6] H. Rucker (William[5] B., George[4], John[3], John[2], Peter[1]) (Dec. 14, 1835-Aug. 25, 1908), m. July 29, 1856, Marianna[7] Rucker (James[6] Monroe, Jonathan[5], George[4], John[3], ——) (Oct. 15, 1838-June 8, 1888), of Bedford. He lived in Amherst Co., near Salt Creek, where all of his children were born, and where his wife died. Later he moved to Buena Vista where he

was Clerk of Rockbridge Co. until his death. The farm in Amherst is now owned by Joe Watts, and formerly by Martin Parks.

1. Parks[7] M. Rucker.
2. Laura[7] Rucker.
3. George[7] Hilton Rucker.
4. Daniel[7] Henry Rucker.
5. Albon[7] McDaniel Rucker.
6. Sudie[7] M. Rucker.
7. Henry[7] Smith Rucker.
8. Marinda[7] James Monroe Rucker.
9. Ella[7] Blanche Rucker.
10. Margaret[7] Virginia Rucker.

1. Parks[7] McDaniel Rucker (Daniel[6], William[5] B., George[4], ———) (Apr. 27, 1857-Jan. 25, 1918), m. Dec. 7, 1879, Katherine Louise Eubank, b. Feb. 11, 1895, Amherst. They lived at his father's home in Amherst, after his removal to Rockbridge.

1. Annie[8] Byrd Rucker, b. May 4, 1881, m. J. W. Brown, 1902.
2. John[8] Eubank Rucker, b. Dec. 17, 1884, m. Margaret B., 1912.
3. Daniel[8] H. Rucker, b. Sept. 17, 1886, m. Eva Bruffy, 1910.
4. George[8] Anna Rucker, b. Feb. 23, 1888, m. Margaret Witt, 1914.
5. Elizabeth[8] Rucker, b. Oct. 5, 1890, m. C. T. Rice, 1916.
6. William[8] Williams Rucker, b. Mch. 21, 1892, m. Hazel Quick, 1917.
7. Henry[8] English Rucker, b. Nov. 30, 1896, m. Bertha Alder, 1918.
8. Robert[8] Rucker, b. July 27, 1898, m. Gladys Pritchett Detwiler, 1920.

2. Laura[7] Rucker (Daniel[6], William[5] B., ———), b. Aug. 30, 1858, m. Joseph Cunningham, of Amherst.

1. Mary[8] Rucker, m. Dr. Pitt Edward Tucker, of Buckingham.
2. Lelia[8] Vixella Rucker, m. Dr. Joseph M. Brown, of Amherst.
3. John[8] Daniel Rucker.
4. Joseph[8] H. Rucker.

3. George[7] Hilton Rucker (Daniel[6], ———) (May 28, 1862-Aug. 24, 1919), m. June 29, 1892, Elizabeth Council, b. Mch. 24, 1871.

1. Mariamna[8] Councill Rucker, b. Apr. 21, 1893, m. Norris Loring Bowen, Apr. 5, 1914.

   1. Carey[9] Bell Bowen, b. Feb. 16, 1915.
   2. Norris[9] Loring Bowen, Jr., b. Aug. 18, 1917.
   3. George[9] Haldane Bowen, b. May 25, 1919.

2. Claudia[8] White Rucker, b. Nov. 6, 1894, m. Feb. 5, 1916, William Morrell Stone.

   1. Elizabeth[9] Wyllys Stone, b. Aug. 9, 1917.
   2. William[9] Leete Stone, b. Oct. 6, 1923.

4. Daniel[7] Henry Rucker (Daniel[6], ———) (Aug. 25, 1866-June, 1924), m. Feb. 12, 1902, Beulah Schermerhorn, of Hampton, Va.

1. Catherine[8] Ann Rucker.
2. Beulah[8] L. Rucker.

5. Albon[7] McDaniel Rucker (Daniel[6], ———), b. May 4, 1868, m. Apr. 23, 1898, Catherine Kennon Williams, d. 1929.

1. Katherine[8] Kennon Rucker.
2. Albon[8] Mack Rucker, Jr., of Buena Vista, Va.

6. Sudie[7] Margaret Rucker (Daniel[6], ———), b. May 4, 1870, m. Nov. 23, 1898, Frank Davies Cunningham.

7. Henry[7] Smith Rucker (Daniel[6], ———) (Mch. 9, 1813-Jan., 1930), m. Dec. 12, 1906, Verna May Hodges, b. Oct. 5, 1875.

1. Georgia[8] Marianna Rucker, b. Nov. 28, 1909.
2. Henry[8] Smith Rucker, Jr., b. Aug. 15, 1913.

8. Marinda[7] James Monroe Rucker (Daniel[6], ———), b. Feb. 16, 1876, m. Nov. 16, 1904, Dr. Clarence Porter Jones, of Newport News, Va.

1. Clarence[8] Porter Jones, Jr., b. Aug. 10, 1909.
2. Sudie[8] Elizabeth Jones, b. May 14, 1914.

9. Ella[7] Blanche Rucker (Daniel[6], ———), b. Feb. 7, 1879, m. Nov. 16, 1904, N. A. Rees, b. Apr. 17, 1871. Live at Clarendon, Va.

Issue:

1. Margaret[8] Virginia Rees, b. May 18, 1909, m. Tracy Elmer Strevey, Dec. 27, 1930.
2. Elizabeth[8] Ann Rees, b. Nov. 1, 1911.

10. Margaret[7] Virginia Rucker (Daniel[6], ———), b. Jan. 13, 1881, m. Jan. 8, 1908, Ashton C. Jones (nephew of Dr. Clarence Porter Jones), b. July 9, 1879.

1. Ashton[8] C. Jones, Jr., b. July 21, 1909.
2. John[8] Rucker Jones, b. May 8, 1914.

2. Susan[6] Margaret Rucker (William[5] B., George[4], John[3], ———) (June 1, 1838-1920), m. July 28, 1852, Dr. Henry Smith, d. June 17, 1888, and lived at Nimrod Hall, Bath County.

1. Mary[7] Willie Smith, d. young.
2. Annie[7] Byrd Smith, m. Edward A. Watson, of England.

3. William[6] Ambrose Rucker (William[5] Ballenger, George[4], John[3], John[2], Peter[1]), was born in Amherst County, Aug. 20, 1840, and died in Richmond, Nov. 7, 1822. On Nov. 28, 1862, with the Rev. Thaddeus Herndon officiating, he married Annie Chappelear, who was born June 7, 1838, near Flint Hill, Rappahannock County (see Chappelear line), and died in Richmond, May 16, 1922. She was married at her father's home, "Woodside", in Fauquier County. William Ambrose took his bride to his old homestead at Pleasant View, in Amherst County. There they lived about five years. On May 19, 1884, he sold his farm of 373 acres on Horsley's Creek, given him by his father, having already moved to Fauquier County, to "Ridgeville", near Delaplane, on a farm given to his wife by her father, Benjamin Chappelear. "Ridgeville", now owned by William's youngest son, Bayard Ambrose Rucker, is a mile distant from "Woodside".

William A. Rucker joined the army at the beginning of the war and was sent at once to Fairfax. He was in the 2nd Virginia Cavalry, Company E, under Col. Radford, later under Col. Thomas E. Mumford. The original officers were Edgar Whitehead as captain; Thomas Whitehead and Valentine Rucker, 1st and 2nd lieutenants, and William Ambrose Rucker, sergeant of company E. William A. Rucker was in both battles of Manassas and in the Valley Campaign under Stonewall Jackson.

He was a Master Mason, belonging to the Warren Lodge, No 33, of Amherst County. The writer has his letter of transfer from this lodge, dated Apr. 29, 1872, to Fauquier Co. (See Chappelear).

1. William^7 Ballenger Rucker.
2. Benjamin^7 Chappelear Rucker.
3. Mary^7 Matilda Rucker.
4. Dana^7 H. Rucker.
5. Claude^7 Pendleton Rucker.
6. Sudie^7 S. Rucker.
7. Annie^7 Lee Rucker.
8. Bayard^7 Ambrose Rucker.
9. Lillian^7 Eliza Rucker.

1. William^7 Ballenger Rucker (Wm.^{6} A., Wm.^{5} B., George^4, John^3, John^2, Peter^1), b. Nov. 3, 1863, in Amherst County, d. in Urbanna, Va., Apr. 16, 1924; will dated Dec. 2, 1908, probated in 1924, m. Beulah Parrish, of Urbanna, Sept. 8, 1902; lived for a while in Loudoun Co., then Middlesex(see p. ——). No heirs.

2. Benjamin^7 Chappelear Rucker (Wm.^{6} A., ———) (May 30, 1865-Aug., 1929), moved to San Francisco, and there he 1st m. Mch. 10, 1888, Pauline Stockhouse, d. June 8, 1889, 2nd m. Ozeita Staniford, of Berkley, Calif.

Issue (by 1st mar.):

1. C.^{8} W. Rucker, unmar.

Issue (by 2nd mar.):

2. Virginia^8 Rucker.
3. Bayard^8 Ambrose Rucker, graduate of University of California.

3. Mary^7 Matilda Rucker (Wm.^{6} A., ———), b. Dec. 28, 1866, m. Rev. Benjamin R. Hudson, July 20, 1895.

1. Garnet^8 R. Hudson.

4. Dana^7 H. Rucker (Wm.^{6} A., ———), b. Jan. 28, 1868, m. Oct. 10, 1895, Lucy E. Harrison, dau. of Edmund^8 Harrison (professor of Latin at old Richmond College for 29 years), and his wife, Kate Steger, dau. of Major John Overton Steger and his wife, Mary Jane Gaines. Edmund^8 Harrison was son of Prof. William^7 Henry Harrison, of Wigwam, Amelia, son of Edmund^6 Harrison, of "The Oaks", Amelia, son of Nathaniel^5, b. at Berkly, son of Benjamin^4, Benjamin^3, Benjamin^2, Benjamin^1 Harrison. Dana is principal of William Fox School in Richmond, a graduate

of Staunton Military Academy, received his B. A. at Richmond College, and M. A. at Columbia University, N. Y.

1. Edmund[8] Harrison Rucker.
2. Dana[8] H. Rucker.
3. William[8] Harrison Rucker.
4. Kate[8] Stegar. Rucker.

1. Edmund[8] Harrison Rucker (Dana[7], Wm.[6] A., ———), b. Feb. 18, 1898, graduate of University of Richmond, served as lieutenant in the World War, m. Oct. 16, 1924, his 1st cousin, Elizabeth Harrison, dau. of Dr. Edmund Harrison and Marguerite Conoway, his wife, of Greensboro, N. C.

1. Marguerite[9] Rucker, b. Nov. 5, 1926.
2. Edmund[9] Harrison Rucker, Jr., b. 1929.

2. Dana[8] H. Rucker, Jr. (Dana[7], ———), b. Oct. 2, 1900, yeoman in the World War, m. June 4, 1925, Lilla Campbell, of Jackson, Miss.

1. Dana[9] H. Rucker, III, b. July 29, 1926.
2. Robert[9] Campbell Rucker, b. Feb. 18, 1928.

3. William[8] Harrison Rucker (Dana[7], ———), b. Apr. 18, 1903, graduate of University of Richmond, m. July 12, 1924, Myrtle Traylor.

1. Allen[9] Harrison Rucker, b. 1925.

4. Kate[8] Stegar Rucker (Dana[7], ———), b. Oct. 15, 1905, graduate of Westhampton College, m. Sept., 1927, Frank Beasley, a lawyer, of Bowling Green, Va.

1. Lucy[9] Harrison Beasley, b. Jan. 1, 1931.

5. Claude[7] Pendleton Rucker (Wm.[6] A., ———), b. Apr. 18, 1869, in Fauquier Co., now living at Mattoax, Va., unmar.

6. Sudie[7] S. Rucker (Wm.[6] A., ——), b. Dec. 18, 1871, attended for 3 years the Luray Female Institute, m. July 3, 1901, William Price Wood, b. Sept. 28, 1865, in Newark, England, son of T. W. Wood and wife, Elizabeth Price. They live in Richmond, Va. (See Wood and Price, Part III.)

Issue:

1. Sudie[8] Elizabeth Wood, b. Dec. 26, 1903, graduate of Devon Manor School of Devon, Pa., m. Dec. 12, 1925, Roger L. Mann.
   1. Sudie[9] Rucker Mann, b. Sept. 15, 1926.
   2. Roger[9] LaFayette Mann, Jr., b. Sept. 13, 1929.
2. William[8] Price Wood, Jr., b. Apr. 3, 1905, received B. S. at Virginia Polytechnic Institute and M. S. at Cornell.
3. Lillian[8] Lee Wood, b. Dec. 18, 1906, graduate of Sweet Briar College.
4. Jean[8] Wood, b. June 22, 1908, graduate of Collegiate School, afterwards attended Ward-Belmont, Nashville, Tenn.
5. Garland[8] Ambrose Wood, twin, b. Feb. 17, 1913, now attending V. P. I.
6. Thomas[8] Ward Wood, twin, d. Aug. 29, 1913.

7. Annie[7] Lee Rucker (Wm.[6] A., ———), b. June 23, 1873, m. Oct. 10, 1894, Hugh Garland[6] Skinker, b. Feb. 1, 1867, son of Thomas[5] Julian Skinker and Ann Hite, his wife, descendant of Jost Hite. Thomas[5] was the son of Samuel[4] Hampson Skinker, of Oakly, and his wife, Margaret Wilson Julian, dau. of Dr. John Julian, a surgeon of Rev. Service. Samuel[4] was the son of William[3] Skinker, b. 1738, and his wife, Mary Pawlett, widow Sills. William[3] was the son of Maj. Samuel[2] Skinker, b. 1677, in England, who m. Diana Thorpe, son of Thomas[1] Skinker, of Bristol, Eng. See Hite, Rose, Madison, Taylor).

1. Garland[8] Ambrose Skinker (Oct. 28, 1895-Nov. 22, 1910).
2. Julian[8] Hampson Skinker, b. Feb. 12, 1897, m. Apr. 11, 1925, Evelyn Burr, b. Aug. 6, 1905, of Dallas, Texas, dau. of Alexander Burr and his wife, Mary Elizabeth Cammack. They live in San Antonio, Texas.
   1. Julian[9] Hampson Skinker, Jr., b. Aug. 30, 1928.
3. Sudie[8] Hite Skinker, b. June 23, 1899, m. Nov. 5, 1919, John R. Benner, b. Oct. 31, 1898. They live in Warrenton, Va.
   1. Anne[9] Rebecca Benner, b. June 29, 1922.
   2. John[9] R. Benner, Jr., b. Dec. 18, 1923.

8. Henry[7] Smith Rucker (Wm.[6] A., ———) (Sept. 25, 1875-June 9, 1876).

9. Bayard[7] Ambrose Rucker (Wm.[6] A., ———), b. July 28, 1877, m. Dec. 19, 1908, Minnie Varner, dau. of John and Lelia Ramey Varner, of Delaplane, Va. (See Varner line).

1. Margaret[8] Ramey Rucker, b. Mch. 17, 1911.
2. Bayard[8] Ambrose Rucker, Jr., b. Apr. 22, 1914.
3. Lelia[8] Varner Rucker, b. Feb. 5, 1916.
4. John[8] William Rucker, b. May 11, 1921.

10. Lillian[7] Eliza Rucker (Wm.[6] A., ———), b. Apr. 26, 1880, m. Apr. 28, 1906, Dr. Henry Cowles Rucker, b. Apr. 3, 1878, son of Benjamin and Sally Parks Rucker. They live at Mattoax, Va.

1. Henry[8] Cowles Rucker, Jr., b. Jan. 28, 1907.
2. Benjamin[8] Ambrose Rucker, b. Nov. 13, 1911.
3. Sarah[8] Ann Rucker, b. Nov. 17, 1916.

4. Addison[6] Clay Rucker (Wm.[5] B., George[4], John[3], ——) (Feb. 19, 1843-Oct. 10, 1905), m. Apr. 1, 1868, Lucy Lyle Snead (Nov. 25, 1850-July 8, 1911). Addison was a civil engineer, and a private under Col. John S. Mosley, 1861-65, during the Civil War.

1. William[7] Ballenger Rucker, b. Mch., 1870, m. 1898, Mattie Rawlings.
2. Robert[7] Snead Rucker (May 10, 1872-Sept. 30, 1895).
3. Mary[7] Ann Dawson Rucker, b. Aug. 27, 1874, m. A. R. McNeil, 1899.
4. Henry[7] Smith Rucker, b. Jan. 10, 1876, m. 1900, Lola Hillis.
5. Charles[7] Manly Rucker, b. Feb. 22, 1878, m. 1905, Charlotte Goodwin.
6. Addie[7] Clay Rucker, b. Mch. 29, 1880, m. 1902, P. D. Payne.
7. Edgar[7] Parks Rucker, b. Mch. 27, 1882, m. 1905, Bertie Bowman.
8. Lyle[7] Wilson Rucker, b. Apr. 13, 1890, m. 1909, Persa Morton, an attorney living in Los Angeles, Calif.

6. William[4] Rucker (John[3], John[2], Peter[1]) (1756-July 24, 1826), m. Mch. 7, 1782, Sarah North, b. in Bedford, Jan. 10, 1762, d. Aug. 23, 1845, dau. of Abraham. A certificate is dated

Mch. 1782, given by Rev. James Rucker of the marriage between William Rucker and Sally North (D. B. 7, p. 342, Bedford).

Among the Amherst Co. Rev. Service Claims in the Archives at Richmond, Va., is the following, to "William Rucker—for 531 lbs. of pork furnished to the British Prisoners", Feb. 14, 1782.

His father, John Rucker, of Amherst, bought and deeded to him land in Pleasant Vale, Bedford, adjoining the land of his brother, George[4], between Nobusiness, Rocky, and Buck Mts. on Elk Creek.

William Rucker bought 258 a. of land on Elk Creek on Feb. 22, 1813, for $100 from Edward G. Watkins (D. B. 13, p. 823).

On Apr. 24, 1819, William[4] and wife, Sally, sold to the heirs of George Rucker, dec'd, for $40, 14¼ acres on Elk Creek, "part of the land where William lives." Again on Oct. 10, 1822, they sold to Barnett Rucker for $2,300, 233 acres, willed to William, Sr., by his father; said William resides on 60 acres and sold all to Barnett (D. B. 17, p. 341).

William[4] moved Oct. 15, 1822, to Murfreesborough, Williamson Co., Tenn., where he died, leaving a will probated July 24, 1826.

I, William Rucker of Williamson County, Tenn., leave to my wife, Sarah, the plantation; to my dau. Susanna Early, son Bernard, dau. Nancy Douglass, son John, son William, dau. Sally Downing, to dau. Lucy Hatcher the tract of land containing 100 acres on which my son-in-law, William Hatcher now lives; to dau. Malinda Rucker, dau. Keturah Burrus, dau. Elizabeth Rucker (unmarried, afflicted). That my sons, John and William, and son-in-law, Benjamin Rucker, to take care of her as her guardians.

Executors: Sons John and William Rucker, son-in-law, Benjamin Asbury Rucker.

Issue:

1. Susanna[5] Rucker.
2. Bernard[5] Rucker.
3. Nancy[5] Rucker.
4. John[5] Rucker.
5. William[5] Rucker.
6. Sally[5] Rucker, d. Aug. 23, 1845, m. ——— Downing.
7. Lucy[5] Rucker, m. William Hatcher.
8. Malinda[5] Rucker, m. Benjamin[5] Asbury Rucker (John[4], John[3], ———).
9. Keturah[5] Rucker, m. ——— Burruss.
10. Elizabeth[5] Rucker.

Will of Abraham North (W. B. 2, p. 269, Jan. 22, 1800, Bedford, Apr. 28, 1800). To grandson, William North, son of William (dec'd), sons, David and John, daus. Sarah Rucker, Susanna Robertson, Betty Miller, Nancy Austin, Patty Jones. Executors: wife and son-in-law, William Rucker and son, David.

An earlier Abraham North obtained a license to marry Sarah Rowzie (Essex Co., Record Book 1692-1695, p. 235).

1. Susanna^{5} Rucker (Wm.^{4}, John^{3}, ———), m. Jan. 6, 1801, Thomas Early, of Bedford, son of Joshua and Mary Leftwich Early, son of Jeremiah and Elizabeth Buford Early, of Middlesex. Thomas and Susanna moved to Pa. before 1812.

1. Rachel^{6} Early, m. 1812, Philip Steckman.
    1. Christine^{7} Steckman.
    2. Jane^{7} Steckman.
    3. Betsy^{7} Steckman.
    4. Valentine^{7} Steckman.
    5. Robert^{7} Steckman.
    6. James^{7} Steckman.

1. Christine^{7} Steckman (Rachel^{6} E., Susanna^{5}, Wm.^{4}, ——, Rucker), b. 1818, m. Elijah Huggard.

1. Mary^{8} Huggard.
2. Sadie^{8} Huggard.
3. Philip^{8} Huggard.
4. Arthur^{8} Huggard, m. Daisy Ernest, of Bedford, Pa.
    1. Marion^{9} Huggard.
5. Mark^{8} J. Huggard, m. Annie Wooster, no children.

1. Mary^{8} Huggard (Christine^{7}, Rachel^{6}, Susanna^{5}, Wm.^{4} Rucker), m. John Witlong, Confederate soldier. She lived and died in Miskogee, Okla.

1. Ada^{9} Witlong, m. Ed. Smith.
2. Minnie^{9} Witlong, m. ——— Johnson.
3. Frank^{9} Witlong.
4. Sadie^{9} Witlong, m. ——— Smith.
5. John^{9} E. Witlong.

2. Sadie^{8} Huggard (Christine^{7}, ———), m. William Baxmeyer, of Holden, Mo.

Issue:

1. Charles[9] Baxmeyer, of California.
2. Bert[9] Baxmeyer, of Kansas City, Mo.
3. Edith[9] Baxmeyer, of Holden, Mo.
4. Ralph[9] Baxmeyer, of Kansas City, Mo.
5. Roy[9] Baxmeyer.

3. Philip[8] Huggard (Christine[7], ———), m. Wilhelmina Cromwell.

1. Earl[9] Huggard.
    1. Ruth[10] Huggard, m. William Smith.
    2. Pearl[10] Huggard, m. William Schwehl.
    3. Katie[10] Huggard.
    4. Daisy[10] Huggard.
    5. Ellen[10] Huggard, m. Harold Stuckey.

2. Daisy[9] Huggard, m. 1916, John H. Jordan, U. S. Attorney for Western Pa.

3. Pearl[9] Huggard, m. Thomas J. Rouey, of Pittsburgh.
    1. William[10] Rouey, lieutenant in World War, m. Marie Potillo, of Atlanta.
    2. Margaret[10] Rouey, m. Leo R. Smith, served in World War.
    3. Thomas[10] J. Rouey, Jr., served in World War.

2. Jane[7] Steckman (Rachel[6], Susanna[5], Wm.[4], ——— Rucker), b. 1820, m. Wayne Mower, of Bedford, Pa.

1. Georgie[8] Mower, d. unmar.
2. Zora[8] W. Mower, d. unmar.
3. Boyd[8] Mower, d. unmar.

5. Robert[7] Steckman (Rachel[6], ———), b. 1824, m. Christiana Morgort.

1. William[8] Steckman.
2. Harry[8] Steckman.
3. Myrtle[8] Steckman.
4. Elsie[8] Steckman.
5. Lillie[8] Steckman, m. 1st Servell Right, 2nd Joseph Gervin.

6. James[7] Steckman (Rachel[6], ———), m. Amanda Morgort, of Lancaster, Pa.

1. Charles[8] Steckman.
2. Carrie[8] Steckman.
3. Ella[8] Steckman.

2. Bernard^{5} Rucker (Wm.^{4}, John^{3}, ———) (May 17, 1785-Dec. 12, 1884), m. in Campbell Co., Oct. 30, 1813, Polly Russell (see Robert Russell, p. ——). He inherited his father's homestead in Pleasant Vale on Elk Creek, Bedford.

On Aug. 24, 1813, he bought 64 acres from Littleberry Hawkins for $548 (D. B. 15, p. 403, Bedford Co.).

Oct. 26, 1840, Bernard gave 164 acres of land on Flat Top Mts. to Alfred and James H. Rucker. This had been given him by his father, William, and was adjoining the land of George Rucker, dec'd.

1. Lucy^{6} E. Rucker.
2. Dr. Alfred^{6} C. Rucker, m. Nov. 2, 1848, Susan Gaddy (dau. of Wm.). They moved to Texas. No heirs.
3. Dr. James^{6} H. Rucker, moved to Tenn.
   1. Mrs. Patty^{7} Kirby.
4. Sarah^{6} Ann Rucker, m. Nov. 20, 1833, Nelson Lowry.
5. William^{6} Rucker, d. unmar. in Bedford, 1885.

1. Lucy^{6} E. Rucker (Bernard^{5}, Wm.^{4}, John^{3}, ———) (June 24, 1824-Oct. 3, 1909), m. 1st Dr. John^{5} Cephas Rucker (Reuben^{4}, Isaac^{3}, John^{2}, ———), June 12, 1843. He died the same year from an injury received by a fall from his horse. An inventory was taken of his estate in 1844. Lucy m. 2nd Thomas W. Moore, Feb. 15, 1848, and moved to Texas.

Issue (by 1st mar.):

1. John^{7} Cephas Rucker, Jr.

Issue (by 2nd mar.):

2. Betty^{7} Moore, b. Dec. 24, 1848, m. John L. McKinney.
3. Charles^{7} Bernard Moore, b. Sept. 6, 1850, m. Nov. 11, 1881, Clara Baltyeger, b. Apr. 21, 1850. Live in Lubbock, Texas.
4. Alice^{7} J. Moore, m. D. A. Pace.
5. James^{7} B.
6. Cora^{7} V.
7. Mary^{7} H.
8. Pattie^{7} Lula.

1. John^{7} Cephas Rucker, Jr. (Lucy^{6}, Bernard^{5}, Wm.^{4}, John^{3}) (Apr. 9, 1844-Apr. 19, 1914), m. Mch. 13, 1876, Marinda Rucker (James^{6} M., Jonathan^{5}, George^{4}, John^{3}, ———).

1. Lodowick^{8} Rucker.
2. Roberta^{8} Eva Rucker.
3. Fleda^{8} Rucker.

1. Lodowick^{8} Rucker (John^{7}, Lucy^{6}, Bernard^{5}, ———), b. Dec. 8, 1877, m. Dec. 29, 1909, Annie Woody.

   1. Annie^{9} W. Rucker.

2. Roberta^{8} Eva Rucker (John^{7}, Lucy^{6}, ———), m. James C. McDaniel, Mch. 31, 1897.

   1. La Fayette^{9} McDaniel.
   2. Lillian^{9} O. McDaniel.
   3. Virgie^{9} H. McDaniel.
   4. Fleda^{9} Russell McDaniel.
   5. June^{9}.
   6. Rucker^{9}.
   7. Waller^{9} Penn.

3. Fleda^{8} Rucker (John^{7}, Lucy^{6}, ———), b. Feb. 22, 1884, m. Marion Douglass Cunningham.

   1. Marion^{9} Douglass Cunningham, Jr.
   2. Russel^{9} Rucker Cunningham, b. May 3, 1925.

8. Pattie^{7} Lula Rucker (Lucy^{6}, Bernard^{5}, ———), b. Dec. 6, 1862, m. R. P. Littlepage, Dec. 29, 1881.

   1. Erie^{8} Littlepage, m. H. H. Hackler.
   2. R. L.^{8}, Tahoka, Texas.
   3. Walthall^{8}, San Antonio, Texas.
   4. Fred^{8} P., San Antonio, Texas.

3. Nancy^{5} Rucker (Wm.^{4}, John^{3}, John^{2}, Peter^{1}), m. John Douglass, Dec. 25, 1803, in Bedford, her uncle, Rev. George Rucker, officiating. They lived in Virginia.

   1. Alfred^{6} Douglass.
   2. Marelia^{6}.
   3. Nancy^{6}.
   4. Robert^{6}, moved to Mo.
   5. Murphy^{6}.
   6. Catherine^{6} Willis Douglass.

1. Alfred^{6} Douglass (Nancy^{5}, Wm.^{4}, George^{3} Rucker), m. 1st Agnes Paxton, Rockbridge; 2nd widow Jones, née Watts, of Bedford; 3rd Lucy Spriggs, of Lancaster Co., Va.

Issue (by 1st mar.):

   1. Edward^{7} Douglass, d. 1904, unmar.
   2. Agnes^{7} Douglass, m. ——— Davidson.

3. Nancy^{6} Douglass (Nancy^{5}, Wm.^{4}, George^{3} Rucker), m. Robert Holmes, of Rockbridge, and moved to Johnson Co., Mo.

5. Murphy^6 Douglass (Nancy^5, ———), m. Katherine Luster, of Natural Bridge.

1. Nan^7 Douglass, m. ——— Hammitt.
2. Will^7 Douglass.

6. Catherine^6 Willis Douglass (Nancy^5, ———), b. Jan. 6, 1806, m. Nov. 3, 1825, Jonathan Wood Eads, of Louisa.

1. William^7 H. Eads (Sept. 13, 1826-Jan. 9, 1829).
2. Mary^7 Francis Eads.
3. John^7 Drury Eads (Mch. 8, 1830-Nov. 30, 1852), single.
4. James^7 M. Eads, } twins.
5. Edwin^7 Rutherford Eads, } twins.
6. Martha^7 Pendleton Eads.
7. Sarah^7 Agnes Eads.
8. Catherine^7 Elizabeth Eads.
9. Robert^7 H. H. Eads, b. 1841, moved west.
10. Isobel^7 J. Steele.
11. Lucile^7 Michie Eads (June 12, 1846-June 22, 1920).
12. William^7 Alfred Franklin Eads (Jan. 27, 1849-Mch. 29, 1925).
13. Drury^7 Saunders Eads (Jan. 2, 1851-1909), m. 1878, Mary Louise Ruff, of Lexington, Va.

2. Mary^7 Francis Eads (Catherine^6, Nancy^5, Wm.4 Rucker), b. Mch. 27, 1828, m. Nov. 13, 1850, James R. Saunders, of White Stone, Lancaster Co., Va.

1. Lelia^8 Saunders, m. Dr. Mathew Bruce, of Prince George.
2. William^8 Lucas Saunders, White Stone.
3. Charles^8 Saunders, m. Mollie Yerbey, living in Baltimore.
4. Lula^8 Saunders, m. Robert Dunaway, White Stone.
5. Ellis^8 Saunders, m. C. Y. Yerbey, of White Stone.
   1. Robert^9 Yerbey.
6. Gaylord^8 Moose Saunders, m. Laurie Hubbard, d. 1926, White Stone.

4. James^7 M. Eads (Catherine^6, Nancy^5, Wm.^{4}, ———), b. June 8, 1832, m. Sallie Montgomery, of Rockbridge. No children.

5. Edwin^7 Rutherford Eads (Catherine^6, ———), b. June 8, 1832, m. Jan. 26, 1860, Bettie B. Taylor, of N. C.

Issue:

1. Anna[8] Eads, m. ——— Hines, of Boydton.
2. Laura[8] Eads, m. John Miller, of Bluefield, W. Va.
   1. Douglas[9] Eads.
   2. Ralph[9] Eads.
3. Bessie[8] Eads, m. Marion E. Bolinger, Los Angeles, Calif.

6. Martha[7] Pendleton Eads (Catherine[6], ———) (Nov. 11, 1834-1916), m. John H. Coffman, June 25, 1856.

   1. Samuel[8] Miller Coffman, d. 1918.

7. Sarah[7] Agnes Eads (Catherine[6], ———) (Nov. 26, 1836-1887), m. June 5, 1859, Dr. Charles E. Lauck.

   1. Charles[8] E. Lauck, Jr. (Feb. 14, 1862-1926), no issue.

8. Catherine[7] Elizabeth Eads (Catherine[6], ———) (Oct. 4, 1843-1905), m. 1858, Samuel S. Miller.

   1. William[8] Eads Miller, m. 1892 Minnie V. Painter, of Ivanhoe, Va., d. 1927, no issue.
   2. Baker[8] Miller, d. unmar.
   3. Ida[8] Steele Miller, d. unmar. 1926.

10. Isabel[7] J. Steele Eads (Catherine[6], ———) (Oct. 4, 1844-Sept. 25, 1899), m. Feb. 8, 1867, Major J. E. Moose, of N. C.

   1. William[8] Russell Moose, b. Jan. 23, 1869, m. Nov. 19, 1902, Julia Evelyn Gerow, of Glasgow, Va.
      1. William[9] Gerow Moose, b. Sept. 18, 1904.
      2. William[9] Russell Moose, Jr., b. Jan. 23, 1907.
      3. Morrison[9] Travis Moose, b. Mch. 28, 1908.
   2. John[8] Douglas Moose, b. Oct. 4, 1872, m. June 8, 1899, Margaret Elizabeth Wright.
      1. John[9] Douglass Moose, Jr., b. Sept. 6, 1901.
      2. Tyree[9] Wright Moose, b. Mch. 11, 1903.
      3. Frances[9] Moose, b. Nov. 28, 1910.
   3. George[8] Francis Moose, b. Jan. 17, 1874, unmar.
   4. Catherine[8] Mary Moose, b. Mch., 1876, unmar.
   5. Willie[8] Elizabeth Moose, b. Mch. 5, 1880, unmar.

4. John[5] Rucker (Wm.[4], John[3], John[2], Peter[1]), was in the war of 1812 under Capt. James Leftwich, with his first cousin, William B. Rucker.

5. William[5] Rucker (Wm.[4], John[3], ———) (Feb. 1, 1792-Mch. 24, 1868), m. Mary Jane Pillow (Mch. 22, 1811-June 19,

1894), dau. of Abner, of Maury Co., Tenn. They moved to Texas.

Sept. 1, 1825, Abner North in debt to William Rucker, the executor of the estate of William Rucker, dec'd, gives a Deed of Trust to Bernard and James Rucker, on a lot in Lynchburg, on Lynch Station and 6th Ally.

1. Capt. William[6] P. Rucker.
2. Elizabeth[6] Rucker, m. Joseph Gentry.
3. John[6] Rucker.
4. Van[6] Rucker, m. ——— Battle.
5. Alonze[6] Rucker, m. ——— Moore.
6. Jennie[6] Rucker, m. Charles Miller.
7. Laura[6] Rucker, m. Robert Jordan.
8. Abner[6] Rucker, m. Laura Wilson.

1. William[6] P. Rucker (Wm.[5], Wm.[4], John[3], ———), b. Nov. 11, 1828, killed Feb. 3, 1863, at 2nd battle of Fort Donelson, m. 1858, Rachel Steele.

1. William[7] Steele Rucker (Jan. 1, 1862-Nov. 25, 1913), m. Dec. 9, 1885, W. Cowles Anderson.
    1. Mary[8] Rucker, b. Nov. 18, 1886, m. Mch. 31, 1915, John C. North.
    2. Cora[8] A. Rucker, b. Feb. 17, 1888.
    3. Thomas[8] P. Rucker, b. Aug. 24, 1889, m. Mary Alice Moore, Oct. 7, 1917.
        1. Thomas[9] Rucker, b. Aug. 12, 1918.
        2. William[9] M. Rucker, b. May 27, 1920.
        3. Mary[9] A. Rucker, b. Mch. 30, 1922.
    4. Fannie[8] Rucker (May 9, 1891-1904).
    5. Moses[8] Steele Rucker, b. Apr. 1, 1896.
    6. Frank[8] Anderson Rucker, b. Dec. 7, 1897.
    7. William[8] Steele Rucker, b. Apr. 15, 1899.

3. John[6] Rucker (Wm.[5], Wm.[4], John[3], ———), m. ——— Thomas.

1. Sarah[7] Rucker, m. ——— Manier.
    1. J.[8] W. Manier, Hudson, Mass.

7. Betty[4] Rucker (John[3], John[2], Peter[1]), m. David North, son of Abraham A. North, of Bedford.

8. Isaac[4] Rucker (John[3], John[2], Peter[1]), b. 1760, in Amherst Co., d. in Kentucky in 1835, age 75. Dr. Isaac Rucker served in

the Revolutionary War, enlisted at the age of seventeen, and later served as a corporal. After the war he studied medicine and practiced in Amherst. His father left him half of 318 acres of land and the remaining half at the death of his mother, Eleanor. In 1798, Isaac paid taxes on the entire 318 acre tract, but sold it in 1800, because he had been living in Jessamine Co., Ky., since 1793, and paying a personal tax.

He came back in 1806 to marry Minty Ogden. Marriage bond in Amherst signed Mch. 25, 1806. Witness: Isaac Rucker and James Pendleton. Attached is the following: "Isaac Rucker of Jessamine Co., Ky., son of John Rucker"; consent given by Henry Ogden, James Ogden and William McDaniel. Minty O. Rucker d. in Jessamine Co., 1858.

Isaac is spoken of as "Doc" in the tax books, both personal and land, as well as in the county petitions; all in the archives in Richmond, Va.

Will recorded in Versailles, Ky.

Issue:

1. Edward[5] Lewis Rucker.
2. Catherine[5] Rucker.
3. Nancy[5] Rucker.
4. John[5] J. Rucker, b. June 3, 1815, of Lexington, Ky.
5. William[5] Rucker.
6. Elizabeth[5] Rucker.
7. Susan Margaret[5] Rucker, m. James Hudson.
8. Martha Ann[5] Rucker.

9. Nellie[4] Rucker (John[3], ———), m. John Morton in Amherst, and moved to Woodford Co., Ky. He was called by his nephews "Uncle Mote".

A note attached to the marriage bond in Amherst Co., written and signed by Nellie Rucker to the Clerk. "Sir, this shall be your sufficient warrant to issue a license to John Morton to marry me.

Nelly Rucker."

Dated Feb. 6, 1786. Witness: John Rucker and John Rucker, Jr.

Sally, Lucy, and Nancy Morton, children of John Morton, dec'd, and their mother, Nelly Morton, widow and relict of John, sold to Richard Harrison 20 acres of land with a mill on Harris Creek, for £200 on Nov. 10, 1814 (D. B. M, p. 653, Amherst Co.). See Morton.

Issue:

1. Sally[5] Morton, m. William[5] Rucker (John[4], John[3], ———), 1st cousin.
2. Lucy[5] Morton, m. Mch. 23, 1802, Joshua Rucker, of Amherst Co.
3. Nancy[5] Morton.

3. Ambrose[3] Rucker (John[2], Peter[1]) (c. 1725-Dec. 21, 1807), first appears in Orange County in 1745, as a witness, and was living there in 1751 when his elder brother, Peter[3], the executor of his father's will divided the land of their father, John[2].

Ambrose lived on the land patented by his father, John, deeded to him on Nov. 11, 1751, by Peter Rucker, son and executor of John Rucker.

Peter, in compliance with the will of his father, John Rucker, deeded to Ambrose Rucker a tract of land laid off for him in Albemarle County, out of a tract of 5,850 acres taken up by John Rucker, deceased, and patented by Peter, executor, containing 324 acres with the exception of four acres for use of David Rosser, adjoining John Harvie and David Rosser. Witness: John Rucker, George McDaniel and William Miller.

Ambrose's land lay east of the Tobacco Row Mountains, south of Bears Mountains, to the south of Harris Creek on Rucker's Run, a branch of Harris Creek.

The following year, Feb. 27, 1752, Ambrose Rucker was in Orange County, a witness, and was paid £25 for attending Court in a suit of Medley vs. Joseph Eve (W. B. 1, p. 357, Albemarle County).

He moved to Amherst County between the years 1752 and 1766. At this time he produced a commission to be lieutenant of a company of militia from Amherst County. This Commission was entered on the Order Book of Amherst County, June 2, 1766.

"November 24, 1766 (O. B. 1766, p. 1), Amherst County, Va., Ambrose Rucker, Gent., produced a commission as lieutenant of a Company of Militia of Amherst County, and took the oath to his Majesty's person and government and the abjuration oath, repeated and subscribed the test."

In November of 1766, Ambrose Rucker was appointed a Justice of Peace of Colonial Virginia, Amherst Co.

Battaile Harrison, Ambrose Rucker and George McDaniel were ordered to view a way for a road from Daniel Burford's into Stovall's Road, which is between Megans and Tye River Road, Dec. 1, 1768 (O. B. 1766-69, p. 90).

George McDaniel, John and Ambrose Rucker ordered to view a way for a road from the head of Harris's Creek into Harvie's Road and make report (O. B. 1766-69, p. 90), Dec. 1, 1766, Amherst.

The first court at which Ambrose Rucker appeared as a Justice is in the 1st volume of Court orders (preserved). The oath of a Justice was administered to him by William Cabell, Jr., Feb. 2, 1767 (O. B. 1766-69, p. 91).

A certificate according to law from Ambrose Rucker, Gent. a Justice of the Peace presented in court by Benjamin Rucker, certifying that said Ambrose Rucker had weighed for said Benjamin 2676 lbs. of merchantable hemp, water and winter rotted, dry, bright and clear. Ordered certified to the Governor (O. B. 1766-69, p. 101). John Rucker raised 696 lbs. of hemp.

5 May, 1767, Ambrose Rucker, Gent. was appointed to take list of tithables between the Tobacco Row Mountains, Buffalo River, Lynches Road and Fluvanna River (O. B. 1766-69, p. 146).

8 Nov. 1768, Ambrose Rucker administrator of estate of John Goff, deceased, vs. Anne Goff and George McDaniel; said Rucker to recover £24-11 and costs (O. B. 1766-69, p. 435).

June Court, 1783. Ambrose Rucker to take list of tithables in his usual bounds (O. B. 5, p. 127).

March Court, 1783, Ambrose Rucker, Gent. appointed to take list of tithables in the 6th hundred in this county and deliver to the clerk of this county before the 1st Monday in May next (O. B. 1782-84, p. 79, Amherst).

Nicholas Cabell, John Diggs, Ambrose Rucker and Gabriel Penn, Gent. are appointed to collect and state from the best proof the case will admit of, the various losses and injuries both private and public which have been sustained within this county during the war from the Depridations of the enemy in their several invasions, and to state the same under as many different heads as such losses and injuries may consist of, and return their proceedings therein, together with the proofs made in support thereof to the court in order to be by them laid before the next assembly (O. B. 1782-84, p. 96, Mch., 1783).

He was appointed sheriff of Amherst County, 16 March, 1778 (O. B. E, p. 142).

The Auditor's Books paid him for the service of Captain for militia service.

The Tax books of 1782 mention him as "Colonel Ambrose Rucker". In the will of his father-in-law, Edward Tinsley, he is mentioned as "Col. Ambrose Rucker", and frequently in the county records he is mentioned as "Colonel", and also in Revolutionary settlement claims for supplies furnished the armies.

Chalkley's *Abstracts,* Vol. 2, p. 482, 1779-1780: "September 3, 1832 James Harrison of Amherst County made a declaration that he was drafted and had served under Captain Ambrose Rucker of Amherst County.

McAlister's *Virginia Revolutionary Militia,* section 112, p. 112-1832.

Lynchburg Paper, May 20, 1884, a list of Revolutionary Soldiers of Amherst County, prepared by Mr. Alexander Brown, Nelson County:

A. Rucker (Anthony),
Ambrose Rucker,
John Rucker, Sr.
John Rucker, Jr.
Lieut. Isaac Rucker,
John Rucker, died in service,
Reuben Rucker, died in service.

Hardesty's *Historical and Genealogical Ency. of Amherst County* (Archives, Richmond, Va.) gives the same list.

McAlister's *Revolutionary Militia,* p. 17, states that "Captain Ambrose Rucker's Company was out in service."

Virginia Historical Magazine, Vol. 9, mentions Major Rucker of Amherst County, 1779.

Ambrose Rucker served as Captain of the Amherst Militia until 1779, then was promoted to Lieutenant Colonel. (See the public claims of Fluvanna Co.) From these claims it was evident the Amherst and Bedford Co. militia served at Yorktown. All of the following references are to be found in the Archives in the Richmond Library.

Photostats of the originals are in the possession of the author.

At a Court continued and held for Fluvanna County on Friday the 2nd of May, 1783.

"David Ross Gent. is allow'd £18 for Castings furnish'd the 20 Amherst Militia, by order Dan'l Gaines, Col., and Receipt thereon endors'd, specifying these Articles under the Hand James Stevens, Jun'r bearing Date 1st November 1780. Also the farther Sum of £8 for 10 bakeing-Irons, and 7 Kettles, furnish'd the Bedford Militia the 9th Jan'y 1781 by Order of William Campbell Commissary and Receipt endors'd by Jesse Tait: Also the farther Sum of £25 for 10 Dutch Ovens, and 15 Kettles furnished

Bedford Militia the 22nd Feb'ry 1781 as per Receipt signed John Gallaway, Capt. Also the Sum of £21 for 38 Camp Kettles furnish'd the Amherst Militia and 4/9 for Waggoning the same to the River by Order Ambrose Rucker, L. C. Militia, and Receipt endorsed under the Hand Anthony Rucker dated 26th Feb'y 1781. Also the farther Sum of £33 for 50 Camp Kettles furnished Capt. Francis Thorpe 24th March 1781 and Receipt endors'd by Nul Boyl. Amherst County to Wit." (L. C. for lieutenant colonel of the county Militia).

"I hereby Certify to have received of Col. Ambrose Rucker Two Beeves weighing Seven hundred and Twenty Six and half pounds for the use of the public pursuant to an Act of Assembly in that case made and provided Given under my hand this 27th day of Sept. 1781.

2 Beeves 726½ lb.

Credit By 38½ lb. of Beef lent to C. A. Rucker (C. for Colonel).

765
5

A. Rucker, D. C. P.
(Deputy Commissioner of the Provisions).

£3,825

Register of General Assembly of Virginia, by Severn, Sessions May 7, June 23, Oct. 1, 1781 to Jan. 5, 1782, mentions William Cabell and Ambrose Rucker as delegates of Amherst Co.

June 4, 1781, he was in the House of Delegates, as a member of the Legislative Body in Charlottesville when General Tarleton raided the town. The account of his escape is given by his great-granddaughter, Mrs. Ellen Rucker Theisz, as it was told by her grandfather, Isaac Rucker, son of Ambrose Rucker.

"When General Tarleton appeared at Charlottesville, the Legislative body then in session (1781) dispersed rather hastily."

He claimed that his life was saved by his horse, which was a powerful hunter, and trained to jump fences which he did successfully this June day although his rider weighed over 300 pounds.

Ambrose Rucker's name was upon a great many petitions from Amherst County—religious papers division of parishes and counties; for building a town at Lynch's Station or Ferry, which was named Madison. He was also a Trustee to establish an Academy at Warminster.

Hening's Statutes, Vol. 13, p. 296—A petition "That 50 acres of land, the property of John Lynch, adjoining the ferry in Amherst shall be invested in Samuel Meredith, Samuel Jordan Cabell, Ambrose Rucker, Benjamin Rucker, David Woodruff, Powhatan Bolling, and David Tinsley, Gentlemen, Trustees, land to be laid off in lots and establish a town by name of Madison."

Hening's Statutes, 1791. "Benjamin Rucker, Ambrose Rucker, David Tinsley, etc., were selected to find a suitable site for a town in Amherst County, to be called Madison."

Hening's Statutes, p. 315: An act was given to build an Academy at Warminster, Amherst County—Money to be raised; one of the Trustees, Ambrose Rucker."

1791: "A petition was granted to Ambrose and Benjamin Rucker to establish a tobacco warehouse in Amherst County."

June 5 1775: A petition for a ferry in Amherst County over Rivanna River. Signed: Ambrose, Benjamin and John Rucker."

The first Episcopal Church called Rucker's Church built in Amherst County was built by Ambrose Rucker of logs. In the last few years this old log church was pulled down and taken to Sweet Briar College using the logs to build a corn crib.

The location is not far from the above college on land belonging to William Ogden. The sunken graves surrounded by a low wall is in evidence, also the outlines of the church foundation.

Anthony Rucker in his will, 1821, set aside one acre surrounding this church for "Public worship".

Ambrose Rucker was one of the church wardens of St. Mathews Church, June, 1779, Lexington Parish.

At a vestry held for the Parish of Lexington, held at the house of Ambrose Rucker: Gentlement present: Ambrose Rucker, Josiah Ellis, William Horsley, Isaac Tinsley, Isaac Rucker.

Lexington Parish, 1840: Resolved that the salary of $600 be paid to our pastor, John W. Griffin, to be thus proportioned:

New Glascow Church	$167.00
Rucker's Church	166.00
Amherst Court House	167.00
Pedlar	100.00
	$600.00

Rucker's Church was also called St. Mathews Church.

The Parish of Lexington was to be divided into districts: one was to begin at the Parke's Road to Gabrill Penn's Quarter, along Tobacco Row Mountain, and the ridge that divides the waters of the Harris Creek from the waters of Hogs and Rutledge Creeks to Harvey's Road. Isaac Rucker and Daniel Burford, Jr., were to procession one certain district.

Vestrymen of Lexington Parish, 1779-1780, Church Wardens: Richard Ballinger and Gabriel Penn.

Vestrymen: Hugh Rose, Ambrose Rucker, Joseph Goodwin, David Woodroof, James Dillard, Daniel Gaines, gentlemen.

James Higginbothan surveyed for Ambrose Rucker 160 acres 23 Oct. 1766.

William Cabell, Jr. surveyed for Ambrose Rucker 350 acres on branch of Harris Creek on South side of Bear Mountains, 2 Feb. 1765 (Survey Book 1761-1803, Plat Book, Amherst County, Va.).

Ambrose Rucker and wife, Mary, sold to John Houchins of Amherst, 90 acres for £5, land granted to Ambrose Rucker 10 Sept. 1767. Witness: Benjamin Pollard, 7 Nov. 1768 (D. B. B, p. 389), Amherst.

He patented in Amherst County 262 acres of land at head of a branch of Harris Creek, July 20, 1767, adjoining Lunsford Lomax, and 90 acres in Graham Cove the same year. Also 2000 acres in 1781, a Treasury Warrant No. 9117, adjoining George Douglas, William Camden, Jesse Clements, and his own line on Harris Creek (Survey Books, Land Office, Richmond, Va.).

Mch. 14, 1774 Ambrose Rucker had 375 acres of land surveyed for him as "Captain Rucker". This land ran to the top of the Tobacco Row Mountains, adjoining Robert Johnson and Henry McDaniel. It was surveyed by William Cabell and William Pendleton (Survey Book 2, p. 260).

He patented about 4000 acres of land in Va. and 1480 acres in Fayette County, Ky.

Ambrose was one of the twenty-one (21) members chosen from Amherst County on the Committee of Safety in 1775.

Cabells and Their Kin, p. 100, July-August, 1775. The Committees under the Continental Association August 1774 had not been uniformly organized as to their numbers, etc., and there was no definite limit as to their term of service. Therefore, the Convention of July-August ordained that they should thereafter be composed of twenty (20) members to be elected annually, in November, for a one-year term.

The second Committee for Amherst was elected at November Court, which was held the first Monday of the month, 1775. This Committee was composed of twenty-one of the most discreet, fit and able men of the said County, viz:

Colonel William Cabell,	Chairman Hugh Rose
Zacharias Taliaferro,	John Dawson,
Ambrose Rucker,	William Horsley
Alexander Reid,	John Digges,
Roderich McCulloch,	Benjamin Rucker,
Col. James Neville,	Colonel Joseph Cabell,
Daniel Gaines,	Gabriel Penn,
David Crawford,	Lucas Powell,
Col. John Rose	Dr. James Hopkins,
James Dillard	David Shepherd,

Francis Meriwether

George McDaniel and wife, Margaret, and Reuben Harrison and wife, Peggy, sold to Ambrose Rucker for £15, land on North branch of Harris Creek, adjoining Thomas Lucas. 6 July 1778 (D. B. E, p. 5, Amherst).

William Goode of Powhatan sold to Ambrose Rucker of Amherst, 400 acres of land on Rocky Creek of Buffalo River, beginning at John Warren's to James Warren's, all houses gardens, etc., 4 Oct. 1784 (D. B. E, p. 563, Amherst). This 400 acres was given to his son Isaac Rucker.

Ambrose Rucker, executor of Thomas Lucas, dec'd (his widow Martha Lucas gave up all claim to her dower to the eldest son of said Thomas) in 1791 (D. B. G, p. 111).

James Morton of Kentucky and Ambrose Rucker of Amherst sold 83 acres on Rutledge Creek, and Pauls Mountains, 30 Oct. 1793 (D. B. G, p. 327).

Ambrose Rucker was appointed Guardian to Daniel Coleman, orphan of John, with William Tinsley, Jesse Carrell, sec., before William Cabell, Ambrose Rucker, James Dillard and William Warwick, Gentlemen, Justices of Amherst, 22 Apr. 1794 (W. B. 3, p. 297).

Inventory of the estate of Ambrose Rucker, deceased, by Isaac Rucker, 1807 (W. B. 5, p. 549).

To Charlotte Rucker,

To Ambrose Rucker, son of Reuben Rucker, deceased.

To Ambrose Rucker, Jr.

To Margaret Burford, and others.

It is said that Ambrose Rucker married twice, 1st to Mary Headley. He married Mary Tinsley, daughter of Edward (W. B. 2, p. 118, Amherst Co.).

Mary Tinsley, wife of Ambrose Rucker, d. 1818, at which time the estate was divided.

(W. B. 4, p. 479), Amherst County, Virginia: Will of Ambrose Rucker, written, signed and sealed December 3, 1803, probated December 21, 1807.

Item: I give and bequeath to my son, Ambrose Rucker, the new survey, or the upper part on the North side of my Mountain Plantation containing 200 odd acres, with the addition of one hundred acres taken off the land formerly contested between Lucas and myself, which said one hundred acres of land last mentioned is a part of tract left my wife, and all the land on the South and West side of the road that leads from the head of Harris' Creek, with two negroes, viz: Sarah and Crease; the former being now in his possession; with all other things that I have given him heretofore, or let him have, except the Ore Bank on the high peak of the Tobacco Row Mountain, to him and his heirs forever.

The Ore Bank land containing 375 acres, with one other tract adjoining is to be sold at the discretion of my executors and divided equally among my children and grand-children.

I give to my son, Isaac Rucker, three hundred acres of land from the upper side of my Rocky Creek Plantation, running quite across the creek from one side of the creek to the other; also a negro woman named Anna and her children, also Betty and her increase. The said negroes now being in his possession, and also all other things I have heretofore given him, to him and his heirs forever.

Item: I give to my son, Benjamin Rucker, three hundred acres of land, it being the tract of land my son Isaac now lives on, so as not to interfere with the storehouse and my barns, also a horse, saddle and bridle and a good feather bed and furniture; two negroes, viz: Caleb and Rhoda, two cows and calves, two sows and pigs, my rifle gun, and three sheep, to him and his heirs forever.

Item: I give and have given to my son, Reuben Rucker, deceased, equal two hundred pounds; also fifty pounds more in property to his heirs forever.

I give, and do give unto the heirs of Peggy McDaniel, deceased, one hundred pounds in property, and they are to be paid by executors (from my estate) in property, one hundred pounds more to them and their heirs forever.

I do, and have given unto Franky Lee two negroes, viz: Lydia and Creasy, and sixty pounds in property, making in the whole to her two hundred pounds, to her and her heirs forever. I have given to Mollie Burford one negro woman named Solelin, and other things to the amount of one hundred pounds, and my executors are to pay her from my estate one hundred pounds more in property, so that her first portion will be made two hundred pounds to her and her heirs forever.

I give to Elizabeth Marr, and have given her two negroes, viz: Dilsey and Tiller now in her possession, and other things to the amount of one hundred and sixty pounds, and my executors of my estate are to pay her in property, out of my estate, forty pounds more to her and her heirs forever.

I lend to Sophia Rucker, now Sophia Jennings, five negroes, viz: Lelia, Doll, Creasy, Betsa, and Daniel, during pleasure, and at her death they are to go to the heirs and issues of her body forever. Also I give to my daughter, Sophia, fifty pounds cash, which said sum I desire my executors to pay her personally.

I give to my daughter, Caroline Hansford, two negroes, viz: Jane and Nancy, and other things to the value of one hundred and fifty pounds, and my executors are to pay her from the estate and property fifty pounds more, to her and her heirs forever.

I give Matilda Marr two negroes, viz: Anna and Charlie, and other things to the value of one hundred and eighty pounds more, to her and her heirs forever.

I give to Charlotte Rucker two negroes, viz: Caroline and Dicey, a good feather bed and furniture; a horse, saddle and bridle worth twenty pounds, and the said negroes valued at one hundred and twenty pounds, and the bed and furniture valued at fifteen pounds, making in all one hundred and fifty pounds, and my executors are to pay her out of my estate forty-five pounds in property to make her legacy two hundred to her and to her heirs forever, which said legacy is to be disposed of to the use of my daughter at the discretion of my executors.

I give to my daughter, Sallie Marr, two negroes, viz: Delphia and Little Lucy, or Yellow Lucy, at the quarter valued at one hundred and fifty pounds; a horse, saddle and bridle at twenty pounds; a feather bed and furniture valued at fifteen pounds, and other things amounting to one hundred and ninety-nine pounds and nineteen shillings, and my executors are to pay her one shilling to make her legacy two hundred pounds in all to her and to her heirs forever.

And finally all my land and other things not herein willed are to be sold and put to value to pay the legacies. After they are paid the remainder of my estate both real and personal, that is not willed away, is to be equally divided among my children and grand-children, viz; the children of Reuben Rucker one share; the children of Winifred Plunkett one share; the children of Margaret McDaniel one share; Mollie Burford one share; Ambrose Rucker one share; Isaac Rucker one share; Sophia Jennings one share; Caroline Hansford one share; Betsy Marr one share; Sally Marr one share; Charlotte Rucker one share; Benjamin Rucker one share, and their heirs forever.

I give to Benjamin Rucker, Sr.; Anthony Rucker and their heirs, and representatives of Isaac Rucker, deceased, their due share of all lands patented in my name in the State of Kentucky, agreeable to contract to them and their heirs forever.

It is to be observed that I reserve half an acre of land for a graveyard, where the graveyard is now fixed to belong to my family forever. And lastly I do appoint my beloved wife, Mary Rucker, and beloved sons Ambrose Rucker and Isaac Rucker whole Executrix and Executors of this my last will and testament.

In witness whereof I have hereunto set my hand and affixed my seal this 3rd day of December, one thousand eight hundred and three.

Signed Ambrose Rucker (seal).

Signed, sealed and acknowledged in the presence of:—John Cooney, Henry A. Christian, Anthony Rucker, Tinsley Rucker.

MEMORANDUM: 'Tis ordered in my will that the land whereon I now reside be sold to the highest bidder. I hereby direct that it be sold on credit, three annual payments, and the money to be divided agreeable to my will.

Signed: Ambrose Rucker,

Jan. 1, 1807.

At a Court held for Amherst County the 21st day of December, 1807, the last will and testament of Ambrose Rucker was proved by the oaths of John Cooney, and Anthony Rucker, two witnesses thereto, and ordered to be recorded. Isaac Rucker, one of the Executors named in the said will, personally came into Court and qualified according to law and entered into bond with Anthony Rucker, David Tinsley, John McDaniel and Benjamin Rucker, Jr., his sureties, in the penalty of $50,000.00, amount of money conditioned as the law directs. Certificate is granted to him for obtaining a probate thereof in due form.

Issue:

1. Reuben[4] Rucker.
2. Ambrose[4] Rucker.
3. Isaac[4] Rucker.
4. Benjamin[4] Rucker.
5. Winnifred[4] Rucker.
6. Margaret[4] Rucker.
7. Frances[4] Rucker.
8. Mary (Mollie)[4] Rucker.
9. Elizabeth[4] Rucker.
10. Sophia[4] Rucker.
11. Caroline[4] Rucker.
12. Matilda[4] Rucker.
13. Charlotte[4] Rucker.
14. Sarah[4] Rucker.

1. Reuben[4] Rucker (Ambrose[3], John[2], Peter) (Dec. 26, 1755-Jan. 27, 1782), m. 1776 Margaret McDaniel (Apr. 16, 1757-Aug. 16, 1798), dau. of George and Margaret Goff McDaniel. Alexander Brown's statement that Reuben was killed in active service during the Revolution substantiates the tradition handed down by the family.

Reuben bought 322 acres from Robert Cash for £500 on Apr. 1780 (D. B. E, p. 226, Amherst Co.).

Letters of administration were granted to Ambrose Rucker, George McDaniel, Isaac and Anthony Rucker, to settle the estate of Reuben Rucker, dec'd, 4 Mch., 1782 (W. B. 22, p. 36). (Also O. B. 2, p. 36, Amherst).

H. and G. Ency. of Amherst also gives his name among the Revolutionary soldiers.

His name appears in the first tax list of Amherst in 1782, as dec'd and his estate pays on 320 acres.

Nine years after Reuben's death, Margaret, his widow, m. Apr. 14, 1791, Philip[3] Burford, son of John[2] Burford. John's will dated 1807, mentions his son Philip as dec'd but gives the names of his children.

Will of John[2] Burford (dated Nov., 1807, probated Dec. 21, 1807):

Son—Daniel 212 acres of land.

Son—Ambrose.

Grandaughter—Matilda Norville.

Dec'd son—Archibald and his children, Caroline and Powhatan Burford.

Daughter—Martha Crews

Deceased daughter, Mourning Ham and her children, Yancey, Micah, Sally, Ham.

Deceased son—Philip[3] Burford and his children,

1. Cynthia Ann Headley Burford
2. George Burford
3. Philip Burford.

Will of Daniel[1] Burford (May 18, 1787, July 2, 1787):

To Virginia Taylor and her son; John Floyd Burford. To my Granddaughter Mourning Burford Stewart; To my son John[2] Burford, To my son Daniel[2] Burford, To my daughter Milly Crews, To my daughter Frances Goodwin, To my daughter Elizabeth Goodwin, Executors: John[2] and Daniel[2] Burford, John Stewart. Witness: John Crews, Able Blankenship, Noel Blankenship (W. B. 3, p. 48, Amherst County).

John Blackwell and Elizabeth, his wife, of Hanover Co., sold to Daniel Burford Jr. of St. John's Parish, King William Co., for £50, 400 acres of land in Frederickville Parish, adj. William Dashper, land purchased of John Anthony, the patentee, 1726 (D. B. A, p. 166, Louisa Co., Va.), Jan. 22, 1744.

Daniel Burford and Mary his wife of Albemarle Co. sold to Richard Phips, 400 acres of land Adj. Juett on North East Creek at Paulett's line. 27, June 1757 (D. B. B, p. 255, Louisa Co., Va.).

John[2] Burford (Daniel[1], ———). Issue: Philip[3] Burford.

Philip[3] Burford (Daniel[2], John[1]), m. 1st Margaret McDaniel (widow of Reuben Rucker) in 1791, d. 1798. Philip m. 2nd Elizabeth (Tinsley?) Philip, d. 1807, leaving 3 children by the 1st marriage.

Elizabeth Burford, executrix of Philip[3] Burford dec'd, with George Tinsley, David Tinsley and Ambrose Burford security, was appointed guardian to Philip[4] Burford, orphan of Philip, dec'd, 21 Dec. 1807 (W. B. 4, p. 483).

The same day the court appointed Ambrose Rucker (half brother) Guardian to Cynthia H. Burford and George Headley Burford, orphans of Philip[3].

The family Bible of the above Ambrose Rucker is in the possession of his granddaughterfi Mrs. William Wirt Harris, (Alice Rucker) of Lynchburg, Virginia. It contains the names of Reuben Rucker and Margaret Rucker's children as well as her children by the second marriage, also the dates of their births and deaths.

The following is copied from the family Bible: Bible printed by his Majesty's Special Command, Edinburgh, 1791. 1st page: (Inside 1st cover.)

"Margaret McDaniel Burford was born the 16th day of April, 1757, and departed this life on Sunday, the 26th day of August, 1798, about 12 o'clock.

2nd page:

1—Ambrose Rucker, son of Reuben Rucker and Margaret, his wife, was born 2nd September, 1777.

2—Rosamond M. Rucker daughter of Reuben Rucker, was born July 18th, 1779.

3—Lucy Rucker, daughter of Reuben Rucker, was born 5th March, 1781, and died January 18th, 1782.

4—Reuben Rucker, father of the above children, was born December 26th, 1755, and died January 27th, 1782.

(Beg. Psalms)

Philip Burford and Margaret, his wife, were married April 14th, 1791.

1—Cynthia Ann Hedley B., their first child, was born November 11th, 1792.

2—Saint George Burford, their first son, was born 5th April, 1794, and died 22nd day February, 1795.

3—George Henry Burford was born February 27th, 1796.

(Last page of book)

Ambrose Rucker was born on Tuesday morning, 2nd of September, 1777.

Betsy Rucker, wife to the above, was born Sunday night, 25th of May, 1776.

(Back of book)

Ambrose Rucker and Betsy, his wife, married the 1st day of August, 1799.

1—William Parks Rucker, their first child, was born Sunday night, July 13th, 1800.

2—Reuben Daniel Rucker was born Saturday morning, 26th . . . (Day of December, 1801)

3—Edwin Sorrel Rucker, born Friday morning 3rd of ———.

4—Nathan Dawson Rucker was born Sunday evening, 3rd day of March, 1805.

5—Clifton Hedley Rucker was born 31st day of January, 1807, (Saturday)

6—Mary Anne Dawson Rucker was born on Wednesday evening about 6 o'clock, the 11th day of January, 1809. m. William Balanger, R. T. Amherst.

7—Alfred Rucker was born Tuesday about - - - o'clock 25th day of September, 1810.

8—Margaret McDaniel Rucker was born on Wednesday, 6th day of May, 1812, about one hour by sun at night, or rather forty minutes after five o'clock in the evening.

9—Ambrose Barnes Rucker was born Thursday night about twelve o'clock, 11th November, 1813.

(at the bottom of texts)

Ambrose Rucker, 22nd Oct., N. D. 1826.

10—George McDaniel Rucker was born Monday evening, 26th of May, 1817, twenty minutes after four.

William P. Rucker departed this life on Thursday, 13th of August, 1818, being eighteen—18—years and one month old."

Issue, by 1st mar. of Margaret (McDaniel) Rucker:

1. Ambrose[5] Rucker.
2. Rosamond[5] Rucker (July 18, 1779), m. Nov. 19, 1803, William Ware, son of Col. William Ware of Amherst.
3. Lucy[5] Rucker (1781-1782).

Issue, by 2nd mar. of Margaret (Rucker) Burford:

4. Cynthia Ann Headly Burford, b. Nov. 11, 1792.
5. Saint George Burford (April 5, 1794, Feb. 1795).
6. George H. Burford, b. Jan. 27, 1796.
7. Philip Burford.

1. Ambrose[5] Rucker (Reuben[4], Ambrose[3], ———) (Sept. 2, 1777-Feb. 23, 1839), m. Aug. 1, 1799, Elizabeth[4] Parks (William[3], John[2], Thomas[1]) (May 25, 1776-May 5, 1854).

George Goodwin sold to Ambrose Rucker, Jr. 111 acres for £150, land near Daviss's lower ferry, at Henry L. Davis to M. Goodwin's line to Mitchell's land, to Jesse Woodrooff's, 7 Sept. 1799 (D. B. —, p. 592).

Ambrose Rucker and wife, Elizabeth, sold to George McDaniel, Sen. of Amherst, 322 acres for £200, land on the head forks of Pedlar River, adjoining James Smith, 15 Dec. 1800 (D. B. I, p. 179). (This was the land his father, Reuben bought in 1780).

He lived in Graham Cove on the South branch of Harris Creek, on land adjoining his grandfather, Col. Ambrose Rucker. His grandfather George McDaniel also owned land in this cove, which he patented adjoining Duncan Graham.

Ambrose was appointed commissioner of the revenue, Sept. 1811. In 1832 Ambrose and Isaac Rucker were Justices of the Peace of Amherst County.

Isaac Tinsley of Amherst County about "To remove to the state of Tennessee" appointed Ambrose Rucker of Amherst his attorney to sell land on the waters of Otter Creek (D. B. M, p. 272, 1812, Amherst).

In 1804 he was appointed Guardian to William Tinsley, son of William Tinsley, dec'd (his wife's nephew) with Reuben Pendleton and James Waugh.

In 1811 he was appointed Commissioner of the Revenue.

His father died when he was five years old and his mother, Margaret, married again when he was fourteen, after which event he made his home with his grand-father, George McDaniel.

Ambrose[5] attended the Methodist Church at Elon. He and his family are buried on his old home place at the foot of the Tobacco Row Mountains. The old residence was pulled down, after the death of his grand son, Valentine Rucker, and rebuilt, but carved in a twelve inch beam was an "M" possibly for McDaniel, which the writer saw in 1926.

The chimney of the original house is still standing. This tract of land passed out of the possession of the Rucker descendants about 1910, after being in the Rucker family six generations, being part of the 5850 acres, patented by John Rucker, 1739. In the graveyard, enclosed in a rock wall, which is falling into decay, is to be seen the following graves with inscriptions:

Two handsome marble slabs mark the graves of Ambrose and his wife, Elizabeth Parks. Some of plain marble and the others millgranite stones. Some cannot be identified.

"Ambrose Rucker, d. 23rd Feb., 1839, in 62d. yr. of age.

"Elizabeth Rucker, d. 5th June, 1854, in 78th yr. of age.

"Kate P. Rucker b. June 15th, 1839, d. Nov. 17, 1859.

"S. T. D. c., b. 1751, d. 18th Nov. 1811.

"Edwin S. Rucker, b. April 8, 1803, d. May 6, 1859.

"Hilton G. Rucker, b. March 29, 1837, d. Aug. 1, 1860.

"Lucy Jane Rucker, b. April 3, 1813, d. Oct. 28, 1852.

"Emily J. Rucker, b. Jan. 21, 1821, d. Oct. 1, 1866.

"Wm. B. Woodroof, b. May 8, 1839, d. Sept. 9, 1849."

Elizabeth Rucker, wife of Ambrose, owned some interest in the Burke estate (sister Margaret married Samuel Burke) for in 1834 when that estate of 96 acres was sold to Patterson, Elizabeth received a share.

Marriage bond between Ambrose Rucker and Elizabeth Parks.

"Know all men by these presents, that we Ambrose Rucker, (Minor) and Martin Parks are held and firmly bound unto James Wood, Esq., the Governor of Virginia, for the time being and to his successors in office for the use of the Commonwealth in the sum of One Hundred and Fifty Dollars, which payment, well and truly to be made. We bind ourselves and heirs, &c., this the 29th day of July, 1799.

The condition of the above obligation is such that since there is a marriage intended shortly to be had and solemnized between Betsy Parks (Spinster) and the above bound Ambrose Rucker. (Minor) and if there should be no legal cause to obstruct the said marriage, then the above obligation is to be void or else to remain in full force and virtue.

Ambrose Rucker, (Seal)
Martin Parks, (Seal)

On motion of George McDaniel the estate of Ambrose Rucker dec'd was committed to Edmund Penn, high sheriff, to be by him administered according to law, said Rucker having departed this life more than 3 months (W. B. 10, p. 385, June, 1839, Amherst County).

Robert Tinsley, George Hylton, Ambrose B. Rucker and George M. Rucker were administrators of the estate of Elizabeth Rucker dec'd, wife of Ambrose. 19 June, 1854 (W. B. 13, p. 355).

1. William^6 Rucker (July 13, 1800-1818).
2. Reuben^6 Rucker.
3. Edwin^6 Sorrell.
4. Nathan^6 Dawson.
5. Clifton^6 Headley.
6. Mary^6 Ann Dawson.
7. Alfred^6 R.
8. Margaret^6 McDaniel.
9. Ambrose^6 Barnes.
10. George^6 McDaniel.

2. Reuben^6 Dawson Rucker (Ambrose^5, Reuben^4, Ambrose^3, ———) (Dec. 26, 1801-1872), m. Mary Glascock, Dec. 23, 1819, of Pittsylvania County. He was a Baptist Minister.

1. George^7 Rucker.
2. Ambrose^7 Rucker.
3. Sallie^7 Rucker.
4. Corinne^7 Rucker.
5. Elizabeth^7 Rucker.
6. Clifton^7 Rucker (Confederate Soldier).

3. Sallie^7 Rucker (Reuben^6, Ambrose^5, Reuben^4, ———) (Feb. 4, 1831-Apr. 17, 1866), m. Capt. Clayborne Tucker (June 2, 1805-Dec. 8, 1867), who served in the war with Mexico. They lived at Mt. Airy, Pittsylvania County.

1. Sallie^{8} Clayborne Tucker.
2. Reuben^{8} Daniel (Dec. 11, 1852-1907), unmar.
3. Selina^{8} A.
4. Robert^{8} G., d. infancy.

1. Sallie^{8} Clayborne Tucker (Sallie^{7}, Reuben^{6}, Ambrose^{5}, ——— Rucker), b. June 11, 1851, m. Gustave A. Creasy, son of George Clayborne Creasy of Bedford County. He served in the Confederate War, in Pickett's Division, 7th Va. Infantry, and was wounded at Drewry's Bluff.

1. Robert^{9} Tucker Creasy of Houston, Texas.
2. Grace^{9}, m. Dr. Edwin Price.
3. Burton^{9}.
4. Stover^{9} Henry, of Gretna, Va.
5. Myrtle^{9}, m. Robert H. Tredway, Chatham, Va.
6. Olive^{9}.
7. Randolph^{9} Tucker, b. Mch. 5, 1885, D. D. S., Warren Co., Va.
8. Prudence^{9} } twins
9. Talmage^{9} } twins
10. George^{9}, of De Funkia Springs, Fla.
11. Maxwell^{9}.
12. Thomas^{9}.

3. Selina^{8} A. Tucker (Sallie^{7}, Reuben^{6}, Ambrose^{5} Rucker), b. Jan. 16, 1856, m. 1st ——— Collins, 2nd Rev. R. P. Ambler, of De Funkia Springs, Fla.

3. Edwin^{6} Sorrell Rucker (Ambrose^{5}, Reuben^{4}, Ambrose^{3}) (Apr. 8, 1803-May 6, 1850), m. 1st 1830, Lucy Hylton (Apr. 3, 1812-Oct. 28, 1852).

1. Valentine^{7} Rucker.
2. Ambrose^{7} C.
3. Elizabeth^{7}, d. young.
4. Dr. Hylton^{7} G.
5. Washington^{7} Irving.
6. Lucy^{7}.
7. Wilber^{7}, went to Cal.
8. Cora^{7}.

1. Valentine^{7} Rucker (Edwin^{6} S., Ambrose^{5}, Reuben^{4}), m. Arianna West, of Amherst. In the Civil War he served as Captain in 2nd Va. Cavalry, Company E. He entered the army as 2nd Lieut. under Capt. Edward Whitehead. In battle, in a hand

to hand sabre fight, he saved the life of Col. Thomas Whitehead, by being quicker with his sabre than the enemy. He left no heirs. He served under Fitzhugh Lee in Stuart's division, organized Apr. 10, 1861, Captain, Edward Whitehead; 1st Lieutenant, Thomas Whitehead; 2nd Lieutenant, Valentine Rucker. Privates: Washington and Ambrose G. Rucker (his brothers), Marcellus and William Ambrose Rucker (1st cousins), third cousins Henry and Paul Rucker (brothers), also cousins Godfrey, Ike (Isaac) and Richard, three sons of Alexander (Sandy) Marr Rucker. Other Ruckers who served were:

Edward L. Rucker.

W. B. Rucker, wounded and captured at Brandy Station. Imprisoned at Camp Chase.

George Rucker, wounded at 2nd Battle of Manassas.

Booker Rucker, killed at Yellow Tavern. All of Company "E".

William P. Rucker and Joshua Tinsley Rucker, of Bedford, were in Company "G" of same regiment.

2. Ambrose[7] C. Rucker (Edwin[6] S., Ambrose[5], Reuben[4]), known as "Long Ambrose", being six feet seven inches tall, married three times: 1st Emily J. Clark (1821-1860), 2nd ——— Acree, 3rd Sally Mason, who qualified as Executrix of Ambrose C. Rucker, dec'd, 20 April, 1891 (W. B. 23, p. 44, Amherst).

Will of Ambrose C. Rucker, June 14, 1890 (W. B. 22, p. 430, Amherst). To my wife, Sallie, and her five children.

1. Sallie[8] N.
2. Margaret[8] M.
3. Charles[8] Hylton.
4. Mary[8] Massie.
5. Helen[8] B.

3. Dr. Charles[8] Hylton Rucker (Ambrose[7], Edwin[6] S., ———), m. Mary Drean. (No issue).

4. Dr. Hylton[7] G. Rucker (Edwin[6] S., Ambrose[5], Reuben[4]) (1837-1860), d. at a medical college in New York of typhoid fever, unmar.

Valentine Rucker was appointed Administrator of the estate of Hylton G. Rucker, dec'd, 15 Oct. 1860 (W. B. 15, p. 452).

5. Washington[7] Irving Rucker (Edwin[6] S., ———), m. 1st Sarah Knight Jones, daughter of Richard and Polly (McDaniel)

Jones, m. 2nd 1864, Betty E. Shelton (1839-1924). He served in 2nd Va. Cavalry, Co. E.

1. Edwin[8] Rucker.
2. Herbert[8] Rucker, m. ——— Clary.
3. Lucy[8] Mable Rucker, m. 1898, McCoy Wilkerson.
4. Maude[8], m. John Blanks.
5. Irving[8], m. Mary K. Miller, of Rappahannock Co., dau. of R. E. and Mattie Miller. No heirs.

6. Lucy[7] E. Rucker (Edwin[6] S., Ambrose[5], ———), m. Andrew J. Porter, 1872, son of John and Mary Porter.

1. Edwin[8] S. Porter.
2. Lucy[8] Porter, m. Robt. Motley.
3. Andrew[8] J. Porter, Jr.

8. Cora[7] Rucker (Edwin[6] S., Ambrose[5], ———), d. Aug., 1931, at Maidens, Va., age 76, m. Wm. Binford (2nd wife).

1. Henry[8] Binford, m. Belle Johnson.
    1. Francis[9] Binford.
    2. Henrietta[9] Binford.
2. Rucker[8] Binford, m. Rose Short.
    1. Susie[9] Rucker Binford.
    2. Winnie[9] Rucker Binford.
    3. Edwin[9] Binford.
    4. Charles[9] W. Binford.
3. Bernard[8] M. Binford.
    1. Christine[9] Binford.
    2. S.[9] B. Binford.

4. Nathan[6] Dawson Rucker (Ambrose[5], Reuben[4], Ambrose[3]) (Mch. 3, 1805-1884), m. 1st Mary Woodroof, 1859. Only one son, Marcellus Rucker, lived, m. 2nd the widow Wharton, Sallie Thomas, who had a son, Marvin Wharton, a prominent Baptist Minister. Sallie Thomas was born in Louisa County(August 10, 1821-Feb. 10, 1910), in Amherst and is buried in the Elon Churchyard.

Issue:

1. Marcellus[7] Rucker (Nathan[6]), m. Elizabeth Higginbotham, daughter of James and Ann London Higginbotham. Soon after Marcellus married he joined the 2nd Virginia Cavalry, Company "E". When his daughter, Minnie, was born he came home on a fur-

lough. This was the last time he ever saw his family. His company was on picket duty near Robinson River where they were driven back by the advancing Federal forces. When they reached Robinson River it was past fording, but the order was given to swim across. The cape that Marcellus[7] was wearing became entangled in grapevines overhanging, also his horse, which was washed from under him. His cousin, Henry[6] Rucker (Benjamin[5], Isaac[4], Ambrose[3], John[2], Peter[1]) swam his horse after him trying to untangle and save him, but after both becoming endangered, and Marcellus going down, Henry had to follow his company. Marcellus's body was later found by the residents and buried, but later heavy rains washed it up, taking it down the river, and was never recovered.

Issue:

1. Minnie[8] Claude Rucker (Marcellus[7]), m. Stephen Edward Morris, son of Dr. B. P. Morris of Amherst. No issue.

5. Clifton[6] Hedley Rucker (Ambrose[5], Reuben[4]), m. Mary Jane Starke Staples, Jan. 13, 1831, of Stonewall, Appomattox County (Jan. 31, 1807-Mch. 20, 1838). He lived in Amherst and was a tobacconist in Lynchburg. He sold a lot in Lynchburg on 11th Street, October 25, 1835. His will dated January 25, 1835, and recorded May 21, 1835, mentions his two boys, William Parks Rucker and James Staples Rucker. Executors, my three brothers, Edwin Sorrel Rucker, Ambrose Barnes Rucker, George McDaniel Rucker.

Issue:

1. William[7] Parks Rucker.
2. James[7] Staples Rucker.

1. William[7] Parks Rucker (Clifton[6], Ambrose[5], Reuben[4], Ambrose[3], John[2], Peter[1]), m. Margaret Scott, Oct. 28, 1852. He was born in Lynchburg, Virginia, Nov. 9, 1831, and died in Lewisburg, W. Virginia, 1904, at the age of seventy-three. He graduated in medicine from Jefferson Medical College, Philadelphia, Pa., and practiced in Covington, Alleghany County, Virginia, until 1862. He left Covington and joined the Federal Army, and was made Provost Marshal under General Crooks, of U. S. A. He was commissioned Major of the 13th West Virginia Infantry and detailed on the Staff of Crooks and Fremont.

At the end of the war he studied law, and in 1870 moved to Lewisburg, West Virginia, where he was prosecuting attorney for that county and that of Pocahontas. His wife, Margaret Scott, was half sister to his brother James' wife, and daughter of Thomas Hazelwood Scott and his wife, Margaret, of Campbell County, Virginia.

Issue:

1. William[8] Waller Rucker.
2. Hedley[8] Scott.
3. James[8] Thomas.
4. Edgar[8] Parks.

1. William[8] Waller Rucker (William[7], Clifton[6], Ambrose[5] Rucker), m. Fannie Applegate, May 20, 1880. He was made prosecuting attorney, 1886. As a Democrat he was elected to Congress in 1896, from the 2nd District in Missouri. Home in Keytesville, Missouri, b. Feb. 1, 1851, in Covington, Virginia. No heirs.

2. Hedley[8] Scott Rucker (William[7] P., Clifton[6] H., Ambrose[5]), m. Elizabeth Camm, a daughter of Dr. Samuel B. Scott and his wife, Sallie Patteson, of Bedford County, b. Sept. 13, 1852, in Lynchburg, Virginia. He practiced law in Keysville, Mo., but later returned to Huntesville, W. Virginia, and finally moved to Marleston, W. Va.

1. Willie[9] Parks Rucker.
2. Margaret[9] Damon, m. Henry Payne.
3. Jessie[9] Waller, m. Paris Yeager, son William[10] Yeager.

3. James[8] Thomas Rucker (William[7] P., Clifton[6] H., Ambrose[5]), m. Ida G. Riffe, 1882, of Greenbrier County, West Virginia. Settled in Nicholas Co., W. Va., at the close of the Civil War. In 1870 moved to Lewisburg, Greenbrier Co. Entered the Academy there as a pupil, and was later Principal of same school. In 1897 he became Principal of the school for deaf and blind, at Romney, W. Va. James was born in Covington, Virginia, Nov. 22, 1856, d. 20 Aug. 1916, Lewisburg.

1. Roy[9] Waller Rucker, m. Elizabeth G. Estle.

   Issue:

   1. Elizabeth[10] Jane Rucker, b. Sept. 11, 1911.
   2. William[10] Waller, b. Apr. 24, 1914.
   3. Ann[10] Estle, b. Nov. 14, 1918.
2. Anna[9] Parks Rucker, m. Howard[10] Schoew.

Will Book 9, p. 142, Aug. 19, 1916. Will of James T. Rucker.

To my wife, Ida G. Rucker; my daughter, Anna Parks Rucker Schoew, to Elizabeth Jane Rucker, daughter of my son Roy W. Rucker, land located in Romney, Hampshire County, West Virginia, all the farm implements to stay on the original Rucker farm now belonging to my brother, William W. Rucker. My children, Roy W. and Anna Parks Rucker Schoew.

4. Edgar[8] Parks Rucker (William[7] P., Clifton[6] H., Ambrose[5]) (Dec. 23, 1861-Apr. 21, 1908), m. Maude Applegate, Jan. 11, 1888, in Washington. He is buried in Lewisburg, West Virginia. Edgar P. was elected Attorney General for Welch and McDowell Co., West Virginia, in 1896. He was president of Margaret Mining Company, Hursley's Coal Company, Merrimac Coal & Coke Company, Stick Rock Coal and Coke Company and Welch Lumber Company.

Will of Edgar Rucker (W. B. 8, p. 317), dated July 8, 1905, Greenbrier, W. Virginia. My only child Margaret Clarke Rucker; my wife Maude A; my mother Margaret A. to my wife's brother, J. Ernest Applegate; my niece Anna Parks Rucker, daughter of my third brother, James T. Rucker; my wife's sister Mrs. William M. Meredith, of Huntington, West Virginia.

Signed Edgar P. Rucker.

1. Margaret[9] Clarke Rucker, b. Princeton, W. Va., Nov. 4, 1890, m. June 12, 1916, Edward Robert Shannon, Jr.
    1. Margaret[10] Rucker (Peggy), b. July 6, 1917, Cincinnati.

2. James[7] Staples Rucker (Clifton[6], Ambrose[5], Reuben[4] Rucker), m. Nannie Smith Scott. They went to LeCompton, Kansas, but returned to Virginia, in 1861, at which time he joined the Confederate Army near Richmond, Virginia. Nannie S. Rucker died Oct., 1862, leaving her son James Clifton with her father's aunt, Mrs. Susan Staples Yeatman. During the war James Staples Rucker was wounded, taken prisoner and died in Washington in prison in 1863, and was buried in the Congressional Cemetery.

Issue:

1. Walter^{8} Rucker (1859-1862).
2. Ida^{8} Bell (1860-1862).
3. James^{8} Clifton Rucker, b. Mch. 19, 1862; m. Emma Franklin Chockley, of Lewisburg, W. Va., June 30, 1886. In Feb., 1887, they returned to Keytesville, Missouri, where they now live.
    1. Mary^{9} Edgar Rucker, b. Nov. 26, 1888.
    2. William^{9} Ambrose, lived only a few hours.
    3. Maud^{9} Mann, b. Jan. 8, 1891.
    4. Ambrose^{9} Chockley, b. June 16, 1894.
    5. James^{9} William, b. June 7, 1897.
    6. Emma^{9} Clifton, b. Sept. 14, 1902, Brunswick, Mo. was a violinist; m. Nov. 6, 1927, ——— McIlhaney.

1. Mary^{9} Edgar Rucker (James^{8} C., James^{7}, Clifton^{6}, Ambrose^{5}), m. Boyd Taylor Williams, Sept. 14, 1906.

Issue:

1. Edward^{10} Clifton Williams, b. June 18, 1908.
2. Emma^{10} Oretta (Jan. 13, 1910-Oct. 30, 1917).
3. Ralph^{10} Parr, b. July 10, 1912.
4. Allen^{10}, b. Sept. 27, 1914.
5. Mary^{10} Elizabeth, b. Oct. 30, 1917.
6. James^{10} David } twins, b. Jan. 12, 1920.
7. John^{10} Peter } twins, b. Jan. 12, 1920.
8. Margaret^{10} Williams.

3. Maud^{9} Mann Rucker (James^{8}, James^{7} S.), studied music and art at Lexington, Mo., in Stephens College in Mo. and did Red Cross work during the war, in Washington. (Unmarried).

5. James^{9} William Rucker (James^{8}, James^{7}, Clifton^{6} Rucker), m. Ethel Zellman, Oct. 4, 1919. Daughter of Dr. Zellman.
    1. Elizabeth^{10}, b. Sept., 1921.
    2. Jean^{10}.

6. Mary^{6} Ann Rucker (Ambrose^{5}, Reuben^{4}) (Jan. 11, 1809-1863), m. Dec. 25, 1822, William Ballenger Rucker (George^{4}, John^{3}, John^{2}, Peter1), b. 1791, Bedford, d. in Amherst, 1862. (See page ——).

The marriage bond of William Ballenger Rucker and his cousin, Mary Ann Dawson Rucker (dau. of Ambrose), was dated

Dec. 25, 1822. Securities and witnesses were William Ware, Jr., B. Davis and Nathan D. Rucker, Amherst.

7. Alfred[6] Rucker (Ambrose[5], Reuben[4], ———), b. Sept. 25, 1810, m. Elizabeth Byrd, June 17, 1833. Moved to St. Louis, Mo.

8. Margaret[6] McDaniel Rucker (Ambrose[5], Reuben[4], ——), b. May 6, 1812, m. Rev. Pitt Woodroof.

1. Pitt[7] Woodroof, m. Serena Mabell.
    1. Ella[8] Woodroof, m. ——— Dillard.
2. Margaret[7] Woodroof.
3. Clifton[7] Woodroof.
4. Ambrose[7], m. Jennie Pleasants.
5. Victoria[7], d. young.
6. John[7], d. young.
7. David[7], m. ——— Bruster.
8. Alfred[7], m. ———Pleasants.
9. Ella[7], m. James Dillard.

9. Ambrose[6] Barnes Rucker (Ambrose[5], Reuben[4], Ambrose[3]) (Nov. 11, 1813-Mch. 22, 1872), m. Mch. 13, 1851, Sarah Benagh. Will of Ambrose B. Rucker, Lynchburg (W. B. E, p. 584).

1. Benagh[7] Rucker, d. young.
2. Elizabeth[7], m. Judge Wm. Richardson, Congressman from Alabama, 16 yrs.
    1. Sarah[8] Richardson, b. Sledge Tatum, no issue.
    2. Barnes[8] Rucker.
    3. Anne[8], m. 1st William S. Wells, d. 1908; m. 2nd Humes Patten.
        1. Elizabeth[9] Wells, b. July 2, 1914.
        2. Humes[9] Patten.
    4. Elizabeth[8], m. Thomas Burnett Howell, Richmond, Va.
        1. William Richardson Howell, b. Mch. 1, 1912, now attending Washington and Lee University. He is State golf champion, 1929-31, qualified in the National Amateur Tournament, 1931.
        2. Thomas[9] Burnett Howell, b. Jan. 11, 1916.
    5. William[8] Rucker Richardson.

3. Annie[7] Robinson Rucker, m. John Mays.
4. Alice[7] McDaniel Rucker, m. William Wirt Henry Harris, who owns the Rucker Bible.
    1. Barnes[8] Rucker Harris.
    2. William[8] Wirt Henry Harris.
    3. Alice[8] Rucker.
    4. Benagh[8] Rucker.
    5. Ambrose[8] Rucker, m. Virginia Porter.
    6. Valentine[8] Rucker Harris, m. Guy Cabell.
5. Barnes[7] Mitchell Rucker.

10. George[6] Henry McDaniel Rucker (Ambrose[5], Reuben[4], Ambrose[3]) (May 26, 1817-1884), m. 1st Catherine Mundy Pettyjohn, Dec. 29, 1846, m. 2nd Mrs. Susan Pannill Martin, Feb., 1865. Lived in Lynchburg, a large merchant and tobacconist, d. at the home of his daughter, Lelia (Mrs. C. J. Mathews), Reidsville, N. C., May 30, 1884.

Issue (by 1st mar.):

1. Kate[7] Mundy Rucker.
2. Nancy[7] Pettyjohn Rucker.
3. Carrie[7] Allison, d. young.
4. Betty[7], d. young.
5. Lelia[7] Josephine.
6. George[7] McDaniel, d. young.
7. Georgiana[7] Parks.
8. Margaret[7] McDaniel.

Issue (by 2nd mar.):

9. Banks[7] Rucker.
10. Pannill[7] Rucker.
11. Stuart[7], d. young.
12. Susan[7] Maria Rucker, m. John Herbert Hawkins.

1. Kate[7] Mundy Rucker (George[6], Ambrose[5], Reuben[4], ———), m. Green Penn (Dec. 31, 1843-1927), b. at Penn's Store, Patrick County, Va., son of Thomas Jefferson and Catherine L. Penn. He entered Randolph-Macon College, 1860. At the outbreak of the war, he volunteered in Co. ——, 42 Virginia Regiment, a company formed in Patrick County under Col. Jesse Burks, of Bedford. Later this regiment became a portion of 2nd Virginia Brigade, under Stonewall Jackson. Green was

wounded at the battle of Chancellorsville, was promoted to Captain. He fought in the battles of the Wilderness, Cedar Run, etc.

1. Rucker[8] Penn.
2. Annie[8] Virginia, d. young.
3. Harry[8] Jefferson.
4. Barnes[8] Rucker Penn.
5. Willie[8] Green, d. young.
6. George[8] Rucker Penn.
7. Jefferson[8] Penn, d. young.
8. Holmes[8].
9. Howard[8].
10. Ellis[8] M.
11. Ethel[8], d. young.
12. Kate[8], d. young.
13. Greenville[8] (May 10, 1874-July, 1929), unmar.

1. Rucker[8] Penn (Kate[7], Geo.[6], Ambrose[5], ———), b. Nov. 21, 1866, m. Cordelia Wills, Louisville, Ky.

1. Mazie[9] Wills Penn, m. Allen E. Gant, Burlington, N. C.
   1. Cordelia[10] Wills Gant.
2. Cordelia[9] Rucker Penn.

3. Harry[8] Jefferson Penn (Kate[7], Geo.[6], ———), b. Apr. 9, 1870, m. Luola Vaughn, Madison, N. C.

1. Greenville[9] Penn, IV, b. Oct. 21, 1898, m. Susanne Slade, New York, d. Dec. 4, 1930.
   1. Greenville[10] Penn, b. Feb. 24, 1927.
   2. Constance[10] Susanne, b. Apr. 7, 1928.
2. J. Vaughan[9] Penn, b. Jan. 7, 1901, m. Virginia Belvin, Richmond, Va. They live in Larchmont, N. Y.
3. Marian[9] Penn, d. in infancy.
4. Kate[9] Rucker Penn, b. Oct. 11, 1905, m. George C. Mason, Memphis, Tenn.
   1. Kitty[10] Penn Mason, b. Mch. 30, 1930.
5. Casandra[9] Vaughan Penn, b. July 30, 1904, m. Forrest Wright, Winston-Salem, N. C.
   1. Mary[10] Lou Penn, b. Feb. 27, 1929.
6. Harry[9] Lee Penn, b. June 24, 1908, m. Nadine Harriss, Summerfield, N. C.
   1. Margaret[10] Lee Penn, b. Aug. 28, 1928.
7. Edgar[9] Vaughan Penn, b. Oct. 7, 1911, single.

4. Barnes[8] Rucker Penn (Kate[7], Geo.[6], ———), b. Feb. 28, 1872, m. Mary Penn, of Danville, Va.

  1. Elizabeth[9] Penn, m. Everett Carter, of W. Va.
    1. Everett[10] Carter, Jr.

6. George[8] Rucker Penn (Kate[7], Geo.[6], ———), b. Oct. 28, 1875, m. Florence Elder Toomey, of Louisville, Ky.

  1. Richard[9] Toomey, m. Ann Garnett, of Danville, Va.
  2. Florence[9] Elder Penn, m. Benjamin Booth, Danville.

8. Holmes[8] Erwin Penn (Kate[7], Geo.[6], ———), b. May 2, 1888, m. Floyd Young, Europa, Miss.

  1. Floyd[9] Young Penn, m. Howard F. Barbee, Greensboro, N. C.
    1. Howard[10] F. Barbee, Jr.
  2. Winnifred[9] Penn.
  3. Holmes[9] Erwin Penn, Jr.

9. Howard[8] Lethe Penn (Kate[7], Geo.[6], ———), b. Jan. 12, 1882, m. Hilda Wall, Madison, N. C.

  1. Hilda[9] Penn, b. Jan. 4, 1916.

10. Ellis[8] Malone Penn (Kate[7], Geo.[6], ———), b. Sept. 6, 1884, m. Mary Thomas, of Georgia. No heirs.

2. Nancy[7] PettyJohn Rucker (George[6], Ambrose[5], ———), m. Dr. Landon B. Edwards, Jan. 17, 1871, of Richmond, Va.

  1. Katherine[8] Rucker.
  2. Charles[8] Mundy, M. D., m. Lelia LeMoyne Gahagan.
    1. Charles[9] Edwards, m. Apr. 2, 1931, Nancy Blow Rawls.
  3. Agnes[8] Vanculen.
  4. Landon[8] B. Edwards, b. Jan. 13, 1887, m. Jan. 20, 1914, Kathleen[2] Caughy, b. Oct. 11, 1890 (Charles[1] M. Caughy and Alice Higgins, wife).
    1. John[9] Woodbury, b. Dec. 31, 1914.
    2. Landon[9] Beirne, b. Mch. 12, 1916.
    3. Charles[9] Clinton, b. Jan. 28, 1918.
    4. Alfred[9] Caughy, b. Apr. 20, 1922.
    5. Nancy[9] Rucker, b. Jan. 16, 1926.
    6. Norbert[9] Caughy, b. Jan. 11, 1928.

5. Lelia^7 Josephine Rucker (George^6, Ambrose^5), d. June 29, 1931, Reidsville, N. C., m. Captain Cave J. Mathews. Served in the Civil War.

1. Landon^8 Edwards, d. in infancy.
2. Carrie^8, m. J. Walter Lovelace, Reidsville, N. C.
3. Hallie^8 Early, m. Lyle E. Russell, of Russell, Pa.
4. Annie^8 Virginia, d. young.
5. Mary^8 Virginia, m. Norris G. White.
    1. Virginia^9 White, student at Sweet Briar College.
6. Lillian^8 Josephine, m. George D. Hopkins.
7. Catharine^8, m. Edward S. Welborne.
    1. E.^{9} S. Welborne, Jr.
    2. Lelia^9 Rucker Welborne.

6. Georgiana^7 Parks Rucker (George^6, Ambrose^5, ———), m. Richard M. B. Ellington.

1. Margaret^8, d. in infancy.
2. Sadie^8, d. young.
3. George^8, m. Jeannette Burgess.

1. Nellie^8 Green Rives (Margaret^7, George^6, Ambrose^5, ———), b. May 8, 1887, Martinsville, Va., m. Sept. 4, 1921, Frank Earle Anderson, of Pompton Lakes, N. J., now living at Oakland, N. J.

2. Catherine^8 Rucker Rives (Margaret^7, George^6, Ambrose^5, ———), b. Aug. 8, 1888, Roanoke, m. Joseph Conrad Kearfott, Martinsville, Oct. 12, 1910.

1. Clarence^9 Piercall Kearfott, b. Aug. 5, 1911, attending V. M. I.
2. Margaret^9 Rives, b. Feb. 19, 1917.
3. Benjamin^9 Rives, b. Nov. 7, 1919.

8. Margaret^7 McDaniel Rucker (George^6, Ambrose^5, ——), m. Benjamin Allen Rives.

1. Nellie^8 Green Rives.
2. Catharine^8 Rucker.
3. Margaret^8 McDaniel, d. young.

9. Banks^7 Rucker (Geo.^{6}, Ambrose^5, ———), m. Clara Entz.

1. George^8 McDaniel Rucker.
2. Charles^8 Albert.

10. Pannill[7] Rucker (George[6], Albert[5], ———), m. Frank Stevens.

1. Benjamin[8] Stevens, d. age 21.
2. Pannill[8] Rucker, Jr.

2. Ambrose[4] Rucker, Jr. (Ambrose[3], John[2], Peter[1]), b. Dec. 6, 1763, in Amherst, d. Aug. 19, 1827, in Bedford, m. Jan. 25, 1786, Elizabeth Lucas (May 6, 1770-Aug., 1823), Amherst.

He was appointed inspector of the tobacco warehouses in Amherst, 1792, with his father, his security.

He and Robert Garland were appointed Guardians to Frances and Nancy Lucas, orphans of Thomas Lucas, deceased (W. B. 3, p. 240), Amherst, Oct. 15, 1792.

Andrew, Elizabeth, Thomas and Sarah Alexander sold to Ambrose Rucker of Amherst for $390, 300 acres on East side of Shoulder Camp Creek, May 26, 1806 (D. B. 12, p. 99), Bedford Co., Va.

June 20, 1812, Nathaniel Offult and Frances Nicholas, his wife, of Nelson, sold to Ambrose Rucker of Bedford Co. for $140, 351 acres on Wolf's Creek and Flat Top Mountains, formerly Rezier Offult's and a part of Cary's order (D. B. 13, p. 721), Bedford Co.

On Nov. 23, 1826, Ambrose Rucker, Sr., to Ambrose Rucker, Jr., for $5. and father's love and affection, 276 acres on Wolf Creek, adjoining Garland Rucker (D. B. 20, p. 122), Bedford Co.

April 22, 1822, Ambrose Rucker sold to Walter Chewning for $1680, 338¾ acres conveyed to Ambrose Rucker by a deed of trust (D. B. 17, p. 200), Bedford Co.

Dec. 23, 1826, William Wills and wife, Frances, to Ambrose Rucker for benefit of Timothy Rogers for $20., 5 acres on Big Branch (D. B. 21, p. 519), Bedford.

Warrant No. 9117, November 22, 1781: Ambrose Rucker, Jr. patented 226 acres of land in Amherst Co., adjoining Ambrose Rucker, Daniel Burford, Daniel Crawford, William Clements, and William Ware. This land was surveyed and cut off for Ambrose Rucker, Jr. out of tract of 2000 acres patented by his father, Ambrose Rucker, Treasurer Warrant above referred to.

In 1804 Ambrose Rucker paid taxes on the above 226 acres for the first time, and he continues until 1812, then on only 152 acres; that year he was living in Bedford County. His name is listed on the personal tax books as early as 1790 in Amherst County.

Ambrose Rucker was appointed Administrator of estate of James Marr, but dying before Marr, his brother, Anthony[4] was appointed in his place, January, 1833.

Will of Ambrose Rucker, Legatees: "Sons—Tinsley and Garland, land in Kentucky: Anthony, dec'd; Frances Hancock, son-in-law, James Rucker; grand-daughter Emily Rucker; grandson Elisha Hurt; son Ambrose; daughter Nancy. Witness: Richard Hobson, Rawley Rather, Francis Franklin. Personal property $2857.30, 14 slaves, etc" (W. B. F, p. 413), Aug. 27, 1827, Bedford Co.

Will of Lucy Coleman, Aug., 1803, Oct. 1803, Estate "to my sisters and brothers, and to Captain Ambrose Rucker, Jr., as a pledge for his tenderness on me in my sickness." (Legacy not definite). (W. B. 4, p. 134), Amherst Co.

1. Tinsley[5] Rucker.
2. Thomas[5] C. Rucker.
3. Garland[5] Rucker.
4. Anthony[5] Rucker.
5. Nancy[5] L., b. Sept. 20, 1794.
6. Mary[5] F.
7. Frances[5], b. 1797, m. ——— Carter.
8. Elizabeth[5].
9. Ambrose[5] L., d. 1832, Bedford Co., m. Betsy McClure, 1824, dau. of William and wife (Hancock) McClure.
10. Sophia[5], m. ——— Hurt.
    1. Elizah[6] Hurt.

1. Tinsley[5] Rucker (Ambrose[4], Ambrose[3], ———), m. 1st Nancy Ware, Feb. 28, 1804, dau. of William Ware, d. in Bedford Co.; 2nd Nancy Burks, Feb. 9, 1807; 3rd to Julia Meng. Tinsley[5] Rucker and wife, Nancy Burks of Bedford, sold to Alexander McDaniel, of same County, for $2,600. 215¾ acres on Trough Run, adjoining said McDaniel (D. B. 14, p. 510), Bedford Co., Feb. 9, 1817.

Nancy Burks, second wife of Tinsley Rucker, was the daughter of Samuel Burks and his wife, Margaret Parks, of Amherst. Nancy and Tinsley moved to Louisville, Kentucky, where Nancy died, and Tinsley married again.

Will dated June, 1824, probated Oct., 1824, of Samuel Burks, father of Nancy Burks Rucker, left property to her and to her children.

Tinsley Rucker was living in Louisville, and wrote the following letter to his brother-in-law, Martin Parks Burks, of Bedford (letter now in possession of Mrs. H. W. Dillard, of Lynchburg.

"Louisville, Kentucky, Nov. 28, 1830.

Mr. Martin P. Burks—

Dear Sir:

This will inform you that myself and family are all well.

My three boys, Samuel, Ambrôse and Bob are all getting on well, at their trade. Samuel has grown pretty stout. Bob is small for his age, he is something like you, full of fun.

Ambrose has progressed well. I received a letter from Tom dated the first of last month, Shullsburg, Ill. Lead Mines. He had when he wrote a spell of fever and ague.

I have not heard from Samuel Burks for several months. He is residing two or more hundred miles below where Tom is on the Mississippi.

My brother, Garland, sent his little daughter, July, last to my house, where she is at present. He wrote me a few lines in August, since, I have not heard from him. Mary and P. live with me—both in fine health. My Brother's Mary will be full in size; she is much taller than my daughter who is nearly double her age. I would be pleased to hear from you, and how the health of your mother is, and where she resides, of Jane and Robert and how all of the family is getting on.

Please remember me to your mother and all of the family, and accept of my good wishes for yourself.

T. L. Rucker, (Tinsley.)"

Issue (by 1st mar.):

1. Thomas[6] G. Rucker.
2. Mary[6] T., m. 1st ——— Stewart; 2nd ——— Robards, Henderson, Ky.
   1. Mrs. Sterling Price.[7]

Issue (by 2nd mar.):

3. Robert[6] F. Rucker.
4. Ambrose[6] B. Rucker.
5. Samuel[6] B. Rucker.
   1. Anna[7] Phalen.
6. Martin[6] Parks Burks, m. Kate Frank, Louisville, Ky., granddau. Louise[8] Rucker, m. Spalding Tafton, Henderson, Ky.

Issue (by 3rd mar.):

7. Anna[6] Maria Rucker, Covington, Ky.
8. Edmonia[6] Pope Rucker, m. A. W. Hyde, Louisville, Ky.
9. Pauline[6] E.
10. Julia[6] Megginson.
11. Daniel[6] Wilson Rucker.
12. Simeon[6] Goodwill Rucker.
13. Maria[6] Ophelia Rucker.

1. Thomas[6] G. Rucker (Tinsley[5], Ambrose[4]), m. Rose Frank, Louisville, Ky.

1. Joseph[7] Rucker.

4. Ambrose[6] B. Rucker (Tinsley[5], Ambrose[4]), m. girl from New Orleans, La.

1. William[7] Rucker.
2. Thomas[7] Rucker.

2. Thomas[5] C. Rucker (Ambrose[4], Jr., Ambrose[3], ———) (May 18, 1789-Nov. 30, 1860), Bedford, m. Elsie Settle, Jan. 12, 1808, dau. of Newman Settle, b. c. 1790.

Ambrose Rucker and wife, Elizabeth, of Bedford, deeded to their son, Thomas, 309 acres on South side of Wolf's Creek, in Bedford (D. B. 14, p. 522), Mch. 23, 1816.

On Jan. 26, 1820, Thomas Rucker and wife, Alcey, of Bedford, sold this 309 acres to Burkett Gray for $2100.

In 1824 Thomas Rucker owed his brother, Garland, $500., it being secured by his father, Ambrose, taking over some slaves, cattle, household furniture, etc.

In 1826 Thomas evidently took a trip on horseback west, judging from a letter in the possession of Mrs. H. W. Dillard, of Lynchburg, written to his uncle in Bedford:

"Boatyard, Tennessee, June 24, 1826.

Dear Uncle,

This will inform you of my arrival to this place about one hour since, and that I am at present having good health and hoping this will find self and family as such. My horse seems to hold up pretty well so far, and I hope he will be able to perform the journey. I have two hundred and sixty miles yet to travel, for which I hope I shall be able to perform in seven days more, and on my arrival I will again write you. I left Uncle Garland's last Monday morning.

From your obliging nephew,
Thomas C. Rucker.

You will please give my best love and compliments to Mr. Skinner.

Rucker.

Kingsport, Tenn.,
To Martin P. Burks, Esq.,
Bedford City, Va.
Captain Porter will please pass."

Issue:

1. Tinsley^6 S. Rucker.
2. William^6.
3. Anthony^6.
4. Thomas^6.
5. Emily^6.
6. Elsie^6.
7. Ambrose^6.

1. Tinsley^6 S. Rucker (Thomas^5, Ambrose^4), m. Catherine Mills.

Issue:

1. Andrew^7 Jackson Rucker, captured during Civil War, imprisoned at Fort Delaware, d. in prison.
2. Nancy^7 Rucker.
3. Thomas^7 Rucker.
4. George^7 A. Rucker.
5. L.^{7} W. Rucker.
6. Elizabeth^7 B. Rucker.
7. C.^{7} D. Rucker.
8. Mattie^7 Rucker.
9. Samuel^7 Rucker.
10. G.^{7} Rucker.
11. Fanny^7, m. Marcus Pritchett Gerod, of Ill.
12. Charlie^7.
13. Jefferson^7 Lee, lives in Verden, Ill.

5. L.^{7} W. Rucker (Tinsley^6 S., Thomas^5, Ambrose^4), b. April 26, 1847, m. 1st Lula Harris, of Charlotte Co., 2nd Lucy Bryant, of Botetourt Co.

Issue (by 1st mar.):

1. Nannie^{8} Rucker.
2. Emma^{8}.
3. Joe^{8}.
4. S. L.^{8}

Issue (by 2nd mar.):

5. Ida^{8}.
6. John^{8}.
7. Mattie^{8}.
8. Frank^{8}.
9. James^{8}.
10. Buck^{8}.
11. Julia^{8}, m. Park Woods.
12. Bessie^{8}.
13. Arthur^{8}.
14. Retta^{8}.
15. Jesse^{8}.
16. Robert^{8}.

7. Ambrose^{6} Rucker (Tho.^{5}, Ambrose^{4}, Ambrose^{3}) (July 15, 1815-July 17, 1891), m. Dec. 12, 1844, Martha Jane Walker, 1828-1898.

1. Cora^{7} Lee Rucker, b. Aug. 31, 1869, of Amherst, m. Thomas Lee Coleman, June 2, 1890, b. July 26, 1870.
    1. Mary^{8} Virginia Coleman, b. Oct. 8, 1902, Madison Heights, Amherst Co. Now of Washington.

3. Garland^{5} Rucker (Ambrose^{4}, Ambrose^{3}) (June 15, 1791-Nov., 1831), b. Bedford, m. Sally Parks Burks, dau. of Samuel Burks; d. of yellow fever in Donaldson, La. The Sheriff, Thomas Sale, administered upon his estate in Bedford, 1832.

Garland Rucker served under Captain Walter Otey of Bedford Co., as Sergeant, in the war of 1812—10th Virginia Reg., also his brothers, Thomas and Anthony, and cousin William Ballinger Rucker, son of George Rucker, from Bedford.

In 1819 Sallie's brother, Martin Parks Burks, deeds to her: property, slaves, furniture, silver teaspoons, silver tablespoons, and other things.

August 28, 1828, Bedford, Garland Rucker to Martin P. Burks. Ambrose Rucker security. Deed of Trust.

"Garland Rucker of Bedford, Trustee, for a deed of trust executed by Samuel Burks of Amherst County, for benefit of Nancy, wife of Tinsley Rucker, and her infant children, of record in Amherst. It will be of more interest to said Nancy and children to move to some Western part of the country with said property named in deed, and I appoint Walter Leake, of Mississippi: Hon. Powhatan Ellis of Louisiana; Hon. Thomas P. Eskridge of Arkansas, and Thomas Woolridge of Huntsville, Alabama, by lawful agents and attorneys to do all necessary with property named in deed" (D. B. 17, p. 297), Nov. 15, 1822, Bedford.

December 2, 1829, Martin P. Burks of Bedford to Sally P., wife of Garland Rucker, and William P. and Mary T. Rucker, children of Sally P. Rucker, who is sister of Martin P. Burks. Trustees: Samuel Garland and Thomas Davis, to them:—Slave, Winny, and her two children, two feather beds and furnishings, one set of silver tablespoons, tea spoons, and other table furniture to help maintain them in their present destitute condition (D. B. 21, p. 519), Bedford.

Issue:

1. William^{6} Garland Rucker.
2. Mary^{6} T. Rucker.

1. William^{6} Garland Rucker (Garland^{5}, Ambrose^{4}), b. Oct. 28, 1818, m. Mary Fletcher Lee, November 28, 1840.

1. James^{7} Garland Rucker.
2. Samuel^{7} Burks Rucker.
3. Lillie^{7} Lee Rucker.
4. Sallie^{7} Anderson Rucker.

1. James^{7} Garland Rucker (William^{6} G., Garland^{5}, Ambrose^{4}), b. Sept. 14, 1841, m. Lavinia Cox, June 26, 1873, dau. of Thomas and Jane Cox.

1. Lillie^{8} B. Rucker.
2. McFarland^{8} Rucker.
3. Isaac^{8} Reynolds Rucker.
4. Frederick^{8} Rucker.
5. James^{8} Sims Rucker.
6. Julia^{8} Rucker.

2. Samuel^{7} Burks Rucker (William^{6} G., Garland^{5}, ———), b. Mch. 26, 1845, m. Mary Katherine Richeson, Oct. 20, 1869, Lynchburg.

1. Pitticus^{8} Garland Rucker, b. July 24, 1870.
2. Lucy^{8} Lee, b. Oct. 10, 1871.
3. Thomas^{8}, b. Oct. 24, 1873.
4. Mary^{8} F., b. Aug. 12, 1875.
5. Samuel^{8} Burks, Jr., b. June 9, 1877.

6. Henry^{8} Latham, b. Jan. 3, 1879.
7. Nancy^{8} Douglas, b. Mch. 18, 1881.
8. Robert^{8} Craighill, b. Mch. 1, 1883.
9. Otis^{8} Grey, b. Apr. 13, 1885.
10. Kate^{8} Sledd, b. 1887.
11. Kathleen^{8} Kingsley, b. Jan. 6, 1891.

3. Lillie^{7} Lee Rucker (William^{6} G., Garland^{5}, Ambrose^{4}), b. Apr. 12, 1849, m. Ambrose Winston, Sept. 3, 1873.

1. Lucy^{8} Elizabeth Winston.
2. A. Penn^{8} Winston.
3. Lee^{8} Winston.
4. Reanmer^{8} Winston.

4. Sallie^{7} Anderson Rucker (William^{6} G., Garland^{5}, ——), b. Sept. 28, 1852, m. Thomas Varland Richeson, Nov. 30, 1870.

1. Samuel^{8} Hope Richeson.
2. Douglass^{8} Richeson, d. Dec., 1929.
3. Clarence^{8} Richeson, d. 1912.
4. T. Rucker^{8} Richeson.
5. Walter^{8} Richeson.
6. Voorhees^{8} Richeson.
7. Lillian^{8} B. Richeson.
8. Russell^{8} F. Richeson.
9. Katherine^{8} M. Richeson.
10. Mary^{8} Richeson, m. Henry W. Loving.
11. Helen^{8} Richeson, d. young.

8. Russell^{8} E. Rucker (Sallie^{7}, William^{6}, Garland^{5}, ———), m. Dr. Thomas Allen Kirk, Apr. 17, 1917.

1. Thomas^{9} Allen Kirk, Jr.
2. Elizabeth^{9} Allan Kirk.

9. Katherine^{8} M. Rucker (Sallie^{7}, Wm.^{6} , ———), m. Apr. 26, 1911, Dr. Charles B. Maits, Pittsburgh, Pa.

1. Charles^{9} B. Maits, Jr., b. Dec., 1913.
2. Sarah^{9} Lee Maits, b. June, 1915.

10. Mary^{8} W. Richeson (Sallie^{7}, Wm.^{6}, ———), m. May, 1906, Henry W. Loving.

1. James^{9} R. Loving, b. Feb., 1907.

4. Anthony^{5} Rucker (Ambrose^{4}, Ambrose^{3}) (Jan. 18, 1790-Apr. 15, 1858), b. Bedford; m. Jan. 1, 1815, Margaret Hardy, (Dec. 29, 1793-Apr. 7, 1870.)

James Ayres and wife Nancy sold to Garland and Anthony Rucker of Bedford 1109 acres on both sides of Mill Run, a branch of Goose Creek in Bedford Co., in 1816, adjoining Kennett, Leftwich, and Hurt (D. B. 15, p. 24), Bedford. Two years later, April 9, 1818, they sold this land to their Aunt Elizabeth Rucker Marr, widow of James Marr, for $6600.

On Oct. 11, 1817, William Dent and wife, Esther, deed to Anthony Rucker for $2956. 373 acres on Persimmon Fork of Hunting Creek (D. B. 15, p. 329), Bedford.

Anthony Rucker paid a personal tax in Henry County for one year only, 1830.

At the January Court of Amherst County in 1833 the "Court was satisfied" that Ambrose[5] Rucker, administrator of James Marr's estate, was dead, and appointed Anthony[5] Rucker. At the March Court of the same year, Anthony was appointed Executor of Ambrose[5] Rucker's estate.

With the marriage bond of Anthony Rucker to Peggy Hardy, there is a note to the Clerk of the Court to issue the license. This note is signed by William Hardy, father of Peggy Hardy, dated Jan. 1, 1816.

Will of Anthony[5] Rucker, Apr. 14, 1858, probated Oct. 25, 1858. Devisees under will: Wife, Margaret Rucker; Sons, Joseph H. and Moses P.; dau. Ann D. Ambrose C. Rucker; Joseph H. and Moses P. named as Executors. Joseph H. Rucker and Ambrose Rucker qualified (W. B. R, p. 142), Bedford.

Children mentioned:

1. Ambrose[6] C. Rucker.
2. Eliza[6] M.
3. Mary[6] L.
4. Sophia[6].
5. Sarah[6]:
6. Susan[6] H.
7. Joseph[6] H.
8. John[6] H.
9. Damaris[6].
10. Moses[6] Peter.

1. Ambrose[6] C. Rucker (Anthony[5], Ambrose[4], Ambrose[3]), b. June 22, 1817, in Bedford Co., m. Sarah Jane Board, dau. of John Board, Dec. 6, 1842.

1. Bettie[7] M. Rucker, m. J. M. Parker.
2. Anthony[7], moved to Kansas.
3. John[7], moved to Kansas.

4. Joseph[7] A., d. young.
5. Benjamin[7], m. Lillian Hicks, moved to Bedford.
6. Olando[7], m. Juanita Miller, moved to Bedford.

2. Eliza[6] M. Rucker (Anthony[5], Ambrose[4]) (May 25, 1819-1905, b. in Bedford County, m. Dr. Reese, of Franklin Co.

1. Dr. William[7] P. Reese.
2. Mary[7] Reese, m. Major George Helm.

3. Mary[6] L. Rucker (Anthony[5], Ambrose[4]), b. Apr. 18, 1821, Bedford Co., m. Rev. Alfred Norman, Methodist Minister.

1. N. B.[7] Norman, Roxboro, N. C.
2. Wilbur[7] F., California.
3. Susan[7], m. ——— Womack, Reidsville, N. C.
4. Mattie[7], m. ——— Stokes, Reidsville, N. C.
5. William[7] Capers, Minister, d. 1902.

4. Sophia[6] Rucker (Anthony[5], Ambrose[4]) (June 29, 1823-1900), b. Bedford, m. W. H. Thaxton, Dec. 20, 1843.

5. Sarah[6] Rucker (Anthony[5], Ambrose[4]) (June 23, 1825-1908), b. in Bedford, m. J. Benjamin Burroughs, Asheville, N. C.

1. Dr. James[7] Burroughs.
2. Ambrose[7] Hamet, d. 1929, Lynchburg, Va.
3. Susan[7], m. ——— Fields, of McPherson Co., Kansas.
4. Roberta[7], m. ——— Dennis.

6. Susan[6] Rucker (Anthony[5], Ambrose[4]), b. in Bedford County, Dec. 16, 1827, died young.

7. Joseph[6] H. Rucker (Anthony[5]) (Jan. 5, 1832-1908), m. ——— Poindexter.

9. Ann[6] Damaris Rucker (Anthony[5]) (Feb. 8, 1835-1895), m. T. H. Love, Lynchburg, Virginia.

1. Albert[7] Sidney Love.
2. Margaret[7] Love.

10. Moses[6] Peter Rucker (Anthony[5], Ambrose[4]) (Mch. 10, 1837-1926), m. Sallie F. Parker, Feb. 14, 1866, in Franklin Co.

1. Ann[7] Rucker, b. June 6, 1867, m. William Sutherland, Pen Hook, Franklin Co., Va.
2. David[7] H., b. June 22, 1869, m. ——— Hardy, Moneta, Va.

3. Joseph[7] A., b. June 28, 1871, m. Eliza Cauthorn, Apr. 30, 1901.
4. William[7] P., b. Oct. 24, 1873, m. ——— Hardy, Moneta, Va.
5. Moses[7] P., b. June 27, 1876, m. Mary Williams, Bedford City.
6. Sallie[7] M., b. Dec. 20, 1881, m. Thomas Dixon, Alleghany Co., Va.

3. Joseph[7] A. Rucker (Moses[6], Anthony[5]), m. Eliza Cauthorn, Apr. 30, 1901.

1. Eleanor[8] Jordon (Apr. 2, 1902-June 30, 1907).
2. Joseph[8] A., Jr., b. Aug. 21, 1906.
3. George[8] C. (Nov. 20, 1909-Nov. 23, 1914).
4. William[8] V., b. Mch. 29, 1911.
5. Ambrose[8] A. } twins; b. Jan. 24, 1916.
6. Virginia[8] B. }

8. Elizabeth[5] Rucker (Ambrose[4], Ambrose[3], John[2], Peter[1]), m. James W. Rucker, Apr. 24, 1820, in Bedford, moved to Tenn.

The will of Andrew Rucker recorded in Bedford Co., Nov. 25, 1822, names James as the only son, daughters, Sallie Counda, Fanny Goodman, Anna Padgett, Elizabeth McClanahan and Ruth Stanley.

3. Isaac[4] Rucker (Ambrose[3], John[2], ———) (c. 1770-1838), m. 1st Mary Ann Christian, Jan. 12, 1796, 2nd Mary Wingfield, Feb. 3, 1812.

From the Amherst marriage bonds "Isaac Rucker, Jr. bachelor, to Mary A. Christian, Jan. 12, 1796. Signed, Henry Christian, father." Witness: Isaac Rucker, Thomas Woodroof.

Will of William B. Christian of Charles City Co. Executrix: my wife Elizabeth B. Christian and brother Turner Christian and my nephew, John Hunt Christian. To my niece Susanna B. Christian, and my brother, Turner. The debt due me from my brother, Henry Christian, dec'd, shall be for his widow Patsey Christian, during her life, and at her death to her youngest daughters Frances and Martha. To my brother, Turner Christian's three youngest children, named William, John, and Turner. It is my wish that should any money be left in the hands of my executors that they appropriate a sum of money for the education of Isaac Rucker's four sons, namely, Henry, Ambrose, Isaac, and William Rucker not exceeding £50 each. Aug. 21, 1805.

Oct. 17, 1805. Witness: W. Douglas, Charles Word (W. B. 1789-1808, p. 633), Charles City Co.

The following, written by Isaac, is copied from his Bible, in the possession of Mrs. Joe Thomasson, of Lynchburg, Va.

"Mary Ann Rucker departed this life, Jan. 25, 1812. Isaac Rucker and Mary Ann were married Jan. 19, 1796.

Henry Patterson Rucker was born 23rd of April, 1797.
Ambrose Rucker, born April 2nd, 1799.
Isaac Rucker born September 10, 1801.
William Brown Christian Rucker, b. Sept. 20, 1803.
Martha Susana Rucker, born October 17, 1806.
Jonathan Patterson Rucker, born March 26, 1808.
Benjamin Jennings Rucker, born Dec. 3rd, 1809.
Samuel Christian Rucker, born 10 May, 1811. (departed this life Nov. 12, 1812).
Nathaniel Wingfield Rucker, son of Isaac and Mary, daughter of Nathaniel Wingfield, b. March 6th, 1814.
Mary Ann Rucker, b. June 21st, 1815.
Thomas Rucker, b. Jan. 3rd, 1817."

Isaac[4] paid his first land tax on 400 acres in 1807, but paid a personal tax first in 1796.

James Morton of Woodford County, Kentucky and Ambrose Rucker of Amherst, sold to Isaac Rucker, Jr. 91 acres of land on North side of Pauls Mountain, on Harris Creek at Thoroughfare on top of Pauls Mountains, 3 Oct., 1793 (D. B. G, p. 319).

Isaac Rucker and wife, Mary Ann, sold 400 acres of land to Wiley Campbell, Mch. 2, 1811 (D. B. M,, p. 104).

Isaac[4] Rucker with Ambrose Rucker, security, was appointed guardian to Henry[5] P., Ambrose[5], Isaac[5], William[5] B. and C.[5] Rucker, infants of said Isaac[4] Rucker, 16 May, 1814 (W. B. 5, p. 430).

Isaac[4] Rucker deeds to his daughter, Martha P. Rucker, a negro girl, with Samuel P. Christian, Trustee, 19 Oct., 1812 (D. B. M, p. 275).

Ambrose Rucker Sr. to son, Isaac Rucker of Amherst, 400 acres of land on Rocky Run (both sides), adjoining John Campbell and Nathan Wingfield, to Frederick Fultz's, 15 March, 1806 (D. B. K, p. 452), Amherst Co.

Isaac Rucker went security for one of his first cousins, who later failed in the tobacco business and Isaac was forced to sell most of his property. After this his sons, Henry, Ambrose, Isaac and Jonathan went to Ohio. Later William B., another son went to Mississippi and married there. His youngest son, Benjamin[5] Rucker, stayed with his father who had been paralyzed.

Both Isaac and his wife, Mary Wingfield were buried at Mt. Horeb Church, not far from his old home, where he died.

Mary Ann Christian died at the home of her brother, Henry A. Christian, in Lynchburg, while on a visit there with her husband and little daughter, Martha. Mary Ann gave this daughter, Martha, to her brother, Henry, on her death bed.

Mrs. Theisz said that they did not keep in touch with the sons in Ohio, but that after the Civil War, her father, Benjamin learned through Major Glass (Cousin) that Isaac[5] Rucker on account of his southern sentiments found it very unpleasant in Ohio, and moved to Missouri about the beginning of the war. During the Civil War, Major Glass of Lynchburg, received a letter from a son of this Isaac Rucker, saying he was a prisoner at Camp Chase, Ohio, and wanted Major Glass to get him exchanged for an officer of the same rank. He was a major on Gen. Price's staff. Major Glass's mother and the young officer's mother were sisters, also the wife of Major Glass was a first cousin to Isaac[5] Rucker, therefore he appealed to Maj. Glass. However, the young officer died before an exchange was made. His name was Robert Rucker, and his mother's name was Cawthorne, the dau. of Robert Cawthorne.

Thomas Glass settled in Fluvanna Co., m. Lavinia, dau. of Richard and Ann Williamson Cauthorne. Thomas was a captain of the militia during the Revolution.

Issue:

1. Robert Henry Glass, m. Eliza, dau. of Judge Samuel Christian, and gdanddau. of Henry Christian, Revolutionary soldier.

In 1821, Isaac[4] Rucker, a Justice of Peace of Amherst, was appointed adm. of William Clarke's will, and in 1827, June Court, was appointed Guardian to Louise Cawthorne, dau. of Robert Cawthorne. In Apr., 1820, he was the Executor of the will of Ambrose Rucker.

Isaac Rucker sold to David Tomlinson all of his interest in the crops now making, and all of his tobacco to Joseph Dodd, now in the hands of his (Joseph's) mother. Isaac Rucker, Sr. (D. B. Q, p. 393), April 18, 1825.

Bartlett Clements, executor of Ambrose Tomlinson, deceased of Amherst, sold property to Isaac and Henry Rucker, 3, Apr. 1824 (D. B. W, p. 30).

Bartlett Clements appointed Isaac Rucker, Sr., his attorney, both of Amherst, Trustee for "My children Polly, Joicy, and

Nancy Clements, their share of the estate of Ambrose Tomlinson, deceased, which may come to me as Guardian of my children, 1825 (D. B. Q, p. 283).

Issue (by 1st mar.):

1. Henry^{5} Patterson Rucker.
2. Ambrose^{5}, m. Haas, dau. of Jacob, of Ohio.
3. Isaac^{5}, moved to Ohio, then to Missouri.
4. William^{5} Brown, b. Sept. 20, 1803; m. and lived near Vicksburg, Miss.
5. Martha^{5} Susan.
6. Jonathan^{5} Christian.
7. Benjamin^{5} Jennings.
8. Samuel^{5} Christian (May 10, 1812-Nov. 1812).

Issue (by 2nd mar.):

9. Nathan^{5} Wingfield.
10. Mary^{5} Ann.
11. Thomas^{5} Hollewell.

1. Henry^{5} Patterson Rucker (Isaac^{4}, Ambrose^{3}, John^{2}), b. Apr. 23, 1797, m. Judith Lee Glascock of Pittsylvania Co. Moved to Ohio, then to Georgia.

1. Mary^{6} Jane Rucker, d. young.
2. Samuel^{6}, unmar.
3. George^{6} Isaac, m. Matilda Reedy.
    1. Matilda^{7} Rucker, m. Jeptha H. Philips.
        1. Althea^{8} Lee, m. Charles E. Echert.
        2. Mary^{8}, m. Hays Gray of Rome, Ga.
    2. Virginia^{7} Lee Rucker, m. George A. Love.
        1. Virginia^{8} Love, m. Wilbur McWilliams.
    3. Evelin^{7}, m. Andrew H. Thompson.
        1. Judith^{8} Lee Thompson.
    4. G. W.^{7} Rucker, of Greenville, Ohio.

5. Martha^{5} Susan Rucker (Isaac^{4}), b. Oct. 17, 1805, m. Sept. 16, 1833, Edward Isaac Brown, son of Stephen, who came to Henrico Co. from England, 1799.

Marriage contract between Edward Brown and Martha S. Rucker, dau. of Isaac Rucker, dated Sept. 16, 1833. Edward to enjoy the use of two of her six slaves, she to have full benefit and then to pass it to her heirs, Richard H. Toler, Trustee. Isaac Rucker and W. Drummond of Amherst acknowledge same.

Martha grew up in the home of her uncle, Henry A. Christian, as one of his family. The following account is given by Martha's youngest son, Benjamin:

"My father, Edward Isaac Brown m. 1st Elizabeth Godfrey, Nov. 2, 1811, 2nd m. Martha S. Rucker of Amherst County, Sept. 17, 1833. During the war of 1812, Edward was stationed in Manchester, Va.

Issue (1st mar.):

1. Edward[6] Brown, d. young. twins, b. Aug. 22, 1812, Sarah[6] Ann, m. W. B. Rock. Richmond, Va.
2. Thomas[6] Logan Douglas, b. Sept. 17, 1814, in Richmond, Va. Commanded a volunteer company in Mexican War; d. in Mississippi on his way home.
3. Elizabeth[6], m. Henry Benson, Feb. 24, 1817 in Lynchburg, Va.
4. Stephen[6], b. 1819 near Liberty, Bedford Co.
5. Samuel[6] Philips, b. Mch. 30, 1822, in Liberty; was a Surgeon in the Confederate Army; practiced in Cumberland Co., Va.
6. Lucy[6] Ann, m. S. S. Pettit, b. Feb. 18, 1824 in Lynchburg.

Issue (by 2nd mar.):

7. Edward[6] Isaac, b. June 11, 1834, Lynchburg; m. dau. of John Robin MacDaniel.
8. William[6] Henry, b. May 13, 1837, Buckingham Co.
9. Philip[6] Francis, b. June 2, 1842, Halifax Co.; m. Nannie Adams.
10. Mary[6] Frances, b. May 11, 1844, Columbia; m. ——— Fry.
11. Benjamin[6], m. ——— Fry (May 25, 1847-1917).

6. Jonathan[5] Patterson Rucker (Isaac[4], Ambrose[3], John[2]), m. Mch. 26, 1808, Antionette Cawthorne, dau. of Robert, lived in Ohio.

Jonathan P. Rucker and Antoinette, his wife, sold to Jacob Haas personal property (O. B., p. 39), Apr., 1832.

7. Benjamin[5] Jennings Rucker (Isaac[4], Ambrose[3]) (Dec. 3, 1809-Apr. 28, 1889), m. 1836 Eliza Jane Sandidge (1814-1884), dau. of Lindsey and Clara Graves Higgenbotham Sandidge.

Will of Benjamin J. Rucker, dated Jan. 5, 1884, prob. May 21, 1889.

To my dau., Clara G. unmar.; To my son, J. H. Rucker; To my dau., M. Ellen Theisz; To my son, Paul J. Rucker; To my son, Benjamin L. Rucker; To my son, Edwin T. Rucker; To my son, William B. Rucker. To my nephew, J. Mangus Sandidge. Executor: H. Henry Rucker (W. B. 1, p. 145), Amherst.

1. H. Henry^6 Rucker.
2. Mary^6 Ellen Rucker.
3. Paul^6 Jennings Rucker.
4. Benjamin^6 Lindsey Rucker.
5. Clara^6 Graves Rucker.
6. Edwin^6 Timothy Rucker.
7. William^6 Bascom Rucker (Brack) b. Sept. 1853; m. Ida Loving Higginbotham, dau. of Aaron Higginbotham and wife Ann Sandidge.

1. H. Henry^6 Rucker (Benj.^{5}, Isaac^4, ———) (July 6, 1840-Aug. 1, 1906), unmarried.

Henry^6 Rucker at the beginning of the Civil War, joined the 2nd Va. Cavalry, Company E, and served until Lee's surrender at Appomattox, having his horse killed under him at the last charge made there. He went to Texas for a few years, but returned to Virginia.

Paul^5 J. joined the same company with Henry at the age of seventeen, and served until the surrender under Fitzhugh Lee, April, 1865.

After it was known that Lee would have to capitulate, Fitzhugh Lee brought his division of cavalry out from Appomattox with the intention of joining Johnson, but learning that Johnson had also surrendered, Lee disbanded his division at Lynchburg. Paul came home a few days later than Henry, who walked home from Appomattox with the intention of getting another horse, and joining Lee's company at Lynchburg."

2. Mary^6 Ellen (Benj.^{5}, ———), m. John Theisz. She was born April 28, 1842, and lived a long and useful life and died without heir in Dec., 1923.

3. Paul^6 Jennings Rucker (Benj.^{5}, Isaac^4, ———) (Feb. 22, 1843-May 13, 1927), m. Feb. 30, 1878, Blanch T. Higginbotham (Oct. 30, 1850-Dec. 25, 1922), dau. of Benj. and Margaret Carter Higginbotham. Blanch d. in Lynchburg. Paul enlisted in the Civil War at the beginning and served in 2nd Va. Cavalry, Co. E, until the surrender.

1. Edwin^7 Rucker, b. Dec. 8, 1879.
2. Vivian^7 V. Rucker, b. July 7, 1889, m. Robert Hackworth, Oct. 7, 1819.

Issue:

1. Edgar^{8} Rucker Hackworth, b. Nov. 29, 1921.
2. Betty^{8} Frances Hackworth, b. Jan. 3, 1924.

4. Benjamin^{6} Lindsey Rucker (Benjamin^{5}, Isaac^{4}, Ambrose^{3}), m. Dec. 3, 1846, Sally F. Parks, dau. of Burwell and Paulina Davies Parks.

Benjamin entered the Confederate Army in the 19th Infantry. He was captured with his brigade in 1864, on the retreat from Richmond and was taken to Point Lookout where he remained until the following summer. He only weighed 90 lbs. when he returned from the army.

1. Ruth^{7} Eliza, unmar.
2. Benjamin^{7} Parks, m. Florence Dickey.
   1. One son^{8}.
3. Dr. Henry^{7} Cowles, m. Lillian^{7} Rucker (William^{6}, William^{5}, George^{4}, John^{3}, John^{2}, Peter^{1}). (See George Rucker, p. ——).
4. Elizabeth^{7} Palmer, m. Dr. Karl Stahrs.
5. Mary Nell^{7}, m. Wingfield Scott MacGill.
   1. Emma^{8} MacGill.
   2. Scott^{8} MacGill.
   3. Eleanor^{8} MacGill.
6. Clara^{7} Maude, unmar.
7. Sara^{7} Pauline, m. 1st Truman Lanham, 2nd Richard Acres, no heirs.

5. Clara^{6} Graves Rucker (May 4, 1849-1914), unmar.

6. Dr. Edwin^{6} Timothy Rucker (Benjamin^{5}, Isaac^{4}, Ambrose^{3}), (Mch. 13, 1853-Apr. 9, 1918), m. Nov. 18, 1879, Anne Pendleton Pierce, (Dec. 9, 1855-Mch. 3, 1917), dau. of ——— and Maria Claiborne Dabney Pierce. He was a practicing physician in Manchester and Richmond, graduated at a medical college in Ky., practiced for a time in Fairfax where he married.

1. Dr. Marvin^{7} Pierce Rucker, b. Jan. 6, 1881, in Fairfax, m. Nov. 3, 1906, Josephine McCrae, of Richmond, b. July 29, 1885. Practices medicine in Richmond, Va.
   1. Edwin^{8} Rucker, b. Aug. 13, 1907.
   2. George^{8} Scott, b. Mch. 17, 1909.
   3. Josephine^{8} Pierce, b. Sept. 14, 1910.
   4. Douglas^{8} Pendleton, b. Nov. 15, 1914.

2. Anne^{7} Clayborne, b. Sept. 6, 1882, m. James Fleet Ryland, Richmond, Nov. 18, 1908.
    1. James^{8} Rucker Ryland, May 4, 1912.
    2. Anne^{8} Pendleton, Apr. 26, 1915.
    3. Charlotte^{8} Hawes, Oct. 27, 1920.

9. Nathan^{5} Wingfield Rucker (Isaac^{4}, ———) (6 Mch. 1814-Oct., 1862, m. Frances Jones, dau. of William Richard Jones and wife, Polly McDaniel (8 Oct. 1824-Feb. 3, 1898).

1. William^{6} Rucker.
2. Mary^{6} J. Rucker.
3. John^{6} Thomas Rucker.
4. Nannie^{6} E. Rucker.
5. James^{6} Monroe Rucker.
6. Henry^{6} W. Rucker.
7. Frances^{6} O. Rucker.
8. Nathan^{6} Rucker.

1. William^{6} Rucker (Nathan^{5} W., Isaac^{4}, Ambrose^{3}, ——) (Nov. 13, 1840-Jan. 25, 1870), served in the Confederate Army, Co. H, 19th Va. He was wounded 1864 at Fort Canton, captured and imprisoned at Camp Chase. He was promoted to First Lieut. just before the close of the war.

2. Mary^{6} Jane Rucker (Nathan^{5} W., Isaac^{4}), m. Joseph Watts, 1st cousin.

1. Nicholas^{7} Watts, m. 1st Shepherd, 2nd Wilkinson.
2. James^{7}, m. 1st ————, 2nd Lena Hicks (cousin).
3. William^{7}, m. ———— Brown.
4. Lillian^{7}, m. ———— Taylor.
5. Rosa^{7}, m.
6. Mary^{7} Frances, single.
7. Joseph^{7}, Jr.
8. Edna^{7}, m. ———— Taylor.

3. John^{6} Thomas Rucker (Nathan^{5} W., Isaac^{4}, ———), b. June 12, 1847, m. Sarah Ellen Ballew Ogden, Dec. 8, 1875 (July 23, 1844, Mch. 26, 1921).

1. Lillian^{7} Snead Rucker.
2. Mary^{7} Jackson Rucker.
3. Eleanor^{7} Burks, d. Mch. 23, 1921.

1. Lillian^{7} Snead Rucker (John^{6} T., Nathan^{5} W., Isaac^{4}), b. July 3, 1877, m. Sept. 13, 1905, Rufus Gilliam.
Issue:

1. Thornton^{8} Elwood, b. May 12, 1906.
2. Kathleen^{8} Rucker.

4. Nannie^{6} E. Rucker (Nathan^{5} W., Isaac^{4}, ———), m. George Hicks, 1874, son of Leroy and Parmelia Hicks.

1. William^{7} Hicks.
2. Lena^{7}.
3. Frank^{7}.
4. Joseph^{7}.

5. James^{6} Monroe Rucker (Nathan^{5} W., Isaac^{4}, ———), m. Janie Duff.

1. Pearl^{7} Rucker, m. ——— Feagans.
2. Minnie^{7}, m. ——— Boswell.
3. James^{7}, Aviator in World War.
4. Ruth^{7}, m. ——— Paris.
5. Louis^{7}.
6. James^{7} W.
7. Warner^{7} A.
8. Warren^{7}.
9. Cecil^{7} G.
10. Vivian^{7} M.

6. Henry^{6} W. Rucker (Nathan^{5} W., Isaac^{4}), m. 1887 Elizabeth B. Bethel, Salt. Lake City, Utah.

1. William^{7} Rucker, m. Rucker.
2. Lizzie^{7}, m. Rucker.

8. Nathan^{6} J. Rucker (Nathan^{5} W., Isaac^{4}), m. 1890 Nannie Duff, dau. of Preston and Martha Duff.

1. Charles^{7} Rucker, served in World War.
2. Bernard^{7}, served in World War.

10. Mary^{5} Ann Rucker (Isaac^{4}, Ambrose^{3}, John^{2}, ———), b. June 25, 1815, m. Robert W. Watts, 1835.

1. Nicholas^{6} Watts, d. young.
2. Almira^{6}.
3. Edna^{6}.
4. Joseph^{6}, m. Mary^{6} Jane Rucker, 1st cousin. See Nathan^{5}, Isaac^{4}, Ambrose^{3}, ———).
5. Mary^{6}, d. young.

6. Julia[6], d. young.
7. Rebecca[6], m. George W. Higginbotham, b. 1874.
8. Robert[6], m. Ida Burford, lived in Lynchburg.
    1. Robert[7] Watts.
    2. Willie[7], m. Joseph Thomasson, Lynchburg.
    3. Harry[7], m.
    4. Carrie[7].
    5. Hattie[7].
    6. Lawrence[7], a minister.

11. Thomas[5] Hallowell Rucker (Isaac[4], Ambrose[3], John[2]), m. Nancy Sandidge, daughter of Lindsey and Clara Sandidge.

1. William[6] L. Rucker, m. Mary Ware, dau. of William Ware.
2. Emma[6], m. ——— Atkins, of N. C.
3. Tekoa[6], m. ——— Keister, of Charlotte, N. C.
4. Nathan[6], d. unmar.

4. Benjamin[4] Rucker (Ambrose[3], John[2], ———), m. Sallie Harris, Nov. 22, 1813, of Amherst Co. Marriage bonds signed by Ambrose Rucker and William Lee Harris. Benjamin served in the War of 1812. In 1785 Land tax books he begins paying on 320 acres of land in Amherst.

5. Winifred[4] Rucker (Ambrose[3], John[2], ———), d. c. 1791, m. Benjamin Plunkett, son of John and Mildred Plunkett of Orange and Amherst. (See Isaac[3], John[2], Peter[1] Rucker). Benjamin Plunkett m. later Frances[4] Ham, dau. of Stephen Ham and Mildred[3] Rucker (John[2], Peter[1]). See Plunkett and Higginbotham lines.

Issue (by 1st mar.):

1. Ambrose[5] Plunkett.
2. Sally[5] Plunkett.

Issue (by Benjamin's 2nd mar.):

3. Jonathan[5] Plunkett.
4. Willis[5] Rucker Plunkett.
5. Milly[5] Rucker Plunkett.
6. William[5] Rucker Plunkett.

1. Ambrose[5] Plunkett, m. Tabitha Hall, bond signed Jan. 13, 1792, with consent of "Father, Benjamin Plunkett" (see Plunkett). Teste: Anthony Rucker, Richard Rucker, Bartlett Ham.

2. Sally^5 Plunkett, m. James Wickersham, bachelor, bond signed Jan. 17, 1773, by Benjamin Plunkett, "father", both of Amherst.

6. Margaret^4 Rucker (Ambrose^3, John^2, Peter^1), d. 1785; m. c. 1769 John^4 McDaniel (George^3, John^2). Will of John McDaniel dated 1835, probated 1839, Amherst. (See McDaniel line). After Margaret's death he m. Lucy^5 Rucker (Benj.^{4}, Ambrose^3, ———).

Issue (by 1st mar.):

1. William ^{5} McDaniel.
2. George^5 McDaniel.
3. Mary^5 McDaniel.
4. Judith^5 McDaniel.

Issue (by 2nd mar.):

5. Ambrose^5 McDaniel.
6. Lindsey^5 McDaniel.
7. Gideon^5 McDaniel.
8. Elizabeth^5 Davis McDaniel.
9. Margaret^5 Ware McDaniel.
10. Sophia^5 Strange McDaniel.

7. Frances^4 Rucker (Ambrose^3, John^2), m. Jan. 25, 1806, James Lee, of Caswell County, N. C.

8. Molly^4 Rucker (Ambrose^3), m. ——— Burford.

1. William^5 Burford.
2. Ambrose^5.
3. Betsy^5.
4. Mary^5 Tinsley Burford.

2. Ambrose^5 Burford (Molly^4, Ambrose^3 Rucker), m. Nancy, daughter of David Tinsley, Amherst Co., Jan. 19, 1796.

Inventory and appraisement of estate of Ambrose Burford, 3 Dec. 1835 (W. B. 9, p. 214), Amherst Co.

Division of his estate:

To Nancy Burford, widow. Her dower as by will.

1st and 2nd lots to Sylvester and Gustavus Burford.

3rd lot to Benjamin McCray in right of his wife.

4th and 5th lots to Martha and Amanda Burford.

Lot 6th to Micajah Clark in right of his wife Belilah.

Lot 7th to James C. Burford.

Lot 8th to Thermuthis Burford. She was given a slave named Mary, worth $275, and money and bonds worth $34.61, total $309.61.

Lot 9th to the infant children of Matilda Tinsley, dec'd.

Lot 10th to Archelus Cox in right of his wife Juliana.

Signed, Wiatt Pettijohn, Robert Ridgway, Isaac R. Reynolds. At a court for Amherst Co. 21 Nov. 1836, this report of the division of the personal estate of Ambrose Burford, dec'd. having been returned and ordered to be for exceptions and no exceptions being filed thereto, was confirmed and ordered to be recorded. Teste, Robert Lindsay, clerk of Amherst Co. Court (W. B. 9, p. 253).

Nancy Burford, William Tucker, and Willis McReynolds gave bond for administration of Ambrose Burford's estate, 16 Nov. 1835 (W. B. 9, p. 135).

Nancy Burford deeded property to James C. Burford and wife, Clementine, in 1837, Amherst Co.

4. Mary[5] Tinsley Burford (Molly[4] Rucker), m. Robert Scott McAlpin.

  1. James[6] Burford McAlpin, whose granddau., Georgia[8] E., m. Dr. Wills.

9. Elizabeth[4] Rucker (Ambrose[3], James[2], Peter[1]), m. James Marr, of Orange. Witness: Isaac Rucker, Alexander Marr, Jan. 3, 1791, in Amherst Co. In 1818 she bought land of her nephew in Bedford Co., 1109 acres on Mill Creek.

Garland Rucker and his wife, and Anthony Rucker and his wife sold 1109 acres to Elizabeth, the widow of James Marr, on Mill Creek, a branch of Goose Creek; adjoining Leftwich, Apr. 9, 1818 (D. B. 15, p. 380), Bedford Co. James Ayres and his wife, Nancy, sold to Garland and Anthony Rucker of Bedford 1109 acres for $4430.00, on both sides of Mill Creek adjoining Kenneth Robinson, Leftwich and Hurt, Mch. 24, 1816.

Land Office, Richmond, Va., Warrant No. 960 (John Marr), a warrant for 50 acres to Daniel Marr, son and heir of John Marr land due unto Daniel for military services performed by the said John Marr, as a soldier in the late war between Great Britain and France, 1763, granted 1780.

10. Sophia[4] Rucker (Ambrose[3]), m. Robert Jennings, Dec. 23, 1791.

11. Caroline[4] Rucker (Ambrose[3]), m. John Hansford in Amherst. The marriage bond was signed Nov. 23, 1793, by her father, Ambrose. Isaac Rucker, J. Callaway and James Wichersham were Witnesses.

12. Matilda[4] Rucker (Ambrose[3]), m. Alexandria Marr; witness: Isaac Rucker. Marriage bond dated Dec. 27, 1796, Alexandria Marr, Bachelor of Amherst to marry Matilda Rucker, Spinster. Signed Ambrose Rucker. Teste: Isaac Rucker.

(One Alexander Marr declared his importation from Great Britain in Caroline County, Mch., 1743 (O. B., 1741-46) (possibly father).

13. Charlotte[4] Rucker was not married when her father Ambrose made his will, 1803.

14. Sarah[4] Rucker (Ambrose[3]), m. John Marr, Aug. 9, 1802. Witness: Reuben Rucker and Alexandria Marr.

4. Benjamin[3] Rucker (John[2], Peter[1]) (c. 1720-1810), of Amherst, was an Attorney at Law, Sheriff of Amherst Co., Justice of the Peace (*Cabells and Their Kin*), a Trustee of the Warminster Academy (*Hening*), a vestryman of Rucker or St. Mathew's Church, a church built by Col. Ambrose Rucker in Lexington Parish, and a member of the committee of Safety of Amherst County (*Cabells and Their Kin,* p. 100) (D. B., p. 24, Oct. 6, 1769), Amherst Co. Peter Rucker of Orange deeds to Benjamin Rucker of Amherst 526 acres of land, beginning at Benj. Rucker's corner to Robert Rose's corner. Witness: Anthony Rucker, John Rucker, and Ambrose Rucker. He lived near the Tobacco Row Mountains, near the Bennetts. In 1789 he is paying taxes on 4430 acres in Amherst, but begins the next year to divide and sell, paying on 617 acres in 1809. In 1783 he is paying on 17 whites, 18 blacks and 8 horses.

Benjamin Rucker of Amherst Co. on Feb. 22, 1773, bought from Bowling Clarke and W. Winifred of Bedford, for $266, 532 acres on Naked Mountain on a creek (D. B. 5, p. 54, Bedford Co.). This land was deeded to son, James Rucker, of Campbell Co. (formed from Bedford in 1784) land on Blackwater Creek adj. said James Rucker, Edmund and Henry Tate, Samuel Scott, Jesse Burton and William Terrell, June 2, 1795 (D. B. 3, p. 535, Campbell). However, the land was not relinquished until Apr. 14, 1810, by Benjamin and wife, Betty Rucker.

In the meantime James and Nancy, his wife, had sold the same 532 acres for £1100 to Richard Chilton of Culpeper in 1798

(D. B. 4, p. 509, Campbell). Nancy, wife of James Rucker, relinquished her rights to the land at the June Court of 1799. Benjamin paid taxes on this land until 1795, then James began paying until 1811.

Maj. Samuel Scott bought 400 acres of land on both sides of Turkey Branch, adjoining Henry Tate, lying between Benjamin Rucker and Chiles Terrell, in Amherst.

Among the unindexed Revolution claims in the Archives in Richmond paid in 1781 for provisions impressed or taken for the use of the army appears:

To Benjamin Rucker for 49½ lbs. of bacon, for the militia of Gen. Green on Feb. 24, 1781; To Benjamin Rucker for Publick Service 270 lbs. of beef, 462 bushels of flour to the troops on the march to Gen. Green; Bacon for Washingtons Dragoons, July 1781; Also numbers of others.

The first tax list in 1782 mentions "Capt. Benjamin Rucker" paying on about 1100 acres of land.

Division of Estate:

To James Rucker 3340 lbs. sterling.

To Thomas Rucker 3340 lbs. sterling.

To Gideon Rucker from the Brown's Estate in all 3340 lbs. sterling.

To Bennett Rucker the same amt.

To Lucy McDaniel the same amt.

To Sophia Burrus the same amt.

To Milly Brown.

Legatees of Benjamin Rucker dec'd Oct. 8, 1810 (W. B. 5, p. 18).

Will of Benjamin Rucker, dated Nov. 20, 1808, probated Feb. 22, 1810, mentions: wife Betty, and children, James, Thomas, Gideon, Lucy McDaniel, Willie Brown, Millie, Sophia Burruss and Bennett Rucker. Witness: Richard, Anthony and Armistead Rucker (W. B. A, p. 123).

1. James[4] Rucker.
2. Thomas[4] Rucker.
3. Gideon[4] Rucker.
4. Lucy[4] MacDaniel.
5. Millie[4] Brown.
6. Sophia[4] Burruss.
7. Bennett[4] Rucker.

For most of the following data, we are indebted to Gen. Edmund Winchester Rucker, Mr. William Harrison Rucker, Mr. Abbott C. Rucker and Mr. John Boddie.

1. James[4] Rucker (Ben.[3], John[2], Peter[1]), b. 1758 in Amherst Co., d. Sept. 10, 1819 in Rutherford Co., Tenn; m. 1st May 31, 1781, Euphan Tate, d. Dec., 1786 (dau. of Henry Tate of Campbell Co., will probated Sept. 3, 1793). James m. 2nd, Jan. 31, 1788, Nancy Reed (dau. of William Reed, will probated in Bedford Co., 1798, mentions: wife Joanna; and children: daughters Nancy Rucker, Sally Rucker, Joyce Rucker, Joanna Reed, Elizabeth Miller, Mary Anderson; and Executors: sons Samuel Reed and James Rucker).

James Rucker purchased from James Reed and Wife, Ann, for £252, 252 acres of land on Blackwater Creek, Sept. 6, 1787 in Campbell Co.

James was made Inspector of tobacco at Lynches Warehouse in Campbell Co., Oct. 1791. He was a Methodist minister. He may have served in the Revolutionary War. The Order Book of Campbell Co., states "James Rucker Furnished supplies to Christopher Irvine Commissioner of the Provision Law, 450 lbs. of beef, two diets at the rate of one Shilling each. Three barrells of corn at six Shillings. Order certified Sept. 1781 (Campbell Co. O. B., 1782-85, p. 53). The will of James[4], dated July 1819, probated Apr. 12, 1820, in Rutherford Co. Tenn. (W. B. 4, p. 199): To my wife, Nancy Rucker; Daus. Betsy Donalson, Lucinda Miller; Sons: Jonathan, Henry Tate, James, Jr., Benjamin, and William Rucker; Dau. Johanna Price; Son Western Rucker; Dau. Joice Rucker; Sons Jack W., Joseph Burrus and Robert Rucker. Executors, sons, James, William, Samuel and Benj. Rucker.

Issue (by 1st mar.):

1. Henry[5] Tate Rucker.
2. Elizabeth[5].
3. Lucinda[5].
4. Jonathan[5].

Issue (by 2nd mar.):

5. James[5] Rucker.
6. Benjamin[5].
7. William[5].
8. Samuel[5].
9. Joanna[5].
10. Western[5] Tennessee.
11. John[5] Wyatt.

12. Joseph[5].
13. Robert[5].
14. Joice[5].

1. Henry[5] Tate Rucker (James[4], Benj.[3], John[2]), b. Dec. 6, 1786, in Campbell Co., Va., d. Apr. 19, 1866, in Rutherford Co., Tenn.; m. Nancy Kavanaugh, dau. of Dr. Charles Kavanaugh, of De Soto, Miss.

1. Mary[6] E. Donelson Rucker.
2. Francis[6].
3. Cynthia[6].
4. Abbott[6] Coleman, of Ripley, Miss.
5. Lindsey[6] Pork, m. ——— Travis, a minister of Brenham, Texas.
6. Dr. Charles[6] Covington.
7. William[6] J. Knox.

1. Mary[6] E. Donelson Rucker (Henry[5], James[4]) (Feb. 24, 1819-1893), m. 1841, James Munford Spight, of Whitesville, Tenn., b. July 5, 1808, in Jones Co., N. C., d. Mch. 10, 1861, in Ripley, Miss.

1. Thomas[7] Spight.
2. Francis[7] Spight, m. Joseph Pearce.
3. James[7] Spight, d. young.
4. Simon[7] Reynolds Spight.
5. Lindsey[7] Donelson Spight.
6. Julia[7] Ann Spight.

1. Thomas[7] Spight (Mary[6], Henry[5], James[4] Rucker), m. 1st Virginia Barnett, 1st cousin; 2nd Mrs. Theda Moore. He served as Captain in the Confederate Army, was a graduate of law and for 25 yrs. was a congressman from Ripley, Miss.

Issue (by 1st mar.):

1. Mattie[8] Spight.
2. Mamie[8] Spight.
3. Allen[8] Spight.
4. Lillian[8] Spight.
5. Henry[8] Spight.
6. Lynn[8] Spight.

4. Simon[7] Reynolds Spight (Mary[6], Henry[5], ———), m. Julia Ann Welch.

1. Lizzie[8] Spight.
2. Minnie[8] Spight.

3. Pearl[8] Spight.
4. Willie[8] Spight.
5. John[8] Spight.
6. Frank[8] Spight.

5. Lindsey[7] Donelson Spight (Mary[6], ———), b. Nov. 11, 1847, Ripley, Miss.; m. 1st Margaret V. Littleton, Oct., 1868, m. 2nd Emma Hill, of Trenton, Tenn.

Issue (by 1st mar.):

1. James[8] Burwell Spight.
    1. Lindsey[9] Spight.
    2. Prudence[9] Spight.
2. Fannie[8] Lamira Spight.
3. Nannie[8] Spight, d. in Texas.
4. Harrison[8] Robins Spight, d. in Tenn.
5. Thomas[8] Spight.
6. Julia[8] Ann Spight.

2. Fannie[8] Lamira Spight (Lindsey[7], Marie[6] Rucker), m. F. E. Chumbler.

1. Virginia[9] Spight Chumbler.
2. Gladys[9] Chumbler.
3. Gerald[9] Chumbler.
4. Leonard[9] Chumbler.
5. Julia[9] Chumbler.

5. Thomas[8] Spight (Lindsey[7], ———), m. Ella Vivian Fallas, of Oregon. He was a missionary to Argentina, South America, for 14 yrs.; served in the Spanish war in 1898; d. at Tampa, Fla. His children live in Los Angeles, Calif.

1. Julia[9] Spight.
2. Isabel[9] Spight.
3. Lindsey[9] Spight.
4. Thomas[9] Spight.

6. Julia[8] Ann Spight (Lindsey[7], ———), m. Aug. 24, 1893, John Robert Johnson.

1. Robert[9] Inman Johnson.
2. Horace[9] Spight Johnson.
3. May[9] Lois Johnson.
4. Edgar[9] Mullins Johnson.
5. John[9] Thomas Johnson.
6. Julian[9] Johnson.
7. Virginia[9] Catherine, b. Sept. 28, 1914.

1. Robert^9 Inman Johnson (Julia^8, Lindsey^7, Mary^6, ——), of Gibson Co., Tenn., b. May 19, 1895. Graduated at Richmond College, Richmond, Va., and the Baptist Theological Seminary, studied voice culture in Italy and in Louisville, Ky. He m. Louise Bave in Italy in 1922.

2. Horace^9 Spight Johnson (Julia^8, ———), b. in Tenn. (June 24, 1897-Feb. 26, 1899), buried at Cave Hill Cemetery, Louisville, Ky.

3. May^9 Lois Johnson (Julia^8, ———), b. Aug. 21, 1899; m. July 12, 1924, James Roscoe Holbrook, of Marysville, Tenn. She is a graduate of Westhampton College, Richmond, Va. She now lives in Orlando, Fla.

4. Edgar^9 Mullins Johnson (Julia^8, ———), b. in Nelson Co., Ky., Feb. 21, 1902, m. Ann Lucile Smith, June 24, 1927, Richmond, Va. He graduated at Richmond College, then Yale, and now is secretary of Religious Education, in Bridgeport, Conn.

5. John^9 Thomas Johnson (Julia^8, ———), b. in Nelson Co., Ky., Apr. 30, 1904; graduated at Marysville College, Tenn., and at the University of Ill., at Urbanna, Ill., and is an instructor there.

6. Julian^9 Johnson (Julia^8, ———), b. July 3, 1906, in Ky., graduated at Marysville College, and now in 1928, is a medical student at the University of Penna.

2. Francis^6 Rucker (Henry^5, James^4, Benj.^{3}, ———), m. ——— Barnett.

1. Virginia^7, m. Thomas Spight.
2. Albert^7, m. ——— Guerney.
3. Henry^7, m. Dolly ———.

3. Cynthia^6 Rucker (Henry^5, ———), m. 1st ——— Comiselle; 2nd ——— Keenan.

Issue (by 1st mar.):

1. Thomas^7 Comiselle.
2. Frankie^7 Comiselle.

Issue (by 2nd mar.):

3. Lydia^7 Keenan.
4. Cynthia^7 Keenan.

4. Abbott[6] Coleman Rucker (Henry[5], ———) (Dec. 16, 1822-1906), m. Emiline M. Prince.

1. W. Henry[7] Rucker, m. Pink Thorn, Gulfport, Miss.
2. Charles[7] A. Rucker.
3. Richard[7] Prince Rucker, unmar.
4. Thomas[7] Coleman Rucker, m. Nellie Whitten.
5. Frank[7] P. Rucker.
6. Mary[7] J. Rucker, m. Andrew Simpson.
7. Abbott[7] Coleman Rucker, Jr., m. Annie Coombs. He was mayor of Ripley, Miss., in 1902.

2. Elizabeth[5] Rucker (James[4], Benj.[3], John[2], ———) (Jan. 8, 1782-Mch. 31, 1828), m. 1801, Severn Donelson, b. in Va. in 1773, d. in Tenn., 1818 (brother of Rachel Donelson, the wife of Gen. Andrew Jackson, and son of Col. John Donelson and his wife, Rachel Stockley, of Va.)

1. Andrew[6] Jackson Donelson, adopted by Gen. Andrew Jackson.
2. Thomas[6] Jefferson Donelson, b. Dec. 4, 1804.

3. Lucinda[5] Rucker (James[4], ———), m. Sept. 8, 1803, Simon Miller.

4. Jonathan[5] Rucker (James[4], ————) (Apr. 18, 1785-1816), m. 1807, Polly S. Reed.

1. Thomas[6] Rucker.
2. Matilda [6] Barton.
3. Benjamin[6] Franklin Rucker.
4. Francis[6] Heard, of Galveston, Texas.

5. James[5] Rucker (James[4], Benj.[3], ———) (Dec. 25, 1788-Sept. 27, 1850), m. 1st in June, 1811, Lucy L. Bedford, in Rutherford Co., Tenn.; 2nd, Lucy's sister, Mrs. Mary N. Johns. Lucy and Mary Bedford were daughters of Col. Bedford and his wife, Mary Reed, dau. of Clements Reed, of Charlotte Co., Va. *The Enquirer* dated July 2, 1819, gives the names of Col. Bedford's children: Mary, Wife of John Johns, Lucy, Wife of James Rucker, Robert Bedford, Clements Bedford, and Frances Ann Bedford.

Will of Isaac Reed, of Charlotte Co., Va. My eldest son, Clem, not of age; My wife Sarah, and the child she goes with; My three children. Executors, wife Sarah, my relation and friend Coll. Thomas Reed and John Coleman. Witnesses, Jonathan Reed, George Carrington and William Dobbs. The will is not dated, but was probated Mch. 2, 1778, at the court held in Charlotte Co., July 2, 1838 (W. B. 1765-91, p. 175). On motion of Clement Reed it was shown that Clement Reed was son of Col. Isaac Reed, dec'd, who died in the service of the Va. line of Cont'l Soldiers established 1776. On Jan. 10, 1839, the heirs of Isaac Reed were allowed land for his services as colonel for 1 yr., 7 months and 7 days. Warrant number 8674, for 1766 acres, issued 29 Jan. 1839 (Book 3, p. 465, Charlotte Co., Va.).

Issue:

1. Mary^6 Rucker, m. Baxter Ragsdale.
2. Robert^6 Bedford Rucker.
3. James^6, d. in the Mexican War.
4. Samuel^6, m. Mary Hall.
5. Lucy^6, m. Dr. Smith, Waco, Texas.
6. Joyce^6, m. ——— Connerly, San Marco, Texas.

2. Dr. Robert^6 Bedford Rucker (James^5, James^4, Benj.^{3}, ———), b. Dec. 21, 1818, Murfreesboro, Tenn., m. Feb. 25, 1845, Mary Harrisson, Athens, Ala. (Jan. 12, 1822-Dec. 24, 1866), d. Rutherford Co., Tenn., dau. of Joshua Harrisson.

1. James^7 Joseph Rucker.
2. Sophia^7, b. 1848, m. Joseph Bates Blooming, of Ill.
3. Lucy^7, b. 1849, m. John T. Wells.
4. William^7 Harrisson Rucker.
5. Fannie^7, b. 1862, m. Howard Wiles, of Marysville, Calif.

1. James^7 Joseph Rucker (Robert^6, James^5, ———), b. Nov. 15, 1846, Murfreesboro, Tenn.; m. Jan. 9, 1879, Minnie Jenkins; graduated from the U. of Penna. in 1869, was president of the Rutherford County Fair, also president of the Rutherford Medical Assn.

4. William^7 Harrisson Rucker (Robert^6, James^5, ———), b. Jan. 25, 1861, Bedford Co., Tenn.; m. Feb. 24, 1887, Blanch Dorman, of Lawrence, Ind., b. June, 1870; is the editor of the Itta Bena Times, Itta Bena, Miss.

1. James^8 D. Rucker, b. Jan. 29, 1888, m. Paulina Bowman.
2. Robert^8 B. Rucker, b. Feb. 24, 1890.
3. Eleanor^8 Rucker, b. Mch. 7, 1901.
4. William^8 Frances, b. Sept. 22, 1911.

6. Benjamin[5] Rucker (James[4], Benj.[3], ———), b. in Amherst, June 2, 1790, d. Feb. 29, 1866, in Rutherford Co., Tenn.; m. 1st Sarah Alexander, 2nd Temperance Bass, and 3rd Eliza Wharton.

Will of Benjamin[5] Rucker, of Rutherford Co., probated Feb., 1866. To my: daus. Josephine Amanda Neill, and Sophia, wife of William Betty, and grand Daus., Ann Brian, wife of John Brian, and Anne, dau. of W. H. Snead. All of my land to Samuel J. Rucker. Executors: Samuel J. Rucker, James J. Neoll, and William Betty (W. B. 22, p. 150).

The following statement was made by James Hudson, of Versailles, Ky., who was an eye witness to the incident, "During the Civil War, when the Confederate soldiers were stationed near Appomattox C. H., a soldier was asked to volunteer to set on fire the Court House, to prevent its being captured by the Federal Troops. A man from a Tennessee company by the name of Benjamin Rucker volunteered, he succeeded in setting the house on fire, but being in full view of the enemy he was immediately shot. We do not know to which family the above Benjamin belongs, but are placing it here hoping some day to hear from the descendants of the above soldier.

Issue: by 1st mar.

1. Sarah[6] Rucker, m. W. H. Snead.
    1. Anne[7] Snead, m. Judge D. Bryan, of Nashville, Tenn.

By 2nd mar.

2. Josephine[6] Amanda Rucker, m. James J. Neill.
    1. Sophia[7] Neill.
    2. June[7] Neill.
    3. Benjamin[7] Neill.
    4. John[7] Neill.
3. Sophia[6] Rucker, m. William Betty.
4. Eliza[6] Rucker.

7. Dr. William[5] Reed Rucker (James[4], Benj.[3], ———), b. Lynchburg, Va. (May 20, 1792-Aug. 8, 1861), m. Susan Childres, Nov. 11, 1819, Murfreesboro, Tenn., the only sister of Sarah Childres, wife of James K. Polk. The two sisters were educated at the Moravian School at Winston-Salem, N. C. Dr. Rucker was a surgeon, and served in the war of 1812, in active service at the battle of New Orleans.

1. Elizabeth[6] Rucker, m. Robert Black.
    1. Elizabeth[7] Black.

2. Sarah[6] Polk Rucker (Sept. 7, 1825-June 18, 1850), m. James Philips. No issue.
3. Joanna[6] Lucinda Rucker.
4. Sarah[6] C. Rucker.
5. Joel[6] Childres Rucker.
6. William[6] H. Rucker, d. young.
7. W.[6] Reed Rucker.

3. Johanna[6] Lucinda Rucker (William[5], James[4], ———) (Sept. 19, 1822-Oct. 15, 1856), m. Robert Jetton. She and her sister Sarah spent much time at the White House when their aunt, Mrs. James K. Polk, was the "First lady of the land".

7. William[6] Reed Rucker (William[5], ———), m. Elizabeth Seary Smith, Fayetteville, Tenn.

1. Joel[7] F. Childres Rucker, m. Rebecca Pigg.
2. Susan[7] C. Rucker.

8. Samuel[5] Reed Rucker (James[4], Benj.[3], ———) (Jan. 21, 1794-Dec. 3, 1862), m. 1823, Martha B. Martin. He patented land in 1820 in Rutherford Co., Tenn.

1. Roseline[6] Rucker, d. young.
2. Robert[6] Martin Rucker, m. ——— Cowan.

9. Joanne[5] Rucker (James[4], ———) (Apr. 19, 1796-Feb. 6, 1822), m. John Price.

1. Mary[6] R. Price.
2. Joanna[6] Jones.

10. Western[5] Tennessee Rucker (James[4], ———) (July 16, 1798-Dec. 7, 1831), m. Apr. 15, 1823, Frances Foote Savage.

1. Samuel[6] Rucker (July 29, 1825-Sept. 10, 1903), d. in Texas; m. 1st, Mary Mitchell of Florence, Ala., dau. of David; 2nd Addie Mitchell, dau. of William and Mary Ledbetter Mitchell.

Issue (by 2nd mar.):

1. S.[7] J. Rucker.
2. Ada[7] M. Rucker.
3. Frances[7] Rucker.
4. Anna[7] G. Rucker.

1. Rev. Samuel[7] James Rucker (Samuel[6], Western[5], James[4], ———), b. Aug. 8, 1868, in Tenn., m. Beth Foster, dau. of William Foster, of Georgetown, Texas, Nov. 9, 1897. He was edu-

cated at Southwestern University, Texas, and Vanderbilt, Nashville, Tenn. He has 3 children.

11. John^{5} Wyatt Rucker (James^{4}, Benj.^{3}, ———), b. Mch. 28, 1802, d. Yazoo, Miss., m. Maria Keeble.

1. William^{6} Rucker, d. Canton, Miss.
2. Sallie^{6} Lambert, of Greenville, Miss.
3. Annie^{6} Bell.
4. Josephine^{6} Rucker.
5. Amanda^{6} Rucker.
6. Kate^{6} Rucker.

12. Joseph^{5} Rucker (James^{4}, ———), b. Dec. 9, 1805, lived in Rutherford Co., Tenn.

1. Benjamin^{7} Rucker, m. ——— Morton, Nashville, Tenn.
2. Western^{7} Tennessee Rucker.
3. John^{7} Frank Rucker.
4. Eliza^{7} Kens.
5. Lucy^{7} Neill.
6. Joseph^{7} S. Rucker.

13. Robert^{5} Rucker (James^{4}, ———) (Feb. 2, 1808-Sept. 10, 1827).

14. Joyce^{5} Rucker (James^{4}, ———), b. Jan., 1801, m. 1823, Thomas^{5} Sidney Rucker, son of Gideon^{4} and Joyce Reed Rucker (double 1st cousin).

1. Joanna^{6} Alfred Rucker.
2. Robert^{6} Powhatan Rucker.
3. Thomas^{6} Rucker.
4. William^{6} Rucker.

2. Thomas^{4} Rucker (Benjamin^{3}, John^{2}, Peter^{1}), b. c. 1759, in Amherst, d. 1843, in Rutherford Co., Tenn., m. Jan. 3, 1793, Sallie Reed, of Bedford Co., Va., dau. of William Reed. Thomas lived in Tenn. on the road between Murfreesboro and Jefferson. In 1798 he was paying taxes in Amherst Co. on 350 acres of land. He was one of the commissioners appointed to divide Rutherford Co., and was one of the first judges of that county. The first court was held at his house on January 3, 1804, at which session Thomas presided. One Thomas Rucker of Tenn. served in the war of 1812. There was a Thomas Rucker who married in Amherst Co. in 1787 Hannah Philips, dau. of Conyers Philips.

Could this Thomas have married twice? The land and personal tax books show only one Thomas Rucker. Thomas and his wife, Sally, sold their land in Amherst Co., Apr. 15, 1799 (D. B. K., p. 99, Amherst Co., Va.). He bought the 350 acres of land from Thomas Bragg and wife Lucy for £15, land on Stovalls Cr. adjoining Benjamin Rucker on 18 Apr. 1796 (D. B. G., p. 704, Amherst Co., Va.).

The will of Thomas Rucker was dated Nov. 2, 1839, and probated Mch. 10, 1843, in Rutherford Co., Tenn. To my wife, Sally, the home tract of 400 acres, also 250 acres; sons Thomas, Jr., Edmund, and Samuel Rucker; and dau. Catherine Porter. Executors; Thomas Rucker. Witness; Robert S. Morris, William Gilliam and M. W. Rucker (W. B. 12, p. 309).

1. Thomas[5] Rucker, Jr.
    1. Edmund[6] Rucker.
    2. Thomas[6] Rucker.
    3. Gideon[6] Rucker.
    4. Benjamin[6] Rucker.
    5. Isabella[6] Rucker.
    6. Eleanor[6] Rucker.
2. Dr. Edmund[5] Rucker.
3. Samuel[5] C. Rucker.
    1. Elizabeth[6] Leiper.
4. Catherine[5] Porter.

2. Dr. Edmund[5] Rucker (Thomas[4], Benj.[3], ———), b. in Rutherford Co., d. Nov., 1861, in Magengo Co., Ala., m. Louise Winchester, dau. of Gen. James Winchester, of Revolutionary

1. Josephine[6] Rucker (1827-Oct. 4, 1888), m. Oliver Bennett Boddie, of Ala.
2. Maphia[6] Rucker, m.. James York, Nov. 5, 1856, Tex.
3. Napoleon[6] Rucker, d. young.
4. Oliver[6] Rucker.
5. Edmund[6] Winchester Rucker.
6. Alexander[6] Rucker.
7. Sarah[6], m. Dr. Charles Gale, of Texas.

5. Edmund[6] Winchester Rucker (Edmund[5], Thomas[4], Benj.[3], ———), b. July 22, 1835, in Rutherford Co., Tenn., m. 1st Mary Woodfin, Nov. 11, 1873, of Marion, Ala., d. 1883; 2nd Mary T. Bentley, of Maury Co., Tenn., Nov. 30, 1886. He lived 5 miles north of Murfreesboro near Stone River. Gen. Rucker served throughout the Civil War in Gen. Forrest's cavalry. He was serving as colonel of the regiment at the battle

of Brentwood near Nashville in which engagement he lost his arm. Later he was brevetted brigadier general for other distinguished services. After the war he owned and operated large coal and iron mines in Ala. He resided in Birmingham.

1. Louise^{7} Winchester Rucker, m. Walter C. Agee.
    1. Edmund^{8} R. Agee.
    2. Walter^{8} C. Agee.
    3. Louise^{8} Agee.
    4. Elizabeth^{8} Agee.
    5. George^{8} Bentley Agee.
2. Mary^{7} Rucker, m. Dr. George H. Stubbs.
    1. Edmund^{8} Rucker Stubbs.
    2. George^{8} H. Stubbs.
3. Edmund^{7} Winchester Rucker m. 1st Lona Lewis, 2nd Lillian Hill.

6. Alexander^{6} C. Rucker (Edmund^{5}, Thomas^{4}, Benj.^{3}, ———), b. Dec. 7, 1842, m. Oct., 1877, Anna M. Stults, b. Aug. 16, 1857, of Martinsville, Henry Co., Va., dau. of W. P. Stults and his wife, Nancy Wells. Alexander is a lawyer living in Louisville, Ky.

1. Edmund^{7} P. Rucker, b. July 11, 1878, m. Laura Creder.
2. Oliver^{7} Hazard, b. Nov. 8, 1880, m. Edith Arms; live in St. Louis.
3. Maude^{7} Winchester, b. Dec. 29, 1886, m. Hannan Gardner, of Gulfport, Miss.
4. Mabel^{7}, b. Nov. 27, 1889, m. Lawrence C. Turnock.
5. Annabel^{7}.
6. Henrietta^{7} Radford, m. Dr. Bird, of Porto Rico.

William Winchester was born in Westminster, England, c. 1708, d. at Westminster, Carroll Co., Maryland, Sept. 2, 1790, m. Lydia Richards, d. Feb. 19, 1809. He founder the town of Westminster in Maryland, served in the French and Indian War. His son James, b. Feb. 6, 1752, m. Susan Black, of Sumner Co., Tenn. He enlisted from Maryland in the Third Regiment in 1776, he was made a lieutenant in 1778, a captain in 1782, and was in the battles of Guilford Court House, Eutaw Springs, Yorktown and others. He moved to Cragford, Sumner Co., Tenn., in 1785. In 1794 he was appointed by President Washington to be a member of the legislative council of the Territory south of the Ohio. In April 8, 1812, he was commissioned brigadier general and served with the army of the Northwest.

The three men who founded Nashville were Gen. Winchester, Gen. Andrew Jackson and Judge Overton.

1. James Winchester, m. Mary House.
2. Louise Orville, m. Edmund[5] Rucker.
3. Maria, m. James N. Breedlove, of New Orleans.
4. Selma, m. William Lors Roveson, of New Orleans.
5. Caroline, m. Orville Shelby, of Kentucky.
6. Almira, m. Col. Alfred R. Wynne, of Penna.
7. Helen, d. young.
8. Marcus Brutus, d. 1856.
9. Lucelius, m. Amanda Bledsoe.
10. Valerius, m. Samuel Price.
11. George Washington, m. Melvina Gaines.
12. Napoleon, d. 1825. (Copied from Mr. John Boddie's Book).

3. Gideon[4] Rucker (Benj.[3], John[2], Peter[1]), m. Joyce Reed, Dec. 25, 1793, dau. of William Reed, of Bedford Co., Va. He began to pay taxes in 1798 on 179 acres of land in Amherst Co. In 1804 he paid on 547 acres, continuing until 1815 when he sold and moved to Cannon Co., Tenn. Gideon and his wife Joyce sold 573¼ acres of land on Rutledge Creek on Lynch's Road, Amherst Co., Va., Apr. 17, 1815 (D. B. M, p. 718).

1. Thomas[5] Rucker.
2. James[5] Rucker.
    1. Thomas[6] Rucker.
    2. Joseph[6] Rucker.

4. Lucy[4] Rucker (Benj.[3], John[2], Peter[1]), m. Jan. 11, 1786, Zachary Dawson, son of Martin Dawson, the marriage bond was signed by Benj. Rucker with Benjamin Plunkett as witness, in Amherst Co. Zachary patented land in Tenn. in 1821, near Murfreesboro where they settled and where he died. After Zachary's death Lucy's first sweetheart, John MacDaniel, of Amherst, came to Murfreesboro and stayed until she finally consented to marry him. John took Lucy and her children back to Amherst Co., Va.

Issue (by 1st mar.):

1. Benjamin[5] Dawson, Clergyman.
2. Martin[5] Dawson.
3. Nelson[5] Carter Dawson.
4. Lewis[5] Dawson.
5. Susan[5] Haskins.

Issue (by 2nd mar.):

6. Ambrose^{5} Dawson, m. Olive Sandidge, Nov. 25, 1804.
7. Lindsey^{5} Dawson.
8. Gideon^{5} Dawson, m. ——— Strange.
9. Elizabeth^{5} Dawson, m. Kempis Davies.
10. Margaret^{5} Dawson, m. ——— Ware.
11. Sophia^{5} Burgess Dawson, m. Thomas Strange.

5. Mildred^{4} Rucker (Benj.^{3}, John^{2}, Peter^{1}), m. ——— Brown, moved to Tenn.

1. Aaaron^{5} Vain Brown.

6. Sophia^{4} Rucker (Benj.^{3}, John^{2}, Peter^{1}), m. Jan. 9, 1792, Joseph Burruss, of Amherst Co., marriage bond was signed by Gideon^{4} Rucker and John Franklin. They moved to Rutherford Co., Tenn.

1. W.^{4} C. J. Burruss.
2. Phillip^{5} Burruss.
3. Fayett^{5} Burruss.
4. James^{5} Rucker Burruss.
5. Sophia^{5} Burruss.
6. Sallie^{5} Burruss.

7. Bennett^{4} Rucker (Benj.^{3}, John^{2}, Peter^{1}), m. Joanna Reed, dau. of William Reed, of Bedford Co., b. Sept. 6, 1802. He paid taxes in 1809 on 170 acres, in 1812 on 844 acres, he inherited 335¼ acres from his father's estate. Bennett and his wife Joanna sold 490¾ acres of land to Richard Harrisson, Apr. 26, 1815 (D. B. M, p. 717, Amherst Co., Va.).

5. Reuben^{3} Rucker (John^{2}, Peter^{1}) may not have married. He paid no taxes on land or personal property, nor made any land transfers in Orange or Amherst. Peter, the executor of his father's will, did not deed any of his father's land to him, according to his father's will.

He signs a deed along with his eleven brothers and sisters in 1769, the order in which they sign was Peter, John, Sarah, Ambrose, Winifred, Benjamin, Reuben, Isaac, Anthony, Mildred, Phoebe, and Margaret Smith.

Another deed, 1781, conveying land, ten of the children sign, but neither Reuben's, nor Margaret Smith's name appears. Reuben may have left Va. very early leaving no record.

6. Isaac^{3} Rucker (John^{2}, Peter^{1}), b. before 1740, Orange Co., d. 1798, Amherst; m. Mildred (Hawkins) Plunket, c. 1761 (widow of John Plunket). Isaac received 404 acres of land in Amherst Co., Va., part of 5,850 acres patented by his father,

John. Stephen Ham sold 100 acres to Isaac in 1778, Amherst. In 1782, he is paying on 404 and 100 acres of land in Amherst. In 1788, 100 acres of this is charged to Moses Rucker's account.

In 1787, Isaac Rucker, Sr., is paying a personal tax on himself and John Rucker "over" 21 years of age.

He pays taxes on 300 and 77 acres of land until 1798, then the "Estate" pays on these two tracts until 1803, at which time his widow, Mildred, begins paying on 170 acres until her death, 1812, Richard having bought 97 acres in 1800, and Reuben in 1802, 100 acres.

His brother, Anthony Rucker, bought 2 tracts of land, 103 and 14 acres from Isaac in 1795, but Anthony does not pay upon this land until 1798. A witness to the sale was his dau., Elizabeth Rucker.

In 1790, "Isaac Rucker Sr." signed a number of county petitions, one to establish a tobacco warehouse in Amherst, opposite Lynchburg, "as the cost is too great to take the casks over the ferry and up the banks."

In 1797 the petition to divide the county was signed by 917 men. Five Isaac Ruckers signed. "Isaac Sr.; Isaac Minor; Isaac Doc.; Isaac, Jr.; and Isaac, Jr."

June 20.th 1785.

At a Board of the Field Officers & Magistrates of the County of Amherst (Pursuant to an Act, entitled "An act for amending several laws for regulating & disciplining the militia & guarding against invasions and insurrections") for the purpose of recommending fit & proper persons to be Captains & Subalterns of the s'd County.

Present.

Samuel Jordan Cabell County Lieut

Magistrates	Field Officers.
William Cabell.	Patrick Rose Lieut Colo.
Hugh Rose.	James Franklin
Ambrose Rucker.	James Pamplin Majors.
Nicholas Cabell.	

The Board after taking the oath prescribed by Law, proceeded to divide the County into Regimental & Compy Districts and to number the said Districts by lot. They then proceeded to recommend by ballot the most able and fit persons to be Captains, Lieutenants, & Ensigns, to each of the s'd Company Districts when the following Gent. were unanimously recommended. Viz.

1st Regt commanded by Lt Colo. Gabriel Penn.

No	*Districts*	*Captains*	*Lieutenants*	*Ensigns*
1.	....	Hendrick Arnold.	Nathl Mantiply.	James Man.
2.	....	James Ware.	Charles Taliaferro.	Charles Ison.
3.	....	Isaac Rucker.	Isaac Tinsley.	Anthony Rucker.
4.	....	John Christian.	James Grisham.	Elijah Christian.
5.	....	Charles Burrus.	Will: Tucker.	Wyatt Powell.
6.	....	Josiah Ellis.	Charles Ellis.	William Haynes.
7.	....	George Penn.	Lindsay Coleman.	Geo. Phillips.
8.	....	Richd Harrison	Thomas Powell.	David Tinsley.
9.	....	William Ware.	Peter Carter.	Valentine Peyton.

He was in the Rev. War. *Hardesty's H. and G. Ency.* mentions him as a lieutenant of the county militia under Col. Daniel Gains. June 21, 1781, they were ordered to join LaFayette at Yorktown.

Mch. Court, 1786. Isaac Rucker is recommended to his Excellency, the Governor, as a proper person to execute the office of Captain of a Company of Militia of this County in the room of Benjamin Rucker, who hath resigned and Anthony Rucker is recommended as Ensign (O. B. 1784-87), Amherst Co., Va.

Isaac Rucker, Sr. may have been a lawyer, for so many Treas. warrants were delivered to him from other people (Land Office Ref.).

Will of John Plunket dated June 11, 1758, probated July 27, 1758, mentions wife, Mildred, children and "father". Exec. wife, Mildred, Rush Hudson and John Morton (W. B. 2, p. 273), Orange Co., Va.

Isaac was appointed Guardian to Benjamin and Sally Plunket, and administrator to settle the estate of John Plunket, dec'd, Aug. 27, 1761 (W. B. 2, p. 447), Orange.

In the meantime he had married the widow of John, Mildred Hawkins Plunket. Ten years later the two children being of age, Isaac brings the Guardian's account to court, making a report, Mch. 26, 1772. "The estate of John Plunket, dec'd, debtor. to Isaac Rucker, Guardian.

Cash paid to Audrey Shepped	£27- 5
Cash paid to Benjamin Porter	0- 7
Cash paid to Edward Thomas	2- 2
Cash paid to John Morton, Esq.	2-17

Cash paid to Benjamin Hawkins	5- 7
To schooling and maintaining 2 children, 11 years, at £4 per year	44-
To Isaac Rucker, for his wife's part of the negroes hire	2- 2
To my third of the estate, that was sold	5- 8
Balance due	£ 114-14

August 27, 1761, on motion of Isaac Rucker, one of the Executors of the will of John Plunket dec'd, it was ordered that Thomas Jameson, Alex. Waugh, Joseph Thomas, Jr., and John Bremham do examine and settle and divide the estate, according to the will, and set apart the wife's share of the same, and make returns at the next court (O. B. 1761, p. 599), Orange Co.

Mildred Hawkins m. 1st John Plunket, d. 1758, and 2nd Isaac Rucker.

Issue (by 1st mar.):

1. Sally Plunket, m. John[4] Rucker (John[3], John[2]).
2. Benjamin Plunket, m. Winnifred[4] Rucker (Ambrose[3], John[2]).

Inventory of the Estate of Mildred Rucker returned by William Knight, Reuben Pendleton and James Pettit, 18 Apr., 1814, valued at $1,425.00 (W. B. 5, p. 434), Amherst.

Aug. 16, 1813, Reuben Rucker was appointed administrator of estate of Isaac Rucker, dec'd, after death of his mother, Mildred with Ambrose Rucker, Richard Rucker, Richard Harrison and Achelaus Reynolds, security (W. B. 5, p. 371).

Rev. Ahmed[5] Rucker, son of Sarah Plunket and John[4] Rucker (John[3], John[2]) states in his memoirs that John[4] was born 1775 in Amherst, d. in Ky., that he knew his grandmother, Mildred, very well; that she was the widow of John Plunket, and speaks of her as an "Excellent woman".

Isaac Rucker d. before Sept., 1799, for in Sept. Court Order, we read, "The Last Will and Testament of Isaac Rucker, deceased, was produced in Court and proven by oath of Thomas Rucker, subscribing witness thereto and ordered to lie for further proof" (O. B. 1799-1800, p. 63).

Issue:

1. John[4] Rucker.
2. Moses[4].
3. Reuben[4].

4. Richard[4].
5. Susanna[4], m. James Tinsley.
6. Elizabeth[4].
7. Isaac[4], Jr. (not mentioned in will) d. in Rev. service. *Hardesty's H. & G. Ency.* of Amherst Co. Mr. Alexander Brown's list of Rev. soldiers.

John Rucker and wife, Nancy; Moses Rucker and wife, Elizabeth; Reuben Rucker and wife, Elizabeth; Richard Rucker and wife, Margaret; James Tinsley and wife, Susanna; Archelaus Reynolds and wife, Elizabeth; sold to Philip Thurman, Jr. all of Amherst, 91 acres of land in Amherst, lying on North side of Pauls Mountains, adjoining John McDaniel, Edmund Winston et als, to the top of said mountain, then East to John McDaniel's line (D. B. 1, p. 400), Oct. 20, 1800.

John and Nancy, Moses and Elizabeth, Richard and Margaret Rucker, James and Susanna Tinsley, and Archelaus and Eliz. Reynolds sold 100 acres to Reuben Rucker (D. B. J, p. 226), Oct., 1802.

John and Nancy, Moses and Elizabeth, and Reuben and Elizabeth Rucker, and James Tinsly and Susanna Tinsley, and Archelaus Reynolds and Elizabeth Reynolds for £60, sold to Richard Rucker 97 acres of land adjoining Reuben Rucker's (D. B. I, p. 222), Oct. 1, 1800.

1. John[4] Rucker (Isaac[3], John[2], ———) (1762-1812), m. Mch. 12, 1788, Nancy Shelton, daughter of Richard, b. Aug., 1728, of King William County) (Jan. 3, 1767-Jan. 12, 1860), b. Amherst Co.

In 1785, John, "son of Isaac", is listed among the personal tax payers. In 1806, John Ellis deeds land to Moses and John Rucker.

John Rucker's estate was appraised 1812, by James Ware, Samuel Burks, and Ambrose Pendleton, value $4,000, Amherst.

Will of Richard Shelton, Nov. 3, 1818, probated June 15, 1821, mentions the children of my dau., Jane Ellis, dec'd; John; Charles; Richard; Jonah; Joshua; Powhatan Ellis; Jane Eubank, and Mary Hunter. To my grand-daughter, Mary Montgomery, infant dau. of Mary W. Montgomery, dec'd, 1/9 of my estate. To Son-in-law George Lee, who married my dau., Elizabeth, 1/9 of my estate. To son, John, 1/9; to daus. Sally Chappell, and Nancy Rucker, each, 1/9; to the children of Nancy Rucker, Willis, Jane E., Elizabeth Moreland, Susanna T., Richard F., and John D. L.; to Martha and John, infant children of Sally G. Wills, dec'd, Nancy Rucker's dau., Mary Edwards; to my son, William, 1/8 part; to grand-son, Ralph Shelton; to daughter-in-law, Polly, widow of son, Joshua Shelton (W. B. 9, p. 205).

Nancy was appointed Administratrix of the estate of John Rucker, with Willis Rucker, Armistead Rucker, Samuel Burks, William Shelton, and James Ware security. July 20, 1812 (W. B. 5, p. 175), Amherst.

October 19, 1812, Nancy was appointed Guardian to Susanna and Jane Rucker, orphans of John Rucker. Also at the division of John Rucker's property, Nancy was allowed 3 slaves, valued at $740, with a balance due her of $73.33, May 20, 1817 (W. B. 5, p. 684), Amherst. In 1822, Nancy began paying tax on 600 acres of land.

Issue:

1. Willis[5] Rucker.
2. Mollie[5] Shelton.
3. Sarah[5] S.
4. Jane[5] Ellis.
5. Elizabeth[5] Lee.
6. Susanna[5] Tinsley Rucker.
7. Richard[5] Fleming Rucker.
8. John[5] Dabney L. Rucker.

1. Willis[5] Rucker (John[4], Isaac[3], John[2]), b. July 6, 1789, m. 1st Permela Cole, 2nd Tabatha Arnold. Willis Rucker, of Amherst, on March 5, 1854, deeds to Beverly Arnold of Campbell for $400 all interest said Willis Rucker and wife, Tabatha, have in the lands of John Arnold, lately dec'd, in both real and personal. In 1833, Willis 1st paid land tax on 100 acres of land.

Issue (by 1st mar.):

1. Cole[6] Rucker.

Issue (by 2nd mar.):

2. Martha[6] A., m. Preston H. Duff, 1852.
3. Matilda[6] J., m. Leyton Peter, 1852.
4. Sue[6] E., m. John Stinnet, 1865, Fincastle.

2. Mollie[5] Shelton Rucker (John[4], Isaac[3]) (Feb. 25, 1791-1834), m. John M. Edwards, Aug. 20, 1804, of Amherst.

3. Sarah[5] S. Rucker (John[4]) (Mch. 25, 1793, d. before 1821), m. John Wills, Feb. 3, 1812. Witnesses to marriage were Willis Rucker and John M. Edwards.

1. Martha[6] Wills.
2. John[6].

4. Jane[5] Ellis Rucker (John[4]) (Sept. 19, 1794-1875), d. in Mo., buried at Sturgeon.

5. Elizabeth[5] Lee Rucker (John[4]) (May 21, 1796-1868), m. 1811 Andrew Moreland, in Amherst Co., b. 1784. He intrusted to Richard F. Rucker for the benefit of Elizabeth Moreland, both real and personal property, Apr. 16, 1832 (O. B. 1832-33, p. 38), Amherst Co.

Andrew Moreland was appointed guardian to an Elizabeth Rucker, orphan of Elizabeth. 21 Sept. 1812, in Amherst.

Sec. Andrew Moreland, James Ware, Willis Rucker, James M. Edwards (W. B. 5, p. 179).

1. Isabel[6] P. Moreland, b. 1812, Amherst, d. Aug. 29, 1905, buried Hopewell, Mo., unmarried.
2. John[6] Rucker Moreland, b. March 17, 1819, Richmond, Va., m. Adeline Ivy Din.
3. William[6], d. in infancy.
4. William[6] Fleming, b. 1826; b. 1st Comford Parks; 2nd Peggy Williams, buried at Hopewell, Mo.
5. Sally[6], m. ——— Coleman, Va.
6. Mary[6] Jane, buried Hopewell, Mo.
7. Elizabeth[6] Susan.
8. Frances[6] Virginia (Sept. 16, 1836-Feb. 18, 1882), m. Jim Townley.

7. Elizabeth[6] Susan Moreland (Elizabeth[5] L., John[4], Isaac[3] Rucker), b. Sept. 14, 1831, Lynchburg; d. June 29, 1917, Versailles, Mo.; m. 1st, July 25, 1848, William Carroll Gunn (July 28, 1814-Apr. 14, 1855), b. Robinson Co., Tenn., d. Versailles, Mo. Elizabeth was his third wife. She m. 2nd, Jan. 24, 1875, Shores Price Hunter (Jan. 28, 1807-May 7, 1882), b. Franklin Co., Va. William Carroll Gunn, m. 1st Catherine Gunn Oct. 1, 1840 (dau. of his 1st cousin, Starting Gunn), b. Mch. 6, 1822, in Tenn.; 2nd Dec. 15, 1846, Mathilda Beauland (Aug. 29, 1830-Aug. 10, 1848); 3rd Elizabeth Susan Moreland.

Issue (by 1st mar.):

1. Cyrus Gunn (Dec. 7, 1842-Apr. 23, 1915), b. Mo.; d. Soldiers Home, Fort Deposit, Ala.
2. John Allen Gunn (Oct., 1844-Oct. 8, 1848).

Issue (by 2nd mar.):

3. Mathilda W. Gunn, b. Mch. 21, 1847, Versailles, Mo.

Issue (by 3rd mar.):

4. Florentine[7] Gunn.
5. Mark[7] (Aug. 14, 1851-Aug. 23, 1865).
6. Adele[7] Ann (Feb. 10, 1853-June 16, 1891, m. William H. Blanks, Sept. 6, 1868.
7. Elizabeth[7] W. (posthumous) (May 16, 1855-1860).

4. Florentine[7] Gunn (Elizabeth[6] S., Elizabeth[5] L., John[4]) (June 9, 1850-Oct. 27, 1926), d. Chicago, Ill., m. 1st, Dec. 16, 1866, Louis Langley Horsley, Versailles, Mo., b. Feb. 6, 1845, Louisville, Ky., d. Mch. 17, 1883, El Paso, Tex.; 2nd, Dec. 3, 1883, Baron Ferguson Deal, of El Paso, Tex. (Dec. 19, 1857-May 16, 1885), b. in Scott Co., Iowa.

Issue (by 1st mar.):

1. Ella[8] Lee Horsley, b. Jan. 27, 1868, Versailles, Mo., d. Jan. 21, 1927, in New York; m. Apr. 7, 1893, Thomas Joseph Ryder, Washington, D. C.
2. Clara[8] Horsley, b. June 26, 1876, Versailles, Mo., m. Apr. 25, 1906, William James Tollerton, St. Louis, Mo., b. Jan. 2, 1870, St. Paul, Minn., d. March 3, 1926, Chicago, Ill.
   1. Frances[9] Lee Tollerton, b. Feb. 7, 1909, Chicago.
   2. Robert[9] William Tollerton, b. June 27, 1911.

6. Susanna[5] Tinsley Rucker (John[4], Isaac[3], John[2], ———), b. Mch. 26, 1801; m. Sept. 7, 1819, Constantine Brown, bond signed by Nancy Rucker, Teste: Jane E. Rucker, and John M. Edwards.

7. Richard[5] Fleming Rucker (John[4], Isaac[3]), b. Jan. 13, 1807, d. young, in Tex.

In 1833, he pays tax on 120, 65, and 52½ acres, the last land transferred from his mother, Nancy, in Amherst Co., Va.

8. John[5] Dabney Lewis Rucker (John[4]) (Dec. 3, 1811-1869), m. Lucy Jane Tinsley, Dec. 20, 1837, and lived at Cedar Grove, Amherst Co., d. in Sturgeon, Mo. Lucy Jane (Apr. 1,

1820, July 10, 1853), was the dau. of Edward and Sarah Dawson Tinsley. John D. L. Rucker 1st paid taxes in Amherst, 1833, on 74 acres of land and in 1742, he is paying taxes on 264½ acres. He moved 1st to Kentucky, then to Mo., 1867. In 1843, John D. L. Rucker of Amherst, went security for James M. McDaniel.

1. Capt. John[6] Fleming Rucker.
2. Sallie[6] (Feb. 17, 1840-1854), unmarried.
3. Edward[6] Lewis, b. Nov. 5, 1841; killed 1863; served under Col. Fitzhugh Lee in Civil War.
4. Nancy[6] Shelton, m. ——— Spratt, Sturgeon, Mo. (May 27, 1843-Mch. 19, 1910).
5. Elizabeth[6], m. Richard Preston Hopkins.
6. Mary[6] Francis, b. Feb. 9, 1847; m. James Jackson.
7. Rhoderick[6] Dawson, b. May 7, 1849, m. Lula Duesenbury, Sturgeon, Mo.
8. Cornelia[6] Alice, b. Apr. 25, 1851, m. James A. Tanner (his 2nd wife).

Will of Edward Tinsley, dated 14 Sept. 1858, probated 18 July, 1859. To my dau. Judith A. Hendricks; my dau. Lucy J. Rucker; my dau. Sarah Shelton and her dau., Sally Wm. Shelton; my dau. Nancy Powell; my dau. Virginia P. Love; my son Chapman J. Tinsley, and my son Edward M. Tinsley. To John D. L. Rucker, Trustee, for my dec'd dau. Lucy J. Rucker; To Monroe Love, for my daughter Virginia (W. B. 15, p. 207), Amherst.

1. Capt. John[6] Fleming Rucker (John[5], John[4], Isaac[3]), b. Sept. 19, 1838, Amherst, d. Dec. 28, 1889, in Mo., m. 1st Aug. 29, 1867, Julia[5] Rucker (June 18, 1843-Mch. 30, 1879), Sturgeon, Mo. (dau. of William[4] Early Rucker, John[3], Ephraim[2], Peter[1]) m. 2nd Frances Dingle. John was a captain in the Confederate army.

Issue (by 1st mar.):

1. Booker[7] Hall Rucker.
2. Guy[7] Lockridge Rucker (Oct. 3, 1870-Dec. 24, 1894).
3. Early[7] Dabney Rucker, b. Mch. 2, 1873, m. Nov. 20, 1904, Mable Mae Alburn.
    1. Andrew[8] A. Rucker, b. Mch. 6, 1807.
    2. John[8] B., b. July 12, 1909.
4. Ray[7] Fleming Rucker (Oct. 5, 1874-Oct. 12, 1909), m. Elsie Gordon.
    1. Elsie[8] Rucker.
    2. Julia[8].
5. Horace[7], d. young.

Issue (by 2nd mar.):

6. Grace^{7} Preston Rucker, b. Dec. 2, 1883, m. Jan., 1907, Harold Buckner.
7. Fannie^{7} Dingle, b. Oct. 3, 1888.

1. Booker^{7} Hall Rucker (John^{6}, John^{5}, John^{4}, Isaac^{3}), b. Aug. 14, 1868, m. Margaret Barrow Southgate.

1. Ray^{8} Southgate, b. Apr. 6, 1905.
2. Booker^{8} Hall, Jr., b. May 8, 1909.

5. Elizabeth^{6} Rucker (John^{5}, John^{4}, ———), b. Apr. 27, 1845, m. Richard Preston Hopkins.

1. Lucy^{7} Lillian Hopkins.
2. Cornelia^{7} Crenshaw, b. Jan. 24, 1870.
3. Hallie^{7} Ellis, b. 1872, d. young.
4. Mary^{7} Cheatwood, b. July 11, 1874, unmar.
5. Dolly^{7} Rucker (Sept. 8, 1786-1904), m. B. H. Downing.
    1. Benjamin^{8} Hopkins Downing, b. July, 1902.
6. Annie^{7} Lee, b. Dec. 17, 1880, m. Roy Skiles.
7. Edna^{7} Elizabeth, b. Apr., 1883, single.
8. Richard^{7} Fleming (June 4, 1885-July, 1920), single.

1. Lucy^{7} Lillian Hopkins (Elizabeth^{6}, John^{5} Rucker), b. Apr. 21, 1868, m. Aug. 24, 1892, J. C. Crockett.

1. Ray^{8} Hopkins Crockett, b. July, 1893.
2. Ellis^{8} Carter, b. Aug., 1895, m. Lizzie Walker.
3. David^{8} Kirkpatrick, b. Jan., 1897.
4. Nannie^{8} Elizabeth, b. Aug., 1900.
5. Alice^{8} Rucker, b. Jan., 1903.
6. Richard^{8} Preston, b. July, 1908.

1. Ray^{8} Hopkins Crockett (Lucy^{7}, Elizabeth^{6}), m. Myrtle Dungan.

1. Razel^{9} Crockett.
2. Roy^{9} Crockett.

3. David^{8} Kirkpatrick Crockett (Lucy^{7}, Elizabeth^{6}, John^{5}, John^{4}, Isaac^{3}), m. Eula Kessler.

1. Lewis^{9} Carter Crockett.
2. David^{9}, Jr.

2. Moses[4] Hawkins Rucker (Isaac[3], John[2], Peter[1]), d. 1835; m. Elizabeth Thurman Parks, widow of John Parks; date of mar. bond, Dec. 27, 1786, Amherst Co.; mentions him as "Bachelor".

His uncle, Col. Ambrose Rucker, wrote this note to the Clerk of Amherst Co.

Dec. 28, 1786.

Sir:

You may with safety join Elizabeth to Moses Rucker, it being consented to by his parents, no more at present, but I and my family are in good health, and I hope you and your family enjoy the same blessing. I am dear sir your most obedient servant.

Ambrose Rucker.

In 1785 he begins to sign petitions (county) and to pay land tax in 1788, on 100 acres, and continues until 1804, then pays on 170 acres.

In 1813, and until his death in 1835, Moses pays tax on 464 acres on Tarrapin Creek, land adjoining Arthur Davis.

The May Court of Campbell County of 1790, pays Moses Rucker for 3 days attendance "travelling twenty miles twice, crossing two ferries at Lynchs" (O. B. 2).

Thomas Moore, Reuben Pendleton, John Ellis, Nelson Crawford, Lewis Dawson and James Ware sold to Moses Rucker "3 certain tracts of ½ acres each, land in the town of Bethel, lots No. 10, 11, and 16". Oct. 18, 1806 (D. B. K, p. 556), Amherst Co.

Mch. 16, 1835, on motion of Peter Rucker, the court appointed Thomas N. Eubanks Sheriff, Administrator to settle the estate of Moses Rucker, dec'd, since 3 months (W. B. 9, p. 60), Amherst Co.

There was a law suit over a negro slave owned by Moses's wife, Elizabeth (Thurman) Parks left to her by John Parks, Jr., her 1st husband, and after Elizabeth's death, claimed by Benjamin Parks, son of John Parks, Jr., by a former marriage.

Issue:

1. Elisha[5] Rucker.
2. Stapleton[5] Rucker.
3. Mildred[5] Rucker.
4. Reuben[5] Rucker.
5. John D.[5] Rucker.
6. Nancy[5] Rucker.

7. Sally^{5} Rucker.
8. Stephen^{5} Rucker, moved to Henry County, Ky.
9. Isaac^{5} Rucker.
10. Peter^{5} Rucker.

1. Elisha^{5} Rucker (Moses^{4}, Isaac^{3}, John^{2}), settled at De Foe, Ky., c. 1830; owned land in both Shelby and Henry Counties, Ky. In 1841, pays a tax on 363 acres of land in Amherst Co., adjoining Charles Ellis.

Archelus P. Mitchell to secure a debt of $65 to Elisha Rucker, mortgaged 221 acres of land to Peter Rucker, 20 Dec. 1820, land adjoining Wm. Hannah (D. B. P, p. 74).

2. Stapleton^{5} Rucker (Moses^{4}, Isaac^{3}).
   1. Moses^{6} Hawkins, settled at De Foe, Henry Co., c. 1830.

3. Mildred^{5} Rucker (Moses^{4}, Isaac^{3}), m. Landon Tuley, son of John, June 18, 1810, in Amherst Co. She d. 1870; buried in Marion, Mo.; he d. 1839, in Ky. They moved from Kentucky to Mo., taking all of their children except their dau., Permelia Tuley Foree.
   1. Permelia^{6} Lambert Tuley.
   2. Elias^{6} Tuley.
   3. Elisha^{6} Tuley.
   4. Landon^{6} Tuley.

1. Permelia^{6} Lambert Tuley (Mildred^{5}, Moses^{4}, Isaac^{3}), b. 1811, m. Thomas Jefferson Foree, of Shelby Co., Ky.
   1. Mildred^{7} Foree.
   2. Rebeca^{7} Jane Foree.
   3. Pauline^{7} Hawkins Foree.
   4. Lemuel^{7} B. Foree.
   5. Permelia^{7} Lambert Foree.
   6. Sarah^{7} Ware, m. Reuben Shaddock, of South Hampton, Eng., in Shelbyville, Ky.
      1. Permelia^{8}, m. ——— Hughes, of Pleasureville, Ky.

4. Reuben^{5} Rucker (Moses^{4}, Isaac^{3}, John^{2}), settled c. 1830 in Clarke Co., Ky., founded the town of Ruckerville.
   1. Nathan C.^{6} Rucker.
      1. B.^{7} J. Rucker, of Warrenburg.

5. John[5] D. Rucker (Moses[4], Isaac[3]), b. in Va. 1795, d. 1867, Henry Co., Ky., m. Belinda Hudson, of Woodford Co., Ky., 1826. He owned land in Shelby Co., Ky.

1. Martha[6] Rucker.
2. Kitty[6].
3. Sarah[6].
4. Richard[6].
5. Permelia[6].
6. Puss[6].
7. John,[6] Jr.

7. John[6] Rucker (John[5], Moses[4], Isaac[3]), b. 1836, in Henry Co., Ky. Was killed Mch. 12, 1871 in Ky. His wife moved to Iowa where she later married, and moved to Calif.

1. Squire[7] Rucker, d. young.
2. Isabella[7].
3. Pryor W.[7]
4. John[7], d. young.

6. Nancy[5] Rucker (Moses[4], Isaac[3], John[2]), m. Finny Bryant, Dec. 5, 1812, in Amherst. (Marriage bond "dau. of Moses".

7. Sally[5] Rucker (Moses[4], Isaac[3]), m. Aug. 24, 1815, Patterson P. Mitchell, in Amherst. Marriage bond signed by Landon Tuley.

9. Isaac[5] Rucker (Moses[4]), m. Mary Higginbotham, no issue; marriage bond dated Jan. 29, 1793; signed by John Higginbotham, "father".

On motion of Thomas G. Hill, the court committed the estate of "Isaac Rucker, son of Moses", to James Powell, sheriff, to be by him administered. Apr. Court, 1844 (W. B. 11, p. 222), Amherst.

10. Peter[5] Rucker (Moses[4]) (c. 1787-1859), m. Sept. 5, 1810, Jane Haynes, dau. Harden Haynes, dec'd. Marriage bond signed by Edith Haynes, "Mother". Edith was dau. of Charles Ellis and his wife, Susanna Harding, dau. of Thomas Harding. Bond signed Sept. 5, 1810.

The records do not show that Peter was the son of Moses. We find no will of Moses, therefore are not sure but the many transactions between this Peter and Moses suggest father and son. Moses signed the marriage contract of Peter Rucker and Peter asked the court to appoint the sheriff to settle Moses's estate in 1839.

In 1820 there was a business transaction between Peter and his brother (?), Elisha Rucker. (See Elisha, p. 141).

My father, Wm. Ambrose Rucker, who was born in Amherst County, in 1840, d. 1922, said he was a young man when "Old Cousin Peter Rucker died, and remembered him very well," that Peter was a neighbor on the West side of Tobacco Row Mountains. He was a very wealthy man. Father did not remember the degree of kinship.

He paid his 1st personal tax in 1809, on one horse, which would indicate he was just of age. He paid his 1st land taxes in 1824 on 100 acres of land transferred to him from the estate of William Schofield, adjoining Godfrey Toler. Two years later he acquired 100 acres more. In 1834 he owns 616 acres of land in Amherst, on the Pedlar River, on the West side of Tobacco Row Mountains. Same adjoined Job Carter. In 1845 he paid taxes on 1,504 acres.

He continued buying and selling until 1859, making at least 80 transactions, some to Charles H. Rucker, George T. Pleasants, Samuel W. Fuller, Lindsey Burks, and Samuel M. Garland.

Peter Carter and wife, Elizabeth, sold to Peter Rucker 16 acres for $50, land on West side of Bannister Mts., on Pedlar River, Sept. 29, 1825 (D. B. R, p. 187), Amherst.

William Jopling and wife, Sarah, sold to Peter Rucker 200 acres for $275, land on West side of Tobacco Row Mts. and on East side of Horsley Creek, 24 Jan. 1832 (D. B. U, p. 2), Amherst. He was appointed at the June Court 1831 to serve as constable in the 2nd hundred of Amherst Co., again in 1834.

He bought all the property, household goods, stock, orchards, houses, of John Rowsey, 10 Apr., 1838.

On Dec. 1832, 66 acres more adjoining Joshua Sandidge (D. B. W, p. 287), Amherst. In 1841, 280 acres from Robert Tinsley.

On motion of Peter Rucker, the estate of Moses Rucker was committed to the sheriff to be settled, Moses being dec'd 3 months, 1835.

Will of Jane Rucker of Amherst, dated May 27, 1860, probated Aug. 20, 1860.

To: my son, Charles H. Rucker; my dau., Elizabeth P. Millner; my grand-son, Ambrose R. Henderson. To William Rucker Pryor. To all children of: Barnett Toler, of Martin E. Henderson, of Charles H. Rucker and of Ely P. Millner. Executor Charles H. Rucker (W. B. 15, p. 326).

Charles H. Rucker appraised the estate of Peter Rucker, Jan. 2, 1860 (W. B. 15, p. 314).

Will of Peter Rucker of Amherst.

To my wife, Jane; to my grand-son, Ambrose R. Henderson with Charles H. Rucker, his trustee; to my children: dau. Brunetta J. Toler $1,835; dau. Martha E. Henderson, wife of Robert B. Henderson; to my daus.: Elizabeth P. Millner, wife of William S. Millner; Mary A. Pryor, widow of John Pryor, Jr.; Edith E. Pryor, wife of James N. Pryor; and Sarah A. Rhoads, wife of Reuben Rhoads. Executor, Charles H. Rucker. Nov. 22, 1859, Dec. 19, 1859 (W. B. 15, p. 323), Amherst Co. Issue:

1. Charles[6] Harden Rucker.
2. Brunetta[6], m. 1st 1832, W. P. Toler, 2nd ——— Burks.
3. Martha[6] E., m. 1834 Robert Henderson, Amherst.
4. Elizabeth[6] P., m. 1840 W. S. Millner, Amherst.
5. Mary[6] Ann, m. John Pryor, Jr.
6. Edith[6] E., m. 1853 James N. Pryor.
7. Sarah[6] A., m. Reuben Rhoads.

1. Charles[6] Harden Rucker (Peter[5], Moses[4], Isaac[3], ——), b. 1818; m. 1847, Lucy D. Richeson, dau. of Capt. Jesse. He paid taxes in 1845 on 100 acres, transferred from Peter Rucker.

1. Henrietta[7] Rucker, m. Samuel A. Patterson.
   1. Lucy[8] Patterson, m. Frank West.
2. Victoria[7] Rucker, m. Samuel A. Patterson, after the death of her sister, Henrietta.
   1. Henrietta[8] Patterson, m. Henry West.
   2. Thomas[8] R.
3. Charles[7] Thomas Rucker, m. 1880, Nannie L. Taliaferro (dau. of Dr. James).
   1. Thomas[8] Earl Rucker, m. Elizabeth Shockey, of Lynchburg.
      1. Dr. Earl[9] Rucker.
   2. Lucy[8] Ethel Rucker, m. R. Lee Lynn, of Roanoke, Va.

3. Reuben[4] Rucker (Isaac[3], John[2], Peter[1]) (1772-Aug. 18, 1844), m. 1st Elizabeth Carter Dawson, Aug. 7th, 1792, in Amherst Co., dau. of Martin Dawson and wife, Elizabeth[2] Carter (Job[1] Carter). Marriage bond signed by Nelson C. Dawson, with consent of Isaac Rucker, dated above. Witness: Anthony and Moses Rucker.

Reuben m. Nancy Hubbard, June 19, 1827. With Joseph Wilson, Sec. in Campbell County.

He was appointed Administrator of the estate of Isaac Rucker, and qualified Aug. 13, 1813. Security: Ambrose Rucker, Richard Rucker, Richard Harrison and Archeleus Reynolds.

Reuben Rucker sold 16 acres of land for $400 to Edmund Wood, land on North-east side of South Fork of Falling River. Elizabeth, his wife, signed the deed (D. B. 11, p. 509), Aug. 25, 1818, Campbell.

He and wife, Elizabeth, deeded to Ambrose Rosser 50 acres for $1.00, land on South Fork of Falling River, Campbell Co., Va., Jan. 20, 1821.

He was appointed 2nd inspector of tobacco at Blackwater Warehouse. Security John Rosser, Thomas Dixon and John Cardwell, Campbell Co., Oct. 18, 1822. He was appointed inspector of tobacco at the Spring Warehouse, Mch. 13, 1826, commission dated Sept. 28, 1825. Names signed to bond were Reuben Rucker, Thomas Dixon, Joshua Rucker and John Rosser (D. B. 15, p. 279), Campbell Co.

Reuben Rucker and wife, Nancy, of Campbell, sold 80 acres of land to Wm. H. Plunkett, assignee of John Hubbard, Jr. James A. Farmer, Jesse and Mariah Hubbard, of Pittsylvania Co., Va.

He deeded 268 acres of land to Isaac Martin Rucker, of Campbell, for love and affection, land on Naked Creek adjoining Wm. Torrence Reece, Evans and Jonathan Martin, etc. May 10, 1840 (D. B. 23, p. 215), Campbell.

He was appointed inspector of tobacco at Martin's warehouse in Lynchburg, March 9, 1841.

1. Isaac^5 Martin Rucker.
2. Joshua^5.
3. Dr. John^5 Cephas, m. Lucy^6 Rucker (Bernard^5, Wm.^{4}, John^3, John^2).
4. Nelson^5 Carter, Methodist Minister, m. Dec. 18, 1828, Louisa Layne (dau. of Benjamin, of Campbell).
    1. Isaac^6 Rucker.
    2. Elizabeth^6.
5. Elizabeth^5 Carter, m. Haythe (Heath).
6. Susan^5, m. ——— Richerson.

1. Isaac^5 Martin Rucker (Reuben^4, Isaac^3, John^2) (May 25, 1809-Dec. 29, 1889), m. Adeline Virginia Tweedy, Nov. 14, 1855 (Apr. 16, 1836-Dec. 19, 1920). He was an accomplished musician, playing violin, clarinet and flute, also had a cultivated baritone voice.

Isaac M. Rucker of Campbell County, gave to the President and their successors of the Literary fund 2 acres of land for the district school, Dec. 23, 1841 (D. B. 24, p. 92), Campbell.

1. John^{6} Isaac Rucker.
2. Virginia^{6}.
3. Lucy^{6} Dabney.
4. Milton^{6} Mattaugh.
5. Mary^{6} Elizabeth.
6. Allen^{6} Tweedy.
7. Laura^{6} Jane.

1. John^{6} Isaac Rucker (Isaac^{5} M., Reuben^{4}, Isaac^{3}), of Concord, Va., b. Sept. 18, 1856, m. Sept. 3, 1879, Lillian Virginia Franklin, b. May 30, 1860.

1. Reva^{7} Rucker.
2. John^{7} Hammer.
3. Allen^{7} McToy.
4. Thomas^{7} Dabney.
5. George^{7} Martin.
6. Robert^{7} I.
7. Joshua^{7} Smith.
8. Nena^{7}.
9. Laura^{7} Elizabeth.

1. Reva^{7} Rucker (John^{6}, Isaac^{5}), m. Joseph Torrence.

1. Eleanor^{8} Torrence.
2. William^{8} Dawson.
3. Lucille^{8}.
4. Jake^{8}.
5. Clyde^{8}.
6. Ashby^{8}.
7. Frank^{8}.
8. Reva^{8} Ward.

3. Allen^{7} McToy Rucker (John^{6},), m. Annie M. Jones.

1. Mina^{8} C. Rucker.
2. Franklin^{8} J.
3. Dorothy^{8} Evans.

4. Thomas^{7} Dabney Rucker (John^{6}), of Steubenville, Ohio.

1. Marguerite^{8} Jean Rucker.
2. Thomas^{8} Donald.
3. Martha^{8}.

8. Nena^{7} Rucker (John^{6}), m. Russell A. Tibbs.
    1. Rucker^{8} A. Tibbs.
    2. George^{8}.
    3. John^{8} Russell.

2. Virginia^{6} Rucker (Isaac^{5} M., Reuben^{4}, Isaac^{3}), b. Sept. 19, 1859, m. Dec. 23, 1884, George C. Rosser (June 3, 1853-Mch. 4, 1925).
    1. Mary^{7} Virginia Rosser, d. in infancy.

3. Lucy^{6} Dabney Rucker (Isaac^{5} M., Reuben^{4}), b. Oct. 6, 1861, m. May 19, 1886, Oba Crawford Jenkins, educated, New Concord Institute; b. Sept. 21, 1859, in Appomattox Co., Va.
    1. Oba^{7} Rucker Jenkins, b. Mch. 29, 1887, educated at Virginia Polytechnic Institute, m. Nov. 26, 1910, Mattie B. Becker, b. Sept. 1, 1891, educated at Cincinnati Conservatory of Music.
        1. William^{8} Becker Jenkins, b. May 21, 1915.
    2. Lucy^{7} Gladys Jenkins, b. Feb. 4, 1889, educated at Hollins College, Va., m. June 20, 1917, Charles W. Scott (June 26, 1890, Nov. 10, 1925).
        1. Charles^{8} Wesly Scott, Jr., b. Oct. 10, 1921.
        2. Oba^{8} Jenkins Scott, b. Mch. 8, 1924.
    3. Mary^{7} Virginia Jenkins, b. Oct. 15, 1890, educated at Hollins College.

4. Milton^{6} Mattaugh Rucker (Isaac^{5} M., Reuben^{4}), b. Aug. 31, 1864, m. Nov. 4, 1891, Evie Kate Flagg, b. Nov. 26, 1871.
    1. Nettie^{7} V. Rucker.
    2. Annie^{7} Laurie.
    3. Milton^{7} M., Jr.
    4. Lucy^{7} Kate.
    5. Jett^{7}.

5. Mary^{6} Elizabeth Rucker (Isaac^{5} M.), b. Nov. 1, 1857, m. 1st, Oct. 3, 1888, Robert Owen Rector (Jan. 19, 1856-Sept. 19, 1902), m. 2nd S. F. Calhoun.
    1. William^{7} Bayless Rector.
    2. Virginia^{7} Dove, m. Dan Dickerson.
    3. Robert^{7} O.
    4. Allen^{7} Rucker.
    5. Alfred^{7}.
    6. John^{7} Parish, m. Frances Wright.
    7. Lucille^{7}, d. young.

6. Allen^{6} Tweedy Rucker (Isaac^{5} M.), b. May 8, 1870, m. July 5, 1894, Mary Frances Plunkett, b. Oct. 11, 1873.

1. Lieut. Allen^{7} Willis Rucker, b. July 23, 1897.
2. Jerry^{7} Chariton, b. Oct. 22, 1898.
3. Mary^{7} Virginia, b. June 22, 1900.
4. Harriet^{7}, b. Sept. 8, 1902.
5. Vance^{7}, b. Sept. 1, 1904.
6. John^{7} Isaac, b. Mch. 19, ...
7. Berkeley^{7}, b. Mch. 30, 1909.

7. Laura^{6} Jane Rucker (Isaac^{5} M.), b. April 6, 1873, m. Feb. 6, 1901, John B. Chilton, b. June 3, 1871.

1. Mary^{7} Virginia Chilton.

2. Joshua^{5} Rucker (Reuben^{4}, Isaac^{3}, John^{2}), m. Emily Tinsley (dau. of ———— Tinsley and wife, McDaniel). Lived in Bedford.

Joshua Rucker and wife, Emily, of Bedford, sold to Balda McDaniel 147 1/8 acres for $500, land on the waters of Ivey Creek, July 21, 1836. Served in war of 1812. *Hardesty's H. and G. Ency.*

1. Joshua^{6} Tinsley Rucker, Jr.
2. Susan^{6} E.
3. Mildred^{6} m. Albert Millner.
4. Angelina^{6} m. Mahali Dameron.
5. Margaret^{6} m. Zackaria Dameron.

1. Lieut. Joshua^{6} Tinsley Rucker, Jr. (Joshua^{5}, Reuben^{4}, Isaac^{3}, ———), b. Apr. 12, 1837, Bedford, a Confederate Soldier under Kirkpatrick; was wounded; m. Louisa Harris, of Nelson County, 1872.

1. Walton^{7} T. Rucker, b. 1873, of West Virginia.
2. Emily^{7}, b. 1875, m. Thomas Oglesby.
3. William^{7} H., b. 1877, m. ———— Merriwether.
4. John^{7} T., b. 1879; m. ———— Dawson, of Bedford, Va.
5. Frank^{7}, of W. Va.

2. Susan^{6} E. Rucker (Joshua^{5}, Reuben^{4}), m. William Ogden, Aug., 1843, son of John Ogden.

1. Charles^{7} Sydnor Ogden, b. Aug. 1, 1844, Jefferson Co., Mo., m. May 9, 1882, Mary Martha Ogden (1st cousin).
    1. Harry^{8} M. Ogden.
    2. Charles^{8} Glenn.
    3. M. Isabelle^{8}.
2. Wellington^{7} Ogden.
3. Emma^{7} Josephine.
4. Mildred^{7}.
5. Sallie^{7}.
6. Robert^{7}.

5. Elizabeth^{5} Carter Rucker (Reuben^{4}, ———), m. Gilbert Haythe, Jan. 2, 1828, in Lynchburg, the son of Thomas Haythe and wife, Martha Gilbert, dau. of Benjamin Gilbert, and wife, Martha Preston. (Thomas Haythe was a Rev. Officer.)

1. Pauline^{6} Rucker Haythe, m. Joseph Layne.
    1. Mattie^{7} Layne.
    2. Joseph^{7}.
    3. Carter^{7}.
2. Victoria^{6} Haythe.
3. James^{6} Gilbert.

2. Victoria^{6} Haythe (Elizabeth^{5}, Reuben^{4}, Isaac^{3}), b. 1833, m. John A. Tanner.

1. Elizabeth^{7} Tanner, m. 1st Robert Robinson, 2nd Mitchell Seate.
2. Dr. John^{7} A. Tanner, m. Carylen Littlefield.
    1. Virginia^{8} Tanner, m. Laurence Green.
3. Alice^{7} M. Tanner, m. Robert Lewis.
    1. Elizabeth^{8} Sterling Lewis.
    2. Robert^{8}.
    3. John^{8}.
    4. Pemela^{8}.
4. Rev. James^{7} G. Tanner.
5. Victoria^{7}.
6. Cornelia^{7}.
7. Willie^{7}, m. W. Fairfax.
8. Charles^{7} Tanner, m. Lena Whately.
    1. Whately^{8} Charles Tanner.
    2. John^{8}.

9. Nannie[7] Tanner, m. Charles Alex Scott.
    1. Charles[8] Alex Scott, Jr. (A. E. F.)
    2. Estelle[8], m. James B. Gallespie.
        1. Billy[9] Gallespie.
        2. Nannie[9].

4. Rev. James[7] G. Tanner (Victoria[6], Elizabeth[5], Reuben[4] Rucker), Presbyterian minister from Bedford, m. Ida Baskerville Seate (dau. of Sophia Fley and ——— Seate) Lexington, Va. She died Mch. 19, 1930, in New Haven, Conn., buried in Lynchburg. They moved to Texas.

1. Frank[8] Baskerville Tanner, m. Ruby Williams, of Dallas, Tex.
    1. Frances[9] B. Tanner.
    2. Elizabeth[9] Carter Tanner.
2. Edith[8] V., m. Arthur Woodson, of Roanoke.
3. Paul[8] A., of Georgia.
4. Elvis[8] Mitchell Tanner.
5. Grace[8] Kinnear Tanner.

5. Victoria[7] Tanner (Victoria[6], Elizabeth[5], Reuben[4]), m. William Kinnear.

1. Wm.[8] Kinnear.
2. Tanner[8].
3. Jean[8].
4. Clarence[8], m. May Gale, Walterson, Tenn.
5. Robert[8].
6. Belle[8].
7. Victoria[8], m. Austin Quick.

4. Richard[4] Rucker (Isaac[3], John[2], Peter[1]), d. 1817, Amherst; m. 1st Patsy Hudson, Mch. 22, 1795; 2nd Margaret Marr, July 10, 1798. Patsy Hudson was the dau. of Joshua Hudson, whose will 1801 mentions Patsy as dead. Marriage bond signed by Joshua Hudson.

Marriage bond of 2nd wife, Margaret Marr, was signed by Alexander Marr.

After Richard[4]'s death, his widow, Margaret, and her sister, Elizabeth Marr, and children, moved near Pedlar Mills.

Feb. 5, 1839, Margaret Rucker, widow of Richard Rucker, dec'd; Alexander M. Rucker and wife, Mary, Sarah R., Elizabeth and Ann, children of Richard Rucker, sold to Richard Ellis for $180, 280 acres of land in Campbell Co., at head of Naked Creek (D. B. 22, p. 488), Campbell.

Richard was signing county petitions, in 1796, in Amherst and in 1801 was paying land tax on 97 acres; in 1814, was paying land tax on 100 acres of land adjoining Burford.

He died 1817, intestate, and Oct. 20, Benjamin Rucker was appointed Administrator with Armistead Rucker and Alexander Marr, his security. The estate was appraised 1818.

Richard Rucker was in the war of 1812, under Capt. Cornelius Sale, 8th Va. Regiment of Amherst, a substitute for John Penn of Amherst for 5 months (Va. Pay Roll, Archives). Richard was cross-eyed.

1. Alexander ^{5} Marr Rucker.
2. Sarah^{5} Willis, unmar.
3. Elizabeth^{5}, unmar.
4. Ann^{5}, unmar.

1. Alexander^{5} Marr Rucker (Richard^{4}, Isaac^{3}, John^{2}), d. 1871, m. 1st Mary Toler of Amherst, dau. of Godfrey Toler (widow Johns), 2nd m. Elizabeth J. Camden, 1859.

Jan., 1890. Will of Godfrey Toler mentions "My five children" (W. B. 22, p. 360), Amherst Co.

Edmond M. Ware qualified as Administrator of the estate of Alexander M. Rucker, 20 Nov. 1871 (W. B. 18, p. 145), Amherst.

Issue (by 1st mar.):

1. Godfrey^{6} Rucker.
2. Isaac^{6} Willis (Ike) was in Co. E, 2nd Va. Cavalry; m. Susan Milner.
    1. Emma^{7} Rucker, m. Willis Rucker.
3. William^{6} was in Co. E, 2nd Va. Cavalry.
4. Sarah^{6} Jane, b. 1831, m. Robert Hudson, 1853.
5. Ann^{6} C., m. James W. Reynolds, 1858, Amherst.
6. Margaret^{6} E., 1st m. ——— Davis, 2nd ——— Smith, 3rd Archie Cox.

Issue (by 2nd mar.):

7. Annie^{6} L. Rucker.

1. Godfrey^{6} Rucker (Alexander^{5}, Richard^{4}, Isaac^{3}), b. Feb. 22, 1831; m. Mary Jane Ould, May 1, 1860, dau. of George W. and Jane (Watts) Ould. Godfrey Rucker was in Co. E, 2nd Va. Cavalry, and was wounded at 2nd battle of Manassas.

1. Allie^{7} V. Rucker, b. 1869, m. J. J. Watts, 1888.
2. Annie^{7}, b. 1870.

Issue:

3. Mary[7] Ellen, b. 1872.
4. George[7] M., b. 1873.
5. William[7] Godfrey, m. Sallie E. Layne, 1898.
    1. T. D.[8] Rucker.
    2. Lucy[8].

6. Elizabeth[4] Rucker (Isaac[3], John[2], Peter[1]), b. Oct. 14, 1777; m. Sept. 9, 1797, Archelaus Reynolds (July 27, 1776-Dec. 4, 1863), of Amherst Co., son of Charles and Ann Taylor Reynolds. Elizabeth's marriage bond in Amherst, signed by Isaac Rucker, Obediah Reynolds and Richard Rucker.

The following is copied from the Bible of Elizabeth[4] Rucker Reynolds, now in the possession of a descendant, James A. Wood:

"Charles B. Reynolds, b. Sept. 11, 1802; Nancy T. Reynolds, b. Nov. 20, 1805, m. Geo. W. Pettyjohn; Obediah Reynolds, b. May 13, 1804."

Issue:

1. Willis[5] Reynolds.
2. Isaac[5] Rucker, m. July 30, 1833, Sarah Parks Burks (dau. of Samuel and Margaret) and widow of Garland Rucker.
3. Charles[5], b. Sept. 11, 1802.
4. Obediah[5], b. May 13, 1804.
5. Nancy[5] T., b. Nov. 20, 1805, m. Geo. W. Pettyjohn.
    1. John[6] Pettyjohn, m. 1st ——— Ould, 2nd ——— Watts, dau. of Abbott Watts.
    2. Sally[6].
    3. a daughter[6], m. Stephen Watts.

2. Sally[6] Pettyjohn (Nancy[5], Elizabeth[4], Isaac[3] Rucker), m. Charles Pettyjohn.

1. Charles[7] Pettyjohn.
2. Clarence[7].
3. Joseph[7].
4. Kate[7].
5. Susie[7].
6. Ann[7].
7. Caunie[7].
8. Maude[7].
9. Carrie[7].

1. Willis[5] Reynolds (Elizabeth[4], Isaac[3] Rucker) (June 5, 1799-Apr. 18, 1876), m. 1st, Oct. 10, 1822, Jane Dawson, d. Jan. 1, 1845, dau. of Rev. Lewis Dawson, m. 2nd Camilla McElroy, Sept. 14, 1848.

Issue (by 1st mar.):

1. John[6] P. Reynolds (1823-1862).
2. Charles[6].
3. Archelaus[6].
4. Francis[6] Marion Reynolds (Jan. 19, 1822-Sept., 1910), m. Nov. 4, 1856, Sarah Frances Buchanan (June 15, 1830-Jan., 1908).
    1. Corbin[7] Miller Reynolds (Oct., 1857-Apr. 1885).
    2. W.[7] Joseph, b. Sept. 15, 1859.
    3. Stella[7] Jane, b. April 16, 1863.
    4. Katherine[7] (Dec., 1865-Nov. 16, 1918), m. George D. Chason.
        1. George[8] R. Chason.
    5. Marietta[7], m. Edwin Muldew.
        1. Camilla[8] Muldrew.
        2. Mary[8].
        3. Fannie[8].
        4. Laura[8].
        5. Hugh[8].
        6. Bettie[8].
        7. William[8] P.
        8. Allen[8] P.
        9. Minnie[8].
    6. Elizabeth[7] Reynolds.
    7. Amy[7].
    8. Joseph[7] Dawson.
    9. Robert[7] Harvey Reynolds (1840-Sept. 30, 1910), m. Apr. 14, 1865, Mollie Verdun.
        1. Charles[8] Reynolds, Waukegan, Ill.
        2. Maggie[8].
        3. Edward[8].
        4. Callie[8] m. Henry DeKay, Plattsburg, N. Y.
        5. Minnie[8].
        6. Bettie[8], of Waukegan.

Issue (by 2nd mar.):

5. William[6] Isaac Reynolds, b. July 13, 1850, m. Georgie Ella Turner, 1894, Salin, Oregon.
6. Alice[6] (1852-1874), m. Edward E. Brown.

7. Mary[6] Jane, b. May 1853, m. Mch. 23, 1786, Thomas D. Philips, Oregon.
   1. Emma[7] Philips, b. Nov., 1877.
   2. Ira[7], b. Feb. 17, 1880.
   3. Eloise[7], b. Sept. 26, 1881.
   4. Eugenia[7], b. Aug. 22, 1883.
   5. Marietta[7], b. Aug. 27, 1885.
8. Edward[6], b. Sept. 19, 1855, Amarillo, Tex., (15 children).
9. Benjamin[6] Watkins, b. Jan. 29, 1859, of Mo.

7. Anthony[3] Rucker (John[2], Peter[1]) d. Feb. 17, 1821, m. Rebecca Burgess. He received his share of his father's land, patented in Amherst Co., Va. (D. B. G, p. 7) Jan. 22, 1781.

In 1781 the following children of John[2] Rucker sold to Anthony Rucker 100 acres of land in Amherst, land beginning at Isaac Rucker's. Deed signed by Peter Rucker, Alexander Marr, John Rucker, John Lee, Ambrose Rucker, Benjamin Rucker, Isaac Rucker, Stephen Ham, Anthony Rucker, James Morton.

Anthony was not of age when the estate of his father was divided in 1751, but in 1782 he is paying on 384, and 100 acres in Amherst Co., the 384 acres "whereupon he lives" on Harris Creek. In 1798 he bought 104, and 9 acres of land from his brother Isaac. In 1806 he is paying on 589, and 213 acres.

Anthony Rucker was Deputy Commissioner of Provision Law for this County for year 1781. Allowed 50 lbs. sterling for same (O. B. 1782-84, p. 207).

7 Oct., 1782, Anthony Rucker is allowed the sum of £47 for 63 days as Commissioner in valuing lands in the Upper Battallion in this county, which sum the sheriff is to pay out of the taxes when collected (O. B. 1782-84, p. 32).

May Court, 1783. On motion of Anthony Rucker the Court doth certify that the said Rucker served as a Commissioner of the Provision Law for this county for the year 1781, and that he found himself writing paper for the said business.

Anthony Rucker was granted 677 acres, part of entry made Mch. 2, 1789, on Treasury Warrant No. 1923, lying in County of Fayette, on waters of Four-Mile Creek, opposite John Rucker, etc. (D. B. D., p. 305).

Fayette Co., Ky., Dec. 7, 1791, Anthony Rucker, of Amherst Co., Va., "finds it inconvenient to come to Kentucky, and appoints James Rucker, my worthy friend", his attorney, to sell his lands in Kentucky. Witness: John Morton, Jeremiah Morton,

Benjamin Moor, James Morton, James Rucker. (D. B. B., p. 101) Woodford Co., Ky.

Revolutionary Service reference: Augusta Abstracts, Vol. 2, p. 492—Shumaker's declaration that he was to guard the Albemarle Barracks under Captain Anthony Rucker. *Hardesty's H. & G. Ency.* of Amherst County.

Calendar of State Papers: Vol. II, p. 406, of Amherst Co., Sept. 9, 1781—a letter written by Anthony Rucker to Colonel Davies, head of the War Department, in reference to carrying out instructions given by him regarding the collection of supplies, saying "Bacon is scarce on account of shortage of salt", and about establishing a magazine at Lynch's Ferry. Anthony was Deputy Commissioner of the Provision Law of Amherst.

From the Diary of Col. Landon Carter, Sabin Hall, Richmond Co., Va., that he had sent a letter by "Captain Rucker, victualer to the regiment" just before Gen. Washington came to Yorktown.

Anthony Rucker bought from Isaac Rucker 14 acres of land on Harris Creek adjoining Captain Benjamin Rucker, 5 Aug., 1795. Witness: Richard, Elizabeth and Patsy Rucker. (D. B. 9, p. 608).

Thomas Burgess and wife, Elizabeth, William Stuart and wife, Nancy; Martin Hardin and wife, Mary; Anthony Rucker and wife, Rebecca (Burgess); Joseph Rodgers and wife, Elizabeth; sold to William Burgess 740 acres of land for $104, land adjoining Thomas Carter, William Price and William Burgess. (D. B. 11, p. 434) Apr. 1, 1799, Pittsylvania Co.

December 17, 1792, Anthony Rucker was appointed a tobacco inspector in Amherst Co., secured by Ambrose Rucker.

"By Gone Days" from a Richmond newspaper of one hundred years ago, 1821: "The public is hereby notified that a patent has been secured for the heirs of Anthony Rucker and Benjamin Rucker, the original inventors of the James River batteau, or tobacco boat, the exclusive right to use and vend to others, etc. The following is in reference to a tobacco boat patented by Anthony and Benjamin Rucker, copied from Amherst Deed Book: "Having confidence in the ability of Edmund Rucker, of Rutherford County, Tenn.; Nelson C. Dawson and Ambrose Rucker, of Amherst, patentees and trustees for the heirs and devisees of Benjamin and Anthony Rucker, the original inventors of the Batteaux or tobacco boats now used on the James River and other waters of the U. S., appoint the said Edmund Rucker our agent in the State of South Carolina, Georgia, Kentucky, Tennessee, Alabama. Patent issued 3 Apr., 1821." (D. B. P., p. 6).

In 1813 Anthony sold 674 acres to his brother Benjamin, on Harris Creek. In 1819 he sold 213 acres to David Tinsley. He died in 1820, leaving 359 acres, adjoining W. R. Roane, upon which his estate paidtaxes in 1822. The following year it paid on 479 acres.

Rebecca's name does not appear upon the tax books until 1822, after which time she pays on 125 acres, adjoining W. R. Roane, a life interest. In 1840 Anthony's estate is still paying on 482 acres.

The following is copied from The Lynchburg Press, Friday, Feb. 23, 1821:

"Died, at his residence in Amherst on the 27 ult., Anthony Rucker, Esq., in the 81st year of his age. He was one of the few surviving patriots of the Revolutionary struggle, and none represented more fully the characteristic honesty and simplicity of manners, of the virtuous age. As he was pure and unsullied in life, so was he constant and intrepid in Death. A living example of rectitude.

"Few men have rendered more important services to their country in the subordinate departments of usefulness than the deceased.

"The offices in the gift of his country, he filled with great credit to himself and satisfaction to his constituents. None have transmitted a more unspotted reputation for honesty to posterity, than old Anthony Rucker. Long will his name be remembered with patriarchal reverence."

Will of Anthony Rucker, Sr. Dated 20 Apr., 1820, recorded 17 Feb., 1821: "To wife, Rebecca, the home with 125 acres of land, slaves. To son, Absolom Rucker, 100 acres on the road, 1 acre of land to be reserved where the church now stands for a place of worship. My estate to be equally divided in six parts: To sons: Abner, Armistead, and Absolom; to dau., Agnes Ogden, 200 acres of land; to the children of my deceased daus.: Ann Eades, and Amelia Richardson. Land on Four-Miles Creek, Ky. Executors: Nelson Carter Dawson, Sr., Ambrose Rucker, son of Reuben Rucker, dec., Isaac Rucker. Witness: John Coleman, Edwin T. Rucker, Nathan D. Rucker, David Tinsly, Sr. (W. B. 6, p. 210) Amherst.

Codicil: to Benjamin Ogden 213 acres to make my daughter Agnes have an equal share.

Inventory of the above estate by Nelson C. Dawson, Sheriff, 31 Dec., 1832, (W. B. 8, p. 324) Amherst.

Issue:

1. Abner^4.
2. Armistead^4.
3. Absolem^4.
4. Agnes^4.
5. Ann^4, m. Bartlett Eads, Apr. 12, 1795; bond witnessed by Sophia and Aggy Rucker.
6. Amelia^4.

1. Abner^4 Rucker (Anthony^3, John^2) (1770-1839). 1st, m. Feb., 1793, Nancy Morton, d. 1827; 2nd, m. Nancy ———, Lexington, Ky. He served in the War of 1812.

He was signing petitions in Amherst Co., Va., in 1790; moved to Ky. and lived upon land taken up by his father, Anthony, by Treasury warrant No. 1923, 677 acres in Fayette Co., on Four-Mile Creek, opposite John Rucker's land. (D. B. D., p. 305). In 1789-1810 he is paying taxes on land in Woodford Co., Ky.

He married Nancy Morton, dau. of Jeremiah Morton, of Woodford Co., Ky., whose will dated 1823, mentions his daughter Nancy, wife of Abner Rucker, and her children, Betsy, Agatha, Anthony, Jeremiah, Jefferson, Julius, Jonathan M. Rucker.

Abner Rucker left a will dated Jan. 24, 1837, recorded Feb., 1839, in Fayette Co., Ky. (W. B. O., p. 109) also in Amherst Co., Va., (W. B. 10, p. 205): "I, Abner Rucker, of Lexington, give to my wife, Nancy Rucker, one dollar only in consequence of her unkindness to me. My estate both real and personal divide amongst all of my children. Should two of my daughters by my present wife, Rebecca and Sally, when they come to years of discretion abandon me and remain with their mother against my will, after I have provided a home for them, in that event I duly leave them a dollar each. . . ."

Issue (by 1st mar.):

1. Betsy^5 Rucker.
2. Agatha^5.
3. Anthony^5, d. Casey Co., Ky.
4. Jeremiah^5, d. 1870 in Ill., m. Lucy Tanner, Feb. 3, 1795.
5. Jefferson^5, d. Shelby Co., Ky. (Woodford Co., Ky.)
6. Julius^5.
7. Jonathan^5 M., d. 1832, Woodford, Ky.
8. Morton^5, buried at old home place near Versailles, Ky.

Issue (by 2nd mar.):

9. Rebecca^5, m. John S. McDaniel, Amherst, Va.
10. Sally^5.

2. Agatha[5] Rucker, (Abner[4], Anthony[3], John[2]) b. 1804, m. c 1818, Isaac[5] Rucker. (John[4], John[3], John[2]), who served in the War of 1812, d. 1856.

1. Edward[6] Rucker went to Ill.
2. Jane[6].
3. Martha[6], m. Charles Ware (no children).
4. Susan[6], m. James Hudson in 1861.
   1. Henry[7] William Hudson.

2. Armistead[4] Rucker (Anthony[3], John[2], Peter[1]) m. Elizabeth Richeson, Dec. 28, 1803. In 1814 Armistead was paying taxes on 100 acres in Amherst, and continued until 1820, when he moved to Pittsylvania Co. He paid a personal tax in Henry Co. from 1820 to 1828. In 1817 he was appointed one of the administrators of the estate of Richard Rucker, 1st cousin. After the death of Armistead, Elizabeth took her children to St. Louis to live, but her son, John, returned to Amherst, Va.

1. John[5] Rucker.
2. Lee[5].
3. Anthony[5].
4. Thomas[5].
5. Anne[5].
6. Cassie[5], m. Loch, of St. Louis.

1. John[5] Rucker (Armistead[4], Anthony[3], John[2]) m. Elizabeth Stevens Duval (duVal) Aug. 14, 1835. John owned land in Campbell Co., near the Court House; also property in Lynchburg, Va. He lived on Diamond Hill in a house formerly owned by Dr. Duval. On Feb. 18, 1836, John and Elizabeth Rucker sold a lot in Lynchburg on Sixth Street. On April 23, 1850, they sold the Blackwater Tobacco Warehouse with 4½ acres of land, and a 40-foot alley for $4,000.

1. Anne[6] Elizabeth Rucker, m. 1st Dr. Lemuel A. Williams, Oct. 17, 1853; 2nd, ——— Sully.

Issue (by 1st mar.):

1. dau[7], m. James Hancock, of Okla.

Issue (by 2nd mar.):

2. Julia[7] Sully, President of the Woman's Club, Richmond, Va., 1923-25, 29-31.

3. Anthony[5] Rucker (Armistead[4], Anthony[3], John[2]), lived at Cedar Grove, Amherst Co.

Issue:

1. Richard^{6}, m. Sophia Harrison, moved to Tex.
2. John^{6}, m. Mary Tinsley, of Bethel, moved to Mo.
    1. John^{7} Rucker.
        1. Mayor^{8} Rucker, living in Sturgeon, Mo.
3. Jane^{6}, unmar.

From the marriage bonds of Amherst County, "Anthony Rucker to marry Rebecca B. Eads. The license requested by Ambrose Rucker, 21 Aug., 1821". Was this the above Anthony Rucker^{2} If so he was very young.

3. Absolem^{4} Rucker (Anthony^{3}, John^{2}) (Aug. 19, 1781-Dec. 12, 1867), d. Amherst Co., m. Nancy ———, d. Dec. 21, 1856.

Jan., 1822, he and his wife, Nancy, of Amherst, gave a deed of trust to Chiswell Dabney, Trustee, for Galt & Bullock Co., merchants, on 160 acres of land, left to him by his father, Anthony Rucker. (D. B. P, p. 36).

Appearing on the tax books in 1822, the year after the death of his father, Absolem was paying on 160 acres, adjoining W. R. Roan's and his mother's land. He lived about 2 miles south of Sweet Briar College on the land now owned by Mr. Ogden, who is a grandson of Agnes Rucker and Benjamin Ogden. Upon this land the first Episcopal Church in Amherst County was built by Col. Ambrose Rucker, c. 1780.

In Apr., 1822, James Gilbert gave to Absolem Rucker power of attorney.

Absolem sold to Samuel Garland and Archibald Robertson "4 negroes and their children, and other personal property of every description, and all of my undivided interest in the whole of my father, Anthony Rucker's, estate, land, stock, etc. . . ." to secure a note owed to Archibald Robertson. (D. B. P., p. 153), Aug. 19, 1822, Amherst, Va.

1. Anthony^{5} Thomas Burgess Rucker.
2. James^{5} Barber, never married.
3. Jackson^{5}, m. Mrs. Maria Louise Jones (nee Dillard).
    1. Pattie^{6} Rucker, m. Watts.
    2. Nannie^{6} L., m. Cooley, Williamsburg, Ky.
    3. Daniel^{6} Warwick.
4. Agnes^{5}, m. Cochran.
5. Rebecca^{5}, m. Wright.
6. Amanda^{5}, m. Nimrod B. James.
7. Susan^{5}, m. Bocock.
8. Amelia ^{5}, m. Couch of Appomattox, Va.

1. Anthony[5] Thomas Burgess Rucker (Absolem[4], Anthony[3], John[2]), b. Mch. 13, 1806, Amherst Co., d. Feb. 3, 1892, Campbell Co.; m. 1st, Aug. 15, 1832, Elizabeth Wilson, of Pittsylvania Co., Va. d. June 23 1835.

He was a tobacconist for many years in Lynchburg, Va.; failing, he sold and moved to a farm in Campbell Co.

He married 2nd Dorothea Perrow (Feb. 6, 1815-Apr. 15, 1891), b. Campbell Co., dau. of Stephen Perrow and Dorothea Cox (dau. of Benjamin), who were married in Campbell Co., June 7, 1805, by Rev. W. P. Martin (W. B. I, p. 217), Campbell Co., Va. (See Perrow, Part III).

For further reference see (D. B. 24, p. 432), Dec. 31, 1842, Campbell Co.. Va.

"Anthony[5] Thomas Burgess Rucker of Lynchburg, Virginia, of the first part; Samuel Garland and Pembroke Garland, of the second part; Robert Tinsley, Commissioner, Robinson Rucker and James D. Brown, of the third part.

Said Anthony Thomas Burgess Rucker purchased at auction of Robert Tinsley, as Commissioner, a family of slaves for $885.00; J. D. Brown, security, and mortgaged the slaves to the Garlands, and his (Anthony Thomas Burgess Rucker's) interest in the estate of Anthony Rucker, deceased, which Anthony Thomas Burgess Rucker claims as having been transferred of his father—Absolem Rucker."

March 5, 1844, Anthony Thomas Burgess Rucker and Dorothea, his wife, of Lynchburg, Va., made a deed of trust to William B. Averett, "a lot of ½ acre; four grown slaves, with four children". The above to be sold, and the residue applied to the support of Dorothea Rucker, and her present children; Edward P., Sarah Jane, and any future issue.

Mch. 22, 1860, Anthony Thomas Burgess Rucker of Campbell Co., sold to Charles R. Slaughter his wife, Dorothy's, interest in the estate of Stephen Perrow, dec'd, both real and personal to secure debts (D. B. 32, p. 141), Campbell.

July 18, 1863, Anthony and wife, "Dolly", sold to James T. Wright, for $2,000 all the interest they have in 82 a. of land belonging to Dolly's parents, land on Opossum Creek, which was alloted to Dorothea, wife of Stephen Perrow, dec'd, from her father, Benjamin Cox's estate, Campbell Co. (D. B. 2, p. 8).

Issue:

1. Edward[6] Perrow Rucker.
2. Sarah[6] Jane, b. July 16, 1843, m. Benjamin Rush Gilbert, of Amherst.

3. John[6] McCabe (Aug. 14, 1844-Feb. 4, 1846).
4. Gertrude[6] (Jan. 9, 1846-Feb. 9, 1847).
5. John[6] R. McDaniel, b. Dec. 24, 1847, a Methodist minister, m. Nannie Smith, of Richmond, Va.
6. Rose[6] Armistead (June 21, 1850-Feb. 18, 1876), m. Jackson Kable (?), Methodist minister.
7. Ellis[6] Otway (Mch. 16, 1852-June 16, 1853).
8. James[6] Anthony (Sept. 12, 1853-Mch. 8, 1898), m. Callie Mason (Jan. 5, 1850-Feb. 26, 1916), of Campbell Co.
    1. Gertrude[7] Rucker, m. Wilkerson Thornton Whitten.
        1. Helen[8] Rose Whitten.
    2. Helen[7], dec'd.
    3. Robert[7] Maurice, dec'd.
    4. Roberta[7], m. Elbert Gibbons Crews; they adopted Helen Rose Whitten, dau. of their dec'd sister, Gertrude.
    5. Ernest[7] Eugene.
    6. William[7] Anthony.
    7. Claude[7] Lee.
9. Gaston[6] Green, b. Dec. 2, 1855, m. Rose McKinnel, of Lynchburg, Va.
10. Florence[6] Nightingale, b. Feb. 6, 1858, unmar.
11. Ester Hamlet[6], b. Mch. 18, 1861.

1. Edward[6] Perrow Rucker (Anthony[5] T. B., Absolem[4]) (Apr. 16, 1842-1906), d. in Lynchburg; was a sergeant in the Rifle Grays of Lynchburg, Va. He was captured and imprisoned at Fortress Monroe during the Civil War, and studied medicine while in prison, under the surgeon. After his release he married Mary Elizabeth Saunders, dau. of Littleberry Saunders, of Bedford Co., but soon rejoined his regiment and served until the surrender. In 1877 he moved west.

1. Mary[7] Lillian, m. Wm. L. Deering, of Bedford Co.
2. Thomas[7] Saunders Rucker.

2. Thomas[7] Saunders Rucker (Edward[6], ———), b. July 13, 1866, Campbell; m. 1st Mary Ellen Marion (grand niece of General Francis Marion, of Charleston, S. C.), Oct. 11, 1892; 2nd, Sept. 9, 1931, Annie Yow (dau. of George H. Yow), of Thomasville, N. C.

He started very young as a tobacconist in Lynchburg, but moved to Winston-Salem, N. C., in January, 1884, and is still in the tobacco business.

In 1915 he formed a partnership with J. Turner Farish in the Stock, Bond and Real Estate Insurance business, and later studied law.

Issue:

1. Richmond[8] Rucker, b. May 10, 1896, Winston-Salem, studied at Tinsley Military Institute; Yeaton Preparatory School, Lancaster, Pa.; Trinity College of Harvard. He joined Company "B" in training at Harvard, Mch., 1917; with the company when mustered into Federal service on July 25, 1917; went into camp a member of Co. "B", 101st M. G. B., A. E. F., landed in England, October, 1917, and in February went into action at Chemin des Dames, Chateau Thierry, St. Miels; the battle of the Meuse, etc., under the command of Morgan G. Buckely, Jr., of Harvard.

4. Mary[4] Agnes Rucker (Anthony[3], John[2], ———), m. Benjamin Ogden, son of Henry Ogden (see Ogden, Part III), Oct. 15, 1807 (1782-1846), d. Amherst Co.

Will of Agnes Rucker Ogden:

"I, Agnes Ogden, being of sound mind and memory do make this my last will and testment in the following manner: First: I give and bequeath unto my two sons, Anthony Rucker and James M., my slaves: Reuben, Jim, Perlina and Betsy, with their increase.

I give unto Francis I. Woody a bed and $100.00 to be divided equally between Nancy E. McDaniel, her two brothers and her sister. The money issued to be raised by the sale of stock, crop returns, etc., upon the premises.

If there should be any money from the proceeds of the sale over $300.00, I give it to be divided equally between my two sons, Anthony and James M. Rucker. I hereby appoint my son Anthony Rucker Executor of this my last will and testament, hereby revoking all former wills made by me.
Witness: Samuel Scott, Thomas R. Ogden, Jno. D. Gilbert.
Dated Sept. 1, 1858, probated Jan. 11, 1865."

Anthony Rucker Ogden and James M. Ogden qualified as Executors on Jan. 11, 1865, to the estate of Agnes Rucker Ogden. Estate of $17,741.42 (W. B. 7-8), Amherst Co.

Issue:

1. Anthony[5] Rucker Ogden.
2. John[5] M.
3. Ann[5] E. McDaniel.
4. Albert[5] H., m. Lucinda McDaniel, 1831.
   1. Ambrose[6] Ogden.

5. Sarah[5].
6. James[5] Madison.

1. Anthony[5] Rucker Ogden (Agnes[4], Anthony[3], John[2] Rucker) (Feb. 18, 1811-Aug. 3, 1881), m. Aug. 8, 1837, Eleanor Skidmore (Mch. 10, 1818-June 4, 1889).

Bible in possession of Henry Anthony Ogden, of Gala, Va. Anthony Rucker Ogden and his wife, Eleanor Skidmore Ogden, lived on a part of the old "Skidmore Tract" at Skidmore's Ferry, Botetourt Co., Va., near Rocky Point. This land was purchased from the Indians, and is now in the hands of John Thomas Rucker, a son-in-law.

1. Infant[6], b. Aug. 6, 1838.
2. Cynthia[6] Mary Virginia Ogden (July 27, 1840-Nov. 27, 1906), m. Capt. William D. Burks.
3. Infant[6], b. Mch. 17, 1843.
4. Sarah[6] Eleanor Ballew, b. July 23, 1844.
5. Infant[6], b. Feb. 18, 1847.
6. Frances[6] Jane Rebecca Allie (June 15, 1848-Aug. 16, 1887), unmar.
7. John[6] Randolph (Mch. 26, 1851-Oct. 22, 1867).
8. James[6] Benjamin Allison (Oct. 17, 1853-Oct. 5, 1862).
9. Henry[6] Anthony, b. Mch. 7, 1858; m. Mary Schaeffer; reside at Gala, Va.
   1. George[7] Washington Ogden, d. young.
   2. Frances[7], d. young.
10. Edwin[6] David, b. Sept. 30, 1861; m. Florence Bradford; d. Apr. 1, 1927; lived at Natural Bridge Station, Va.
    1. Gladys[7] Ogden.
    2. Earl[7].

4. Sarah[6] Eleanor Ballew Ogden (Anthony[5], Agnes[4], ——), (July 23, 1844-Mch. 26, 1921) m. Dec. 8, 1875 John[6] Thomas Rucker (Nathan[5] W., Isaac[4], Ambrose[3], John[2], ——), b. June 12, 1847; lived in Rocky Point, Va.

1. Lillian[7] Snead Rucker.
2. Mary[7] Jackson, graduate of Piedmont College.
3. Eleanor[7] Burks, d. Mch. 24, 1920, unmar.

1. Lillian[7] Snead Rucker (Sarah[6], Anthony[5], Agnes[4], ——), b. July 3, 1877; m. Sept. 13, 1905, Rufus Gilliam (Apr. 6, 1881-Dec. 30, 1914), reside at Rocky Point.

1. Thornton[8] Elwood Gilliam.
2. Kathleen[8] Erma (July 20, 1911-Sept. 4, 1912).

2. John^{5} M. Ogden (Agnes^{4}, Anthony^{3}, John^{2} Rucker).
   1. William^{6} Ogden, m. Aug., 1843, Susan^{6} E. Rucker (Joshua^{5}, Reuben^{4}, Isaac^{3}, John^{2} Rucker).
      1. Charles^{7} Sydnor, m. 1st cousin, Mary Martha Ogden.
      2. Wellington^{7} Ogden.
      3. Emma^{7} Josephine.
      4. Mildred^{7}.
      5. Sallie^{7}.
      6. Robert^{7}.

6. James^{5} Madison Ogden (Agnes^{4}, Anthony^{3}, John^{2} Rucker) (Sept. 30, 1816-Jan. 20, 1890), m. Mary Attaway Gilbert.
   1. Benjamin^{6} A. Ogden (May 23, 1844-Apr. 29, 1845).
   2. William^{6} Henry (Oct. 1, 1842-Jan. 10, 1918), m. Sallie G. Ramsey.
      1. Raymond^{7} Fairfax Ogden.
      2. Alma^{7}.
   3. James^{6} Marshall (Feb. 8, 1848-1926), m. Nannie J. Arthur.
      1. Lou^{7} Vernon, m. William Farmer.
      2. Lizzie^{7}, m. ——— Arthur.
   4. Albert^{6} Jackson.
   5. Thomas^{6} Clifton, b. Apr. 30, 1854, bachelor.
   6. John^{6} Wyatt.
   7. Lafayette^{6} Warren.
   8. Walter^{6} Stanley (Aug. 8, 1859-Oct. 11, 1917), m. Georgia A. Bennette.
      1. Bessie^{7} Scott Ogden, m. Olin L. Blankenship.
   9. Robert^{6} Marion.
   10. Frank^{6} Russell.
   11. Mary^{6} Agnes (Mch. 2, 1846-Feb. 4, 1916), m. Joseph Clifton Gilbert.
   12. Sallie^{6} Ellen Anne (Jan. 22, 1853-1923), m. William Walter Gilbert.
   13. Frences^{6} Jane, b. Sept. 27, 1857, m. Wilbur Franklin Amonette.

Mary Attaway Gilbert was the dau. of Wm. Gilbert and wife, Mary Bollin, whose children are:

1. Henry Claiborne Gilbert, m. Sarah Gilbert.
2. John Dabney Gilbert, bachelor.
3. William Wyatt Gilbert, m.MildredAnneBoswell.
4. Clifton Ludlow Gilbert, m. Mary Anne Gilbert.
5. Powhatan Marshall Gilbert, bachelor.

6. Martha Anne Gilbert, m. ——— Coppedge.
7. Mary Attaway Gilbert, m. James Madison Ogden.
8. Sarah Ellen Gilbert, died young.
9. Frances Cornelia Gilbert, spinster.

4. Albert[6] Jackson, b. Jan. 3, 1850, m. Jennie E. Sprouse.
1. Sidney[7] Ogden.
2. William[7].
3. Florence[7] Virginia.
4. Minnie[7] Jackson, m. Samuel Arthur.
5. Pearl[7].
6. Mamie[7].

6. John[6] Wyatt Ogden (James[5], Agnes[4] Rucker) (May 5, 1851-July 31, 1919), m. Celecia A. Gilbert.
1. Thomas[7] Warren Ogden, m. Jurgurtha White.
2. Harry[7] Marvin, m. Buelah Booker.
3. Rose[7] Virginia, m. Samuel H. Ewers.
4. Nannie[7] Wyatt, m. Leroy Milton Lane.
5. Lucy[7] Dora, m. John Robert Hill.

7. Lafayette[6] Warren Ogden (James[5], ———) (Dec. 1, 1855-Nov. 18, 1896), bachelor; was a prominent architect in his day, having designed many buildings of importance throughout the middle west. He died in Parkersburg, W. Va., of fever.

9. Robert[6] Marion Ogden (James[5]), b. Sept. 30, 1863, m. Mary Katherine Myers, b. May 18, 1864.
1. Ruby[7] Myers Ogden, b. Oct. 9, 1889, m. Volney S. Holt, Oct. 2, 1917, b. Nov. 22, 1888.
2. Mary[7] Emma, b. Sept. 16, 1895, m. W. Dewey Curd, June 2, 1923, b. Aug. 11, 1899.
3. Karl[7] Vellemonte, b. Apr. 15, 1898, m. Lucile Wheeler Mills, Aug. 22, 1925, b. Feb. 10, 1903.
4. Robert[7] Willard, b. Jan. 2, 1902.

10. Frank[6] Russell Ogden (James[5]) (June 5, 1867-1924), m. Clara L. White.
1. Hazel[7] Frank Ogden.
2. Newman[7] Russell, m. Frankie Vaughan.
3. Mary[7] Sue.

6. Amelia[4] Rucker (Anthony[3], John[2], Peter[1]), m. Capt. Jesse Richeson, Jan. 12, 1801. Marriage bond has the consent

of Anthony Rucker. Witness: Anthony, Armistead and Absolem Rucker.

1. John[5] Richeson, m. Susan[5] Rucker (Reuben[4], Isaac[3], John[2]).
2. William[5].
3. Josephine[5], m. James M. Millner, 1852, Amherst.
4. Lucy[5], m. 1847, Charles[6] H. Rucker (Peter[5], Moses[4], Isaac[3], John[2]).

8. Sarah[3] Rucker (John[2], Peter[1]), m. Jan. 5, 1757, Alexander Marr, in Orange Co. Several children.

Issue:

1. Margaret[4] Marr, m. 1798, Richard[4] Rucker (Isaac[3], John[2]).
   1. Alexander[5] Marr Rucker, m. ——— Toler.
      1. Godfrey[6] Rucker, m. Mary Old.
      2. Isaac[6] (Ike).
      3. Richard[6].
      4. Ann[6], m. ——— Reynolds.
      5. Margaret[6], m. 1st ——— ———; 2nd ——— Davis; 3rd ——— Smith.
2. Elizabeth[4] Marr.

9. Winifred[3] Rucker (John[2], Peter[1]), m. John Lee, of Culpeper.

10. Mildred[3] Rucker (John[2], Peter[1]), d. in Amherst Co., m. Stephen Ham. Stephen patented land in Amherst on Stovall Creek. The military accounts (Vol. 22, p. 8), mentions Stephen Ham as being paid for Revolutionary Service. Stephen d. in Amherst, will dated Sept. 1, 1810, probated Feb. 17, 1812.

1. John[4] Ham, m. Dec. 18, 1787, Betsy Gatewood.
2. Frances[4].
3. James[4].
4. Ambrose[4], m. Oct. 5, 1790, Tabatha Gatewood.
5. Lucy[4], m. Nov. 25, 1795, James Turner.
6. Elizabeth[4], m. Feb. 24, 1787, Osmond Knight.
7. William[4].
8. Samuel[4].
9. Susanna[4], m. Sept., 1806, Robert Douglas.
10. Polly[4], m. Dec. 25, 1803, David Douglas.
11. Bartlett[4].
12. Sally[4], m. Nov. 29, 1802, Richard Turner.

2. Frances[4] Ham (Mildred[3], ———), m. July 16, 1792, Benjamin Plunkett, widower. On Dec. 16, 1796, Benjamin Plunkett and wife, Frances, of Campbell Co., sold 177 acres of land on Stovall Creek to Madison Hill by Benjamin's line, for $800 (D. B. H, p. 135), Campbell Co. (See Plunkett, p. ....).

Witness: John and Charles Wingfield, Stephen Robinson.

1. Jonathan[5] Plunkett.
2. Willis[5] Rucker Plunkett.
3. Milly[5] Rucker Plunkett.
4. William[5] Plunkett.

2. Willis[5] Rucker Plunkett (Frances[4], Mildred[3], John[2], ———) (Mch. 2, 1796-Aug., 1883), m. 1st July 23, 1818, Margaret Finley Shields (Mch. 27, 1801-Apr. 2, 1831), dau. of James Shields and wife, Elizabeth Higginbotham, who were m. Mch. 2, 1793. James was son of John Shields and wife, Margaret Finley, m. June 26, 1768. Margaret was dau. of Capt. John Finley and wife, Thankful Doaks. Willis m. 2nd Mahala Robertson Dillard.

Issue (by 1st mar.):

1. Angelina[6] Elizabeth Plunkett (June 14, 1819-Nov. 28, 1898), m. Feb. 7, 1849, Joseph[4] Cabell Higginbotham (Joseph[3], James[2], John[1]).
2. Eliza[6] Frances (Sept. 9, 1821-Aug. 7, 1908), m. Dec. 10, 1840, Alexander[5] Brown Higginbotham (Aaron[4], Aaron[3], Aaron[2], John[1]).
3. James[6] Shields, b. Sept. 18, 1824.
4. William[6] Ham (Sept. 27, 1825-1864).
5. Mary[6] Ann (Apr. 2, 1827-Nov. 28, 1896).

Issue (by 2nd mar.):

6. Casandra[6], b. Mch. 1, 1833; m. July 1, 1866, John Collins.
7. Joseph[6] Marion (Apr. 15, 1834-1862).
8. Jonathan[6] Dillard, b. Sept. 27, 1835, m. Clinton Plunkett, first cousins.
9. Pauline[6] E., b. Oct. 31, m. Van Buren Camden, Aug. 10, 1853.
   1. Belle[7] Camden, m. Herbert Maurey.
   2. Benjamin[7] Camden, m. ——— Dillard.
10. Margaret[6] Watts, m. Nov. 25, 1866, W. W. Goodwin, twin of Pauline.

Issue:

1. Thomas^7 J. Goodwin, b. Dec. 25, 1867.
2. Kemmie^7, m. Thomas Mays.
3. John^7 Overton, m. Mary Dell McLain.
4. Geter^7 } twins.
5. Charles^7 } twins.
6. Henry^7.
7. Alma^7.

11. Thomas^6 Pettis (Sept., 1845-1862).
12. David^6 Willis, b. Oct. 2, 1848.

3. James^4 Ham (Mildred^3, John^2, Peter^1), m. first Mourning Burford, Dec. 1, 1787; m. second Nancy Crews, Feb. 20, 1796; m. third Peggy Tinsley, dau. of David, July 24, 1802. The marriage bond was signed by her father David. (Will of David Tinsley, Amherst, 1826:

To grand son David Tinsley, son of George; to dau. Matilda McCan; to sons David, Edward, George and Anson Tinsley; to Saluda Busby deceased; to dau. Lucy Tinsley; to dau. Nancy Burford; to dau. Ruth Burford; to grand dau. Nancy Davidson, dau. of Peggy Ham deceased. Witness: James Bennett, John T. Tinsley, Zachary Tinsley.

8. Samuel^4 Ham (Mildred^3, ———), d. 1856, wife Elizabeth.

1. Mary^5 Ham.
2. Mildred^5 Ham.
3. Stephen^5 Ham.
4. Samuel^5 Ham.

11. Phoebe^3 Rucker (John^2, Peter^1), m. James Morton, of Orange Co., they moved to Amherst, then to Ky. James Morton of Ky. and Ambrose Rucker of Amherst sold 82 acres of land in Amherst on Rutledge Creek and Paul Mts. 30 Oct. 1793 (D. B. G, p. 327), Amherst Co., Va.

Ambrose Morton and James Morton sold 100 acres of land to Jesse Woodroof, to the thoroughfare 4 Oct. 1791 (D. B. G, p. 89).

12. Margaret^3 Rucker (John^2, Peter^1), m. Isaac Smith, of Orange. She was mentioned in the will of her father, John Rucker, in 1742, "To my dau. Margaret Smith one Shilling", John may have given some property to her before, later her

mother, Susanna and brother, Peter, the executors of the will of John, deeded property to Isaac and Margaret Smith. The will of Isaac Smith dated 1802, does not mention the name of his son Benjamin, who died in 1796, unmarried, but left property to the children of his sister, the wife of William Rucker, naming the children mentioned in the will of William[3] Rucker (Thomas[2], Peter[1]).

Will of Isaac Smith, 1801, recorded Aug. 26, 1802. Madison Co., Va.

"In the name of God, Amen. The last will and testament of Isaac Smith, Senor, of the County of Madison, being in perfect senses and memory; after all my just debts are paid, I do give the rest of my Estate as followeth:

Item—I give and bequeath to my son, William Smith, one shilling sterling together with what he has had.

Item—I give and bequeath to my grandson, William Smith, son of D. Smith, one negro man by the name of Senor to him and his heirs forever.

Item—I give and bequeath to my grand daughter, Susanny Underwood, a certaine tract of land containing one hundred and seventy three acres lying and joining Michael Wallis and Reuben Clark and Jobe Breadin and one feather bed and furniture to her and her heirs forever.

Item—I give and bequeath to my grand Daughter, Sary Rucker, daughter of William Rucker, a certain tract of land containing One Hundred & thirteen Acres lying and joining Jeremiah Rucker and Joel Graves and Jobe Breadin & John Delaney to her and her heirs forever.

Item—I leave all the rest of my estate to be sold at publick auction for twelve months credit the purchasers giving bond and approved Security the money so arising from the sale thereof to be occupied by the executors and then to be so divided as followeth—

Item—I give and bequeath to my grand daughter Elizabeth Fleshman, Five Pounds to her and her heirs forever.

Item—And the remainder part to be equally divided between my grandson Jarvis Rucker and Nelly Rucker and Fanny Rucker and my granddaughter, Elizabeth Underwood to them and their heirs forever.

I do constitute my two grandsons William Smith & Downin Smith my executors. August 18th 1801.
Signed, sealed and delivered in presence of:

Joel Grayson
John Berry
Ana X Broyles
mark

At a court held for Madison County on Thursday the 26th day of August 1802, the last Will and Testament of Isaac Smith Senor was Exhibited into Court and proved by the oaths of Joel Grayson, Acey Smith and Anny Broyles, witnesses thereto and ordered to be recorded. Upon the motion of William Smith and Downing Smith the Executors therein named approval thereof in due form is granted them, they having made oath thereto and entered into Bond with Security according to Law.

Teste:

John Walker, Jun'r. C. M. C.

Issue:

1. William^4 Smith.
2. Downing^4 Rucker.
3. dau.^{4}, m. William Rucker (see p. 229).
4. dau.^{4}, m. ——— Underwood.
5. dau.^{4}, m. ——— Fleshman.
6. Benjamin^4, d. 1796, Madison Co., leaving a will.

2. Downing^4 Rucker Smith (Margaret^3, John^2, Peter^1 Rucker), d. in Madison Co., leaving a will dated Feb. 26, 1826.

1. Susanna^5 Smith, m. Feb., 1791, Isaac Smith, Jr.
2. Benjamin^5.
3. William^5, d. before 1826.
4. Downing^5.
5. Asa^5.

4. Downing^5 Smith (Downing^4, Margaret^3, John^2 Rucker), m. Mch. 28, 1803, Elizabeth Bush, d. 1839, dau. of Joshua.

1. Frances^6 Smith, m. Oct. 25, 1824, William D. Cave, son of Abner Cave.
2. Jane^6, m. Dec. 23, 1822, Lewis Powell.
3. Thomas^6, m. Oct. 25, 1824, Polly Cave, dau. of Abner.
4. St. Clair^6, m. Mch. 26, 1827, Rhoda Powell, dau. of Lewis G. Powell.
5. Downing^6.
6. William^6.

5. Downing[6] Smith (Downing[5], Downing[4], Margaret[3] Rucker) (1811-1891), m. Nov. 25, 1828, Sara Powers Gibson (1804-1881), dau. of John Gibson and wife, Elizabeth Harvey. (See Gibson, p. ....).

1. Elizabeth[7] Smith.
2. Joseph[7].
3. Susan[7].
4. Downing[7].
5. Mary[7] Catherine.
6. Benjamin[7] Franklin.

1. Elizabeth[7] Smith (Downing[6], Downing[5], ———), b. 1830, m. Nov. 5, 1856, John D. Maupin.

1. Bee[8] Maupin.
2. Henry[8].
3. William[8].
4. Elizabeth[8].
5. Sally[8].

2. Joseph[7] Smith (Downing[6], Downing[5], ———), m. Mildred Harris.

1. Newton[8] Smith, m. 1st Ellen Gibson; 2nd Eva Harris.

   Issue (by 1st mar.):

   1. Mollie[9] Smith.
2. John[8] Augustine Smith, m. Cynthia Elliott.
   1. Nettie[9] Augusta Smith, m. Lacy Burgess.
   2. William[9], m. Sallie Harrison.
   3. Julia[9] Margaret.

3. Susan[7] Smith, m. Pitman Gibson.

1. Ellen[8] Gibson, m. Newton Smith.
   1. Mollie[9] Smith.
2. Selina[8] Smith, m. George Ergenbright.
   1. George[9] Ergenbright.
   2. Ellen[9].
3. Ida[8] Smith, m. Edgar Marshall.
   1. Virginia[9] Marshall, m. Dr. John Powell Williams.

4. Downing[7] Lemuel Smith (Downing[6], Downing[5], ———) (Jan. 22, 1846-Sept. 8, 1924), m. Dec. 22, 1874, Willie Minor Marshall, b. May 24, 1853, dau. of James T. Marshall and Jane Frances Gibson, his wife.

Issue:

1. Dr. John[8] William Rosser Smith.
2. Sarah[8] Jane Smith, b. Mch. 30, 1879.
3. Susan[8] Pocahontas Smith, b. Dec. 1, 1881.
4. Eva[8] Minor, b. July 10, 1883, m. Sept. 7, 1910, Dr. Emanuel Swedenborg Gregory, son of E. S. and Amanda Martin Gregory.
5. James[8] Downing.
6. Ruth[8] Catherine.
7. Judge Lemuel[8] Franklin.
8. Dr. Joseph[8] Hamilton, b. Sept., 1893, m. Sept. 10, 1925, Hester J. McLarren.
   1. Hester[9] Jane Smith, b. Feb. 17, 1928.
9. Mary[8] Elizabeth, b. July 29, 1896.

1. Dr. John[8] William Rosser Smith (Downing[7], Downing[6], ———), b. Sept. 13, 1875, m. Sept. 9, 1908, Bessie Tranquilla Omohundro.

   1. Virginia[9] Smith, b. Dec. 30, 1909.
   2. Katherine[9], b. Dec. 15, 1911.
   3. James[9], b. Oct. 14, 1918.

5. James[8] Downing Smith (Downing[7]), now serving as a commander in the U. S. Navy, b. Oct. 8, 1884, m. July 22, 1911, Charlotte Elizabeth Greene.

   1. Edward[9] Downing Smith, b. June 12, 1915.

6. Ruth[8] Catherine Smith (Downing[7]), b. June 16, 1888, m. Dec. 22, 1922, George Elmer Mortenson.

   1. Ruth[9] Catherine Mortenson, b. Oct. 19, 1923.
   2. George[9] Elmer, b. Feb. 18, 1825.

7. Judge Lemuel[8] Franklin Smith (Downing[7]), b. Apr. 21, 1891, m. Oct. 27, 1916, Grace Stulting.

   1. Downing[9] Lemuel Smith, b. Aug. 12, 1917.
   2. James[9] Doyle, b. Jan. 27, 1921.
   3. Minor[9] Marshall, b. Mch. 10, 1923.

5. Mary[7] Catherine Smith (Downing[6]), m. George William Fuller.

   1. George[8] William Fuller.
   2. Mable[8] Catherine Fuller.
   3. Marshall[8] T. Fuller.

6. Benjamin[7] Franklin Smith (Downing[6]), m. Willie Ann, dau. of Elijah Dunn and wife Susan Ann Sandridge, she was the dau. of Benjamin Carr Sandidge and wife, Selina Elliott.

Issue:

1. Sally[8] Moss Smith, m. Rev. Dr. Arthur Rowbotham.
    1. Sarah[9] Kirk Rowbotham.
    2. Marjorie[9] Lee Rowbotham.
2. Emma[8] Lee Smith, m. Dr. Carl Clifford White.
3. Ann[8], m. Rev. Horace Pettus Read.
    1. Charles[9] Lewis Read.
    2. Thomas[9] Lee.
    3. Benjamin[9] Franklin.
    4. Pettus[9].
    5. Anne[9] Smith Read.
4. Benjamin[8] Franklin Smith, m. Florine Guilbert.
    1. Benjamin[9] Guilbert Smith.
    2. Betty[9] Grey Smith.
    3. Anne[9] Dunn Smith.

CHAPTER THREE

Peter Rucker

2. Peter[2] Rucker (Peter[1]) was mentioned in a deed in 1707 by Frederick Coghill, of Essex. "For love and affection to John , Thomas and Peter Rucker, sons of Peter Rucker. In 1734 his brother, John, deeded to their parents, "Peter Rucker and his wife, Elizabeth, their natural lives, 420 acres and after their death to Peter Jr. and Ephraim land whereon they now live."

We find nothing more of him. He left no will. If he married and had children, he divided up what property he may have had. There are no deeds recorded. His father did not mention him in his will, nor did his brothers.

CHAPTER FOUR
Thomas Rucker

3. Thomas[2] Rucker (Peter[1]), d. in Culpeper, 1763; m. Elizabeth[3] Reynolds (Cornelius[2], Cornelius[1]), of Essex Co.

Will of Martha Reynolds Mch. 10, 1753, Sept. 18, 1753,

To son, Cornelius; to dau.s: Elizabeth Rucker, Ann Beazley, Margaret Leandall, Mary Goodloe; to grandson, Cornelius Reynolds, son of William Reynolds, dec'd. Executors: Son, Cornelius Reynolds; Son-in-law, Thomas Rucker. Witness: David Dishman, Thomas Reynolds, William Moore (W. B. 9, p. 246), Essex Co., Va.

Will of Cornelius[2] Reynolds, Apr. 15, 1734, Feb. 18, 1734.

To sons: William Reynolds, Cornelius Reynolds; to dau.s: Sarah, Annie, Margaret, Mary; To my wife, Martha. Witness: Broumfield Long, Samuel Bizwell, John Long (W. B. 5, p. 320), Essex.

Inventory of estate of Mr. Cornelius Reynolds by his wife, Margery, Executrix, 9th Feb. 1685 (W. B. 6, p. 88), Old Rappa. Co., Va.

Thomas Rucker of St. Anne Parish, Essex, bought 100 acres of land from James Taylor of St. Stephen Parish, King and Queen Co., May 27, 1725 (D. B. A, p. 143), Spotsylvania Co.

In 1727 he sold this land to Henry Downs of St. George Parish, Spotsylvania Co. Thomas was then living in King and Queen.

In 1730 he patented 876 acres of land in Spotsylvania. 476 acres of this patent he sold in 1732 to his brother, John Rucker, land in St. Marks Parish, wife Elizabeth, signed the deed. Witness: Thomas Chew, Joseph Hawkins, Robert Turner.

In 1739 he bought from John Rucker 539 acres of land on the North side of the Rapidan River, on Maple Run.

In a suit against Jarrell, Thomas paid Henry Powell 90 lbs. of Tobacco for one days attendance, coming and going 10 miles to court. Also 30 lbs. of tobacco to James McKenney, and 90 lbs. to Sarah Keaton, all as witnesses (O. B. 1732, p. 276), Dec. 13, 1734, Caroline Co.

He was appointed surveyor of the roads in "Room" of Charles Beasley, May 10, 1730. Four years later he petitioned the court to appoint James ffitch in his "Room."

In 1737 Thomas and wife, Elizabeth, and James Rucker and wife, Margaret, sold land to Charles Beasley. Thomas deeded land to sons, Thomas, Cornelius and Peter, to the other sons he willed land on the North side of the Rapidan (now in Madison Co.)

May 28, 1741, Thomas was appointed constable in Orange in place of William Jackson (O. B. 2, p. 357), Caroline.

Thomas Rucker of Caroline sold land to Robert Taliaferro, 1741. (He moved to Orange before 1747.)

Thomas Rucker of Orange, St. Thomas Parish, sold 123 acres of land to William Rucker, for £25, Aug. 22, 1747. Witness: Bartho. Vawter, Nathan Underwood, Ephraim Rucker.

The same year he sold 90 acres to Thomas Coffee both of Orange. He patented 347 acres of wash land in 1754, adjoining his own land, and Captain Henry Downs. Witness: Zachary Taylor, Charles Hoomes.

Lewis Herndon and wife, Frances, of Caroline, sold 100 acres for £40 to Thomas Rucker of Culpeper, land on both sides of Stanton River.

Thomas Rucker of Culpeper on July 16, 1761, sold to Michael Erhart of same, for £12, 240 acres of land in Culpeper, adjoining Julius Christy, Samuel Angels and Thomas Rucker on Rapidan River (D. B. C, p. 534), Culpeper Co. Witness: William Lightfoot, Thomas Chew, Benjamin Chew.

Elizabeth, the widow of Thomas Rucker, died in Culpeper in 1788.

Thomas left his plantation and two slaves to her, and to his son, George after her death.

In 1782, Elizabeth was paying on 200 acres of land in Culpeper. She continued until 1788.

Her son, George, in 1782, was paying on 136 acres. In 1788 he began paying on three hundred and thirty-six acres (his mother's land).

Will of Thomas Rucker, June 11, 1763, Oct. 20, 1763.

"In the Name of God, Amen. June the eleventh day in the year of our Lord One Thousand Seven Hundred sixty three.

I, Thomas Rucker of Blumfield Parish in the County of Culpeper, having my sound and Perfect Sense of mind, and memory Thanks to the Almighty God for the same, and Calling to mind the mortality of mankind and that all men must die, Therefore as Touching such Worldly Estate that it hath Pleased God to Bless me in this world with I do give and Bequeath in manner and form following.

Imprimis. First and Principally I Bequeth my soul to the almighty God that gave it to me, and my Body to be Buried in a christian like manner at the Direction of my Executors.

Item: I give and Bequeth unto my well beloved son John Rucker all that Tract or Parcel of Land situate, lying and Being in Culpeper County and Bound between Cornelius Ruckers line, Peter Ruckers Line, Michael Eharts Line, Thomas Ruckers Jun. his line, and the road that now parts it from the Land I now live on to him and his heirs forever.

Item: I give and bequeth unto my beloved son George Rucker the Land and Plantation I now live on, it being Bounded by the Road that now is Thomas Rucker Jun. his line, the river and William Craford's line which said land and plantation I give to my son George and his heirs for ever.

Item: But and in case my son John Rucker should die without heir then his Part as above mentioned shall be and I give the same unto my son William Rucker and if in the like case my son George Rucker should die without heir that the part laid off for him above mentioned shall be and I give the same to my son Muldin Rucker, the above two Parcels of Land shall be to my two said sons William and Muldin and their heirs for Ever if Either of the forementioned John Rucker and George Rucker should die without heirs as above mentioned.

Item: I will and Desire that my wife, Elizabeth Rucker shall have the work and I do lend her the two negroes, as shall be here mentioned (viz) Jack and Hannah which said negroes I do lend to my wife Elisabeth for and during her Natural Life and no Longer and After the Decease of my said wife Elisabeth then the said Negroes and future increase of the said Negroes Hannah if any shall be at the *Decease* of my said wife shall return to my Estate and shall be as I shall hereafter mention.

I lend unto my wife Elisabeth my *manner* Plantation I now live on For and During her Natural Life and no Longer and at the Decease of my said Wife Elisabeth then the said Lands and Plantation to return to my son George as above mentioned.

Item: I lend to my wife Elisabeth all and Every of my Estate that Remaineth and Every of my Estate Personal and all and Every Negro shall be sold and then the money arising thereby shall be Equally Divided Between my Children as shall be hereafter named, Thomas, Peter, Mary, John, Elisabeth, Martha, William, Muldin, Isaac, Easter, Franky, George.

Item: I constitute Nominate and appoint my Two sons Peter and John to be the Executors of this my last Will and Testament, utterly Revoking, Disallowing and Disannuling all former and other Wills, Testaments, Bequests, Legacies by me formerly made and Done and allowing this and only this to be my last will and Testament. In Testimony whereof I do hereunto set my hand and Seal the Day and Year above written. Signed Thomas Rucker (W. B. A, p. 350), Culpeper Co.

Issue:

1. John[3] Rucker.
2. George[3].
3. Thomas[3], Jr.
4. Cornelius[3].
5. Peter[3].
6. William[3].
7. Mauldin[3].
8. Mary[3].
9. Elizabeth[3].
10. Martha[3].
11. Isaac[3].
12. Easter[3] (Estha).
13. Frankey[3].

1. John[3] Rucker (Thomas[2], Peter[1]), born in Orange (later Madison), sold his share of his father's land and moved across the river Rapidan into Orange (later Greene), and founded Ruckersville. He died there in 1794, leaving his wife land on Rippins Run, on the South side of the Rapidan River.

He married Mary[2] Burton (May[1] Burton), who died in Orange (Greene), 1823, leaving a will (Sept. 23, 1822, prob. Feb. 24, 1823), which mentions children: Milly Head, the wife of Marshall Head; Mary Graves, wife of Walter Graves, and Joel Rucker.

Witness: John White, William Collins, William H. Mansfield (W. B. 6, p. 66), Orange Co.

Mary paid tax on 120 acres in Orange, in 1802, land on Rippins Run, continuing until her death, 1823.

John Rucker and wife, Mary, of Orange Co., sold 150 acres for £20 to George Rucker (brother). Land in Culpeper on Maple Run (his share of his father's estate).

Witness: William Rucker, Michael Ehart, Robert Sherman (D. B. H, p. 602), Culpeper.

John[3] of Orange Co. bought 200 acres of land in Orange from Ambrose Burton and wife, Caty, in 1779 (D. B. 17, p. 271).

He bought from Mathew Hambleton both of St. Thomas Parish, Orange, 185 acres of land Mathew had purchased from Dr. John Fothergill of London, Apr., 1787. 1788 John Rucker sold to Hambleton 200 acres of land adjoining "Twyman's in Orange".

In 1782 John is paying taxes on 400 acres and 200 acres of land in Orange.

In 1786 he adds 185 acres more, and sold the 200 acres in 1788, but continues to pay on the 400 acres and 185 acres until his death, in 1794. Land on Rippins Run (later Greene County).

In 1782 he payed personal taxes on slaves named Giles, Hog, Ishel, Rachel and Adams (personal tax book).

1780 John Rucker of Orange was mentioned as "Ensign".

He signs a great many county petitions (to be found in the Archives, Richmond, Virginia).

In 1801 his widow Mary Burton with her sisters and brothers sold their share of their father's estate. "Mary Rucker; Ambrose Burton, May Burton, James Burton; Ambrose Medley and his wife, Frances; William Burton and Joseph Burton legatees of the estate of May Burton deceased, late of Orange, sold land to John Head of same. Witness: Tavernor Head, John Rucker, Ezekiel Rucker, Belfield Cave." Oct. 27, 1801 (D. B. 22, p. 331), Orange Co.

Will Oct. 12, 1788, June 23rd, 1794. Executrix: Wife Mary, and friend May Burton (W. B. 3, p. 309), Orange Co.

Issue:

1. Joel[4] Rucker.
2. Frankey[4].
3. Milly[4], m. Nov. 11, 1789, George Marshall Head, Orange Co.
4. William[4].
5. Jeremiah[4].
6. James[4].
7. John[4].
8. Mary[4].
9. Nancy[4].
10. Burton[4].

1. Joel[4] Rucker (John[3], Thomas[2], Peter[1]) (1767-1833), b. and d. Orange, m. Dec. 20, 1786, Nancy Oliver, same county.

In May, 1802, Joel Rucker of Orange, Thomas and Amos Ladd and Samuel Parsons of Richmond, Va., made a note to secure a payment of $529.50, due to Ann Fothergill, and John Chorley, Executors of Dr. John Fothergill, dec'd, of Great Britain, Joel to hold the land.

In 1787 he pays his 1st personal tax, but does not pay on land until 1792, then upon 296 acres of land on Rippins Run.

After the death of his father, Joel bought a tract of 300 acres of land belonging to his father, which land was not deeded to him until 1824, after the death of his mother, Mary, land adjoining his uncle, May Burton, Minor Rucker, William Henderson, Edward Cason, Mary Rucker, dec'd, and John Head; called "Beverly Tract". Jan. 16, 1824. (D. B. 30, p. 396), Orange.

He deeded to his son, Blyfield, 178 acres of land in Orange on the Richmond Road, Nov. 18, 1824. Joel Rucker bought 45½ acres from John Head.

The appraisers of the estate of Joel Rucker, dec'd, were Robert Cave, George Stephens and Edward Cason. They met at the home of Captain Minor Rucker. Estimated value at $4,667.25 on Apr. 16, 1833 (D. B. 7, p. 595), Orange.

Will of Joel Rucker, dated July 21, 1831, mentions, son, Minor Rucker, all lands and slaves. To son, Blyfield Rucker, $10. To my grandchildren, heirs of Elzy Rucker, dec'd, Kitty, Joseph and Edmund Rucker, $30. each. John Rucker was one of the Executors (W. B. 7, p. 559), Orange.

Issue:

1. Minor[5] Rucker.
2. Blyfield[5].
3. Elzy[5].

1. Minor[5] Rucker (Joel[4], John[3], Thomas[2]), m. 1822 Harriett Head. He received land in Orange from his father. In 1814 he paid taxes on 195 acres of land on Rippins Run.

In Sept., 1834, Minor and wife, Harriett of Orange, sold their land to Larkin Rucker. November of the same year, they have moved to Missouri. In 1841 they sold to his brother, Blyfield, of Greene Co., "A tract of land willed to me by my father, Joel Rucker" for $250 on the North side of Mine Road, from Cartersville to Ruckersville, 6 acres and 46 acres, two tracts adjoining Rucker and William White.

On Nov. 3, 1838, Minor Rucker and wife Harriett of Missouri, sold to Larkin Rucker of Greene Co., 60 acres for $500 (D. B. 37, p. 319), Orange.

2. Blyfield[5] Rucker (Joel[4], John[3]), d. Apr., 1849, Greene Co.; m. 1890 Nancy White. He bought land from his brother, Joel, on the Richmond Road.

Will dated Apr., 1849 (W. B. 1, p. 409), Greene Co., mentions children:

1. Albert[6] G. Rucker, m. Sarah Parrott, 1831, Greene Co. He received land from the estate of Thomas G. Parrott, 1832; moved to Randolph Co., Mo., and sold to Charles Parrott in 1833.

2. William^{6} E., d. in Greene Co., leaving his estate to his brother, Willis (W. B. 2, p. 143).
3. Willis^{6} W.
4. Minor^{6} B. Rucker, wife Sarah joined in selling land, 1838.
5. Virginia^{6} Pittman.
6. Frances^{6} Ann Mitchell.
7. Allen^{6} O. Rucker in 1836 m. Harriett Pritchett.
   1. Mary^{7}, m. L. C. Estes.
   2. Lucy^{7} Catherine.
   3. Martha^{7}.
   4. Ann^{7}.
   5. Sarah^{7}.

3. Willis^{6} W. Rucker (Blyfield^{5}, Joel^{4}, John^{3}), d. Greene County. Will dated Dec. 15th, 1900. Mentions W. W. Cold, Lindsey Rucker Cold; to the children of my sister Virginia Pittman, and Frances Ann Mitchell; to my nieces Mary Ellis and Sally Dunn (W. B. 2, p. 213), Greene Co.

3. Elzy^{5} Rucker (Joel^{4}, John^{3}, Thomas^{2}), b. 1783, m. Jan. 16, 1809, Mary, daughter of Joseph Burton of Culpeper. They moved to Greenway Co., Ky. On Oct. 17, 1814, Elzy Rucker of Orange sold to John Lucas several slaves, to pay a note of £10 to Reuben Twyman of Orange (D. B. 26, p. 177), Orange.

1. Kitty^{6} Rucker.
2. Joseph^{6} Rucker.
3. Edmund^{6} Rucker.

One Elzy Rucker enlisted in the war of 1812, a sergeant, died in Carters Co., Ky.

2. Frankey^{4} Rucker (John^{3}, Thomas^{2}, ———), m. July 28, 1785, Joel White. Security George Tomlinson (Marriage bond), Orange.

1. Durett^{5} White.
2. Galin^{5}.
3. Ambrose^{5}.
4. Jeremiah^{5}.
5. Elizabeth^{5}.
6. Joel^{5}.

(George Tomlinson m. Nov. 24, 1785, Elizabeth, dau. of Henry White of Orange. Security David Cave. Marriage bond, Orange Co.).

4. William[4] Rucker (John[3], Thomas[2], ———), b. Aug. 26, 1769, Orange; m. Dec. 25, 1794, Katy Taliaferro Thornton in Orange, b. Aug. 18, 1775. Moved c. 1827 to Monroe Co., Mo.

1826 George Thornton of Orange mentioned in his will my dau. Katherine Rucker, wife of William Rucker, and their children, Thornton, Frances, John, Lucy, William T., Anthony G., Kittie, Annie, and James N. Rucker, all of Albemarle Vo., Va. Issue of William Rucker:

1. Rev. Thornton[5] Rucker.
2. William[5] Taliaferro.
3. Frances[5], m. 1820, Henry Marr, of Orange; William Rucker signed m. bond.
4. John[5].
5. Lucy[5].
6. Anthony[5] G.
7. Kittie[5].
8. Anne[5].
9. James[5] N.
10. Margaret[5], m. John H. Sherman, 1822 (William Rucker signed bond).
11. George[5].

1. Rev. Thornton[5] Rucker (William[4], John[3], Thomas[2], ———), b. Sept. 22, 1797, buried in Heath Creek Church yard in Salino, Mo.; m. 1819 Martha Sydner (Oct. 7, 1802-Aug. 30, 1843), of Orange Co., dau. of Michael Sydner. They moved to Columbia, Mo., after selling his land in Orange, Va., to Daniel Miller in 1824.

Will of Michael Snyder, dated Jan. 27, 1815, mentions children: Sarah, m. Joel Wayland; James, m. Sarah Ann Aylor; Lydia, m. John Peyton; Betsy, m. Peter Thornton; Martha, m. Thornton Rucker; John, m. Malvira Yeager; Charlotte, m. William Taylor; William; Lucy, m. Adron Fray; Polly, m. Zachary Taylor; Nancy, m. Ephraim Fray.

Issue:

1. Lucy[6] Ann Rucker, m. Joseph Campbell.
2. George[6] Thornton, m. Eliza Howe.
3. William[6] Michael.
4. John[6] Sherman, m. Mary Harlan.
5. James[6] Jefferson.
6. Mary[6] Frances, m. Milton Davis.
7. Thomas[6] Fristoe, d. young.
8. Henry[6] Anthony.
9. Martha[6] C., m. Frank Wilson.

10. Eliza[6] Margaret, m. Y. C. Blakey.
    1. dau.[7], m. T. M. McKinley, Bronsville, Mo.
11. Bettie[6] Jane, m. Jasper Harvey.
    1. Mary[7] Harvey, Bronsville, Mo.
12. Susa[6] Taliaferro.

3. William[6] Michael Rucker (Thornton[5], William[4], John[3], ———), m. Eliza Bridgwater of Culpeper; they moved to Mo.
   1. Charles[7] T. Rucker, b. Sept. 3, 1837, of Blackwater, Mo.
      1. James[8] Rucker, m. Lula Irwine.
         1. Martha[9] Rucker.
         2. Ray[9].
         3. C.[9] T., of Baltimore.
         4. Ruth[9].
      2. Lydia[8] Rucker, m. J. N. Sims.
         1. John[9] Rucker Sims, graduate of Missouri State College, Columbia.

5. James[6] Jefferson Rucker (Thornton[5], William[4], ———), m. Sept. 10, 1855, Mary Allison. He was president of Georgetown College, Ky., for 50 years.
   1. Eugene[7] Rucker.
   2. Alice[7], m. ——— Bristoe.

8. Henry[6] Anthony Rucker (Thornton[5], ———), b. June 11, 1834, Monroe Co., Mo., d. May 27, 1902, Marshall, Saline Co., Mo.; m. Dec. 27, 1855, America Fry Ferguson (June 19, 1834-Sept. 9, 1886), of Cooper Co., Mo.
   1. William[7] Henry Rucker.
   2. Thomas[7] Douglas, m. Celeste Simpson.
   3. Mary[7] Eliza, m. William Davis.
   4. Fannie[7] Louise.
   5. Sarah[7] Allen, m. Frank Bane.
   6. Charles[7] Blakey.
   7. Bertie[7] Shelby.

1. William[7] Henry Rucker (Henry[6], Thornton[5], William[4], ———), b. Sept. 25, 1859, at Camp Cole, Benton Co., Mo.; m. Oct. 25, 1882, Fannie H. Lukens, Columbia, Boone County, Mo., b. Nov. 5, 1862.
   1. Lucile[8] Rucker, b. Jan. 31, 1884, Pilot Grove, Cooper Co., Mo.

2. William^5 Taliaferro Rucker (William^4, John^3, ———), b. Mch. 20, 1809, m. Jan. 4, 1831, Verenda S. Taylor in Va. They moved to Monroe Co., Mo.

1. Joseph^6 Edmundson Rucker, b. Dec. 21, 1831, in Mo., moved with his father to Calif. in 1852.
   1. Joseph^7 H. Rucker, San Francisco, Calif.

5. Jeremiah^4 Rucker (John^3, Thomas^2, Peter^1), m. Dec. 9, 1799, Henrietta, dau. of Susanna Stanley. From 1792 until 1796 he pays taxes on 63 acres of land in Orange Co. In 1797 he bought 120 acres of land in Orange from William Stanard (D. B. 21, p. 207).

In 1802 Jeremiah and wife, Henrietta of Orange, sold this land to Mary Rucker of Orange, for £20 (D. B. 22, p. 336), now Greene.

In 1800, Jeremiah and wife, Henrietta of Orange, bought from Isaac Smith, Jr., of Madison, 64 acres for £3, land in Madison Co., on the Rapidan River. Witness: Francis Blunt, Tavenor and Sally Rucker (D. B. 2, p. 446), Orange.

Oct. 31, 1810, Jeremiah Rucker and wife, Henrietta, of Madison Co., Kentucky, sold 60 acres of land in Madison Co., Virginia, to Thomas Graves (D. B. 5, p. 69, Madison Co.).

Jeremiah and Henrietta Rucker and Susanna Stanley sold for £180 196 acres of land in Orange Co.

He appears in the personal tax books of Monroe Co., West Virginia, for one year only, 1801.

8. Mary^4 Rucker (John^3, Thomas^2), married 1st ——— Miller, and 2nd Walter Graves, June 12, 1805. On May 12, 1824, Walter Graves of Orange Co., bought 223 acres of land in Orange for $1,115 from Joel Rucker, land inherited from his father after the death of his mother, Mary (D. B. 30, p. 397), Orange Co. This land Walter Graves sold in 1833 to Belfield Cave.

10. Burton^4 Rucker (John^3, Thomas^2), b. in Orange (now Greene Co.), moved to Elbert Co., Ga., c. 1785, later to Alabama, then to Mansfield, Louisiana.

1. Wilton^5 Rucker, has granddau., Mrs. Jett Willis Rucker, living in Kenston, Ala.
2. John^5 P.
3. Willis^5.

2. John^5 P. Rucker, m. Emily Williamson in Bibbs County, Alabama; left fifteen children.

Issue:

1. Andrew^{6} William Rucker, b. 1844; confederate soldier of 56 Ala. Regiment, Co. A; m. Jane Benson of South Carolina, Jan. 11, 1866, dau. of G. W. Benson.
    1. Anson^{7} Rucker.
    2. William^{7} A.
    3. Mary^{7} E.
    4. Roger^{7}.
    5. Thomas^{7}.
    6. J. Ross^{7}.
    7. Myra^{7}.
    8. Sadie^{7}.
    9. Maurice^{7}.

3. Willis^{5} Rucker (Burton^{4}, John^{3}, Thomas^{2}, ———), d. 1834; m. Milly Alexander, 1809, in Elbert Co., Ga.

Will of Willis Rucker: "I give and bequeath to my loving daughters Mary and Margaret Rucker, two negroes, Washington and Sam to be held jointly by them until one of them marries and then to be valued and an equal part assigned to each of them. If either of my daughters Mary or Margaret, die before they marry or become of age, it is my wish and desire that such part of the above Washington and Sam as would be assigned to such deceased be assigned to my two sons Jerry and Peter Rucker. I wish for my daughters to have a bed and furniture each of them, the beds are in the possession of Jacob M. Cleavland. I give and bequeath to my two sons Jeremiah and Peter all of my property not herein bequeathed. I appoint my beloved friend Peter Alexander my executor. dated July 29, 1834. Willis Rucker.

Codecil: To my remaining 3 children, Fermelia Cleavland, Jeremiah Rucker and Peter Rucker. Ordinary, Elbert Co. (B. O, folio 419-480), Jan. 15, 1835.

Peter Alexander exec. to the will of Willis Rucker dec'd makes the following return to the court of Ordinary, July 1835.

Cash in hand	$25.00
A note on David Daniel for the use of Mary and Margaret Rucker minors, of the said dec'd for hire of negroes	$60.25
A note on Peter Rucker for the amt. of sale of Perishable Property	$72.62½
Paid Peter Rucker	$ 8.62½

Received of Peter Alexander exec. of the estate of Willis Rucker dec'd, $8 in part of my distribution share of said estate April 2,

1835. Signed: Peter Rucker. Ordinary Office (B. P, folio 94-95), Aug. 4, 1838, Elbert Co.

2. George[3] Rucker (Thomas[2], Peter[1]), was born and lived in what is now Madison Co. His father, Thomas, left him his "Manor Plantation", after the death of his mother, Elizabeth.

In 1777, for £20, George bought 150 acres of land in Culpeper, now Madison, from his brother, John and wife, Mary Rucker, of Orange Co., land on Maple Run, on the North side of the Rapidan. Witness: Thomas Rucker, Michael Ehart, Robert Sherman, and William Rucker (D. B. H, p. 602), Culpeper Co.

In 1782 he is paying tax on only 136 acres, continuing until 1788, at which time he inherited the 200 acres of his mother, Elizabeth, dec'd. The following year, 1789, George sold both tracts of land to George Anderson (D. B. J, p. 309), Culpeper. The land books of 1792, Madison, charges George Anderson with 336 acres, formerly George Rucker's land.

George was in the Revolutionary War. He may have married late in life. His widow and three children moved to Wilkes Co., Ga., and settled upon land reserved for Revolutionary War soldiers. George married Catherine Ehart.

Her father, Abraham Ehart, died, leaving a will, dated May 7, 1788. In this he mentions: My wife, Catherine, my dau.s: Christine Bruce, Catherine Rucker, Susanna Herndon, my sons, Abraham, Michael, Adam, and Jacob John Ehart. It also speaks of land purchased from Peter Rucker (W. B. C, p. 332), Culpeper Co.

George Rucker and wife, Catherine, sold to William Alexander, all of Wilkes Co., Ga., 122 acres of land on the Savannah River adjoining John McGowen Aug. 13, 1790. Test: Thomas Keyes and Daniel Matkin. George and Catherine signed a deed in Franklin Co. in 1809.

The will of George Rucker: wife, Catherine, son George Jr. Indy, Nancy, Simeon, Susanna, Elizabeth, Mary and Frances Rucker. Executors: Son George, and Robert Barnwell. Signed Sept. 5, 1810, prob. Nov. 6, 1815, Franklin Co., Ga.

(One Nancy Rucker m. William Martin May 29, 1817, in Franklin Co. One Cinthia Rucker m. Samuel Johnson Jan. 6, 1825, Franklin Co.)

Issue:

1. George[4] Rucker.
2. Indy[4].
3. Nancy[4].
4. Simeon[4] Bluford.

5. Susanna[4].
6. Elizabeth[4].
7. Mary[4].
8. Frances[4].

1. George[4] Rucker (George[3], Thomas[2], Peter[1]), moved to Franklin Co., Ga. The census of 1850 gives his age as 69, a farmer, and having been born in Va. Lucy may have been his wife, age 66, born in Ga.; some of those listed may be the children of George. See following census of 1830, 1840, and 1850 of Franklin Co.

1830 Census.

George Rucker, age under 50, woman age under 50.
Simson Rucker.
Katherine Rucker.

1840 Census.

Jeptha Rucker, age under 40, woman, age under 40.
George Rucker, age under 60, woman, age under 60.
Aznon Rucker, age under 30, woman, age under 30.
Elliott Rucker, age under 30, woman, age under 30.
Tabner Rucker, age under 60, woman, age under 50.

1850 Census.

Armor Rucker, age 25, Farmer. Value of property $1200, b. in Ga.
Amanda Rucker, age 20.
Sarah L. Rucker, age 1.
George Rucker, age 69 m. Farmer. Value of property $10,000, b. in Va.
Lucy Rucker, age 66, f.
J. W. C. Rucker, age 25, m. farmer, Value of property, $2,500, b. in Ga.
Azmon Rucker, age 37, m. farmer, value of property, $1,100, b. in Ga.
Rebecca Rucker, age 37, f. b. in Ga.
James W. Rucker, age 10, b. in Ga.
Milissa C. Rucker, age 9, f. b. in Ga.
Wiley Rucker, age 6, m. b. in Ga.
Moses Rucker, age 4, m. b. in Ga.
Jepthia Rucker, age 35, Farmer, Value of property, $1,000, b. in Ga.
Alsey Rucker, age 33, f.
John Rucker, age 13, m. b. in Ga.
George Rucker, age 11, m. b. in Ga.
Lindsey, age 10, m. b. in Ga.

Elizabeth, age 8, f. b. in Ga.
Cynthia, age 3, f. b. in Ga.
Emily, age 1, f. b. in Ga.

A Nancy Rucker married James Hamilton July 30, 1812. Mrs. Milly Rucker married Larkin Johnson July 19, 1827 (Elbert Co., Ga.).

Administrators and Guardians Bonds; Will Book 1809-1812; Elbert Co., Ga.: Nancy Rucker gave bond as Admrs. of Azmon Rucker, John Rucker and John Jones, Jr. Securities Jan. 6th. 1812 (p. 267).

Autograph Signatures Georgia Militia for the War of 1812. Azmon Rucker, Major (p. 35-36).

Land Lottery: Elbert Co. 1806. Cap't. Duston Blackwell's District. Azmon Rucker 1 draw.

1806. John Rucker 1 draw. Capt. Dunston Blackwell's District.

1827. John Rucker, 1 draw. Capt. Allston's District. Orphs of.

1827. John Rucker, h. of f. & r. s. 3 draws. Capt. Blackwell's District.

4. Simeon[4] Bluford Rucker (George[3], Thomas[2], ———), d. Aug. 6, 1881; m. Jane Barnwell (Apr. 9, 1801-Sept. 5, 1879). He moved to Milton, Ga., in 1833, and built there his home which is still standing. He took with him his mother, Catherine, his sister, Julia, the widow of Benjamin Vaughan, and her child, his wife and several children. He and all of his family to the present day are buried in Milton.

1. George[5] Elsie Rucker.
2. William[5] Derrell.
3. Nancy[5] (Apr. 10, 1822-Nov. 25, 1895), m. ——— Moore.
4. Joel[5].
5. Julia[5] (Mch. 29, 1825-Apr. 2, 1864), m. John Rainwater.
6. Mary[5] (May 8, 1830-Oct. 10, 1904), m. ——— Stewart.
7. Simeon[5] (Jan. 17, 1835-Jan. 11, 1915), m. Martha Manning (Feb. 16, 1837-May 26, 1914).
8. Russell[5] J. (Aug. 1, 1837-July 23, 1913), m. 1st Adeline[2] Mayfield (Giley[1]), 2nd m. Jan. 17, 1881, Mary[2] Ellen James (John[1] S.), b. Nov. 3, 1841.
9. John[5].

1. George[5] Elsie Rucker (Simeon[4] B., George[3], Thomas[2], ———) (Jan. 10, 1819-Aug. 15, 1898), m. Emily S. Rainwater (Oct. 10, 1820-Jan. 29, 1901), dau. of Joseph Rainwater of Anderson Co., S. C.

   1. Mahala[6] C. Rucker (July 25, 1842-Feb. 20, 1880), m. ——— Kent.
   2. Joseph[6], b. Dec. 24, 1843; killed during Civil War in Battle of King's School House, June 25, 1864.
   3. George[6] M. (Oct. 1, 1846-July 26, 1874).
   4. Martha[6] L. (April 6, 1849-Mch. 21, 1920), m. William Mosteller.
   5. John[6] G. (1851-May 25, 1894).
   6. Elizabeth[6] Rucker, b. Dec. 9, 1856.
   7. Goldston[6] P. Rucker (Aug. 28, 1860-Oct. 9, 1901).

2. William[5] Derrell Rucker (Simeon[4] B., George[3], Thomas[2], ———) (Aug. 25, 1820-Oct. 17, 1903), m. Permelia C. Dorris (Mch. 17, 1831-Jan. 17, 1910), lived in Griffin, Ga.

   1. Robert[6] B. Rucker, b. Feb. 14, 1848.
   2. James[6] J., b. Apr. 27, 1850.
   3. Joel[6] W., b. Feb. 5, 1852.
   4. Nancy[6] Jane.
   5. Roxie[6] Ann.
   6. Simeon[6] Newton.
   7. Dora[6] I.
   8. Cora[6] A.

4. Nancy[6] Jane Rucker (William D.[5], Simeon[4], George[3], ———), b. June 21, 1854, m. Dec. 21, 1876, William Norman Manning.

   1. Zedora[7] J. Manning (Oct. 16, 1877-1884).
   2. Nettie[7] A., b. July 15, 1879.
   3. Robert[7] Derge, b. Jan. 5, 1881, m. Lizzie Tatum.
   4. Simeon[7] A., b. Sept. 21, 1882; m. Asa Bush, Apr. 19, 1906.
   5. Lillian[7] Manning.
   6. Joel[7] (Dec. 2, 1885-Dec. 26, 1907), m. Ella Hunnicutt.
   7. William[7] J., b. Dec. 10, 1887.
   8. Ambrose[7] H., b. Reb. 15, 1890.
   9. Roxie[7] L., b. Dec. 31, 1891; m. Nov. 15, 1919, E. F. Striblin.
   10. Dessie[7] H., b. Oct. 23, 1893.
   11. Norman[7] Pryor, b. Aug. 14, 1896.
   12. Roy[7] Barnett, b. Feb. 26, 1901.

5. Lillian^{7} Manning, b. Feb. 26, 1884; m. Nov. 26, 1908, Claud E. McLendon.

- 1. William Marion^{8} McLendon, b. Sept. 13, 1909.
- 2. Nettie^{8}, b. May 13, 1911.
- 3. Joseph^{8} Terrell (Sept. 27, 1912-1913).
- 4. Hiram^{8} Warner, b. July 31, 1914.
- 5. Dora^{8} (July 12, 1917-1918).
- 6. Etta^{8} Carolyne, b. Oct. 3, 1919.
- 7. Claud^{8} Early, Jr., b. Oct. 28, 1920.

5. Roxie^{6} Ann Rucker (William^{5} D., Simeon^{4}, George^{3}, ———), b. Nov. 15, 1856; m. William W. Watkins.

- 1. Oliver^{7} C. Watkins, b. Oct. 13, 1878, m. Dora Adams.
  - 1. Elsie^{8} Watkins.
  - 2. Eva^{8}.
- 2. Walter^{7} E. Watkins, b. Sept. 29, 1880, m. 1st Laura Wade, and 2nd Lizzie Kirkade.

  Issue (by 1st mar.):
  - 1. Anne^{8} Watkins.
  - 2. Lucile^{8}.
  - 3. Walter^{8}.

  Issue (by 2nd mar.):
  - 4. Charles^{8}.
  - 5. James^{8}.
  - 6. Elizabeth^{8} Kirkade.
- 3. Annie^{7} May Watkins, d. young.
- 4. Daisy^{7} Maude, b. Jan. 6, 1884, m. Reuben Black.
  - 1. Evelin^{8} F. Black.
- 5. Gloria^{7} / 6. Flora^{7} } twins, b. Apr. 16, 1886. m. 1st Joseph Reed and 2nd Roy McChes-key.

  Issue (by 1st mar.):
  - 1. Pauline^{8} Reed.
- 7. William^{7} Ware Watkins, b. Nov. 21, 1888; m. Sallie Dobbs.
  - 1. Janette^{8} Watkins.
  - 2. William^{8} Ward.

6. Simeon^{6} Newton Rucker (William D.^{5}, Simeon^{4}, George^{3}, ———), b. May 28, 1859; m. May 28, 1881, Bettie B. Crisler, b. Aug. 3, 1862.

- 1. Pearl^{7} Rucker, b. Apr. 29, 1883, m. Apr. 29, 1803, Joseph W. Fowler.
  - 1. Joel^{8} Fowler.
  - 2. Dorris^{8}.

2. Lloyd[7] C. Rucker, b. June 1, 1885, m. July 7, 1913, Cynthia Wardlaw.
    1. Margaret[8] Rucker.
    2. Bettie[8].
3. William[7] Rucker, d. in infancy.
4. Cliff[7] Rucker, b. Sept. 23, 1899; m. Nov. 3, 1918, Jessie Moffett.
    1. William[8] Newton Rucker.
    2. Jane[8].
    3. David[8] M.

7. Dora[6] I. Rucker (William D.[5], Simeon[4], ———), b. Dec. 9, 1861, m. Joseph L. Gillespie, Dec. 9, 1880.

1. Lola[7] B. Gillespie, b. Dec. 18, 1881; m. William H. Brooke, Oct. 3, 1897.
    1. Isla[8] Brooke.
    2. Audrey[8].
2. Minnie[7] Lee.
3. Jessie[7] Velma.
4. William[7] G., b. Apr. 26, 1890.
5. James[7], b. Jan. 30, 1884.
6. Annie[7] Myrtle (1892-1912).

2. Minnie[7] Lee Gillespie (Dora[6], William D.[5] Rucker), b. Mch. 10, 1886; m. Carl Black, July 31, 1905.

1. Homer[8] Derrell Black.
2. Lucy[8] G.
3. Andrew[8].
4. Hubert[8].
5. Maggie[8].
6. Emery[8].
7. Carl[8].
8. Lola[8].

3. Jesse[7] Velma Gillespie (Dora[6], William D.[5], Rucker), b. May 20, 1888; m. May 30, 1906, William Moreland Lancaster, b. Nov. 8, 1883.

1. Dorothe[8] Lancaster (Apr. 3, 1907-1908).
2. Wesly[8] Moreland (Apr. 6, 1908-1909).
3. Ophella[8] (May 23, 1909-1910).
4. David[8] Dudley, b. Aug. 13, 1910.
5. George[8] Marvin, b. Feb. 22, 1913.
6. Carlos[8] Newton, b. Mch. 18, 1915.

Issue:

7. Luther^{8} McCazer, b. Apr. 7, 1917.
8. Lesbia^{8}, b. Mch. 3, 1919.
9. William^{8}, b. Dec. 9, 1920.

8. Cora^{6} A. Rucker (William D.^{5}, Simeon^{4}, George^{3}, ——), b. Mch. 9, 1864; m. Nov. 23, 1882, James Simeon Reed.

1. Inah^{7} Mae Reid, b. Nov. 25, 1885; m. Oct. 16, 1918, Fred Thomas.
2. Sarah^{7} Henryetta, b. Apr. 9, 1887, m. William F. Upchurch.

4. Joel^{5} Rucker (Simeon^{4}, George^{3}, Thomas^{2}, ———) (Nov. 10, 1823-July 18, 1889), m. Dec. 29, 1857, Miriam Elizabeth (Mch. 26, 1843-Apr. 20, 1913), dau. of Pinkney and Sara E. Rainwater.

1. Joella^{6} May Rucker (May 24, 1863-Oct. 9, 1904), 1st m. Oct., 1878, William J. W. Letson (Mch. 11, 1857-Sept. 20, 1881), m. 2nd Frank M. Ramsey.
   1. Lola^{7} Letson.
2. Rinnie^{6} Kiturah Rucker, b. July 18, 1865; m. Charles Turner Letson (Dec. 27, 1859-Apr. 7, 1885).
   1. Earle^{7} Letson.
   2. Lonnie^{7} Letson.
3. George^{6} Derrell Rucker.
4. Louis^{6} Isabella Rucker.

3. George^{6} Derrell Rucker (Joel^{5}, Simeon^{4}, George^{3} Rucker), b. July 25, 1867; m. June 19, 1889, Florence Meander Teasley, dau. of Alfred Hunt and Laura E. Teasley, b. Sept. 16, 1867. He was a great student. In 1890 he established a newspaper, "The Alpharetta Free Press", which he owned and edited for more than 30 years. He was the county school superintendent, Secretary of the Rucker Cotton Seed Company, Postmaster of the village, President of the Milton County Bank, which he organized, and steward in the Methodist Church. He died Feb. 18, 1922, of blood poisoning.

1. Blanche^{7} Valine Rucker, b. Nov. 12, 1890, m. Sept. 8, 1915, Cincinnattis Emerson Maddox, son of Dr. C. C. Maddox, b. Apr. 2, 1883.
   1. Anne^{8} E. Maddox, b. Aug. 5, 1917.
   2. George^{8} Emerson Maddox, b. Nov. 13, 1919.
2. Von Teasley^{7} Rucker (Nov. 12, 1892-1893).
3. Ruth^{7} Elizabeth, b. Sept. 14, 1894, educated Wesleyan College.

4. Lois^{6} Isabella Rucker (Joel^{5}, Simeon^{4}, George^{3}), b. Dec. 19, 1872, m. Holliday Kelley, moved to Texas.

1. Vivian^{7} Kelley.
2. Madge^{7}.
3. Lois^{7}.
4. Bernice^{7}.
5. Jessie^{7} May, and possibly others.

9. John^{5} Rucker (Simeon^{4}, George^{3}, ———) (Dec. 23, 1842-Feb. 1, 1918), m. Sarah Jameson, widow of Thomas Jameson (Jan. 5, 1844-Feb. 3, 1896).

1. Joel^{6} Jackson Rucker.
2. William^{6} David.
3. John^{6} Simeon.

1. Joel^{6} Jackson Rucker (John^{5}, Simeon^{4}, George^{3}, ———), b. Dec. 17, 1880, m. Dec. 25, 1906, Nora^{2} Rusk (Henry^{1} Rusk), b. June 24, 1878.

1. Sarah^{7} Dorcas Rucker, b. Mch. 28, 1908.
2. Margaret^{7} Lee, b. Oct. 5, 1910.
3. Julia^{7} Josephine, b. Dec. 8, 1913.
4. Joel^{7} John, b. Jan. 15, 1917.

2. William^{6} David Rucker (John^{5}, Simeon^{4}, ———), b. Feb. 16, 1872; m. Sept. 20, 1891, Melissa Princella Broadwell. He was one of the three partners of the Rucker Cotton Seed Company. The cotton which was first used was grown on the farms of the Rucker's in Georgia.

1. Troy^{7} Rucker, b. Dec. 16, 1892; m. Elizabeth Copeland, Nov. 18, 1916.
2. Mary^{7} Ruth, m. U. A. Murdock, Oct. 9, 192.......

3. John^{6} Simeon Rucker (John^{5}, Simeon^{4}, ———), b. Apr. 10, 1877; m. Feb. 25, 1902, Emma A. Cox, b. Aug. 15, 1881.

1. Malcolm^{7} Everetta Rucker, b. Mch. 2, 1908.
2. Martha^{7} Edith, b. Nov. 13, 1912.
3. Marion^{7} Neal, b. Aug. 5, 1914.

1. ——— Rucker (possibly George^{3}, Thomas^{2}, Peter^{1}), of Va., m. Frances Wayne; they moved to Wilkes Co., Ga. The connection of this branch with the cousins in Va. and Ga. has not been established, but we know they are descended from Peter the emigrant. (Could he have been George, Jr., son of George^{2}, son of Peter^{1}, mentioned in 1810 in his father's will).

Issue:

1. Willis² Rucker.
2. Judith².
3. Elizabeth², m. ——— Page.
4. Lucy², m. Philip Henley.
   1. John³ James Henley.
   2. Winnie³.
   3. Eliza³.
   4. Judith³.
   5. Nancy³.
   6. Amelia³.
5. Mary² Rucker, m. ——— Brown.

1. Willis² Rucker (———¹ Rucker), of Elbert Co., Ga., m. Sept. 12, 1790, Jane Pope.

1. Fielding³ Rucker.
2. Lucy³, b. Aug. 31, 1792.
3. Narcessa³, b. Mch. 27, 1793, m. ——— Henderson, no issue.
4. Gideon³ P., b. Jan. 31, 1797.
5. Levinia³, b. Sept. 8, 1798.
6. Niah³ W.
7. Willis³ P., b. Oct. 20, 1801.

Census of Elbert Co., Ga., 1820, lists a Gideon Rucker, age under 26.

1. Fielding³ Rucker (Willis², ———¹ Rucker), b. Aug. 5, 1791; m. July 14, 1815, Louisa Villers, b. Aug. 25, 1801.

1. Jett⁴ Willis Rucker (1816-1817).
2. Almeda⁴ Jane.
3. Sarah⁴ Louise, b. Feb. 17, 1821.
4. Jett⁴ Willis, b. Oct. 29, 1823; m. Mary Jane Powell.
5. John⁴ Pope (Nov. 13, 1825-July 1, 1838).
6. Lucy⁴ Ann, b. Oct. 29, 1828, m. Milton Glass.
   1. Lucy⁵ Glass.
   2. Charles⁵.
7. Nina⁴ Narcissa.
8. Mary⁴ Ann Elizabeth.
9. Fielding⁴ Presley, b. Oct. 25, 1836.
10. Gideon⁴, b. 1841, m. Sue Daniels.
11. Martha⁴ C. Josephine Rucker.

The above births copied from a Bible in the possession of Mrs. Mary E. Martins.

2. Almeda[4] Jane (Fielding[3], Willis[2], ————[1] Rucker) (Sept. 28, 1818-Jan. 28, 1843), m. John Henson.

1. Lelia[5] V. Henson, m. William S. Pains; no issue.
2. Charles[5] A., m. Nannie Nichols.
    1. Harry[6] Henson.
    2. Frank[6].
    3. Charles[6].
    4. Annie[6] L.
3. Jett[5] C. Henson, m. Millie Stovall.
    1. Dorothy[6] C. Henson.
4. Annie[5] Mae, m. William Bang.
5. Moray[5].
6. Fielding[5] P., b. Jan. 4, 1841, m. Annie Monger.
    1. Lelia[6] V. Henson.

7. Nina[4] Narcissa Rucker (Fielding[3], Willis[2], ———) (May 14, 1831-May, 1907), m. 1st ——— Kidd, 2nd ——— Archer.

1. Lizza[5] Kidd, m. H. L. Crawford.
2. Julia[5] Kidd, m. W. A. Jones.
    1. Maude[6] Jones.
    2. Cora[6] Bell Jones.
3. Tinie[5] Kidd, m. ———— Ewell.
    1. Lewilla[6] Ewell, m. John McCarter.
4. Lewella[5] Kidd, m. 1st John Stell, 2nd W. A. Davis.

Issue (by 1st mar.):
1. Alaine[6] Steel, m. B. P. Q. Edwards.
    1. Thomas[7] Edwards.
    2. Corine[7].

Issue (by 2nd mar.):
2. Mignom[6] Davis.
3. Nina[6].

8. Mary[4] Ann Elizabeth Rucker (Fielding[3], Willis[2], ——), b. Feb. 9, 1834, m. John G. Martin.

1. Julia[5] Martin, m. C. V. Tutwiler.
    1. Jesse[6] Tutwiler.
    2. Ethel[6].
    3. Horace[6], m. L. Petty.
        1. Martha[7] Tutwiler.
        2. Julia[7] Tutwiler.

11. Martha^{4} C. Josephine Rucker (Fielding^{3}, Willis^{2}, ——), b. Jan. 10, 1843; m. 1st ————Stein; 2nd ———— Meynel, no issue by 2nd mar.

Issue (by 1st mar.):

- 1. Carolyn^{5} Stein, m. 1st ———— Templet, of Louisville, Ky.; 2nd H. H. Cameron.
    - 1. Louise^{6} Templet, m. Allen Bates.
        - 1. Bettie^{7} Bates.
        - 2. Henry^{7}.
    - 2. Henry^{6} Rucker Templet; no issue.

6. Niah^{3} W. Rucker (Willis^{2}, ————^{1} Rucker), b. Apr. 5, 1800, m. Philip Orr.

- 1. Aramenta^{4} Orr.
- 2. Camilla^{4}, m. ———— Brown.
- 3. John^{4}.
- 4. Niah^{4}.

1. Aramenta^{4} Orr (Niah^{3}, Willis^{2}, ———), m. Nov. 29, 1838, Robert W. Simms.

- 1. John^{5} B. Simms.
- 2. Philip^{5}.
- 3. Eugenia^{5} Anna, m. Mch. 21, 1867, Jefferson La Fayette Richmond.
    - 1. Zella^{6} Eugenia Richmond.
    - 2. Lelia^{6}.
    - 3. Erskine^{6}.
    - 4. John^{6} La Fayette, m. Effie Taylor Stafford.
        - 1. John^{7} L. Richmond, Jr., Chicago, Ill.
- 4. Susan^{5} Robert Simms, m. Robert P. Trippe.
    - 1. Allee^{6} Eugenia Trippe, m. Samuel Coombs Poter.
    - 2. John^{5} Richmond.

1. Zella^{6} Eugenia Richmond (Eugenia^{5}, Aramenta^{4}, ——), m. Jan. 5, 1887, Alonzo Richardson.

- 1. Claudia^{7} Dill Richardson.
- 2. Edward^{7}, m. Manella Brewster.
- 3. Capt. Weaver^{7}, serving in the U. S. Army, m. Virginia McLean, Tex.
- 4. Lelia^{7} Eugenia, m. James Coleman Brown, Tex.
- 5. Dr. Jefferson Richmond.

2. Lelia^{6} Richmond (Eugenia^{5}), m. Sept. 9, 1891, George W. Forrester, Albany, Ga.

1. Robert[7] Richmond Forrester, served in World War as a Lieutenant; was wounded at St. Mihiel, d. 1920.
2. George[7] W. Forrester, Jr., b. 1907.

3. Erskine[6] Richmond (Eugenia[5], ———), m. Jan. 17, 1894, Dr. William Calvin Jamagin.

1. Calvin[7] Jamagin.
2. Susan[7].
3. Erskine[7], m. Oct. 10, 1920, Samuel Walton Forgy, Jr., Elkton, Ky.

2. Judith[2] Rucker (———[1] Rucker and Wayne or Wynne?), b. in Lincoln Co., Ga., moved to Wilks Co., Ga., moved to Ala. in 1845, d. in 1873; m. John B. Wiseman, d. in 1862, in service during Civil War.

1. Lucy[3] Wiseman, d. young.
2. Betty[3], m. John Stokes.
3. Mary[3] Brown.
4. Martha[3], d. young.
5. Willis[3], d. young.
6. Wilson[3], d. young.
7. John[3] Wayne, m. ——— Lawton, moved to Terrell Co., Ga., 1840, then to Ala.
8. Isaac[3], b. Lincoln Co., Ga., d. 1850, m. ——— Woolbright.
    1. Green[4] Wiseman.
    2. Martha[4].
    3. Isaac[4].

3. Mary[3] Brown Wiseman (Judith[2], ———[1] Rucker) (Oct. 12, 1808-July 27, 1873), m. July 2, 1829, William Baird Norman.

1. Julia[4] Norman (1832-Jan. 27, 1872), m. Apr. 30, 1851, James Argyle Norman (3rd cousin).
    1. Sarah[5] Louise Norman.

1. Sarah[5] Louise Norman (Julia[4], Mary[3], Judith[2], ——— Rucker), of Montgomery, Ala., m. Jan. 21, 1872, John Bascom Jobson.

1. J. Norman[6] Jobson, b. Dec. 22, 1872; m. July 31, 1901, Emma B. Gill.
    1. Sarah[7] E. Jobson, b. Apr. 6, 1903; m. Oct. 10, 1925, Hubert Nichols Hart, b. June 19, 1903, Brooklyn, N. Y.

2. Eugene^6 Moffett Jobson, b. Feb. 3, 1875.
3. Frances^6 Sheers, b. Jan., 1878; m. 1908, Belle Daunts.
4. Philip^6 Neil, b. 1882, m. Dec. 4, 1901, Nellie Jobson.
    1. Philip^7 Neil Jobson, Jr., b. Jan. 3, 1903.
    2. Frances^7 Marion Jobson, b. Nov. 23, 1904.
5. Frederick^6 Harris, b. Sept. 21, 1885; m. Aug. 5, 1906, Frances Parks.
    1. Frederick^7 Harris Jobson, Jr., b. Mch. 9, 1907.
    2. Adele^7 Parks Jobson, b. Jan. 2, 1910.
    3. John^7 Norman, b. Aug. 12, 1914.
    4. Robert^7 Bruce, b. Aug. 24, 1920.
    5. Sarah^7 Norman (July 30, 1927-Aug. 1, 1927).
6. John^6 Bascom Jobson, II, b. June 15, 1888, m. Mch. 31, 1913, Elizabeth Philips.
    1. John^7 Bascom Jobson, III, b. 1914.
7. Columbus^6 Drew Jobson, b. Mch. 28, 1891, m. Feb. 18, 1915, Margaret Wemple, b. July 27, 1894, in New York.
    1. Caroline^7 Norman Jobson, b. Mch. 26, 1916.
    2. William^7 Wemple (Feb. 15, 1918-Apr. 9, 1918).
    3. Nancy^7 Pope Jobson, b. June 12, 1919.
    4. Margaret^7 Alice, b. June 29, 1922.
    5. Thomas^7 Wooten, b. Feb. 23, 1925.

3. Thomas^3 Rucker (Thomas^2, Peter^1), d. in Madison County, 1805. Wife, Elizabeth.

Thomas lived in Madison County. Paid land and personal tax until 1805, but he also owned land on the South side of the Rapidan, in Orange County (now Greene).

His father, Thomas, deeded to him 235 acres, land on the Rapidan River, March 15, 1759 (D. B. C, p. 171, Culpeper), and the other land he bought, owning about 2,000 acres. In 1792 he paid on only 190 acres, his estate paid on this until 1814, and his widow Elizabeth until her death in 1827.

On Dec. 4th, 1770, Thomas Gully and wife, Mary, of St. Thomas Parish sold to Thomas Rucker, 100 acres at 100 lbs. Sterling, land on the river. Witness: William Rucker, Peter Rucker and May Burton (D. B. 15, p. 265, Culpeper County).

In 1784, Aug. 24, he bought from Harry Beverly's estate 372 acres, land on Robinson River (D. B. 18, p. 277, Culpeper Co.).

The next year Thomas sold 172 acres of this tract to Captain Belfield Cave, land on Rapidan River.

Thomas made a deed Jan. 7, 1794, in Madison County (D. B. 20, p. 322), to his grandchildren:— "The household furniture and stock on my plantation in Orange (Greene) whereon my son, Wisdom, now lives, and from which he will soon move, to Wisdom and his children, Mary Elizabeth and Thomas Rucker. Witness: George Eve, Sarah Rucker and Tabatha Rucker.

Thomas Rucker of Madison, in 1800, June 23, bought from Belfield Cave and wife, Milly of Orange, 155 acres for 155 lbs. Sterling, land in Orange (Greene), on South side of Rapidan, adjoining William Herndon, May Burton, on Pole Cat Run (D. B. 22, p. 36, Madison Co.).

In 1793 Thomas Rucker, John Rowzee and Edward Herndon were appointed to appraise the estate of William Crawford, deceased (O. B. 1, p. 15, Madison Co.).

The adjustment of Revolutionary claims for provisions taken during the Revolutionary War for Culpeper County, 16 oct., 1781:—

To Thomas Rucker, for 650 lbs. of beef, 8 lbs. Sterling 2s 6d.

Received from Thomas Rucker 425 lbs of beef for which payment at the rate of two pence—5 lbs. Sterling 6—3, 16 Oct. 1781.

Will of Thomas Rucker, dated Jan. 7, 1805, probated June 23, 1808 (W. B. 2, p. 29, Madison Co., Virginia).

In the name of God, Amen. I, Thomas Rucker, of the County of Madison and State of Virginia, being of sound mind and memory thanks be to Almighty God for the same and calling to mind the precariousness of this transitory life and the certainty of death, do make and constitute, order and declare this to be my last Will and Testament, and First I give my soul to Almighty God who gave it and my body to the earth to be decently buried and whereas it has pleased Almighty God to bless me with this world's wealth I give and dispose of the same in manner and form following.

Item. I lend to my dear loving wife Elizabeth Rucker all my estate both real and personal during her natural life or widowhood but if in case she should marry my will is that all my estate both real and personal shall be divided as hereafter directed, that is, first my lands both in Madison and Orange shall at the death or marriage of my dear wife Elizabeth Rucker be divided and laid off in lots as many as I have children hereafter named except my son Wisdom Rucker. I cut him off with one dollar and he is not to inherit no more of my estate than the named six shillings and he the above named Wisdom Rucker stands at this time indebted to me in the sum of forty-four pounds, but it is to be understood that all the children that my son Wisdom has or shall have by his present wife Rozanna Rucker they shall and I do by these presents give unto them to be equally divided among them all the part of my estate that I intended for their father Wisdom Rucker, which said estate is to be in the hands of my executors and as my son Wisdom Rucker's children come to age they may and shall draw it out of the hands of my executors hereafter named and apply it to the uses they so cause and as I intend the said Wisdom Ruckers children shall have a lot in the land as I intended for their father, my executors hereafter named may and shall and has by these presents fully authorized and impower to sell the said lot of land and after public notice sell to the best advantage they can and make a good and lawful right to the same in behalf of my son Wisdom Ruckers children so that each lot shall have as equal number of acres as the other as near as can be laid off and these lots to be valued by three respectable free holders and each lot to be numbered and the value of every lot to be set on each ticket with its number and all the tickets thrown in a hat or box and they shall draw for the lots beginning at my eldest child and so on to the youngest except my son Wisdom Rucker, his children as above named shall receive his part in every instance in my estate as above directed and a bystander shall draw for them and it shall be lawful and good and he or she or my son Wisdom's children gets of more value than the other shall pay to the other in proportion so that every lot may be of equal value to the owner. But let it be remembered that if any of my children, they or their husbands bargain and sell the above named lots of land or their supposed rights it is my will and desire that he or she be it which it may they shall and are by these presents cut entirely off from having any share or lot in the above named land and their part shall return to those who do not sell, the intent and meaning of the above disinheritance is that if they sell before a general division, after a general division they are at liberty to do as they please.

Item. My will and desire is that the rest of my estate, namely my negroes, my stock of every kind that with my household furniture and everything else belonging to the said estate too tedious here to mention shall be sold to the highest bidder for ready money and that my grandson Morning Rucker is to have a good horse saddle and bridle or twenty pounds cash which he chooses, but if he dies without heirs it shall return and be equally divided among all my children.

Item:—If either of my children namely Sarah Rucker or Ezekiel Rucker should be single at my death they shall receive thirty pounds each as a free gift before a division takes place.

Item:—My will and desire is that after the death or marriage of my dear wife Elisabeth Rucker that my estate be sold as above directed and the money arising from the sale after paying all my just debts and the legacies above named by dividing equally among my children, namely Mary Herndon, Sarah Rucker, Ann Herndon, Wisdom Rucker's children, as above directed, Tabitha Loyd, Catey Burruss, John Rucker, Ezza Anderson, Ezekiel them should die without heir their part of the estate shall return and be equally divided among the rest of my children according as already directed.

Item;—My will and desire is that all the expenses which arises at the said sale shall be paid off before the division takes place.

Item:—Some of my children have already received property of me namely Mary Herndon one negro girl Dafney valued at fifty pounts: Ann Herndon one negro boy Willis valued at fifty pounds: Tabitha Loyd one negro boy Jeremiah valued at forty-two pounds: Ezza Anderson one negro girl named Hannah valued at fifty pounds: Elisabeth Phillips one negro girl, Grace valued at forty-two pounds; John Rucker has received in cash of me forty seven pounds, two shillings and six pence; Caty Burruss one negro girl Lucy valued forty pounds: Ezekiel Rucker has received of me in cash forty two pounds, which said valuation in money is to be.

(Signed) Thomas Rucker.

The following is taken from the division of Thomas Rucker's Estate:

"Eve's mill house South bank of Rapidan river 43 acres in Orange, E. side of branch, to widow Ahart's land at mouth of Rapidan adjoining Geo. Anderson, to fork of road leading to Aharts old ford and to Rucker's ford, adjoins Ezekiel Rucker, on north side of road to Jas. Collins in Madison 1632 acres. Also Jack, Robert, Caty and her child Esther for widow's dower in the slaves amounting to two pounds 10 shillings more than her dower.

Witness: May Burton, Belfield Cave, Joseph Brock Jr., John Bradford. Statement of division of estate, 23 June, 1808 (W. B. 2, p. 173).

To Leroy Canady for surveyor's fees.
To Morning Rucker, Legacy per will 20 lbs.
To Ezekiel Rucker, Legacy per will 30 lbs.
To Sarah Rucker, Legacy per will 30 lbs.
To Elisabeth Rucker, 1/3, etc.

11 distributees:—William Herndon, Edward Herndon, Jr. Robert Loyd, Jacob Anderson, Zach Phillips, John Rucker, Sam-

uel Burruss, Ezekiel Rucker, Sarah Rucker, Winslow Rowzie and Wisdom Rucker's children, 120 lbs. each.

Division of property after the death of Elizabeth, widow (W. B. 5, p. 201). Thomas Rucker, dec'd. Division of Land By decree of Madison Court, 28 August, 1828, bounded by Eheart's road on the north; by the Rapidan River on the East; the Rapidan on the West; the Orange road runs through south west corner; Rucker's ford of Rapidan on West; the Orange Mill Run empties into the Rapidan River on the land and so does a branch on the north; adjoins lands of John White, Michael Eheart, the estate divided into 77 lots, 18 2/3 acres each, each valued at $121.09.

Wisdom Rucker's children, Lot 1, valued at $60.00. Wil- Herndon in right of wife Mary, Lot 2, valued at $86.00. Edward Herndon in right of wife Nancy Lot 3, valued at $250.00. Sarah Furneyhough Lot 4, valued $180.00.

Robert Loyd in right of wife Tabitha, Lot 5, valued $200.00. John Rucker's children, Lot 6, valued $160.00.

William Rowzie in right of wife Frances Lot 7, valued $170.00. Samuel Burriss as tenant by courtesy, remainder of his children in fee simple by his wife Kitty formerly Kitty Rucker, Lot 8, valued at $72.00.

Ezekiel Rucker, Lot 9 valued $60.00.

Zachariah Phillips in right of his wife Elisabeth Lot 10, valued at $61. Jacob Anderson as tenant by the courtesy of remainder of his three children in fee simple by his wife Esther Lot 11, valued at $73.00.

Appraisement made October 23, 1828 by Michael Eahart, John White, William Walker and recorded 25 Dec. 1828.

William Herndon, Administrator of Thomas Rucker, rented land to James Herndon with negroes. Recorded July 24, 1829 (W. B. 5, p. 258).

Will of Elisabeth Rucker, of Orange County.

I, Elisabeth Rucker of the County of Orange and State of Virginia, being of a disposing memory do constitute and make this my last disposition of property.

Item.—All the property which my four (youngest) children now have in possession, namely Ezekiel Rucker, Sarah Furneyhough, Molly Herndon and Tabitha Lloyd, I do hereby give to them in fee simple, to them and their heirs forever.

Item:—All the property which I have in possession I give and bequeath the same to my daughter Molly Herndon to her and her heirs forever.

Item:—All the other to be in money either in hand or outstanding at my decease then my wish is after my just debts are satisfied that the remainder be equally divided among my four children heretofore named, to them and their heirs forever.

Item:—I do constitute Joseph Cave executor to this my last disposition of property.

As witness my hand and seal this 26th day of April, 1826. Teste: Alex A. Bradford, Elisabeth Rucker, Henry Herndon.

Elizabeth Rucker paid tax on 190 acres until 1828. Land of her husbands in Madison but she lived in Orange (Greene) until her death. The tax book "Elizabeth of Orange" paid on 190 acres in Madison.

Will of Elizabeth, W. B. 6, p. 501, Orange Co., dated April 20th, 1826, probated 24 Sept. 1827.

Issue:

1. Wisdom[4] Rucker,
2. Mary[4].
3. Nancy[4].
4. Sarah[4].
5. Tabitha[4].
6. John[4], Jr.
7. Frances[4].
8. Caty[4].
9. Ezekiel[4].
10. Elizabeth[4].
11. Ezza[4] (Isabel).
12. James[4].

1. Wisdom[4] Rucker (Thomas[3], Thomas[2], Peter[1]), of Orange Co., m. Rosanna Burruss, Sept. 29, 1787, a daughter of Mary Burrus of Orange, who left a will in 1794, lending to her daughter Rosanna the wife of Wisdom Rucker and their three children, Mary[5], Elizabeth[5] and Thomas[5] her household furniture. The same year Wisdom[4] Rucker's father, Thomas, made a deed leaving household furniture, stock, etc., to the same three children, stating that Wisdom is "about to move". Wisdom[4] was living on a plantation in Orange, belonging to his father, Thomas[3], and in moving is leaving his children. So their grand parents are "lending" them household furniture, pigs, cow and calf, corn, meat, rye and other necessary things. Wisdom moved to Tennessee.

1. Mourning[5], m. Julia Lloyd, May 13, 1811.

He paid a personal tax in 1815 in Madison County, only one year.

In 1805 Madison County there was a guardian bond made by "Robert Lloyd to pay to Mourning Rucker, $500.00" security Belfield Cave (D. B. 2, p. 59, Nov. 28, 1805, Madison County).

2. Mary[4] Rucker (Thomas[3], Thomas[2], Peter[1]), b. 1763, Culpeper, d. 1835. Married William[2] P. Herndon, b. Feb. 28th,

1764, son of Edward[1] Herndon, Sr. William was one of the administrators of the will of his father-in-law.

Issue:

1. Thomas[5] Herndon.
2. Edward[5] Herndon.
3. James[5] Herndon.
4. Ezekiel[5] Herndon, b. Dec. 7, 1790.
5. Mary[5] P.
6. Elizabeth[5].
7. Abner[5].
8. Rachel[5].
9. Henry[5].
10. William[5].
11. Manson[5].
12. Joel[5].

3. Nancy[4] Rucker (Thomas[3], Thomas[2], Peter[1]), b. Culpeper, d. Ga., 1822, m. Aug. 18, 1791, Edward[2] Herndon, Jr., b. 1768 (Edward[1] Herndon), of Culpeper, d. 1827. Moved to Georgia, 1803.

Edward Herndon, Jr., sold his wife's interest in 187 acres of land to Robert Lloyd in 1806, Culpeper.

Issue:

1. Ezekiel[5] Herndon, b. Dec. 7, 1791.
2. Mary[5] Gaines Herndon.
3. Thomas[5] Rucker Herndon, d. 1820.

4. Sarah[4] Rucker (Thomas[3], Thomas[2], Peter[1]), m. Thomas Furneyhough Feb. 23, 1806. She received Lot No. 4 valued $180. from her parents estate. Her mother signed her marriage bond, Jan. 16, 1806.

Jan. 15, 1806 Sarah Rucker, Ezekiel Rucker, Edward Herndon and John Rowzie Jr. of Madison County and Zachariah Philips and his wife, Elizabeth, of Amherst County sold to Robert Lloyd of Orange for 305 lbs. 187 acres, part of land of which Thomas Rucker, deceased, of Madison County died seised of.

5. Tabitha[4] (Thomas[3], Thomas[2], Peter[1]), m. Robert Lloyd, Mch. 17, 1794, Madison Co. Her father Thomas signed the marriage bond.

Robert Lloyd was appointed in 1805 Guardian to Mourning Rucker (son to Wisdom), to pay him $500.00 out of the estate of Thomas Rucker, security Belfield Cave.

6. John[4] Rucker, Jr. (Thomas[3], Thomas[2], Peter[1]), b. in Culpeper. Died in Tennessee before 1827, his heirs receiving his share of his mother's estate in 1828. Madison County.

John married in Amherst, Hannah Philips, daughter of Zachariah. Marriage bond dated March, 1799.

Witness: Thomas Phillips and Conyer Phillips.

Zacharia Phillips left a will in Amherst, dated June 11, 1807, probated Dec. 1817, in which he left to my friends Hawes Coleman and Captain John Harvie fifty pounds sterling in trust for my daughter Hannah Rucker and his children (W. B. 4, p. 470, Amherst County).

1797 James Tinsley is paying on 105¾ acres of land, formerly of John Ruckers (Tax books), Madison.

This land John Rucker bought from Benjamin James Powell in 1796, land on Elk Run, Madison Co. He paid a personal tax until 1800, then on an "Overseer". John went to Amherst before moving to Tennessee, and lived on Rucker's Run in Amherst (now Nelson), for a year.

He was living in Amherst Co. in 1806, having sold his land, his wife, Hannah, signing the deed, land in Madison Co. Paying no further personal tax in either county.

A deed recorded in Madison, Jan. 15th, 1806, Jacob Anderson and his wife, Ezza, of Orange, John Rucker and his wife, Hannah, of Amherst, sold 76 acres in Madison (D. B. 24, p. 79, Madison).

After the death of his mother in 1828, John received his share of her estate, 18 2/3 acres, living in Humphrey Co., Tenn. His heirs appointed Robert Bumpas of that county and state their attorney to sell this 18 2/3 acres of land in Madison Co. (D. B. 10, p. 532), Jan. 9th, 1830.

Zacharia Rucker, Thomas and Nancy Rucker of Tennessee appointed Robert Bumpas of same their attorney to sell the 18¾ acres of land in Madison County, Virginia.

(D. B. 10, p. 523), 30 May, 1831, Madison Co., Virginia. Robert Bumpas, attorney for Elizabeth Rucker; Frances Tilley, wife of Henry; Susan Allman, wife of James; John Rucker, Polly Rucker and James Rucker of Wilson County, Tenn.; also attorney for Zacharia Rucker; Thomas Rucker and Nancy Rucker of Humphrey Co., Tenn., children of John Rucker, deceased. One of the devisees of Thomas Rucker deceased, of Madison County, sold to James Herndon of Madison County, Virginia, 18 2/3 acres, for $160.00. Land of Thomas deceased inherited by the heirs of John Rucker, deceased.

Issue:

1. Zachary^{5} Rucker.
2. Thomas^{5} Rucker.
3. Nancy^{5} Rucker.
4. Elizabeth^{5} Rucker.
5. Frances^{5}, m. Henry Tilley.
6. Susan^{5} Rucker, m. James Allman.
7. John^{5} Rucker.
8. Polly^{5} Rucker.
9. James^{5} Rucker.

Will of James^{6} P. Rucker, 1875, mentions brother S. B. Rucker, brother J. H. Rucker, mother Elizabeth (Wilson Co., Tenn.).

1. Zachary^{5} Rucker (John^{4}, Thomas^{3}, Thomas^{2}, Peter^{1}), b. in Madison County, m. 1830, Susan Pope, at Huntsville, Alabama.

1. William^{6} Jasper Rucker, b. Dyersburg, Tenn., d. 1864 in the confederate service, m. Louise Adams, d. 1890.
    1. Susan^{7} Jane Rucker, b. Dyersburg, Tenn., m. Dr. George Dalton, lived Walden, Mo.
        1. Zetta^{8} Rucker Dalton, Rutland, Tacoma, Washington.
2. Newton^{6}, d. 1916.
3. Taylor^{6}.
4. Sarah^{6}.
5. Emily^{6}.
6. Mary^{6}.
7. Delia^{6}.

7. Frances^{4} Rucker (Thomas^{3}, Thomas^{2}, Peter^{1}), m. Mch. 22, 1803, Winslow^{2} Rowzie (John^{1}). Her father, Thomas, signed the marriage bond, March 19, 1803, m. 1805, Dec. 4 (D. B. 24, p. 80, Orange County). Winslow Rowzie and wife, Frances, of Elbert County, Georgia, sold to John Rowzie of Madison County 37½ acres, their part of Thomas Rucker's estate in Orange County. (John Rowzie Jr. sold this land in 1806, to Robert Lloyd of Orange.)

Winslow Rowzie received 18 2/3 acres of land, after the death of Frances's mother Elizabeth, in 1827.

(Will of Edward Rowzie, dated Dec. 26, 1674, probated Jan. 6, 1677).

To my wife Mary, Executrix,

To my son, Edward, 400 acres of land at the head of Occupasia Cr. when of age.

To my son, Lodowick, land whereon I live, when of age.

To daughters Sarah and Elizabeth 1000 acres in the freshies of the Rappahannock River, on South side. Witness: Robert Pley, George Bruce (W. B. 7, p. 13, Old Rappa. Co.).

Ralph Rowzie was a French Huguenot (Maury's *Huguenot Emigrants,* p. 34). Ralph and Edward Rowzie were in Essex County, 1704.

8. Caty[4] Rucker (Thomas[3], Thomas[2], Peter[1]), m. October 29, 1788, Samuel Burruss of Culpeper.

9. Ezekiel[4] Rucker (Thomas[3], Thomas[2], Peter[1]), lived in Madison County, moved west after 1807. He bought a tract of 50 acres from George Anderson, on South side of Ehart Mill Dam, about three miles below the junction of Elk Run and the Rapidan River. Land in Madison Co. This land he sold to James Collins for 100 lbs. sterling in 1803 (D. B. 5, p. 373, Mad. Co.).

He bought 50 acres from John Walker, Jr. Same location, and 75 acres from George Anderson, 1807. He sold 76 acres to James Colliers for $608.00 land adjoining John Ahart, and Thomas Rucker (D. B. 4, page 361, Madison County).

Ezekiel sold to John White of Madison for $28.00 4 acres, land received from his father Thomas's estate. Dec. 2, 1828 (D. B. 10, p. 200, Madison). Witness: John W. White and Henry White.

The land tax book of 1829 charges to Ezekiel's account 14 2/3 acres (inherited from his mother, Elizabeth).

In 1806 Ezekiel and some of the other heirs of Thomas[3] Rucker sold 187 acres of land to Robert Lloyd.

10. Elizabeth[4] Rucker (Thomas[3], Thomas[2], Peter[1]), m. Zacharia Philips, Feb. 26, 1797, his second wife. The marriage bond was signed by her father Thomas. They moved to Amherst County. The will dated December 21st, 1807 in Amherst of Zacharia Philips in which he left 50 lbs. sterling and two negroes to his daughter, Johanna Rucker and her children. John Rucker married Johanna Phillips, 1799 in Amherst County (marriage bond).

Zachary Phillips and his wife, Elizabeth, of Amherst County, sold to Robert Lloyd their share of 187 acres, land of her father Thomas Rucker, deceased (Orange County), 1806.

11. Isabel[4] Rucker (Thomas[3], Thomas[2], Peter[1]), m. Mch. 7, 1794, Jacob[2] Anderson (son of George[1] Anderson), d. 1807, in Madison Co., the marriage bond was signed by her father, Thomas.

Jacob Anderson and his wife, Ezza, of Orange Co., and John Rucker and his wife, Hannah, of Amherst Co., sold to May Burton 76 acres for £88. Part of the land inherited from Thomas Rucker, deceased. Witness: Ezekiel Rucker (D. B. 24, p. 79, Jan. 15, 1806, Madison County).

12. James[4] Rucker (Thomas[3], Thomas[2], Peter), died in Culpeper Co., 1784, leaving his wife, Mildred, and no children. Therefore was not mentioned in his father's will. He married 1782, died 2 years later, leaving a will, which mentions wife, Milly, Brother Wisdom and Father Thomas Rucker.

Executors, Father Thomas Rucker and John Tinsley (W. B. C, p. 86, Culpeper County). He appears in the personal tax list, 1782.

Will dated May 31, 1784, recorded Nov. 15, 1784. Mildred was the daughter of John and Sarah Tinsley of Madison. After James death she married Jonathan Franklin. Mentioned in her father John Tinsley's will, dated 1797 in Madison County. "To my wife Sarah, to Son William Tinsley, daughter Sarah Falkner, daughter Joanna Vernon, daughter Mary Alexander, daughter Agge Rucker, daughter Betsy Rucker, daughter Milly Franklin and grand daughter Sarah.

4. Cornelius[3] Rucker (Thomas[2], Peter[1]), b. before 1735, Orange Co., d. 1761 Culpeper, m. Mary[3] White (daughter of John[2] and Anne (Wisdom) White, son of Conyer[1] and Mary White).

In 1759 his father deeded to him 283 acres of land in Culpeper—"where he now lives"—1753 a negro girl named Sarah belonging to Cornelius Rucker was by the court adjudged, ten years old, Orange.

Will of Cornelius Rucker, dated March 28, 1761, probated July 16, 1761 (W. B. 1, page 253, Culpeper).

I lend to my loving wife, Mary, all of my estate both real and personal during the time she continues to be a widow, and no longer.

I will and desire that if my loving wife should either die or marry again, that my estate shall be equally divided among my three children, Joseph, Anne and John. I appoint my loving brothers, John Rucker and Conyers White, my sole executor.

Witness, Richard Quinn, Thomas Quinn, Peter Rucker.

Issue:

1. Joseph[4].
2. Ann[4].
3. John[4].

1. Joseph[4] Rucker (Cornelius[3], Thomas[2], Peter[1]), b. 1758 in Culpeper Co., Va., d. in Ruckersville, Elbert Co., Ga., m. Agnes[2] Tinsley (John[1] and Sarah Tinsly).

Will of John Tinsly, Sept. 10, 1797, Aug. 27, 1798 of Madison Co., Virginia.

"To my wife, Sarah, all of my estate at her death to be sold, and divided among my children, William Tinsley; Mary Alexander; Agge Rucker; Betsy Rucker; grandaughter, Sarah, daughter of Jonathan and Milly Franklin.

Executors, son William Tinsley and Joseph Rucker, Witness: Frances Blunt, Sarah Vernon and William Rucker.

John Tinsly furnished supplies for the Revolutionary Army, 16th Oct. 1781, certificate in the archives, Richmond, Virginia.

In 1782 Joseph[4] was paying taxes on 283 acres of land in Culpeper Co., land given to his father, Cornelius, by his grandfather, Thomas, in 1759. This 283 acres, Joseph and his wife Aggie sold to Bartlett Bennett of Albemarle Co., Va., Oct. 22, 1789 for 169 pounds sterling. Land in Culpeper.

Witness: May Burton, Jr., John Miller and Francis Collins (D. B. P, page 536, Culpeper Co., Va.).

On Oct. 19, 1789, Joseph andd Aggie sold 10 acres of land in Culpeper to William Crawford, on the Rapidan River—now in William Crawford's possession for several years (D. B. P, page 212, Culpeper). In 1791 he sold 20 acres more to William Crawford. Land in Culpeper.

In 1798 Joseph appears in Elbert Co., Ga., receiving a grant of 42 acres of land. In Culpeper County he paid taxes on slaves named "Sal, Harry, Jack, Jerry, and Dinah".

Issue:

1. John[5] Rucker.
2. James[5] Rucker.

1. John[5] Rucker (Joseph[4], Cornelius[3], Thomas[2], Peter[1]) a merchant of Ruckersville, Georgia.

The records of Elbert Co., May, 1801, John Rucker appointed Thomas Collins, of Madison Co., Va., his attorney to collect his share of John Tinsley's estate from the executor, Sarah Tinsley.

1. Amanda[6] B. Rucker, b. Ruckersville, Georgia, m. Elbert, Co., Willis B. Jones, July 14, 1829, moved to Alabama, 1836.
    1. John[7] E. Jones, b. in Georgia. Lived at Robinson Springs, Alabama.
2. Mildred[6] Rucker, m. White, of Elbert Co., Georgia.

2. James[5] Rucker (Joseph[4], Cornelius[3]), b. in Madison Co., Va., d. in Elbert Co., Ga., left no heirs. The inventory of his estate was returned by Tavner and William Rucker, May 2, 1828 (Adms. & Guards. Accts. B. N., pages 73, 427, Elbert Co.)

The will of James Rucker dated June 28, 1828, prob. Sept. 7, 1829, leaves his property to his nieces Amanda B. and Milly Rucker sole heirs.

Exec.: Thomas A. Banks. Test: James F. White and Westley S. Bailey (W. B. N, page 38).

3. John[4] Rucker (Cornelius[3], Thomas[2], Peter[1]), b. 1759, Culpeper Co., d. Ruckersville, Georgia, m. May 28, 1780, Betsy Tinsley, daughter of John and Sarah. It is said that John married three times:

First, ——— Fielding.
Second, Betsy Tinsley.
Third, Mrs. Hudson, née Garr.

On March 3, 1783, John Tinsley and his wife, Sarah, sold to John Rucker, 200 acres for 100 pounds sterling. Land in Culpeper (now Madison) (D. B. M, page 38).

Wit.: John Walker, William Roberts, Joseph Rucker.

This 200 acres, John and Betsy sold to John Walker for 157 pounds sterling, land on Robinson River, adjoining William Walker and William Alexander, Jr., Oct. 16, 1786 (D. B. N, page 390, Culpeper Co.)

In 1799 he patented land in Elbert Co., Ga.

Served in the Revolutionary War from Culpeper Co., Va., then moved to Wilkes Co., Ga.

1. Fielding[5] Rucker.
2. Joseph[5] Rucker.
3. Martha[5] Rucker.
4. James[5] Rucker.
5. John[5] Rucker.
6. William[5] Rucker.
7. Judith[5] Rucker.
8. Zachary[5] Rucker.
9. Elizabeth[5] Rucker.
10. Mildred[5] Rucker.
11. Margaret[5] Rucker, m. William Garr.
12. Polly[5] Rucker, m. George Garr.

1. Fielding[5] Rucker (John[4], Cornelius[3], Thomas[2], Peter[1]). Married in Benton Co., Ga. Nancy Beasley, b. 1770, d. July 7, 1845, daughter of Richard and wife, Jane (Yarbrough) Beasley.

They moved from Wilks Co. to Muscogee Co., Ga., where he died in 1813 (see Beasley, p. ——).

1. Arden^{6} Somers Rucker.
2. Jane^{6} Beasley Rucker, b. 1797, d. Feb. 6, 1862, m. Jesse Stalling (no children), Taylors Co., Ga.
3. Richard^{6} Rucker.
4. Mary W.^{6} Rucker, b. Feb. 7, 1802, d. Jan. 14, 1865, m. Rev. Saunders Durham (no children).

1. Arden^{6} Somers Rucker (Fielding^{5}, John^{4}, Cornelius^{3}), b. Feb. 26, 1795, in Wilkes Co. Ga., moved to Monroe Co., Ga., d. 1895 in Taylor Co., Ga., m. Ann Pope, of Upson Co., born July 5, 1800.

1. Adrian^{7} Matilda Rucker.
2. Virginia^{7} Rucker, m. McLendon.
3. Mary^{7} Rucker, m. ———— Crawford.
4. Missouri^{7}, m. ———— McLendon, moved to Florida.
5. Royland^{7} Beasley (called Bee), moved to Texas.
6. Martha^{7} Frances Rucker.

1. Adrian^{7} Matilda Rucker (Arden^{6}, Fielding^{5}, John^{4}), b. July 20, 1821, m. 1836, George W. Davis, lived in Upson Co., Ga.

1. Thomas^{8} Watts Davis, b. Sept. 2, 1841.
2. James^{8} Ryland Davis, b. 1844.
3. Wilson^{8} Somers.
4. Marianna^{8}.
5. George^{8} Doggett, b. 1854.
6. Merit^{8}.
7. Matilda^{8}, b. April 1, 1861.
8. S. Emma^{8}, b. 1865.

3. Wilson^{8} Somers Davis (Adrian^{7}, Arden^{6}, Fielding^{5}), b. 1848, m. 1st, Mattie Cobb, m. 2nd, 1912, Emma Murry. Issue (by 1st marriage):

1. James^{9} Ryland Davis, b. May, 1880, m. Carrie Allison.
   1. James^{10} Davis.
   2. Matilda^{10} Davis.
   3. Virginia^{10} Davis.
2. Clara^{9} E. Davis, b. Aug. 7, 1882, m. J. W. Adams, d. 1915.
   1. Clara^{10} Adams.
   2. John^{10} Adams.
3. George ^{9} Wilson Davis, b. Feb., 1884.

4. Marianna[8] Davis (Adrian[7], Arden[6], Fielding[5], ———[4] Rucker), b. June 13, 1851, m. J. T. Dozier.

1. George[9] Iguatur Dozier, b. Nov. 18, 1877, m. Georgie Fink.
2. A. Rosa[9] Dozier, b. Jan. 2, 1880, m. Andrew J. Shell.
3. Gertrude[9] Anna Dozier, b. Feb. 15, 1882, m. James Love Brooks.
    1. Dozier[10] B. Brooks, b. 1903.
    2. Anna[10] R. Brooks, b. 1906.
    3. Clifford[10] M. Brooks, b. 1909.
    4. Esther[10] F. Brooks, b. 1912.
    5. Sue[10] G. Brooks, b. 1915.
    6. James[10] Love Brooks, Jr., b. 1918.
4. Warren[9] Clifford Dozier, b. Sept. 8, 1886, m. Annie Bridges.
    1. Warren[10] C. Dozier, Jr.
5. Matilda[9] R. Dozier, b. March 15, 1889, m. William W. Bennett.
    1. Thomas[10] Waring Bennett.
    2. William[10] Walter Bennett, Jr.
6. Fannie[9] Dean Dozier, b. Sept. 2, 1892, m. John Carl Bland.
    1. John[10] Carl Bland, Jr., b. 1915.
7. Susie[9] Clyde Dozier, b. July 20, 1894.

6. Merit[8] Davis (Adrian[7], Arden[6], Fielding[5] — Rucker), b. 1858, m. Lucile Womble.

1. May[9] Ida Davis.
2. Merit[9] Davis.
3. A. Matilda[9] Davis.
4. Cecil[9] Davis.

6. Martha[7] Frances Rucker (Arden[6], Fielding[5], John[4]), b. Mch. 19, 1835, d. Mch. 2, 1914, m. 1st, Robert Spier, killed in Civil War, m. 2nd, James Taylor Evers, b. July 10, 1849, d. 1885.

Issue (by 1st marriage):

1. Mary[8] Luda Spier, b. Dec. 11, 1855.
2. Missouri[8] Ann Spier.
3. Cullen[8] Pope Spier.
4. Robert[8] Beasley Spier.
5. Allison[8] H. Spier.

Issue (by 2nd marriage):

6. Frances[8] Virginia Evers, b. 1869, m. July, 1891, Charles O. Burts.
    1. Melvine[9] Burts, b. 1895.

7. Rowenia[8] Lee Evers.
8. Minnie[8] Rucker Evers.
9. Mary[8] E. Evers.
10. Annie[8] E. Evers.

7. Rowena[8] Lee Evers (Martha[7], Arden[6], ——— Rucker), b. Sept. 6, 1871, m. Jan 30, 1891, Samuel Edwards Mays, b. Dec. 19, 1864.

1. Miriam[9] Rowena Mays, m. Oct. 4, 1916, William Edwards Lee, b. Feb. 8, 1891.
2. Katherine[9] F. Mays, b. Jan. 18, 1902.
3. Samuel[9] E. Mays, b. Oct. 21, 1905.
4. James[9] Arden Mays, b. Mch. 1, 1910.

8. Minnie[8] Rucker Evers (Martha[7], Arden[6], —— Rucker), b. Mch. 31, 1874, m. June 12, 1894, Luther R. Waver, b. June 4, 1868.

1. Lorena[9] Rosamond Waver, b. 1895.

9. Mary[8] Emma Evers (Martha[7], Arden[6], Fielding[5] —— Rucker), b. May 3, 1876, m. Mch. 23, 1892, Wade Hampton Reed, b. Mch. 14, 1867, of Washington, D. C.

1. Jessie[9] E. Reed, b. Nov. 4, 1896, m. George Whitney Stephenson.
2. May[9] Ina Reed, b. Feb. 2, 1890.
3. Wade[9] H. Reed, Jr., b. Jan. 11, 1893, m. Mildred Odum, Jan. 1, 1915.
   1. Gerald[10] Hampton Reed, b. 1915.

10. Annie[8] Elizabeth Evers (Martha[7], Arden[6], Fielding[5] —— Rucker), b. Oct. 25, 1878, m. June 13, 1897, Elbert Osborn, of St. Petersburg, Fla., b. Dec. 10, 1878.

1. Gladys[9] Osborn, b. May 6, 1900.
2. Elsie[9] L. Osborn, b. Feb. 10, 1902.
3. Frances[9] M. Osborn, b. June 6, 1906.
4. Elizabeth[9] V. Osborn, b. May 25, 1911.
5. Miriam[9] Osborn, b. July 24, 1912.
6. Morris[9] Osborn, b. Jan. 7, 1899.
7. Earl[9] E. Osborn, b. Feb. 14, 1908.
8. Eugene[9] H. Osborn, b. June 2, 1914.

3. Richard[6] Beasley Rucker (Fielding[5], John[4], Cornelius[3]), b. June 4, 1799, Wilkes Co. Ga., d. Jan. 5, 1861, Taylor Co., Ga.,

m. Sept. 20, 1820, Cerena Williamson, b. Jan. 2, 1806, d. Feb. 15, 1885, at Atlanta, Ga.

1. Mary^{7} Jane Rucker.
2. William^{7} Rucker, b. 1823, d. young.
3. James^{7} Arden Rucker.
4. Rebecca^{7} Ann Rucker.
5. Lucenda^{7} Elizabeth Rucker.
6. Louisa^{7} Matilda Rucker, b. June 4, 1832, m. 1st, Aug. 21, 1851, John P. Durham, d. Sept., 1851, m. 2nd, Jan. 5, 1854, W. S. Johnson.
    1. George^{8} Flewellyn Johnson, of N. C.
    2. Charles^{8} Johnson, d. young.
    3. Richard^{8} Newton Johnson.
7. Fielding^{7} Saunders Rucker.
8. Virginia^{7} Frances } twins — b. July 27, 1836, d. young.
9. George^{7} Granberry } twins — d. Dec. 24, 1886, Atlanta, Ga., m. Sarah Flanagan.
    1. George^{8} G. Rucker, Jr.
    2. Joseph^{8} Rucker, of N. Y.
10. Richard^{7} Z. Rucker.
11. Zachariah^{7} Gordon Rucker, moved to West.
12. Julia^{7} M. Rucker, d. young.
13. Ella^{7} Serena Rucker.
14. Ambrose^{7} Beasley Rucker, d. Nov. 20, 1849.

1. Mary^{7} Jane Rucker (Richard^{6}, Fielding^{5}, John^{4}, Cornelius^{3}, ———), b. June 22, 1821, m. May 21, 1836, W. H. Greer.

1. Mildred^{8} Greer.
2. Richard^{8} Greer.
3. Cerena^{8} Greer, m. 1st D. Poole, m. 2nd Eldridge Cook.
    1. Thomas^{9} Poole, m. 1st ——— Ogburn, m. 2nd ——— Baltman.
    2. Clara^{9} Cook.
4. Rebecca^{8} Greer, m. ——— Cook.
    1. Alice^{9} Cook.
    2. Rebecca^{9} Cook.
5. William^{8}, m. ——— Hays.
6. Durham^{8} Greer, m. Mary Hawks.
    1. Carrie^{9} May Greer.
7. Ella^{8} Greer, m. Jere Cartledge.

1. Matilda^9 Cartledge, m. J. S. Willis.
   1. Neal^{10} Willis.
   2. Julia^{10} Willis.
2. Julia^9 Cartledge, m. J. M. Webster.
   1. William^{10} Webster.
   2. Joseph^{10} Webster.

1. Mildred^8 Greer (Mary^7, Richard^6, Fielding^5, ——— Rucker), m. Franklin Singleton.

1. Oscar^9 S. Singleton, m. 1st Eulah Beal, m. second Louisa B. Singleton.
2. Cora^9 Singleton.
3. Lola^9 Singleton, m. Jere Cartledge.

Issue:
   1. Mildred^{10}, m. Luthur H. Medlock.
4. Nell^9 Singleton, m. John Mansfield.
   1. Franklin^{10} R., m. ——— Wise.
   2. Carrie^{10} Mansfield, m. Jackson Davis.
   3. Earl^{10} Mansfield.
   4. Dreer^{10} Mansfield.
   5. Russell^{10} Mansfield.
5. Annie^9 Singleton, m. Dr. W. Pumpelly.
6. William^9 Singleton.
7. Bess^9 Singleton.

3. James^7 Arden Rucker (Richard^6, Fielding^5, ———), b. Oct. 28, 1825, d. in the Battle of Sharpsburg, m. Jan. 30, 1845, Virginia King.

1. Emma^8 Rucker, d. unmarried.
2. James^8 Richard Rucker, went west.
3. Meula^8 Rucker, m. James Ely (seven children).

4. Rebecca^7 Rucker (Richard^6, Fielding^5, ———), b. Feb. 16, 1828, m. Dec. 23, 1845, Andrew Polkill Mitchell.

1. Alice^8 Judson Mitchell.
2. Mary^8 Virginia Mitchell.
3. Laura^8 T. Mitchell.
4. Sanders^8 D. Mitchell.
5. Edgar^8 P. Mitchell.

1. Alice^8 Judson Mitchell (Rebecca^7, Richard^6 Rucker), b. March 7, 1847, m. Dec. 13, 1875, Allen W. Walker.

1. Mary^9 Allen Walker, m. C. H. Monk.

2. Edwin[9] B. Walker, m. Mary Phelps.
    1. Allen[10] Phelps Walker.
3. Emmet[9] Walker.
4. Allen[9] Mack Walker.
5. Hugh[9] Walker.
6. Grady[9], m. Annie Thomasson.
7. Luther[9] Cary Walker.

2. Mary[8] Virginia Mitchell (Rebecca[7], Richard[6], Fielding[5], ——— Rucker), b. Sept. 24, 1849, m. Thomas Chapman.

1. Lila[9] May Chapman.
2. Augustus[9] Chapman, m. Harriot Medlock.
    1. Dorothy[10] Chapman.
    2. Sarah[10] Chapman.
    3. Augustus[10] M. Chapman, Jr.
    4. Joseph[10] M. Chapman.
3. Herbert[9] Clifton Chapman, m. Adah Williams.
    1. Herbert[10] C. Chapman, Jr.
4. Harry[9] DeWitt Chapman, m. Annie Clara Wynn.
    1. Anna[10] Clara Chapman.
    2. Harry[10] DeWitt Chapman, Jr.

3. Laura[8] T. Mitchell (Rebecca[7], Richard[6], Fielding[5], ——— Rucker), b. April 1, 1852, m. James R. Rawls.
Issue:

1. Matilda[9] Rawls.
2. J. Roy[9] Rawls, m. Nellie Lord.

    Issue:

    1. Allen[10] Rawls.
    2. Albert[10] Rawls.
    3. Polhill[10] Rawls.
3. Polhill[9] Rawls.

5. Edward[8] Denard Mitchell (Rebecca[7], Richard[6], Fielding[5], ——— Rucker), b. Nov. 19, 1858, m. Augusta Jones.

1. Lila[9] Mitchell.
2. Jones[9] Mitchell.

5. Lucinda[7] Elizabeth Rucker (Richard[6], Fielding[5], ———), b. April 5, 1830, m. Aug. 30, 1847, J. P. Illges.

1. Florence[8] Illges.
2. Charles[8] Illges, m. ——— Gates.
    1. Anne[9] Illges.

2. Raymond^{9} Illges, m. William Lanford.
    1. Richard^{10} H. Illges.
    2. George^{10} Illges, m. Violet Trippe.
    3. Ruby^{10} Illges.
    4. Paul^{10} Illges } twins.
    5. Pearl^{10} Illges } twins.
3. George^{8} Illges.
4. Lucile^{8} Illges, m. Patten Tollman.
    1. Florence^{9} Tollman.
    2. Charles^{9} Tollman, m. Filia Dawson.
    3. Pauline^{9} Tollman, m. Leo Jones.
        1. Lucile^{10} Jones.
        2. Dorothy^{10} Jones.
    4. Mary^{9} Tollman, m. John Metcalf.
    5. Richard^{9} M. Tollman.

7. Fielding^{7} Saunders Rucker (Richard^{6}, Fielding^{5}, ———), b. Talbot Co., Georgia, July 20th, 1834, d. July 6, 1894, Rome, Ga., m. Oct. 20, 1858, Mary Elizabeth Wynn (daughter of Thomas Harrison Wynn and wife, Temperance Huff, of Georgia).

1. Irene^{8} Julia Rucker, m. Dec. 28, 1882, James Thomas Tisinger, a lawyer of Thomaston, Ga.
    1. Louis^{9} Fielding Tisinger, m. Nov. 18, 1906, Matilda^{2} McCullen (Bryan^{1} McCullen and wife, Matilda, of Richmond, Va.
        1. Matilda^{10}, b. July, 1911.
2. Lucy^{8} Eloise Rucker, m. Aug. 11th, 1887, Azor Warner Van Hoose, president of Shorter College, Rome, Georgia.
3. Mary^{8} Alice, b. 1867, d. 1882.
4. Adelaide^{8} Rucker, m. Oct. 15, 1895, Herbert Black Tingley of New Brunswick, Canada.
    1. Mary^{9} Alice Tingley, b. 1896.

10. Richard^{7} J. Rucker (Richard^{6}, Fielding^{5}, John^{4}, ———), b. July 7, 1836, m. Emma Nance, Columbia, Georgia.

1. Lizzie^{8} H. Rucker, m. 1888, Edgar A. Story.
    1. John^{9} Latham Story.
    2. Augusta^{9} Story.
    3. Edgar^{9} A., Jr.
    4. Margaret^{9} Story.
    5. Elizabeth^{9} Story.

2. Laura[8] Eugenia Rucker.
3. Charles[8] L. Rucker.

13. Ella[7] Cerena Rucker (Richard[6], Fielding[4], ————), b. May 31st, 1849, m. Henry H. Caldwell in 1869 of Butler, Taylor Co., Georgia.

1. Eulah[8] M. Caldwell, b. Taylor County, Georgia, Nov. 1870, m. May 27th, 1888, J. S. Fuller.
   1. Richard[9] Fuller, d. in infancy.
   2. Henry[9] Grady, b. Nov., 1891.
   3. Cerena[9] A., b. 1894.
   4. Herbert[9] C., b. 1897.
   5. J.[9] C. Fuller, b. 1900.
   6. Eulah[9] M., b. 1903.
2. Ambrose[8] Beasley Caldwell, b. March 18th, 1873, m. 1892, ———— Austin of Columbus, Georgia.
   1. W. May[9] Caldwell, b. Mch. 15th, 1904.
   2. Eugene[9] E. Caldwell, b. Apr. 15th, 1907.
   3. Lila[9] M. Caldwell, b. Mch. 20th, 1910.
3. Henry[8] Fielding Caldwell, b. Oct. 29th, 1875.
4. Annie[8] Cerena Caldwell, b. Oct. 9, 1878, m. William Norman Sayer, 1908.
   1. Myriam[9] C. Sayer, b. September 10th, 1906.
   2. William[9] Norman Sayer, b. May 24th, 1909.
5. Julia[8] Rucker Caldwell, b. July 29th, 1880, m. 1st M. R. Eldridge, Jan., 1901, m. 2nd George D. Tuma, Nov., 1906.
   1. Maurice[9] Olga Eldridge, b. 1902.
   2. Drew[9] H. Tuma, b. Dec. 10, 1907.
6. Lucy[8] Eloise Caldwell, b. Jan. 22, 1883, m. Dec. 24, 1900, S. T. Gray of Butler, Georgia.
   1. Rucker[9] Gray, b. Sept. 2, 1902.
   2. Thelma[9] Gray.
7. Caddie[8] Beasley Caldwell, b. Jan. 26, 1886, m. 1906, C. E. Thornton, Columbus, Georgia.
   1. Carl[9] E. Thornton, b. April 17, 1907.
8. Richard[8] Rucker Caldwell, b. November 5th, 1888.
9. Lora[8] Belle Caldwell, b. Oct. 3, 1890, m. March 9, 1912, H. M. Cole of Birmingham, Alabama.

2. Joseph[5] Rucker (John[4], Cornelius[3], Thomas[2], Peter[1]), b. Jan. 5, 1788, d. Aug. 27, 1864, in Ruckersville, Georgia, at his home, Cedar Grove, m. Jan., 1812, Margaret Houston Speer of

Abbeville District, South Carolina, daughter of William Speers of Cherokee Falls, d. Sept. 5, 1864. Joseph Rucker was the first millionaire in Georgia, it is claimed.

The records of Elbert County of 1803 show that Joseph of Georgia appointed Benjamin Head of Madison, his attorney to collect his share of his grandfather's (John Tinsley) estate, from Sarah Tinsley, the Executor. See census of Elbert County, 1830-40.

He was the administrator under the will of his brother, Zachary Rucker, in 1835, Elbert County. Joseph was a banker.

Issue:

1. Tinsley[6] White Rucker.
2. Catherine[6] Rucker.
3. Martha[6] Rucker.
4. Mary[6] Rucker.
5. John[6] Rucker, graduated at University of Georgia in 1844. Moved to Florida, d. May 11th, 1850. Buried in Bonaventure, Savannah, Georgia.
6. William[6] Rucker, b. June, 1820, d. Ruckersville, Georgia.
7. Elbert[6] Marion Rucker.
8. Alexander[6] Randolph Rucker.

1. Tinsley[6] White Rucker (Joseph[5], John[4], Cornelius[3], ———), b. 1813, m. Sarah Elizabeth Harris, daughter of General Jeptha Harris, of Athens, Georgia. Graduated at the University of Georgia, 1833, and was a member of the State Legislature in 1836.

His plantation, Farm Hill, is very lovely.

1. Sarah[7] Margaret Rucker.
2. Jeptha[7] Rucker.
3. Georgia[7] Rucker.
4. Katie[7] Rucker.
5. Tinsley[7] Rucker.
6. Alexander C.[7] Rucker.

1. Sarah[7] Margaret Rucker (Tinsley[6], Joseph[5], John[4], Cornelius[3]), m. Augus McAlpin.

1. Ellen[8] McAlpin.
2. Georgia[8] McAlpin.
3. Florence[8], m. H. W. Johnson.
4. Sallie[8].

2. The Honorable Jeptha[7] H. Rucker (Tinsley[6], Joseph[5], Johu[4], Cornelius[3]), of Athens, Georgia, m. Virginia Lyon.

3. Georgia[7] Rucker (Tinsley[6], Joseph[5], John[4], Cornelius[3], ———), m. first: James M. Hall. Second: Dr. DeSaussure Ford, of Augusta.

Issue (by 1st mar.):
1. Dr. James[8] Meriwether Hull.
2. Asbury[8] Hull.

Issue (by 2nd mar.):
3. Frank[8] Gualdo Ford, m. George L. Baker, of Columbia, S. C.
4. Rucker[8] Ford.
5. DeSaussure Ford, Jr.

1. Dr. James[8] Meriwether Hull (Georgia[7], Tinsley[6], Joseph[5], ———), Athens, Georgia. Educated at Richmond Academy, Georgetown University and Bethany College. Graduated in Medicine at University of Georgia, 1879. Studied in Berlin and Vienna, m. May, 1916, Mary Lyon of Augusta.
1. Asbury[9] Hull.
2. James[9] M. Hull.
3. Mary[9] Hull.
4. Frank[9] Hull.
5. Lamar[9] Hull.
6. Georgia[9].

1. Asbury[9] Hull (James[8], Georgia[7], Tinsley[6], Joseph[5] Rucker), m. Martha Miller.
1. Katherine[10] Hull.
2. Mary[10].

2. James[9] M. Hull (James[8], Georgia[7], Tinsley[6], Joseph[5] Rucker), m. Marie Phinizy.
1. Stewart[10] Phinizy Hull.
2. Mary[10] Baldwin Hull.
3. James[10] M. Hull, III.

3. Mary[9] Hull (James[8], Georgia[7], Tinsley[6], ——— Rucker), m. Earle M. Kaminer of Columbia, South Carolina.
1. Frank[10] Gualdo Kaminer.
2. Mary[10] Hull.

4. Frank[9] Hull (James[8], Georgia[7], Tinsley[6], ——— Rucker), m. Marie Brooks.
1. Caroline[10] Lamar Hull.

6. Georgia[9] Hull (James[8], Georgia[7], Tinsley[6], ——— Rucker), m. R. Beverley Herbert, of Columbia, South Carolina.

   1. R. Beverly[10] Herbert, Jr.
   2. James[10] Hull Herbert.
   3. Georgia [10] Hull Herbert.
   4. Mary[10] Baldwin Herbert.

2. Asbury[8] Hull (Georgia[7], Tinsley[6], ——— Rucker), m. Alice Sibley.

   1. Emma[9] Georgia Hull, d. 1929, m. Andrew Perkins.
      1. Emma[10] Perkins.
      2. Andrew[10] Perkins.
   2. Jeptha[9] Hull.
   3. Alice[9] Hull.
   4. Asbury[9] Hull.

4. Rucker[8] Ford (Georgia[7], Tinsley[6], ——— Rucker), m. Laura Whisenant.

   1. Rucker[9] Ford, a daughter.

5. Tinsley[7] White Rucker, II (Tinsley[6], Joseph[5], John[4], Cornelius[3], ———), m. Sarah[3] M. Cobb (daughter of General Howell[2] Cobb, son of John[1] Cobb and Mildred Lewis), d. ———, 1926. He graduated at University of Georgia and represented his district in Congress.

   1. Tinsley[8] W. Tucker, III, Athens, Georgia, m. Elon Cason.
      1. Tinsley[9] W. Rucker, IV.
      2. Cason[9] Rucker.
      3. Embey[9] C. Rucker.
   2. Lamar[8] Rucker, m. Nita Black.
   3. Mary[8] Ann Rucker.
   4. Kate[8] B. Rucker, m. William Larkin Smith.

6. Alexander[7] C. Rucker (Tinsley[6], Joseph[5], ———), m. Carrie Simpson, Athens, Georgia.

   1. Sarah[8], m. Lamar Lyndon.
      1. Elizabeth[9] Lyndon.
      2. Moselle[9] Lyndon.

2. Catherine[6] Rucker (Joseph[5], John[4], ———), m. David S. White, moved to Mississippi.

   1. Eleanor[7] (d.)

2. Bertha[7] White, m. Thomas M. Durrett.
 1. Thomas[8] Durrett.
 2. Richard[8] Durrett.
 3. Agnes[8], m. William David Gilchrist.
  1. Mamie[9] Gilchrist.
3. Sara[7] Shelton White, m. R. M. Ruffin.
4. Margaret[7] White, m. Thomas Ruffin.

3. Martha[6] Rucker (Joseph[5], John[4], Cornelius[3], ——— Rucker), m. Richard Durrett.

1. Douglas[7] Durrett.
 1. William[8] Durrett.
 2. Thomas[8] Durrett.
2. Thomas[7] Joseph Durrett, m. Elizabeth Price.
3. Fannie[7] Margaret Durrett, m. William Harper.
 1. Richard[8] Harper.
 2. William[8] J. Harper.
 3. Ann[8] Yancy Harper.
 4. Thomas[8] S. Harper.
 5. Mary[8] E. Harper.
 6. Sallie[8] T. Harper.
 7. Alston[8] Harper.

2. William[8] J. Harper (Fannie[7], Martha[6], ——— Rucker), m. Genevieve Dean.

1. Marguerite[9] Harper.
2. Edwin[9] Harper.
3. Joseph[9] Rucker Harper.
4. Genevieve[9] Harper.
5. Edward[9] Harper.

4. Thomas[8] S. Harper (Fannie[7], Martha[6], ——— Rucker), m. Mattie Moon.

1. Edwin[9] J. Harper.
2. Addie[9] Harper.

5. Mary[8] E. Harper (Fannie[7], Martha[6], ——— Rucker), m. Irvine Denby.

1. Henry[9] Denby.
2. Marshall[9] Denby.

4. Kate[7] Rucker (Tinsley[6], Joseph[5], ———), m. Richard B. Baxter.

Issue:

1. John[8] S. Baxter, m. Mary Lawton.
2. Edgeworth[8] Bird, m. Ella B. Alexander.
   1. Vera[9] Baxter.
   2. Lucy[9] Baxter.
3. Sarah[8] E. Baxter, m. Lane Mullalley.
   1. Richard[9] B. Mallalley.
4. R.[8] B. Baxter, Jr., m. Sarah Cobb.
5. Georgia[8] Baxter, m. James Reid Boylston.
   1. Kate[9] Baxter.
   2. C.[9] DuBose Baxter.
   3. Elizabeth[9] Baxter.
6. Thomas[8] W. Baxter, m. Susan Boylston.
   1. Hallowell[9] Baxter.

4. Mary[6] Rucker (Joseph[5], John[4], Cornelius[3], Thomas[2], Peter[1]), b. Aug. 23, 1833, at Cedar Grove, d. Jan. 29, 1804, m. James S. Lamar, June 19, 1856, of Augusta, Georgia. They lived first at Cedar Grove, then in Augusta, where two of the children were born. (Later James S. Lamar married Sarah May Ford, daughter of Dr. Lewis Ford, of Augusta).

1. Joseph[7] Rucker Lamar.
2. Philip[7] Rucker.
3. Mary[7] Rucker.

1. Joseph[7] Rucker Lamar (Mary[6], Joseph[5], ——— Rucker), b. Oct. 14, 1857, d. 1916. He attended Bethany College, West Virginia, where he married, Jan. 30, 1879, Clarinda H. Pendleton, dau. of Dr. William K. Pendleton, president of the college. They lived there one year. In 1880 he returned to Augusta to practice law, making his home at "Sand Hills". In 1886 he was elected representative to the State Legislature. In 1902 he was appointed a justice of the Supreme Court of United States by President Taft. He died in Washington, Jan. 2, 1916, and was buried in Augusta.

1. Philip[8] Lamar, b. 1880, in West Virginia.
2. William[8] Pendleton Lamar, b. Oct., 1882.
3. Mary[8] Lamar, d. young.

7. Elbert[6] Marion Rucker (Joseph[5], John[4], Cornelius[3], ———) (June 15, 1828-Sept. 9, 1906), m. Nov. 3, 1853, Sarah Frances Harrison Whitner (Mch. 21, 1832-Jan. 24, 1924), dau. of Judge Joseph N. Whitner, of South Carolina. A graduate of the University of South Carolina, a signer of the Ordinance of Secession. Elbert was a member of the Southern Rights Con-

vention held at Milledgeville in 1851. Judge in South Carolina, lived at Ruckersville, Ga., and Anderson, S. C. A soldier of the Confederacy.

1. Elizabeth[7] Whitner Rucker.
2. Joseph[7] Rucker.
3. James[7] Harrison Rucker.
4. Elbert[7] Marion Rucker, Jr.
5. Guy[7] Glover Rucker, m. Lucia Herndon Hicks.

1. Elizabeth[7] Whitner Rucker (Elbert[6], Joseph[5], John[4], ———), m. David Sloan Taylor, Anderson, South Carolina.

1. Marion[8] Taylor.
2. Lucia[8] Taylor.
3. Tallulah[8] Eubank Taylor.
4. Rucker[8] Taylor.
5. Frank[8] Glover Taylor.

1. Marion[8] Taylor (Elizabeth[7], Elbert[6], ——— Rucker), m. John T. Ligon.

1. David[9] Ligon, m. Anne Wells.
2. Francis[9] Ligon, m. Lemuel Lawson.
3. John[9] Ligon.

2. Lucia[8] Taylor (Elizabeth[7], Elbert[6], Joseph[5], John[4], ——— Rucker), m. W. A. Hudgens, Captain U. S. A., A. E. F., killed in action Oct., 1918.

1. Elizabeth[9] Hudgens.
2. Margaret[9] Hudgens.
3. Wilma[9] Hudgens.
4. Lucia[9] Hudgens.
5. Thomas[9] Hudgens.

4. Rucker[8] Taylor (Elizabeth [7], Elbert[6], ——— Rucker), m. Nellie Harper.

1. Elizabeth[9] W. Taylor.
2. Anna[9] H. Taylor.

5. Frank[8] Glover Taylor (Elizabeth[7], Elbert[9], ——— Rucker), m. Sara Thornton.

1. Eubank[9] Taylor.
2. Joseph[9] Taylor.
3. Frank[9] Taylor.

2. Joseph[7] Rucker (Elbert[6], Joseph[5], John[4], ———), m. Addie Nash, Elbert Co., Georgia.

Issue:

1. Earle[8] Rucker.
2. Harley[8] Rucker.
3. Marion[8] Rucker.
4. Joseph[8] Rucker.
5. Genevieve[8] Rucker, m. ——— Fin Cannon.
6. Kathleen[8] Rucker, m. Robert Ingram.
7. Annie[8] Lee Rucker, m. Cliff Wheatley.

3. James[7] Harrison Rucker (Elbert[6], Joseph[5], John[4], ———), m. Elizabeth Wall (Elbert Co.)

1. Ella[8] Rucker.
2. Tacoa[8] Rucker.
3. Marion[8] Rucker.
4. James[8] Harrison Rucker.
5. William[8] Rucker.
6. Guy[8] Rucker.
7. Sara[8] Rucker, m. Duncan McIntyre.
8. Bessie[8] Rucker.
9. George[8] Rucker.
10. Lee[8] Rucker.
11. Juanita[8] Rucker.
12. Edith[8] Rucker.

4. Elbert[7] Marion Rucker (Elbert[6], Joseph[5], John[4], ———), b. Mch. 15, 1866, d. Aug. 16, 1926, m. Dec. 15, 1886, Susan Elizabeth Kinard, b. May 30, 1862, d. Sept. 22, 1923, A. B. and L. L. B. of University of South Carolina, a member of Chi Psi and Phi Beta Kappa Societies. A member of the General Assembly of South Carolina, 1900-10. Special associate justice of Supreme Court of South Carolina. Professor of law at University of South Carolina, 1910-26. He married second Mary Martin, Florence, Alabama.

Issue (by 1st marriage):

1. Elizabeth[8] Rucker, m. George Rainsford Norris, of Columbia, South Carolina.
   1. Grace[9] Waller Norris.
2. Louise[8] Rucker, m. William Webster Moore, Danville, Virginia.

8. Alexander[6] Randolph Rucker (Joseph[5], John[4], Cornelius[3], ———), m. June 22, 1859, Aurelia Calhoun, b. Sept. 22, 1836, Abbeville, South Carolina, daughter of John and Sarah Woodward Calhoun. No issue.

3. Martha[5] Rucker (John[4], Cornelius[3], ———), b. July 15, 1815, d. Oct. 11, 1847, buried at Ruckersville, Georgia.

6. William^5 Rucker (John^4, Cornelius^3, ———), m. Miss Manguin.

1. Mildred^6 Rucker, m. William Bowling White, Senator from Georgia.
   1. Tinsley^7 Rucker White.

1. Tinsley^7 Rucker White, d. Apr. 28, 1930, age 86, in Atlanta, and was buried in the cemetery at Van's Creek Church, at Ruckersville, Elberton Co., Ga. He m. Mary Mathews.

1. Cora^8 White, m. Lundy Harris. She has become very renowned through her clever writings, depicting human nature.
   1. Faith^9 Harris, now deceased.
2. Hope^8 White.

7. Judith^5 Rucker (John^4, Cornelius^3, ———), m. William B. Clark.

1. William^6 Joseph Clark.
2. Rebecca^6 Clark.

1. William^6 Joseph Clark (Judith^5, John^4, Cornelius^3, ———), m. Mrs. Allen, née Isabella Blackwell.

1. Elizabeth^7 M. Clark, m. Carr, Clarksburg, West Virginia.
2. W.^{7} P. Clark.
3. Overton^7 Tate Clark.
4. Mary^7 Frances Clark.
5. Joseph^7 Cornelia Clark.

4. Mary^7 Frances Clark (William^6, Judith^5, John^4, Cornelius^3, Rucker), m. William Willis Adams, of Elberton, Georgia.

1. William^8 C. Adams, m. Lou North.
   1. Emma^9 T. Adams.
2. Raymond^8 Adams.
3. Moses^8 Fleming Adams.
4. Marshall^8 M. Adams.
5. M. Willis^8 Adams.
6. Richard^8 Park Adams.
7. Samuel^8 Justice Adams.
8. Louis^8 F. Adams.
9. J.^{8} Freeman Adams.

2. Rebecca^6 Clark (Judith^5, John^4, Cornelius^3 Rucker), m. Overton Tate.

Issue:

1. William[7] Tate, m. Georgia Harper.
2. Asberry[7] Tate, m. Cora Thomas.
    1. Mary[8] Tate.
    2. Rebecca[8] Tate, m. B. J. Conyers.
        1. Benjamin[9] Conyers.
        2. Tate[9] Conyers.
3. Jane[7] Tate, m. Robert Wright.
    1. F.[8] T. Wright.
    2. Tate[8] Wright.
    3. Norma[8] Wright, m. H. E. Hawes.
    4. Robert,[8] Wright, Jr., m. Thelma Wright.
4. Mary[7] Mildred Tate, m. Eugene Hewitt.
    1. Sallie[8] M. Hewitt, m. L. A. Harper.
        1. William[9] Harper.
        2. Augustus[9] Harper.
        3. Hewitt[9] Harper.
        4. Sarah[9] Harper.
        5. Rebecca[9] Harper.
        6 Madge[9] Harper.

8. Zachary[5] Rucker (John[4], Cornelius[3], ———), d. in Elbert Co., Georgia, in 1835. Leaving children. His brother, Joseph, was appointed administrator of his estate. From the following court record we know he had at least one son, Joseph[6] Rucker, further search may prove other children.

Joseph Rucker, Administrator of Estate of Zachary Rucker, deceased, 1835, made the following returns to court:

To William White, $63.43¾; William B. White, $40.00; Johnson Mabry, $3.00; John Beck, $11.00; Thomas F. Gibbs, $5.00.

Paid Charles Reynolds by Joseph Rucker, Guardian for Joseph Rucker, a Minor, of Zachary Rucker, deceased, $4.75 for schooling, which is in full, 31st July, 1835.

Ordinary Office, Book P, folios 134, 135, 136, Elbert Co., Georgia.

9. Elizabeth[5] Rucker (John[4], Cornelius[3]), m. William Hinton Alston, Jan. 25, 1820.

1. Elizabeth[6] Alston, m. William E. DuBose.
    1. Mary[7] Ellen DuBose, m. Perry Spencer.
    2. Adelle[7], m. Donaldson Huff.
2. Amanda[6] Alston, m. Col. Edward S. Ott.
    1. Anna[7] Ott, m. Agustus H. Alston.

2. Elizabeth[7] Ott, m. James H. Drake.
   1. James[8] H. Drake.
   2. Edward[8] Ott Drake.
   3. Mary[8] F. Drake, m. J. I. Pritchett.
   4. John[8] C. Drake.
   5. Amanda[8] A. Drake, m. James M. Cecil.
   6. Nicholas[8] Drake.
3. Mildred[7] Ott, m. Dr. David Miller.
4. Charity[7] A. Ott, m. John Tavner.

10. Mildred[5] Rucker (John[4], Cornelius[3], ———), m. James M. Blackwell.

1. Cornelia[6] Blackwell.
2. Elizabeth[6] Blackwell.
3. Joseph[6] Blackwell.
4. Sarah[6] Rebecca Blackwell.
5. Kate[6] Blackwell.
6. Jane[6] Blackwell.

5. Peter[3] Rucker (Thomas[2], Peter[1]), b. Orange Co., Va., d. Mississippi. Thomas Rucker deeded to "Son Peter of Culpeper Co., 122 acres in Culpeper, land whereon Jacob is now living." 15 Mch., 1759 (D. B. C, p. 169) Culpeper.

Peter Rucker and wife, Sarah, of Bloomfield Parish, Culpeper Co., sold to Michael Ehart, of the same, for £45, 181 acres in Culpeper, "whereupon Jacob Hubbard now lives," adjoining Joseph Henderson, James Alexander, Joseph Rucker, George Rucker, and Michael Ehart. Signed, Peter Rucker, Sarah Rucker. Witness: William Walker, John Gibbs, Jonathan Underwood, James Finney. Feb. 10, 1775 (D. B. I, p. 415) Culpeper. Recorded May 15, 1775.

Peter evidently did not live on the above land owning others, from a deed recorded, 1775, he sold the land he resided on adjoining William Offells, Ephraim Rucker and Isaac Tinsley (D. B. B, p. 301) Culpeper.

Henning's statutes mentioned Peter Rucker, of Culpeper, as furnishing supplies to the county militia of Culpeper in 1755. Also, on Apr. 14, 1757, the General Assembly of Virginia mentions "services rendered by Peter Rucker".

In the French and Indian War, Peter Rucker and William Nalle, Jr., served under Captain Robert Slaughter. They were paid for services rendered, September, 1758. (*Virginia Colonial Militia*).

On Jan. 25, 1773, Peter Rucker, of Culpeper, mortgaged 185 acres to John Rucker, of Orange, (brother), for £50, to secure a debt. The mortgage was paid the next year. Witness: May Burton, Jr., William Rucker, George Rucker.

Peter Rucker served in Pennsylvania at Fort Pitt, during the Revolutionary War. Afterwards he and wife, Sarah, moved to Mississippi and settled on the River Mississippi below Natchez.

1. Jonathan[4] Rucker.
2. Katherine[4].
3. Susanna[4].
4. William[4].

1. Jonathan[4] and wife, Ann Rucker, patented 255 acres of land on Pearl River, Louisiana.

4. William[4] Rucker was granted 500 acres in Feleciona Parrish, La., to the "heirs of William Rucker, out of Public Lands. 4 Aug., 1806". (Survey No. 6).

6. William[3] Rucker (Thomas[2], Peter[1]), d. May 20, 1819, in Madison Co., Va., m. ———[4] Smith, dau. of Isaac Smith and wife, Margaret[3] Rucker, of Madison Co. (See p. 170).

William[3] Rucker bought 150 acres of land from Stephen Southern and wife, Margaret, of Culpeper Co., and Francis Vawter, land in Culpeper on the forks of Conway and Stanton Rivers, adjoining William Kirtley and Francis Conway. Witness: George Anderson, Isaac Smith, William Smith, Downing Rucker Smith. (D. B. F, p. 332), Sept. 12, 1771, Culpeper. Later he bought more land in the same place.

In the land and personal tax books of Culpeper, he is mentioned as "William Sen", "William Jaw Bones", "William, son to Thomas[1]" and "William (J. Bones) Sen"; to distinguish him from his 1st cousin, "William, son to William". See the tax list copied from the original tax book of Culpeper in Richmond, Va., given under (William[3], William[2], Peter[1] Rucker, p. 243).

In 1782 he is paying on 300 acres, but in 1794 John Leatherer is paying on 33 acres of William Rucker's and William is paying on only 267. He continued to pay on the 267 acres until his death in 1819.

Will of William[3] Rucker, May 20, 1818, Sept., 1820. He directs his land and all of the rest of his estate to be sold, and after all of his debts are settled, the money to be divided among his children: sons, Joel, Benjamin, Jarvis; daus., Fannie and Eleanor. "My two daughters, Sally Warren and Nancy Carter, having received legacies from their grandfather, Isaac Smith, and Benjamin Smith, their uncle, amounting to more than I have given to my other children, I have thought proper to give them no part of my estate." Executor: George H. Allen. Witness: Robert

Briggs, William Burnett, Charles Hume (W. B. I, p. 1) Madison.

George H. Allen, administrator of the estate of William Rucker, dec'd, gave bond with William Early, Sec. Dec. 16, 1819.

Ambrose[4] Booten (Tomagen[3], Ephraim[2], Peter[1] Rucker), bought all of William Rucker's land, Jan. 8, 1826, for $3,057,45. He sold 59½ acres of it to Jarvis Rucker, son of William, for $589, land adjoining Henry Rose (D. B. 9, p. 105), Madison Co. Henry Rose bought 100 acres of the above land of William Rucker.

1. Joel[4] Rucker.
2. Benjamin[4], m. July 10, 1795, Mrs. Nancy (Herndon) Carter.
3. Jarvis[4].
4. Sally[4].
5. Fanny[4].
6. Nancy[4].
7. Nelly[4].

1. Joel[4] Rucker (William[3], Thomas[2], Peter[1]), m. Amy Young, 1791, in Culpeper Co. He paid a personal tax in Madison from 1793 for 2 years. In 1795 he appears in Bath Co., until 1807, and paying a land tax on 75 acres of land until 1815.

This 75 acres was deeded to Joel in 1803, by Samuel Young, of Bath, for $1.00, land lying on the branches of the Greenbriar River, being a part of a patent of 468 acres, made by Samuel Young and wife, Mary. (D. B. 2, p. 555), Bath.

In 1807 he appears on the personal tax books of Kanawha Co., West Virginia, and continues there. On Feb. 28, 1815, Joel Rucker, of Kanawha Co., of State of West Virginia, sold to James Young, of Bath, for $100.00, 75 acres being part of 116 acres, land in Bath on the Swego Creek, branch of Great River, land patented by James Young. (D. B. 4, p. 472) Bath.

Joel was in the war of 1812, enlisted from Kanawha Co., under Capt. John Willson's Co. of Riflemen, under Col. John Ambler, 2nd Regiment, 1st Brigade. Discharged in Richmond, Va., Dec. 1814 (*History Of Kanawha County,* by Atkinson, p. 332).

3. Jarvis[4] Rucker (William[3], Thomas[2], Peter[1]) (1779-1837), m. June 10, 1810, Mildred Grayson (dau. of William), d. 1862. Jarvis bought 59½ acres of his father's land from Ambrose Booten in 1826. He lived, died and was buried on this place, near Hood, Madison Co., Va. He paid his first personal tax in 1804.

1. Peachy[5] Rucker.
2. Ambrose[5].
3. Smith[5].
4. Julia[5].
5. Mary[5].
6. Frank[5].
7. John[5].

1. Peachy[5] Rucker (Jarvis[4], William[3], Thomas[2]) (Aug. 13, 1811-Aug. 30, 1899), m. 1st, Powell; 2nd, Wilhoit

Issue (by 1st mar.):

1. Gabriel[6] Powell.
2. Susan[6].

Issue (by 2nd mar.):

3. Henry[6] Wilhoit.
4. Eliza[6].
5. Mary[6].
6. Martha[6], m. Roberts.
7. Henrietta[6], m. Van Winkle.
8. George[6].

2. Ambrose[5] Rucker (Jarvis[4], William[3]), m. Sept. 28, 1843, Catherine Ruth Karon.

1. Sarah[6] Elizabeth Rucker, b. Aug. 14, 1844.
2. James[6] Henry, b. Dec. 24, 1849.
3. Benjamin[6] Franklin, b. Dec. 27, 1851.
4. Martha[6] Ophelia, b. Nov. 18, 1853.
5. Walter[6] Raleigh, b. Apr. 15, 1855.
6. Lee[6] Madison, b. Apr. 24, 1857.
7. Owen[6] Dale, b. Jan. 6, 1859.
8. Louise [6] Virginia, b. May 10, 1861.
9. Ida[6], b. Aug. 17, 1863, m. Roberts.

3. Smith[5] Rucker (Jarvis[4], William[3]) (June 15, 1815-Mch. 27, 1906), m. Ellen Anderson.

1. James[6] F. Rucker, b. Feb. 29, 1840.
2. Emma[6].

4. Julia[5] Rucker (Jarvis[4]), b. Mch. 15, 1813, m. June 5, 1836, Frederick Lane.

1. Francis[6] Lane (Apr. 20, 1837-1922).
2. Thomas[6] J., b. Feb. 7, 1841.
3. John[6] Westly.
4. Clara[6] W., b. May 16, 1844, m. Bently.

Issue:

5. Alice[6] A., b. Mch. 20, 1846.
6. O.[6] P., b. May 7, 1848.
7. Peachy[6] Ellen, b. Dec. 10, 1849.
8. Mary[6] Agnes, b. Oct. 5, 1851.
9. Parthenia[6] Maud, b. Sept. 2, 1853.
10. Frank[6], b. Jan. 12, 1856.
11. Julia[6] Ann, b. Mch. 25, 1859.

3. John[6] Westly Lane (Julia[5], Jarvis[4], William[3] Rucker) (Sept. 11, 1842-Nov. 21, 1923), m. Martha J. Richards.

    1. Julia[7] Lane, m. E. M. Harter.
        1. Westly[8] Harter.
        2. Richard[8].
        3. Alice[8].
        4. Dorothy[8].
    2. Arthur[7] Lane.
    3. Bertha[7], m. Rev. M. L. Webb.
        1. John[8] Lane Webb.
    4. Leon[7] Lane.
        1. Edward[8] Lane.
        2. Martha[8].

4. Clara[6] W. Lane (Julia[5], Jarvis[4], William[3] Rucker), m. ——— Bentley.

    1. Nettie[7] Bentley, b. Mch. 12, 1865, m. ——— Shepardson.
        1. Mildred[8] Shepardson.
        2. Grayson[8].
    2. Maude[7] Agnes, b. Dec. 12, 1867.
    3. Alice[7], b. Apr. 3, 1870, m. ——— Rendlen.
    4. John[7] Williams, b. Jan. 23, 1880.
    5. Bess[7], b. July 7, 1882.

5. Mary[5] Rucker (Jarvis[4], William[3]), m. George Footney.

    1. Lutie[6] Footney.
    2. Annie[6].

6. Frank[5] Rucker (Jarvis[4]) (1820-Nov. 5, 1890), m. Sarah A. Herndon.

    1. William[6] W. Rucker, b. Sept. 6, 1854.
        1. Edith[7] Rucker.
    2. John[6] W.
    3. Ann[6] Maria, b. Mch. 15, 1859.
    4. Thomas[6] F., b. May 20, 1861.

5. George[6] A., b. Dec. 22, 1863.
6. Robert[6] E. L., b. Aug. 15, 1865, m. Mattie ———.
    1. John[7] Rucker.
    2. Mary[7].
7. Walter[6].
8. Mary[6] Susan.
9. James[6] Clinton, b. Apr. 2, 1873.
10. Joseph[6] C.

2. John[6] W. Rucker (Frank[5], Jarvis[4], William[3]) (July 20, 1854-May 9, 1893), m. Matilda Stockdale.

1. Percy[7] Rucker.
    1. Ethel[8] Rucker.
2. Elizabeth[7] Rucker, m. 1st ——— Downey, 2nd ——— Ward of Newark, N. J.
    1. Gladys[8].
    2. Irene[8].
    3. Earl[8].

7. Walter[6] Rucker (Frank[5], Jarvis[4]), b. Oct. 22, 1867, m. Ada ——— of Shenandoah, Va.

1. Frank[7] Rucker.
2. Lee[7].
3. Beulah[7].
4. Blanch[7].

8. Mary[6] Susan Rucker (Frank[5]), b. Aug. 17, 1870, m. Apr. 6, 1893, Charles Osborn.

1. Margaret[7] Osborn, m. ——— Dolley.
    1. Ruth[8] Dolley.
2. Charles[7] Osborn.

10. Joseph[6] C. Rucker (Frank[5]), b. July 25, 1874, m. Sudie Eppard.

1. William[7] Rucker.
2. Everett[7], of Washington, D. C.
    1. George[8] Rucker.
3. Lucille[7].
4. Rosalyn[7].
5. Ray[7].
6. Joseph[7].

7. John[5] Rucker (Jarvis[4], William[3], Thomas[2]) (Mch. 24, 1826-Mch 24, 1887), m. Dec. 24, 1849, Mary Jane Smith.

1. Mary[6] Rucker.
2. Sarah[6], m. Sept. 21, 1853; m. John Bernhart.
    1. Bertie[7] Bernhart.
    2. Annette[7].

3. Virginia^{6}, b. June 2, 1856;m. Apr. 9, 1872, Alexander Smith.
   1. Ethel^{7} Aurora Smith, b. Mch. 19, 1876, m. Oct. 26, 1905, William W. Johnson, Jamestown, Ohio.
4. Clinton^{6}.
5. William^{6}.
6. Rose^{6} (July 23, 1868-1892), m. John^{6} W. Bolton.
7. Alice^{6}.
8. Lee^{6} Franklin, d. 1889, m. Lucy Culver.
9. Birdie^{6} Maye (Nov. 15, 1871-June 11, 1920), m. ———— McBride.
10. Annie^{6} Laurie, b. Sept. 15, 1873, m. Leary White Parker.

1. Mary^{6} Rucker (John^{5}, Jarvis^{4}, William^{3}), b. Jan. 6, 1851, m. 1st Jessie Ellis, 2nd A. J. Crow.

   1. Ora^{7} Jay, b. Sept. 25, 1869; m. 1st May Hartzeer, 2nd Velma Wright of Kansas, Mo.
   2. Grace^{7}, b. Oct. 26, 1882, m. Jan. 3, 1903, Charles Johnson of Danville, Ill.

4. Clinton^{6} Rucker (John^{5}, Jarvis^{4}), b. Mch. 11, 1858, m. Sadie Drummond, Warrenburg, Mo.

   1. Grace^{7} Rucker.
   2. Pearl^{7}.
   3. Mable^{7}.
   4. Drummond^{7}.

5. William^{6} Rucker (John^{5}), b. May 5, 1860, m. 1st ——— Watkins, 2nd Ellen Wheeler.

   1. Willard^{7} Rucker.
   2. El^{7} Mae.
   3. Wheeler^{7}.
   4. Fay^{7}.

7. Alice^{6} Rucker (John^{5}, Jarvis^{4}, William^{3}) (Mch. 30, 1863-1889), m. Henry^{7} Hitt (Mary^{6}, Henry^{5}, Sally^{4}, Wm.^{3} Rucker).

   1. Charles^{7} Leslie Hitt, b. May 16, 1883, m. May 16, 1917, Caroline May, lived in Baltimore, Md.
      1. Alice^{8} May Hitt.

4. Sally^{4} Rucker (William^{3}, Thomas^{2}, Peter^{1}), m. Feb. 20, 1808, James Warren.

Will of Isaac Smith dated Aug. 18, 1801, bequeathed to "My grand daughter, Sara Rucker, daughter of William Rucker, a tract of 113 acres adjoining Jeremiah Rucker, Joel Graves, Job Breeden, and John Delany" (W. B. 1, p. 344), Madison Co., Va.

Will of Benjamin Smith, dated May 20, 1808, Madison County, mentions "My nephews and nieces", Jarvis, Joel, Benjamin, Sally, Fannie, Ellen, and Nancy Rucker.

Issue of Sally Rucker Warren:

1. Pamelia^{5} Warren.
2. Henry^{5}.

1. Pamelia^{5} Warren (Sally^{4}, William^{3}, Thomas^{2} Rucker), m. Abraham Taylor.
   1. Lou^{6} W. Taylor, m. ——— Fletcher.
      1. Irma^{7} Fletcher. 2. Mamie^{7}. 3. Wilber^{7}.
   2. Alvin^{6} Taylor, m. Mattie ———.
      1. Corra^{7} Taylor.
   3. Jennie Taylor, m. ——— Dimond.

2. Henry^{5} Warren (Sally^{4}, William^{3} Rucker).
   1. Mary^{6} Warren, d. 1891, m. ——— Hitt.
      1. Henry^{7} Hitt, m. Alice^{6} Rucker (John^{5}, Jarvis^{4}, Wm.^{3}) (see p. ....).

5. Fannie^{4} Rucker (William^{3}, Thomas^{2}), m. Oct. 22, 1815, Henry Rose in Madison Co.
   1. Ellen^{5} Jane Rose, m. John Gallihugh.
      1. Lavassa^{6} B. Gallihugh.
      2. John^{6} Catlett.
      3. William^{6} E. (Feb. 11, 1855-Sept. 10, 1923), m. Sept. 8, 1881, Mattie Huckstep.
   2. William^{5} Rose, d. 1846.

6. Nancy^{4} Rucker (William^{3}, Thomas^{2}), m. June 26, 1798, Thomas^{7} Carter, Madison Co. Her uncle, Benjamin Smith left her a legacy in his will, also her grandfather, Isaac Smith.

7. Eleanor^{4} Rucker (William^{3}, Thomas^{2}), m. Feb. 28, 1817, DeWitt Rucker (of line of James^{2}), and lived in Greenbrier Co., W. Va.

7. Mulden^{3} Rucker (Thomas^{2}, Peter^{1}), is only mentioned in the Orange or Culpeper records twice: (1) as a witness to a deed in 1764, "Thomas Chew sold 11 acres of land to Thomas Rucker of Culpeper for ten shillings." This land Thomas Sr. verbally gave to his son, Thomas Jr. Witness: William Rucker and Mulden Rucker; (2) in his father's will.

12. Estha^{3} Rucker (Thomas^{2}, Peter^{1}), d. June 2, 1779, leaving her property to her sister, Frances Rucker; her brothers, William and James were executors (W. B. B, p. 343), Culpeper.

13. Frankey^{3} Rucker (Thomas^{2}), m. William Alexander, Aug. 21, 1782. George Eve was the minister officiating. Culpeper Co., Va. He may have moved to Ga.

CHAPTER FIVE

Elizabeth Rucker

4. Elizabeth[2] Rucker (Peter[1]), married James Pierce. James died in 1778. Will in Orange County mentions wife, Elizabeth, and children, July, Edith, Jeremiah, Francis, Peachy and Elizabeth. Executor, Minor Rucker (W. B. 5, p. 213, Orange County, Va.).

Issue:

1. July[3] Pierce.
2. Edith[3] Pierce.
3. Jeremiah[3] Pierce.
4. Francis[3] Pierce.

CHAPTER SIX

Margaret Rucker

5. Margaret[2] Rucker (Peter[1]), b. in Essex Co. Va. was living in 1776, m. Isaac Tinsley a neighbor, they lived in what is now Madison Co. Va. and later moved to Amelia Co. Va., in 1758. Thomas Jackson of Spottsylvania sold to Isaac Tinsley of King and Queen, 100 acres of land adjoining the land of Sarah Tinsley (mother?) bought by Jackson of Joseph Berry of King and Queen Co., Apr. 17, 1727 (D. B. 18, p. 298, Spots. Co.).

John Rucker of Orange deeded to Margaret 100 acres in Orange Co. 17 May, 1730 (D. B. I, p. 270, Orange Co.). Thomas Jackson of St. Marks Parish sold to Isaac Tinsley of same county, 100 acres of land at Crawford's Corner on the Rapidan River, June 17, 1735 (D. B. 5, p. 47, Orange).

Peter Rucker devised to his dau. Margaret Tinsley a slave named Yorkshire, ten years later after the death of Elizabeth this slave Yorkshire was delivered to Isaac Tinsley. On March 14, 1759 Isaac Tinsley of Amelia Co. deeded to Isaac Tinsley of Brumfield Parish Culpeper "For love and Affection to my son" 100 acres of land in Culpeper on the Rapidan River (D. B. C, p. 338, Culpeper).

On the same day Isaac sold to Ephraim Rucker 100 acres of land on Elk Run in the forks of the Rapidan and Robison Rivers. David Parish of King William Co. sold to Isaac and Thomas Tinsley of Rawleigh Parish, Amelia Co., 200 acres of land in Amelia Co., adjoining William Shem Cook, James Hurt, and Hester Truley, "To the said Isaac and Thomas Tinsley and to the heirs of said Thomas." Feb. 26, 1756 (D. B. 5, p. 405, Amelia Co.). One of Margaret's son born in Orange Co., in 1749 was a minister and had a charge in Albemarle Co. in 1770, later moved to Savanna Ga. settling near Augusta, where he died in 1801.

Will of Isaac Tinsley of Amelia Co. Va. "A member of the Baptist Church of Christ, on Sandy Creek", being well stricken in Years. To my wife Margaret Tinsley three negroes named Yorkshire and Nannie his wife, and old Jane, the rest of my property to be divided among my Children. Executors: William Ford. Joseph Jackson. Joshua Chaffin.

Wit: David White, Samuel Allen, David Tinsley. Dated 13 Mch. 1776. Probated 22 Aug. 1777.

CHAPTER SEVEN

William Rucker

6. William[2] Rucker (Peter[1]), was born in Essex County, and died in Amelia, 1794. In 1734, Essex County, he witnessed a deed between Richard Mauldin of Spotsylvania Co., and Edward Tinsley, of King and Queen Co.

In June of the same year, his brother, John, of Spotsylvania County, deeded to him two hundred acres of land in St. Mark's Parish, Spotsylvania Co.

In 1737 William Pierce sold to William Rucker one hundred acres of land in St. Marks Parish, Orange Co. in line of the patent granted to John Rucker adjoining George Eastham and Thomas Rucker. (William Rucker sold this land to John Powell in 1741.)

September, 1737, John Garth paid to William Rucker five hundred and thirty pounds of tobacco for coming as a witness, "80 miles twice," to Caroline Co. Court.

In 1742 William and his wife, Honar, sold land in Elk Run, Orange Co. to Michael Holt.

The next year he sold one hundred acres to William Henderson which consisted of land adjoining John Rucker's in St. Thomas Parish in the Little Fork between Rappahannock and Robinson Rivers on Muddy Creek. Witness: Ephraim Rucker (D. B. 7, page 231, Orange).

William bought one hundred and twenty-three acres of land from Thomas Rucker, both of St. Thomas Parish, Orange Co., on Aug. 22nd, 1747. Witness: Bartholomus Vawter and Ephraim Rucker (D. B. 11, page 18, Orange Co.).

In 1749, he sold one hundred and ninety-three acres of land to William Twyman, "Land received by inheritance". Wife, Honar, joins in the deed (D. B. A, p. 117, Culpeper Co.).

1750 Henry Downs and Thomas Jackson sold to William Rucker, of Culpeper, One hundred acres of land, lying in Culpeper, also a grist mill on the Rapidan River.

William, of St. Marks Parish, Culpeper, bought two hundred acres of land in Rawleigh Parish, Amelia County on July 27, 1758, from Micajah Turner of Southam Parish, Cumberland Co. (D. B. 6, p. 367, Amelia Co.).

In 1758 Tesiah Meador of Cumberland Co. sold to William Rucker of St. Marks Parish, Culpeper Co., fifty acres of land in Rawleigh Parish (D. B. 6, p. 370, Amelia Co.).

In 1762 William and Honar of Amelia, sold to James Collins two hundred acres of land in Culpeper, on the Rapidan River.

In 1767 Thomas Munford sold to William Rucker of Amelia Co., three hundred and fifty acres of land on Sandy Creek, adjoining Bently and Thomas Munford.

William and Honar begin in 1771 to sell their land. First they sell one hundred acres in Amelia to Benjamin Hendrick which was the land "Gidion Rucker lived upon".

The same year he sold forty acres to Judith Bently (D. B. 11, p. 373, Amelia). Witness: Elisha Rucker, Joshua Rucker, Sarah Rucker.

He also sold one hundred and fifty acres to Joseph Jackson, and sixty acres to William Claybrook.

In 1779 he sold to William Gray of Powhatan, One hundred and twenty acres of land on Sandy Creek, adjoining Joshua Rucker's land.

The following year, "William for love and affection" deeds to son, Joshua, one hundred and thirty acres of land adjoining William Winston. William paid a personal tax until 1788, but did not die until 1794.

The first personal tax of Amelia mentions in 1782 William, Pleasant, Mordecai, and Joshua Rucker. Some of the sons and grandsons lived in N. C. and S. C.

William left no will, therefore it is impossible to know exactly which are his sons. Some of his descendants have family records to prove their descent. The Ruckers of the proper age, living in Amelia, we are supposing to be his sons. With that supposition we have:

Issue:

1. Gideon[3] Rucker.
2. Joshua[3] Rucker.
3. William[3] Rucker.
4. Elisha[3] Rucker.
5. Mordecai[3] Rucker.
6. Joseph[3] Rucker.
7. James[3] Rucker.

A Benjamin Rucker of Amelia served in the war of 1812 as Lieutenant under Captain Samuel B. Jeter's company of artillery, 7th regiment (18 August, 1814).

1. Gideon[3] Rucker (William[2], Peter[1]), born in Orange in 1737. Married in Amelia, Feb. 9, 1762, Elizabeth Cook, daughter of John Cook, security James Tinsley (she may have been his

cousin). Later Gideon and the Cooks moved to Pittsylvania (D. B. 4, page 43, Pittsylvania Co.). "John Cook deeded to Gideon Rucker, son-in-law for love and affection, one hundred acres of land on Crab tree Forks of Snow Creek, July 28th, 1774. Pittsylvania Co.

They lived at first in Amelia County. (D. B., page 188), of Amelia County states "William and Honar Rucker sold to Benjamin Hendricks, Jr. 100 acres of land in Amelia Co., the same upon which Gideon Rucker lately lived. Jan. 23, 1771. Witness: James Rucker.

Gideon was paid for three rifles, sold to Captain Dillards for his "Minute Men" (Revolutionary War, 1410, Virginia Historical Magazine, Vol. 12).

In 1777 Gideon Rucker of Henry County took the oath of Allegiance, September 13th, age 40 years.

2. Joshua[3] Rucker (William[2], Peter[1]), born in Culpeper. In 1780 William[2] Rucker deeded one hundred and thirty acres to his son Joshua[3]. This land Joshua sold to Richard Webber, land on Sandy Creek, in 1784. In 1807 Joshua[3] deeded to his son Reuben[4] twenty-eight acres of land in Amelia County. Witness: Pleasant Rucker (D. B. 22, page 313, Amelia County).

Nov., 1809. The heirs of Joshua[3] Rucker deceased, sold to Reuben Rucker (son of Joshua) for $25.00 each, their share in their father's land, one hundred and twenty-two acres. Signed: Lemuel Rucker, wife Polly, Pleasant Rucker, wife Elizabeth, John Martin, wife Sally, Jesse Martin, wife Christiana, William Butler, wife Martha, Lucy. Joshua Rucker, moved to South Carolina.

Joshua Rucker of Amelia bought 150 acres of land for 1500 lbs. of tobacco, of Moses Morris, land adjoining Pauline Anderson, William Tarpley, Benjamin Hendricks and Tabitha Morris. 13 Oct. 1785 (D. B. 17, p. 357, Amelia).

The tax receipts of 1782 of Amelia, charges Joshua Rucker with one hundred and fifty acres of land.

The census of that year finds him paying tax on "9 whites" and one slave.

This Joshua[3] served in the Revolutionary War. (See Auditors Accounts, Virginia 22, page 77, Archives, Richmond, Virginia). Settlement of Joshua's estate, 10 Jan. 1809 (W. B. 7, p. 445).

1. Reuben[4] Rucker.
2. Polly[4] Rucker.
3. Pleasant[4] Rucker.

4. Sally^{4} Rucker, m. John Martin, 1804, Amelia Co.
5. Christiana^{4} Rucker, m. Jesse Martin, 1805, Amelia Co.
6. Martha^{4} Rucker, m. Wm. Butler (2nd wife), 1805.
7. Lucy^{4} Rucker, m. John Milton, 1814, Amelia Co.
8. Joshua^{4} Rucker.

1. Reuben^{4} Rucker (Joshua^{3}, William^{2}, Peter^{1}), m. Dec. 20, 1793, in Amelia Co. Susanna^{2} Kelley (Elisha^{1}). Security John Rucker.

In 1807 he bought twenty-eight acres of land for fifty-three pounds sterling from his father, Joshua (Amelia Co.). Witness: James Hendricks, Jr., Pleasant Rucker.

In 1810 he bought the stock and house-hold furniture from his brother-in-law, William Butler (D. B. 22, page 313, Amelia Co.).

In 1809 Reuben bought from his sisters and brothers, one-hundred and twenty-two acres, the remaining tract of land owned by his father, Joshua (D. B. 23, page 133, Amelia Co., Virginia).

Four years later he sold to his brother, Pleasant, the one-hundred and twenty-two acre tract bought from his brothers and sisters. Land in Amelia.

He paid his first personal tax in 1793‘.

From the census of Amelia Co., 1810, Reuben's age was under 45.

Sally Rucker's age, under 26, Lemuel Rucker's age, under 45.

2. Polly^{4} Rucker (Joshua^{3}, William^{2}, Peter^{1}), married Lemuel Rucker, 1st cousin (son of William^{3}, William^{2}, Peter^{1}), Dec. 8, 1792. Security Joshua Rucker, Amelia Co.

They lived for a while in Amelia. Dec. 22, 1803, Levi Deaton's estate was settled, and in the report it was stated that on April 6, cash had been paid to Lemuel Rucker of Amelia.

Lemuel was paying a personal tax in Amelia in 1793. He died before the will was made by his father, William of Georgia in 1834, which mentions "Heirs of Lemuel deceased."

3. Pleasant^{4} Rucker (Joshua^{3}, William^{3}, Peter^{1}), d. June, 1860. The will of Pleasant Rucker mentions having married twice, and having two lots of children, but does not give their names (W. B. 18, page 389, Amelia Co., Virginia).

In settling his estate June 27, 1860, cash was paid to his son, Harvey.

Pleasant bought from his brother, Reuben, one hundred and twenty-two acres of land for $337.00, whereon Reuben now resides (D. B. 23, p. 559, Amelia Co.).

On Feb. 6, 1823, Pleasant Rucker and wife, Nancy, sold to Herbert Eans, forty acres of land, adjoining Pleasan's. Four years later Pleasant sold sixty-three acres more to Herbert Eans, land in Amelia. He married 1st: 1808, Betsy Farly; 2nd: 1833, Nancy^{2} Walden, dau. of John Walden.

Issue:

1. John^{5} Harvey Rucker (son of Nancy Walden), possibly others.

1. John^{5} Harvey Rucker (Pleasant^{4}, Joshua^{3}, William^{2}, Peter^{1}), of Amelia County, m. 1st, at the age of 26, Martha M. Hendrick, Jan. 11, 1860 dau. of Walter and Mary Hendrick. He m. 2nd at the age of 39 Ellen E. Scott, dau. of Edwin and M. E. Scott.

1. Nannie^{6} A. Rucker, m. Oct. 5, 1887, A. S. Barden, age 26, son of T. W. and F. N. Barden.
2. Wallace^{6} Rucker, of Petersburg.
3. Eugene^{6} Chester Rucker.
4. Alfred^{6} Rucker.
5. Dora^{6} M. Rucker, m. Dec. 27, 1908, S. F. Meadow, age 24, son of Thomas and Alice Meadow.
6. Effie^{6} T. Rucker, m. Nov. 1, 1904, W. A. Burton, age 35, son of Alfred and Julia Burton.
7. R.^{6} E. Rucker, m. at the age of 34, Lillian Thompson, dau. of S. P. and A. E. Thompson, Oct. 14, 1914.

3. Eugene^{6} Chester Rucker (John^{5} Harvey, Pleasant^{4}, Joshua^{3}, William^{2}), served in the World War. He was trained at Camp Lee, transferred to France, served with the famous 80th Division, and lost his life in the battle of Chateau-Thierry, July 18, 1918.

3. William^{3} (William^{2}, Peter^{1}), b. Sept. 28, 1744, in Orange Co., Va., d. in Georgia in 1835, wife, Elizabeth, may have been a Tavernor or a Barden; both families were living in the same county, William sold his land to James Collins in 1803 and his father William sold land to a James Collins in 1762.

In the first land tax book of Culpeper, 1782, he is paying on one-hundred acres. Later it mentions this one hundred acres as lying on White Marsh Run, adjoining George Harrison's, Culpeper Co., Virginia.

In the personal tax of 1782 he pays on one slave named Harry. William is called "Jr." and later "Long Nose" (Personal tax books), also "William Son to William" to distinguish him from his first cousin, who was called "William, son to Thomas", "William Sen.", "William Jaw Bones".

Nov. 2, 1803 William Rucker and wife, Elizabeth, sold to James Collins 100 acres of land in Madison Co. adjoining James Collins, John Walker and Ambrose Powell for $216.00. Witness: John Plunkett and Tavernor Head (D. B. 5, p. 371, Madison Co.). The 1810 Land tax Book of Madison Co. James Collins paid tax on this 100 acres "formerly William Rucker's".

Revolutionary War Record of William Rucker. From the papers in the Revolutionary War pension claims. File No. 16520, it appears that William Rucker was born September 28th, 1744, in Culpeper County, Virginia, and was living there when he served as a private in the Virginia Troops, as follows:

For two months, in 1781, under Capt. Phinks and Col. James Slaughter.

For one month, in 1781, under Capt. Slaughter and Col. Slaughter.

For four months in 1781, under Capt. Beall and Col. Finney.

He was allowed pension, on his application Jan. 18th, 1833, while living in Elbert Co., Ga.

Copy of *Culpeper* land tax book, taking the two William Ruckers.

1782 Wm. Rucker, Sen. 300 acres.
1782 Wm. Rucker, 100 acres.
1790 Wm. Rucker, Sen. 267 acres, having sold 33 acres.
1790 Wm. Rucker, 100 acres.

Madison County:

1793 Wm. Rucker, Sen. 267 acres.
Wm. Rucker, 100 acres.
1810 Wm. Rucker, Sen. 267 acres.
1810 Wm. Rucker (having sold and moved to Georgia).
1820 Wm. Rucker, Dec'd 267 acres.

Culpeper Personal:

1785 Wm. Rucker, paid on 1 white, 1 negro.
1785 Wm. Rucker (son to William), paid on 1 white.
1789, Wm. Rucker (son to Thomas), paid on 2 whites.
1789, Wm. Rucker (Tavernor & Benjamin), paid on 3 whites.
1792, Wm. Rucker, Sen. 2 whites, and 2 negros.
1792, Wm. Rucker Jun. 1 white, and 2 negros.
1801, Wm. Rucker, "Jaw Bones", Sen. 2 whites, and 2 negroes.

1801, Wm. Rucker, "Long Nose," 2 sons, 3 whites and 2 negros.

1804, Wm. Rucker, "Jaw Bones", Sen. 1 white and 2 negros.

1804, nothing more of "Long Nose".

1820—Census of *Elbert Co.,* Georgia.

William Rucker and wife, both over 45, four children.

James Rucker, age under 26.

1830—Catherine Rucker, age under 60.

Joseph Rucker, age under 50, woman under 50.

Barden Rucker, age under 50, woman under 50.

Lemuel Rucker.

Alexander Rucker, age under 30, woman under 30.

1840—Wm. Rucker, age over 60.

Catherine Rucker.

Joseph Rucker.

Tinsley W. Rucker, age under 30, woman under 30.

Peter Rucker, age under 30, woman under 30.

Mary Rucker, age under 30.

1850—P. Rucker, age 37, m. Farmer, born Ga.

M. Rucker, age 32, f. born Ga.

J. Rucker, age 10, M. born Ga.

M. Rucker, age 8, f. born Ga.

E. Rucker, age 6, f. born Ga.

J. Rucker, age 1, f. born Ga.

JosephRucker, age 62, M. Farmer, valuation of property $68.00, born in Ga.

A. Rucker, age 18, Farmer, born in Ga.

M. Rucker, age 58, F. born in Ga.

E. M. Rucker, age 21, M. Born in Ga.

B. Rucker, age 65, M. Farmer, valuation of property, $1,200.00.

A. Rucker, age 59, F. Born in Ga.

B. Rucker, age 23, M. Farmer, born in Georgia.

W. Rucker, age 14, M. Born in Georgia.

F. Rucker, age 16, F. Born in Georgia.

Wm. Rucker, age 60, Farmer, Valuation of property, $250.00, born in Va.

A. Rucker, age 27, M. Farmer, Valuation of property $700.00 born in Ga.

M. Rucker, age 18, F. Farmer, Born in Georgia.

Wm. died in 1835 in Elbert County, Ga., and was buried in the old Rucker Cemetery in the rear of what is now the home of Rev. Thomas J. Rucker, one of the descendants of William Rucker, in Elbert County, Ga.

Will of William Rucker, dated Aug. 5, 1833, probated Jan. 5, 1835, Elbert Co. Ga. (W. B. 1830-35, p. 447).

All of my property real and personal to my children and grand children Viz; Barden, Tavener and William Rucker, to Frances Rucker now Frances Jones and her heirs, to my two grand children, William Rucker Childs and Susanna Serepta Childs, children of John and Elizabeth Childs, and the heirs of Lemuel Rucker. Friend David Dobbs to take charge of the property.

Executors, Sons, Barden and Tavener.

Test; John Harris, Reuben Thornton and John Highsmith.

Tavener Rucker, William Rucker, and Jesse Wallis were witness to the will of James Highsmith of Elbert Co. Ga., will dated Dec. 25, 1819, Prob. Mch. 10, 1824 (W. B. M, p. 335).

The division of the slaves of William Rucker Jan. 5, 1935. Legatees: Tavener, William and Barden Rucker, William and Susan Childs, the children of 'Lemuel Rucker and Francess Jones (Administrators and Guardians Accounts, 1830-38, p. 487, Elbert Co.).

In the list of those entitled to draw lottery tickets for land in Georgia for 1827 was William Rucker, R. S. (Revolutionary Soldier) two draws (p. 253).

In a sale of personal property of the estate of William Rucker, deceased, Feb. 26, 1835, things were bought by the following: William, Tavener, and Barden Rucker, Joshua and Benjamin Teasley, John G. Higginbotham and others. Frances Jones bought "the large Bible" (Ordinary's Office, Book P, Folio 138-141; Oct. 15, 1835, Elbert Co., Georgia).

Issue:

1. Barden[4] Rucker.
2. Tavenor[4] Rucker.
3. William[4] Rucker, Jr.
4. Lemuel[4] Rucker.
5. Frances[4] Rucker, married Standley Jones, July 24, 1823.
6. Elizabeth[4] Rucker.

1. Barden[4] Rucker (William[3], Wm.[2], Peter[1]), b. in Culpeper Co. 1785; d. in Elbert Co., Ga. m. Frances Alexander (dau. of William). (The Administrators and Guardian Bonds W. B. 1809-12, p. 156) gives a receipt of Barden Rucker to Peter and Nancy Alexander for his share of the estate of William Alexander, dec'd. Jan. 1811.

Will of Barden Rucker dated 10 July 1836, prob. 1856. To my wife Frances Rucker, Serepta Rucker Maxwell, Sarah Rucker Brown, Alexander Rucker, Burton Rucker, Frances Rucker Nelms, and William B. Rucker (W. B. 1835-60, p. 156).

1. Alexander[5] Rucker, m. Mary Hall.
2. Burton[5] Rucker.
3. William[5] B., m. Sarah C. Maxwell.
4. Thomas[5].
5. Serepta[5], m. William Maxwell.
6. Sarah[5] Ann.
7. Frances[5], m. Willis Nelms.

6. Sara[5] Ann Rucker (Barden[4], William[3], William[2], ——) (Feb. 7, 1823-Nov. 11, 1899), m. Sept. 12, 1839, Andrew Jackson Brown (Mch. 11, 1816-Au., 1889).

1. A.[6] Rucker Brown, m. Martha Thornton.
2. Elzie[6], m. Amanda Cunningham.
3. Jefferson[6], m. Phronie Teasley.
4. C.[6] H. N., m. Samanthia Cunningham.
5. E. Jackson[6], m. Nancy Johnson.
6. Fannie[6], m. John Glenn.
7. Elizabeth[6], m. E. P. Jenkins.
8. Lucie[6], m. Martin Teasley.
9. Amanda[6] Jane.
10. Cassie[6], m. George E. Herndon.
11. Leon[6], m. Columbus Glenn.
12. Phelitie[6], m. W. T. Johnson.

9. Amanda[6] Jane Brown (Sarah[5], Barden[4], ———), b. Sept. 1, 1851-Apr. 2, 1902, m. Apr. 27, 1871, Isham Jefferson Teasley.

1. John[7] Eston Teasley (Apr. 2, 1872-Aug. 12, 1898), single.
2. William[7] Elzie Teasley (Jan. 7, 1874-Dec., 1895), single.
3. Benager[7] Columbus Teasley, M. D.
4. Hailey[7] Isham Teasley (Oct. 29, 1877-Feb. 12, 1898), single.
5. Lucy[7] Ann Teasley (June 21, 1881-May 27, 1907), single.
6. George[7] Allen Teasley (Mch. 28, 1883), m. Dec. 27, 1911, Ellen Coggin.
    1. Cecil[8] Amanda Teasley, b. Jan. 21, 1913.
    2. Cornelia[8] Allen Teasley, b. July, 1910.

7. Sidney^{7} Ewell Teasley (May 27, 1885-Jan. 27, 1908), single.
8. Sallie^{7} Elizabeth Teasley, b. June 12, 1888.
9. Drucilla^{7} Cecil Teasley (Aug. 20, 1892-July 4, —), m. Dec., 1913, Ernest Bacon.

3. Dr. Benager^{7} Columbus Teasley (Amanda^{6}, Sarah^{5}, Bernard^{4}, ———), b. Jan. 21, 1876; m. Dec. 10, 1901, Effie G. Adams (b. Nov. 12, 1881).

1. Dr. Harry^{8} Eugene Teasley, b. Sept. 29, 1902, Denver, Col.
2. Dr. Gerald^{8} Haynes Teasley, b. June 30, 1907, Atlanta, Ga.
3. Benager^{8} Columbus Teasley, Jr., b. Mch. 16, 1913.

2. Tavener^{4} Rucker (William^{3}, William^{2}, Peter^{1}), b. Jan. 12, 1777, in Culpeper Co. Va., d. 1855 in Cobb Co. Ga. m. Elizabeth Wade, 1793, d. in Missouri in 1864. His father paid his personal tax in Culpeper in 1789, the next year he paid his own tax. Tavener went to Greenbrier Co., W. Va. where he paid a personal tax from 1796 to 1816, then living in the Anthony Creek district. From there he moved to Elbert Co. Ga. where he may have conducted a school, for in 1819 he gives to James Haley a receipt for Tuition (Administration and Guardian Acc'ts, B. M, p. 133). Also in 1820 he gives a receipt to John Johnson for tuition (A. & G. Acc't, B. L, p. 446). From there he moved to Franklin Co. The Census of that county of 1840 lists him as over 60 and female over 50. Tavener is not mentioned in the census of that county in 1850.

3. William^{4} Rucker (William^{3}, William^{2}, ———), d. 1851, m. ——— Alexander of Elbert Co. His children moved to Tenn., then to Mo. The Census of Elbert Co. lists William in 1850 as a farmer age 60, "born in Virginia".

1. J.^{5} W. E. Rucker.
2. Joel^{5} Shelton.
3. Frances^{5} M. A.
4. Anna^{5} M. A.
5. William^{5} Childes.
6. James^{5} Clements.
7. Lemuel^{5}.

4. Lemuel^{4} Rucker (Wm.^{3}), b. in Culpeper Co. evidently visited his grandfather William Rucker in Amelia Co., where he married his 1st cousin Polly (dau. of Joshua), Dec. 8, 1792

(Mar. bond). In the will of his father, Lemuel is mentioned as dec'd.

There was another Lemuel Rucker who married Priscilla Teasley in Elbert Co., Aug. 11, 1825. This Lemuel may be the son of William and nephew of Lemuel above.

6. Elizabeth[4] Rucker (Wm.[3]), m. John Childs, Dec. 20, 1812.

1. William[5] Rucker Childs.
2. Susanna[5] Sarpena Childs.

4. Elisha[3] Rucker (William[2], Peter[1]), b. in Orange, settled in 96 District, Greenville Co., S. C., before 1791 (census). Some of his descendants went to Tennessee, Illinois, Texas and Arkansas. Elisha was a witness to a sale of land in Amelia 1771, his father selling 40 acres of land to Judith Bently.

5. Mordicai[3] Rucker (William[2], ———) (1755-1845), b. in Culpeper Co. The 1st census of Amelia Co., Va., lists Mordicai among the heads of families, with seven whites, males. He moved 1st to Greenville Co., S. C., 96 District, then to Rutherford Co., N. C. (see census later), later to Tenn.

He m. 1st Susanna Bailey, 2nd ——— Martin.

Issue (by 1st mar.):

1. James[4] Rucker, b. 1772.
2. Elliot[4], b. 1777.
    1. John Wingfield[5] Scott Rucker, b. 1823.
        1. Emma[6] Rucker, m. ——— Morton.
            1. Gertrude[7] Morton, m. J. Guy Huff, Nashville, Tenn.
                1. Hadley[8] Terrell Huff, b. 1926.
3. Wilford[4] Rucker, b. 1779.
4. Elisha[4].

Issue (by 2nd mar.):

5. William[4] Martin Rucker, b. 1797, m. Elmira Lynch (sister of Sally).
    1. Dr. James[5] Saxton Rucker, m. Betty Fanning of Amelia (dau. of Rev. Frank).
        1. William[6] Fanning Rucker, m. Elizabeth Hoyle of Charlotte, N. C.

The Mordicai who went to Greenbriar County, W. Va., and m. Susanna Rucker may be a son of the above Mordicai. He later moved to Tenn. See the Greenbriar County Records under the James[2] Rucker line.

1. James^4 Rucker (Mordicai^3, William^2, Peter^1) (1772-1839), d. near Athens, Tenn., m. ——— Wheeler. He lived for a while near King's Mountains, N. C., moved to McMinns Co., Tenn., near Chattanooga.

1. John^5 Rucker, moved to Ill.
2. Mordicai^5, moved to Ill., 1853; settled near Decatur.
3. William^5.
4. Wilford^5.
5. Matilda^5.
6. Emily^5.
7. Rachel^5.
8. James^5.
9. Jesse^5.

3. William^5 Rucker (James^4, Mordicai^3, William^2), b. 1804; lived for a while in Tenn., moved to Ill. in 1853; d. Nov. 29, 1886 in Decatur, Ill.

1. Mary^6 Rucker.
2. James^6.
3. John^6.
4. Nathaniel^6.
   1. Mary^7, m. E. D. Horton.
5. Ann^6 Rucker.
6. Sarah^6.
7. Rachel^6.
8. Margaret^6.
9. William^6 T. Rucker, of Blackwell, Okla.

7. Rachel^6 Rucker (William^5, James^4, Mordicai^3), b. June 26, 1844, near Athens, Tenn.; d. Decatur, Ill., Oct. 11, 1892; m. Hiram Hamilton Carter.

1. Mary^7 Carter.
2. Sarah^7 Ellen.
3. William^7 Jasper.
4. Ida^7 Ann.
5. Cora^7 Ellis.
6. E. Jane^7.
7. Homer^7 Elmer.
8. Eddie^7 Winston.
9. Nancy^7 Nellie.
10. Grover^7 Cleveland.

3. William^7 Jasper Carter (Rachel^6, William^5, James^4 Rucker), b. Jan. 4, 1867, near Decatur, Ill., m. Bertha Maude Patton.

Issue:

1. Russell[8] W. Carter, b. Dec. 5, 1897, of La Place, Ill.; m. Ruth Rockwell, of Aurora, Ill.
   1. Russell[9] W. Carter, Jr.
2. Rachel[8] Carter, b. Mch. 12, 1899, of La Place, Ill., m. Philip McCutchon, of Decatur, Ill.
   1. Carter[9] McCutchon.

8. Winston[7] Carter (Rachel[6], William[5] Rucker), m. June 27, 1821, Susanna ————, b. Nov. 14, 1801.

1. William[8] Martin Carter.
2. James[8] Elbert.
3. Luther[8] Neal.
4. Madison[8] Lafayette.
5. Hiram[8] Hamilton.
6. Elizabeth[8] Jane.
7. Hugh[8] Gaines.
8. George[8] Winston.
9. Polly[8] Ann.

6. Joseph[3] Rucker (William[2], Peter[1]), bought 150 acres of land in Amelia Co. from Moses Morris, for 15,000 lbs. of tobacco, Oct. 15, 1785; land adjoining William Farley and Benjamin Hendricks. Witness: Zacharia Morris, Thomas Morris, William Burton (D. B. 17, p. 357), Amelia.

7. James[3] Rucker (William[2], Peter[1]), was a witness to a sale of land that his father sold to Benjamin Herrick in 1771, land Gidion formerly lived on in Amelia.

The following are of the family of William Rucker of Amelia, Va., 1790; Census of Wilkes Co., N. C.

Colby Rucker paid on 2 males over 16, & 5 females 1800. Colby Rucker age over 26, wife over 26, & 7 children.

1790 Burke Co., N. C.

Joseph Rucker, 3 whites over 16, 2 females.

1790 Rutherford Co., N. C., Morgan District. William Rucker, 1 white over 16, 2 females.

1800 William Rucker age over 26, woman 26. Mordecai Rucker age 45, woman 45.

1790 Greenville Co., S. C., 96 District. Mordecai Rucker, 3 whites, 2 females.

Elisha Rucker, 2 whites, 4 females, 1 slave.

1790 Orangeburg District. Gaspard Rucker, 1 white male, 2 females.

Michael Rucker, 1 white male, 2 females.

1820 Wilkes Co., Ga. Gideon Rucker, age 26.

CHAPTER EIGHT
Mary Rucker

7. Mary² Rucker (Peter¹), married William Offill. Her brother, John, deeded 100 acres of land to her. William Offill patented 2000 acres of land in Orange, Rockingham and Page Counties.

In 1752 after the death of Elizabeth, William Offill received a negro out of Peter Rucker's, deceased, estate (D. B. 1, p. 400), 21 Feb. 1752, Culpeper.

In 1755, Nov. 4, William Offill and wife, Mary of Broomfield Parish, Culpeper, sold to John Offill for 10 lbs. sterling, 100 acres, part of the patent made by John Rucker, adjoining Ephraim Rucker, Isaac Tinsley, Richard Vawter, Jeremiah Early and Peter Rucker (D. B. B, p. 301), Culpeper.

CHAPTER NINE

James Rucker

8. James[2] Rucker (Peter[1]), b. in Essex, d. in Greenbrier County, m. Margaret ———.

He sold all of his land in Culpeper before 1770 and in 1782 appears on George Poage's list of Heads of Families of Bath County: "James Rucker, Sr., James Rucker, Jr. and Wyatt Rucker on the Greenbrier River Section."

James Rucker, Sen., patented and bought land in Augusta and Bath (later Greenbrier) on the Middle fork of Greenbrier River, some of which he deeded to his sons.

To the East of the river, near the South-west corner of Bath County, is a pass called "Rucker's pass", through the Al-leghany Mountains, into Greenbrier County. We find no will of James Rucker, Sr. Therefore we do not know all of his children, but the Ruckers of the next generation living on the middle fork of Anthony's creek, we are taking for granted to be children of James, Sr., every available clue having been fol-lowed, and all of the records studied with the following result, which is very meagre.

Issue:

1. James[3] Rucker, Jr.
2. Ephraim[3] Rucker.
3. Lemuel[3] Rucker.
4. Wyatt[3] Rucker.
5. Samuel[3] Rucker.
6. Elzaphem[3] Rucker.
7. Augustine[3] Rucker.
8. Mildred[3] Rucker, m. ——— Underwood, of Cul-peper.
9. Ambrose[3] (?).

James Rucker, Jr., and Wyatt Rucker are in the census of 1783, owning land in Bath County.

Lemuel Rucker, in the Augusta County tax list, is paying on land formerly of James Rucker, Sr. (Anthony Creek).

Ephraim Rucker received 100 acres of land from James Rucker, Sr. (Anthony Creek). Later Ephraim sold this land adjoining his "brother Lemuel." Samuel received 145 acres from James Rucker, Sr. "Now in Samuel's possession."

Mildred Underwood's two sons, James and Berryman, were deeded land by James Rucker, Sr., for the use of their "Mother".

Elzepham Rucker was in the Revolution. Pay received by James Rucker. Elzepham, Samuel and Lemuel Rucker were in the 8th Virginia Regiment (War D. 19, 6). Their cousins in Culpeper were in the 1st Virginia Regiment.

Francis Kirtley of Culpeper deeded to James Rucker of same county. "All that tract in Culpeper County, whereon the said James Rucker now resides, on Gartle's Run—to F. Kirtley's line—to the river, the walnut trees not to be disturbed except by the said Rucker—to saw into plank, to the use of Tenement liberty, given to said Rucker with all houses, buildings etc., for the term of 99 years." May 8th, 1750. Witness: Martin Dewit, Charles Neale and William Henderson (D. B. A, page 171, Culpeper County).

James bought 376 acres from John Powell of Culpeper of Broomfield Parish. Land on Great Mountains, adjoining Francis Conway's, and over the Great Mountains to Captain John Frogg. Witness: Thomas Rucker, Russell Hill, Barthelomew Vawter (D. B. A, page 448, Oct. 19th, 1752).

Lewis Herndon, and wife, Frances, of Caroline, sold to James Rucker, of Bluefield Parish, Culpeper County, 100 acres for 40 lbs. Land on both sides of Stanton River, July, 1759. Culpeper.

May 1750, Orange County, James was paid 110 lbs of tobacco as a witness.

The final settlement of Peter Rucker's estate was completed in 1752. A deed on that date states, "Thomas and William Rucker, William Offill and Shem Cook, agree to the legacies paid by James and Ephraim Rucker, Executors.

To Isaac Tinsley, 1 negro boy, Yorkshire.
To Shem Cook, 1 negro girl, Jenny.
To Ephraim Rucker, 1 negro girl, Phillis.

Signed: Thomas Rucker, William Rucker, Shem Cook, William Offill. Witness: Francis Kirtley and Richard Vawter (D. B. 1, page 400, 21 Feb. 1752, Culpeper Co.).

James Rucker and wife, Margaret of Culpeper, sold to James Griffin of Orange, 120 acres of land in Culpeper, part of a patent of John Powell, dated 1749. Land on top of the mountain running North, Sept. 16th, 1756 (D. B. B, page 498, Culpeper).

The same day, same book, page 500, he and Margaret "sold 250 acres to William Sims of Orange, for 400 pounds of tobacco, between the Stanton and Conway Rivers.

He sold for £91 a tract of 100 acres of land in Culpeper, on Stanton River, adjoining Charles Neale, William Kirtly, Hugh Lenox, and William Scott, also a wagon, four gear horses and mares, buildings etc., — to Hugh Lenox. James Rucker had the privilege to reclaim this if he wished (D. B. F, p. 132, June 28, 1765, recorded Sept., 1774).

James and wife, Margaret, deeded to George Underwood, 180 acres of land in Culpeper Co. on Staunton River, March, 1770 (D. B. F, p. 191, Culpeper Co.).

James Rucker of Greenbrier County, deeded to James Underwood of same county, land on Middle fork of Anthony Creek, 75 acres, part of 400 acres granted to James Rucker 1794, adjoining Robert Armstrong, "In order that his mother, Milly Underwood, may have peaceable possession on this land during her life time." 29 April, 1794 (D. B. 1, page 417, Greenbrier Co.). (Milly Underwood may be a daughter of James Rucker, Sr.)

The same to Berriman Underwood, the same day, for the use of his mother, Milly Underwood.

He patented 345 acres June 10th, 1780, on East branch of Greenbrier River, called "Buck Creek", adjoining William Warrick's line to Jacob Warwick (Vol. H, page 332, L. Gr., Richmond, Va.).

This land James deeds to Lemuel Rucker, who began paying taxes on it in 1782, Augusta, Co.

June 10th, 1780, he patented 361 acres of land on Hospital Run, and the East Branch of Buck Creek on the North Branch of Deer and Warrick Creeks, by right of settlement (Vol. H, page 377, L. Gr., Richmond, Va.).

June 11th, 1783, James Rucker, Sr. patented 345 acres of land in Augusta, on the East branch of Greenbrier River, Buck and Warwick Creeks (L. Grants).

James Rucker sold to Thomas Carvel of Bath for £56 170 acres of land in Bath, (now cut from Augusta) being part of a 345 acre tract, granted to James by patent, June 11th, 1783, on East branch of Greenbrier River, called "Buck Creek", Sept. 9th, 1794 (D. B. 1, page 172, Bath Co.).

James Rucker, Sr. of Greenbrier Co., sold to James Talman of Bath, for £150 195 acres in Bath, granted James Rucker, June, 1783, on Sept. 9th, 1795 (D. B. I, page 173, Bath Co., Virginia).

James Rucker, Sr. of Greenbrier County, deeded to Moses Honchin for £1, 211 acres of land in Bath, granted to James Rucker, June, 1783 (D. B. 1, page 173, Bath Co.).

March 12th, 1793, James Rucker patented 400 acres in Augusta Co., on Anthony Creek of Greenbrier River (L. Gr., B. 29, p. 297, Richmond, Va.).

James deeded 145 acres of the 400 acre tract to Samuel Rucker (both of Greenbrier County), Land on Middle Creek of Anthony. Land patented by James, June, 1783, and now in the possession of Samuel, 1794 (D. B. 1, page 337, Greenbrier Co.).

1794 James Rucker, Sr. deeded to Ephraim Rucker both of Greenbrief Co., 100 acres part of the 400 acres tract patented by James, June, 1783, on Middle and Anthony Creek, on Raccoon and Sugar Runs (D. B. 1, p. 357, Greenbrier County).

Nov. 12th, 1793, Surveyed for James Rucker, 141 acres in Augusta on the waters of Sitlengton Creek at a place called Richland, assigned to Jacob Warwick.

1794, James Rucker, Sr. sold land to Cornule Thomas (D. B. 1, page 192, Greenbrier Co.).

1. James[3] Rucker, Jr. (James[2], Peter[1]), wife, Mary (left no will in Greenbrier Co., W. Va.

He was living in Augusta Co. in 1778, from the following county petition, dated 13 April, 1778, "A petition to cut off a new county, stating, "Their trouble with the Indians had prevented them from addressing the assembly at an earlier date, being settlers west of the Alleghany." Signed: James Rucker, Jr.

He had 285 acres surveyed June 8th, 1780. Land on the East branch of Greenbrier River, a certificate in right of settlement in the county of August (Vol 11, p. 319, Land Grants, Richmond, Va.).

Land near the Warm Spring, Bath Co., was assigned to Wm. Poage, James and Augustine Rucker (Chalkley's *Abstracts*, p. 17).

In 1782 he pays land tax on this 285 acres as land in Augusta. In 1791 this land is paid upon as lying in Bath Co. Tax paid until 1795. He was evidently living in Bath until 1796 from the personal tax. In 1797 he paid personal tax in Greenbrier Co., until 1829.

James Rucker, Jr. and wife, Mary, of Augusta, give power of attorney to Leonard Rucker, to convey a tract of land to Mathew Penn of Amherst, land in Augusta (Chalkley's *Abstracts*, April 26, 1785; D. B. 25, p. 42, Augusta Co.). Leonard may be his son.

In Augusta land tax books, of 1798, James Rucker, Sr. and James Rucker, Jr. both pay personal taxes. In 1802 "James Rucker, Sr., James Rucker, Jr., and James, son of James, Jr." all three pay personal taxes in Greenbrier Co.

In the census of Greenbrier Co. James and Wyatt Rucker are listed as "heads of families", 1783-86.

"James, son of James Jr." began paying a personal tax in Greenbrier Co., 1803. Was still paying in 1806.

Issue:

1. James[4], "son of James Jr."
2. Possibly Leonard[4], of Bath.

2. Ephraim[3] Rucker (James[2], Peter[1]), b. in Culpeper County. Lived in Greenbrier, m. June 25th, 1775, Elizabeth Randall of Orange.

In 1794 he received from his father, James, 100 acres of land on Raccoon and Sugar Runs on the middle fork of Anthony Creek (D. B. 1, page 357, Greenbrier Co.).

29 Aug., 1825, Ephraim and wife, Betsy, of Monroe Co., Ohio, sold to Lemuel Rucker of same county and state, for 1 lb. sterling, land in Greenbrier Co. on middle fork of Anthony Creek, granted to said Ephraim by patent dated June 13th, 1798, beginning at a maple on the east side of a tract of land sold by said Ephraim to John Hoffner—to a corner owned by Lemuel, and since sold by him to Leonard Wade; at the mouth of Raccoon Creek, 50 acres. Witness: Paschal Rucker, Ambrose Rucker (D. B. 10, p. 185, Greenbrier County, Virginia).

Oct. 3, 1818, Ephraim Rucker and wife, Elizabeth, sold to John Horner of Greenbrier County, 226 acres of land on Anthony Creek, for $1,000.00, adjoining Wilson's line—to James Rucker's land, across the old survey line, marking trees "between his brother, Lemuel Rucker and John Hefner" (D. B. 7, p. 361).

Betsy Rucker relinquished her rights to the land sold by "Ephraim Rucker, my husband of the county of Monroe" to John Hefner, on 3 Oct. 1818. Signed 19 August, 1823.

He paid a personal tax in Greenbrier Co. in 1792 on two whites. Continued until 1817.

He was a private in the Revolution from Culpeper Co. on Nov. 13th, 1783, his money was received "By Mr. Stockdale" of the 8th Virginia Regiment (War 4, 328).

3. Lemuel[3] Rucker (James[2], Peter), b. Apr. 15, 1754, in Culpeper Co., Va., d. March 4th, 1842, near Summerville, Ohio, m. 1783 Ann Booten (Dec. 11th, 1763-March, 1845). They moved to Greenbrier County about 1788, then to Ohio after 1817. Settled in Wills Creek about thirty-five miles from Wheeling, where all of his children were born except Julia, the eldest, born in Greenbrier Co.

He was paying a personal tax in Augusta in 1782 on himself and three slaves, until 1788. He then paid on five slaves until 1817 in Greenbrier. In the land tax books of Augusta in 1782, 345 acres are transferred from "James Rucker, Sr." to "Lemuel Rucker's" account. The latter paid on this tract until 1789, at which time he sold 200 acres of it to John Slaving, paying on the remaining 145 acres mentioned in the tax books of 1791, as land lying on Anthonys Creek. He continues to pay on this land until 1817.

Bath Co. records, April 14th, 1795, Lemuel Rucker of Greenbrier sold to William Hanken of Bath, 127 acres for £90 land in Bath granted by patent June 9th, 1783, to James Rucker. Witness: Thomas L. Lewis, Reuben Lunsford and Andrew Moore (D. B. 1, page 217, Bath Co.).

17 Sept. 1825, Lemual Rucker, and wife, Anna, of Monroe Co., Ohio, sold to Leonard Wade of Greenbrier Co. for $1200.00 land in Greenbrier on middle forks of Anthony Creek, out of a tract containing 400 acres granted to James Rucker by patent, and conveyed by said James Rucker to said Lemuel by deed, dated 29 April, 1794, at mout of Raccoon Branch, 150 acres. Also a certain tract in the same county and place, granted to Ephraim Rucker by patent, and conveyed by said Ephraim to Lemuel Rucker, 29 August, 1825, on east side of land conveyed to John Haffner, 50 acres, this he sold to Leonard Wade (D. B. 10, page 214, Greenbrier Co.).

5 Nov. 1825, Lemuel Rucker sold to Leonard Wade, 75 acres for $1.00 land on Middle fork of Anthony Creek being part of a tract of 400 acres, granted to James Rucker by patent dated 28th Dec. 1793 (D. B. 10, p. 205).

24 April, 1809, James Underwood of Greenbrier Co. sold to Lemuel Rucker of same county, for £120, 75 acres of land on Anthony Creek, west of Ruckers. Witness: Merriman Rucker, Dewit Rucker, James Jeffres (D. B. 4, p. 182).

Lemuel served in the Revolution. Enlisted 1776. Served two years as a private, then as a sergeant, under Captain George Slaughter, of the 8th Virginia regiment, under the "Fighting Parson", Col. Muhlenburg. The pay roll of May 25th, 1776, mentions him as a private. In 1778, as "sick and in the hospital". Mr. Strother received his pay.

He applied for a war pension, Jan. 7th, 1820, which was granted (No. 340372). He was living in Monroe Co., Ohio, age 66 years at that time. Military references.

War 4, 331.334.

W. D. 181,1-8th Va. Reg.

Special Reports of 1911 of the Department of Archives and History of Virginia, p. 385, Rd., Va.

Census of Pensions, 1840, p. 177.

April 30th, 1785. The pay of Lemuel Rucker of Culpeper was received by Eppa Hubbard.

In the same company were Elzaphan and Samuel Rucker.

He was discharged at Valley Forge, Pa., sick.

The records of Monroe Co., being burned, we have only Bible and family records to prove Lemuel Rucker's children.

Issue:

1. Julia[4] Rucker, b. Oct. 9, 1784, m. ——— Rogers, of Greenbrier Co.
2. Ambrose[4] Rucker.
3. Paschal[4] Rucker.
4. John[4] Jackson Rucker.
5. Ephraim[4] Rucker.
6. Lemuel[4] B. Rucker.
7. Catherine[4] Rucker.
8. Garlin[4] (Garland).
9. Edward[4] Rucker.

2. Ambrose[4] Rucker (Lemuel[3], James[2], Peter[1]), b. March 17, 1787, d. Aug. 23, 1871, Iowa. Married 1st, Dec. 22, 1808, Sarah Steele, d. Dec. 16, 1826, m. 2nd, Oct. 16, 1828, Rachel Stephens. Ambrose paid tax in Bath County for one year only, 1809. "Ambrose Rucker and wife, Sarah, of Bath County, sold to Edith Steele of same county for $100.00 land belonging to Edith's father, James Steele, Sr. deceased, land on Jackson River, 1809 (Bath County, D. B. 3, page 379), adjoining Abram Evans, William H. Cavandish, Moses McClintock.

Issue (by 1st mar.):

1. Lemuel[5], borne June 10, 1809, died Feb., 1852.
2. Polly[5] Wise, born Dec. 17, 1810, died Feb. 27, 1846.
3. Eddeth[5], born Nov. 6, 1812, died Sept. 18, 1821.
4. Samuel[5], born Sept. 1, 1814, died Aug. 21, 1819.
5. Jahn[5], born May 25, 1816, died Aug. 29, 1855.
6. James[5], born Jan. 18, 1818, died March 17, 1906.
7. William[5], born Oct. 3, 1819, died July 8, 1897.
8. John[5], born April 21, 1821, died March 24, 1845.
9. Sarah[5], born June 22, 1823, died March 24, 1845.
10. Elizabeth[5], born 1825, died March 8th, 1845.

Issue (by 2nd mar.):

11. Levi[5], born Nov. 30, 1829, died June 22, 1864.
12. Marriann[5], born June 26, 1831, died Oct. 16, 1849, Ohio.
13. Stephen[5], born 1833, Centre Point, Iowa, died Iowa.
14. Phoebe[5], born Oct. 6, 1834, died Apr. 16, 1854.
15. Nelson[5], born Jan. 29, 1837, died March 17, 1852.

16. Ambrose[5], born March 12, 1839, died Soldiers' home in Marshaltown, Iowa.
17. Rev. Aaron[5], born July 14, 1841, died Oct. 22, 1916, Spences, Iowa.
18. Wesley[5], born Jan. 16, 1844, died Jan. 31, 1899, Hot Springs, S. D.
19. Rachel[5], born Sept. 14, 1845, died Oct. 10, 1889, Toledo, Ohio.
20. Amy[5], born March 26, 1848, died June 30, 1889, Central Point, Iowa.

6. James[5] Rucker (Ambrose[4], Lemuel[3], James[2], Peter[1]), b. Jan. 18, 1818, near Summerfield, Ohio, Monroe County, d. March 17, 1906, Hampton, Iowa, m. Margaret Baker, 1838, b. 1816, Monroe Co., Ohio, d. May 29, 1882, Blaine, Washington, Iowa.

1. Maria[6] Elizabeth Rucker.
2. Pricella[6] Equilla Rucker.
3. Mary[6] Rucker.
4. Harriet[6] Ann Rucker.
5. Susan[6] Ellen Rucker.
6. Jasper[6] Newton Rucker.

1. Maria[6] E. Rucker (James[5], Ambrose[4], Lemuel[3]), m. William J. Shroyer, Hampton, Iowa.

1. Everett[7] Shroyer, deceased.
2. Ella[7], m. V. J. Kratz, Hampton, Iowa.
3. Cora[7] Shroyer.
4. Minnie[7], m. L. B. Appleby, Geneva, Iowa.
5. William[7] Wooster, Hampton, Iowa.

2. Priscilla[6] Equilla Rucker (James[5], Ambrose[4], Lemuel[3]), m. Jasper N. Lindsey, Buena Vista, Iowa.

1. Laura[7] Lindsey.
2. Eddie[7].
3. J. M.[7] Lindsey.
4. Fred[7] Lindsey, Blaine, Washington.
5. Baker[7] Lindsey.
6. Eva[7] Lindsey Root, Marysville, Washington.

3. Mary[6] Rucker (James[5], Ambrose[4], Lemuel[3]), m. John Enders, Buena Vista, Iowa.

1. James[7] Hopkins Enders.
2. Harriet[7].

3. Ethel^{7}.
4. Berthol^{7}.
5. Albert^{7}.
6. Daisy^{7} Murphy, Marcus, South Dakota.
7. Dwight^{7} Hopkins, Sturgis, South Dakota.

4. Harriet^{6} Ann Rucker (James^{5}, Ambrose^{4}, Lemuel^{3}), m. Perry Newell, Ponca, Nebraska.

1.. Myrtie^{7} Newell Sellers (widow), Gaylord, Kansas.

5. Susan^{6} Ellen Rucker (James^{5}, Ambrose^{4}, Lemuel^{3}, James^{2}, Peter^{1}), b. Nov. 2, 1849, Monroe Co., Ohio, m. 10 Mch. 1870, Chauncey F. Ream, Ponca, Nebraska.

1. Myrtie^{7} Ream, b. 1874, m. James A. Quinn, no issue.
2. Frank C.^{7} Ream, b. Oct. 17, 1876, Humboldt, Nebraska, m. Maude Crippen, June 30, 1906.
   1. Dorothy^{8} F. Ream, b. Sept. 1, 1908, Omaha, Neb.
   2. Irvine^{8} R., b. April 9, 1914, Omaha, Neb.
3. Alberta^{7} P. Ream, b. Apr. 13, 1879, m. Raymond W. Hadley, Sept. 10, 1903, Omaha, Neb.
   1. Ronald^{8} W. Hadley, b. May 16, 1904.
   2. Margaret^{8} A. Hadley, b. Aug. 10, 1908.
4. Ida^{7} L. Ream, b. Jan. 9, 1881, m. Erdman S. Parker, Sept. 15, 1909, Omaha, Neb.
   1. Polly^{8} R. Parker, b. July 17, 1910.
   2. Pomeroy^{8} S. Parker, b. Jan. 7, 1913.
5. Ralph^{7} E. Ream, b. Nov., 1887, m. Virginia A. Smith, July 21, 1909, Council Bluff.
   1. Ralph^{8} E. Reams, Jr., b. Mch. 16, 1911, Omaha.
   2. Susan^{8} Matilda, b. May 12, 1916.

6. Jasper^{6} Newton Rucker (James^{5}, Ambrose^{4}, Lemuel^{3}), m. Lizzie Cain, Blaine, Washington.

1. Dwight^{7} Rucker.
2. Eva^{7} Rucker.
3. Ira^{7} Rucker.
4. Edna^{7} Rucker.
5. Minnie^{7} Rucker.
6. Nat^{7} Rucker.
7. Hall^{7} Rucker.

3. Paschal[4] Rucker (Lemuel[3], James[2], Peter[1]), b. Jan. 20, 1790, d. 1867, m. Polly Rodges (sister of Julia Rucker's husband). Lived in Monroe County, Ohio. The following is recorded in Greenbrier County, D. B. 9, page 165, 27 Sept. 1823: "Sarah Philips wife of Isaac Philips, (who died July 1806) leaving no will, Paschal Rucker and Nancy Smith witnesses." They stated that at the death of Sarah, all of their estate was to go to Sally Graham, who was under her care, (Sarah's) at that time. That later the said Sally Graham had married John Rucker.

John and wife, Sally Rucker, of Monroe County, sold the above land for $200.00 to David Desen in Greenbrier County, Sept. 27, 1823. John and Sally Rucker were married Feb. 22, 1814, in Greenbrier County., Rev. McElhany officiating.

Issue:

1. Allen[5] Rucker.
2. William[5].
3. Julia[5].
4. Elliot[5].
5. Nancy[5].
6. Peter[5].
7. Katherine[5].
8. Sarah[5].

1. Allen[5] Rucker (Paschal[4], Lemuel[3], ———), d. in Nodaway Co., Mo., m. Lucretia Blake.

2. William[5] Rucker (Paschal[4], Lemuel[3], ———) (Jan. 21, 1818-1867), Belle Plains, Iowa, m. 1840 Nancy Blake, b. 1825, William Rucker moved with his brother, Elliot to Benton County, Iowa.

1. Col. Cornelius[6] Rucker.
2. Julia[6], m. Thomas F. Greenlee, Iowa.
3. Sarah[6], m. John Cutler Hanby, Colorado.
4. Cora[6], m. Mitchell McCune, Colorado.
5. George[6], m. Minnie Stone, Minneapolis.
6. Thomas[6], d. young.
7. Mary[6].
8. Robert[6].
9. Frank[6], d. young.

3. Cornelius[6] Rucker (William[5], Paschal[4], Lemuel[3]), of Durham, California, m. 1867, Sarah Hanby, of Iowa. They have a son[7] living in Transval, South Africa.

4. Elliot[5] Rucker (Paschal[4], Lemuel[3], James[2], Peter[1]) (1822-Nov. 22, 1867), in Benton Co., Iowa, m. Catherine Ste-

phens (1828-June 30, 1883), in Ohio. Moved to Benton County, Iowa.

1. Dwinna[6] Rucker, m. Mary Myers.
2. Letha[6] Ellen Rucker, m. William Furnace.
3. William[6], m. Nancy ———.
4. Charles[6].
5. John[6], m. Buna Greenley.
6. Cynthia[6], m. Joshua Cole.
7. Lucy[6], m. John Ringler.
8. Colthia[6], m. Marion Crombaugh.
9. Lucretia[6] Ann, m. Francis Richardson.

9. Lucretia[6] Ann Rucker (Elliott[5], Paschal[4], ———), b. June 30, 1836, m. Sept. 14, 1881, Francis Asbury Richardson, b. June 23, 1858.

1. Hibbard[7] Elliot Richardson, m. Ruth C. Ellsworth.
2. Elva[7] Richardson, m. Adonis Howard.
3. Lydia[7] Richardson, m. George P. Jones.
4. James[7] Richardson, unmarried.

4. John[4] Jackson Rucker (Lemuel[3], James[2], Peter[1]), b. Mch. 24, 1794, Greenbrier County, Va., d. 1840, Monroe County, Ohio, m. Sarah Graham, Feb. 22, 1814, in Greenbrier.

Sarah Rucker of Monroe County, Ohio, stated in a petition: "John Rucker late of Monroe County departed this life in 1840. He left the petitioner, Sarah, widow, Ephraim, John, James and Catherine Rucker, who intermerried with Gason Blake, and ——— Rucker who intermerried with George Okey" (D. B. 11, p. 373, Monroe County, Ohio).

1. Ephraim[5] Rucker.
2. John[5] Rucker.
3. James[5] Rucker.
4. Catherine[5] Rucker, m. Gason Blake.
5. ———[5] Rucker, m. George Okey.

5. Ephraim[4] Rucker (Lemuel[3], James[2], Peter[1]), b. April 12, 1796, m. Oct. 22, 1818, Margaret Loughridge in Bath County, Rev. Otho Wade officiating.

He was a private in the war of 1812 (Ref. House of Delegates, 1834, War, 1812, Richmond, Virginia).

1. Lemuel[5] Rucker.
2. Mythias[5] Rucker.
3. Anna[5].

4. Ellen[5] Rucker.
5. Martha[5] Rucker.
6. Jack[5] Rucker.

6. Lemuel[4] Booten Rucker (Lemuel[3], James[2], Peter[1]) (Mch. 9, 1800-Feb. 19, 1852), m. 1827, Lucy Blake (daughter of Daniel Blake, and sister to Sarah, Nancy, and Lucretia, from Kennebunk, Maine), d. July 6, 1861.

1. Louis[5] Booten Rucker.
2. Mary[5] Ann, no heirs.
3. Jane[5], m. Thomas Guilick.
4. Julia[5], m. Washington Kirkbride.
5. Emeline[5].
6. Samuel[5].
7. Lanford[5].
8. Warren[5], m. Amanda Canady.
9. Larkin[5], m. Amanda Lilly of Parma, Idaho.

1. Louis[5] Booten Rucker (Lemuel[4], Jr., Lemuel[3], Sr., James[2], Peter[1]) (Aug. 15, 1828-Jan. 28, 1909), m. March 29, 1849, Margaret Daily (Oct. 16, 1830-Oct. 10, 1922). Moved to Kansas about 1878.

1.. Thomas F.[6] Rucker.
2. Lucy[6] C. Rucker, b. Oct. 30, 1852, m. ——— Garner.
3. John L.[6] Rucker, b. April 19, 1855.
4. Nancy[6] E. Rucker.
5. Louisa[6] V. Rucker, b. Feb. 27, 1862, m. ——— Minter.
6. Mary[6] E. Rucker, b. July 22nd, 1864.

1. Thomas F.[6] Rucker (Lewis B.[5], Lemuel, Jr.[4], Lemuel, Sr.[3], James[2]), b. Jan. 2, 1850 (living in Corning, Kansas), m. Dec. 31, 1875, Mary E. Thomas, b. Dec. 26, 1859.

1. Alva[7] Rucker, b. Nov. 7, 1887.
2. Ethel[7] Rucker, b. Dec. 8, 1892, m. Dec. 10, 1912, Luther Martin Phillips, b. March 4, 1886.
    1. Etta[8] Philips, b. 1913.
    2. Frank[8] Philips, b. 1920.
    3. Catherine[8] Philips, b. 1924.

4. Nancy[6] E. Rucker (Lewis[5], Lemuel[4], ———), b. Oct. 8th, 1857, m. Charles W. Hunt.

1. Jesse[7] Hunt Bender.
2. Archie[7] Hunt.

6. Samuel[5] Rucker (Lemuel, Jr.[4], Lemuel, Sr.[3], ———), b. Nov. 14, 1835, d. Sept. 24, 1865, m. Feb. 17, 1857, Mary E. Allen, b. Oct. 28, 1831, d. Sept. 11, 1912.

1. Charles[6] M. Rucker, b. Sept., 1857.
2. Alva[6] S. Rucker, b. June 11, 1860.
3. Anna[6] V. R. Ogle, b.. 1863.

7. Sanford[5] Rucker (Lemuel, Jr.[4], Lemuel, Sr.[3], ———), b. March 24, 1838, in Ohio, d. March 19, 1902, m. 1859, Ruth Wilson, b. Oct. 18, 1840, d. Aug. 31, 1926, dau. of Thomas Wilson of Virginia and his wife Rebecca of Maryland.

1. William[6] Warren Rucker, b. Ohio, d. Feb., 1821, m. 1st Nancy Pool, m. 2nd Maggie McCampbell.
2. Mary[6] Adelia Rucker, b. Nov. 10, 1861, in Ohio, m 1883, Marian Morris, d. 1889.
    1. Ray[7] Morris, of Ohio.
    2. Sanford[7], of Ohio.
    3. Jesse[7], of Ohio.
3. Albert[6] Rucker, b. Ill., m. L. Williamson.
    1. C.[7] S. Rucker, lawyer of Mo.
4. Sarah[6], b. Mo., m. Frank Trimble.
5. Lily[6], b. Mo., m. John Hayden.
6. Martha[6], b. Mo., m. James Pierce.
7. John[6], b. Mo., m. Leona Blood.
8. Samuel[6], b. Mo., m. Martha Harris.
9. Jennie[6] Dell, b. Mo., m. William Chiffman.
10. Maude[6], b. Mo., m. John Hise.
11. Bessie[6], b. Mo., m. ——— Lanthrop.

7. Catherine[4] Rucker (Lemuel[3], Sr., James[2], Peter[1]), b. July 4, 1802, d. 1885, m. Lemuel[4] E. Rucker, Jr. (Ambrose[3], James[2], Peter[1]), b. 1796, d. April 26th, 1850, age 54.

1. Owen[5] Rucker.
2. Isaih[5] Rucker.
3. Anna[5] Rucker.
4. Nash[5] Rucker.

5. Cyrus[5] Rucker.
6. Elizabeth[5] Rucker.
7. Julius[5] Rucker.
8. Taylor[5] Rucker.
9. John[5] Rucker.
10. Sarah[5] Jane.

1. Owen[5] Rucker (Catherine[4], Lemuel, Sr.[3], James[2], Peter[1]), b. 1825 in Monroe County, Ohio, d. in Civil War in Service, m. Rachel Togel.

Issue:

1. Rachel[6] Rucker, b. Aug. 11, 1863, m. June 15, 1880, Leroy Fraker of Monroe County.

2. Isaih Rucker[5] (Catherine[4], Lemuel, Sr.[3], James [2], Peter[1]), b. Monroe County, Ohio, May 17, 1827, d. Jan. 5, 1891, in Noble County, Ohio, m. Mary Jane Hardesty, Mch. 2, 1854, b. Dec. 9, 1835, d. Jan. 27, 1917.

1. . Isaac[6] Richard Rucker, b. Sept. 25, 1858, m. Oct. 11, 1879, Jane Cunningham.
    1. Mary[7] Quinn Rucker, b. May 16, 1881, m. June 8, 1905, Herbert Barnes Horton.

8. Garland[4] Rucker (Lemuel, Sr.[3], James[2], Peter[1]), b. Apr. 8, 1805, m. Sarah Ann Blake (daughter of Daniel), b. Oct. 14, 1814, in Maine.

He was on his way to the California gold fields in 1849, by way of ship from New York around the South America. The ship was wrecked, and Garland was never heard from.

1. Joseph[5] Rucker, moved to Kansas.
2. Eunice[5] Rucker.
3. Daniel[5], died young.
4. Nancy[5].
5. Martin[5].
6. William[5] Rucker, b. Sept. 30, 1844, Ohio, d. Feb. 22, 1918.
7. Bettie[5] Jane, m. Joshua Blake.
8. Martha[5], m. M. Cornell.
9. Jane[5].

9. Edward[4] Rucker (Lemuel[3], James[2], Peter[1]), born in Greenbrier County, Virginia, and went to Monroe County, Ohio, about 1815 on Wills Creek. Private in War of 1812 (House of Delegates Proceedings of Virginia, 1834—War, 1812, Richmond, Virginia.

1. Ephraim[5].
2. Garland[5].
3. William[5].
4. Lemuel[5].
5. Ambrose[5].
6. Allen[5], moved to Ind., 1855.

1. Ephraim[5] Rucker (Edward[4], Lemuel[3], James[2], Peter[1]), moved to Mo. in 1841. His wife died when her son, G. W., was 2½ years old, and her baby daughter two months old, leaving one son about four years of age. The children were taken back to Ohio, to her people to be reared. Ephraim died 1862. Married twice.

Issue (by 1st mar.):

1. Charles[6] Madison Rucker, m. Bettie Bernard.
   1. L.[7] V. B. Rucker, a newspaper man of Miami, Fla. Miami, Florida.
2. G. W.[6] Rucker, b. March 3rd, 1841. Lived in Brunswick, Mo.
3. Daughter[6].

Issue (by 2nd mar.):

4. John[6] Early Rucker.
5. Edmond[6] W. Rucker, of Fayette, Mo.
6. Thomas[6] Rucker, of Carrolton, Mo.

4. Wyatt[3] Rucker (James[2], Peter[1]). Listed in the census of Virginia in 1783-86 as "head of a family." He paid a personal tax from 1786 to 1789 in Greenbrier County. No longer.

5. Samuel[3] Rucker (James[2], Peter[1]). James Rucker deeded to him 145 acres of land on Racoon Branch of Middle Fork of Anthony Creek out of a tract of 400 acres of land, patented by James Sr. 1783. Now in the possession of Samuel (D. B. 1, page 337, Greenbrier County, April 29th, 1794). 1795 Samuel Rucker sold this land to H. Williams.

(D. B. A, page 158, Bath County), March, 1774, Samuel Rucker, attorney for Mathew Penn of Amherst, sold some land to John Stover. Augusta Abstracts (Vol. 1, p. 330), May 15,

1781, Samuel Rucker of Augusta County was recommended and qualified as Lieutenant in Captain Oliver's company (Rev. war).

Aud. Acct. XXXI, 161, mentions Samuel Rucker of the 8th Virginia Regiment, serving under Captain George Slaughter.

Personal tax books of Augusta, 1783, Samuel paid his personal tax, and on three horses until 1788.

6. Elzaphan^{3} (Elzy) Rucker ((James^{2}, Peter^{1}), b. about 1760. Served in the Revolutionary War with his brothers, all from Culpeper County, under Captain George Slaughter. Later moved to Greenbrier County (Reference W. O. 181-6).

(War 4, p. 332), 16 Dec. 1784. The pay of Elzy Rucker, sergeant, was received by James Rucker.

He applied for a Revolutionary pension living at that time in Carters County, Kentucky, age 57 (from Pension Bureau). We are assuming Elzaphan to be the son of James, only because James received his pay in the Revolutionary War, and because he lived for a while in Greenbrier County (personal tax book) until 1814.

Robert^{4} Rucker (Elzy^{3}, James^{2}, Peter^{1}), b. May 3, 1794, in Greenbrier County. Married Elizabeth Vermilleon, b. Oct. 14, 1794, in Greenbrier County. They moved to Gallia County, Ohio. (It is said Robert was the son of Elzy.)

1. Elliott^{5} Rucker, b. Jan. 15, 1815, m. Margaret Elaeson.
2. Nancy^{5}, b. Sept. 15, 1816, William Hatfield.
3. Elzaphan^{5}.
4. Uriah^{5}, b. Sept. 12, 1820, m. Polly Stewart.
5. Elizabeth^{5}, b. Sept. 21, 1822, James Marcure.
6. Polly^{5}, b. Apr. 10, 1825, unmarried.
7. Susannah^{5}, b. April 19, 1827, m. Perry Peyton.
8. Charlotte^{5}, b. Dec. 20, 1830.
9. Lucy^{5} B., b. Sept. 21, 1834.
10. Amy^{5}, b. March 26, 1837, m. J. A. Neal.
11. Rachel^{5}, m. Martin Brown.
12. Basha^{5}, m. Joseph Strait.

1. Elliott^{5} Rucker (Robert^{4}, Elzy^{3}, James^{2}, Peter^{1}), b. May 3, 1794, m. Margaret Eleason.

1. Robert^{6} Rucker.
    1. Cora^{7} Rucker, m. ————Vance, of Westerville, Ohio.
    2. Robert^{7} Rucker.

2. John^6 Rucker.
   1. Earl^7 Rucker.
   2. Pearl^7 Rucker of New York.

3. Elzaphan^5 Rucker (Robert^4, Elzy^3, James^2, Peter^1), b. June 8, 1818, m. Mary C. Arthur, Feb., 1844. Lived in Laurence County, Ohio.

   1. Elizabeth^6 Rucker, b. Jan. 8, 1845, m. James Waddle.
   2. Wingate^6 James.
   3. John^6 Robert, b. June 17, 1848.
   4. Elliott^6 Jackson, b. June 26, 1850, Tulsa, Oklahoma.
   5. Mary^6, b. April 30, 1852, m. James Adkins.
   6. George^6 Washington, b. July, 1855, m. Martha Vance.
   7. William^6 Henry, b. Jan. 28, 1858, m. Charlotte Cryder.
   8. Sarah^6, b. Feb. 7, 1860, m. Jack Kayler.
   9. Amy^6, b. April 24, 1862, m. James Goleanor.
   10. Nancy^6, b. June 17, 1864, m. Lewis Huffman.
   11. Susie^6, b. Oct. 5, 1865, m. Tamner Given.

2. Wingate^6 James Rucker (Elzaphan^5, Robert^4, Elzy^3, James^2, Peter^1), b. August 9, 1846, m. Rutha Jane David.

   1. Charles^7 Edward Rucker, b. July 4, 1875, m. Martha Huffman.
   2. Amos^7 Wilson, b. April 22nd, 1877, m. Emie Crossland.
   3. Ida^7 Bell, b. January 28th, 1880, m. James Marion Adams.
   4. Howard^7 Sleveland, b. Dec. 7, 1884.
   5. Eva^7 May, b. May 5, 1887, m. 1st Walter Mulkey, second, Samuel Pick.
   6. Robert^7 Hillman, b. Aug. 22nd, 1890, m. Ethel Ivey.
   7. Ivory^7 Alberta Rucker, b. Aug. 16, 1893, m. 1st Parker Edmonson, 2nd Lester Davis.

9. Ambrose^3 Rucker (James^2, Peter^1), moved to Monroe County, about 1800.

   1. Julius^4 Rucker.
   2. Lemuel^4 E. Rucker, b. 1796, d. 1850. (See Catherine^4, Lemuel^3, Sr., James^2, Peter^1 Rucker).

1. Julius^4 Rucker (Ambrose^3, James^2, Peter^1), b. 1801 in Ohio. Was a Methodist minister, m. 1829 Susan Bates (daughter of Timothy).

   1. Wyatt^5 Rucker.
   2. Julius^5 Rucker.

3. Bethel[5] Rucker.
4. Phoebe[5] Rucker.
5. Emma[5] Rucker.
6. Landon[5] Rucker.

1. Wyatt[5] Rucker (Julius[4], Ambrose[3], James[2], Peter[1]), b. 1830, Ohio, m. Jane Morris (daughter of Moses Morris and ——— Stotts of New England).

1. William[6] H. Rucker, Frederickstown, Ohio.
2. Bethel[6] Rucker, Everett, Washington.
3. S. Emily[6], m. ——— Young.
   1. Benjamin[7] Young, Yonkers, N. Y.
4. Susan[6].
5. Roxanna[6].
6. Victoria[6], d. young.
7. W. Jasper[6] Rucker, Everett, Washington, is a very active man for his years. Since his 70th birthday he has traveled 25,800 miles by airoplane. Forty years ago he founded the city of Everett, in Washington. Never married.

The following names are listed in the personal tax books of Pocahontas County, which was cut from Bath in 1822. But by 1849 all by the Rucker name have disappeared.

List:

James, son to James, Jr.,	from 1822 to 1845.
Mordicai	from 1822 to 1829.
William	from 1822 to 1824.
Samuel	from 1822 to 1824.
Benjamin	from 1822 to 1823.
Merryman	from 1822 to 1823.
John	from 1835 to 1849.

Mordicai Rucker (wife Susannna Rader), began paying taxes on Greenbrier Co. in 1805. Continued until 1817. Moved to Pocahontas Co. in 1822. He pays a personal tax there until 1829. Then to McMinn County, Tenn. There were a number of land transfers from 1840 to 1857 by a Mordicai Rucker.

Wilfred Rucker was living in McMinn Co., 1836.

William Rucker and wife, Nancy; Thomas Epperson, Katherine and William Witt; heirs of Nathan Witt; Mordicai Rucker and others sold to Mordicai Rucker, 160 acres of land, McMinn's Co., Tenn., 1841.

John Rucker, Mordicai Rucker, James E. Rucker, Jesse Rucker, Joseph Witt, Matilda Witt, James Gresham and Emily Gresham sold to William Rucker all of the estate of James Rucker, Sr., deceased, 16 acres, McMinn's Co., Tenn., 1830. Could this James[3] have been a son of James[2], son of Peter[1]?

In 1853, William Rucker sold 480 acres to Mordicai Rucker, of McMinn's Co., Tennessee.

Levi Swinford deeded land to Joseph C. Rucker, paid by Merryman Rucker, guardian to Joseph C. Rucker, one of the heirs of Mordicai Rucker, deceased, 1857.

James S. Rucker, one of the heirs of Mordecai, sold land to William A. Rucker, McMinns Co., Tenn.

James C. Rucker sold to Hilton H. Burks (Sarah C. Burks, wife of Hilton. (The above Ruckers were from Pocahontas and Greenbrier counties).

The following are of a young generation and may be grandchildren of James, Sen., living on Anthony's Creek. Dewitt[4] Rucker (———[3], James[2], Peter[1]) (1776-1848) of Madison Co., Va., m. 1817 Eleanor Rucker.

In 1833 he bought 248 acres from Alex Benson. In 1838 he sold 100 acres. In 1845 he sold 140 acres to Liovey. In 1848 he bought 145 acres from George Wach.

Dewitt's name appears first on the Greenbrier personal tax books in 1800.

The estate of Dewitt Rucker was appraised by James Hefner, Aaron Levy, and William Mays, Sr. (W. B. 2, p. 388) Greenbrier Co., Oct. 9, 1898.

Oct. 11, 1838, Dewitt Rucker and wife, Eleanor, of Greenbrier Co., sold to John Kencaid, Mary McColester, Ann Scott, Elizabeth Buzzard, Sarah Rider, Jame Dizard, and Andrew L. Kincaid, heirs of Andrew Kencaid for $600, 100 acres of land on Middle Fork of Anthony Creek. (D. B. 14, p. 519) Greenbrier Co.

Dewitt Rucker deeded to John Rucker, both of Greenbrier Co., "On account of John Rucker's keeping and supporting Dewitt kindly and affectionately during his natural life", 145 acres, delivered to John Rucker, uncle of Dewitt, Jan. 20, 1874; deed recorded Feb. 17, 1853, (mentioned his age as 77 years) (D. B. 20, p. 31) Greenbrier Co.

Samuel Kincaid and wife, Margaret, of Greenbrier Co., deeded to Taverner Rucker, of same, for five shillings, 100 a. on North fork of Anthony Creek, adjoining Jeremiah Hopping.

William Rucker heir at law of Taverner Rucker, deceased, of Greenbrier Co., deeded to Timothy Holcourt, of same, for $1.00, land on North fork of Anthony Creek, 100 acres, being part of 320 acre tract, joining Jeremiah Hopping, 7 Oct., 1826 (D. B. 10, p. 389).

Merryman[4] Rucker (———[3], James[2], Peter[1]) paid his first personal tax in Greenbrier Co., 1797.

In 1818, July 17, he appears in the Bath County (later Pocahontas County) record, selling 100 acres of land to John May, of Bath, out of a 753-acre tract, surveyed in Greenbrier Co. (D. B. 7, page 278, Greenbrier Co.)

February 7, 1827, he sold to William May, of Greenbrier Co., 250 acres for $510.00 out of the same tract, on Anthony's Creek, and another 100 acres to Leonard Buzzer (D. B. 10, page 384).

Sarah, wife of Merryman, of Pocahontas Co., relinquished her dower rights before James Waugh and Samuel Cummings, Justice of the Peace (D. B. 7, page 548, Greenbrier Co.)

Merryman paid personal tax in Pocahontas Co. until 1833.

Dewitt Rucker administered on the estate of Merriman Rucker deceased, Sept. 20th, 1838 (O. B. Bath Co.).

Gideon Rucker, m. Lydia Underwood, daughter of Elijah, Dec. 12, 1804, Madison Co. He paid personal tax in Greenbrier Co. in 1799-1807, living on Anthony's Creek.

Personal tax book of Greenbrier Co.
James, Sen., 1785 to 1806.
James, Jr., 1797-1830.
James[3], 1802-1805.
Wyatt, 1785-1788.
Lemuel, 1789-1817.
Ephraim, 1792-1817.
Taverna, 1796-1816 (Estate).
Merryman, 1797-1815.
Gideon, 1797-1813.
Dewitt, 1802-1848.
Langford, 1805-1835.
Mordicai, 1805-1817.
Elzaphan, 1809-1813.
Ambrose, 1809-1811.
Paschal, 1812-1815.
John, 1815-1816.
Fanny Rucker, 1815-1816.
Lidia Rucker, 1815-1816.
Hannah, 1817-1818.

Susanna Rucker, 1817-1818.

Marriage records of Greenbrier Co.

Mordicai Rucker, m. Susanna Rader, July 21, 1818.

William Rucker, m. Catherine Byers, March 30, 1828.

Andrew J. Rucker, age 21, b. in Pocahontas Co., son of John and Mary G. Rucker, m. Elizabeth Ann Hefner, age 16, of Greenbrier, May 25, 1865.

John R. Thomas, age 28, b. Alleghany County, m. Frances J. Rucker, age 19, b. Greenbrier Co., daughter of Ballard and Matilda J. Rucker, June 2, 1870.

James E. Richey, m. Mary A. L. Rucker, April 30, 1874.

John Rucker, of Greenbrier County, son to M. and Elizabeth Rucker, d. August 22, 1884, age 77 years.

Land office, Richmond, Va., Book 118, page 404, Sept. 1, 1864, John Rucker patented 112 acres of land on Bear Creek, running into Middle fork of Anthony Creek.

James C. Rucker one of the heirs of Mordicai, sold land to William A. Rucker, McMinn's Co., Tenn. James C. Rucker, sold to Hilton H. Burks, (son of Sarah C. Burks, wife of Hilton). (The above Ruckers were from Pocahontas and Greenbrier Counties).

CHAPTER TEN

Ephraim Rucker

9. Ephraim[2] Rucker (Peter), d. Dec. 1796 in Madison, m. Margaret Vawter (daughter of John Vawter and Margaret Noel of Essex.

(Will of John Vawter, May 23, 1748, 1752 in Culpeper Co., mentions "My wife, Margaret". To my daughter Winifred, 150 acres of land inherited of my father-in-law, Daniel Noel.

To my dau., Margaret Rucker, 150 acres at the Great Mountains, part of a patent of 700 acres patented in 1736 by me. Witness: Edwin, Elizabeth and Samuel Vawter. (The above 150 acres of land was deeded by John Vawter to Ephraim Rucker, Feb. 7th, 1750).

(Daniel Noel patented 200 acres of land in St. Anne Parish, Essex Co., adjoining the land of his mother, Nov. 13, 1713 (L. Gr. B. 10, page 188).

Isaac Tinsley and wife, Margaret Rucker, sold 100 acres to Ephraim, land in Culpeper on Elk Run, in the forks of Rapidan and Robinson River, in 1759.

Angus and Ann Vawter of Orange Co., sold to Ephraim and James Barbour 159 acres of land on Pocoaney Fork Mts. being one-half of the land patented by James Lewis and John Harford in 1751 (D. B. 13, page 272, Orange Co.).

23 June, 1776, Ephraim sold this 159 acres to Jeremiah Jarrell.

In 1773 William Twyman and wife, Winifred, of Culpeper, sold to Ephraim 505 acres of land on Elk Run in the forks of Rapidan and Robinson Rivers.

He deeded 150 acres to son, Angus Rucker, in 1775, in the forks of Robinson and Rapidan Rivers; on North side of the court house road near Holt's mountains. The same day Ephraim deeded to Edmund Gaines 150 acres in the same location, to James Davis, 150 acres more in the same location.

The first land and personal tax books of Orange mentions him as "Col. Ephraim Rucker", paying on 63 acres, on eight slaves, names Sambo, James, John, Giles, Hog, Ishal, Rachel, and Adams, and 13 head of Cattle. Ephraim owned this property in Orange (Greene) but he was living on the North side of the Rapidan River in Culpeper (Madison).

The first land and personal tax books of Culpeper Co. mentions Ephraim as paying on 400 acres of land and on 16 slaves, Harry, Ben, York, Cloe, Venus, Diana, Will, Phil, Moll, George, James, Milly, Violet, Phillis, and Frank, and his own personal tax. In 1796 he pays his own and "son Julius".

In 1787 (Culpeper) he pays a personal tax on two sons, Julius and Elliot (both sons being away in Revolutionary service).

When Madison was formed from Culpeper in 1792 he is paying on the same 400 acres, continuing until his death, 1796. His estate continued until 1811 (Tax list). In 1799 Margaret Rucker paid on 7 slaves in Madison. In 1800 she pays on "son" continuing until 1813. This son may be Julius, who was injured in the Rev. Service. Ephraim paid on Julius in 1795, and in 1796 paid on two grand sons.

"Ephraim and wife, Margaret Rucker, paid 30 shillings for the present years schooling of Charles George Cook, and thirty shillings for the next, and for the year following." Sept. 3, 1774 (D. B. H, page 22, Culpeper).

In 1775 Charles G. Cook paid £21 to Ephraim for 60 acres of land, ½ mile above the bridge, which crosses Elk Run.

Revolutionary Service reference. Culpeper Court, Oct. 7, 1777, commissioners appointed James Slaughter, John Slaughter, and Ephraim Rucker as Lieutenant Colonels (Council Journals, 1777-8).

Hammersley's U. S. Army Register 1777-81, mentions Lieutenant Colonel Ephraim Rucker. *Heitman's* mentions the same.

War 23, 1776, mentions Captain Ephraim Rucker of Culpeper Co., Virginia.

Ephraim Rucker's will, dated Sept. 24, 1796, probated Dec. 28th, 1797 (W. B. 1, page 348, Madison Co.).

To my wife, Margaret, my whole estate until her death, then 1/7 to son Angus, and the land whereon he now lives. 1/7 to son Elliott, 1/7 to son John, 1/7 to daughter, Tabitha Gaines, 1/7 to daughter, Mary Vawter, 1/7 to daughter, Tomagen Rucker and her sons John and Ambrose Booten, and her daughters Ann and Elizabeth Rucker.

To my daughter, Margaret Morgan, and her sons, Elliot and Joseph Minor, and her daughter, Mary Early. Witness: James Ridish, George Allen and Joseph Bradford. Executors: Sons, Angus, Elliott and John. Angus and John gave bond in the sum of $10,000.00 Dec. 28, 1797, with William Blakey and Joseph Bradford, security.

Settlement of part of estate April 29, 1809, shows the estate to be in debt to John Rucker, $59.19.

Settlement of some property of the estate of Ephraim by John Rucker only acting executor in 1805 (W. B. 2, page 206).

Paid to Edmund Gaines; To William Morgan; To Julius Rucker; To Augustine Rucker.

In 1815 Angus Rucker, Executor of Ephraim Rucker, sold to Abraham Edden's, of Orange, 400 acres of land, Ephraim died seized with. Land in Madison County, adjoining Dr. William Morgan's, the heirs of Augustine Rucker, deceased, and Captain Joseph Early (D. B. 5, p. 471, Madison County).

1. Angus[3] Rucker.
2. Elliott[3] Rucker.
3. John[3] Rucker.
4. Tabitha[3].
5. Mary[3] Vawter.
6. Tomagen[3] Rucker.
7. Margaret[3] Morgan.
8. Julius[3] Rucker.

1. Angus[3] Rucker (Ephraim[2], Peter[1]), b. 1746 Culpeper, d. 1836, m, Jane Allen, about 1770. The inscription on his tombstone in Madison County states "Departed this life on Sept. 21, 1836, in the 89th year of his age, an officer of the Revolution and for many years a soldier of the cross."

His father deeded 150 acres of land to him May 15, 1775, on the Northside of the Court house road, near Holt's Mountains, in the forks of the Rapidan and Robinson Rivers in Culpeper County.

In 1792 he bought 265 acres near the Rapid Ann meeting house. In 1805 he bought 125 acres from Joseph Early's estate, land on Elk Run. In 1815 he bought 100 acres adjoining Edmund Gaines.

In 1805 he sold 99½ acres to Edmund Gaines for $50.00. Witness: Augustine Rucker, William Gaines and George A. Allen.

1801 Angus Rucker and wife, Jane, sold to Augustine Rucker, 28 acres for £48. Land in Madison. At the same time Angus bought 30 acres from Augustine and wife, Thomsey Rucker.

In 1815 Angus sold to Philip Slaughter a grant of 1,000 acres of land in Indian Territory. Granted for Rev. service.

In 1826, Angus and wife, Jane, sold to Augustine Rucker land beginning at Mrs. Early's Corner, and 24 acres on an old road called the Mountain Road, where it meets the main road, leading from Graves store to Fredericksburg.

Angus volunteered for Rev. service as a private in 1775, from Culpeper Co. 24 June, 1777 he was commissioned 1st Lieutenant in Captain John Nicholas Co. under Col. George Gibson. On the 3rd day of July, 1777, he was made Captain of the same regiment, serving until 1780. In 1781 he was appointed Superintendent of a hospital in Chesterfield Co., and served until the surrender (Pension Department, Washington, D. C.). One of his pension claim numbers is S. 19068, executed February 26, 1830, then a resident of Madison County.

Revolutionary Service References: W. D. 18-6, June 24, 1777; W. D. 1935, Dec. 6. Bounty warrants. Heitman's.

Executive Department, Richmond, Virginia, April 5, 1838.

"The heirs of Angus Rucker are allowed Bounty land for his service as Captain in the state line from Jan. 7, 1783, to Nov. 3, 1783, in addition to quantity heretofore allowed. Land issued to George A. Rucker, devisee and executor of Captain Augus Rucker.

Among the petitions, is one from Norfolk, No. 4283.

"Memorial of the military Officers, and Citizens of the State of Va. on behalf of themselves and the troops under their command, asking exemption from taxation during the War, for themselves and their overseers, as lands and crops deteriorate during absence."

Petition signed at camp, State of New York, Aug. 20th, 1779, Angus Rucker, Captain 1st Virginia.

He was pensioned 1830 as "Invalid" receiving 4000 acres of land in Kentucky (Kemper's Genealogy).

Will of Augus Rucker.

In the name of God—Amen.

I, Angus Rucker, of the County of Madison and State of Virginia, being of sound mind and of disposing memory, and knowing the certainty of death and the uncertainty of life—do hereby declare the following to be my last will and testament:—

Item:—It is my will and desire after my death my executors here in after named of those who may qualify under this WILL shall proceed to sell to the highest bidder upon a credit of twelve months—the purchaser or purchasers giving bond and good security for their respective purchases—the whole of my estate both real and personal. The real estate to be sold upon a credit of one or two years and the money arising from the sale of the said property to be divided equally (after the payment of all my just debts) in the following manner—to-wit:

1st.—One sixth part I give to my daughter Sallie A. Gaines, and her heirs or assigns forever:—

Secondly:—One sixth part I give to my daughter Catherine Early, her heirs and assigns forever:—

Thirdly:—One sixth part I give to my daughter, Margaret Blakey, her heirs and assigns forever:—

Fourth:—One sixth part I give to my son, George A. Rucker, to him his heirs and assigns forever:—

Fifth:—One sixth part I give to my daughter Jane Minor—to be vested in the hands of William Vawter, of the County of Boone, in the State of Kentucky as trustee, for the exclusive use and benefit of my said daughter Jane during her natural live and after her death whatever of said legacy may remain to be equally divided among all her children advanced.

Sixth:—One sixth part of which I give to my son John F. Rucker, or in the event of his death, to be equally divided among all his children deducting from the amount of said legacy the sum of forty dollars being for a horse theretofore advanced.

Item:—Should I make any further advances to my children or any of them between this date and the time of my death it is my will and desire that my executors hereinafter named or those who may act shall deduct the same from his or her part claimed under this will.

I do hereby revoke all wills heretofore made by me and declare this to be my only true last will and testament.

I do hereby ordain—constitute and appoint my son George A. Rucker and my sons-in-law William Early and James Blakey Executors to this my last will and testament—any of whom may act.

In testimony whereof I have hereunto subscribed my name and affixed my seal this 1st day of August in the year 1832.

Angus Rucker, (Seal)

Signed—sealed and acknowledged in the presence of John Harrison, Jr. and Linn Banks.

At a Court held for Madison County the 22nd day of September, 1836, the last will and testament of Angus Rucker deceased was produced into Court and proved by the oaths of John Harrison, Jr. and Linn Banks, witnesses thereto and ordered to be recorded.

On motion of George A. Rucker, executor therein named who made oath thereto and entered into bond and security according to law a certificate for obtaining a probate thereof in due form is granted him.

William Early and James Blakey the other executors in said will in open court refused to take upon themselves the execution of said will.

1. Sallie[4] Allen Rucker.
2. Catherine[4] Early.
3. Margaret[4] A. Rucker.
4. George[4] A. Rucker.
5. Jane[4] Minor.
6. John F.[4] Rucker.

1. Sallie[4] Allen Rucker (Angus[3], Ephraim[2], Peter[1]), b. in Virginia, d. Fayette Co., Indiana. Buried in Webb Cemetery near Alpine, Indiana, m. Oct. 4, 1804, William M. Gaines, b. Jan. 31, 1771, d. Nov. 18, 1836, of Madison Co., Virginia (son of Henry Gaines (1733-1811), and his 1st wife, Martha George). Moved to Boone Co., Kentucky, 1811. (See Gaines, p. ....)

1. Angus[5] Gaines, b. about 1806, Madison Co., Virginia.
2. Henry[5] Thomas Gaines.
3. Richard[5] George Gaines.
    1. Jess[6] Gaines, d. 1928, in Shelbyville, Ind.
    2. John[6] P. Gaines, d. 1929, in Shelbyville, Ind.
4. Mary[5] Jane Gaines.
5. Susan[5] Gaines.
6. Benjamin[5] A. Gaines.

2. Henry[5] Thomas Gaines (Sallie A.[4], Angus[3], Ephraim[2], Peter[1] Rucker), b. Sept. 20, 1810, Madison Co., d. Feb. 20, 1899, m. Aug. 9, 1836, Matilda Willis Cornelius, b. Sept. 3, 1818, of Shelby County, Ky., daughter of George and Elizabeth Willis Cornelius.

In 1838 they moved from Boone Co., Ky., to Shelby County, Indiana, where he died 1897. Matilda after her husband's death moved to Salina, Mo., making her home with her son, William C. Gaines.

1. George[6] Cornelius Gaines.
2. William[6] Currier Gaines, b. February 3rd, 1843.
3. Edward[6] C. Gaines, b. Dec., 1853, d. in infancy.

1. George^{6} Cornelius Gaines (Henry^{5} T., Sally^{4} A., Angus^{3}, Ephraim^{2}, Peter^{1} Rucker), b. Nov. 26, 1840, m. Dec. 3, 1867, Emily Jane Kaster (Dec. 8, 1848-Oct. 8, 1913).

    1. Lulu^{7} Gaines.
    2. Vi^{7} Gaines, died in infancy.
    3. William^{7} H. Gaines.
    4. Matilda^{7} B. Gaines.
    5. Charles^{7} S. Gaines.
    6. Edward^{7} C. Gaines.

1. Lulu^{7} Gaines (George^{6}, Henry^{5}, Sally^{4}, Angus^{3}, Ephraim^{2}, Peter^{1} Rucker), b. Sept. 30, 1868, in Shelby Co., Indiana, m. June 22, 1890, John H. Burkher.

Issue:

1. Ire^{8} Gaines Burkher, b. Mch. 28th, 1891, m. Apr. 30, 1917, May Stens.
2. Frances^{8} Burkher (July 17, 1894-Feb. 25, 1895).

3. William H.^{7} Gaines (George^{6}, Henry^{5}, Sally A.^{4}, Angus^{3}, Ephraim^{2}, Peter^{1} Rucker), b. June 7, 1874, Shelby Co., Indiana, m. Jan. 9, 1898, Ida Carmony.

    1. Justine^{8} Gaines, b. April 2, 1909.
    2. Frank^{8} Gaines, b. Aug., 1914.

4. Matilda^{7} B. Gaines (George^{6}, Henry^{5}, Sally A.^{4}, Angus^{3}, Ephraim^{2}, Peter^{1} Rucker), b. Sept. 19, 1876, m. 1894, Carey Gardner.

    1. H. Marie^{8} Gardner, b. Jan. 25, 1896, m. Jan. 10, 1924, Charles Skinner.
    2. Rema^{8} Gardner, b. May 1, 1898, m. 1915, Clarence Hewitt.
        1. James^{9} Kenneth Hewitt, b. April, 1920.
    3. Tekoa^{8} Gardner, b. Dec., 1899.
    4. Mabel^{8} Gardner, b. Mch. 28, 1901, m. Oct. 2, 1922, Faye Miller.
        1. Richard^{9} Gardner Miller, b. Oct. 15, 1923.
    5. Julia^{8} Gardner, b. 1902, m. Theodora Hurst.
        1. Junior^{9} Hurst.
        2. Harriet^{9} Hurst.
        3. Betty Lou^{9} Hurst.
    6. Floy Dolly^{8} Gardner, b. Oct., 1904, m. Joseph Patterson.
        1. Maxine^{9} Marie Patterson.
        2. Joseph^{9} Patterson.
    7. George^{8} Gardner, b. August, 1906.

5. Charles^{7} S. Gaines (George^{6}, Henry^{5}, Sally A.^{4}, Angus^{3}, Ephraim^{2}, Peter^{1} Rucker), b. Sept. 12, 1878, m. about 1903 Clara Kank.

1. Herbert^{8} Gaines.
2. Garnett^{8} Gaines.
3. Francis^{8} Gaines.
4. Lulu^{8} Bernin Gaines.
5. Woodrow^{8} Gaines.
6. Karl^{8} Robert Gaines.
7. Beulah^{8} Jean Gaines.
8. Eilien^{8} Gaines.
9. Betty^{8} Jane Gaines.
10. Lucile^{8} Gaines.
11. Charles^{8} Gaines.

6. Edward^{7} C. Gaines (George^{6}, Henry^{5}, Sally A.^{4}, Angus^{3} Rucker), b. Nov. 19, 1883, m. Feb. 9, 1911, Jennie S———

1. Howard^{8} Gaines (Mar. 31, 1912).
2. Rosamond^{8} Gaines (Feb. 24, 1920).

2. William^{6} Currin Gaines (Henry^{5} T., Sally^{4} A., Angus^{3}, Ephraim^{2} Rucker), b. Feb. 3, 1843, Shelby Co., Indiana, d. Dec. 15, 1924, Salino Co., Mo., m. Nov. 24, 1868, Pamelia C. Graves, of Boone Co., Ky., b. July 21, 1847, d. Nov. 21, 1910, in Mo., daughter of John W. Graves and Louisa Cave, his wife. They lived in Boone Co., Ky., until 1875, then moved to Salino Co., Mo.

1. Harry^{7} Terrill Gaines.
2. Mary^{7} Elizabeth Gaines.
3. Lulu^{7} Gaines.
4. Edward^{7} Cornelius Gaines, b. Feb. 1, 1878, now living Chicago, Ill.
5. Elis^{7} M. Gaines, b. Dec. 8, 1881, d. Sept. 1, 1882.
6. William E.^{7} Gaines.
7. Bessie^{7} C. Gaines, b. May 8, 1888.

1. Harry^{7} Terrell Gaines (William C.^{6}, Henry T.^{5}, Sally^{4} Rucker), b. June 25, 1871, Boone Co., Ky., m. April 28, 1898, Mary C.. Duggins, daughter of William T. and Anna Pulliam Duggins, in Saline Co., Mo.

1. George^{8} Duggins Gaines, b. Feb. 22, 1899.
2. Harry^{8} T. Gaines, b. June 8, 1900, d. 1901.
3. Margaret^{8} Gaines, b. Jan. 9, 1902.
4. Anna^{8} Pulliam, b. Dec. 17, 1907.
5. Elie^{8} Howard Gaines, b. Dec. 25, 1909.

2. Mamie^{7} Elizabeth Gaines (William^{6}, Henry^{5} T., Sally^{4} A. Rucker), b. Dec. 10, 1873, Boone Co., Ky., m. Oct. 18, 1893, Brick Pomeroy Storts (son of Perry C. and Anne E. Garrett Storts, Saline Co., Mo.), b. May 18, 1867.

  1. Edward^{8} Turner Storts, b. Dec. 25, 1902.
  2. Brick^{8} Pomeroy Storts, Jr., b. Sept. 12, 1905; graduated in medicine 1929, at the Ky. State College at Louisville, is now located in Ajo, Arizona; m. July 14, 1931, Gladys Elizabeth Long of Phoeniz, Arizona.

3. Lulu^{7} Gaines (William^{6}, Henry^{5}, ———), b. Jan. 12, 1876, d. Oct. 16, 1877.

6. William E.^{7} Gaines (William C.^{6}, Henry T.^{5}, Sally A.^{4} Rucker), b. Jan. 4, 1884, Saline, Mo., m. Dec. 25, 1905, Maude Dulaney, daughter of Landon Dulaney and Melinda Brumitt, his wife.

  1. Lila^{8} Louise Gaines, b. Oct. 18, 1913, Saline County, Mo.

7. Bessie^{7} Catherine Gaines (William^{6}, Henry^{5}, Sally^{4}, —), b. at Slater, Saline Co., Mo., May 8, 1888, d. Apr. 9, 1931, at a hospital in Kansas City, Mo.

3. Richard^{5} George Gaines (Sally A.^{4}, Angus^{3}, Ephraim^{2} Rucker), b. April 20, 1814, d. Jan. 20, 1883, Shelby Co., Indiana, m. Sarah Woodard.

  1. Sarah^{6} C. Gaines, Oct., 1842-1923, m. James Nave.
     1. Robert^{7} L. Nave, Acton, Indiana.
     2. Dr. H.^{7} E. Nave^{7}, Fountaintown, Indiana.
     3. Mrs. Viola^{7} Fox, Mountaintown, Indiana.
     4. Alva^{7} Nave, Shelbyville, Indiana.
  2. Mary Jane^{6} Gaines, b. Aug. 17, 1844, d. Mch. 14, 1852.
  3. William^{6} H. Gaines, b. Aug. 22, 1846, d. Sept., 1864.
  4. Matilda^{6} L. Gaines, b. June 22nd, 1849, d. June 16, 1857.
  5. John^{6} P. Gaines, b. 1850, m. Oct. 8, 1873, Isabelle Thompson, daughter of William and Ellen of Shelbyville, Indiana.
  6. James^{6} T. Gaines, b. March 6, 1855, d. 1856.
  7. Jesse^{6} Fremont Gaines, b. Sept. 19, 1856.
  8. Oliver M.^{6} Gaines, b. 1860, d. Feb. 2, 1924.
  9. Wingfield^{6} Gaines, Dec., 1880, m. Ida Oldham.

4. Mary^{5} Jane Gaines (Sally^{4} A., Angus^{3}, Ephraim^{2}, Peter^{1} Rucker), b. April 20th, 1814, Boone Co., Ky., d. Jan. 20, 1894,

m. Oct. 3, 1837, Benjamin F. Conner, b. July 17, 1817, Boone Co., Ky., d. Oct. 12, 1910 (son of Reuben and Uancy Conner).

1. Amanda[6] Gaines Conner, d. young.
2. William[6] Gaines, d. young.

An adopted daughter, Catherine Bitinger.

5. Susan[5] Gaines (Sally A.[4], Angus[3], Ephraim[2], Peter[1] Rucker), b. May 27, 1820, d. Oct. 9, 1861, m. John Hackleman.

1. Amanda[6] Hackleman, d. Jan. 1, 1926, m. ——— Atchison.
    1. Frank[7] Atchison.
    2. Mary[7] Jane Atchison, m. ——— Michels, of Kissimme, Fla.
        1. Fred[8] Michels.
    3. Elsie[7] Atchison.
2. Pink[6] Hackleman, b. 1918, of Tolona, Ill.
3. Lewis[6] Hackleman, b. July, 1921.
4. James[6] Hackleman.

6. Benjamin[5] A. Gaines (Sally[4] A., Angus[3], Ephraim[2], Peter[1] Rucker), b. Sept. 5, 1821, Boone Co., Ky., d. July 14, 1895, Vincennes, Indiana, m. Aug. 3, 1845, Edna Ann Cornelius.

1. William[6] Churchill Gaines, b. April 29, 1847, Indiana, d. Jan. 18, 1866, Richland, Ill.
2. Nancy[6] Ann Gaines, b. Dec. 13, 1848, in Kentucky, d. Dec. 22, 1871, Vincennes, Indiana.
3. John[6] H. Gaines, b. Feb. 4, 1851, in Kentucky, d. Feb. 20, 1877, m. Nov. 21, 1874, Sarah Elizabeth Wills.
4. Mary[6] Jane Gaines, b. Oct. 15, 1855, Jasper County, Ill.
5. Angus[6] Gaines, b. Nov. 22nd, 1861, Lawrence, Ill.

2. Catherine[4] Rucker (Angus[3], Ephraim[2], Peter[1]), b. Oct. 27, 1786, m. Feb. 2, 1804, William Early, Sr., b. Oct. 20, 1773, sister to Juliana Early Rucker, Madison Co., Va.

1. Howard[5] Early, m. Oct. 3, 1826, Tabitha Lewis.
    1. Thomas[6] Early.
    2. Jennie[6] Early.
    3. Catherine[6] Early.

3. Margaret[4] Rucker (Angus[3], Ephraim[2], Peter[1]), m. Nov. 30, 1813, James D. Blakey, of Madison Co., Va. At the age of 92, she travelled with her son, Marcus B., from Louisville to Shelbina, Mo., where she lived a few years.

1. Marcus[5] D. Blakey, of Missouri.
2. Jane[5] Allen Blakey, m. Alfred D. Allmond. Lived near Charlottesville, Virginia, where her children were born.
    1. Angus[6] Allmond.
    2. Marcus[6] Blakey Allmond.
    3. James[6] Mann Allmond.
    4. Alfred[6] T. Allmond.
    5. Harry[6] F. Allmond.

1. Angus[6] Rucker Allmond (Jane[5] Allen, Marbus[4] B., Margaret[3], Angus[3] Rucker), of Denver, Colorado, m. Feb. 6, 1894, Stella Ewing Eakin, of Nashville, Tenn.

1. Stella[7] Eakin Allmond.
2. Rowena[7] Ewing Allmond.
3. Jane[7] Allen Allmond.
4. Angus[7] Rucker Allmond, Lieutenant of 77th Division, 305th Artillery in service in France. Now living in San Francisco, California.

4. George[4] Allen Rucker (Angus[3], Ephraim[2], Peter[1]), m. Anna Marie Vawter (1st cousin).

In 1829 William and Catherine Simpson of Orange sold all of their rights to land in Madison Co. to George Rucker.

In 1835 he was paying a land tax on 4½ a. of land adjoining Sarah Lewis and Angus Rucker, in Madison County.

In 1839 George A. Rucker and wife, Anne M. sold to Elizabeth Yager of Madison Co. 24½ a. for $1500.00, land in Madison, Va. (D. B. 12, p. 125).

William Gully of Augusta County, Va., deeded to Anne M. Rucker for "Love and affection" a negro girl, Marcia, aged 4 years (D. B. 15, p. 297, Madison Co.).

1. Anne[5] Maria Rucker, m. 1832, Louis Hazelton Bascom.
    1. Virginia[6] Bascom.
    2. Henrietta[6] Bascom.
    3. Elizabeth[6] Bascom.

4. Alpheus^{6} Bascom.
5. Endora^{6} Bascom, m. ——— Smith.
    1. Dr. Larz^{7} Smith, San Francisco, Calif.
6. Ray^{6} Bascom.
7. de Wilton^{6} } Bascom twins.
8. Oscar^{6} }
9. Louis^{6} Bascom.
10. Eva^{6} Bascom.
11. Keating^{6} Bascom.

4. Jane^{4} Rucker (Angus^{3}, Ephraim^{2}, Peter^{1}), m. 20 Sept. 1808, Elliott Minor, son of Armistead Minor and wife, Margaret^{3} Rucker (Ephraim^{2}, Peter^{1}) in Madison Co., Va.

They moved to Boone Co., Ky. Jane's interest in her father's estate was left in trust to William Vawter, Boone County, Kentucky, but William refused to act as Guardian. Jane lived "On the Pike" in Boone Co., Kentucky.

1. Allen^{5} Minor, lived in Waldron, Indiana.
2. Owen^{5} Minor.
3. Oren^{5} Minor.
4. Malvina^{5} Minor.
5. Richard^{5} Minor.

The muster roll of the Boone Co. militia, of Ky., 1843, mentions William Minor, Owen Minor, Oren Minor, William Allen and William Graves.

6. John^{4} F. Rucker (Angus^{3}, Ephraim^{2}, Peter^{1}), m. Feb. 19, 1816, Mary Jarrell, Madison Co., Va., daughter of Mary Jarrell (marriage bond).

2. Elliott^{3} Rucker (Ephraim^{2}, Peter^{1}), b. in Orange, d. March 19, 1832, in Shelby Co., Ky., m. May 6, 1789, Nancy Smith, daughter of Benjamin, who deeded to Nancy Rucker a negro boy, Bob, "for love and affection" June 16, 1795, Madison Co. (D. B. 1, page 225). Witnesses: Thomas and Lewis Kirtly.

Elliott of Orange Co. bought 309a. of land on the Rapidan River from the executors of Richard Cave for £53 Apr. 28, 1796 (D. B. 1, p. 364).

Elliot Rucker of Orange bought 54 a. from David Williams and wife, Sally, land in Madison on the Rapidan River, September 2, 1800 (D. B. B, p. 2). Land adjoining John Herndon.

In 1805, Oct. 23, he bought 224 a. from Joshua Quinn, John Morton and Nancy, his wife, Hiram Quinn and Dorandy Quinn, of Madison Kentucky for £521. Land in Madison Co., Virginia.

Elliott lived in Orange Co. on the 63 acres belonging to his father, "Colonel Ephaim", until 1797, then moved across the river into Madison, living on his own land until 1806, then moved to Shelby Co., Ky. He paid a personal tax in Orange until 1797, but no land tax, after which date he paid personal and land in Madison, on 309, 224 and 54 acres of land.

In 1807 he sold 500 acres to John Jackson, land in Madison.

Elliott Rucker was a member of the house of Delegates from Madison Co., Va., 1802-04. In 1805 he was a Justice of the Peace of that county.

He was living in Shelby Co., Ky., when he applied for a pension for Revolutionary service, Nov., 1830. He enlisted in 1775 from Culpeper, serving for one year as a private under Captain John Green. In 1776 he was commissioned ensign under Colonel George Gibson, 1777, later a lieutenant in the same regiment. He became a major in 1781. Elliott remained in the regular army and was sent during the whiskey insurrection to western Pennsylvania to quiet the disturbance. He was raised to the rank of Inspector General then.

He was engaged in the storming of Stony Point. A number of letters are in the possession of one of Elliott's descendants in Kentucky, written by him to his wife, Nancy, while he was in active service there.

Petition No. 8495. Archives, Richmond, Va.

Elliot Rucker was with Col. Patrick Henry when he was in the battle of Williamsburg.

"About the 20th of Sept. 1775, the first regular company in Va. enlisted for a term of twelve months and marched to Williamsburg as a guard to the seat of Government. Elliot Rucker remained there until his term of service expired in the month of Jan. 1777. He was appointed ensign in the 1st Va. State Regiment, commanded by Col. George Green. As soon as they were organized, they were marched north to join Washington."

A petition filed in the Virginia State Archives, No. 8491, from Shelby Co., Ky., dated Dec. 17, 1825, a petition by John Shipman for Revolutionary pension:—"I served in the campaign of 1781 under the command of Major Elliott Rucker, of Va. He commanded a battallion of men, who were styled the "White Squad." I fought under him at the battles of Hot Water, Jamestown and at the siege of York. He was attached to General Wayne's brigade, and belonged to the regular army under Colonel Gibson.

Signed John Shipman.

Another affidavit of the same character concerning Elliot, is in the same folio, written by Angus Rucker.

Revolutionary service references: Aud. Accounts VII, 198; Aud. Accounts XV, 551; War, 5-19, W. D. 29-8, W. D. 29-8; Hammersley's U. S. Register.

He sold his land in Madison and moved to Shelby Co., Ky., where he died in 1832, leaving his widow, Nancy.

Issue:

1. Pricilla^{4} Rucker.
2. George^{4} W. Rucker.
3. Nancy^{4} Rucker.
4. Le Grand^{4} Rucker.

1. Pricilla^{4} Newman Rucker, m. James DeNeal.
    1. John^{5} DeNeal, m. Muriel Rucker.
        1. Caroline^{6}, m. James Pendleton Huggins.
            1. Elizabeth^{7} Huggins, m. John McMillen.
            2. Clements^{7} W. Huggins.

2. George^{4} Washington Rucker m. Maria Vawter, Oct. 6, 1810, in Woodford Co., Ky. Descendants live in San Francisco, California.

4. Le Grand^{4} Rucker, m. Caroline Wooldridge, Nov. 20, 1813, in Woodford Co., Ky.
    1. Elizabeth^{5}, m. Daniel Polk.
        1. Ellen^{6} Polk, m. Herman Ruff, of Denver.
            1. Alice^{7} P. Ruff, m. Frank P. Dellinger.
        2. Louis^{6} Polk.
        3. Alice^{6} Polk, m. W. Crow Hill, Denver.
            1. William^{7} Hill.
                1. Alice^{8} P. Hill.

3. John^{3} Rucker (Ephraim^{2}, Peter^{1}), d. 1811, Woodford Co., Ky., m. Juliana^{5} Early (Joseph^{4}, Jeremiah^{3}, Thomas^{2}, Peter^{1} Early), b. 1763, d. 1851.

In 1775 Ephraim Rucker deeded to his son, John, 150 acres. In 1795 John bought 30 acres from William Simpson and wife, Frankey, of Broomfield Parish. In 1797 John bought 12 acres from Thomas Stockdale, Sr., and wife, Elizabeth (D. B. 2, p. 52, Madison Co.)

April, 1805, John Rucker and wife, Judy, Paschal Early, William Early, Mary Newman and Joseph Early, heirs of Joseph Early, deceased, sold to John Rucker 125 acres of land on Elk

Run. Witness: George Alexander, William Gaines and Whitfield Jarrell. (D. B. 4, p. 119, Madison Co.).

Land tax books of Madison Co., 1792, mentions "John Rucker, son to Ephraim, paying on 150 acres. 1795, John Rucker, son to Ephraim, 150 acres and 130 acres, formerly of Jeremiah White's". 1797, "30 acres formerly of William Simpson" and "12 acres formely of Stockdale." In 1795, Feb. 10th, Jeremiah White, Jr., and wife, Rachel, of Madison, sold 130 acres to John Rucker, land adjoining Cornelius Wayland's (formerly Isaac Smith's), Merry Walker's, William Simpson's and John Rucker's, George Eastham's, Thomas Stockdale's and Francis Collins, on the east side of Neal's Mountain, for £300. Witness: Merry Walker, William Kirtley, William Morgan, Elliot Minor.

Oct., 1797, Ephraim for "natural love and affection, which I bear to my son, John Rucker, one negro boy, Frank, now in John's possession. (D. B. 2, p. 132).

John Rucker and wife, Judy, sold 396 acres to Richard Booten, Oct., 1810. (D. B. 5, p. 43, Madison Co.).

The land tax books of 1806. John Rucker paid on 150, 30, 30 and 12½ acres (of Elizabeth Rucker's). This one-half acre John sold in 1807 to Joseph Brock, Jr.

1799, John and his wife, Judy Rucker, sold to Francis Collins 100 acres for $100.00 land in Madison Co.

He paid taxes in Madison Co. until 1810, having already moved to Woodford Co., Ky., where he died, 1811, leaving a will dated March 12, 1811, recorded April, 1811, in Versailles, Woodford Co., Ky. (D. B. "C", p. 234). Will mentions wife, Julianna. To son, Joseph Rucker. To son, John Rucker. To daughter, Mary H. Rucker. To son, Paschal Rucker. To son, William Early Rucker. To son, James Rucker. To daughter, Jane Rucker. To son, J. Alfred Rucker. Executors: Wife, Julianna, and sons, Joseph E. and John S. Rucker. Witness: William Vawter, Elliot Rucker.

Issue:

1. Joseph[4] Rucker.
2. John[4] Rucker.
3. Mary[4] H. Rucker.
4. Paschal[4] Rucker.
5. William[4] Early Rucker.
6. James[4] Rucker.
7. Jane[4] Rucker.
8. J.[4] Alfred Rucker.

3. Mary[4] H. Rucker (John[3], Ephraim[2], Peter[1]), m. Churchill Gaines (Henry and Sara Churchill Gaines, of Madison Co.) (See Gaines, p. —.)

1. Edwin[5] M. Gaines.

The following letter speaks for itself:

Burlington, Boone Co., Ky.,
Oct. 7, 1856.

Mr. Bellfield Cave,
Madison, Virginia.

Dear Sir:

Edwin M. Gaines, of our County, only heir of Mary Gaines, late Mary Rucker, daughter of Juliana Rucker, widow of John Rucker. Said Juliana Rucker was sister to Capt. Joseph Early, of your County. Said Edwin M. Gaines, son of Churchill and said Mary Gaines, is a grand nephew of said Joseph Early, and as such claims to be a devisee and heir of the estate of Early. He has been informed that there is an attempt being made to cut out the grandnephews and nieces,, perhaps some proceedings now pending to settle the question whether they are devisees.

At Mr. Gaines' request I enclose you a power to act as his agent in the premises, to attend to his interest promptly. Mr. Gaines is a very worthy citizen and a gentleman who will promptly pay for any and all expense incurred in the premises and for services.

Please attend to it for him if convenient, if not appoint some one to do so, and advise me of proceedings, etc.

Respectfully yours,
John Cave.

5. William[4] Early Rucker (John[3], Ephraim[2], Peter[1]), b. March 5, 1797, m. Nov. 7, 1822, Clarissa Rodges, d. March 15, 1900.

1. Sarah[5] Ann, b. March 7, 1824, m. Jack Hutchinson.
2. Addison[5], b. August 20, 1826, m. 1st, Hudgens; 2nd, ————.
3. Horace[5], b. August 30, 1828, unmarried.
4. Alfred[5], b. May 1, 183—, m. Cheneweth.
5. John[5], b. August 7, 1833, m. Margaret Ireland.
6. Mary[5], b. July 1, 1836, m. William Smith.
7. Andrew[5] Jackson, b. October 25, 1841, d. April 29, 1907, unmarried.

8. Julia^{5}, b. June 18, 1843, d. December 31, 1931, age 88, m. John^{6} Fleming Rucker (John^{5} D. L., John^{4}, Isaac^{3}, John^{2}, Peter^{1}).
   1. Booker^{6} Hall Lewis Rucker.
   2. Roy^{6} Fleming Rucker.
   3. Early^{6} Rucker.

4. Tabitha^{3} Rucker (Ephraim^{2}, Peter^{1}), m. Edmond Gaines, d. 1815, lived in Madison Co., adjoining Angus Rucker.

In 1796, Madison Co., Edmund Gaines was appointed by the court "To pay to Elliott Minor, orphan of Armistead Minor, deceased, the amount due him when of lawful age, out of the estate of John Rucker, deceased." (W. B. 1, p. 109).

In 1805 he bought 99½ acres from Angus Rucker.

His father-in-law, Ephraim, deeded to him 150 acres in Culpeper Co., on Elk Run, in the forks of the Rapidan and Robinson Rivers, May 15, 1775.

5. Mary^{3} Rucker (Ephraim^{2}, Peter^{1}), m. June 4, 1784, William^{4} Vawter (David^{3}, John^{2}, John^{1}) (marriage bond in Orange Co. Security James Staples). William, b. 1758, d. Nov. 27, 1823.

They moved to Woodford Co., Ky., in 1788, then to Burlington, Boone Co., Ky.

In 1803, William and Mary sold land in Fayette Co., Ky., between the years of 1805 and 1809, also land in Jessemine and Gallatin Counties, Ky.

William was appointed by Angus Rucker, of Madison Co., trustee for his daughter, Jane Minor, wife of Elliott Minor, of Boone Co., Ky. William refused to act.

William Vawter served in the Revolution. Enlisted Jan. 17, 1779, under Captain John Champ, of the 1st Virginia Regiment, under Colonel George Gibson. Later became a lieutenant. At a court of appeals held at the Capitol in Richmond, Va., Sept., 1791, in a suit, the Commonwealth against William Vawter, late lieutenant in the 1st Va. Regiment—Case was dismissed.

William Vawter's name appears in the first census of Kentucky, 1790.

1. William^{4} Vawter, Jr.
2. George^{4} M. Vawter.
3. Herman^{4} Vawter.
4. Edmond^{4} Vawter.
5. Thomas^{4} Vawter.
6. Virginia^{4} Vawter.

1. William[4] Vawter, Jr. (Mary[3], Ephraim[2], Peter[1] Rucker), b. April 4, 1795, Woodford Co., Ky., d. March 31, 1858, Fulton, Mo., m. 1st, Sarah Neave, b. 1807, Manchester, England, d. 1839; m. 2nd, Amanda Poage, b. 1813, d. 1860, Fulton, Mo.

Issue (by first marriage):

1. Jane[5] Neave Vawter, b. Jan. 16, 1837, Monroe Co., Mo., d. Sept. 1, 1922, Salino, Mo., m. J. Carter Kirtly, of Mt. Leonard, Mo., b. March 4, 1931, Rolls, Mo.
   1. Irving[6] W. Kirtly, b. June 20, 1858.
   2. Herbert[6] Kirtly.
   3. Flora[6] Kirtly.
   4. Ella[6] Kirtly.
   5. George[6] Kirtly.
   6. Roland[6] Kirtly.

Issue (by second marriage):

2. Alfred[5] Fleming Vawter, d. 1928, Los Angeles, Calif.
3. James[5] Vawter, d. 1915, Memphis, Tenn.
4. Pierce[5] Vawter.
5. William[5] Franklin Vawter.

2. Herbert[6] Rucker Kirtly (Jane[5], William[4] Vawter, and Mary[3] Rucker), b. June 2, 1862, d. Feb. 19, 1921, m. 1896, Hattie Tinker, of Plymouth, Mass., lived in Michigan City, Ill.

1. H.[7] Rudolph Kirtly, m. Hilda Gillow, of New York.
2. Madeline[7] Kirtly, b. 1898, m. Robert Fitz, Feb., 1925.
3. Frank[7] Kirtly, b. 1900, m. Myrtle Tasker.
4. Edward[7] Kirtly, b. 1902, m. Clara Schultz.
5. Jane[7] Neave Kirtly, b. April 11, 1908.

3. Flora[6] Kirtly (Jane[5], William[4] Vawter, and Mary[3] Rucker), b. Dec. 3, 1863, d. single, Mt. Leonard, Mo.

4. Ella[6] Kirtly (Jane[5], William[4] Vawter, and Mary[3] Rucker), b. Aug. 28, 1866, m. Oct. 31, 1892, George Buchanan, El Pasa, Texas.

1. Evelyn[7] Buchanan, b. Sept. 19, 1893, at San Antonio, Texas, m. Murry Kyle, son William[8] M. Kyle, b. Aug., 1916.
2. Percy[7] C. Buchanan, b. Aug. 26, 1898, Del Rio, Texas.
3. Frances[7], b. Jan. 16, 1907, San Antonio, Texas.

5. George[6] E. Kirtly (Jane[5], William[4] Vawter, and Mary[3] Rucker), b. Dec. 30, 1868, a Presbyterian minister of Newman, Ill.

6. Roland[6] Kirtly (Jane[5], William[4] Vawter, and Mary[3] Rucker), b. June 1, 1877, d. Oct. 25, 1919, m. 1904, Mary Tuttle, Denver, Colo.

1. Sue[7] T. Kirtly, b. May 15, 1905, New York City.
2. Ralph[7] D. Kirtly, b. Jan. 9, 1910, of Denver, Colo.

6. Tomagen[3] Rucker (Ephraim[2], Peter[1]), m. 1st, ——— Booten. 2nd, Augustine[3] Rucker (James[2], Peter[1]).

Her father, Ephraim, mentions four of her children in his will, 1796. John and Ambrose Booten, and Ann and Elizabeth Rucker. "Polly Rucker, daughter of Augustine, m. April 13, 1802, Thomas Parrott, Madison Co., marriage bonds." Whether she was a daughter of Tomegen or by a former marriage is not shown.

Augustine bought 28 acres for £45 from Angus Rucker and wife, Jane, Dec. 24, 1801.

Augustine Rucker and wife, Thomsey, sold 30 acres for £25 to Angus Rucker in Dec., 1801. (D. B. 3, p. 126, Madison Co.).

In the land tax books of Culpeper, 1782, Augustine[3] Rucker is paying on 200 acres and continues until 1815 in Madison, land on Conway River, which was divided between his two sons, Ephraim and Larkin Rucker. In the first personal tax books, Augustine paid on four slaves, by name, "Fan, Rachel, Phillis and Ezekiel".

In 1807 he pays poll tax on "step-son", O.[2] A. Booten, and 1800 on one "son", 1807 on "2 sons". Will of Augustine Rucker, dated 1814, probated Feb. 23, 1815, mentions, "to son, Larkin, a negro; to son, Ephraim, 1 negro, and they to have the residue of my estate, wife Thomsey." Executors: My sons, Larkin and Ephraim. Witness: Richard C. Booten, Joseph Early and Ambrose Crisler. (W. B. "B", p. 97, Madison Co.)

It cannot be located from the records which son of Peter[1] Rucker was the father of Augustine, not having found the wills of William and James, it is impossible to know. But Augustine was associated with James Rucker, Jr., in a land deal in Bath Co. This land had been patented by Lewis, near the Warm Springs, on the Cowpasture River, and 260 acres of the tract had been assigned to George Poage, James Rucker, Jr., and Augustine Rucker, 1793. (Augusta Co. Abstracts). Augustine did not pay a land or personal tax in Augusta, Bath, nor Greenbriar Counties.

Issue (by 1st mar.):

1. John^{4} Booten.
2. Ambrose^{4} Booten.

Issue (by 2nd mar.):

3. Ann^{6} Rucker.
4. Elizabeth^{6} Rucker.
5. Ephraim^{4} Rucker.
6. Larkin^{4} Rucker.
7. Polly^{4} Rucker.

2. Ambrose^{4} Booten (Tomagen^{3}, Ephraim^{2}, Peter^{1} Rucker), owned 173 acres of land adjoining Jarvis Rucker.

5. Ephraim^{4} Rucker (Tomagen^{3}, Ephraim^{2}, Peter^{1}), b. about 1778, in Culpeper Co., d. in Anderson Co., Ky., m. Jan. 4, 1816, Rosamond Wright, in Madison Co., Va., daughter of Captain Wright, of Revolutionary service. His land adjoining William Morgan's. He and his wife, Rosanna G., sold to his brother, Larkin Rucker, 100 acres for $700.00. Land conveyed to Ephraim by the will of his father, Augustine Rucker, deceased. (D. B. 6, p. 199, Madison Co., Sept. 11, 1817).

1. John^{5} Rucker.
2. Ambrose^{5} Rucker.
3. Charles^{5} Rucker.
4. Willis^{5} Rucker.
5. Legrand^{5} Rucker.
6. Lizzie^{5} Rucker, m. Rains.
7. Mary^{5} Rucker, m. Dawson.
8. Rosa^{5} Rucker, m. Jerry Harrison.
9. Joseph^{5} Rucker, b. 1828 in Ky., d. Aug. 16, 1915, moved to Chariton, Mo., in 1850, m. Eliza F. Robinson, Jan 16, 1855, at Roanoke, Mo., they lived at Salisbury, Mo.
    1. Mary^{6} Rucker.
    2. Ennie^{6} Rucker.
    3. J.^{6} W. Rucker.
    4. William^{6} L. Rucker.
    5. Ambrose^{6} S. Rucker.
    6. Ernest^{6} J. Rucker.
    7. Annie^{6} E. Rucker.
    8. Graves^{6} T. Rucker, m. Mary Scott, Oct. 5, 1884.
    9. Georgia^{6} Rucker.

1. Mary^{6} Rucker (Joseph^{5}, Ephraim^{4}, Tomagen^{3}), b. May 7, 1858, m. J. C. Robertson, lived at Yate, Mo.

2. Ennie^{6} Rucker (Joseph^{5}, Ephraim^{4}, Tomagen^{3}), m. Nov. 8, 1883, J. C. Hurt, Salisbury, Mo.

   1. O.^{7} O. Hurt.
   2. Lieut. Paul^{7} E. Hurt.

3. Joseph^{6} Wiley Rucker (Joseph^{5}, Ephraim^{4}), a Baptist minister of LaFayette, Ga., m. Jesse Deberry. No children.

4. William^{6} L. Rucker (Joseph^{5}, Ephraim^{4}), b. Nov. 19, 1867, was the treasurer of Liberal Co., Mo., m. Molly Burton, Dec. 24, 1895.

5. Ambrose^{6} S. Rucker (Joseph^{5}, Ephraim^{4}), b. Aug. 12, 1872, a banker in Salisbury, Mo., m. Minnie E. Easton, Dec. 20, 1891.

   1. Lieut. Joseph^{7} E. Rucker, of the U. S. Navy, b. Oct. 1, 1899, m. Oct. 27, 1922, Olive Walker.
   2. Ambrose^{7} J. Rucker, b. Jan. 6, 1910.
   3. Frances^{7} Elizabeth, b. Sept. 19, 1916.

6. Ernest^{6} J. Rucker (Joseph^{5}, Ephraim^{4}), b. Sept. 11, 1894, a farmer of Salisbury, Mo., m. Nannie Damenon.

   1. Dr. L.^{7} C. Rucker, of Moberly, Mo.

7. Annie^{6} E. Rucker (Joseph^{5}, Ephraim^{4}), b. Aug. 8, 1877, m. J. T. Morressy, of Clifton Hill, Mo.

   1. Thurman^{7} Morressy.
   2. Forrest^{7} Morressy.
   3. Carson^{7} Morressy.
   4. Euradice^{7} Morressy.
   5. Hellen^{7} Morressy.

9. Georgia^{6} Rucker (Joseph^{5}, Ephraim^{4}), b. Jan. 23, 1881, m. Dr. Achilles Eubank, Kansas City, Mo., June 24, 1908.

   1. Hellen^{7} Eubank.
   2. Ruth^{7} Eubank.

6. Larkin^{4} Rucker (Tomagen^{3}, Ephraim^{2}, Peter^{1}), m. Feb. 21, 1815, Lucy Terry, daughter of John and Rachel Terry (D. B. 10, p. 7, Madison Co.) On June 4, 1839, power of attorney

was given to Larken to sell land of Sarah Terry, sister of Lucy. Larkin was given 100 acres of land by his father, Augustine.

Sept. 11, 1817, Larkin Rucker bought the 100 acres of lnad of his brother, Ephraim—the tract conveyed to Ephraim by will of his father, Augustine Rucker, deceased (D. B. 6, p. 199, Madison Co.)

Larkin and wife, Lucy, of Madison Co., sold to Richard C. Booten, of same, 200 acres for $1,000.00, land adjoining Thornton Harrison and Joseph Early, Sept., 1828, (D. B. 10, p. 170). William Burton and Sarah, his wife, sold to Larkin Rucker, of Madison, 360½ acres for $1,800, land in Orange Co. This land Larkin sold in 1837 to William Pence for $2,000.00.

1837, Sept. 15, Larkin Rucker bought land from Minor Rucker and his wife, Harriet, of Orange, land adjoining Minor Rucker, William Herndon and Blyfield Rucker.

1842, Sept. 1, Larkin Rucker sold land to R. D. Sims, land in Greene Co. (Orange). Witness: Larkin G. Rucker.

Issue:

1. Margaret[5] Rucker, m. Dr. Terrill, moved to Kentucky.
    1. Felix[6] Terrell, moved to Texas.
2. James[5] Rucker, d. 1827.
3. Larkin[5] Grandison Rucker.
4. Sarah[5] Ann Rucker.

3. Larkin[5] Grandison Rucker (Larkin[4], Tomagen[3]), b. 1810, m. ——— Davis, moved to Patrick Co., Va. He was Clerk of the Court for 50 years. The writer has a letter written by Larkin G. Rucker, dated Aug. 10, 1866, to a Mr. R. G. Rucker, of Columbia, Ga., some parts of which will be given here. "My father, Larkin Rucker, married Lucy Terry, of Madison County, leaving four children. My mother, my brother and my sister have died. When a boy of 16 I moved to this county (Patrick). At the same time my father and sister moved to Kentucky. I have seen none of my family since, my home has been among strangers. I married at the age of 17, and have three children, a son, now of the age of 21, who entered the Confederate Army, at the age of 16 at the beginning, and served to the close, spending the last 14 months in prison at Fort Delaware. I have a daughter eight years of age, and a son five.

Very respectfully,

L. G. Rucker."

Issue:

1. Wooster^{6} Rucker.
2. Sallie^{6} Rucker.
3. William^{6} T. Rucker.
4. Sarah^{6} Ann Rucker.

1. Wooster^{6} Rucker (Larkin^{5}, Larkin^{4}, Tomagen^{3}, Ephraim^{2}, ———), b. 1845, m. ——— McCanloss. He was a Confederate soldier.

   1. Dudley^{7} Rucker.
   2. Lucean^{7} Rucker.

2. Sallie^{6} Rucker (Larkin^{5}, Larkin^{4}, Tomagen^{3}, Ephraim^{2}, ———), b. 1859, m. Judge J. R. Moore, of Patrick Co.

   1. Carrie^{7} Moore.
   2. Jessie^{7} Moore.
   3. Rucker^{7} Moore.
   4. Cora^{7} Moore.

3. William^{6} T. Rucker, b. 1861, m. 1892, ——— Gray, of Culpeper.

4. Sarah^{6} Ann Rucker (Larkin^{5}, Larkin^{4}, Tomagen^{2}, ———), d. Aug., 1839, m. April, 1838, John A. Miller, of Greene Co.

   1. Lucy^{7} Miller, b. 1839, m. Dec., 1859, Hiram Parrott, of Quinque, Va.
      1. Sarah^{8} E. Parrott, m. June, 1893, B. T. Douglas.
         1. Annie^{9} Jennings Douglas.
      2. Otto^{8} Jennings Parrott, m. Sudie Parrott, Oct., 1911.
         1. Annie^{9} Buford Parrott.
         2. Brightberry^{9} Parrott.
         3. Edward^{9} R. Parrott.
         4. O.^{9} J. Parrott, Jr.
         5. Starnell^{9} Parrott.

7. Polly^{4} Rucker (Augustine and Tomagen^{3}, Ephraim^{2}), m. April 13, 1802, Thomas Parrott, marriage bond dated above, states: "Polly daughter of Augustine Rucker".

7. Margaret^{3} Rucker (Ephraim^{2}, Peter^{1}), m. twice (from her father's will), m. 1st, Armistead Minor, d. before 1791; m. 2nd, William Morgan.

The land tax books of Culpeper of 1785 charges Armistead Minor's account with 326 acres of land, formerly Turner Richardson's. Armistead's estate in 1791 was paying on 205 acres of land.

1. Mary[4] Early.
2. Joseph[4] Minor.
3. Elliott[4] Minor, m. Jane[4] Rucker (Angus[3], Ephraim[2], Peter[1]), Sept. 20, 1808, in Madison Co., Va. John Rucker, Edmund Gaines and James Barbour were appointed trustees for Elliott Minor, orphan, of Armistead Minor, deceased, June 23, 1796 (W. B. 1, p. 109, Madison Co.)

8. Julius[3] Rucker (Ephraim[2], Peter[1]), was a Revolutionary soldier, auditor's account, 15, 551.

War 4, p. 327, mentions him as Sergeant, an "Invalid Soldier".

In 1782 Ephraim paid a personal tax on son Julius. Also in 1795.

1807 Margaret Rucker paid on "son". Nothing further.

CHAPTER ELEVEN
Ann Rucker

10. Ann[2] Rucker (Peter[1]), wife of Shem Cook.

In 1752, they received a negro girl named Jenny out of the estate of Peter Rucker, deceased. In 1758 they sold and moved to Amelia Co., Va.

Shem Cook sold 200 acres for £80 to James Seay, land in Amelia Co., adjoining William Foster, John Butler and Thomas Wingo on Hunt Creek.

(Signed) Shem Cook.

Witness: William Ford, William Hurt and Edmund Booker. 30 Oct., 1766 (D. B. 8, p. 702, Amelia Co.)

Shem Cook left no will in Amelia Co. William Shem Cook owned land in Amelia, adjoining Isaac Tinsley, in 1756.

The following names on marriage bonds have not been located in this work:

Henry Allen, m. Phoebe Rucker, Jan. 25, 1790, Culpeper Co., Va.

Angus Rucker, m. Mary Susanna Graves (daughter of Thomas Graves and wife, Sarah Delaney, daughter of John Delaney and wife, Frances Stanton), Aug. 24, 1806, Madison Co., Va. (Thomas Graves was son of John Graves and wife, Susanna).

Robert Rucker, m. 1806, Oct. 9, Sallie Graves, Culpeper Co., Va.

Richard Rucker, m. Sallie Gaines, daughter of Richard, Culpeper Co.

James R. Rucker, m. Mary Terrell, 1782, Culpeper.

Moses Rucker, m. Elizabeth Thomas, April 20, 1781, Orange, Va.

Gideon Rucker, m. Lydia Underwood, Dec. 13, 1804.

George M. Rucker, m. Almira Burford, Lynchburg, Va., 1842, Oct. 4.

Richard H. Rucker, m. Sophia Harrison, 1842, Oct. 4, Amherst, Va.

Who is this Benjamin Rucker?

Benjamin Rucker, of Culpeper, served in the Revolution, under Captain Sale, of the 8th Virginia Reg., 4th Brigade. (Stubbelfield's Orderly Book, Archer's Rd., Va.)

War 22, p. 92—"The following sum sent by Capt. Richard Taylor to Capt. James Taylor, of Orange," to pay the ——— Benjamin Rucker, deceased, Stephen Ham and others.

War, 22, p. 2—March 9, 1776—Cash to Benjamin Rucker.

PART II.

HERALDRY

Rücker

Rucker Family Coat of Arms

The first coat of arms of the Rucker name was used by Johan Von Rücker, of Vienna, a crusader A. D. 1096. In the records he is called "Sir Knight Crusader," see Feyerabend's *Geschichte Der Kruzzüge,* a history of the Crusades and Crusaders, the first printed book published in Frankfort, A. D. 1583.

This armorial is shown in the famous compilation (54 volumes) entitled, *Grosses und Allgemines Wappenbuck,* by Von J. Siebmacher; *Enthaltent Zwei Tausend Historisch Begründete Familien Wappen,* etc. Nurnberg, 1857, (General book of coat armor by Siebmacher). Also see Helmer's *Erneuertes und Vermehrtes Wappenbuch,* Nurnberg, 1699, section—Ritter und Adels Personen, on Knights and Nobility. The Rücher name appears first in Vienna branching off to Livonia, Bavaria, Holland, France, England and later to America. There are fifteen coat of arms of the name and the shields of fourteen of these granted later are differenced upon the first, used in 1096, that is each one of the fourteen has one or more of the designs used on the original. All of them have wings for their crest, and all have wings, six pointed stars or crescents on the shields, all of which are used on the original by John Von Rücher.

The French and English authorities on Heraldry are very emphatic on one point, never to place color on color nor metal on metal, but the study of the arms of the crusaders, discloses the fact, that it was very frequently done by the crusaders. They were going to Palestine to reclaim it for Christ from the Turks, and each crusader used a star, crescent, cross or some emblem of the church on their standard or arms.

The following is from Nesbit's *Heraldry*:

"Those 'Justing' in the military exercises were obliged to hang up their shields some days before the time of exercise, near the place of action, if in the field, upon trees, pavillions or barriers of the place. They who were to fight on foot hung their shields by the right corner, and they on horseback by the left. This position is called pendant very frequently all over Europe from the eleventh to the fourteenth century. All the Shields pendant that I have seen of the sons of the royal families were pendant by the sinister, and very few from the dexter, the shield pendant when lying on the right side was then a mark, that the owner thereof had formerly been exercised in Tournaments, into which none were admitted but those that were truly noble."

These references for the following coat of arms are to be found in the New York Library:

Wade's *Symbolisms; Forstman; Furgoson;* Fayerabend's *Geschichte der Kruzzuge Rosenthal,* Munich; Siebmacher; Reiststap; Helmer; Planche's *de l'Armorial General.*

Number 1. This coat of arms of Johan Von Rücher of Vienna the crusader, in 1096, carries a blue shield with a silver point in which is a six pointed gold star; at the sides of the point are two gold crescents. The helmet is of silver, surmounted by a male figure in blue, with silver wings holding a gold star in each hand. The mantling is of blue and gold. (Siebmacher).

No. 2. Rücker, Rothenburg, Bavaria, granted 1647. D'argent à une ètoile d'or; le champ chapé d'azur, a deux croissant adossé d'or.

C:un jeune homme iss., hab. d'àzur, ailé d'arg. supp. de chaque main une étoile d'or.

L.; d'or et d'àzur. (Siebmacher Book 5, p. *Der Burgerlichen Wappen.*)

(This is the same shield used by Johan Von Rucher of Vienna in 1096, this Rucker may be an heir of Johan's eldest son, and is making a re-patent of it in Bavaria in 1647.

No. 3. This patent was granted to Rücker of Frankford, 24 Juillet 1515. (Nob. du St. Empire).

Coupé; au I bandé d'azur et d'or, de quatre pièces; au d'azur à un croiss. Versé d'or en chef et une étoile du mème en p.

C:une étoile d'or entre un vol d'azur, chaque aile ch. d'un croiss, d'or celui à dexter cont., celui a sen. tourné. (Rietstap; Helmer, book I, p. 211, published 1605; Ciebmacher).

No. 4. From a seal which carries coat of arms of the above Rücker families divided, namely Rotenburg and Frankfort (No. 3). The upper in blue with 3 gold bands. The lower in blue over a gold star, a silver moon, in the other a gold moon. Over the gold helmet a gold star between open wings with a moon in each. (Helmer, book 5, p. 250.)

No. 5. Rücher of Bavaria (Conf. de la Nob. du St. Empire), patented 28 Sept. 1689.

Ec; Aux I et 4 d'azur à trois étoiles d'or, au 2 et 3 d'or à trois bandes azur.

C.: une étoile d'or, entre un vol aux armes du 2 (sur l'aile dextre les bandes sont transformées en berras (Rietstap, book 2, p. 628; Helmer, b. 2, p. 23; Siebmacher).

No. 6. Was granted to Rücher of Livonia (similar to the one of Bavaria). In the Livonian nobility book is found registered "Edgar Rücher of Unnipecht, with district certificates to the convention of deputy nobles for March 1894, by Third Class. He was son of the councilor Otto George Von Rücher, broker and lord of Waimel Nanhof estate gained through purchase. The entrance by Third class points to the Russian Nobility through civil distinction, although the family is found to have come from Vienna in 1689, sprung from Johan Michael Rücker of Imperial nobility, whose descendants are also registered in Bavaria."

It carries a coat or arms divided into four parts, first and fourth blue with three gold stars; second and third gold with three blue bands.

Crest: a gold star between open gold wings with one blue band in each. Helmet.

No. 7. Was granted to Rücher, Von Vinstingen, Effensche. Alsace, 1690.

De qu. à l'aigle ep. d'arg., bq. et m. d'or. C.; un demi vol aux arms de l'écu. (Reitstap; Helmer, b. 2, p. 128.)

No. 8. Is the same as number 7, except the shield of one is red and the other is blue bearing a double headed eagle.

No. 9. Rücher, Hamberger Familie Von der 1767-1844, Vier Personen als Rothsherren vorkommen. Wappen; (Siebmacher Book 5, p. 3. *Der burgerlichen Wappen.*)

No. 10. Was granted to three brothers of Hamburg (Siebmacher). To Dr. John Michael Rücker, Daniel Rücker, Jeremiah Frederick Rücker.

Gen. D. H. Rucker, U. S. Army, now deceased, was of this family. The shield bears a woman with flowing hair standing on an anchor holding a dove (wings). The crest has the same figure.

No. 11. There is another Rucker coat of arms very similar to number ten (Siebmacher).

There are several other Rucker coat of arms, some of German and one of English, but every one has wings, stars or crescents differenced upon the earliest arms used by the Crusader in 1096.

The following Ruckers came from Holland to England and were naturalized:

John Anthony Rucker, naturalization number 25.
Daniel Henry Rucker, naturalization number 29, in 1775.
John Gotthelf Rucker, naturalization number 78, in 1772.
John Anthony Rucker, Jr., naturalization number 267.
Conrad Rucker, naturalization number 80, in 1772.
John Peter Rucker, naturalization number 6, in 1764.
Journal of the House of Lords.

June 2, 1794, The petition of Daniel Henry Rucker next of kin and natural guardian of John Anthony Rucker, the infant son of Theoplies Rucker and Louisa Dorthea, his wife, born in Hamburg.

An act for naturalization of John Anthony Rucker, an infant.

Peter Rucker was born in Hamburg, son of Diederick Christian and Anna Catherine.

George Rucker, Burger of Rothernburg, married Margaret Blasius, March 1, 1573.

Michael Rucker published a book in 1573.

Jeremiah Frederick Rucker, b. Nov. 18, 1655, d. in Buringer 1703, a senator. He married Maria Elizabeth Bansch.

John Michael Von Rucker, b. Oct. 6, 1653, d. Aug. 7, 1712, m. Maria Sibylla Hambergern, b. 1657, d. Apr. 23, 1732.

Christian Frederick Rucker, b. at Winshein, Aug. 25, 1689, d. Oct. 19, 1763, m. July 31, 1714, Ann Maria Steinbrenner.

Rücker aus Spandau stammend.

Bastian Rüttger war 1491 Bürgermeister in Spandau; 1506 werden sie zuerst Rücker genannt. Seit etwa 1700 zu Hamburg ansässig; s. Teil 111. s. 67.

In der Zeit von 1767 bis 1869 wurden fünf Mitglieder des Geschlechts in der Senat gewahlt, ein Mitglied wurde Oberhalter. (Hamburger Geschlechterbuch Band V.)

Wappen: in W. auf g. Boden ein Weib in gr. Gewande mit blonden Haar, auf der rechten Hand eine zugekehrte r. Taube haltend, die Linke auf einem # Ankerstutzend (die Hoffnung). Helm: auf g.—beflügelter g. Kugel stehend ein gewandloses Weib (die Glücksgotten) mit blonden flatterndein Haare, mit beiden Händen eine wehende r. Flagge haltend. Decken: gr. w. (Mitt. d. Hr. Reg. R. Dr. Koerner). Siebemacher's Wappenbuch, Vol. 5-10, p. 49.

(Translation)

Rucker originally of Spandau.

Bastian Ruttger was in 1491 Burgermaster of Spandau; in 1506 for the first time named Rucker. In 1700 were domiciled in Hamburg. (See part 3, page 67.)

In the time from 1767 until 1869, five members of the family were elected to the Senate, one member was Oberhalter. (Hamburger Geschlechterbuch, Vol. V.)

Coat-of-Arms: Shield a woman in a green gown with blond hair holding in the right hand a dove facing her on the left leaning on an anchor (Hope).

Crest: On a winged ball an undraped female figure (Goddess of Luck) standing with flowing blond hair holding in both hands a waving flag.

Hall's Deutsche Family notes.

The following is found in the Eleventh Edition of the *Encyclopaedia Brittanica,* Vol. 21, p. 564, giving an account of the harpischord and the makers, of Antwerp.

"Fortunately there is an harpischord existing with a double keyboard, unaltered dated 1638 made by Jean Rucker, also Hans Rucker, the great clavisengel maker of Antwerp." Also Vol. 13, p. 16. See further about Hans Rucker, his son Jean and grandson Jean Couchet of Antwerp, makers of harpischords.

In the *International Studio, published* Aug. 1, 1922, is an article written by Karl Freund, From Harp to Harpischord. On page 375 is a picture of a Double Spinet made by Hans Rucker, the elder, and decorated by Peter Paul Rubens, "One of the only known instruments of its kind, it is composed of a large and small portable Spinet with separate action, the interior of the cover is painted with a scene of Apollo and Marsyus . . . ." Another decorated Harpischord made in Antwerp in 1600, by Hans Rucker, the elder, remade in France in 1750.

The Virginal, spinet and clavicitherium, supplied one string to each key, the harpischord two, three or more tuned in unison, until Rucker's added the octave string to the action of the spinet. A Double Spinet by Rucker bearing date 1579 has the maker's initials in a carved and gilded rose, made by Hans (Johannes) Rucker, of Antwerp (now in Mrs. Skinner's collection), not only remarkable for its appearance and rarity, but for its place as a milestone in the progress of keyboard music.

"From the beginning of the 17th Century, the Rucker family, Johannes the father, and his equally gifted sons, Franc, Andreas, Hans, and Anton, seemed to have supplied an ever increasing demand for their instruments, presented to their patrons with unfailing taste, in cases of extraordinary beauty.

Reubens, Nicolas, Maes, Tenier, Brill, Wouverman, Palamedes, are mentioned among the Dutchmen and Flemish employed to trim their cases with the most pleasing compositions their minds could invent. In the Metropolitan Museum, No. 2362, a double keyboard harpischord made by Jean Couchet, a nephew of Hans Rucker, the younger, is of a very fine quality."

In a sale of a "Ruckers-Taskin Harpischord", which took place in Paris about 1775, it brought the stupendous price of 6240 livres.

5
6
4

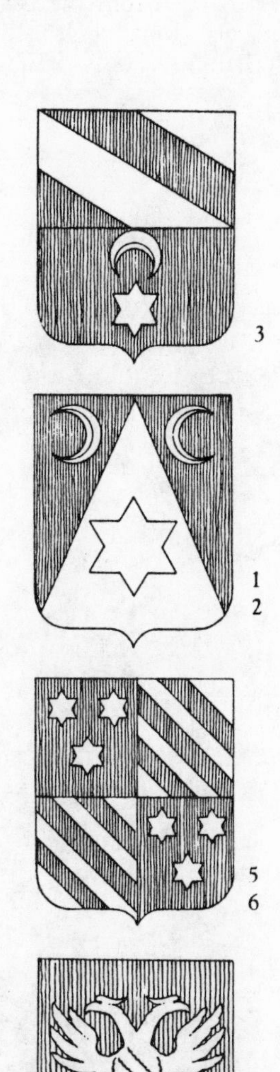
3
1
2
5
6
7
8

PART III.

AUXILIARY LINES

Coghill

The Coghill family came to Virginia in 1664. James[1] Coghill lived in Essex Co. below Fredericksburg on Cockleshell and Potobacco Creeks. He died there in 1685, leaving a will in which he mentions his wife, Mary, who later married ——— Dusberry, she died in 1715, leaving a will. Her granddaughter, Susanna Coghill, may have married John Rucker, son of Peter[1], as Frederick Coghill deeded to John Rucker 56 acres of land for "love and affection". John and Susanna Rucker later sold this land, formerly of James Coghill's. Or Peter[1] Rucker may have married Elizabeth, the daughter of James Coghill. Since the above land was leased to Peter before it was deeded to son, John, James's will does not mention a daughter, Elizabeth.

Thomas Powell, of Rappahannock Co., and wife, Mary, sold for "Nyne Barrells" of Indian corn already received, to James[1] Coghill, of Sittingbourne Parish, all of his interest in 30 acres of land in the freshes of the Rappahannock River on the north side, 30 Sept., 1662 (D. B. 2, p. 125 Rappahannock Co.)

James bought 110 acres from Valentine Allen and wife, Mary, for 1200 lbs. of tobacco, 2 Mch., 1664(D. B. 5, p. 131).

James Coghill patented 246 acres of land in the county of Rappahannock in the freshes, beginning at Mr. Lucas's creek, along the line of trees formerly belonging to Valentine Allen, . . . to Hendrick Lucas's line, to Daniel Gaines, to Peter Cornwell's, due to Coghill for transporting 5 persons, Mch. 24, 1664-5 (L. Gr. B. 5, p. 470).

He bought two-thirds of the land of Rorah Macrah, of Rappahannock Co., land Macrah bought of William Gibson, Dec. 1, 1666 (D. B. 4, p. 28).

Jan. 21, 1667, James Coghill sold to Timothy Pell land formerly belonging to William Wilton on the east side of Beaver Dam, toward the head and on the north side of Allen's Creek (D. B. 2, p. 133, Rappahonnock Co.)

On April 17, 1667, he patented 600 acres on south side of the Rappahannock River.

James patented 1050 acres of land one mile from the head of the eastward branch of Potobacco Creek, April 17, 1676 (L. Gr. B. 6, p. 61).

James and Mary Coghill sold to William Brown, Jr., all interest in the land bought of Valentine Allen (D. B. 6, p. 271, Rappahannock Co.)

Will of James[1] Coghill, of Sittingbourne Parish; Rappahannock Co., dated Oct. 5, 1684, probated Sept. 2, 1685:

To my wife Mary the plantation and etc.
To my eldest son William 124 acres of land.
To my son James 224 acres, my gun, sword, and etc.
To my son David 200 acres, and my gun at the age of 18.
To my son ffrederick 200 acres.
To the unborn child.
To my dau. Margaret.
To my dau. Mary.

Witness: W. O. ffenley and Christopher Man (W. B. 6, p. 80, Rappahannock Co.).

Essex Co. O. B. 1692-1695. Reverse of book p: 68. David Coghill deeds to Richard Booker of Gloucester 250 acres adjoining the plantation of James Coghill. July 20, 1692.

P. 241. John Powell and Margaret, his wife, sell to John Battaile 300 acres patented by James Coghill in 1667 and left by said Coghill's will to his two daughters, Margaret and Mary. Margaret, now wife of John Powell, Nov. 14, 1691.

Will of Mary (Coghill) Dusberry dated Apr. 21, 1715, probated Dec. 20, 1715 (W. B. 14, p. 428, Essex Co.) of St. Ann Parish.

"Unto Susanna Coghill, Thomas Coghill and Mary Coghill, children of my son ffrederick Coghill.

To my daughter Mary Willis all of my clothes.

The rest of my estate to be divided between my son ffrederick, my daughter, Mary Willis and my son George Dusberry.

To my son-in-law John Willis."

Will of George Dusberry dated Nov. 5, 1715, probated Dec. 26, 1715 (W. B. 14, p. 430, Essex).

To Susanna Coghill, eldest daughter of my brother ffrederick Coghill my plantation should she die without heir, to go to Richard Booker.

To John Dusberry.

Issue of James[1] Coghill:

1. William[2] Coghill.
2. James[2] Coghill.
3. David[2] Coghill.
4. ffrederick[2] Coghill.
5. child[2] unborn.
6. Margaret[2] Coghill, m. John Powell, of Essex Co., Va.
7. Mary[2] Coghill.

Coghill coat of arms: Gules, on a chevron, argent, 3 pellets; a chief sable. Crest: on a mount vert a cock with wings expanded or. Motto: Non dormit qui custodit.

William[2] and James[2] Coghill of Rappahannock Co. "sons of James Coghill" state in a deed (Essex Co., B, 1682-92) that they moved from Charles county, Maryland in 1664. William moved back to Maryland. He died there and left a will. (Possibly he married twice.)

William[2] and James[2] Coghill of Charles Co. Maryland sold 250 acres out of a 1000 acre patent, land in Virginia, to Johanna Hudson, widow, land lying at the head of Potobacco Creek, in Rappahannock Co., called James Coghill's plantation which is now in the possession of Johanna Hudson, all household goods, etc.

Signed: William Coghill and wife, Susanna.
James Coghill and wife Ann.

Later a second wife of James[2], Elizabeth signed another deed to 190 acres of land in Prince George Co. Md. (Land Office). James later moved back to Essex Co., Va.

Issue:

1. Zacharia[3] Coghill.
2. Susanna[3] Coghill.
3. Ezra[3] Coghill.
4. Priscilla[3] Coghill.
5. Gideon[3] Coghill.

Feb. 18, 1734, James was living in South Farnhem Parish Essex Co. Va., at which time he deeded to his brother Frederick Coghill "For brotherly love and Affection" all rights of inheritance from his father.

4. Frederick[2] Coghill (James[1]) m. Sarah ———. He patented 613 acres of land in St. Mary's Parish, Essex Co. three miles from the Rapahannock River, lying within the boundaries of a patent granted to James Coghill deceased on Potobacco Creek for transporting 13 persons Oct. 20, 1704 (L. Gr., Vol. 11, p. 644).

Richard Booker of Abingdon Parish Gloucester Co. sold to Frederick Coghill 105 acres land formerly patented by James Coghill deceased. Oct. 27, 1707 (D. and W. B. 13, p. 51, Essex).

Johanna Hudson of St. Charles Co. Maryland, sold land in Essex Co. to Richard Booker of Gloucester Co. Aug. 18, 1691 (D. B. 9, p. 264, Rappahannock Co.).

witness: Mary Ducksbury.
Cornelius Buthell
David Coghill
Rowlin Porwin.

Richard Booker deeded land to John Pemberton for "Love and affection" land near Peter Rucker's line 1723 (Essex B. 1721-24).

American Heraldica, p. 114. John Coghill, the emigrant, was son of Marmaduke Coghill of Tintergate, York Co., England, came to Virginia before 1664. He descended from the Coghills of York. The Coghills lived in York, England. On their paternal side they trace their ancestors to Knarlsborough, 1378, and on the maternal side to Slingsby of Scriver Hall, 1135.

Mr. Playfair in his *British Family Antiquary,* Vol. 7, p. 226, says the name Coghill probably is derived from a place called Cockle Hall, now Coghill Hall, where they resided in the county of York in the reign of Henry IV, 1378-1413. (The emigrant James Coghill came to Virginia and settled on Cockleshell Creek, now Essex Co.). Wingfield's *History of Caroline.*

Warren

John Warren appears in Old Rappahannock County as early as 1676, wife Rachel. John left no will, but Rachel died in 1707 in Essex County, leaving a will in which she mentions her children.

Cornelius Noell, of Rappahannock Co., for 150 lbs. of tobacco sold to Richard West and John Warren all of his interest in a tract of land in Sittingbourne Parish, 1097 acres situated 4 miles from the river backwards, patented 25 Sept. 1665, near Occupatia Creek, sold 28 Jan. 1667 (D. B. 2, p. 135, Rappa. Co.).

Cornelius Noell, Henry Jarman and William Coppin patented 1097 acres of land on the south side of the Rappahannock River in the freshes of the same, about four miles from the river on the main branch called Occupatia Creek over the Chickahominy Path, due for transporting 22 persons Sept. 25, 1665 (L. Gr. B. 5, p. 469).

Richard West and William Fogg patented 444 acres of land on the south side of the Rappahannock River at a white oak tree beyond the Mills and John Watkins, due for transporting 9 persons, July 25, 1660 (L. Gr. B. 5, p. 448).

John Warren, of Rappa. Co., for 1200 lbs. of tobacco. Sold to Richard West, my interest in a parcel of land bought by Richard West and said Warren, 6 Mch. 1668 (D. B. 4, p. 482, Rappa. Co.).

Witness: Wm. Fogg
Wm. Preasley

Acknowledged by Thomas Page, Attorney for said John Warren.

William Presley patented 1150 acres of land in Northumberland Co. Va. on the Potomac River between Chingeham Cr. and Presley's Cr. for transporting 20 persons, namely: John February, Robert Cralle, William Hicks, John Warren, John Butler, John Chappel, Thomas Spalding, Humps, Blackman and others. Oct. 14, 1649 (B. 2, p. 186, Land Office, Rd. Va.).

Deed from John Hawkins and Elizabeth, his wife, to Rachel Warren conveys fifty acres of land in St. Annes Parish adjoining Edward Martin. Dated September 20, 1698. Book 9, pg. 258.

Deed from John Hawkins and Elizabeth, his wife, to John Warren: conveys fifty acres of land in St. Annes Parish adjoining the lands of Rachel Warren. Dated Sept. 20, 1698. Book 9, pg. 259.

Will of William Sergent of Rappahannock Co. dated Feb. 15, 16—probated Apr. 4, 1683, To my son George Sergent certain of my land when he becomes Twenty.

To William Wheldridge son of John Wheldridge — — land

In case of the death of my son George — — I give to William Warren son of John Warren 100 acres of land adjoining William Wheldridge and Richard Mathews.

To Henry son of A. Field — —
To William son of William Griffin — —
To Mr. Daniel Gaines — — and to others.

Signed: Will Sergent.

(W. B. 6, p. 215, Rappa. Co.). Inventory of estate of Wm. Sargent, in which it shows John Warren owing the estate—9 May, 1683 (W. B. 6, Rappa. Co.).

John Warren may have married Rachel, daughter of William Sergent.

William Sergent and Edmund Pagget patented 707 acres of land on the south side of the Rappahannock River, on Mills Creek alias Tignor's Creeg, beginning at John Dangerfield's, formerly Andrew Gilson's, to Lt. Col. Guttridge's, to Thomas Ranson's, for transporting 15 persons, Oct. 20, 1666 (L. Gr., b. 5, p. 661).

Mrs. Alice Parke in her will dated Feb. 15, 1683, left land to William Sergent.

Rachel Warren was a witness in Essex in a suit between Capt. Arthur Spicer and Edwin Martin (O. B. 2, p. 12, 1695-99, Essex Co.).

Will of Rachel Warren of Essex.
To son, Wm. 50 acres land he now lives on
To my eldest son, Thomas Warren
To my gr. dau., Mary Parker
To my gr. daus., Jean & Margaret Martin
Elizabeth Martin to live on the plantation
To Mary Parker & Ann Warren, my gr. daughters

Witness: Thomas Harris
Margaret Cary
Mary Warren (W. & D., b. 12, 1704-7, Essex).

Issue:

1. Thomas² Warren.
2. Wm.² Warren.
3. Elizabeth² Martin.
4. ————² Parker.

1. Thomas² Warren (John¹).

Will of Thomas Warren of Spots. Co. 13 Apr. 1749—4 Dec. 1750 (W. B. B., p. 56).

To son, Hackley Warren 95 acres land I formerly gave to dau. Rachel.

To my daughter, Rachel Haskins
To my daughter, Elizabeth Brook
To my daughter, Mary Buford
To my daughter, Rosanna More

To my son, Samuel Warren all the land of the plantation I live on, and negroes at the death of my wife, Mary.

Executors: Wife Mary, and son, Hackley

Witness: Robert Huddleston
Abraham Rogers
Barbara Rogers

His sons, Lancelot and Thomas, were not mentioned in will.

Spots. D. B. A, p. 169, 2 Nov. 1725.

Thomas Warren of Spots., deeded to my daughter, Rachel Askew, the wife of John Askew, 95 acres land on south side of Middle River, in Spots. at John Rogers. Signed: Thomas Warren

Witness: Austin Elles
Jacob Brook
John x Elson

Colonial Militia (O. B. 1724-30, p. 332, Spots. Co.).

Capt. Wm. Johnson and his officers, one of whom was Thomas Warren, were commissioned 5 Aug. 1729.

(O. B. 1724-30, p. 41), 2 Mch. 1724-5, Spots. Co.

Petition of Henry Goodloe Gent. for a road from his house to the new church that is built on the river, Ta, alias Middle River. Wm. Warren, Thomas Warren and Mark Wheeler to lay out the said road.

(O. B. 1, p. 424), June 1736, Spots. Co.

Thomas Warren having been presented to grand jury for absenting himself from his parish church, sent a letter in excuse that he was a Quaker, but it not appearing that he was one of the people called Quakers, he is ordered to pay 5 shillings, or 50 lbs of tobacco, fine.

(O. B. 1738-49, p. 61), Caroline Co., 6 Nov. 1739.

Petition of Thomas Warren to be discharged as overseer of the road from Mattopany Church road to the Caroline Co. line and Wm. Warren is ordered to serve in his stead.

Issue:

1. Hackley[3] Warren.
2. Rachel[3] Hoskin.
3. Elizabeth[3] Brooks.
4. Mary[3] Buford.
5. Rosanna[3] Moore.
6. Samuel[3] Warren.
7. Lancelot[3] Warren.
8. Thomas[3] Warren.

1. Hackley[3] Warren (Thomas[2], John[1]), m. Sarah Shipp (Caroline O. B. 1741-46, p. 300), Aug. 10, 1741. Land was sold by the following heirs of Thomas Shipp:

John Willson
Ann Willson
Hackley Warren
Sarah Warren
Margaret Shipp

The said Ann Willson and Sarah Warren being examined acknowledge their deed and lease of land sold to Thomas Shipp.

6. Samuel[3] Warren (Tho.[2], John[1]), bought 303 acres of land in Spots Co. 1762.

Thomas Graves and wife, Ann, of Spots. St. Geo. Parish sold to Samuel Warren of same, land adjoining land formerly belonging to Humphrey Bell adjoining Robert Goodloe's—to Thomas Dillard's—to Robert Stubblefield's. 2 April 1770 (Spots. Co. D. B. G, p. 343).

(Spots. Co., Va., B. E, p. 364), 3 Sept. 1779, 19 Oct. 1780.

Will of Samuel Warren of Beckley Parish:

To my son, Wm. Warren, land whereon I live, including my house and plantation.

To my son, James Warren, 100 acres adjoining my son, William, including the Plantation where James Ross now lives.

To my son, Samuel, the remainder of my tract of land I bought of Thomas Coats.

To my son, John Warren, the tract of land I bought of Thomas Graves.

To my dau., Letty Humphes

To my dau., Elizabeth Rash

To my dau., Ann Warren

To my gr. son, Tho. Shackleford, son of my dau., Rebecca.

Executors: Sons Wm. and Samuel Warren.

Witness: John Major
John Johnson
Peter Mason

Issue:

1. Wm.[4] Warren.
2. James[4] Warren.
3. Samuel[4] Warren.
4. John[4] Warren.
5. Letty[4] Humphes.
6. Elizabeth[4] Rash.
7. Ann[4] Warren.
8. Rebecca[4] Shackleford.

1. John[4] Warren (Samuel[3], Tho.[2], John[1]), d. before 1785, at which time his brother, Wm., sold land devised to him by his "brother, John, dec'd, son of Samuel".

(O. B. 1730-33, p. 494), 3 May 1737).

John Warren is to be overseer of the road to Mr. Henry Goodloe's, to Mattapony church road. (1765 Halifax Co., Va.). Goodloe Warren of Orange Co., N. C., sold to Wm. Atkinson of Henrico Co., Va., 350 acres of land at Gideon's corner Oak.

2. William[4] Warren (Samuel[3], Tho.[2], John[1]). John Sutton figured in a suit against Wm. Warren, 13 June 1740 (O. B. 1732, p. 613).

In 1785, 1 June, Wm. Warren, and wife, Katy, of Spots. Co. sold 78 acres land in Spots. Co., devised to said Wm. by his father, Samuel Warren, dec'd, and part devolved upon him as heir of his brother, John Warren, dec'd (Crozier's).

1785—Wm.[4] Warren and wife, Catherine, and Samuel Warren of Spots. Co., sold to Durett of Caroline, 190 acres of land in Spots. Co. Nov. 5, 1785. 1785 Wm. Warren of Spots. and wife, Katy, sold 25 acres of land (Crozier's).

(Spots. D. B. K., p. 547), 5 Nov. 1785.

Wm. Warren sold to John Lehone, both of Spots., for £20, 25 acres land whereon Lehone now lives.

(Signed) William Warren,
Katy (mark) Warren.

7. Launcelot[3] Warren (Thomas[2], John[1]) and wife, Margaret, of Orange, sold to Jeremiah Morton, of same county, for £22, 20 acres of land in Orange—part of a tract once owned by Andrew Harrison, deceased, 22 Nov. 1753. (D. B. 12, p. 198, Orange Co.).

In 1750 his brother, "Thomas, son and heir of Thomas Warren, dec'd," deeded 210 acres of land, belonging to their father, to Launcelot.

Lancelot[3] Warren, of Spots., and wife, Margaret, sold to William Waller, of same, for £100, all of that tract of land that Lancelot lives on, 210 acres in St. George Parish on south side of the Middle River on the Mattaponi, adjoining Wm. Waller, to Thomas Waller's, to Hackley Warren's, formerly Haskin's in John Roger's line except the 10 acres where his parents are buried and the old orchard devised by his father to his brothers, 5 June 1750. Signed: Lancelot Warren.

Margaret (mark) Warren.

Witness: Richard Tutt
Geo. Stubblefield
Robert Mickleborough

(O. B. B., p. 533, Spots. Co.)

8. Thomas[3] Warren (Thomas[2], dec'd, late of Spots. Co., deeded 210 acres of land to Lancelot Warren, son of Thomas, dec'd, who died seized of the 210 acres of land in St. George Parish, 31 Jan. 1750, Spots. Co.

Witness: Wm. Warren
Hackley Warren
Robert Moore
James Ham

Sept. 3, 1742, Eusobie Stone, of Caroline, sold 400 acres of land to Thomas Warren, Jr., of Spots., in Orange Co., adjoining Joseph Hawkins, for £23.

Witness: Henry Franklin (Orange Co. Records, D. B. 8, p. 218).

(D. B. 12, p. 57), 14 Oct. 1751, Orange Co.

Thomas Warren, of Orange, sold to Wm. Lucas, of same, land formerly granted to Eusobie Stone, of Caroline, 400 acres.

The Warrens left Spottsylvania about 1750 and moved to North Carolina.

1759, John Warren, of Granville Co., bought 179 acres of land from Wm. Byrd, of Charles City Co., land in Halifax Co., Va., on the line.

Goodloe Warren, of Orange Co., N. C., bought 350 acres in Halifax in 1765.

James Warren, Sr. and Jr., were both living in Halifax in 1766.

John Warren, Sr., deeded to his sons, Timothy, Hackley, William, and Archibald, land in Halifax. Some of the sons moved to Roan, some to Caswell, and some to Person Co.

2. William[2] Warren (John[1]), b. c. 1660 in Rappa Co., d. in Spotsylvania in 1727. He was mentioned in the will of Will Sergent in 1683, to whom 100 acres of land was left "should his son George Sergent not live," the land adjoined Richard Mathews.

In Feb., 1701, William Warren, of Essex, sold 100 acres to Giles Mathews, of Richmond Co., land in Richmond Co. for 1800 lbs. of tobacco.

Nov. 5, 1722, Wm. Warren and wife, Elizabeth, deeded to Samuel Ham 100 acres on south side of Middle River of Mattapony River, part of a patent of 1525 acres of land, St. George Parish. (D. B. A, p. 89, Spots. Co.) (Crozier's).

Deed dated Nov. 18, 1717, from William Warren, of St. Annes Parish, to Samuel Ellett, of same parish, conveys two tracts of fifty acres each, being the same land conveyed to John Warren and Rachel Warren, dec'd, by two deeds dated Sept. 20, 1698. (Deed Book, No. 15, p. 112).

(Spots. Co., Va., W. B. B, p. 61), 21 Feb. 1750, 2 Apr. 1751. Will of Elizabeth Warren.

To my son, James Warren, a negro girl named Catie.

To my son, Samuel Warren, the money John Farish owes me.

To my daughter, Mary Warren.

Executors: Son, Samuel, and son-in-law, Thomas Burges.

Witness: John Farish
James Ham
Mary Ham

Will of William Warren, of St. George Parish, dated 1726, probated 1727.

To sons, John, Samuel, William and James.

Issue:

1. John[3] Warren.
2. Samuel[3] Warren.
3. William[3] Warren.
4. James[3] Warren.
5. Daughter[3], m. Samuel Ham.
6. Daughter[3], m. Thomas Burgess.

Aug. 5, 1740, John Rogers, of Drysdale Parish, sold land to Thomas, John, William and Samuel Warren.

2. Samuel[3] Warren (William[2], John[1]).

Deed dated Dec. 7, 1749, between William Warren and Samuel Warren, of Spotsylvania Co., and Anthony Samuel, of St. Annes Parish, Essex Co., conveys two tracts of land, the same tracts which were conveyed by John Hawkins to John Warren and Rachel Warren by two deeds dated Sept. 20, 1698.

Issue:

1. William[4] Warren, m. Anne Wilcox, moxed to Kentucky, 1782.

 Issue:

 1. John[5] Warren, m. Judith Swann Boswell, dau. of George Boswell and wife, Judith Swann Fauntleroy, of Northern Neck, Va.

 Issue:

 1. Nancy[6] Wilcox Warren, m. Evan Shelby, son of Gov. Isaac Shelby, of Kentucky.

Issue:

1. John[7] Warren Shelby, m. Mary Humphries Knight.

Issue:

1. William[8] R. Shelby, m. Mary Kenedy Cass.

Issue:

1. Cass[9] Knight Shelby, m. Letitia Hol. combe Landis, 534 Hickory St., Hollidaysburg, Pa.

3. Wm.[3] Warren (Wm.[2], John[1]), wife, Alice Seems. (Caroline O. B. 1732, p. 613), 13 June, 1720, John Sutton and William Warren brought suit.

Action of debt between Jonathan Gibson against Wm. Warren, 8 Oct., 1736. (O. B. 1732, p. 376, Caroline).

Action of debt brought by John Sutton against Wm. Warren and Ham Hendricks, 13 June, 1740. (O. B. 1732, p. 611, Caroline Co.)

(Orange Co., D. B. 12, p. 38), 6 Oct., 1751, Wm. Warren and wife, Alice of Orange, sold 50 acres of land to Thomas Graves, of Orange, for £20, land conveyed by deed of gift to said Warren by Joseph Seems, 50 acres to Thomas Graves and wife, Isabella.

1786, Wm. Waller's will, of Spots. Co., mentions land formerly bought from Wm., John, Samuel and Lancelot Warren. (Crozier's).

4. James[3] Warren (Wm.[2], John[1]), b. c. 1700, in Essex Co., Va., was in Goochland as early as 1734, being a witness to a deed of Robert Lewis to his children. (Robert Lewis deeded to his children land bought from his father-in-law, Nicholas Meriwether —(children named Robert, John, Nicholas, Elizabeth, Jane and Anna Lewis).

Witness: Charles Lynch
James Warren
Richard Johnson

(Hanover B. 1733-35, p. 54, 25 Apr. 1734).

James[3] Warren was paid for one wolf's head, certified by James Shelton on Nov. 25, 1735. (O. B. 4, Goochland).

He brought suit against Charles Lynch in Nov., 1735. (O. B. 4, p. 22, Goochland).

James Warren patented 100 acres of land in the county of Goochland, on the north side of Rivanna River, beginning at the Hanover Co. line, by the river, and crossing the river at the mouth of Ivy Creek, Sept. 12, 1738. (L. Gr. Vol. 18, p. 100).

At the April court of 1742, on the motion of James Warren, he is levy free. (O. B. 5, p. 28, Goochland).

June, 1742, Cabell vs. Warren—"In the action of debt between Wm. Cabell, plaintiff, and John and James Warren, defendants, at May court, a conditional judgment was granted against the defendant, James Warren, and Charles Coffrey, his security. The defendant, James, now failing to appear on the motion of the plaintiff, the said judgment is confirmed and it is therefore considered that the plaintiff do recover against the defendant, James Warren, and Charles Coffrey, his security, 2608 pounds of sweet scented tobacco and cask, the suit is to be discharged on the payment of 1304 pounds of like tobacco and cask, with interest, therefore, after the rate of 5% per annum, from XXXth day of March DCCXXXV (1735), till the same shall be paid together with the cost of this suit and a lawyer's fee. The sheriff, having returned that the defendant, John Warren, is not an inhabitant of this county, the suit as to him is dismissed." (O. B. 5, p. 73, Goochland).

Charles Coffrey patented 300 acres of land on both sides of Moor's Creek, a branch of the Rivanna, 10 June, 1737. (Land Grant B. 17, p. 338).

At the Oct. court, 1742, James Warren, Sen., was paid for one wolf's head, certified by Charles Lynch.

In 1746, James and wife, Elizabeth, sold land in Albemarle Co. to Thomas Chambers.

He patented 276 acres of land on the meadows, on north side of Buffalo Ridge in Sept., 1748. (L. Gr. Vol. 28, p. 418).

On Sept. 5, 1747, James Warren patented 400A. in Albemarle on both sides of Stoney Run at Buffalo Ridge. (L. Gr. Vol. 27, p. 441).

He also patented 400 acres on both sides of Arthur's Creek, a branch of Slate River, 9 Nov. 1747, surveyed. (Survey Book 1744-70, p. 50, Land Office).

James Warren patented 100 acres on a branch of Mechum River, called Rich Cove, March 10, 1750. (L. Gr. Vol. 32, p. 688).

In 1764, Martha and Margaret Fry patented 1160 acres of land adjoining James Warren's and Joshua Fry's (L. Gr. Vol. 35) on Buffalo River.

On June 20, 1766, James Warren, Sr., mortgaged 205 acres on Stoney Creek of Buffalo Ridge, whereon John and said James Warren now live adjoining Christian's and Dillard's land. (D. B. B., p. 126, Amherst Co.)

At the Sept. court 1766, was recorded a mortgage between James Warren, Sen., and McPherson Mingee, merchant, endorsed by Thomas Reed, Gabriel and Wm. Penn. (Order Book).

Will of James Warren, of Amherst, dated 1769, recorded July 3, 1769, in Amherst. (W. B. 1, p. 137).

To my son, John Warren, all of my estate, real and personal.

To my daughter, Elizabeth Whittle, 175 acres of land between Col. Braxton's and Christian's Orphans.

Signed: James Warren.

Executors: Mathew and John Whittle.

Witness: Eleazer, Ralph and Sarah Lemaster.

Albemarle Co. (D. B. 1, p. 164, March 25, 1748).

"John Warren, of St. Annes Parish, Albemarle County, is bound unto James Warren, of same, James Warren, the younger, of Lunenburg County, Betty, wife of Mathew Whittle, Sarah, wife of Charles Coffrey, Eleanor, wife of John Rucker and Grace Warren, the four last named being of St. Annes Parrish, of Albemarle County, in the sum of 1000 pounds, to be paid in equal proportions to said James Warren, and James Warren the yonger, Betty Whittle, Sarah Coffrey, Eleanor Rucker and Grace Warren, their attorneys, executors or assignees to which payment I bind myself and my heirs. The condition of this obligation is such that if the above bounder, John Warren, shall pay or cause to be paid unto the above James, etc., six-eighths parts (6/8) in equal proportions, one-eighth (1/8) to each, of the neat produce of all mines and minerals that now are or hereafter shall be discovered on a tract of 276 acres of land surveyed for said John Warren on north side of Buffalo Ridge, in aforesaid Parish of St. Annes, Albemarle County, the charge of working the said mines and minerals and sum of 200 pounds only excepted. During the term of their natural lives and shall afterwards for the space of 1000 years to be completed and ended from the death of the survivor of them, the said James Warren, etc., pay or cause to be paid yearly and every year at the day of the Feast of St. Michael, to the heirs of the aforesaid James Warren, etc., lawfully issuing of their body's the above mentioned proportion of one-eighth part of the clear or neat produce of the aforesaid mines and minerals to the heirs of each of them, according to their parent stocks, then this obligation to be void and of none effect otherwise to remain in full force and virtue.

John (his mark) Warren.

Witnesses: Joshua Fry, John Harvie, John Coffrey.

At Court February 13, 1749. This Bond proved by Joshua Fry and John Harvie, two of witnesses."

Aug. 4, 1763, Joseph Crews and Agnes, his wife, of Amherst, sold to Wm. Dillard, of Hanover, 195 acres of land lying on both sides of Rocky Run, a branch of Buffalo Ridge, being part of a tract of 400 acres of land James Warren, Sr., now lives on.

Witness: James Dillard
Thomas Robertson
Mary Ann Tenison.

Issue:

1. John[4] Warren.
2. James[4] Warren, Jr.
3 Betty[4] Warren.
4. Sarah[4] Warren.
5. Eleanor[4] Warren.
6. Grace[4] Warren.

(O. B. p. 520), 7 Aug., 1769, Amherst Co., Va.

Will of James Warren further proved by Eleanor Lancaster, and ordered recorded.

John Whittle, one of the executors named in will, qualified, but Matthew Whittle refused. Bond $200.
Sureties: Matthew Whittle, Ambrose Jones and James Gossett.

1. John[4] Warren (James[3], Wm.[2], John[1]), born in Spots., wife, Susanna.

He patented 276 acres of land in Albemarle Co. on the north side of Stony Run of Buffalo Ridge on the Meadows at James Warren's line, adjoining Capt. John Harris, Sept. 20, 1748. (L. Gr. Vol. 28, p. 418). Survey by Joshua Fry, 9 Nov. 1747. Mathew Whittle and James Warren chain carriers. (Survey Book, Albe. Co., 1744-90, p. 29).

John sold the Mineral right to the above 276 acres in Feb. 13, 1749, and sold the land to Chiswell in May, 1749.

John Warren and wife, Susanna, of St. Anne's Parish, Albemarle Co., sold to John Chiswell, of Hanover Co., merchant, for £200, 276 acres of land patented by said Warren, 20 Sept., 1748. Said deed was delivered to Capt. Charles Lynch, and if said "Chiswell is pleased" with the land, to accept and work the minerals. May 3, 1749. (D. B. I., p. 85, Albe. Co.)

John Chiswell, of Albemarle Co., sold 2000 acres of land on Rockfish River to John Robinson, of King and Queen Co., also 7/8 part of a copper mine, which land he bought of John Warren. (Hening's Vol. 8, p. 270).

John Warren patented 400 acres in Albemarle Co. on Rocky Creek of Buffalo Ridge, beginning at James London's corner, extending to Col. Braxton's line to the branch of Rocky Creek and to Christian's line—1755. (L. Gr. B. 31, p. 673). Surveyed 14 Oct., 1749, by Thos. Turpin. (Albe. Survey Book 1744-90, p. 107).

He sold 400 acres to Charles Christian of Goocrland, for £16, land in Albemarle, on the branches of Buffalo Ridge, 9 Oct., 1764. (Albe. D. B. 2, p. 348).

He patented 192 acres of land in Lunenburg on the back side of Flatt Creek, beginning at David Irvin's, crossing the creek thus to his own line, then to Christopher Irvin's line, 10 Jan., 1760. (L. Gr. B. 34, p. 553).

John Warren, of Albemarle Co., sold to Stephen Goggin, of Bedford Co., for £25, 192 acres of land on Flatt Creek, adjoining David Irvin's.

Witness: Luke Murphy
Thomas Sulter
James Burrus Whittle.

The tax books of Amherst Co. of 1782 charges John Warren with 276 acres of land, this may be the land left to him by his father. Both James and John patented 276 acres of land adjoining in 1748. John sold his in 1748, asked to be relieved of paying a levy.

(Amherst Co., O. B. 766-69, p. 254), 8 Dec., 1767, upon the petition of John Warren, an infirm man, it is ordered that he be exempted from paying the county levy.

John Warren, Sr., of Amherst, to Benjamin Warren, of same, for £7, 25 acres of land, beginning at Harvey's land on the Road, to Wm. Dillard's. (D. B. F., p. 205, Oct. 20, 1786).

2. James[4] Warren (James[3], Wm.[2], John [1]). (L. Gr. Vol. 28, p. 153), James Warren, Jr., bought 217 acres of land in Albe. on south side of Rivanna River, a branch of Moose Creek, adjoining David Lewis, 20 Aug., 1747.

(W. B. 2, p. 61), Mch. 10, 1755, Albe. James Warren, Jr., was appointed with others to value the estate of General Fry, dec'd.

Amherst Co., Jan. 26, 1763, James Warren, Jr., and John Warren, Jr., were witnesses to a deed from Elias Dehart to Wm. Duiguid.

James[2] Warren sold 99 acres to Alexander Spiers and others, land on Owen's Cr., land said Warren had bought of Thomas Bibee, 29 Feb., 1775, Amherst. (D. B. C., p. 361).

Wm. Goode, of Powhatan, sold to Ambrose Rucker, of Amherst, 400 acres of land on Buffalo Ridge, beginning at John Warren's, to James Warren's. 14 Oct., 1784. (D. B. 3, p. 563). Some of the descendants of the Warrens moved to Lincoln Co., and to Fayette Co., Ky., after selling land in Amherst Co., Va.

3. Betsy[4] Warren (James[3]), married Mathew Whittle, son of John.

8 May, 1747, Matthew Whittell and Betsy, his wife, of Louisa Co., sold to Thos. Chambers, of Albe. Co., for £30 cur. money, 300 acres with plantation whereon said Matthew Whittell lived, lying on north fork of James River, to the county line and crossing the river.

Matthew Whittell,
Betsy (her mark) Whittell.

Witness: Beasell Maxwell
Nath. Chambers
John Maxwell.

(Louiso Co. D. B. A, p. 289).

Surveyed for Mathew Whittel 400 acres under Buffalo Ridge, 2 Dec., 1747. (Albe. Survey B. 1744-90, p. 29).

Mathew Whittle, of Amherst County, to son, Joseph Whittle, of Amherst, 200 acres at the upper end of tract I now live on in Amherst.

Witness: Martin Dawson and wife, Elizabeth.

May 5, 1777 (D. B. D, p. 432).

John Whittle and wife, Sarah, Mathew Whittle and wife, Elizabeth, to Charles Wingfield, 400 acres granted to Mathew Whittle under Buffalo Ridge on Rocky Run and Christian's Path to Moses Higginbotham's Mill; same land conveyed by said Mathew Whittle to his sons, Joseph and John Whittle, adjoining Colonel Chiswell, John Warren and Joyner. Jan. 21, 1780 (D. B. E., p. 215).

4. Sarah[4] Warren (James[3]), m. Charles Coffrey. He patented 300 acres of land in the county of Goochland on both sides of Moore's Creek, a branch of the Rivanna River (Trees the only boundary) 10 June, 1737. (L. Gr. B, 17, p. 338).

5. Eleanor[4] Warren (James[3]), m. John[3] Rucker (John[2], Peter[1]).

Morton

Will of Wm.[1] Morton, of Orange, dated Dec. 8, 1747, prob. July 28, 1748:

To my wife, Ann (Motherhead).

To my son, Elijah.

To son-in-law, Andrew Browne.

To George Morton, son of Elijah.

To my granddaughter, Frances Christopher, who married Francis Browne, of Ky. (W. B. 2, p. 131), Orange Co.

The children of Wm. Morton, given by Dr. W. R. Brown, of Murry State College, Murry, Ky.:

1. Jeremiah[2] Morton, m. Earah Street.
2. Elijah[2] Morton, m. Elizabeth Hawkins.
3. Ann[2] Morton, m. Henry Browne.
4. Elizabeth[2] Morton, m. Thomas Newman.
5. Mary[2] Morton, m. ——— Minor.
6. Jane[2] Morton, m. Andrew Browne.
7. John[2] Morton, under 21 when will was made.
8. dau.[2], m. Christopher.

7. John[2] Morton (Wm.[1]), d. in Woodford Co., Ky., will dated Apr. 21, 1807, prob. Oct., 1810:

To my wife, Sarah (Browne).

1. To my dau., Lucy[3] Haden.
2. To my dau., Ann[3] Rucker, m. Rev. James[4], (John[3], John[2], Peter[1]).
3. To my dau., Frances[3] Watts.
4. To my son, James[3].
5. To my son, Jeremiah[3].
6. To my son, John[3], m. Nellie[4] Rucker (John[3], John[2], Peter[1]).
7. To my son, Benjamin[3].
8. To my son, William[3].
9. To my son, Thomas[3].

   Granddaughter, Lucy[4] Morton, dau. of Wm.[3]

Executors: Sons, Jeremiah, Wm. and wife, Sarah.

Witness: Spencer Gill
George Hubbard
Wm. Christopher

(W. B. C., p. 282, Woodford Co., Ky.)

Will of Sarah Morton, dated Nov. 23, 1826, prob. Sept., 1828.

After all debts are paid, the remainder of my property to be divided into 6 parts:

Two parts to son, Jeremiah[3].
Two parts to son, Wm.[3]
One part to son, Thomas[3].
One part to the heirs of son, John[3].

Executors: Jeremiah and Wm. Morton.

Sarah, in her will, mentions the date of the death of her husband as being Sept. 12, 1810.

Witness: Thomas Coleman
Jeremiah Morton, Jr.

6. John[3] Morton (John[2], William[1]), was born in Orange Co., Va., moved to Amherst, with the Ruckers, Hawkins, Plunketts, and other families; later, after the Revolution they moved to Ky., Woodford Co. He married Feb. 7, 1786, Nellie[4] Rucker, in Amherst, daughter of John[3] Rucker and Eleanor Warren. He died 1810.

1. Sally[4] Morton, m. 1st cousin, Wm.[5] Rucker (John[4], John[3], John[2], Peter[1]).
2. Lucy[4] Morton, m. Rucker.
3. Nancy[4] Morton.

There was surveyed for this John Morton, 3,000 acres of land on Licking River, Ky., on treasury Warrants No. 2854, 55, 56, 57, 62, 63, in 1786.

John Morton's brothers, William and Thomas, were Rev. soldiers, receiving bounty lands in Woodford County in 1810. In the settlement of John[2] Morton's estate, his son, William, was paid expenses "for two business trips to Virginia in 1806-1807.

5. Jeremiah[3] Morton will dated July 7, 1823, prob. Apr. 1827, m. 1st, Rosamond; 2nd, Judith Moore, 1819.

Will mentions, my wife, Judy.

To my daughter, Lucy[4] Wilson.

To the children of my deceased daughter, Nancy[4] Rucker, namely:

Betsy[5] Rucker.
Agatha[5] Rucker and her children.
Anthony[5] Rucker.
Jeremiah[5] Rucker.
Jefferson[5] Rucker.
Junius[5] Rucker.
Jonathan[5] Rucker.

Executors: Thomas Bullock
Isaac Wilson
Wm. Morton.

Codicil written by Wm. Christopher, Sr., Wm. Dale, witness.

3. Nancy[4] Morton Rucker, the deceased daughter of Jeremiah[3] Morton, married Abner[4] Rucker (Anthony[3], John[2], Peter[1]), in Amherst Co., Va.

Will of Judith Moore Morton, dated Oct. 20, 1829, prob. 1829, mentions my three sisters:

Hannah Hiett
Elizabeth Morton
Sally Morton
To my sister, Eliza Morton.

Executors: Allen Hiett and Reuben Morton.
Witness: Jacob Smith and Middleton David.

(D. B. H., p. 327, Woodford Co., Ky)

5. Jeremiah[3] Morton and wife, Rosamond, sold to Peter C. and John L. Buce a piece of land lying in the town of Mortonsville, called Ruckers Big Spring, designated in the plan of the town as lot No. 4, which is 48 ft. on the main street, 138 ft. back and 52 ft. on the back line, Feb. 7, 1812. (D. B. F, p. 192), Woodford Co., Ky.

8. Wm.[3] Morton's will dated June 29, 1826, prob. June, 1826, Woodford Co., Ky.:

My wife, Elizabeth.
To my son, Reuben, $300 in cash.
To my dau., Sally, $200 in cash.
For the care of their aged parents.

The rest of my property to be divided among my children, Reuben, Simon, Sally, Anne, James, Hawkins, Elijah, Joseph, Jeremiah, and daughter, Lucy White.

Executors: Elijah Reuben Morton and Thomas H. Vance.

Witness: Issac Boone
James Smith
Lemuel Hammond.

(W. B. "G.", p. 400).

6. Capt. John[3] Morton, of Clarke Co., Ky. (1758-1837), m. 1788, Tabitha Tinsley (1754-1858), of Spotsylvania Co., Va.

Pre-emption warrant No. 2590 entered Oct., 1784, in Fayette Co., Ky., land surveyed for John Morton on the north forks of Licking Creek, Nov. 15, 1784 (D. B. D, p. 216).

Issue:

1. Wm.[4] Morton, b. Clarke Co., Ky., 1790, d. 1858, m. Rebecca Didlake (no issue).
2. Quinn[4], a minister, died in Alabama.
3. Richard[4], a minister.
4. Elder[4] John, b. 1800-1853, Lexington, Ky.
5. David[4], m. Sallie Wagner.
6. Tazitha[4], m. John Golston.
7. Lucy[4], m. David Owen.
8. Betty[4], m. 1st, Joseph Craig; 2nd ———.
9. Susan[4], m. 1st, Thomas Lane; 2nd, Wm. Webb.

Capt. Moses Hawkins, of the 14th Va. Reg., was killed at Germantown, Oct. 4, 1777, his sister married ——— Morton, of Orange. They (Hawkins), Ruckers and Mortons moved first to Amherst, then to Woodford Co., Ky. For this family of Mortons, the town of Mortonsville, Ky., was named. (Most of the Morton data was furnished by Mrs. Wade Hampton George, of Ky.)

Tucker

Francis Tucker, with his family, evidently moved to Prince George Co. about 1712. The first land patents are made on 8 May, 1712, surveyed and deeded to his 8 sons; 200 acres to son, John, on the east side of the Great Branch of Namoseen Creek, called Ellington.

141 acres to son, Robert, on west side of Namoseen Creek, on both sides of the river path, adjoining Col. Francis Eps, in 1725.

On May 8, 1712, the following surveys were made in Prince George Co.:

100 acres to son, William, on west side of Namoseen Creek.
100 acres survey for son, Joseph, on Namoseen Creek.

100 acres survey, Francis, on west side of Whiphonock Creek. (Prince George B. 1, p. 750) adjoining Henry Mayes.

In 1720, 99 acres were surveyed for Mathew Tucker, son of Francis, land on west side of Whipponock Creek. (Prince George 1713-28, p. 745). Now Dinwiddie Co.

In his will Francis left land to his sons, Henry and Abram. Eight sons are mentioned. In July 10, 1717, Francis Tucker, Sr., patented 289 acres on both sides of Whipponock Creek in Prince George Co., on the Great Branch of said creek, adjoining Herbert (L. Gr., b. 10, p. 339).

Prince George 1713-28, p. 160, 14 May, 1717, Robert Tucker, of Bristol Parish, Prince George Co., sold to David Crawley, of same, for £20, 200 acres in Prince George, to the Appomattox River on the west, south to Maj. Robert Bolling, north to John Coleman's, to Maj. Robert Munford's. Signed, Robert Tucker.

Prince George, 1713-28, p. 231, 10 June, 1718, Francis Tucker, the elder, of Bristol Parish, Pr. Geo. Co., sold to John Crawley land in Bristol Parish, 100 acres ——— south to Crawley's land, west to Barto. Crowders, to John Butler's. Wife, Mary, signed the deed.

Evidently Robert and Francis sold the land they had inherited, for there is no record of land being patented by Robert. Possibly they were brothers.

Robert Bolling petitioned for an acre of land on Tucker's Run, belonging to David Crawley, to build a water mill, March 17, 1718. (O. B. 1711, p. 236, Pr. Geo.)

(Vol. 1, p. 663, Pr. Geo. Co.). Will dated Dec., 1722, prob. 10 Dec., 1723, of Francis Tucker, of Bristol Parish. "To my son, Francis Tucker, that part of the land on the east side of Whipponock Creek, at the lower end as I have marked the same out to him.

To son, John Tucker, that part of land on the north side of Whipponock Creek, adjoining Henry May's, already purchased for him.

To son, Henry Tucker, part of land between Francis and John Tucker's, the plantation whereon I live, being part of said land.

To son, Abram Tucker, that part of my land on north side of Whipponock Creek, joining on my son, Henry, and Thomas Mitchell.

To son, Mathew Tucker, that part of my land adjoining Thomas Mitchell, already surveyed for him.

All goods and chattels to be equally divided between all of my children, and unto my wife, Mary, one child's part. She to be my sole extrx.

Witness: Mathews Mays, Henry Mays, John Powell.

Mary, the extrx., being deceased before the will was probated, it was presented in court by the son, Francis Tucker.

Issue:

1. Francis[2] Tucker.
2. John[2] Tucker.
3. Henry[2] Tucker.
4. Abram[2] Tucker.
5. Mathew[2] Tucker.
6. Robert[2] Tucker.
7. William[2] Tucker.
8. Joseph[2] Tucker.

2. John[2] Tucker's (Francis[1]) wife was Catherine, of Bristol Parish.

On 8 May, 1712, 200 acres were surveyed for John[2] Tucker on Namazine Creek on the east side of Ellington Creek (Survey B. Pr. Geo., Arch. Dept.).

On July 15, 1717, John Tucker patented 200 acres on Namazine Creek and Ellington Cr., Pr. Geo. Co. (B. 10, p. 338, L. Gr.). He also patented 100 acres on the west side of Whipponock Creek, adjoining Nancy Mays, in his own line, 13 Nov. 1721 (L. Gr., b. 11, p. 77). He sold this 100 acres to Patrick Dorum, 13 Jan. 1723, on the Whipponock Creek for eleven pounds. Signed, John Tucker, 13 Jan. 1723 (B. 1, p. 671, Pr. Geo.).

Witness: William Cureton
William Short
Joseph Renn

Inventory of the estate of John Tucker, 6 May, 1727, by John Tally, administrator (Pr. Geo., 1713-28, b. I, p. 1016). John Cordle, Robert Tucker and William Coleman, appraisers. One fiddle is mentioned in the inventory. The Bristol Register gives: "Drury, son of John and Catherine Tucker, born 24 Sept., 1719, bapt. 24 Oct., 1720".

Issue:

1. Drury[3] Tucker.

1. Drury[3] Tucker (John[2], Francis[1]), was born in Prince George 24 Sept., 1719, and baptized 19 Oct., 1720 (Bristol Parish Register); died in Amherst Co. 1801. He married first, Susanna

Douglas; second, 6 Apr., 1769, Frances (Penn) Lee, widow of Ambrose Lee of Amherst Co., formerly of Amelia Co. Drury lived near the "Oaks" in Amherst.

(L. Gr., b. 26, p. 119). Drury Tucker patented 400 acres on branches of Hasel and Ware Rivers Oct. 1, 1747.

10 Jan., 1746, Drury Tucker patented 400 acres on north side of Fluvanna River, adjoining Seven Islands, Goochland Co. (L. Gr., b. 12, p. 479).

Drury Tucker, of Albemarle County, sold to Abraham Childers for 1000 lbs. Tobacco and cask, 200 acres of land on Rockfish Creek, parting Ezekiel Davidson and Abram Childers, purchased by said Tucker of Robert Walton.

Signed: Drury Tucker.

Witness: Mathew Tucker
Lucresha Tucker
Ez. Davidson

(3 Mch. 1749-50, D. B. 1, p. 204, Albe. Co.).

Drury Tucker sold to Abraham Childers for 50 lbs., 400A. on the river at Cannon's Corner and Amos Ladd's line. Susanna, wife of Drury, relinquishing her dower (D. B. 1, p. 433, Albe. Co., 10 Nov. 1751).

(D. B. 1, p. 152, Amherst Co., 25 Mch. 1763). A bond of Pearce Wade and Joshua Fowler, to Drury Tucker.

Land Tax Books: Drury Tucker paid tax on 374 acres in 1782. In 1799, Drury Tucker paid tax on 374 acres, 10 acres, 100 acres and 26½ acres, in Amherst Co.

Will of Drury Tucker of Amherst County, dated 24 Feb. 1798, prob. 2 Sept. 1801:

"To my son, Isaac Tucker; my son, Littleberry Tucker; my son, Zachariah Tucker; my son, Pleasant Tucker; to my wife, Franky Tucker 1/3 of the rest of the estate. The remainder to be divided equally between my children as follows: To Mary Douglas; to William T; Daniel; Martha Rucker; Milly Harrison; Mathew Tucker; Robert Tucker; Isaac Tucker; Littleberry Tucker; Zachariah and Pleasant Tucker. Executors: Daniel and Littleberry Tucker.

Witnesses: George Dillard
Henry Camden
William Penn, Jun.
Charles Burrus
Beverly Williamson

(W. B. 4, p. 25, Amherst).

William Coleman, Mathew Tucker, Wickers Watson and Richard Harrison gave bond as security for William Coleman administrator of the estate of Drury Tucker, dec'd, 20 June 1803, Amherst (W. B. 5, p. 85-119, Amherst).

The estate of Drury Tucker, dec'd, was divided according to his will: each devisee to draw a number from a hat. Lot No. 1 fell to Littleberry; No. 2 to Mathew, as near equal value as possible. Lot No. 3 to George Douglas and wife, Mary; Lot No. 4 to Robert Tucker; Lot No. 5 to Richard Harrison and wife, Milly; Lot No. 6 to Daniel Tucker; Lot No. 7 to Isaac Tucker; Lot No. 8 to William Tucker; Lot No. 9 to Littleberry Tucker; Lot No. 10 to George Rucker and wife, Martha; Lot 11 to Zachariah Tucker. Returned by David S. Garland, Leonard Henly and John McDaniel.

It is not certain that Drury Tucker served in the revolutionary war, but he furnished supplies, as shown by following:

Certificate No. 26: "Received of Drury Tucker, 1 beef weighing 500 pounds, for the use of the public, 14 Jul. 1781". Signed: A. Rucker, D. C. P. Also: 650 lbs. of beef. Certificate signed by Gabriel Penn, C. A. C.

Issue:

1. Mary^4 Tucker.
2. William^4 Tucker.
3. Daniel^4 Tucker.
4. Martha^4 Tucker.
5. Milly^4 Harrison.
6. Mathew^4 Tucker.
7. Robert^4 Tucker.
8. Isaac^4 Tucker.
9. Littleberry^4 Tucker.
10. Zachary^4 Tucker.
11. Pleasant^4 Tucker.

1. Mary^4 Tucker (Drury^3, John^2, Francis^1), m. George Douglas 13 Apr. 1769. (See Douglas.)

2. William^4 Tucker (Drury^3), m. Nancy, daughter of Ambrose Lee.

    1. Dandridge^5 Tucker.

3. Daniel^4 Tucker (Drury^3), bachelor, m. Judith Coleman, widow, 15 Sept. 1792. Robert Coleman, bondsman. Daniel's son, George, moved to Missouri.

4. Martha[4] Tucker (Drury[3], ———), m. George[4] Rucker (John[3], John[2], Peter[1]).

5. Mildred[4] Tucker (Drury[3], John[2], Francis[1]), m. Richard Harrison. They sold their share of her father's estate to Mathew Tucker for $100, land now in the possession of Frances Tucker in Amherst.

Witness: Colby Tinsley
Patrick Burton
Wm. Shelton

6. Mathew[4] Tucker (Drury[3]), sold his share of his father's estate to his brother, Daniel Tucker, for a horse named "High Flyer" Dec. 2, 1801 (D. B. I, p. 369, Amherst Co.).

Witness: Zach Tucker
L. berry Tucker
Pleasant Tucker

7. Robert[4] Tucker (Drury[3], ———), m. Phoebe, daughter of Joseph Ballinger and wife, Sarah Franklin, of Bedford County Aug. 14, 1791.

9. Littleberry[4] Tucker (Drury[3], ———), d. 1812, wife Sarah. Littleberry was one of the executors of his father's will; he brings in a bill for expenses, going to Kentucky on Sept. 19, 1803. "Littleberry Tucker was paid for his expenses going to Kentucky to sell land" of Drury Tucker's—paid £22—1 shilling (D. B. 4, p. 113, Amherst). Sarah Tucker was administratrix for Littleberry Tucker, dec'd, 15 Jan. 1812 in Powhatan Co. Va. (W. B. 4, p. 31, Powhatan).

10. Zachary[4] Tucker (Drury[3], ———), m. Pattie Craig of Stanford, Ky.

11. Pleasant[4] Tucker (Drury[3], ———), m. Sally Craig.

Issue:

1. Caleb[5] Tucker.

John and Robert Tucker may be brothers, both were living in Prince George as early as 1711, and Francis Tucker patented land in the same locality in 1712. They may have come from Norfolk Co.

In 1716 both sold land to David Crawley land lying on Tucker's Run, in Prince George Co.

In 1712 Robert Tucker "of Prince George" was paid for one wolf's head in Norfolk Co. John died in Pr. Geo. Co. in 1716, and Robert was appointed his attorney.

(O. B. Pr. Geo. 1711-20, p. 88). Edward Wyatt, Benj. Rix, James Bell and Marshall Talbott, or any others were ordered to appraise the estate of John Tucker, dec'd—Ann Jackson to return the inventory, 13 Nov. 1716.

(Pr. Geo. O. B. 1711-20, p. 88). The will of John Tucker, dec'd, was proved by Ann Jackson, the executrix, therein named, and proved by Thomas Daniel, and Elizabeth Jackson. Witness: Wm. Jackson security. 13 Nov. 1716. Ann may be John's sister.

Prince George (D. B. 1713-28, p. 133). Nov. 13, 1716, prob. Nov. 2, 1716. Will of John Tucker:

To God Dau., Elizabeth Jackson
To Ann Jackson
To Mary Thornhill
To Thomas Daniel
To James Craig
To Wm. Smith
Ann Jackson, exec.

Same book and page as above, Prince George Co. Robert Tucker of Norfolk, attorney for John Tucker.

Nov. 13, 1716. Power of Attorney from Robert Tucker (Attorney of John Tucker, attorney to Mrs. Ann Millner, administratrix of Isaac Millner of London, Dec'd, and Mr. Peter Pagan) to Capt. John Worsham (O. B. 1711-20, p. 88), Pr. Geo. Co.

(P. 355, 14 Mch. 1720), Pr. Geo. Co. The Sheriff of Princess Anne County—to pay Robert Tucker 2285 lbs. of Tobacco—which was levied on said County by the General Assembly in 1717—and ordered paid to this County for wolves heads, etc. In consideration whereof, Robert Hall Gent, in behalf of said Tucker, appears in Court and assumes to pay to this County 4 shillings per hundred for said tobacco.

(Order Book 1714-20, p. 186), May 13, 1718, Pr. Geo. Robert Tucker, a juryman. (Possibly brothers of Francis.)

1720—for wolves killed by Joseph Tucker and Robert Tucker of Prince George Co. (O. B. 1711-20).

(O. B. Pr. Geo. 1711-20, p. 354). Thomas Walke's letter of attorney to Francis Lightfoot was proved by Robert Tucker 14 Mch. 1720.

(Pr. Geo. 1713-20, p. 466). 20 May 1719, Mrs. Mary Mathews, relect of Mr. Jonathan Mathews, late merchant of London, appointed Mr. Robert Tucker, merchant, her attorney to collect ________.

(Pr. Geo. 1713, 28, p. 530). Tho. Withers and Tho. Harrison, both of Barbadoes, merchants, app. Mr. Robert Tucker, merchant of Virginia, their attorney to collect a bill against the estate of Mr. John Baylor, merchant.

Arms: Azure, barry wavy of ten Argent and Azure on a chevron embattled and counter embattled, between three sea horses naiant of the first.

Crest: a lion gaunt erased gules charged with three billets of Azure and or, holding a battle ax or, head blue.

Douglas

The county records having been destroyed of Charles City, of New Kent, King and Queen, King William and Hanover, it is impossible to trace the Douglas family, but since Susanna, John, George, and Robert are found to be living in the same community at the same time, we are including all the records to be found on these names. Edgar Wood's *History of Albemarle County,* p. 180, says: a family of Douglass was living in the Cove neighborhood as early as 1751, two of which family, James and George, probably brothers, were among the first members of the Cove Presbyterian Church. George d. 1785.

1. Susanna[2] Douglas, b. c. 1720, m. c. 1740 Drury Tucker (see the Tucker line). She d. before 1767.
2. John[2] Douglas.
3. George[2] Douglas.
4. Robert[2] Douglas.

2. John[2] Douglas pat. 430 a. of land on both forks of Licking hole Swamp, by Wood's Road, Goochland Co., 6 July 1741 (L. Gr., b. 19, p. 1031).

The estate of Robert Holt was Appraised 5 Nov. 1735 by Charles M. Moorman, Anthony Pale, and John Douglas in Hanover Co. Benjamin Alsop of St. Pauls Parish Hanover Co. sold to John Douglas 150 acres of land in Hanover adjoining John Ragland in line with Clark, to Gilbert Gibson's line, to the River, houses, orchards, etc., for £12, 3 Sept. 1735 (Hanover Book 1733-35, p. 312).

Witness: John Minor.
Anthony Pouncy.
William Hundley.

John Douglas patented 129 acres of land on the west branch of Bear Creek of the Fluvanna River 20 Nov. 1745 (L. G., b. 24).

George Nicholas of Dinwiddie Co. sold to Daniel Scott of Cumberland Co. for 400 lbs. sterling, 500 acres granted to George Nicholas, dec'd, late of Williamsburg, in Jan. 1729, lying on the north side of the Fluvanna River, on the river, at John Douglas' house. Witness: James Claiborne, Gideon Marr, and Samuel Jordon. May 26, 1752 (D. and W. B. 1, p. 467, Albemarle Co.).

John Douglas on Sept. 10, 1755, patented 400 acres of land on both sides of Rockfish Creek, at William Matlock's, to Robert Walton's, Abraham Childer's, 175 acres being formerly granted to said John Douglas Aug. 20, 1748, and 225 acres never before having been granted (L. G., b. 31, p. 733).

The 175 acres on Rockfish Creek was surveyed for John Douglass by Thomas Turpin (Survey Book of Albemarle, 1744-90, p. 29).

John Douglas paid a land tax in Amherst, in 1782, on 108 acres.

3. George[2] Douglas (   ) of Albemarle Co. bought from Charles Lewis Sr. for 4 lbs. sterling 400 acres of land in the Rich Cove patented July 6, 1741, by said Lewis, sold June 12, 1759 (D. B. 2, p. 131, Albemarle Co.). Witness: James Douglas, Michael Smith, William Maxwell, John Adkins.

George Douglas Sr. of Albemarle Co. sold to Wiloughby Pugh of Amherst, land on Hickory Creek of Rockfish River. This had been surveyed for Capt. Charles Lewis Oct. 5, 1772 (Amherst Co., D. B. C, p. 417).

George Douglas Sr. and wife, Mary, of Albemarle Co., and son, James Douglas of Amherst Co. sold to George Blane of Amherst Co., 400 acres of land on Hickory creek which had been bought by George Douglas Sr. from Charles Lewis Sr. On the same day, Oct. 5, 1772, they sold for 80 lbs. sterling 8 acres on Hickory Creek, granted to James Douglas, 6 Sept. 1767 (D. B. C, p. 412, Amherst Co.).

On Dec. 9, 1774, George bought 148 acres of land in Amherst from William Goolsby of Albemarle Co. (D. B. D, p. 330, Amherst). Witness: Mathew Tucker, Ambrose Rucker, John Merritt.

He sold this 148 acres on Hoop Creek of Hickory Creek to William Leach on Oct. 15, 1792, his wife, Mary, signing the deed (D. B. G, p. 181, Amherst Co.).

He paid taxes on 147 acres of land in Amherst in 1782.

Ambrose Rucker patented land in Amherst, 1797, adjoining on the south George Douglas' land (Survey B. 5, p. 24, Amherst Co.).

Issue:

1. George[3] Douglas.
2. James[3] Douglas.
3. David[3] Douglas.

1. George[3] Douglas (Geo.[2], ———[1]), m. Mary Tucker, dau. of Drury, Apr. 13, 1769, Amherst. One of the witnesses to the marriage bond was James Douglas. George died in Bedford Co.; will probated in 1812. Executors: wife, Mary; son, Murphy; and Waddy Cobb.

George Douglas served in the Rev. war in the 7th Va. Regiment. He enlisted April 10, 1775, and served from June 1777 to March 1778.

Issue from the will:

1. Lucinda[4] Clayton.
2. David[4] Douglas.
3. Susanna[4] Douglas.
4. John[4] Douglas.
5. Murphy[4] Douglas.
6. Polly[4] Ballard.
7. Sally[4] Coward.
8. William[4] Douglas.

1. Lucinda[4] Douglas (Geo.[3], Geo.[2], ———[1]), m. Mch. 21, 1797, John Willis Clayton Jr.

1. Mary[5] Polina Clayton, m. Thomas Turpin in 1818.
    1. Lucy[6] Douglas Turpin, m. William Ackerly.
        1. John[7] Paul Ackerly, m. Conna Blount White.
            1. Mary[8] Denham Ackerly, Lexington, Va.

2. David[4] Douglas (Geo.[3]), b. Feb. 26, 1776, m. Nov. 12, 1801, Sally White, b. Aug. 18, 1787, dau. of Jacob and Hannah (Spiers) White of Bedford Co.

Issue:

1. James[5] Douglas, b. Oct. 31, 1803.
2. Nancy[5] Douglas, b. Nov. 19, 1804, m. James Sledd.
    1. William[6] Sledd, m. Arabella Hobson.
        1. Prof. Benjamin[7] Sledd, Wake Forest.
        2. William[7] Sledd.
        3. Eliza[7], m. ——— Cornelius.
        4. Nannie[7], m. ——— Campbell.
        5. James[7] Sledd.
        6. Ida[7] Sledd.
        8. Samuel[7] Sledd.
3. George[5] W. Douglas, b. 22 Nov. 1806.
4. Elizabeth[5] Douglas, b. 13 Mch. 1808, m. 24 Sept. 1827, Alexander H. Logwood.
    1. Mary[6] Logwood.
    2. Nannie[6] Logwood.
    3. James[6] Logwood.
5. William[5] B. Douglas, b. 27 Jan. 1810.
6. Louisa[5] Jane, b. Oct. 20, 1811, m. Milton Hatcher.
7. Edward[5] A. Douglas, b. 14 May 1813.
8. Mary[5] Ann L., b. 21 Oct. 1816, m. ——— Hatcher.
9. Martha[5] Ann Douglas, b. Apr. 5, 1819, m. David Witt.
10. Lamira[5] Douglas, b. Mch. 1, 1821.
11. Sarah[5], b. Jan. 21, 1823, m. Robert Douglas (cousin).
12. Edatha[5], b. Feb. 7, 1826, m. Benjamin Hobson.
13. Robert[5] H. W. Douglas.
14. Edna[5] A. Douglas, b. Aug. 11, 1830.
15. Catherine[5] H. Douglas, b. Aug. 20, 1833, m. Spotswood A. Major.

13. Robert[5] H. W. Douglas (David[4], George[3], George[2]), b. Mch. 1, 1828, m. Bettie Major.

1. Lemma[6] Douglas, m. Billy Burks.
2. Pate[6] Douglas, m. Frank Parks.
3. William[6] Douglas, m. M. Parks.
4. Sallie[6], m. Edward Burks.
5. Jesse[6] Douglas, m. first, Lottie Turpin; m. second, Mrs. Yoder.
6. J. Letch[6] Douglas, m. Georgie Penn.

4. John[4] Douglas (Geo.[3], Geo.[2]), m. 25 Dec. 1805 Nancy Rucker (William[4], John[3], John[2], Peter[1]). See Rucker.

4. Robert[2] Douglas bought 295 acres of land of James Blevin in Goochland on the north side of the James River on Muddy Creek at Ashford Hughes corner, 13, Aug. 1743 (Goochland Co. D. B. 4, p. 218).

Robert Douglas was a witness of Albemarle to be payed for coming 30 miles, 150 lbs. of tobacco, 1745. To Goochland Court (Goochland Co. O. B. 6, p. 520).

Taken from St. Peters Parish Register. Children born and baptized of Robert Douglass:

George son of Robert baptized April 9 168—
Robert son of Robert baptized Feb. 5 168—
William son of Robert baptized Oct. 24 168—
Mary dau. of Robert baptized Nov. 9 169—
Copied from Greer's *Emigrants.*

John Douglas, 1655, imported by Lt. Col. Thomas Swann of Surry Co. Thomas, George and James were Imported in 1650 by Richard Tye and Charles Sharren of Charles City Co.

William Lee Douglas in 1655, by Maj. William Lewis of New Kent; Archibold Douglas in 1652, by Col. George Ludlow of Gloucester; Dan Douglas in 1650, by Edmund Bowman.

From Stanard's *Emigrants.* James Douglas in 1724 to Prince William Co. son of James Campbell Douglas of Mains Scotland and brother of Margaret who d. 1704, m. Archibald, Duke of Douglas.

From Hotten's *Emigrants.* Living in Va. at Charles Cittie Feb. 10, 1623 William Douglas. In 1626 he patented 250 acres of land in Charles Cittie.

Capt. Douglas, Commander of the Primrose, from London to Va., 24 Oct. 1635.

Hugh Douglas on the Constance age 22, 1635.

Thomas Douglas was sworn as constable in Merchant's Hope Parish (Charles City Co., B. 1655-65, p. 276).

Taken from the Land Grants of Virginia.

James Douglas pat. 380 acres in the upper parish of Nansemond on Bennets Creek on Mare Branch, for transporting seven Persons, 26, Apr. 1704 (B. 9, p. 600).

George Douglas pat. 180 acres of land lying between William Morris and William Rawlins in King William Co., for transporting four persons: Anne Glover, John Symond, Robert Abbott and Amey, his wife. 23 Oct. 1703 (B. 9, p. 559).

George Douglas and William Dutton pat. 400 acres in King William Co. on Caudle's Branch, 27 Oct. 1727 (B. 13, p. 401).

Robert Douglas pat. 150 acres in King and Queen Co., 16 April 1704, in Pamunkey Neck in St. John's Parish (B. 9, p. 600).

William Douglas pat. 275 acres in King William Co. on the south side of the Mattaponi River, 1710 (B. 10, p. 225).

Penn

George[1] Penn lived in Carolina Co., Va., died there in 1749 —"his will presented to court by Ann Penn, his wife, 8 Sept. 1749—the executrix with John Rogers and Giles—" (Caroline O. B. 1746-54, p. 172). He owned land in Amherst, where his wife and children moved after his death. The will was again "presented to court" in Caroline Co. by Moses Penn, one of the executors, Feb. 1756 (Caroline O. B. 1756, p. 137).

The division of his estate in Caroline was not recorded until 1758—Dec. 14 (O. B. 1758, p. 415) by Edmlund Pendleton, Frances Taylor and Eusebrius Stone.

The division of his property in Amherst, "According to his will", was made by William Cabell, Moses and Aaron Higgenbotham, 12 Nov. 1762 (O. B. 1759-62, p. 387, Amherst).

George Penn patented 1000 acres of land in Spotsylvania Co. at the foot of Great Mts., beginning at Zachary Taylors, to Octunie Hill, of Drysdale Parish, Sept. 28, 1728 (Land Gr., b. 12, p. 450).

His widow, Ann, later married ——— Dudley, possibly of Caroline. They moved to Amherst where her children were already living, and where she died in 1794, leaving a will which mentions five children, two having died before this date, leaving wills. George Penn's brother Moses presented the will in 1758 for probate. This Moses was the father of John Penn, the signer of the Declaration of Independence, who later moved from Caroline Co., Va. to North Carolina.

The will of Ann Dudley dated June 16, 1794 Amherst:

1. My dau., Frances[2] Tucker.
2. My son, George[2] Penn.
3. My son, Philip[2] Penn.
4. My son, Gabriel[2] Penn.
5. My son, Abraham[2] Penn.
6. My son, Wm.[2] Penn.
7. My son, Moses[2] Penn.

The following is taken from the Penn family Bible:

George Penn b. Dec. 13, 1737
Philip Penn b. Jan. 27, 1739
Gabriel Penn b. July 17, 1741
Abraham Penn b. Dec. 27, 1743
Frances T. b. Jan. 9, 1735
Wm. Penn b. Apr. 7, 1746
Moses Penn b. Jan. 13, 1748

1. Frances^{2} Penn (George^{1}), m. 1st Ambrose Lee, son of Wm. and Rachel Lee of King and Queen Co. and Amelia. (See will of Wm. following): Frances married 2nd Drury Tucker (widower) in Amherst 1767. Ambrose Lee died in Amherst 1764. Will dated 23 Oct. 1764, prob. 5 Nov. 1764, mentioned:

My wife, Frances Lee.

1. son Frank^{3} Lee.
2. son, George^{3} Lee.
3. son, Richard^{3} Lee.
4. dau., Elizabeth^{3} Lee.
5. dau., Jeane^{3} Lee.
6. dau., Sucky^{3} Lee.
7. dau., Nancy^{3} Lee.

Executors, George and Gabriel Penn
Wm. Lee
and wife Frances
(W. B. I, p. 44, Amherst Co.).

1. Francis^{3} Lee (Frances^{2}, George^{1} Penn), m. Nancy^{2} Penn (John^{1}) 1 Nov. 1786, died, leaving will dated 3 Oct. 1791, leaving children:

1. Wm.^{4} Lee.
2. Sophia^{4} Lee.

2. George^{3} Lee (Frances^{2}, George^{1} Penn), m. Jan. 21, 1772, Elizabeth^{2} Shelton (Richard^{1}) formerly of King Wm. Co. They moved to Ky. (1791) where George died 2 Aug. 1825.

Issue:

1. Ambrose^{4} Lee, b. 1773, m. Hanna Blaine.
2. Permela^{4}, b. 1774, m. John Welch.
3. Richard^{4}, b. 1777, m. ——— Montgomery.
4. Mary^{4} Wright, b. 1779, m. Thomas Montgomery.
5. Lewis^{4}, b. 1781.

3. Richard[3] Lee (Frances[2], George[1] Penn), m. 4 Dec. 1786 Frank Harrison.

2. George[2] (George[1]) Penn was a Captain in Revolutionary Service. He was chosen guardian of George Lee, orphan son of Ambrose Lee, dec'd Nov. 1771. He left two sons:

1. Wm.[3] Penn.
2. George[3] Penn, Jr.

He was paying on 400 acres of land in Amherst in 1782 (Land Tax Book).

3. Philip[2] Penn (George[1]) paid tax in Amherst in 1782 on 200 acres of land.

4. Col. Gabriel[2] Penn (George[1]), b. July 1741 in Caroline Co., m. Sarah Callaway, dau. of Col. Richard. He was one of the committee of Safety from Amherst County 1774 (*Cabells and Their Kin,* p. 101). He was paying tax on 2000 acres of land in Amherst in 1782. Will mentions wife, Sarah, and children.

1. James[3] Penn.
2. Edmund[3].
3. Elizabeth[3] (m. 1st James Calaway; m. 2nd Wm. Lorrey).
4. Sophia[3] (m. Wm. Crawford).
5. Pamelia[3] (m. Thomas Haskins).
6. Matilda[3] (m. Abner Nash).
7. Fannie[3] (m. ——— White).
8. Nancy[3] (m. ——— McCredie).
9. Sarah[3] (m. ———Crews).
10. Catherine[3] (m. ——— Holder).

(Chalkley's *Augusta Records*).

5. Col. Abraham[2] Penn (George[1]), b. in Caroline Co., m. Ruth Stovall in Amherst Co. with Daniel Gaines security. He moved to Henry Co., and was a Justice of Peace 1778. Served in the Revolution at Yorktown.

1. George[3], b. Jan. 7, 1770, m. ——— Gordon, moved to New Orleans.
2. Lucinda[3], b. 1771, m. Samuel Staples of Patrick Co.
3. Gabriel[3], b. Nov. 3, 1773, m. Jincy Clarke.
4. Horatio[3], b. Nov. 14, 1775, m. Nancy Parr, moved to Mo.

5. Polly[3], b. 1777, m. ——— Foster.
6. Greenville[3], b. 1779, m. (1st ——— Leath; 2nd Matilda Read).
7. Thomas[3], b. 1781, m. 1st Martha Leath; 2nd Mary Christian Kennerly.
8. Abraham[3], b. 1783, m. Sally Kreitz.
9. James[3], b. 1785, m. 1st ——— Leath; 2nd Mary Shelton.
10. Edmund[3], b. 1789, m. Polly Ferris.
11. Philip[3], b. 1792, m. Louise Briscoe.

6. Wm.[2] Penn (George[1]), b. 7 Apr. 1746. Served in the Revolution, may have died unmarried in service. Will dated 13 Aug. 1776, probated 1777, mentions himself as "Going into Service", he also mentions "My brothers, George, Philip, Gabriel and Abraham Penn". He was commissioned 1st Lieut. June 16, 1776, and Captain on March 15, 1777. (Heitman's *Register of Continental Soldiers*).

7. Moses[2] Penn (George[1]), b. 13 Jan. 1748, left a will dated Aug. 3, 1774, prob. Oct. 3, 1774, mentions "My brothers, Philip, Gabriel, George and Wm. Penn, my nephews, Frank and Richard Lee, my niece, Nancy Lee. Wm.[1] Lee patented 100 acres of "Escheat land of Thomas Ware" on West Side of Mattapony River, in St. Stephens Parish, adj. Taylor, Mrs. Ann Willshire, to Thomas Camp's line 16 Dec. 1714 (Land Gr., b. 10, p. 214). Anthony Gholston, Jr., of Spotsylvania Co. sold to Wm. Lee of King and Queen Co. for £50, 500 acres of land in St. George Parish, June 7, 1742.

Wm. Lee, or Lea, of King and Queen Co., sold to Anthony Garnett of Spotsylvania Co., for £55, 500 acres of land in St. George Parish. (Wm., father of Frances Lee). Rachel, wife of Wm. Lee, signed the deed (D. B. D, Spotsylvania Co., 2 Oct. 1744). Witness James Brock
Thomas Foster
John Coffrey

William[1] Lee moved to Amelia Co., Va., died there 1770 (W. B. 24, p. 328). Mentions: Wife Rachel.

1. My dau. Sarah[2] Penn.
2. My dau. Elizabeth[2] Clark.
3. My dau. Ann[2] Bennett.
4. My dau. Milly[2] Dudley.
5. My dau. Lucy[2] Lee.
6. Wm.[2] Lee.

7. Joseph[2] Lee.
8. Andrew[2] Lee.
9. John[2] Lee.
10. Ambrose[2] Lee, dec'd and his seven children.

(Wm. writes his name Lea, yet spells his sons, Lee.)

Will of John[2] Lee of Amelia probated 6 Jan. 1783 in Charlotte Co. (W. B. 1765-91, p. 320).

I give to my nephew, George Lee, 10 shillings.

My horses to my brother, Joseph Lee.

To my brothers and six sisters, Wm. Lee, Joseph Lee, Andrew Lee, Elizabeth Clark, Mary Walden, Ann Bennett, Sarah Penn, Nielly Ellcott, and Lucy Green.

Executors: Brothers, Wm. and Joseph Lea, and friend, Abraham Hackett.

Wit.: Milner Bennett, Ann Brimore, Richard Bennett.

Goodwin

Robert[1] Goodwin, of London, m. Jane Dollin, daughter of Anthony Dollin, of Chenault, Flanders. (See *Wm. and Mary Quarterly,* Oct., 1897).

Son, Peter[2] Goodwin, d. 1633, m. Sara Highlord.

Son, Major James[3] Goodwin, b. 1618 in London, d. 1678 in York Co., Va., m. Rachel (1630-1688). He was a member of the House of Burgesses.

Son, Peter[4] Goodwin, d. 1731 in York Co., m. Rebecca Tiplady, d. 1748.

Son James[5] Goodwin, d. 1758, m. Elizabeth Chapman, d. 1783.

Daughter, Elizabeth[6] Goodwin, d. 1828, m. Nov. 15, 1765, at Crab Neck, York Co., Va., Robert Blackwell (1730-1789), Captain of the Infantry of Lunenburg Co., during the Revolutionary War. (See Auditor's Accts.)

Issue:

1. Robert[7] Blackwell, m. Juicy Jones.
2. Thomas[7] Blackwell, b. Dec. 18, 1771, m. 1st, Anne Sydnor; 2nd, Maria B. Bridgeforth.
3. Christianna[7] Blackwell, m. Robert Jones.
4. Nancy[7] Blackwell, m. Peter Hawthorne, Jr.

5. Chapman[7] Blackwell, m. 1st, Polly Hatchett; 2nd, Prudence Jeffrees.
6. John[7] Blackwell.
7. Joel[7] Blackwell, m. 1st, Sally E. Gunn; 2nd, Martha F. Dance.
8. Elizabeth[7] G. Blackwell, m. Cannon F. Green.
9. James[7] Blackwell, d. young.

(See *Old Free State,* written by Bell).

6. John[7] Blackwell, d. 1832, m. Mary Polly Edmundson, 1796, they lived in Lunenburg, Va.

Daughter, Elizabeth[8] Blackwell (1799-1876), m. 1815, Robert Blackwell Jones (1797-1866).

Son, John[9] Robert Jones (1822-1901), m. 1846, Ann Elizabeth Blackwell Manson (1829-1914).

Son, Dr. Clarence[10] Porter Jones, b. 1874, m. 1904, Marinda[7] Rucker (Daniel[6], William[5], George[4], John[3], John[2], Peter[1]).

Issue:

1. Clarence[11] Porter Jones, Jr.
2. Sudie[11] E. Jones.

Chappelear

Louis[1] Chappelear and his wife, Simone Rous, lived in Uzes, Languedoc (Gard), France. (*Huguenot Society of London,* Vol. 7, p. 179).

Issue:

1. Isaac[2] Chappelier came to London after the revocation of the Edict of Nantes. He was naturalized in London, May 25, 1702, as "son of Louis Chappelier . . . of Uzes, Languedoc." He m. Oct. 28, 1696, Anne Arnaud, a native of Tremblale (Saintouge), dau. of Elie Arnaud and Madeline De Valan, his wife. (*Huguenot Society of London,* Vol. 7, p. 179).

Isaac and Anne Chappeliar made "temoiguag" at the Jesuit church at Threadneedle Street, London, Oct. 10, 1697, age 25, a surgeon.

He was "ancien et secretaire" to the Jesuit church of Crispin Street, London. He signed an entry there, on July 30, 1699.

Isaac had a son, Isaac Chappelier, bapt. at Threadneedle Street Church, on Mch. 16, 1698. Witnesses, Eli Arnaud and

Anne Chataigner. Isaac's dau. named Narionne, was bapt. Jan. 21, 1700. She evidently died, as another with same name was bapt. Jan., 1701, dau. of Isaac Chappelear, Apotecary, and Anne, his wife, of Crispin St., Stepney. (Vol. 3, p. 171).

Other children of Isaac and Anne Chappelier were: Son, Arnaud, b. Aug. 9, 1702; dau., Etienne, b. Mch. 11, 1705; and Louis, b. Dec. 23, 1706.

Mr. C. E. Lart, authority on the Huguenot migration and Huguenot families, says: "Isaac Chappelier evidently left France for the sake of religion."

Will of Isaac Chappelier, of London:

In the name of God Amen. I, Isaac Chapalier, Surgeon of H. M. Ship Canterbury, being in bodily health and disposing mind and memory considering the perrills and dangers of the sea and other uncertaintyes of this transitory life doe for avoiding controversies after my decease make publish and declare this my last will and testament in manner and form following: First, I give my soul to God that gave it and my body I committ to the Earth or Sea as it may please God to order and as for and considering all my worldly estate I give bequeath and dispose thereof as followeth Item I give unto Mr. Thomas Guppy for his great care and paines he took of me in the time of my sickness 8 dollars.* Item I give unto my servant Daniell Barrow 4 dollars with all my old clothes that are not of any service to my widdow and children. Item I give unto John Hill 2 dollars with one old coat and all and singular such wages two pences sume or sumes of money lands goods chattells and estate whatsoever as shall be anywayes due owing of belonging unto me at the time of my decease I do give devise and bequeath the same unto my loving wife Anne Chapalier and my two children Isaac Chapalier and ——— Chapalier the child being born since my being abroad and I don't know the Christian name. All my estate equally to be divided between my said wife and two children and in case of the death of either of them the survivor to have the deceased partyes dividend and I do hereby nominate and appoint Peter Gambo merchant liveing in St. Martin's lane by London Sole Executor of this my last will and testament for the whole use and behoofe of my said wife and children. My hand and seal 18 Jan. 1706/7 on board said ship at sea in America.

---

* Spanish money.

Witnesses: G. Walton, Captain Henry Lawson, Lt. Philip Tucker, Master John White, clerk.

Proved in Prerogative Court of Canterbury, Will 103, Poley, London, 10 May, 1707, by Peter Gambo alias Cambauld.

Issue:

1. Isaac[3] Chappelier.
2. Marionne[3] Chappelier.
3. Arnaud[3] Chappelier.
4. Etienne[3] Chappelier.
5. Louis[3] Chappelier.

1. Isaac[3] Chappelier (Isaac[2], Louis[1]), bapt. Mch. 16, 1698, Threadneedle Street, London, came to settle in Maryland, in Saint Mary's county. Wife, Rachel.

The records of that county are destroyed, so it is not known just when he emigrated, but there is an inventory filed at Annapolis: "Inventory of the estate of Isaac Chappelear, late of St. Mary's Co., Md., deceased, taken and appraised by Baptist Barber and Richard Wainright, thereunto appointed and sworn, this 24th day of Mch., 1741." (Children under age, names not given). Inventories 27, p. 54, Land Office, Annapolis, Md.

Edward Briscoe and Rachel, his wife, made oath as to having produced all goods of Isaac Chappelear for appraisement, July 6, 1742. (Same book as above).

Land Office, Annapolis, Maryland. Liber 19, folio 441. (1742-1743).

Being the account of Rachel Brisco of the estate of Isaac Chappelear. "Sureties are Thomas Reader and James Wood, of St. Mary's County, Ball disposed of a third to the deceased's widow, the Residue to Elias Arnold Chappelear and James Chappelear, Orphans of the Decd."

Issue:

1. Elias[4] Arnold Chappelear.
2. James[4] Chappelear.

1. Elias[4] Arnold Chappelear (Isaac[3], Isaac[2], Louis[1]), of St. Mary's Co., Md., appears in the Debt Book of that county as owning in 1774, 292 acres of land, part of Underwood, now called Wood's Pleasure.

This land was patented by Abraham Wood in the year 1731, part of it lying in St. Mary's and part in Charles counties. He moved to Culpeper Co., Va., after 1783, paying a personal tax there in 1787, on two white and two black persons.

In 1788, he bought 100 acres of land from James Monroe in Culpeper Co., and paid on this land until 1797. (Land Tax Book, Arch. Dept., Va. State Lib.)

In 1791 Elias Chappelear leased land from Presley Thornton, in Culpeper Co. In 1791, he paid personal tax on 3 whites and 2 blacks: mentioned "William and Zack" sons.

In 1795 William Chappelear paid personal tax on "father" —(2 taxes).

In 1797, William paid only his own tax. We suppose Elias to be deceased. He left no will, but his widow, Ann, began paying tax in 1799 on one slave.

Ann Chappelier was supposed to have been a Brammell or Bramwell, of Pennsylvania, daughter of William Brammell or Bramwell. One of Ann's granddaughters (the daughter of her son, George) was named Ann Brammell.

The following is copied from a note in possession of John Williams, son of Adaline Chappelear Williams, daughter of Benjamin Chappelear, son of William, son of Elias Chappelear. (Notation of outside of note, "Elias Chappelear's bond for four thousand pounds of tobacco.")

"Elias Chappelear of St. Mary's make unto Mary Hilton, of said county; eight thousand pounds of crop of tobacco to be paid —said Mary Hilton her certain allowance. E. Goodman, administrator. 8 Jan., 1783, 4000 lbs. of tobacco. Elias Chappelear. Witness, Henry Chappelear."

A deed from Thomas Haynie, of Culpeper, to Mrs. Ann Chappelear, for life, then to revert to her children: Thomas Haynie, William, James, Samuel, Zachariah, Presley and George Chappelear. (D. B. CC, p. 332, Culpeper Co., Va.)

Elias left no will.

Issue:

1. James^5 Chappelear.
2. Margaret^5 Chappelear.
3. William^5 Chappelear.
4. Zachary^5 Chappelear.
5. Samuel^5 Chappelear, moved to Georgia.
6. John^5 Chappelear, probably died in infancy.
7. Presley^5 Chappelear, probably died in infancy.
8. George^5 Chappelear.

1. James^5 Chappelear (Elias^4, Isaac^3, Isaac^2, Louis^1) was born in St. Mary's Co., Md., 25 May, 1760, died in Ohio. He married in Maryland, Margaret Cook. Margaret's father, Alex-

ander Cook, of St. Mary's Co., left two negroes to his "daughter Margaret Chappelear, to have the use of during her life." The negroes were "by no means to be disposed of by her husband, James Chappelear." A true extract from the will of Alexander Cook, late of St. Mary's Co., Md., deceased. The will is dated 14 day of April, 1809; proved 24 Oct., 1811. Signed, James Forrest, Register of Wills, St. Mary's Co., Md. Copy-teste, James Forrest. The above will is recorded in Culpeper Co., Va., 10 Dec., 1811.

There is a petition in the Arch. Dept., Va. State Lib., dated 14 Dec., 1809, from James Chappelear, of Culpeper Co., to the Assembly, to permit these slaves to be brought out of the State of Maryland into Virginia. See Petition No. 5462-A and 8495.

Will of Alexander Cook. (W. B. F., p. 313, St. Mary's Co., Md.): "I give to the children of my daughter, Margaret Chappelear, one negro woman named Tender and one girl named Mary."

James[5] Chappelear moved to Sunday Creek, Perry Co., Ohio, in 1823. He paid his first personal tax in Culpeper Co. in 1793.

1. John[6] Chappelear.
2. William[6] Chappelear.
3. Charles[6] Chappelear.
4. George[6] Chappelear went West.
5. Elliott[6] Chappelear.
6. Ann[6] Chappelear.

1. John[6] Chappelear (James[5], Elias[4]) served in the War of 1812, with his brother, William. He moved to Ohio with his father, James. The Census of Pike Township, Perry Co., Ohio, of the year 1850 gives:

John C. Chappelear, b. in Virginia, age 54.

Elizabeth Chappelear, b. in Pennsylvania, age 51.

John Grule Chappelear, b. in Ohio, age 10.

2. William[6] Chappelear (James[5], Elias[4]) served with his uncle, George, and brother, John, as a Private in the 34th Regiment of First Militia from Culpeper Co., in the War of 1812, under the command of Captain Charles Shackelford. (Adj't. Genl's. Office, Washington, D. C.)

1. James[7] Washington Chappelear.
2. Johnson[7] Chappelear.
3. Charles[7] Chappelear.
4. Jackson[7] Chappelear.

1. James^{7} Washington Chappelear was born in Ohio, m. Mary, daughter of Isaac Murphy, b. May 15, 1821, d. 1906, at Mount Pleasant, Mich.

   1. Nancy^{8} Chappelear, b. Aug. 19, 1861, in Morgan Co., Ohio, m. Jan. 6, 1880, Arthur Wright, son of Moses Wright and Fanny Peirce. (June 10, 1854-Apr. 28, 1911).

      1. Blanche^{9} Wright.
      2. Clyde^{9} Wright.
      3. Grace^{9} Wright.
      4. Lucile^{9} Wright.
      5. Wilbur^{9} Wright.

1. Blanche ^{9} Wright (Nancy^{8}, James^{7}, William^{6} Chappelear) was b. at Corning, Perry Co., Ohio, June 12, 1883. She m. at Corning, Roy Walke, of Michigan.

   1. Margaret^{10} Jane Walke.

2. Clyde^{9} Wright (Nancy^{8}, James^{7}, William^{6} Chappelear), b. Aug. 27, 1885, m. Edna ———, of Los Angeles, Cal.

3. Grace^{9} Wright (Nancy^{8}, James^{7} ———), b. Dec. 27, 1887, at Charleston, W. Va., m. Arthur Rother, of Michigan.

4. Lucile^{9} Wright (Nancy^{8}, James^{7} ———), b. Aug. 4, 1890, m. Walter ———.

5. Wilbur^{9} Wright (Nancy^{8}, James^{7} ———), b. Jan. 14, 1893, m. Katrina Stout and lives in Corsicana, Texas.

   1. Katrena^{10} Wright.
   2. Vixian^{10} Wright.

3. Charles^{6} Chappelear (James^{5}, Elias^{4} ———), Census of Hopewell Township, Muskingum, Ohio, 1850, records:

   Charles Chappelear, age 46, b. Virginia. Grocer.

   Althea A. Chappelear, age 35, b. Virginia.

   William M. Chappelear, age 16, b. Ohio.

   Sarah A. Chappelear, age 14, b. Ohio.

   Susanna M. Chappelear, age 10, b. Ohio.

5. Elliott^{6} Chappelear (James^{5}, Elias^{4} ———), of Hopewell Township. Census of 1850, records:

Elliott Chappelear, b. in Virginia, age 38.
Elizabeth Chappelear, b. in Virginia, age 32.
William Chappelear, b. in Ohio, age 10.
Samantha Chappelear, b. in Ohio, age 8.
Isaiah Chappelear, b. in Ohio, age 5.
Howard Chappelear, b. in Ohio, age 3.
Rozettha Chappelear, b. in Ohio, age 1.

2. Margaret^5 Chappelear (Elias^4, Isaac^3, Isaac^2, Louis^1) was born near Flint Hill. She married 20 Dec., 1789, Thomas Haynie, of Winchester, Va.

(Fauquier records) in 1808 Thomas Haynie deeded land to Mrs. Ann Chappelear. (Deed B. CC, p. 332, Culpeper Co.)

3. William^5 Chappelear (Elias^4, Isaac^3, Isaac^2, Louis^1) was born 20 June, 1770, in St. Mary's Co., Md. Died in Rappa'ck Co. 1851; was buried by his wife, Honar Garner, on his farm which is now owned by his gr. gr. dau., Jesse Huffman, near Flint Hill, Va.

My mother (Annie Chappelear Rucker) said that her grandmother's name was Honar, but not liking her name she called herself Ann. The marriage license granted to William has Honar Garner, dated 28 Nov. 1795, but the returns were not made by the minister for a year, 28 Nov. 1796, and Ann Garner was written instead of Honar. The name of Honar Chappelear was on the tombstone by which William was buried.

William Chappelear's Bible, now in the possession of Joseph Williams, of Flint Hill, has some items written by William:

"William removed to Culpeper, 26 Dec., 1804."
"William died in the year of our Lord, 22 Dec. —— (worn)."
"Mariah Chappelear was born ye December, April 7, 1800."
"Benjamin Chappelear was born March 22, 1803."
"William Chappelear was born 27 June, 1770."
"Honor, his wife, was born ——— 17, 1771."
"William Chappelear and his wife, Honor, were married ye December 6, 1795."
"Mary Chappelear, his daughter, was born 20 Sept., 1797."
"Elizabeth Chappelear was born ye 10 Sept., 1806."
"John Chappelear was born 29 August, 1808."
"Armistead was born 18 July, 1810."
"Elias and Ann (twins) were born 22 March, 18—."

The last page of the book gives the births of their slaves, and a cure for the disease called Gravel.

October 13, 1803, William Chappelear rented his land in Culpeper Co. to his brother, James. The land was to continue in the possession of James until 25 Dec., 1804; James to pay to William 700 pounds of tobacco. One of the witnesses to this transaction was Thomas Haynie.

William began paying land tax in 1792 on twelve acres, formerly of John Thomas. He paid in the same year on 106 acres of land, formerly of James Faygens.

In 1817 William Chappelear bought of William Norman 337 acres of land on Crooked Run. He owned land on the north side of Hickman's Run.

In 1814 he was living on land near Flint Hill and owned land at Gaines Cross Roads.

Elias Chappelear paid personal tax, 1791, for "sons, William and Zack."

William Chappelear in 1794 paid personal tax for "self and father."

The following is from an old Prayer Book, dated 1751; owned by Dr. Fred. D. Chappelear, of Hughesville, Md.:

"William Chappelear and Honor, his wife, were married 6 Dec., 1795. Mary Chappelear, his daughter, was born 23 Sept., 1797."

On another page of the same book: Margaret Bramms.

James Chappelear, son of Elias and Ann, his wife, was born the 25th day of May, 1766.

Margaret Chappelear was born ——— day of ————.

William Chappelear was born the 23rd day of June, 1770.

Zachariah Chappelear was born the 31st day of July, 1772.

On another page of same book: George Chappelear was born in the year of our Lord, 5th May, 1788.

James Chappelear ——— ——— ———.

Samuel Chappelear was born the 4th day of December in the year 1776.

———risa Chappelear was born the 4th of March in the year 1779.

Margaret Chappelear was born the 23rd of June, 1768 (?).

From another page of same:

James Chappelear was born the 25th day of May, 1766.

Margaret Chappelear was born the 29th day of May, 1768. (Very clear).

From another page of same:
William
William born March was born the Nineteenth day.
1751 Jems born
1761
Elias Chappelear, Ann Chappelear, his wife."

Ann, the widow of William, lived some years upon the 250 acres of land left to her; the taxes being paid by her son-in-law, John Palmer.

Her son, Benjamin, was living at that time in Fauquier Co.

(Culpeper Deed Book 00, p. 142, Feb. 1, 1822): William Garner, of Culpeper, to secure the payment of the sum of 1200 dollars: to William Chappelear, did by note, bearing date 1 Feb., 1822, as well as for the one dollar paid by Zachary Chappelear, have sold unto the said Zachary, negroes, Pomfrey, Mary, Polly, Jacob and Johnson, one horse, saddle and bridle, my chest of tools and all my interest in my deceased father's and mother's estate, real and personal. Justices Charles Shackelford, George Detherage. 14 Sept., 1822.

Will of William Chappelear, dated 17 June, 1846; probated 25 Sept., 1851:

"I, William Chappelear, of the county of Rappahannock, I give to my beloved wife, Ann Chappelear, the farm upon which I now live, 250 acres, together with such farming utensils, horses, stock, etc.

To my daughter, Mary Welch, one-ninth part during her natural life, the same to go to her daughter, Anne Best.

The residue of the estate given to my wife, Ann, for life, then to be divided among my children. To my son, Benjamin, one-fourth part; to my daughter, Maria Palmer, one-fourth part; to my son, Elias, one-fourth part; to my daughter, Anne Raeger, and to my son-in-law, Henry Raeger, one-fourth part, but should my daughter, Anne Raeger, die without heir, her part to be divided among the above named children in such proportions as above named, so that my daughter, Elizabeth de Latourandais, and her heirs shall receive an equal share with my son, Benjamin, my daughter, Maria Palmer, and my son, Elias. My daughter, Mary Welch, to receive only one-half a share during her life and at her death to go to her daughter, Anne Best, and her heirs.

But my desire to be expressly understood that my daughter, Elizabeth de Latourandais, and her heirs are not to receive any other portion of the estate given to my wife, Anne Chappelear, except that part given my daughter, Nancy Raeger. My estate both real and personal to be divided among my following named children: my daughter, Mary Welch; my son, Benjamin; my daughter, Maria Palmer; my son, Elias Chappelear; my daughter, Nancy Raeger; my daughter, Elizabeth de Latourandais. I charge my daughter, Maria Palmer, with the sum of 253 dollars; my son, Benjamin, the sum of 363 dollars; my daughter, Mary Welch, the sum of 130.25 dollars; my son, Elias, with the sum of 642.85 dollars; my daughter, Nancy Raeger, with the sum of 961.13 dollars.

I desire my ex'ors. to pay to my daughter, Elizabeth, for her sole and separate use, the sum of 400 dollars, 250 dollars is to be paid out for building her a dwelling house, to be erected upon land set aside for her by a deed of trust. My son, Benjamin, my sole ex'or."

Signed, William Chappelear (seal).

Witnesses: A Turner, Robert Deatherage and J. W. Fletcher.

Division of the estate showed that William owned 477½ acres of land and twenty-one slaves (W. B. A, p. 47, Rappa'ck Co.).

Children of William Chappelear:

1. Mary[6] Ellis Chappelear.
2. Maria[6] Chappelear.
3. Benjamin[6] Garner Chappelear.
4. Elizabeth[6] Chappelear.
5. John[6] Chappelear.
6. Armistead[6] Chappelear.
7. Elias[6] Chappelear, d. Jan. 8, 1894, unm. } twins.
8. Nancy[6] Chappelear, d. Feb. 13, 1901, m. Henry Raeger. } twins.
9. James[6] Pendleton Chappelear.

1. Mary[6] Ellis Chappelear (William[5], Elias[4]) was born 23 Sept., 1797. She married first, Hiram Ellis. Married second, 4th March, 1816, William Welch and had issue: Anne[7] Welch, who married ——— Best.

2. Maria[6] Chappelear (William[5], Elias[4]) was born 7 Dec., 1800; married John Palmer.

John Palmer sold some corn to a produce merchant in Alexandria for a Mrs. Mary Chappelear at Warrenton P. O., Va.

Issue:

1. Melville[7] Palmer, mar. Dr. David Stephenson, of Fauquier Co., Va.

Issue:

1. Senora[8] Stephenson, mar. Mr. Huffman.
   1. William[9] Huffman.
   2. Joseph[9] Huffman.
   3. Jesse[9] Huffman.
2. Dora[8], mar. George Davis, of Marshall.
3. Mrs. J. S.[9] Clothier, of Poolsville, Md., and other children.

3. Benjamin[6] Garner Chappelear (William[5], Elias[4]) was born 3 March, 1803, Culpeper Co.; died 23 May, 1895 (tombstone), and was buried in the Fletcher burying ground, upon the farm owned by Robert Fletcher. Benjamin married 17 August, 1817, Matilda Fletcher (Robert[2], Joshua[1]), of Fauquier Co. They resided for a while near Flint Hill, then near Markham, and in the year 1842 he bought Woodside (the old Armistead homestead) near Piedmont, now Delaplane. Here they lived until their death. Matilda died twenty years before her husband, Benjamin.

In the Fall of 1822, Benjamin went with a number of friends and relatives from Culpeper Co. to Ohio, crossing the mountains with caravans of covered wagons, leading all manner of animals, to make their homes in new lands. Among the number were his uncles, James and George. Benjamin spent the winter near Zanesville and taught school, but in the following Spring rode back to Virginia.

Upon his return he became overseer for Basil Gordon, the first millionaire of America, under whose tutelage, he became a good business man. During his life he amassed a large fortune for that time. His wife, Matilda, inherited her father's business qualities, and helped her husband invest, spend and save, at the same time to give their children a good education. As a girl, Matilda's hair was red, but after an illness from typhoid fever, her hair fell out, but was replaced with abundant tresses of black. As children we loved to hear Benjamin (my grandfather) tell of his trip across the mountains and his experiences while in the employ of Basil Gordon.

Benjamin met Matilda Fletcher in Rappahannock Co. while she was visiting her uncle, Dr. John Fletcher. She was horseback riding with her cousin, John Dillon, and coming to a brook where the water was deep, they rode in. Into the same brook rode Benjamin Chappelear, and it chanced that he saw Matilda for the first time, going to a camp meeting.

Children of Benjamin and Matilda Chappelear:

1. Laura^{7} Chappelear.
2. Adeline^{7} Chappelear.
3. Pendleton^{7} Chappelear.
4. Eliza^{7} Chappelear.
5. Armistead^{7} Chappelear.
6. Annie^{7} Chappelear.
7. George^{7} Warren Chappelear.
8. Emily^{7} Chappelear.
9. Roberta^{7} Chappelear.

1. Laura^{7} Chappelear (Benjamin^{6}, William^{5}, Elias^{4}), died unmarried, 17 May, 1891.

2. Adeline^{7} (Benj.^{6}, William^{5}, Elias^{4}), was born 13 April, 1830; died 7 March, 1907; mar. 15 June, 1869, Dr. William Williams; b. 17 Jan., 1824; d. Mar., 1905.

1. Joseph^{8} Williams.
2. John^{8} Catterton Williams.

1. Joseph^{8} Williams (Adeline^{7}, Benjamin^{6}, William^{5}, Elias^{4} Chappelear) was born 15 May, 1870, (living). Married 7 June, 1899, Agnes Grace Hart, at Carter's Run Church, Fauquier Co., Va.

1. Edwin^{9} Goodwin Williams, b. 10 Mch., 1900; mar. Gladys Bradley, 12 Jan., 1924.
2. Agnes^{9} Sanford Williams, b. 28 Mch., 1901.
3. William^{9} Chappelear Williams, b. 25 Apr., 1903.
4. Nellie^{9} Garner Williams } twins, b. 20 Nov., 1906.
5. Marian^{9} Hart Williams }
6. Grace^{9} Huskeil Williams } twins, b. 6 July, 1909.
7. Minnie^{9} Woodson Williams }

2. John^{8} Catterton Williams (Adeline^{7}, Benjamin^{6}, William^{5}, Elias^{4}) was born 7 Dec., 1872; married Miss Gore. No issue.

3. Pendleton^{7} Chappelear (Benjamin^{6}, William^{5}, Elias^{4}) served as a Private in the Civil War under Col. Richard Dulaney, of Fauquier Co. While on a furlough he went on a scouting party of Col. Mosby's men, and was killed near Drainsville, Va., on 22 Feb., 1864, at the age of thirty-one years, two months and

eleven days. (Tombstone on the Fletcher burying ground). He served with his two brothers under Gen'l. Payne. He was much beloved, and my mother spoke of him as the "Peacemaker".

4. Eliza[7] Chappelear (Benjamin[6], William[5], Elias[4]) was born 29 July, 1834; died 10 Dec., 1909; mar. Daniel B. Cheatwood; b. in Bedford Co., 10 Feb., 1830; d. 14 Dec., 1908. They lived at Pedlar Mills, Amherst Co., Va. Daniel B. Cheatwood was a son of Hiram and his wife, Harriett, (McDaniel) Cheatwood. Harriett was the daughter of Baldy, and granddaughter of George McDaniel, of Pittsylvania Co., Va.

Hiram was the son of Daniel Cheatwood and his second wife, Miss Porter. Daniel B. Cheatwood served in the Civil War, first under Kirkwood, later in Company H, of the Eleventh Infantry.

Issue:

1. Pendleton[8] Chappelear Cheatwood (1863-Jan., 1907); married 4 Apr., 1895, Mary Alice Ackerly, at Lynchburg, Va.
2. Hiram[8] Chappelear, born 1867; married Jennie Hewitt, at Wildwood, N. J.
3. Annie[8] Cheatwood, born 1870; mar. 15 Feb., 1894, Dudley D. Williams.
    1. Ernest[9] Williams, served in the World War.
    2. Dudley[9] Cheatwood Williams, Jr., b. Jan., 1904.
    3. Harry[9] Williams, b. 22 Aug., 1908, Graham, Va.
    4. Daniel[9] Williams.
    5. Eliza[9] Williams.

5. Armistead[7] Chappelear (Benjamin[6], William[5], Elias[4]) was born 1 Dec., 1835; died 1 June, 1916; married Amanda (Tea) Edmonds. He and his brother attended school at Hallowell Academy at Alexandria. Armistead resided after his marriage near Paris, in Ashley's Gap, Va. He was attending Emory and Henry College when the war began. With his two brothers he served under Gen. Payne. Armistead was a farmer and a great student.

Issue:

1. Harry[8] Chappelear.
2. Zulime[8] Chappelear, died 1922, unmarried.
3. Clayton[8] Chappelear, married Bertha Hackley.
4. Curtis[8] Chappelear, married Gladys[8].
5. Elizabeth[8] Chappelear.

6. Annie^{7} Chappelear (Benjamin^{6}, William^{5}, Elias^{4}), was born 7 June 1838; died 16 May 1922; married William Ambrose Rucker of Amherst County, 27 Nov. 1862. Annie and William Rucker are both buried in the Upperville cemetery, near the home where they had lived and the church they had attended with their nine children. Annie attended Mrs. Archer's boarding school at Oak Hill, and later attended Mrs. Butler's boarding school in Fairfax, at the same time her two brothers were at school in Alexandria.

Issue:

1. William^{8} B. Rucker.
2. Benjamin^{8} Chappelear Rucker.
3. Mary^{8} Matilda Rucker.
4. Dana^{8} Rucker.
5. Claude^{8} Pendleton Rucker.
6. Sudie^{8} Rucker.
7. Annie^{8} Lee Rucker.
8. Bayard^{8} Ambrose Rucker.
9. Lillian^{8} E. Rucker. (See Rucker excursus.)

7. George^{7} Warren Chappelear (Benjamin^{6}, William^{5}, Elias^{4}), was born 8 Sept. 1842, died 5 Nov. 1922 (12:30 A. M.); married Nancy O. Barrett of Amherst Co. George Warren was attending the Episcopal school at Alexandria when the Civil War began. He returned home, joined Company H, of the 6th Va. Cavalry, under the command of Col. Dulaney. He was only sixteen years of age. He was special courier for Gen. Cook at the battle of Fredericksburg, and was present at the wounding of Gen. Cook, and witnessed the death of Gen. Cobb. He was wounded at the battle of Appomattox. He was not at the first battle of Manassas, but joined soon after, and served until the surrender.

It was said by his comrades that "there was no braver soldier in the army than George Warren Chappelear."

Issue:

1. Benjamin^{8} Chappelear, married 27 Mch. 1910, Mrs. S. H. Perkins (nee Higginbotham).
2. Mamie^{8} Chappelear, mar. 2 Oct. 1909, Dr. Charles Peyton Greyer.
3. Mattie^{8} Chappelear, mar. 17 Oct. 1907, Clayton Ayre.
4. Lyle^{8} Chappelear, mar. 13 Dec. 1919, Miss Johnston.
5. Sadie^{8} Chappelear, mar. 11 April 1906, L. T. Jeffries.
6. Gladys^{8} Chappelear, mar. 30 Oct. 1926, Curtis Chappelear (1st cousin).
7. George^{8} W. Chappelear.

7. George[8] Warren Chappelear (Geo.[7], Benj.[6]), b. Aug. 23, 1889, in Fauquier Co. m. Nannie Binford, dau. of Ballard Williams Binford and Evelyn Archer (Leake) Binford on June 7, 1917.

George received his B. S. at the Virginia Polytechnic Institute in 1912, and his M. S. in 1913, during which session he served as instructor of Agronomy. From 1913-1918 he was instructor in science and mathematics at the Miller School of Albe., and is now the head of the department of Biology at the State Teachers College of Harrisonburg.

Issue:

1. Nancy[9] Chappelear, b. Nov. 25, 1918.
2. Gladys[9] Georgiana Chappelear, b. Dec. 18, 1921.

8. Emily[7] Chappelear (Benjamin[6], William[5], Elias[4]), b. 1840; d. 1904 at Delaplane, Va.; m. Elisha D. Kincheloe, b. 1837; d. 1918. They resided in the home of her parents at "Woodside". Elisha D. Kincheloe represented Fauquier Co. in the House of Delegates from the year 1871-72.

Issue:

1. Winston[8] Kincheloe, m. Belle James, 7 July 1909, no issue.
2. Bertha[8] Kincheloe, m. 27 Nov. 1902, Dixey Welfley of New York.
3. Pendleton[8] Kincheloe, m. 23 Oct. 1913, Ruth Shacklett.

9. Roberta[7] Chappelear (Benjamin[6], William[3], Elias[4]), died Apl. 1909; mar. 22 Oct. 1868 Thomas Browning of Rappa'ck Co., Va. where they lived until his death 22 Mar. 1916.

Issue:

1. James[8] Browning, d. unmar. 23 Aug. 1903.
2. Benjamin[8] Browning, d. unmar. Sept. 1910.
3. Maude[8] Browning, d. unmar. 28 Nov. 1919.
4. Emmett[8] Browning, mar. Bessie Ramey June 1910.
5. Sue[8] Browning, mar. Harvie Clifton Churn 25 Apl. 1906.
6. George P. Browning, b. 18 Jan. 1884; m. Mable Newman Miller of Baltimore, 21 Feb. 1914 at Flint Hill, Rappa'k Co. though her home at the time was in Baltimore.

4. Elizabeth[6] Chappelear (William[5], Elias[4]), born 10 Sept. 1806; m. 11 Apr. 1829 Joseph de la Tournandais of Rappa'k

County, Va., born 1 May 1802; died before 1853 (Tax books). Joseph was a Frenchman, born in San Domingo. During an insurrection on that island, his parents were killed. A faithful servant concealed two of the children on board a ship bound for America. They were brought to Baltimore and there placed in a Catholic home. The servant had brought a basket of the family silver. The son Joseph came to Virginia, and the daughter made her home in Baltimore, where she married. Elizabeth Chappelear's father William left her property, in trust, with her brother Benjamin as trustee. "William Chappelear and wife Ann of Rappa'k Co. to Benjamin Chappelear, trustee; for Elizabeth Latournandais, the wife of Joseph, for love and affection which he bears to his daughter Elizabeth".

Issue:

1. William[7] de la Tournandais, b. 22 Mch. 1830; died young.
2. Burwell[7], born 3 May 1832; m. 11 Apr. 1878 Julia Duncan. No issue.
3. Mary[7] Emily, born 3 May 1834; m. J. R. Miller 5 Aug. 1879.
4. Maria[7], born 20 Feb. 1837; died young.
5. Nancy[7] Jane, died in infancy.

5. James[6] Pendleton Chappelear (William[5], Elias[4]), born 27 Aug. 1808 in Culpeper Co. lived in Rappa'k Co., died unmarried before his father, and is not mentioned in the will of William Chappelear.

6. John[6] Armistead Chappelear (William[5], Elias[4]), born 18 July 1810; died 2 Nov. 1875 at Paynesville, Pike county, Mo., unmarried. His brother Benjamin was appointed administrator of his estate (W. B. 40, 41, 42, Fauquier Co.). The legatees mentioned: William Welch, Henry Raeger, Burwell W. la Tournandois and Elias Chappelear. (See also W. B. 36, p. 8, Fauquier Co.)

The following letter was written by Armistead to his brother John Chappelear, Gaines Cross Roads, Rappa. Co. Va.

Paynesville, Pike Co., Mo., 5 Apr. 1840. Dear Brother: "I have met Mr. Palmer's people. The old man has chills. I have been to see Mr. Thornton Nelson. Mr. Palmer is settling his business in Rappahannock. Tell father to stay where he is. I have visited Ohio, Illinois, Indiana, Kentucky and Missouri, and do not like them. There are chills everywhere. Help Elias and Benjamin to get a farm for me in Rappahannock Co., I do not want my sisters to know where I am. I expect to keep a grocery store here. Signed, Armistead Chappelear. He states that he has opened a cash Grocery business; that he went twice a year to New Orleans for his groceries, bought cattle and sheep to take down the Mississippi river and brought back his wares. The trip took him six weeks. He mentions his niece Melville and his brother Benjamin. He signs his name "Art Chappelear".

4. Zachary[5] Chappelear (Elias[4], Isaac[3], Isaac[2], Louis[1]), born 31 July 1772; m. Lyna Settle, 9 Aug. 1799, in Culpeper Co., Rev. John Puckett officiating. In 1799 Zachary leased land from John Minor. Zachary Chappelear signed a petition, in the year 1791 with his brothers, George and James. He began paying personal tax in the year 1792, his father Elias paid his tax in 1791, yet in 1800, Zachary, "a minor", paid tax on 12 acres. This 12 acres he sold to his brother, William in 1808 (D. B. C, p. 143, Culp. Co.).

Zachary moved to Ohio (D. B. A, p. 124, Rappa'k). Zachary Chappelear of Culpeper Co., sold land to Daniel McGower and to W. J. Menefee in 1831. In January of the year 1823, Zachary, George and James moved to Perry Co., Ohio.

They settled on Sunday Creek, near Lexington Township, about twelve miles south east of Zanesville. Hanson, son of Zachary, moved to Clayton Township, Perry county.

Elliott, Charles and John O., sons of James Chappelear, William Woods, son of Zachary Chappelear, all moved north to Hopewell Township, Muskingum Co., Ohio. Henderson, son of Zachary, remained in Perry county.

Issue:

1. Hanson[6] B. Chappelear.
2. Henry[6] Chappelear, moved to Texas as a young man.
3. Hedgeman[6] Chappelear.
4. William[6] Woods Chappelear.
5. Samuel[6] Chappelear.
6. Nancy[6] Gray Chappelear.
7. Catherine[6] Chappelear.

1. Hanson[6] Brammell Chappelear (Zachary[5], Elias[4]), m. Elizabeth Morehead in Culpeper Co., Va. In 1826 he was living there and was paying personal tax. He was then between twenty and thirty years of age. He moved to Clayton township, later to New Lexington township, Perry Co., Ohio. (See Census of 1850.)

Hanson B. Chappelear, listed in this census (1850) as being 47 years old. Others listed are possibly his wife and children. They are:

Elizabeth, b. in Virginia, age 39.
Cordelia, b. in Virginia, age 20.
Charles C., b. in Ohio, age 18.
Elleanor, b. in Ohio, age 16.
Melville, b. in Ohio, age 14.
Thomas Henry, b. in Ohio, age 10.
Susan E., b. in Ohio, age 8.
Mary F., b. in Ohio, age 6.
Hanson B., b. in Ohio, age 4.
Joseph W., b. in Ohio, age 1.

The foregoing named are of 7th generation and are children of Hanson^6 Chappelear; Elizabeth, his wife.

3. Charles^7 C. Chappelear (Hanson^6, Zachary^5, Elias^4, Isaac^3), born 1832 in Ohio; died 1859; m. Elizabeth Forgrove.

1. Charles^8 C. Chappelear, born at Thornville, 1858. He was State senator. Editor and publisher of Union Herald of Centreville, Ohio. Married Nettie White, daughter of Dr. White. Children.

4. Thomas^7 Henry Chappelear (son of Hanson^6), Dana, Indiana.

1. Charles^8 Chappelear, Greenville, Ill.
    1. Dr. Claude^9 Chappelear, Dean of Illinois College, Jacksonville, Ill.

3. Hedgeman^6 Chappelear (Zachary^5). Lyna Chappelear, widow of Zachary, lived the last years of her life with this (Hedgeman) son, at his home on Sundays Creek.

1. Josephus^7 Chappelear.
2. Thomas^7 Chappelear.

4. William^6 Woods Chappelear (Zachary^5), born 13 Mch. 1818, at Gaines Cross Roads. Moved to Ohio in the year 1823 to Sunday Creek. In 1850 he removed to Missouri with his wife and five small children. He m. first, Miss Ewing who was born in Va. He married secondly, Miss Beymer. The census of Hopewell township, Muskingum Co., Ohio, of 1850, gives:

William W. Chappelear, b. in Va. Age 32. Tradesman.
Elizabeth Chappelear, b. in Ohio. Age 27.
Henry S. Chappelear, b. in Ohio. Age 9.
Mary A. Chappelear, b. in Ohio. Age 6.
Julia C. Chappelear, b. in Ohio. Age 5.
Matilda Chappelear, b. in Ohio. Age 3.

Issue:

1. Henry[7] Stuart Chappelear.
2. Mary[7] A. Chappelear.
3. Julia[7] Chappelear.
4. Matilda[7] Chappelear.
5. Emma[7] Chappelear.
6. Minnie[7] Chappelear.
7. Alice[7] Chappelear.

1. Henry[7] Stuart Chappelear (William[6] W.), b. 1841; d. 1916; m. Clara Evans, b. 1853; d. Feb. 1927. Moved to Texas.

1. Col. Louis[8] S. Chappelear of U. S. Army. Living in Los Angeles, Cal. Married 1st, Florence Peabody who died in San Francisco. Married 2nd, 18 Jan. 1922, Mary Barrett Cosby of Santa Barbara.

2. Mary[7] A. Chappelear (William[6] W.), b. 1844; m. L. A. Ross. Their daughter, living in Los Angeles, is a graduate of Stanford University.

8. George[5] Brammell Chappelear (Elias[4], Isaac[3], Isaac[2], Louis[1]). Born near Flint Hill, Va., May 1788; m. Susan Jones of Va., who was b. 28 Apr. 1791; d. 27 Mch. 1880. Moved to Perry Co., Ohio. Some of his children appear to be married prior to 1850, for the census of New Lexington of that year (1850) gives:

George B. Chappelear, b. in Va., age 62. Tavern Keeper.
Susan Chappelear, b. in Va., age 59.
Ann Chappelear, b. in Va., age 29.
John Chappelear, b. in Va., age 23.
William Chappelear, b. in Ohio, age 28.
Eliza Chappelear, b. in Ohio, age 22.
Thomas P. Chappelear, b. in Ohio, age 2.

Other children had moved elsewhere. George Chappelear served as a Rifleman in the War of 1812 under Capt. Charles Shackleford of Culpeper Co. from Aug. 1812 to Aug. 1814. He moved with his brothers and friends, in the Fall of the year 1823, to Sundays Creek, near Zanesville. In 1837 he wrote a letter to his nephew, John Chappelear (son of William) of Gaines Cross Roads, Rappa. county, dated 14 May. He was living at Somerset, Perry county at this time. The letter was addressed to "Dear Nephew" and signed, "Your uncle, G. Chappelear. The letter relates of the part he had taken in the war of 1812, with two of his nephews, John and William, sons of "Brother James of Sundays Creek. He also mentions his brothers James and William, and says that his nephew Benjamin had visited him at his place of residence, and "On account of the vast improvements in their neighborhood, Benjamin could not recognize it". He writes of the children of his brother William, giving their names: "Benjamin, Elias, Armistead, Polly, Mariah and Nancy". At the close of the long letter, he adds: "Your Aunt Sucky wishes to be remembered". This letter is in the possession of Bessie Chappelear of Delaplane, Va.

Issue:

1. Sally[6] Chappelear.
2. Henderson[6] Chappelear.
3. William[6] A. Chappelear.
4. Ann[6] B. Chappelear.
5. Juliet[6] C. Chappelear.
6. John[6] B. Chappelear.

1. Sally[6] Chappelear (George[5], Elias[4]), b. 2 Nov. 1814; d. 3 July 1893; m. Smith Wartman, no children.

2. Henderson[6] Chappelear (George[5]), b. 22 July 1817 in Va.; d. 16 Mch. 1894; m. Lucinda ———, b. in Va. Moved to Pike Co., Ohio.

1. Lyde[7] Chappelear.
2. George[7] Chappelear.
3. William[7] H. Chappelear, b. 1848 in Ohio; d. 4 Jan. 1929, Illinois.
    1. Dell[8] Chappelear.
    2. Fred[8] W. Chappelear.
    3. Charles[8] C. Chappelear. Has sons William[9] and Lawrence[9].
    4. Frank[8] Chappelear.
    5. Roy[8] Chappelear.
    6. Flo[8] Chappelear.
    7. Anna[8] Chappelear.
4. Samuel[7] Chappelear resides in Los Angeles, Calif.

3. William^{6} A. Chappelear (George^{5}, Elias^{4}), b. 21 May 1819 in Va.; d. 21 Jan. 1887 in Ohio.

1. Charles^{7} V. Chappelear, b. 15 Oct. 1850, Illinois. Has sons: Walter^{8}, Willie^{8} Chappelear.

4. Ann^{6} Brammell Chappelear (George^{5}, Elias^{4}), b. 18 May 1821; d. 1911; m. ———— Parker. No children.

5. Juliet^{6} Chappelear (George^{5}, Elias^{4}), b. 16 Aug. 1823; m. ———— Wolf.

6. John^{6} Chappelear (George^{5}, Elias^{4}), b. 23 Jan. 1827; d. Mch. 1895.

1. Edward^{7}, died in infancy.
2. Samuel^{7}, b. 27 Oct. 1863; m. Laura E. Monroe of Leesburg, Va.
    1. Rose^{8}, b. 28 July 1885.
    2. Monroe^{8}, b. 24 Feb. 1898.

The following from the census, probably refers to John, though the birth dates do not agree. Hopewell Township, Muskingum Co., Ohio.

John B. Chappelear, b. in Va., age 34.
Melville Chappelear, b. in Va., age 32.
Sarah D. Chappelear, b. in Va., age 10.
Harvey Chappelear, b. in Va., age 8.

2. James^{4} Chappelear (Isaac^{3}, Isaac^{3}, Louis^{1}), lived in St. Marys Co., Md., where he died, leaving a will, dated 20 Sept. 1808; prob. 10 Oct. 1808 (W. B. JJ-3, p. 183, St. Marys). "To my daughters living in Virginia, $100 each: Mary Harrison, Rebecca Dent, Cassandra Riley and Ann Chappelear. To my sons Henry and George Chappelear and to my granddaughters Rebecca and Elizabeth Chappelear. To my son John. To my grand son Thomas Edwards. To Elkanah, the ex'or. of Nathan Chappelear's estate. To my son Henry Chappelear, residing in the state of Georgia, $40. To sons John and Benjamin, the residue of the estate.

Issue:

1. Nathan^{5} Chappelear.
2. John^{5} Chappelear.

3. Benjamin^5 Chappelear, m. 9 Dec. 1797, Mary Wood.
4. Henry^5 Chappelear.
5. Rebecca^5 Chappelear, m. 14 Oct. 1799, Thomas Dent, St. Marys.
6. Mary^5 Chappelear, m. Joseph Harrison, moved to Culpeper, Va.
7. Cassandra^5 Chappelear, m. James Riley, moved to Culpeper, Va.
8. Ann^5 Chappelear.
9. Elizabeth^5 Chappelear.
10. George^5 Chappelear.

1. Nathan^5 Chappelear of St. Marys Co., Md. Will 14 Nov. 1809 (W. B. JJ-3, p. 157).

"To my father James Chappelear; To my brother Henry Chappelear; To Richard Chappelear; To Elizabeth Chappelear; To Rebecca Dent, wife of Thomas Dent. The residue of my estate to be divided equally between John Chappelear, Benjamin Chappelear, Ann Chappelear, Elizabeth Edwards, Rebecca Dent, Cassandra Riley, wife of James Riley, and Mary Harrison, wife of Joseph Harrison."

2. John^5 Chappelear (James^4, Isaac^3, Isaac^2, Louis^1).
   1. Harry^6 Chappelear.
   2. George^6 Chappelear.
   3. Eliza^6, unmarried.
   4. Rebecca^6, m. ——— Cartwright.

1. Harry^6 Chappelear (John^5, James^4, Isaac^3, Isaac^2, Louis^1).
   1. William^7 Chappelear.
      1. Harry^8 Chappelear.

2. George^6 Chappelear (John^5, James^4), b. 1800; m. Jan. 2, 1834, Elizabeth Tycer.
   1. John^7 Chappelear.
   2. George^7 Chappelear.
   3. James^7 D. Chappelear.
   4. Franklin^7 Chappelear.
   5. Annie^7 Chappelear.
   6. Nathan^7 Chappelear.
   7. Emily^7 Chappelear.
   8. Mary^7 Chappelear.

1. John^{7} Chappelear (George^{6}, John^{5}, James^{4}) (1835-1918), m. 1st Elizabeth Johnson; m. 2nd Josephine Tycer; m. 3rd Susan Canter.

1. Thomas^{8} Chappelear.
2. Lansing^{8} Chappelear.
3. Eva^{8} May Chappelear.
4. Annie^{8} Chappelear.
5. Robert^{8} Chappelear.
6. John^{8} Chappelear.

1. Thomas^{8} Chappelear (John^{7}, George^{6}, ———).

1. Andrew^{9} Leo Chappelear, m. Annie Herbert.
    1. Leo^{10} Chappelear.
    2. James^{10} Chappelear.
    3. Imogene^{10} Chappelear.
    4. Thomas^{10} Chappelear, m. Bessie Stennett.
        1. Thomas^{11} Chappelear.
        2. Ellen^{11} Rose Chappelear.
        3. Mary^{11} Virginia Chappelear.
        4. Flavers^{11} Chappelear.
        5. Frances^{11} Chappelear.

2. Lansing^{8} Chappelear (John^{7}, George^{6}).

1. John^{9} Chappelear.

4. Annie^{8} Chappelear (John^{7}, George^{6}), m. Dudley Davis.

1. Gertrude^{9} Davis, m. Mark Markin.
2. Eileen^{9} Davis, m. Will Irvin.

6. John^{8} Chappelear (John^{7}, George^{6}), m. Dora V. Davis.

1. John^{9} A. Chappelear.

2. George^{7} Chappelear (George^{6}, John^{5}, ———), d. at age of 56; m. Mary Emily Montgomery who d. at age of 82. Lived in Hughesville, Md.

1. George^{8} Edwin Chappelear, m. Angie Herbert.
    1. George^{9} Herbert Chappelear.
    2. Edwin^{9} Chappelear.
    3. Angela^{9} Chappelear.
    4. Alma^{9} Chappelear.
2. Dr. Harry^{8} Chappelear, m. Edith Cox.
3. Dr. Fred^{8} Chappelear, m. Katherine Hughes.

4. William^{8} G. Chappelear, m. Irene Booy.
   1. William^{9} Chappelear.
   2. Virginia^{9} Chappelear.
5. Ella^{8} Chappelear, m. 1st Henry Chappelear (son of William), 2nd William Douglas.

Issue, by 1st m.:

1. Elizabeth^{9} Chappelear.
2. Erla^{9} Chappelear.

Issue, by 2nd m.:

3. Lawrence^{9} Douglas.
4. Lee^{9} Douglas.
5. Ruth^{9} Douglas.

3. James^{7} Chappelear (George^{6}, John^{5}, James^{4}), d. at age of 80 years; m. Ella Canter.

1. Leroy^{8} Chappelear, m. Miss Henderson.
   1. Dorothy^{9} Chappelear.
   2. Fay^{9} Chappelear.
   3. James^{0} Chappelear.
   4. Leroy^{9} Chappelear.
2. Albert^{8} Chappelear, m. Ethel Lacey.
   1. James^{9} A. Chappelear.
   2. Elizabeth^{9} Chappelear.
3. Edith^{8} Dent Chappelear, m. Reuben Acton.
   1. Helen^{9} Acton.
   2. Reuben^{9} Acton, Jr.
4. Irene^{8} Ella Chappelear, m. Martin Shrone.
5. Adrian^{8} Chappelear.
   1. James^{9} Chappelear.

4. Franklin^{7} Chappelear (George^{6}, John^{5}, ——), d. aged 69; m. Anna Burch.

1. George^{8} Chappelear, m. Verena Mattingby.
   1. George^{9} Chappelear.
   2. Louise^{9} Chappelear.
2. Lewis^{8} Chappelear.
3. Susie^{8} Chappelear.
4. Etoile^{8} Chappelear.
5. Martha^{8} Chappelear.

3. Susie^{8} Chappelear (Franklin^{7}, George^{6}, ——), m. Jeff Tennyson.

Issue:

1. Lynette[9] Tennyson.
2. Anna[9] Tennyson.
3. George[9] Tennyson.
4. Etoile[9] Tennyson.
5. Loretta[9] Tennyson.

4. Etoile[8] Chappelear (Franklin[7], George[6]), m. Kendrick Thompson.

1. Franklin[9] Thompson.
2. Doris[9] Thompson.
3. Katherine[9] Thompson.

5. Martha[8] Chappelear (Franklin[7], George[6]), m. Elijah Yates.

1. Jack[9] Yates.
2. James[9] Yates.
3. William[9] Yates.

5. Annie[7] Chappelear (George[6], John[5], James[4]), d. aged 75; m. Robert Johnson who also d. at age of 75.

1. John[8] Johnson, m. Mary Chisman.
   1. Roland[9] Johnson.
2. Joseph[8] Johnson, m. Irene Corbin. He d. in Spanish War.
3. Theodore[8] Johnson.
4. Julia[8] Johnson, m. John Sinclair, d. age 55.
5. James[8] Johnson.
6. Lina[8] Johnson.
7. Emma[8] Johnson, m. William Bailey.
   1. Howard[9] Bailey.
8. Mary[8] Johnson.
9. Olive[8] Johnson, m. Howard Norris.

6. Nathan[7] Chappelear (George[6], John[5], ———), killed by lightning, aged 50; m. 1st Jennie Burch; m. 2nd Columbia Canter.

Issue, by 1st m.:

1. Maude[8] Chappelear.
2. Cora[8] Chappelear, m. ——— Acton.
   1. Benjamin[9] Acton.
3. Benjamin[8] Chappelear.
4. Mamie[8] Chappelear.

Issue, by 2nd m.:

5. Leby[8] Chappelear, m. 1st Herbert Holmes; m. 2nd ——— Lee.

Issue, by 1st m.:

1. Lillian[9] Holmes.

6. Nellie[8] Chappelear, m. Benjamin Shafer.

8. Mary[7] Chappelear (George[6], John[5], ———), m. William Woodburne.

1. George[8] Woodburne.
2. Elizabeth[8] Woodburne.
3. Alice[8] Woodburne.

1. George[8] Woodburne (Mary[7], George[6], ———), m. Marie Canter.

1. Mary[9] Woodburne.
2. Clarence[9] Woodburne.
3. George[9] Woodburne.

2. Elizabeth[8] Woodburne (Mary[7], George[6], ———), m. Elsion Canter.

1. Mazie[9] Canter.
2. Clara[9] Belle Canter.
3. William[9] Canter.

9. Elizabeth[5] Chappelear (James[4], Isaac[3], Isaac[2], Louis[1]), mar. Elkanah Edwards, 19 Dec. 1801.

1. Thomas[6] Edwards.

Elkanah Edwards married 2nd, Mary Chappelear. He was executor of Nathan Edwards' estate.

Marriage records of Maryland.

1798. Feb. 5, John Chappelear m. Jane Bean.
1798. Feb. 5, John Chappelear m. Dorothy Legar.
1825. Jan. 17, Henry Chappelear m. Catherine Sothoron.
1851. Mch. 31, Eliza Chappelear m. Alex. W. Carthright.

Arnaud

During the French Revolution Isaac Le Chapelier, a lawyer, became famous. He was one of the eight men of the Constitutional Committee who was selected to draw up the new French Constitution on July 14, 1789.

The following is taken from the Huguenot Society of London. Jean A. Arnaud, son of Jean A. Arnaud, and Esther, his wife, was baptized Oct. 26, 1709; witness Margaret Arnaud.

Louis Arnaud, son of Jean A. and wife Ester, bapt. Mch. 21, 1711.

Jaque François Arnaud, son of Jean A. and wife, Ester, bapt. Oct. 1714.

Madelaine Arnaud, a witness, Jan. 25, 1719, to a baptism.

Vol. 7, b. 26. Etienne Arnaud, son of William Arnaud, and Margaret, his wife, was bapt. Sept. 1. 1715. Mr. Renauet officiating in the absence of Mr. Dee Cassé.

Francoise Arnaud m. Jean Budit Jan. 17, 1730.

Vol. 7. Suzanne Arnaud, wife of Abraham Tabois, merchant, a native of Jonzac, Xaintonge, France.

Will of Elias Arnaud.

In the name of God the Father and Holy Ghost, Amen. I Elias Arnaud knowing that nothing is more certain than death and the uncertain hour thereof, being of sound mind, memory, and understanding Do make my last will and testament in manner and form following: First, I recommend my soul to God the Father Son and Holy Ghost three persons and only one God And in regard to my temporal estate as well movables as immovables that shall be found after my death I will and intend that my wife Magdalen take possession of all immediately after my decease to enjoy and dispose of them according to her direction as she shall be advised to do all acts of justice as shall be thought proper for recovery of them and for possessing of them and also to dispose of my said goods or Estate to our children by testament or otherwise as she shall judge convenient to be received and possessed by them in such manner as she shall order. I will also that in case anyone of our heires shall controverse the Execution of this my said will he shall be excluded of any part of my said goods or Estate and shall be reduced to one shilling My wife to be sole executrix of this my last will and testament. Signed and sealed 14 Sept 1724.

Arnaud LS (sic)

Wit: Antonio Chabrol, Gabriel Doller.

Substantialiter translatum per

Robt. Bogg jun. Notary Public

Proved in P. C. C. London 4 Feb. 1725/26 by Magdalen Arnaud alias Davellaud relict, the executrix named in the will. 16 Plymouth.

The wills of the parents of Anne Arnaud the wife of Isaac Chapelier, whose will was probated in London, 1707.

Will of Madalen Arnaud.

In the name of God Amen, I, Madalen Arnaud, widow, living in Spittlefields Middlesex, very Ancient, but by God's Grace, of sound mind and memory, make my testament and disposition of my last will, in the manner following. Imprimis, I Recommend my soul to God my Creator, in the name and by the Merits of his most dear only Son, Jesus Christ, my Sole Saviour and redeemer, and as concerning my temporal goods after the discharge of my lawful debts, if there be any due and the charges of my funeral and execution of my present will, I give and bequeath to my grandson Peter Arnaud in consideration of the service which he has done me, all my Household goods, beds, cloaths and linen belonging to my house. Item, I give and bequeath to my son Elias Arnaud, at Gosport, County Southampton, one entire Third part of all the residue of goods Chattels, rights and credits and other things without exception that shall be found belonging to me at the time of my death. Item I give one third to my two granddaughters Mary Magdalen Arnaud and Susanna Arnaud, daughters of my late son John Arnaud, by equal portions between them both. Item, I give the remaining third part of my said goods and effects to my grandson Isaac Chapellier, and nominate and constitute for executor and executrix of my present testament my said son Elias Arnaud and my granddaughter Mary Magdalen Arnaud, and my will is that they do deliver and remit to the said Isaac Chapellier the third which I have heretofore bequeathed to him of my estate in manner and form following vitz; 50 lbs. Sterling within two years after my decease and the like sum of 50 lbs. Sterling two years after the said first term, if said portion can produce the said two sumes, and if it produces more than that sum, the surplus and residue of the said portion shall be paid and delivered to him one year after the said last term but my executor and executrix shall not be obliged to pay interest of the portion of the said Isaac Chapellier during the delays here laid down for the deliverance thereof and in case the said Isaac Chapellier should dye before he has received the said thirds entirely, in case he leaves any lawful children alive, what shall be left of the said third shall be delivered to them, as soon as they come of age, and in the meantime the interest that shall be produced therefrom after the expiration of the term here before set forth shall be for their use in and in case of the decease of the said Isaac Chapellier. Without lawful issue or of the decease of such issue before the age of majority, what shall remain of the said thirds shall go and belong, viz: one moity to my said son, Elias Arnaud, or to his representatives, and the moiety to the said two granddaughters, Mary Magdalen Arnaud and Susannah Arnaud, or to the representatives thereof. I made void and annull all other Testaments by me heretofore made, and do declare this to be my last will. In witness whereof I have signed and sealed my said present Testament at London this 16th day of October in the year of Grace one thousand seven hundred and thirty. Magdalen Arnaud her mark signed and sealed published and declared by the said Magdalen for to be her last will and Testament in presence of us, who have subscribed in presence of the said testatrix. Stephen Benee, Isaac Norman, Ben Bonnett.

Substanialiter Translatum est' Londini hoc vicesimo tertio.

Februarii 1730/31 per me Pet. St. Eloy N. P.

Probatum apud London 20th day of February 1730/31 juramento Mariae Magdalene Arnaud salutae unius executoris in dicto testamento nominat. Reservata potestate similem commissionem facendi Elie Arnaud alteri executori cum venerit eandem petiturus.

(P. C. C. Isman 23). (Translated from the original will which was written in French).

Issue:

1. Elias Arnaud or Arnold.
2. John Arnaud.
3. Anne Arnaud.

Fletcher

1. Joshua[1] Fletcher, b. March 20, 1750, d. April 27, 1811, in Fauquier Co., m. about 1773, Agnes Hutchins, of Maryland, d. Oct. 1821.

The first we know of him is from the Auditor's Account, 18, p. 115, in 1781, when he is paid for Revolutionary Service, a private under Captain Morehead. (Ref. Aud. Accounts, Richmond, Virginia, Archives).

In 1791 he leased land from John Carter, but it was not settled until 1794 (see the lease), 200 acres of land northwest of Goose Creek. Carter exacted that he should build a house of stone (see lease) which is still standing in good condition. The spring is up on the hill by the house, flowing so bold and freely that Joshua called the place "Fountain Hill". It is a ten-room house, the old stone "meat" house and another outhouse is still there. "Fountain Hill" farm has recently been bought by Dr.

Carey Grayson, of Washington. The farm is about a mile from Upperville.

After the death of Joshua and Agnes, their son, Joshua, and wife, Marcia Lanham, lived on this farm.

Agnes, b. 1755, the widow of Joshua, died before October 30, 1821. On that date an inventory of the estate of Joshua appears. (W. B. 8, p. 114, Fauquier Co.)

(D. B. 17, p. 792, Fauquier Co., 25 July, 1810). A receipt from Joshua Tidball and Elizabeth, his wife, of Fauquier Co., to Joshua Fletcher, of same, for $2,500.00, paid by Joshua Fletcher, land whereon the said Fletcher now lives on the waters of the Goose Creek. On a road on the north side of the said Fletchers Spring branch in George Carter's line, on the east side of a branch in Charles L. Carter's line, thence with the line of Charles Carter and Moore F. Carter, on the west side of the road in Moore F. Carter's line, 125 acres. Also one other tract, on the waters of the Goose Creek, on the west branch of Goose Creek, corner at George Carter's to a stone in Hugh Whiteford's line, to Benjamin Glascock's line, to a Spanish oak, marked "M. F. C.", containing 130 acres granted by Elizabeth Tidball, formerly Elizabeth W. Carter, in the division of the estate of the late John Carter, deceased.

1813, Agnes Fletcher, widow of Joshua, paid taxes on 225 acres of land, adjoining George Carter and Daniel Mitchell. Also 130 acres, adjoining Hugh Whiteford, on Goose Creek (Fauquier Land Tax Books).

Lease:

This indenture made this 11 day of April, 1794, between Mrs. Jane Carter, Landon Carter, Jr., of Bull Run, and Robert Carter, of the same place, for himself, and as guardian of Miss Ann Carter, Miss Jane Carter, Miss Elizabeth Carter, Miss Matilda Carter, John Carter, the son of John, George Carter, also the son of John, Fitzhugh Carter and Edward Carter, of the one part, and Joshua Fletcher, of the County of Fauquier, of the other part.

Whereas, John Carter, deceased, did, in his life time, promise and obligate himself and his heirs that he and they should give the said Fletcher a lease for his lot of land hereinafter more particularly described, for their lives, and on the terms hereinafter expressed, and whereas the said Joshua Fletcher demands a lease for the aforesaid lot of land, agreeable to the said John's promise and contract with the said Fletcher, and refuses to pay rent, unless the aforesaid lease is duly and legally executed, and whereas the said demand appears to the aforesaid Carter just and reasonable, they therefore have consented to comply with the same, and that the lease may be binding to all parties interested, the said Robert Carter consents for his aforesaid wards and hereby grants for them, by and in consequence of the authority and power vested in him as their Guardian.

Now this indenture witnesseth, that the said Mrs. Jane Carter, Landon Carter, Robert Carter, as well as for himself, as for Miss Ann Carter, Miss Jane Carter, Mrs. Elizabeth Carter, Miss Matilda Carter, John Carter, George Carter, Fitzhugh Carter, Edward Carter, for and in consideration of the rents and covenants hereinafter mentioned, on the part and behalf of the said Joshua Fletcher, hath demised, granted and to farm let, and by these presents, doth demise, grant and to farm let unto the said Joshua Fletcher a certain tract or parcel of land, whereon he now liveth, lying and being in the County of Fauquier and bounded as follows: (metes and bounds given), containing Two Hundred acres under the reservations hereinafter mentioned.

To Have and to Hold the afore mentioned lands, together with every appertenance thereunto appertaining unto the said Joshua Fletcher and his wife, Agnes, and his son, Joshua Fletcher, and the longest liver of them yearly and paying unto the said Miss Jane Carter, unto the said Robert Carter, Landon Carter, John, George, Fitzhugh, Edward, Miss Ann, Miss Jane, Miss Elizabeth, Miss Matilda and the heirs and assigns of them, two hundred acres of land, he to build a good dwelling house, 20 feet long, by 16 feet wide, of brick or stone chimney, for and during their natural lives of him the said Joshua Fletcher and his wife, Agnes, and his son, Joshua Fletcher, and the longest liver of them, and paying unto the the said parties yearly, and every year on the first day of January, during the said term, the rent of Fifteen pounds current money of Virginia, together with the land taxes.

Signed:

Janet Carter,
Robert Carter,
Landon Carter,
Joshua Fletcher.

Recorded April 28, 1794 (D, B. 11, p. 509, Fauquier Co.)

WILL AND CODICIL OF JOSHUA FLETCHER
(W. B. 5, p. 115, Fauquier Co., Va.)

In the name of God, Amen. I, Joshua Fletcher, of the County of Fauquier and Commonwealth of Virginia, knowing the uncertainty of this mortal life, and being of sound and perfect mind and memory, blessed be the name of God for the same, do make and constitute this my last will and testament in manner and form as follows, that is to say:

First. That all my just debts be paid by my executors. Next I give and bequeathe to my beloved wife, during her natural life, the tract of land whereon I now reside, containing One Hundred and twenty-five acres, be the same more or less, with appurtenances thereto, belonging, also all my horses, cows and hogs, and all my live stock of whatsoever nature with all implements of every kind which are now used for cultivating the farm. Also all of my negroes of every description, and all household furniture of every species which I am now in possession of, all and singular, which land, goods and chattels to occupy and enjoy during her natural life as above unless my said wife, Agnes Fletcher, should after my death intermarry with some other person, in which case it is my will she should deliver up to my executors all of the above property except the said land and appurtenances, which she shall or may continue on during aforesaid term or rent it out and receive the annual proceeds therefrom as she may see proper.

I also will and bequeathe to my three Grandchildren, namely, Joshua Dillon, Harriet Dillon and John Hopper, and to the children of Robert Martin and Elizabeth, his wife, namely, Agnes Martin and John Martin (My Grand children) to each the sum of Fifty pounds, Virginia currency, to be paid them by my executors, viz., to the girls as they arrive at the age of eighteen years, and to the boys as they arrive at the age of twenty-one years. I also wish the said Grandchildren raised and to have reasonable schooling at the expense of my children. I also bequeathe and devise to my five sons, namely, Robert, William, John, Joshua and Benjamin Fletcher, the remaining part of my landed property, with all appurtenances to the same, belonging at my decease and at the death of my wife all the land and movable property of whatsoever kind or nature which is hereinbefore willed and bequeathed to my said wife, Agnes Fletcher. I give in like manner to my five sons, as also all debts, dues, demands, interests, goods, chattels, commodities and heraditaments not hereinbefore bequeathed, all of which to be equally divided among my said sons, provided nevertheless my said sons shall first pay to said estate or discount such sums out of their said dividends respectively and individually as they so separately stand charged with on my books, reference being thereunto had. They paying first to Samuel Dillon and Samuel Hopper the sum of One Dollar each, and provided my wife, said Agnes Fletcher, should hereafter intermarry as before mentioned, it is my will that such property and interests thereby relinquished all claim to shall be divided in like manner among my five sons.

And lastly, I nominate, constitute and appoint my two sons, Robert and William Fletcher, my executors to this my last will and testament, hereby revoking all former wills made by me.

In witness whereof I have hereunto set my hand and affixed my seal this 25th day of March, in the year of our Lord, 1811.

Joshua Fletcher. (Seal)

Signed, sealed and acknowledged by Joshua Fletcher to be his last will and testament in the presence of John Carr, Daniel Glascock, Samuel Turner and William Penquite, William Gore.

I, Joshua Fletcher, of the County and Commonwealth aforesaid, do this 26th day of April, 1811, make and publish this codicil to my last Will and Testament in manner and form following, that is to say, I give and bequeathe to my above named five sons a certain tract of land, lying and being in the county of ———, in the Commonwealth of Kentucky, containing 2953 acres as will more fully appear by a certificate of the Register of the Virginia Land Office bearing date of the 10th day of November, 1799, reference being thereto had. And lastly, it is my desire that this my present codicil be annexed to this my last Will and Testament as a part thereof to all intents and purposes.

IN WITNESS whereof, I have set my hand and affixed my seal.

Joshua Fletcher. (Seal)

Signed, sealed and acknowledged by Joshua Fletcher in the presence of William Penquite, Daniel Glascock, William Gore. Probated in Fauquier County Court, July 22nd, 1811.

Inventory of the estate of Joshua Fletcher (W. B. 5, p. 244), appraisers: Messrs. John B. Armistead, Glascock and Charles Adams (Sept. 7th, 1811).

A few of the articles included, valued at $10,712.

1 Walnut leaf table (the writer owns)
1 Square walnut leaf table
18 Pewter plates
5 quart pewter basin
5 large pewter dishes
1 pewter tea pot
1 candle stand (the writer owns)
6 Windsor chairs
6 Arm chairs
1 Tea tray, etc.
1 Walnut chest.

Issue:

1. Robert[2] Fletcher.
2. Ann[2] Fletcher (Nancy).
3. Agnes[2] Fletcher.
4. Elizabeth[2] Fletcher.
5. William[2] Fletcher.
6. John[2] Fletcher.
7. Joshua[2] Fletcher.
8. Benjamin[2] Fletcher.

Joshua may have come to Va. from Pennsylvania.

The Goose Creek Baptist Church was formed from the church in Philadelphia in 1775 (from the records of this church). The name of Joshua Fletcher appears on the records as a representative of Goose Creek Church to the yearly convention in 1792. Joshua may have been a member of this church before he left Philadelphia, the name of his wife Agnes and son John also appear, later in the records. In April of 1805 the members subscribe $792, to build a new church, to be of stone or brick to be 44 by 43 feet in dimension "for the Baptist Society of Goose Creek", of this sum Joshua Fletcher gave $50 (church records). William Martin, Walter Lanham and Jonathan Gibson also contributed.

In Aug. of 1825 the name was changed from Goose Creek Baptist Church to Upperville Baptist Church, the new church having been built in the village.

1. Robert[2] Fletcher (Joshua[1]), b. Oct. 16, 1777, in Fauquier County, d. 18 Aug. 1845, married Elizabeth Whiteford about 1803 from near Baltimore, b. Dec. 1784, d. April 27, 1841, daughter of David Whiteford and wife, Miss Cummings.

They lived at Oak Spring farm, only a few miles east of Fountain Hill, which house is still standing, but was not built by Robert F. In the yard is a wonderful stone spring house used by the Fletchers, with a very bold spring, running through the yard. On the hill near the house is the Fletcher burying ground, within the walls of which were once buried Robert, his wife, Elizabeth, and all of his children and grandchildren. But about 25 years ago, the descendants of his son, Joshua, moved the remains of their family to a new burying ground in Upperville, leaving Agnes Robinson, Matilda Chappelear, Anne Lake, Elias Fletcher, Benjamin and William Fletcher's families buried there.

Agnes Robinson left a notebook to her daughter, Betty, in which book Agnes had written the names of her mother and her six aunts, and five uncles. It states that Elizabeth Whiteford's mother was from Baltimore (near), and her name was Miss Cummings. The following is also from the same note-book: Children of the Whiteford and Cummings marriage. (Book in the possession of Mrs. Mary Bucknor of Winchester, a great granddaughter of Robert F.).

Nancy Whiteford, m. ——— Stephens, of Monongaha, West Virginia.

Ann Whiteford, m. ——— Isgrig, of Baltimore.

Pegg Whiteford, m. Johnston.

Polly Whiteford, m.

Grace Whiteford, m. ——— Michael.

David Whiteford, m. Margaret Marshal of Bucks County, Penn.

Samuel Whiteford.

James Whiteford, m. Tipton of Maryland.

John Whiteford.

Hugh Whiteford (leased land 1791 from John Carter, adjoining Joshua Fletcher).

Daniel Michael, Joseph Johnson, and Joshua Fletcher leased adjoining tracts of land in Fauquier County, North of Goose Creek in 1794. Hugh Whiteford leases a tract also from the heirs of John Carter in the same part of the county (Fauquier Co. Records).

Robert Fletcher built a barn in 1833, the corner stone was cut with that date. About 1915 the barn being in bad condition. George Slater, the owner, built another, using this old marked stone in its construction.

George Stater married Tacie Fletcher, a great grand daughter of Robert and Elizabeth Fletcher.

Robert[2] was a cripple, and not being able to enlist in the war of 1812 sent a substitute. He was very fastidious in his personal appearance, being always so well dressed that he was called "Broadcloth Fletcher", so his grand daughter, Annie Chappelear Rucker, states.

21st July, 1809. John Wren of Fauquier County, sold land to Robert Fletcher of same (D. B. 17, p. 507, Fauquier Co.).

Where as John Carter, deceased, of Loudon County, of Sudley Farm did in his life time promise to give a lease to said Wren of a tract of land. Landon and Robert Carter being sons of said John Carter, deceased, grant the lease according to the contract, for $250.00. They assign the land to Robert Fletcher, that tract of land with all houses, buildings, 126 acres of land adjoining Thomas Urton's on the banks of Plum Run, during the natural lives of said John Wren and Hannah, his wife, and James Wren, their son.

Signed, John Wren.

John B. Armistead and Ann, his wife, sold to Robert Fletcher, for $306.25 land adjoining John Carter's line, and Dennis's, on South side of Plum Run, adjoining Wren's Road, on to John Carter's. 30 June 1809 (D. B. 17, p. 508, Fauquier Co.).

Moore F. Carter and Judith, his wife, leased to William and Robert Fletcher executors of Joshua Fletcher deceased, all of that tract of land now in the possession of William and Robert Fletcher bounded as following: To Daniel Michaels, Benjamin Glascock, to Charles Kempers, 30 acres, lying between Charles and Moore Carter, and John Carter's heirs. 27 Aug. 1811 (D. B. 18, p. 339, Fauquier Co.).

John H. W. Smith and Maria Love, his wife, sold to Robert Fletcher for $737.50 land on Goose Creek, being the remainder of a tract purchased by said Smith of John Wren, surveyed by Aquilla Glascock, 29½ acres, adjoining Edmund Carter, John B. Armistead, near Henderson's spring. 23 May 1820 (D. B. 24, p. 175, Fauquier Co.).

Edward Carter and Fannie, his wife, sold to Robert Fletcher for $405. land Fletcher had leased from Edward Carter, as one of the distributors of the late John Carter of Sudley. 24 Feb. 1821 (D. B. 25, p. 80, Fauquier Co.).

1821 Aquila Glascock leased for ten years to Robert Fletcher land Fletcher had leased from Glascock, lately purchased by Glascock from Edward Carter and John Wren.

Later Acquila Glascock and wife Susanna sold the above land to Robert Fletcher, the two tracts conveyed in 1810 by Edward Carter to John Wren, and by Wren and wife, to Acquila Glascock by deed, 33¾ and 91 acres. 25 Nov. 1820.

1821 John Wren and wife Hannah leased to Robert Fletcher land formerly in the possession of John B. Armistead, now owned by John H. Smith, about 50 or 60 acres.

Robert Fletcher and Elizabeth, his wife, sold to William Fletcher of same, both sons of Joshua Fletcher, in whose will he devised "to my five sons, but now (son) Benjamin, being deceased, unmarried, and Agnes being also deceased. 23 Mch. 1822 (D. B. 26, p. 175). This land Robert and wife, Elizabeth, sold to William Fletcher for $3752.00 all of the interest they (Robert and Elizabeth) have in the estate of Joshua Fletcher, deceased, all of the rights they have in the estate of Benjamin (brother) and in the estate of Agnes Fletcher, deceased.

(Signed) Robert Fletcher,
Elizabeth Fletcher.

In 1837 Nathan Loughborough of District of Columbia sold 1½ acres of land in Fauquier County to straighten out a dividing line to Robert Fletcher.

Surveyed June 8, 1841 for Mr. Robert Fletcher of Fauquier County, three adjoining tracts, one on North side of Goose Creek, the upper or home tract, the middle being the Wren tract, the lower being the Henderson tract.

The upper began at a planted stone in the road from Rectortown to Upperville, corner at Joshua Fletcher, sen, and to Penquite's corner and two tracts to Loughborough's field.

In 1793 Robert's personal tax was paid by his father Joshua

(W. B. 19, p. 298, Fauquier County), date, June 8, 1841, probated 1845, July 4th. Will of Robert Fletcher.

"All of my land on the North-west side of Goose Creek, surveyed by George Love, to be divided:

1st: the manor farm, containing 270 acres,

2nd: the middle tract, containing 158½ acres,

3rd: the Henderson farm, being the lower tract, containing 160 acres.

It is my desire that my son, William Jr., be the purchaser of tract No. 1, the manor or upper farm.

That my son, Joshua Jr., may purchase the 2nd, the Wren or Middle Tract, and also Lot No. 3, the Henderson or Lower Farm.

The valuation being fixed by George Love, Cuthbert Powell, Senior, Joshua Tidball, John H. Carter, William Fletcher, Sen., and Joshua Fletcher, Sen.

Having made an advancement to my following children, viz; William F. Jr., Joshua F. Jr., Elias W., my son-in-law Benjamin Chappalier and my daughter, Matilda, his wife; my son-in-law John G. Robinson and my daughter, Agnes, his wife; which is equal to $2500.00 to each of them.

I give to my Brother, William Fletcher, to my son, Joshua Fletcher, to son William Fletcher or the survivors, the following property in trust, for the benefit of my daughter, Ann Lake, the wife of Richard, which is to be over and above an equal part of the residue of my estate, namely one negro girl, named Caroline, and at my death a boy named George, one wagon team, stock and farm tools, household furniture — — — to equal $1500.00 more, making all advancement to the sum of $2500.00 for the benefit of my daughter Ann Lake.

I give to my daughter, Alcie Fletcher, 1 negro girl, named Catherine, and her daughter, Ellen, a negro boy, James, also a riding Creature, a bay mare, and three young horses, 100 barrels of corn, 1000 lbs. of pork, $60.00 worth of cattle, $65.00 worth of live hogs, and sheep, my sideboard, two tables, two good beds, 1 dozen chairs, and all of my kitchen furniture, and $900.00 in cash, to my daughter, Alcie. To my son, Elias Fletcher, an equal payment. A negro woman, named Charlotte to my daughter, Agnes Robinson, over and above her equal share.

After my death, my estate to be divided into seven equal parts:

1/7 to son William, 1/7 to son Joshua, 1/7 to son Elias, 1/7 to Benjamin Chappelier, 1/7 to daughter Agnes, (in trust) wife of John G. Robinson, 1/7 to daughter, Ann Lake, (in trust) wife of Richard Lake, 1/7 to Alcie Fletcher.

Reserve ½ an acre of land for a burying ground including the present graves.

Executors: Brother, William Fletcher. Sons, William and Joshua. (Signed) Robert Fletcher.

Witness: W. Lufborough, Jun., William Wilkinson, George Ayre, George Love.

A few things in the inventory of the estate, August 25th, 1845 (W. B. 20, p. 136), Fauquier.

1 Carpet, 25 yards,
½ doz. Windsor Chairs, 7 blue Windsor chairs,
1 Small table,
1 Folding leaf table,
1 Large folding leaf table,
1 old chest.

Issue of Robert[2] and Elizabeth:

1. William[3] Fletcher.
2. Matilda[3].
3. Agnes[3].
4. Joshua[3].
5. Elias[3].
6. Alcie[3].
7. Ann[3].

1. William[3] Fletcher (Robert[2], Joshua[1]), b. Jan. 1, 1804, d. Sept. 21, 1886, m. Harriet Lake (daughter of Isaac and Sally Lake, Jan. 3, 1826, b. Oct. 16, 1808, d. July 30, 1857).

Issue:

1. Alphons[4] Fletcher.
2. Eliza[4] V. Fletcher.
3. William[4] H. Fletcher.
4. Sarah[4] Fletcher.
5. Robert[4] Fletcher.
6. Isaac[4] Fletcher.
7. John[4] E. Fletcher.
8. Harriett[4] A. Fletcher.
9. Marion[4] Fletcher.
10. Benjamin[4] Franklin Fletcher.
11. Mary[4] Fletcher.
12. Kate[4] Fletcher.
13. Albert[4] Fletcher.

1. Alphons[4] Fletcher (William[3]), b. 7 Jan. 1827, d. Sept. 10, 1908, m. Dec. 11, 1861, Mrs. Wheatley, of Fauquier, b. 18 Sept. 1830, d. Nov. 15, 1892.

2. Eliza V. Fletcher, b. Oct. 26, 1828, d. Dec. 8, 1887.

3. William[4] Fletcher (William[3]), b. 18 Sept. 1830, d. Nov. 14, 1892, m. Mollie Skinner, Dec. 6, 1865.

4. Sarah[4] Fletcher (William[3]), b. 23 March, 1832, d. 15 Apr. 1917.

5. Robert[4] Fletcher (William[3]), b. May 27, 1833, d. 8 Feb. 1890.

6. Isaac[4] Fletcher, b. 1835, d. Mch. 12, 1906, m. Mollie Castleman, Nov. 7, 1860.

7. John[4] E. Fletcher, b. 9 Apr. 1837, d. 12 Mch. 1906, m. Lou W. Taylor, Jan. 21, 1880.

8. Harriet[4] A. Fletcher, b. Aug. 27, 1839, d. 8 Aug. 1842.

9. Marion[4] Fletcher, b. 20 July 1841, d. 1 July 1881, m. Dec. 4, 1879, M. C. W. Woolf.

10. Benjamin[4] Franklin Fletcher (William[3]), b. Oct. 16, 1843, d. Feb. 11, 1913, unmarried.

11. Mollie[4] Fletcher (William[3]), b. 28 Nov. 1845, d. Dec. 11, 1920, unmarried.

12. Kate[4] Fletcher (William[3]), b. 21 April, 1847, d. 12 Aug. 1922.

13. Albert[4] Fletcher (William[3]), b. Sept. 20, 1850, m. Hannah Brown; m. 1885, no heirs.

2. Matilda[3] Fletcher (Robert[2], Joshua[1]), b. Aug. 28, 1806, d. 1872, m. Benjamin Garner Chappelear (son of William Chappelear and wife, Ann Garner), b. March 3, 1803, d. 1896, buried at the Fletcher burying ground. See Benjamin Chappelear line, page 356.

3. Agnes[3] (Robert[2], Joshua[1]) Fletcher, b. 7 Dec. 1808, d. May 29, 1895, m. John Garner Robinson of Rappahannock County, b. March 24, 1806, d. Aug. 9, 1857 (son of William Robinson and wife. Nancy Garner).

Issue:

1. Robert[4] Robinson.
2. William[4] Robinson.
3. Bettie[4] Robinson, unmarried.
4. Jack[4] Robinson.
5. Milton[4] Robinson.
6. Monroe[4] Robinson.
7. Alice[4] Robinson, d. March, 1907, unmarried.
8. Ida[4] Robinson.

1. Robert[4] E. Robinson (Agnes[3], Robert[2] Fletcher), m. Mattie Davis, Pendleton County, West Virginia.

2. William[4] Robinson (Agnes[3], Robert[2] Fletcher), m. Bettie O'Rear of Clarke County, Virginia. Issue: Milton[5], William[5] and Mary[5], m. Charles Buckner and had one daughter, Marie[6], the wife of Joseph Gibson of Upperville, Virginia.

4. Jack[4] Robinson (Agnes[3], Robert[2], ——— Fletcher), m. Fannie Skinner.

5. Milton[4] was killed in Civil War.

6. Monroe[4] Robinson (Agnes[3], Robert[2], ——— Fletcher), m. Mattie Lockert of Norfolk, Virginia, daughter, Margaret[5] Robinson.

8. Ida[4] Robinson (Agnes[3], Robert[2], ——— Fletcher), b. Aug. 4, 1857, d. 1929, Nov. 12, buried at Upperville, Virginia, m. Robert McCarty, a descendant of Dennis McCarty of Westmoreland County.

Issue:

5 sons[5].

1 daughter[5].

William Robinson (father of John Garner Robinson) of Culpeper, m. Nancy Garner March 28th, 1796, Fauquier County, marriage bonds.

Issue:

1. William Fletcher Robinson, b. Jan. 5, 1804, d. Aug. 18, 1848.
2. Matilda Robinson, b. June 13, 1805.
3. John Garner Robinson, b. March 24, 1806.
4. Agnes Robinson, b. Dec. 7, 1808.
5. Joshua Robinson, b. May 21, 1810.
6. Elias Robinson, b. July 17, 1813.
7. Eliza Robinson, b. March 25, 1819.
8. Alice Jane Robinson, b. Dec. 28, 1820.
9. Ann W. Robinson, b. June 29, 1825.

4. Joshua[3] Fletcher (Robert[2], Joshua[1]), Jr., b. May 21, 1810, d. Mch. 21, 1862, m. Sept. 18, 1834, Eliza A. Fletcher, age 15, daughter of Dr. John and Tacy (Gibson) Fletcher of Culpeper, 1st cousin. They lived at the Maples near Upperville. Born 2 March, 1819, d. June 24, 1893.

1. John[4] Fletcher.
2. Tacy[4].
3. Robert[4].
4. Sarah[4].
5. Mary E.[4]
6. Clinton[4].
7. William[4].
8. Emily[4].
9. Virginia[4]. } twins, b. Sept. 18, 1847, d. unm.
10. Julia[4]. }
11. Joshua[4].
12. Ella[4].
13. Ida[4].
14. Gibson[4].

1. John[4] Fletcher (Joshua[3], Robert[2], Joshua[1]), b. Sept. 25, 1835, graduated from Virginia Military Institute before the Civil War, and at the beginning of the war, was commissioned lieutenant under Capt. Turner Ashby, later became captain. He was

killed leading a cavalry charge at Bucktown Station on May 23, 1862, advancing into the enemy's lines. He died at the age of twenty-seven, unmarried.

2. Tacy^{4} Ann Fletcher (Joshua^{3}, Robert^{2}, Joshua^{1}), b. June 15, 1837, d. Oct. 8, 1907, m. Oct. 11, 1865, W. Seldon Peach, d. June 4, 1890.

    1. Clinton^{5} Miller Peach, b. Aug. 18, 1866, d. Sept. 10, 1926, m. Daisy Richards, Nov. 1, 1893, b. June 29, 1866.
        1. Richard^{6} Seldon Peach, b. June 2, 1897, m. 28 Aug. 1928, Irene Johnston.
        2. William^{6} Fletcher Peach, b. Aug. 29, 1901.
        3. Seldon^{6} Peach, b. 14 Oct. 1904.
    2. Robert^{5} Murphy Peach, b. 19 May 1868, d. March 24, m. 5 July 1891, Zella Dice.
        1. Ann^{6} Eliza, b. 15 Feb. 1892.
        2. Virginia^{6} Calvert, b. 27 Oct. 1896.
        3. Robert^{6} Murphey Peach, b. 6 Dec. 1904.

3. Robert^{4} Fletcher (Joshua^{3}, Robert^{2}, Joshua^{1}), b. Jan. 1, 1839, d. Apr. 20, 1911, age 72, m. June 1877, Tacie Glascock, first cousins, b. 10 Nov. 1844, d. 23 July, 1878, they lived at West View, Fauquier Co. During the Civil War he served in the Cavalry under Captain Welby Carter, at the First Battle of Manassas he was desperately wounded in his right arm, which he would have lost except for the skill of Dr. Thomas Settle of Paris, Va. After recovering and returning to his company he was captured, and spent six months in the Federal prison in Washington, then he was sent to Point Lookout for twelve months, and later exchanged before the end of the war.

    1. Tacie^{5} Glascock Fletcher, b. 15 July 1878, m. 28 June 1905, George Hoffman Slater, of Paris, Va.
        1. George^{6} Robert Slater, b. Dec. 27, 1906.
        2. Thomas^{6} Glascock Slater, b. 14 Aug. 1908.
        3. Bedford^{6} Fletcher Slater, b. Dec. 31, 1911, killed in an auto accident Nov. 27, 1930, driving to Charlottesville to attend a football game. He was attending school at St. Christophers, Richmond, Va.

4. Sarah^{4} Elizabeth Fletcher (Joshua^{3}, Robert^{2}), b. Oct. 11, 1840, d. 1847.

5. Mary^{4} Eliza Fletcher (Joshua^{3}, Robert^{2}), b. June 24, 1842, d. Aug. 1861.

6. Clinton^4 Fletcher (Joshua^3, Robert^2), b. Feb. 12, 1844, d. 1863. He served in the Confederate Army under Col. Richard Dulaney, was killed at Green Gap near Mooresfield, April 25, 1863, age 18. He was studying for the ministry.

7. William^4 Fletcher (Joshua^3, Robert^2), b. 24 Aug. 1845, d. 19 Mch. 1915, m. Annie Glascock, 8 Oct. 1872 of Spring Hill, Rectortown, Va.

1. William^5 Glascock Fletcher, b. 25 May 1877, m. Louise Griffith Mobley May 25, 1929, of Rockville, Maryland, dau. of Walter W. Mobley of Ashley Farm near Derwood.
2. Bedford^5 Fletcher, b. 17 May 1884.

8. Emily^4 Fletcher (Joshua^3, Robert^2, Joshua^1), b. 13 Feb. 1847, d. 1 Nov. 1908, m. George Frazier 28 Oct. 1872, b. Sept. 1844, d. 20 May 1922.

1. Gibson^5 Fletcher Frazier, b. 20 July 1875, m. Margaretta Baggott Gulick 3 Nov. 1904.
    1. Eliza^6 Fletcher Frazier, b. 14 Sept. 1905.
    2. John^6 Withers Frazier, b. 9 Aug. 1909.
    3. Margaretta^6, b. Sept. 1911.
    4. Emily^6 Frazier, b. 2 Dec. 1915.

11. Joshua^4 (Joshua^3, Robert^2, Joshua^1) Fletcher, b. Sept. 5, 1850, d. April 8, 1913, m. 1st Lula Foster, 24 Feb. 1886, d. July 22, 1892; m. 2nd Marian P. Carter, 16 Nov. 1898. Lived at the Maples.
Issue, by 1st m.:

1. Mary^5 Eliza Fletcher, b. Oct. 1888, m. Waugh Glascock, Oct. 1918.
2. Lulie^5 Foster Fletcher, b. 20 July 1891, d. 24 Sept. 1907.

Issue, by 2nd m.:

3. Joshua^5 Fletcher, b. 29, Dec. 1900.
4. Robert^5 Clinton Fletcher, b. 14, July 1902.

12. Ella^4 Fletcher (Joshua^3, Robert^2, Joshua^1), b. Jan. 21, 1852, d. Jan. 1, 1878.

13. Ida^4 Fletcher (Joshua^3, Robert^2), b. 30 Dec. 1853, d. June 23, 1878, m. Bedford^4 Glascock (1st cousin) Feb. 13, 1877, b. Dec. 31, 1849, d. 1929, at his home Bolling Brooke near Upperville. After Ida's death Bedford m. 2nd Lula Richards of Bal-

timore. Bedford[4] was son of Thomas Glascock and wife Emily[3] A. Fletcher (John[2], Joshua[1]).

14. Gibson[4] Fletcher (Joshua[3], Robert[2]), b. 20 May, 1859, d. 1866 Aug. 15.

5. Elias[3] Fletcher (Robert[2], Joshua[1]), b. July 7, 1813, d. Mch. 12, 1854, m. Catherine Foley (Jan. 18, 1821-Sept. 4, 1862).

1. Benton[4] Fletcher, m. Mary Nelson.
2. Lavinia[4] Fletcher, m. Perry Johnson.
3. Maria[4] Fletcher, m. Henry Browning.
4. Lou[4] Fletcher, m. John Thomas.

   1. May[5] Thomas.
   2. Elton[5] Thomas.
   3. Edgar[5] Thomas.
   4. Owen[5] Thomas.
   5. John[5] Thomas.
   6. Vernon[5] Thomas.
   7. Annie[5] Thomas.
   8. Sherman[5] Thomas.
   9. Thomas[5] Thomas.
   10. Katie[5] Thomas.
   11. Lizzie[5] Thomas.
   12. William[5] Thomas.
   13. Washington[5] Thomas.
5. William[4] Fletcher, died unmarried.
6. James[4] Fletcher.
7. Benjamin[4] Fletcher, m. Nannie Smith of Upperville.

6. Alcie[3] Fletcher (Robert[2], Joshua[1]), m. John[3] Gibson Fletcher (John[2], Joshua[1]), first cousin.

7. Anne[3] Fletcher (Robert[2], Joshua[1]), b. June 29, 1825, d. July 11, 1863, m. Richard Lake.

The first four children are buried at the old Fletcher graveyard.

1. Ella[4] B. Lake (b. Nov. 29, 1852, d. Nov. 14, 1856), tombstone).
2. Alice[4] Maude Lake, b. Mch. 19, 1857, d. July 17, ——, m. Neville Bashan.
3. James[4] Robert Lake, b. Dec. 14, 1845, d. Nov. 3, 1869.
4. Maria[4] Theresa Lake, b. Sept. 9, 1849, d. Feb. 1, 1872.

5. Henry[4] Lake, m. Laura Davis.
6. Marion[4] Lake, m. Lizzie Hatcher.
7. Elizabeth[4] Lake, m. Thomas Woolf.
8. Rinaldo[4] Lake, m. Kate Lake.

2. Nancy[2] Fletcher (Joshua[1]), b. Dec. 8, 1779, m. Samuel Dillon, 1805.

1. Joshua[3] Dillon.
2. Harriett[3] Dillon, b. Nov. 27, 1808, m. Wm. Lake, moved to Ill.

They were raised by their uncle, William Fletcher, and called him "Uncle Big Billy."

1. Joshua[3] Dillon (Nancy[2], Joshua[1] Fletcher), b. Oct. 4, 1806, in Fauquier County, managed the estate of his Uncle Dr. John Fletcher, near Flint Hill, d. March 1, 1891, Vesta, Nebraska, m. Elizabeth Samuels Jeffries, Culpeper, March 29, 1829, born Aug. 10, 1808, daughter of Joseph Jeffries and wife, Samuels.

1. William[4] Dillon.
2. Anne[4] Dillon.
3. Sarah[4] Dillon.
4. Joseph[4] Jeffries Dillon.
5. Robert[4] Dillon.
6. Thomas[4] Dillon.
7. Parthenia[4] Dillon.
8. Amanda[4] Dillon.
9. Job[4] Dillon.
10. Harriet[4] Dillon.
11. Mary[4] E. Dillon.

1. William[4] Dillon (Joshua[3], Nancy[2], ——— Fletcher), b. Jan. 31, 1830, in Fauquier Co., Va., m. Apr. 14, 1853, Mary E. Cantrell, of Decatur, Illinois, d. June 1883. (Wm. d. June 9, 1889, at Quincy, Ill.)
Issue:

1. William[5] T. Dillon.
2. Louis[5] E. Dillon.
3. Fannie[5] Dillon.
4. Frank[5] Dillon.
5. Mary[5] Dillon.
6. George[5] J. Dillon.
7. Mary[5] E. Dillon.
8. Robert[5] L. Dillon.

9. Annie^{5} S. Dillon.
10. Parthenia^{5} J. Dillon.
11. Grace^{5} C. Dillon.

7. Mary^{5} Elizabeth Dillon (William^{4}, Joshua^{3}, Nancy^{2}, ——— Fletcher), b. Nov. 30, 1867, m. Geo. M. Reed, Apr. 14, 1887, at Decatur, Illinois.

1. Kenneth^{6} Samuel Reed, b. Feb. 1, 1893.
2. Miriam^{6} Reed, b. Nov. 2, 1898.

3. Agnes^{2} (Joshua^{1}) Fletcher, m. Samuel Hopper.

1. John^{3} Hopper.
2. Benjamin^{3} Hopper.

4. Elizabeth^{2} Fletcher (Joshua^{1}), b. March 30, 1782, m. Robert Martin.

1. Agnes^{3} Martin.
2. Margaret^{3} Martin.
3. John^{3} Martin.

Elizabeth and Robert moved to Missouri, where they died, the children were brought back to Virginia to be reared.

5. William^{2} Fletcher (Joshua^{1}), b. July 13, 1784, d. 1856 in Fauquier County. Never married.

He lived near his brother, Robert Fletcher. Left his land to his slaves, who sold out and moved to Iowa and Ohio.

27 Oct. 1811. Moore F. Carter and wife, Judith sold to William Fletcher land on Goose Creek and Gap Run. Land now in the tenue of Lina Boyal and all of that land situated on Goose Creek now in the occupation of Thomas Urton, for ten years. Reserving for himself (Moore F. Carter) the right to build a mill on the premises, on the waters of Goose Creek or Gap Run, reserving a wagon road to the mill for the public use, from Rectortown to Ashby's Gap. It was also agreed that in case Moore F. Carter should take possession of five acres of land adjoining the mineral spring, there would be a proper abatement of rent (D. B. 18, p. 229, Fauquier Co.).

(M. F. Carter built the mill at the junction of the two creeks. The mill is still in use, 1930.—S. R. W.)

In 1818 William Fletcher bought his brother, Joshua's interest in their father's estate, also interest in their brother, Benjamin's estate, who had lately died unmarried.

In 1820 William bought out the interest his brother, John Fletcher had in the estate of their father, Joshua, also John's interest in the estate of Benjamin, deceased, their brother.

6. Dr. John[2] Fletcher (Joshua[1]), b. 13 Sept. 1786, in Fauquier Co., d. in 1827 in Culpeper Co., m. 1st Tacy Prior Gibson, 2nd Maotilda Baker. Tacy was born at Green Garden near Upperville, Fauquier Co., 1 Mch. 1795, she was of Quaker descent, her grandmother with her seven sons came from Philadelphia. They were very devout, each year the seven sons would ride horseback to Philadelphia to attend a Quaker Meeting. There is a tradition that they would use Aspen branches to urge their horses to better speed, and upon returning home stuck the switches in the ground; they grew, which accounts for the growth of aspens at Green Garden.

Tacy at an early age made a sampler, a map, about two feet square which now is in the possession of her great granddaughter Tacie Fletcher Slater of Rose Hill.

John married second Matilda Baker of Winchester; after John's death in 1827 she married Philip Slaughter of Culpeper Co. (Minute B. 17, p. 92), Aug. 19, 1828, is recorded the settlement of John's estate by his brother Robert, in which it is stated that Matilda had married Philip Slaughter and one third of the property was allowed to her. Robert was appointed guardian to the three children.

John lived near Flint Hill on a farm called Green Garden, Culpeper (now Rappahannock County). Near him also lived his sister, Nancy Dillon, the wife of Samuel.

John Fletcher graduated at a medical college in Philadelphia, and practiced medicine in and around Flint Hill.

He sold his interest in his father's and brother's estate in Fauquier County, in 1820, April 1 (D. B. 24, p. 162, Fauquier Co.).

John Fletcher and Tacy P., his wife of Culpeper County sold to William Fletcher of Fauquier County all their rights in the estate of Joshua Fletcher, deceased, their father. Situated in the neighborhood of Grigsby's and Bogges's Mill, Fauquier County, being subject to the widow of Joshua Fletcher, deceased, and at present in the occupancy of the widow of said Joshua Fletcher, deceased.

(Signed) John Fletcher

Tacy P. Fletcher.

Issue, by 1st m.:

1. John[3] Gibson Fletcher.
2. Eliza[3] Agnes Fletcher.
3. Emily[3] Ann Fletcher.

Issue, by 2nd m.:

4. Mary[3] Fletcher, m. Dr. Garnett of Culpeper.

1. John[3] Gibson Fletcher (John[2], Joshua[1]), b. March, 1818, in Culpeper, d. 16 Feb. 1856, m. April 30th, 1846, his first cousin Alcie[3] Fletcher (Robert[2], Joshua[1]) of Fauquier, b. Dec. 28, 1820. They lived near Flint Hill, at which place they lost one of their children, which is buried in the garden. The tombstone is still standing.

Later Gibson Fletcher sold this farm and bought in Fauquier, near Delaplane, on Crooked Run.

His first cousin, Matilda Fletcher and her husband, Benjamin Chappelear, bought Gibson's farm near Flint Hill, and later Pendleton Chappelear was living there when he volunteered to join the Confederate Army.

1. John[4] Gibson Fletcher (b. Feb. 11, 1847, d. Jan. 1853).
2. Cornelia[4], b. 30 Jan. 1848.
3. Ann[4] Elizabeth, b. 20 Nov. 1849.
4. Tacie[4], b. July 3, 1851.
5. Robert[4] L. Fletcher, b. March 10, 1853, m. Mary Kincheloe.
6. Mark[4] R. Fletcher, b. Dec. 3, 1854, m. Willie Snead of Lynchburg.
7. Alice[4] Gibson Fletcher, b. May 31, 1856.

2. Eliza[3] Agnes Fletcher (John[2], Joshua[1]), m. Joshua[3] (Robert[2], Joshua[1]). See Joshua.

3. Emily[3] Ann Fletcher (May 30, 1821-Jan. 11, 1897), m. Thomas Glascock, b. Apr. 21, 1814, d. July 23, 1895. They lived at Rose Hill.

1. Bedford[4] Glascock, m. 1st his cousin Ida[4] Fletcher (Joshua[3], Robert[2], Joshua[1]), m. 2nd Lula Richards of Baltimore.
    1. Thomas[5] Bedford Glascock.
    2. Burr[5] Richards Glascock.
    3. Emily[5] Glascock, m. John Ramy.
    4. Josephine[5] Glascock.
    5. Eleanor[5] Glascock.

Issue:

1. Thomas⁵ Bedford Glascock m. Mary Moore Howe of East Radford, Va.

1. Mary⁶ Howe Glascock.
2. Lula⁶ Richards Glascock.

2. Burr⁵ Richards Glascock m. 1st Sue Wood Harmon of Charlottesville; m. 2nd Ann Turner of Warrenton, Va.

Issue, by 1st m.:

1. Susan⁶ Harmon Glascock.

Issue, by 2nd m.:

2. Burr⁶ Richard Glascock.
3. Anne⁶ Turner Glascock.

3. Emily⁵ Glascock m. John Thomas Ramey of Marshall, Va.

4. Josephine⁵ Glascock m. Richardson Armstrong Libby of New York.

5. Eleanor⁵ Elizabeth Glascock m. George Richard Thompson III, of Fauquier, Va.

1. George⁶ Richard Thompson IV.

7. Joshua² Fletcher (Joshua¹), b. Oct. 17, 1788, d. Oct. 30, 1862, called "Uncle Big Josh", m. Sept. 24, 1824, Marcia Lanham, Loudoun County, Record Book 1, page 69. She died Aug. 1861.

They lived at the home of their parents, at Fountain Hill, near Upperville, and are buried on the farm in sight of the house.

Dr. Carey Grayson the present owner has built a stone wall around the graves of Joshua and Marcia Fletcher.

Marcia's sisters had a small boarding school for girls in the town of Upperville. Several of the Chappelear sisters (my mother's sisters, Adeline and Elizabeth) boarded there.

Joshua Fletcher of Maples died suddenly Oct. 30, 1862. The following facts are given here as told by Old Uncle George Brewer about the Union soldiers and the death of "Marse Josh":

Uncle George was a young slave who served in the capacity of assistant butler. When the Yankees were stationed near Upperville, three Officers came to Maples, the handsome home of a wealthy land owner, Mr. Joshua Fletcher, to commandeer a good dinner. Mr. Fletcher served mint juleps very freely as was the custom of every Southern gentleman before dinner; after a few rounds of the delicious cooling drink, the officers and their host became four convivial gentlemen. Mr. Fletcher having the constant dread of his property being destroyed by the invading army, began to tell things he would not have otherwise told. He emphatically said where he wanted the "Damned Yankees" to go, and drank a toast to the success of the Confederacy.

When the officers grasped the meaning of the words of their host, they called him a traitor, and left saying they would return to "get him". Later Mr. Fletcher realized what he had said, and their return meant imprisonment for himself, confiscation of his property, and poverty for his wife and children. It so overwhelmed him that his weak heart could not stand the strain, and the following morning he died suddenly of apoplexy.

At noon the officers returned to take Joshua prisoner, the colored boy told them at the door that his master was dead, they of course did not believe him, and demanded to be taken to see his master, which George did. The officers were so much affected by the tragedy that they left the house and gave no further trouble to the family or to the property.

Issue:

1. Prof. Joshua[3] Fletcher of Berryville.
2. Benjamin[3]. Fletcher.
3. Helen[3], m. Marsh Lake.
4. Lemuel[3], b. May 17, 1829, d. 1896, m. 11 Nov. 1857, Lou Ellen Smith.
5. Eliza[3], m. James E. Towson.
6. Carrie[3], m. 1st William Smith (brother to Lou Ellen), three children; married second Charles Buck of Front Royal.

Joshua Fletcher of Fauquier sold to William Fletcher of same.

Whereas Joshua Fletcher, deceased, father of the said Joshua and William devised in his will, to my five sons, Whereas Benjamin is deceased, unmarried and intestate, William bought from his brother, Joshua all of the latter's rights in the estate of their father, Joshua, deceased. 24 April 1818. (Signed) Joshua Fletcher (D. B. 22, p. 308).

James Turner of Fauquier rented to Joshua Fletcher of same, land adjoining the land he now lives on, 100 acres, adjoining Hugh Whiteford, for $60.00 a year. 21 Jan. 1828.

Witness: Joshua Fletcher, William Fletcher, Robert Fletcher (D. B. 30, p. 154).

John Glascock and wife, Agnes, of Fauquier County, in consideration of natural live and affection they have for their connection, Ann Simpson, the wife of John, and her children and also in consideration of one dollar paid to him by Joshua Fletcher, Sr. do confirm unto the said Joshua Fletcher the following real and personal estate one lot of two acres of land, adjoining Alfred Rector and John Glascock, furniture and farm implements. Jan. 11, 1841 (D. B. 40, p. 259).

Skinker

Thomas[1] Skinker, b. in Bristol, England, d. Mch. 11, 1723.

1. Samuel[2] Skinker, b. 1677 in England, settled in King George Co., Va., 1723, d. 1752. He was major of the County Militia, m. Diana Thorp.
    1. Samuel[3] Skinker.
    2. Thomas[3] Skinker.
    3. John[3] Skinker.
    4. George[3] Skinker.
    5. William[3] Skinker.
    6. Sarah[3] Skinker.
    7. Elizabeth[3] Skinker.

5. William[3] Skinker (Samuel[2], Thomas[1]), b. 1738, d. 1812, m. Mary Pawlett (widow ——— Sells), b. 1745, d. Dec. 20, 1798. He owned the land on the north side of the Rappahannock River called Moss Neck.

1. Alice[4] Peters Skinker
2. Samuel[4] Hampson Skinker.

And others.

1. Alice[4] Peters Skinker (William[3], Samuel[2], Thomas[1]), m. 1789 Washington John Washington (of the Samuel Washington line).

2. Samuel[4] Hampson Skinker (William[3], Samuel[2], Thomas[1]), of Oakley (Apr. 5, 1783-Sept. 8, 1856), m. Margaret Wilson Julian, b. Nov. 28, 1803, dau. of Dr. John Julian, a surgeon in a hospital at Fredericksburg during the Revolution.

1. Samuel[5] Wilton Skinker.
2. Thomas[5] Julian Skinker.
3. A dau.[5], m. ——— Knox, no heir.
4. Howard[5], d. without heir.

1. Samuel[5] Wilton Skinker (Samuel[4], William[3], Samuel[2], Thomas[1]), m. Martha Rebecca Washington, dau. of Washington John Washington and Alice Peters Skinker. Samuel lived at Morrisville, Va.

1. George[6] Washington Skinker, d. in Stafford Co., without issue. A Washington family Bible marked "M. Washington" is now in the possession of his cousin, Sudie Hite Skinker Benner, of Warrenton, Va.

2. Thomas[5] Julian Skinker (Samuel[4], William[3] ————), of Oakley, Stafford Co., m. 1848, Anne[5] Eliza Hite. (James[4], Isaac[3], Isaac[2], Jost[1]), of Guilford, Clarke Co., Va.

1. Hugh[6] Garland Skinker.
And others.

1. Hugh[6] Garland Skinker, of Middleburg, Va., m. Annie Lee Rucker, Oct. 10, 1894, of Ridgeville, Fauquier Co., Va. (See p. 55).

Hite

Jost Hite or Hoyte, of Alsace, patented land in 1732 in the valley of Virginia, m. Anna du Bois.

Issue:

1. Col. Isaac[2] Hite, m. 1745, Elenor Ellinge. They lived at Long Meadows, near Strasburg, Va.

1. Maj. Isaac[3] Hite, m. 1783, Nelly Conway Madison, of Montpelier, Va. They lived at Belle Grove, Strasburg, Va. He graduated at William and Mary College, was a member of the "Phi Beta Kappa" Society in 1776, served in the Rev. and while at Yorktown wrote a diary which is still in the family of one of his descendents, the Skinker family. He called it "Ye Trenches at Yorktown".

1. James[4] Madison Hite (Isaac[3], Isaac[2], Jost[1]), b. 1793, m. Caroline[4] Matilda Irvine, 1815, dau. of Samuel Irvine and wife, Anne[3] Fitzhugh Rose (Hugh[2], Robert[1]). James was a graduate of William and Mary College.

1. Anne[5] Eliza Hite, of Guilford, Clarke Co., b. 1830, m. 1848, Thomas Julian Skinker (Samuel[4], William[3], Samuel[2], Thomas[1]), of Oakley, Stafford Co., Va.

Rose

The family histories of Rose, Hite, Madison and Taylor are copied from a note book and private papers belonging to Mrs. Ann Eliza Hite Skinker, the wife of Thomas Skinker, formerly of Middleburg, Va.

1. Rev. Robert^1 Rose, m. Anne Fitzhugh.

Issue:

1. Col. Hugh^2 Rose, m. Caroline Matilda Jordan, a dau. of Col. Samuel Jordan and his wife, Ruth Meredith, a dau. of Capt. Samuel Meredith, of Hanover Co.
    1. Caroline^3 Matilda Rose.
    2. Susan^3 Rose.
    3. Hugh^3 Rose.
    4. Dr. Robert^3 Rose.
    5. Samuel^3 Rose.
    6. Judy^3 Scott Rose.
    7. Annie^3 Fitzhugh Rose.
    8. Lucinda^3 Rose.
    9. Pauline^3 Rose, d. young.
    10. Dr. Gustavus^3 Adolphus Rose.
    11. Emily^3 Rose.

(Will of Robert Rose to be found in Albemarle Co., W. B. 1, p. 24, probated Nov. 12, 1751, mentions wife, Anne; sons, John, Henry, Hugh, Patrick and Charles; daus., Susanna and Margaret; nephew, Robert Rose; brother, Patrick; mother; brother, John; and brother-in-law, Thomas Fitzhugh).

1. Caroline^3 Matilda Rose (Hugh^2, Robert^1), m. Dr. Turpin, of Chesterfield, Va.

    1. Caroline^4 Matilda Turpin, m. Dr. Johnson, of Ky.
        1. Philip^5 Johnson.
        2. Gen. Edward^5 Johnson.
        3. Rosana^5 Johnson, m. ——— Wright, of N. C.

2. Susanna^3 Rose (Hugh^2, Robert^1), m. Gov. James Pleasants.

    1. Mary^4 Anna Pleasants, m. Granville Smith.
        1. Adalaid^5 Smith, m. Dr. Royal.
        2. John^5 Smith.
        3. Susanna^5 Smith.

2. Caroline[4] Matilda Pleasants, m. Dr. Thomas, no issue.
3. John[4] Hampden Pleasants, m. 1st, Ann Eliza Irvine; m. 2nd, Mary Massie.

Issue by 2nd marriage:

1. James[5] Pleasants.
2. Ann[5] Eliza Pleasants.

4. Marcella[4] Pleasants, m. Marcellus Smith.

1. Caroline[5] Smith, m. James Morris, Green Springs, Louisa Co., Va.
2. Marcellus[5] Smith, d. unmarried.

5. Susanna[4] Pleasants, m. Dr. John Morris, Green Springs, Louisa Co., Va.

1. James[5] Morris.
2. William[5] Morris.
3. Mary[5] Morris, m. Charles Morris, son of Richard, of Taylor Springs.
4. Susanna[5] Morris.

6. Hugh[4] Rose Pleasants, d. single.
7. James[4] Pleasants, d. single, in Ky.
8. Ann[4] Pleasants, m. Dr. Elam.

1. Sallie[5] Elam, m. Col. Lindsay Walker, of "Long Tom" fame.

3. Hugh[3] Rose (Hugh[2], Robert[1]), m. ——— Philips, of Georgia, where he lived.

4. Dr. Robert[3] Henry Rose (Hugh[2], Robert[1]), m. Frances Madison, sister of President Madison, also sister of Nelly Conway Madison, the wife of Maj. Isaac Hite.

Issue:

10 children who settled in Louisiana and Texas.

5. Samuel[3] Rose was killed by the Indians in Ky.

6. Judy[3] Scott Rose (Hugh[2], Robert[1]), m. 1st, Landon Cabell; m. 2nd, ——— Tabb, of Lynchburg.

1. Dr. L.[4] R. Cabell, m. Marrian Cabell.
2. Dr. R.[4] H. Cabell, m. Julia Mayo, sister of the wife General Scott.
3. Betsy[4] Cabell, m. William R. Preston, moved to Missouri.

7. Anne^3 Fitzhugh Rose (Hugh^2, Robert^1), m. Samuel Irvine, of Lynchburg.

1. Mary^4 Irvine, m. Samuel Anthony, Dec. 9, 1813.
2. Caroline^4 Matilda Irvine, m. June 2, 1815, James Madison Hite, a nephew of President Madison.
3. John^4 R. Irvine, m. Dec. 21, 1824, Lucy Hobson, of Bedford.
4. Samuel^4 Irvine, m. ——— Isbell.
5. Ann^4 Eliza Irvine, m. John Hampden Pleasants, Mch. 31, 1818.
6. Frances^4 Madison Irvine, m. Dr. John M. Patterson, of Lynchburg, Dec. 29, 1825.

8. Lucinda^3 Rose (Hugh^2, Robert^1), m. Spotswood Garland, of Nelson.

1. Hugh^4 A. Garland, clerk of the House of Representatives, m. Anne P. Burwell.
2. Caroline^4 Matilda Garland, m. Maurice H. Garland.
    1. Brig. Gen. Samuel^5 Garland, C. S. A., was killed Sept. 14, 1862.
3. Landon^4 Cabell Garland, m. Louise F. Garland, dau. of David S. Garland.

10. Dr. Gustavus^3 Adolphus Rose (Hugh^2, Robert^1), m. Jan. 4, 1816, Anne S. Garland, dau. of David S. Garland.

11. Emily^3 Rose (Hugh^2, Robert^1), m. William Copeland, of Lynchburg.

1. Dau., m. Wilcher Lewis.

(The following is a law suit brought by William Copeland, of Lynchburg, and his wife, Emily, against Gusta, Hugh, Robert and Samuel Rose, Landon Cabell and wife, Judith Rose, Spottswood Garland and wife, Lucenda Rose, Samuel Irvine and wife, Anne Rose, John, David, Isaac and Joshua Tinsley. Bill to set aside the will of Caroline Matilda Rose, mother).

Madison

1. John^1 Madison, of Gloucester Co., 1653.
    1. John^2 Madison (John^1), m. Isabella Todd.
        1. Ambrose^3 Madison (John^2, John^1), m. 1721, Frances^3 Taylor.

1. James[4] Madison, Sen., of Montipelier, m. 1749, Nelly Conway.
    1. Nelly[5] Conway Madison, m. 1783, Maj. Isaac[3] Hite, of Belle Grove.
        1. James[6] Madison Hite, of Guilford, Clarke Co., m. Caroline[4] Matilda Irvine, 2 June, 1815, of Lynchburg, dau. of Samuel and Anne Fitzhugh Rose Irvine.
            1. Anne[7] Eliza Hite, m. Thomas Julian Skinker.

Taylor

1. James[1] Taylor, b. 1635, in England, m. 1st, Frances. They certainly had one James[2] by this marriage. He m. 2nd, Mary Gregory.

1. James[2] Taylor.
2. Ann[2] Taylor.
3. Edmund[2] Taylor.
4. Elizabeth[2] Taylor.
5. Mary[2] Taylor.
6. John[2] Taylor.

1. Col. James[2] Taylor (son of James[1] and Frances), m. Martha Thompson, lived at Monte Bello, Orange Co., Va. He was one of the Knights of the Golden Horse Shoe 1716, also a member of the House of Burgess. Great-grandparents of James Madison and Zachary Taylor.

1. Zachary[3] Taylor, m. Elizabeth Lee.
    1. Zachary[4] Taylor, m. Alice Chew.
2. Richard[3] Taylor, m. Sarah Strother.
    1. Gen. Zachary [4] Taylor (President).
        1. Sarah[5] Taylor, m. Jefferson Davis (President of the Confederacy).
        2. Gen. Richard[5] Taylor.
3. Charles[3] Taylor, m. Sarah Conway.
4. James[3] Taylor, m. Alice Thornton.
5. Col. George[3] Taylor, m. Rachel Gibson, they had seven sons who served in the Revolution as officers, ancestor of the Taylors, of Kentucky.
    1. Dr. Charles[4] Taylor.
    2. Col. Frank[4] Taylor.

6. Erasmus[3] Taylor, m. Jane Moore.
   1. Milly[4] Taylor, m. William Morton.
   Possibly others.
7. Frances[3] Taylor.
8. Martha[3] Taylor, m. Thomas Chew.
9. Tabetha[3] Taylor, m. ——— Wild.
10. Hannah[3] Taylor, m. ——— Battaile.
11. Milly[3] Taylor, m. ——— Thomas.

7. Frances[3] Taylor (James[2], James[1]), m. 1721, Ambrose[3] Madison.

1. James[4] Madison, Sen., of Montpelier, Orange Co., m. 1749, Nelly Conway.
   1. James[5] Madison.
   2. Nelly[5] Conway Madison.

1. James[5] Madison (James[4], Frances[3], James[2], James[1] Taylor), President of the U. S., m. the widow (Payne) Todd.

2. Nelly[5] Conway Madison, m. Maj. Isaac[3] Hite, and lived at Belle Grove, Strasburg, Va.

5. Mary[2] Taylor (James[1]), d. 1770, 1st Henry[2] Pendleton (Philip[1]), m. 2nd Edward Watkins (see Pendleton line).

6. John[2] Taylor (James[1]), m. Catherine Pendleton (Philip).
1. Edmund[3] Taylor, m. Annie Lewis.
2. John[3] Taylor, m. ———Lyne, of Caroline.
3. James[3] Taylor, m. Anne Pollard.
4. Philip[3] Taylor, m. Mary Walker.
5. William[3] Taylor, m. ——— Anderson.
6. Joseph[3] Taylor, m. Frances Anderson.
7. Mary[3] Taylor, m. Robert Penn.
8. Catherine[3] Taylor, m. Moses Penn.
   1. John[4] Penn, the signer of the Declaration of Independence.
9. Isabella[3] Taylor, m. Samuel Hopkins.
10. Elizabeth[3] Taylor, m. 1st ——— Lewis, 2nd ——— Bullock.

Will of John Taylor, Granville Co., N. C., dated 16 Mch. 1780 (W. B. 1, p. 275).
Son Joseph
dau. Mary Penn deceased and her children John, Philip, Moses, Thomas, Catherine, and Mary Penn.

gr. children John and Elizabeth, children of son James Taylor deceased.
gr. son John Penn, son of my dau. Catherine.
To the children of my deceased son Philip Taylor, James, and three others.

My children now living Edmund, John, William, Joseph, Isabella, Hopkins, and Elizabeth.

Executors:

Sons Edmund, John, William, and Joseph.

Varner

Philip[1] Varner, b. 1740, the emigrant, d. 1830, m. Barbara Hottel (1751-1812) of German origin, living in Alsace, they came to America, patented land in Page Co., Va.

1. David[2] Varner (Jan. 3, 1782-Apr. 14, 1816), m. 1808 Barbara Hershberger (1789-Dec. 5, 1877).
    1. Samuel[3] Varner (March 21, 1814-May 13, 1898), m. Sarah Ann Varner (Aug. 17, 1820-Jan. 18, 1880).
        1. John David[4] Varner (b. Oct. 24, 1848, d. 1930), m. Mch. 7, 1878, Lelia Mortimore Ramey (Sept. 30, 1856-Nov. 4, 1904).
            1. Minnie[5] Lee Varner, b. Sept. 16, 1879, m. Dec. 19, 1905, at Warrenton, Va., Bayard Ambrose[7] Rucker (Wm.[6] A., Wm.[6] B., George[4], John[3], John[2], Peter[1]), four children.
            2. Harry[5] Varner of El Paso, Texas.

Russell

Robert Russell, Campbell Co., lived on Flat Creek, m. Ann Bard. He died in 1791 leaving a will.

To my wife Ann.

To my children,

1. Robert[2] Russell, Jr.
2. James[2] Russell.
3. Elizabeth[2] Russell.
4. Catherine[2] Russell.
5. Mildred[2] Fleming.

6. Eleanor^2 Robinson.
7. Mary^2 Rowland.
8. Ann^2 Boaz.

2. James^2 Russell (Robert^1), m. Rosanna Rutherford.
   1. Polly^3 Russell, m. Bernard^5 Rucker of Bedford (Wm.^{4}).
   2. Patsy^3 Russell, m. Willis D. Elliott.
   3. Nancy^3 Russell, m. John Halp.
   4. Capt. James^3 Russell, Jr., b. 1800, m. Mary Fitzpatrick.

Tinsley

Thomas^1 Tinsley (d. 1699), first of the name in Virginia, patented 300 acres on West side of Chickahominy River, Dec. 13, 1650. For transporting three persons he patented 111½ acres of land in Essex in 1698, at the foot of Mt. Clayborne Hill on a branch of Portobago, adjoining James Coghill and James Scott (L. Gr., b. 8, p. 25).

In 1699, he administered on the estate of Henry Askill deceased in Essex Co. (W. and D., b. 10, p. 1).

Judgment was given against Maj. William Moseley, late sheriff of Essex Co., for 900 lbs of tobacco for the nonappearance of Thomas Tinsley at the suit of Robert Payne against Thomas Tinsley's estate, June 21, 1699 (O. B. 1695-99), Essex Co., Va.

Thomas^2 Tinsley (Thomas^1), patented 1400 acres in Essex Co. on the Mattapony River, for transporting 28 persons into the colony. Also 1000 acres the same date, 26 Apr. 1704, receiving land on the Mattapony, adjoining Edward Tucker's for transporting 20 persons (L. Gr., b. 9, p. 593-99). The quit rents of Essex of 1704 lists him as paying on 100 acres.

On Dec. 5, 1706, Thomas^2 Tinsley and wife, Sarah, of St. Anne's Parish, Essex, sold 150 acres to Walter Roberts of Middlesex Co. (D. B. 12, p. 309, Essex).

John May and wife, Grace, of Essex, sold 1100 acres to Thomas Tinsley, land on the Rappahannock and Mattapony Rivers, Occopation and Cockleshell creeks, adjoining Charles Brown and John Coleman. Witness: Robert Cooke (D. B. 12, p. 334, Essex).

William Winston, Gent, of St. Anne's Parish in Essex, bought of William Makenne of same, for 2000 lbs. of tobacco and cask, 1100 acres granted to John May, Oct. 20, 1704, and by May conveyed to Thomas[2] Tinsley, and by said Tinsley[2] conveyed to William Makenne. This land adjoined that of Thomas Sneed and Thomas Bell. June 17, 1718 (Essex Co., Vol. 15, p. 197).

The records of Essex do not show the names of the other sons of Thomas[2] Tinsley who died in 1716, but we know that he lived on Cockleshell Creek near Peter Rucker, James Coghill, Cookes, and others who intermarried with the children of Peter[1] Rucker, whose daughter, Margaret[2], married Isaac[3] Tinsley, son of Thomas[2]: Essex.

Will of Thomas Tinsley dated Nov. 5, 1715, probated Feb. 22, 1716, mentions: Wife Sarah. To my sons Thomas and Philip each a horse; to each of my other sons (names not given) a cow; to each of my daughters an ewe (W. B. 14, p. 483, Essex). Witness: James Coghill, James Jameson and Thomas Lee.

Feb. 22, 1716 Sarah Tinsley gave bond as executrix of the will of Thomas Tinsley, deceased. James Coghill and Thomas Jackson Security.

Thomas Jackson of Spotsylvania Co. sold to Isaac Tinsley of King and Queen Co. 100 acres of land bought of Joseph Berry of King and Queen Co. adjoining the land of Sarah Tinsley Apr. 17, 1727 (D. B. 18, p. 298, Essex Co.).

Thomas Jackson deeded to Isaac Tinsley 100 acres of land out of a 732 acre tract at Crawford's Corner, on the Rapidan River, in St. Mark's Parish, June 17, 1735 (D. B. I, p. 47, Orange Co.).

Sarah Tinsley acknowledged a deed of land to David Tinsley of Caroline Co. Mch. 9, 1744 (O. B. 1741-46, p. 256, Caroline Co.

The following may be the children of Thomas and Sarah Tinsley:

1. Thomas[3] Tinsley, Jr., m. Margaret ———.
2. Philip[3] Tinsley.
3. David[3] Tinsley, m. Carterine ———.
4. Edward[3] Tinsley, m. Margaret ———.
5. John[3] Tinsley, m. Sarah ———, lived in Culpeper Co.
6. Isaac[3] Tinsley, m. Margaret[2] Rucker (Peter[1]).

1. Thomas[3] Tinsley Jr. left a will in Essex Co. dated Mch. 7, 1749, probated July 16, 1764, To my wife Margaret, to sons Joshua, John, William and Isaac. My estate to be divided among my seven children (W. B. 12, p. 136).

4. Edward[3] Tinsley (Tho.[2], Tho.[1]), b. c. 1700, d. in Amherst Co. 1783. His wife Margaret was b. c. 1705, was living in 1769, but was deceased in 1783. Edward and Margaret Tinsley bought 100 acres of land from James Taylor both of King and Queen Co., St. Stephens Parish, land in St. George Parish, Spots. Co. Witness: Samuel Lloyd, May 27, 1725 (Crozier's).

Sept. 1726 Edward sold this 100 acres of land to William Crawford, land bought of Col. James Taylor.

Edward Tinsley, John Rucker and Thomas Jackson were witnesses to a sale of land between Thomas Rucker and Henry Downes.

Mch. 27 1734 Edward Tinsley of King and Queen Co. bought 120 acres of land from Richard Mulden, land in Spots Co. Witness: William Rucker.

Edward and Margaret were witness to a deed to Philip Tinsley in Caroline Co. Apr. 14, 1738. Tradition says Margaret was of the Talliaferro family.

Duncan Graham of Caroline Co. and wife, Mary, sold to Edward Tinsley of Amherst Co. for £184, 740 acres of land on Harris Creek near the Tobacco Row Mts. Wit: Battaile Harrison, Reuben Harrison and David Tinsley, Oct. 8, 1766 (D. B. C, p. 139, Amherst).

Edward Tinsley and Margaret, his wife, deeded to John Tinsley 100 acres of land on Harris Cr., Mch. 6, 1769 (D. B. B, p. 403).

Edward[3] Tinsley and wife, Margaret, deeded to their son John Tinsley 100 acres of land on Harris Creek, part of a larger tract purchased by said Tinsley. March 6, 1769 (D. B. B, p. 403, Amherst County).

The same year he bought more land in Amherst (D. B. B, p. 179). Stephen Ham and Ambrose Gatewood sold to Edward Tinsley 126 acres of land in Amherst for £64 (D. B. C, p. 508, Amherst).

Edward[3] Tinsley died in 1783. His estate was divided on Aug. 4. "Among my legal heirs, Elizabeth Pendleton, Wm. Tinsley, Richard Vernon, Edward Tinsley, Isaac Tinsley, John Tinsley, David Tinsley, Joseph Johns, Joshua Tinsley and Col. Ambrose Rucker, each to receive 120 pounds sterling. Estate to be divided by Edmund Winston, John Penn and Richard Shelton (W. B. 2, p. 118, Amherst County).

Issue:

1. Elizabeth[4] Tinsley.
2. William[4] Tinsley.

3. Sarah[4] Tinsley, m. Richard Vernon of Caroline Co.
4. Edward[4] Tinsley.
5. Isaac[4] Tinsley.
6. John[4] Tinsley.
7. David[4] Tinsley.
8. Joshua[4] Tinsley.
9. A daughter[4] Tinsley, m. Joseph Johns.
10. Mary[4] Tinsley, m. Col. Ambrose[3] Rucker.

1. Elizabeth[4] Tinsley (Edw.[3], Tho.[2], Tho.[1]), b. c. 1730, m. c. 1747 William Pendleton (John).

Issue:

1. James[5] Pendleton, b. c. 1748, m. 1769 Sarah[4] Rucker (John[3], John[2], Peter[1]).

McDaniel

The name McDaniel or MacDaniel is claimed to be of the MacDonald, or of the Donald clan. In a catalogue compiled by the Paisleys, Limited, a Company in Scotland, which sell the correct plaids for each clan; statement is made that MacDaniel is of the Clan MacDonald (Clan Donald).

1. George[2] McDaniel (John[1]), married Margaret Goff, daughter of John and Ann Goff.

"George McDaniel Sr. was born 17th. May 1722, and died 15th. Nov. 1821. He was married in his 26th. year to Margaret Goff in her 20th. year. His father was named John whose father was a native of Scotland. Geo. McDaniel Sr. had four brothers, John, William, Jerry, and Henry. Their mother walked straight and well at 102 yrs. old and lived several years after."

(Copied from the old Bible that belonged to Balda McDaniel, the oldest son of Geo. McDaniel and Dolly Waller Robinson. The Bible is now in the possession of Mrs. Robert C. McDaniel, Lynchburg, Va.).

"George the son of John (McDaniel) the elder, was born in King William Co. on Saturday, May 17th, 1722, and died on Thursday, Nov. 15th. 1821, in Amherst Co. on his farm at the foot of Tobacco Row Mt.

In his 26th year he married Margaret Goff who was then in her 20th. year. They had three sons and five daughters. The sons were John, George and William. The daughters were Margaret, Nancy, Francis Lucy, and Phoeby."

(Copied from the diary written by John Robinson McDaniel, the youngest son of Geo. McDaniel and Dolly Waller Robinson, now in the possession of Mrs. Lucy Almond Harrell, Norfolk, Va.)

The McDaniels were born in King William Co., moved to Orange near the Ruckers, Tinsleys and Goughs with whom they intermarried. From the Order Books of Orange the two brothers John and George are living in St. Marks Parish in 1744, about which time George moved to Goochland.

On petition of John McDaniel Jr. it is Ordered that George McDaniel and William DeBoard be added to the list of Tithables for St. Mark's Parish. 25, Dec. 1744 (O. B. 1743-46, p. 228, Orange Co.).

(O. B. 5, p. 510, 1744, Goochland Co.). A suit was brought by Arthur Hopkins against George McDaniel for 700 pounds due him. Thomas McDaniel enters special bail. The defendant appears and confesses judgment, whereon it is considered that the plaintiff "do recover against the defendant the said sum of 700 pounds".

George McDaniel was in Albemarle Co. in 1747. Charles Turnbull brought suit against him. In 1748 he was brought before the grand jury "for profanely swearing two oaths in two months."

George first patented land in Amherst county in 1760. This was 174 acres on the north side of Harris Creek, in a cove of the Tobacco Row Mountains. His grandson Ambrose Rucker and his wife, Elizabeth Parks lived there later. When the old mansion house was torn down, a few years ago, by a stranger who had bought the farm, one of the corner logs had a large "M" cut in the end of it, which suggests McDaniel.

(D. B. B, p. 36, Amherst). 5 Aug. 1765, George McDaniel and his wife, Margaret, sold 136 acres to Baylor Walker, land on the south side of Harris Creek, adjoining the Tobacco Row Mts. The same day he exchanged 500 acres on Stovell's Creek for 153 acres on Harris Creek, "as per agreement with John Goff, dec'd."

In 1767 George bought 300 acres on south side of Harris Cr., on the east side of Tobacco Row Mts. He continues to patent land. In 1771 he sold 165 acres on Harris Cr. to Abraham Penn.

George McDaniel and wife according to agreement with John Goff (now dec'd.) deeded to Leonard, Joseph, Ambrose Goff and Elizabeth Moran, a tract of land granted to Sarah Lynch in 1759, Amherst Co. The home place reserved for the life of Ann Goff, widow of John Goff, dec'd. (D. B. D, p. 36, 1775, Amherst Co.).

In 1775 Leonard Goff, son and heir of John and his wife, Ann Goff, deeded land to George McDaniel, as per agreement between himself and the late John Goff (D. B. D, p. 297, Amherst).

14 July 1775 Ambrose Goff and wife, Ann, deeded to Henry McDaniel 112 acres of land in Amherst county (D. B. D, p. 297).

Richard Ellis and Martin Parks with wife, Nancy Parks, of Amherst Co. sold to George McDaniel, all same, 265 acres for $205. Wits: Ambrose Rucker, James Ware and A. Carter (D. B. M, p. 355, Amherst Co.), 19 May 1813.

The Tax Books of Amherst Co., 1783, mentions: Henry McDaniel; George McDaniel; John McDaniel; George McDaniel, Jr.; Angus McDaniel; Daniel McDaniel and Thomas McDaniel. Written McDonald or McDaniel.

George[2] McDaniel served as a Sergeant in the Revolutionary War. See Eckenrode's List of Rev. Soldiers: War 5, 125, State Arch. Dept. Also Hardesty's H. and G. History of Amherst Co.

In his will, dated 1818; probated 1821, Amherst Co. (W. B. 6, p. 270), he left to Ambrose Rucker, fourteen shares of bank stock for the support of an old negro woman, at her death to be divided among his heirs. Ex'ors. Dabney Ware, James Ware and Nelson Dawson.

Issue:

1. Nancy[3] Tinsley.
2. Sarah[3] Tinsley, dec'd.
3. John[3] McDaniel.
4. George[3] McDaniel.
5. Margaret[3] Burford, dec'd.
6. Lucy[3] Tinsley, dec'd.
7. William[3] McDaniel, died of Smallpox during the Revolution, in 1776. He is not mentioned in the will of his father.
8. Winnie[3] McDaniel m. Thomas Edwards, 6 Jan. 1781. The marriage bond found in Amherst Co.: "Winnie, daughter of George McDaniel, Sr." Signed by Thomas Edwards and Winnie McDaniel. She is not mentioned in her father's will.
9. Frances[3] McDaniel, m. William Tyree, 5 Dec. 1785. Marriage bond signed by George McDaniel. She is not mentioned in her father's will.

3. John^{3} McDaniel (George^{2}, John^{1}), born 1751; died 1831; buried in Amherst County; m. about 1773, first to Margaret^{4} Rucker, daughter of Ambrose^{3} and Mary (Tinsley) Rucker. Margaret Rucker died leaving four children. John McDaniel married second Lucy^{4} Rucker Dawson, daughter of Benjamin^{3} Rucker (John^{2}, Peter^{1}) and widow of Zachary^{2}, son of Martin^{1} Dawson.

From an article filed in the Arch. Dept., Richmond, Va., "John McDaniel was born in Albemarle Co. He had hazel eyes, dark hair and swarthy complexion".

He was in Kentucky during the Winter of 1800, when his fourteen year old daughter Judith married David Woodroof, Jr.

From a letter written by John McDaniel to the clerk of Amherst county, dated 3rd Feb. 1799: "I give my free consent for my daughter Judy McDaniel to marry David Woodroof, Jr." Signed, John McDaniel. Yet this letter does not seem sufficient, for her grandfather Ambrose Rucker wrote another note to the clerk: "Sunday Morning, before sunrise, Jan. 19, 1800. To Mr. William S. Crawford, clerk of Amherst Co., Dear Sir: Mr. John McDaniel is to be absent from this county longer than he expected when he left to go to Ky. I can undertake that you may grant a marriage license for Daniel Woodroof, Jr. and his" (John McDaniel's) "daughter Judy McDaniel, for I know before he left, he much approved of Mr. Woodroof's conduct and person". Signed, Ambrose Rucker.

Will of John McDaniel (W. B. 10, p. 77), Amherst Co. "I desire that all my just debts be paid and the balance of my estate to be equally divided between my children as hereafter named, viz: my sons Ambrose, Sidney and Gideon; Betsy Davies, Peggy Ware and Sophia Strange; my four children hereafter named having had their full share of my estate, thirty odd years ago, viz: William, George, Mary Jones and Judiete Heiskill." Dated 3 June 1835; prob. 18 Feb. 1837.

Issue, by 1st m.:

1. William^{4} McDaniel.
2. George^{4} McDaniel.
3. Mary^{4}, m. 1 Feb. 1797, Richard Jones (m. bond signed by father, John McDaniel).
4. Judith^{4} McDaniel.

Issue, by 2nd m.:

5. Ambrose^{4} McDaniel.
6. Sidney^{4} McDaniel.
7. Gideon^{4} McDaniel.

8. Elizabeth[4] McDaniel.
9. Margaret[4] McDaniel, m. John Ware. Marriage bond signed by John McDaniel, 25 Nov. 1800.
10. Sophia[4] McDaniel.

1. William[4] McDaniel (John[3], George[2], John[1]), b. 22 Feb. 1774; d. 19 June 1857; m. 20 Jan. 1801, Elizabeth[5] Pendleton (19 Dec. 1787-17 May 1835), only child of James[4] Pendleton (William[3], John[2], Philip[1]).

1. Sally[5] Rucker McDaniel, b. 6 July 1802; d. 3 Oct. 1827; m. 16 Oct. 1817, ——— Myers.
2. Peggy[5] McDaniel, b. 25 Oct. 1804; d. 17 Oct. 1826.
3. Catherine[5] McDaniel, b. 27 May 1807; m. 21 Oct. 1824, ——— Glenn.
4. James[5] Pendleton McDaniel.
5. Betsey[5] McDaniel, b. 31 May 1811; m. 17 Nov. 1825, Ogden ———.
6. John[5] Rucker McDaniel.
7. Jane[5] McDaniel.
8. William[5] McDaniel, b. 3 Sept. 1817; m. Mary Thurman, moved to California.
9. Lindsey[5] McDaniel, b. 25 July 1819; m. Martin Glenn.
10. Mary[5] Ann McDaniel, b. 22 Feb. 1821.
11. Philip[5] McDaniel, b. 10 May 1824.
12. Sophia[5] Burrus McDaniel, b. 4 May 1827.
13. Edward[5] Jackson McDaniel, b. 1829; d. 1832.

4. James[5] Pendleton McDaniel (William[4], John[3], George[2], John[1]), b. 19 June 1809; d. 25 July 1877; m. 14 Feb. 1832, Mary Glenn Robinson.

1. John[6] Edwards McDaniel.
2. Jane[6] McDaniel.
3. Lindsey[6] McDaniel, moved to Kentucky after the Civil War.
4. Philip[6] McDaniel, moved to Lebanon, Texas.

1. John[6] Edwards McDaniel (James[5], William[4], John[3], George[2], John[1]), b. 14 June 1833; d. 1881; m. Martha Emily Arthur, 2 July 1857 of Big Island, Bedford Co. She was the daughter of Col. L. C. Arthur and his wife Nancy (Jones) Arthur.

1. Russell[7] McDaniel.
2. James[7] Crawford McDaniel.
3. Penn[7] Arthur McDaniel.

4. Myra[7] Blanche McDaniel, b. 2 Apr. 1868.
5. Sallie[7] Taliaferro McDaniel, b. 3 July 1870, m. Sept. 1895, James Perrow Taylor.
6. Emma[7] Glenn McDaniel, b. 20 Feb. 1875.
7. Edward[7] Bass McDaniel, b. May 1877.
8. Ella[7] Woodroof McDaniel, b. April 1879, m. Oct. 23, 1916, Frank Pollard Austin.

1. Russell[7] McDaniel (John[6] Edwards), m. 15 Jan. 1879, Waller Rucker.

2. James[7] Crawford McDaniel (John[6] Edwards, James[5], ———), b. Dec. 12, 1863, m. 31 Mch. 1897, Roberta Eva Rucker, live at Wynn, Ark.

1. Lafayette[8] McDaniel.
2. Lillian[8] Fleda McDaniel.
3. Virgil[8] McDaniel.
4. June[8] McDaniel.
5. Rucker[8] McDaniel.
6. Waller[8] Penn McDaniel.

3. Penn[7] Arthur McDaniel (John[6] Edwards, James[5], William[4], John[3] McDaniel), b. 15 Apr. 1865; m. 24 June 1891, Lucy Surber, b. 18 Sept. 1873; d. 27 Aug. 1921; m. 2nd Frances Thompson of Potter, Ky., dau. of Judge John Thompson, Jan. 4, 1923.

1. Mabel[8] Mercer McDaniel, b. 11 Jan. 1893.
2. Wilfred[8] Porter McDaniel, b. 12 Mch. 1896; m. 4 July 1923, Olive McGrath.
3. Valrie[8] Shields McDaniel, b. 28 July 1898; m. 16 Dec. 1922, Mattie Shaw.
4. Fern[8] Almeta McDaniel, b. 14 May 1900; m. 20 June 1922, Munsey Runion.
5. Sunshine[8] Elizabeth McDaniel, b. 19 June 1904.
6. Weston[8] Owen McDaniel, b. 26 Oct. 1907.
7. Trula[8] Carmen McDaniel, b. 20 Jan. 1915.

6. Judge John[5] Rucker McDaniel (William[4], John[3], George[2], John[1]), b. 2 Jan. 1813; d. 30 July 1889; m. 1st 9 Sept. 1837, Elizabeth Thurman, no children. He m. 2nd Mary Bowling, b. 1824; d. July 1889

1. James[6] Bowling McDaniel, m. Carrie Grigsby. Two children.
2. Elizabeth[6] McDaniel, m. Dr. Peter Connaughton. No children.

3. William^{6} Pendleton McDaniel, m. Bettie Carson. Eight children.
4. John^{6} Milton McDaniel, m. Annie Hendricks. Eight children.
5. Edward^{6} Wingfield McDaniel, m. Lucy Walker. Five children.
6. Charles^{6} Lewis McDaniel, m. Sallie Arthur. Five children.
7. Samuel^{6} Augustus McDaniel, m. Bettie Glass Hughes. No child.
8. Alfred^{6} Spriggs McDaniel.
9. Mary^{6} McDaniel, m. Alfred S. Burks. Three children.
10. Roslyn^{6} McDaniel, m. Roy Moore. Five children.
11. Ella^{6} McDaniel, died in infancy.

7. Jane^{5} Pendleton McDaniel (William^{4}, John^{3}, George^{2}, John^{1} McDaniel), b. 29 Feb. 1816; d. 17 Apr. 1871; m. 12 Mch. 1833, Henry West Quarles of King William Co., b. 20 Nov. 1795. Their farm was called "West Dale". Henry Quarles died 19 Jan. 1869, a son of Francis West Quarles, and grandson of Col. Merewether Smith of Essex Co.

1. Susan^{6} Elizabeth Quarles, b. 18 Feb. 1834.
2. Lucy^{6} Brockenbough Quarles, b. 10 Nov. 1835; d. 3 Feb. 1858; m. 20 Dec. 1854, Richard G. Davenport.
3. Ann^{6} Dangerfield Quarles, b. 21 Oct. 1837; d. 21 Oct. 1916; m. 21 Aug. 1873, Henry James Dobbs, of High Point, N. C.
    1. Nellie^{7} West Dobbs, unmar.
    2. Joseph^{7} Henry Dobbs.
4. Mary^{6} Henry Quarles, b. 3 Sept. 1839.
5. Virginia^{6} West Quarles, b. 5 Sept. 1841.
6. Susan^{6} Fauntleroy Quarles, b. 24 Apr. 1844.
7. Henry^{6} Francis Quarles, b. 6 Apr. 1847.
8. George^{6} William Quarles, b. 25 Mch. 1848.
9. Ella^{6} Jane Quarles, b. Sept. 1852.

Only two of the nine children married.

8. Alfred^{6} Spriggs McDaniel (John^{5} R., William^{4}, John^{3}), m. 1790, Lizzie Walker.

1. Alfred^{7} Vernon McDaniel, m. 1922, Mabel Marsh.
    1. Elizabeth^{8} Harris McDaniel.
    2. Alfred^{8} Vernon McDaniel, Jr.
2. Mamie^{7} Elizabeth McDaniel.
3. Dorothy^{7} Evelyn McDaniel.

4. Amelia^{7} Walker McDaniel.
5. Lucy^{7} West McDaniel, m. 1925, Harry Lee Brown.
   1. Harry Lee Brown, Jr., b. 1927.
6. Charles^{7} Robert McDaniel, m. 1927, Estelle White.
7. Leslie^{7} McDaniel.

2. George^{4} McDaniel (John^{3}, George^{2}, John ^{1}), m. 18 Dec. 1801, Frances Higginbotham, daughter of Joseph Higginbotham. Wits: Benjamin Rucker, Jr., Joseph Swanson and William McDaniel. 20 July 1820, George McDaniel, Jr. and wife Frances, of Amherst Co. sold 63 acres of land to Henry Saul, Jr. for $10. The land in Bedford Co. They sold 448 acres to John Sledd, land in Bedford Co., adjoining Wade's land.

3. Mary^{4} McDaniel (John^{3}, George^{2}, John^{1}), m. Richard Jones. She died 9 Sep. 1823.

1. Daughter^{5}, m. Bluford Morris.
   1. William^{6} Morris.
   2. Charles^{6} Morris.
   3. Lewis^{6} Morris.
2. Frances^{5} Jones, m. Nathan^{5} Rucker (Isaac^{4}, Ambrose^{3}, John^{2}).
   1. Mary^{6} J. Rucker, m. Joseph Watts (cousin).
   2. William^{6} Richard Rucker, of 2nd Va. Cavalry, Co. E, in Civil War.
   3. Nannie^{6} Rucker, m. George F. Hicks.
   4. John^{6} R. Rucker, m. ——— Ogden of Bedford Co.
   5. James^{6} R. Rucker, m. ——— Duff.
   6. Henry^{6} Rucker.
3. ———^{5} Jones, m. ——— Jackson, no heirs.

4. Judith^{4} McDaniel (John^{3}, Geo.^{2}, John^{1}), b. 1786, d. 4 June 1844, m. 1st David Woodroof, Jr., in 1800, m. 2nd Samuel Haskill. Judith was fourteen years of age when she married Woodroof, her father, John, and grandfather Col. Ambrose Rucker wrote letters to the clerk of Amherst Co. giving consent to her marriage. She died in 1844 leaving a will in which she mentions having received her share of her first husband's estate (David having d. in 1814). Her father's will mentioned her as Judith Heiskell. They are buried at Round Top, Amherst Co.

1. Nancy^{5} Woodroof, m, 1st Thomas Bass, 18 May 1820; m. 2nd Henry Ogden.

2. Mary^5 Woodroof, m. Nathan^6 Rucker (Ambrose^5 Reuben, Ambrose).
3. Winston^5 Woodroof.
4. Pitt^5 Woodroof, m. Margaret^6 Rucker (Ambrose^5, Reuben, ————).

3. Winston^5 Woodroof (Judith^4, John^3 McDaniel), b. 1807, d. 1872, m. about 1827 Frances Jane Higginbotham London, b. 1812, d. 1862.

1. Alphonso^6 Woodroof, b. 1847, d. 1915, m. Susie Graves of Orange Co., b. 1852, still living (1931).
   1. Martha^7 Woodroof, only child.

1. Martha^7 Woodroof, m. June 23, 1909, Philip Wallace Hiden, son of Philip Barbour Hiden and wife Bettie Goodwin.

1. Martha^8 Woodroof Hiden, b. 4 Mch. 1910, m. 25 Nov. 1929, Deleno McKelvey, b. 15 Aug. 1908, son of Charles W. McKelvey and wife Susan Adams Delano.
2. Susanna^8 Elizabeth Hiden, b. 12 July 1911.
3. Georgie^8 Goodwin Hiden, b. 4 Feb. 1915.
4. Philip^8 Wallace Hiden, b. 3 Sept. 1917.
5. Frances^8 Winston Hiden, b. 12 Oct. 1919.

Captain David Woodroof, Sen. died 1817; m. Clara Powell who died Feb. 1825. Both were of Caroline Co., Va.

1. Thomas Woodroof died before 1813, leaving daughters Matilda and Amanda Woodroof.
2. John Woodroof.
3. David Woodroof, Jr.
4. Jessee Woodroof, m. Miss Lee.
5. James Woodroof.
6. William Woodroof.
7. Nancy Woodroof, m. ———— Harrison.

5. Ambrose^4 Rucker McDaniel (John^3, George^2), m. 28 Nov. 1804, Olive Sandidge (daughter of William Sandidge, 26 June 1830, Amherst Co.).

7. Gideon^4 McDaniel (John^3, George^2), m. Miss Strange.

8. Elizabeth^4 McDaniel (John^3, George^2), mar. Kemper Davies, a brother of Dr. Landon Davies of Amherst Co.

1. William^5 Davies, m. Miss Carter.

2. Addison[5] Davies, m. Miss Burks.
3. Nicholas[5] Davies.
4. Charles[5] Davies, m. 1st Miss Glenn; m. 2nd Henrietta Ott.
5. Emily[5] Davies.
6. Arthur[5] Davies, m. Harriet Pierce.
7. Sallie[5] Davies, m. John Ware.
8. Pauline[5] Davies.
9. Mary[5] Frances Davies.

5. Emily[5] Davies (Elizabeth[4], John[3], George[2], John[1] McDaniel), m. 1832, Martin D. Tinsly, Amherst Co.

1. Virginia[6] Tinsly, m. Joseph Harvey.
2. Scott[6] Tinsly, died unmarried.
3. Addison[6] Tinsly, went West.
4. Eddie[6] Tinsly.

8. Pauline[5] Davies (Elizabeth[4], John[3] McDaniel), m. 1st Burwell Parks; m. 2nd ——— Hibbs, s. p.

Issue (by 1st mar.):

1. William[6] Parks, died young.
2. Anne[6] Parks, m. Fletcher Harvey.
3. Arthur[6] Parks.
4. Sallie[6] Parks, m. Benjamin[7] Rucker (Benj.[6], Benj.[5], Isaac[4]).

9. Mary[5] Frances Davies (Elizabeth[4], John[3] McDaniel), m. John R. Cunningham.

1. Joseph[6] Cunningham, m. Laura[7] Rucker (Daniel[6], Wm.[5] B., George[4], John[3].
2. George[6] Cunningham, m. Mamie Richardson.
3. Mary[6] Eliza Cunningham, m. George, son of William Morris.
4. Olie[6] Cunningham, m. Samuel, son of Rufus Higginbotham.

9. Margaret[4] McDaniel (John[3]), m. John Ware, Jr. The marriage bond in Amherst Co., dated 25 Nov. 1800. Signed by John McDaniel; "To permit John Ware, Jr. to marry my daughter Peggy. They were married 5 Dec. 1800.

10. Sophia[4] McDaniel (John[3]), m. 1823, Thomas Strange.

4. George[3] McDaniel, Jr. (George[2], John[1]), b. 12 Mar. 1755 in Albemarle Co.; died Sept. 1848 in Amherst Co. He married 1st 1781 Dolly Waller Robinson (daughter of John Robinson), b. 26 Dec. 1763; d. 16 Feb. 1816. George[3] married 2nd Mary, widow of Mr. Glascock of Chalk Level, Pittsylvania Co. He died there and was buried at Boonsboro, Bedford Co., Va. There were no children by the second marriage. In 1792 he was appointed inspector of the tobacco warehouse at Amherst. John McDaniel was his security.

In 1817, George McDaniel and his wife Mary, of Lynchburg, sold all their rights in land purchased by his father, George, from Seth Wood. He reserved two acres.

Mrs. Howard Willis Dillard, of Lynchburg, has a portrait of this George McDaniel.

Copy of records found in an old Bible that belonged to Balda McDaniel, son of George and Dolly (Robinson) McDaniel. The Bible is now (Apl. 1928) in the possession of Robert McDaniel, of Lynchburg, who is an only son of Samuel McDaniel and Eliza (Crenshaw) McDaniel. Mr. Robert McDaniel is about seventy-five years of age.

Copy from Bible:

George McDaniel, Jr., son of George, Sen. was born 12 Mar. 1755.

Dolly McDaniel his wife was born 26th Dec. 1763.

Their first son Balda McDaniel was born 1st Jan. 1782.

Lodowick McDaniel was born 25 June 1783.

Alex. McDaniel was born 4th March 1785 and died 19 Aug. 1818.

Albon McDaniel was born 18th Aug. 1786.

Florentine McDaniel was born 1st Feb. 1789; died 27 Sept. 1793.

Palentine McDaniel was born 8 Apl. 1793; died 20th March ——.

Cleopatra McDaniel was born 12 Nov. 1794.
Alfred McDaniel 7th June 1796.
John R. McDaniel 9th July 1807.
Elizabeth McDaniel died 18 Dec. 1810.
Lucy Robinson died 2 Oct. 1825.
Lucy Crenshaw, late Lucy McDaniel died on the night of 18 March 1839.
Balda McDaniel died 17th Feb. 1847.
Nancy McDaniel died 11th Dec. 1866.
Balda McDaniel born 1 Jan. 1782.

Nancy McDaniel born 2 July 1786.
——— born 25 Oct. 1802.
——— born 15 Sept. 1803.
Harriet born 2 Oct. 1804.
Elizabeth born 6 Dec. 1806.
Lucy born 27 May 1808.
Martha Ann born 3 Oct. 1810.
Samuel born 29 Sept. 1822.

Issue:

1. Balda[4] McDaniel.
2. Lodowick[4] McDaniel.
3. Alexander[4] McDaniel.
4. Albon[4] McDaniel.
5. Florentine[4] McDaniel.
6. Palatine[4] McDaniel.
7. Cleopatra[4] McDaniel.
8. Alfred[4] McDaniel.
9. John[4] Robin McDaniel.

1. Balda[4] McDaniel (George[3], George[2], John[1]), b. 1 Jan. 1782; d. 19 Feb. 1847; m. Dec. 26, 1801, Nancy Hobson of Bedford Co., formerly of Powhatan Co. In Feb. 1820 Balda sold four negroes to Robert Tinsley (Amherst Co. Rec.).

1. Harriet[5] McDaniel (see below).
2. Elizabeth[5] McDaniel, b. 5 Dec. 1806; d. 1810.
3. Lucy[5] McDaniel.
4. Martha[5] Ann McDaniel.
5. Samuel[5] McDaniel.

1. Harriet[5] McDaniel (Balda[4], George[3], George[2], John[1]), b. 2 Oct. 1804; d. 13 Dec. 1860; m. 1822 Hiram Cheatwood, son of Daniel and Sarah Porter Cheatwood of Powhatan and Amherst Counties.

Hiram and Harriet lived in Bedford county about eight miles from Lynchburg, on a farm of 160 acres. The house stood on a high elevation, affording a splendid view of the Blue Ridge Mountains. (See Lynchburg and Its People, by Asbury Christian, p. 83-86).

1. Lucy[6] Hobson Cheatwood, mar. 1st Richard Edward Preston Hopkins. Issue: three children; mar. 2nd Elisha Carter. One child.
2. Dorothy[6] Waller Cheatwood, mar. John[2] Dabney Burke (Martin[1] P. Burke).

3. Anne^{6} Eliza Cheatwood, mar. Albon Acree. Three children.
4. Sara^{6} Porter Cheatwood, mar.
5. Henriette^{6} McDaniel Cheatwood, mar. George F. Tinsley.
6. Daniel^{6} Benjamin Cheatwood, mar. 1st Sara Patterson Hobson. One child; 2nd Eliza^{4} Chappelear, dau of Benj.^{3} (William^{2}, Elias^{1}).
7. Hiram^{6} Samuel Cheatwood, mar. Julia Margaret Reese. Three children.
8. Nicholas^{6} Leighton Cheatwood.
9. George^{6} Cheatwood.
10. Lodowick^{6} McDaniel Cheatwood.

4. Sarah^{6} Porter Cheatwood (Harriet^{5}, Balda^{4}, George^{3} McDaniel), mar. 1870, William Pleasant Nance; 2nd, Robert Berry.

1. Lula^{7} Preston Nance (Single).
2. Mary^{7} Leighton Nance, m. H. M. Singleton.
    1. 1. Harold^{8} Brown Singleton.
    2. Mary^{8} Middleton Singleton.
    3. Philip^{8} John Singleton.
3. Lillian Vernon Nance, m. 1st, William M. Guy; m. 2nd, Robert Berry.
    1. Porter^{8} Guy.
4. Florence^{7} Royal Nance, m. Oscar DeMott.
    1. May^{8} Amonette DeMott.
5. Julia^{7} Rees Nance (Single).
6. Russell^{7} Nance, m. Martha Wells.
    1. James^{8} W. Nance, m. Marjory Thurman, of Clarksville, W. Va.
    2. Frances^{8} Porter Nance, m. ——— Jamison, of Paynesville, W. Va.

10. Lodowick^{6} McDaniel Cheatwood (Harriet^{5}, Balda^{4}, George^{3} McDaniel), m. Lillian^{3} Vernon Branch (dau, of William Jennings Branch). He was Mayor of Lynchburg for twenty-five years.

1. William^{7} Branch Cheatwood (Single).
2. Sallie^{7} McDaniel Cheatwood, m. Dibrel Henry Oglesby.
3. Vernon^{7} Cheatwood.
4. Harry^{7} Clement Cheatwood, m. Lottie Mosby.
    1. Harry^{8} Clement Cheatwood, Jr.

2. Harriette^8 McDaniel Cheatwood.
3. Lillian^8 Vernon Cheatwood.
4. Mary^8 Elizabeth Cheatwood.
5. Dorothy^8 Waller Cheatwood.
6. Sallie^8 Branch Cheatwood.
7. William^8 Jennings Cheatwood.

5. Elizabeth^7 Jennings Cheatwood, m. Joseph L. Newland.
   1. George^8 Cheatwood Newland.
   2. Joseph^8 L. Cheatwood Newland, Jr.
   3. Lodwick^8 McDaniel Newland.
6. Nicholas^7 Leighton Cheatwood (Single). Was killed in an automobile accident, Jan. 1, 1925.

3. Lucy^5 (Balda^4, George^3, George^2, John^1), b. 27 Nov., 1808; d. 18 Mar., 1839; m. John Crenshaw.

4. Martha^5 Ann (Balda^4, George^3, George^2, John^1), b. 3 Oct., 1810; m. Richard Crenshaw.

8. Nicholas^6 Leighton Cheatwood (Harriet^5, Balda^4, George^3 McDaniel), m. Mary Priscilla Hurt, daughter of Stephen Clifton Hurt and his wife, Maria Frances Crenshaw.

1. Henrietta^7 Hurt Cheatwood (Single).
2. Harriette^7 McDaniel Cheatwood, m. Thomas Hubert Fox.
   1. Mary^8 Clifton Fox, m. R. D. Apperson, Jr.
      1. R.^{9} D. Apperson, III.
      2. Thos.^{9} Fox Apperson.
   2. Thomas^8 Hubert Fox, m. Lucy Chiswell Heald.
   3. Hallie^8 Hamilton Fox, m. Edward Dudley Colhoun.
      1. Edward^9 Dudley Colhoun, Jr.
   4. John^8 Hinton Fox. (Single).
   5. Henrietta^8 Crenshaw Fox. (Single).
3. Frances^7 Crenshaw Cheatwood, m. Thomas Ashby Watts.
   1. James^8 Winston Watts, M. D. (Single).
   2. Thomas^8 Ashby Watts, Jr., m. Emily Langhorne.
   3. Hubert^8 Bruce Watts. (Single).

4. Mary^7 Leighton Cheatwood. Died unmarried, May, 1927, while en route to Europe.

5. Samuel[5] McDaniel (Balda[4]) (Sept. 29, 1822, Dec. 12, 1882). (Son of Balda McDaniel and Nancy Hobson McDaniel), m. Eliza S. Crenshaw (Feb. 25, 1823, Apr. 20, 1883), m. Nov. 9, 1842.

They lived at the home of his father, Balda McDaniel, in Bedford County, Virginia, near Boonsboro, this tract of land having been a grant, and is still held by the family at this time (July, 1929).

1. Ann[6] Priscilla McDaniel, b. Aug. 21, 1843, d. Oct. 13, 1844.
2. Balda[6] McDaniel, b. Apr. 6, 1846, d. June 22, 1848.
3. Lucy[6] McDaniel, b. Apr. 8, 1848, d. Apr. 30, 1848.
4. Lelia[6] McDaniel, b. June 27, 1851, d. Apr. 1, 1870.
5. Ella[6] McDaniel, b. Sept. 11, 1855, d. Mar. 17, 1856.
6. Robert[6] Crenshaw McDaniel, b. Feb. 13, 1858, d. Apr. 9, 1929.

4. Lelia[6] McDaniel (Samuel[5], Balda[4]), m. Dr. Thomas Walker Nelson, Nov. 3, 1869, in her eighteenth year, and died about six months later.

6. Robert[6] Crenshaw McDaniel (Samuel[5], Balda[4]), m. Margaret Timberlake Thornhill, daughter of Dr. and Mrs. George William Thornhill, Nov. 11, 1884. The old McDaniel estate was inherited by him, and used as a summer home, the family living most of the time in Lynchburg, Va.

1. George[7] Thornhill McDaniel, b. Apr. 10, 1886.
2. Eliza[7] McDaniel, b. Nov. 20, 1887.
3. Samuel[7] Marshall McDaniel, b. July 10, 1889.
4. Robert[7] Crenshaw McDaniel, Jr., b. Aug. 5, 1891, d. July 16, 1928.
5. Margaret[7] McDaniel, b. Aug. 17, 1893.
6. Will[7] Harris McDaniel, b. Dec. 30, 1895.
7. Ellis[7] Bibb McDaniel, b. Dec. 30, 1897.
8. Thomas[7] Nelson McDaniel, b. Feb. 5, 1901.
9. Mary[7] Elizabeth McDaniel, b. Mar. 9, 1904.

1. George[7] Thornhill McDaniel (Robert[6], Samuel[5], Balda[4]), m. Jennie Darby Glass, daughter of Mr. and Mrs. Erskine Douglas Glass, of Lynchburg, Va., June 10, 1915. They have one son, George[8] Thornhill McDaniel, Jr., b. May 21, 1916.

2. Eliza[7] McDaniel (Robert[6], Samuel[5], Balda[4]), m. James Edward Cunningham, of Pedlar Mills, Va., Sept. 5, 1911.

Issue:

1. Margaret[8] McDaniel, b. June 24, 1912.
2. Elizabeth[8] Anna McDaniel, b. Feb. 25, 1919.
3. James[8] Edward McDaniel, Jr., b. Mar. 20, 1921.
4. Mary[8] Frances McDaniel, b. June 18, 1923.
5. Ora[8] Jean McDaniel, b. Apr. 2, 1927.

3. Samuel[7] Marshall McDaniel (Robert[6], Samuel[5], Balda[4]), m. Elizabeth Louise Steptoe, daughter of Mr. and Mrs. W. T. Steptoe, of Lynchburg, Va., January 25, 1916.

1. Samuel[8] Marshall McDaniel, Jr., b. Oct. 6, 1916.
2. Ada[8] Byron McDaniel, b. Dec. 15, 1917.
3. Robert[8] Steptoe McDaniel, b. Apr. 15, 1921.

4. Robert[7] Crenshaw McDaniel, Jr. (Robert[6], Samuel[5]), m. Louise Krider, of Salisburg, N. C., Oct. 10, 1925, and lived at the old McDaniel homestead until his death, July 16, 1928.

1. Robert[8] Crenshaw McDaniel, III, b. July 14, 1926.
2. Margaret[8] McDaniel, lives in New York City.

7. Ellis[7] Bibb McDaniel (Robert[6], Samuel[5], Balda[4]), m. Inez Roseman Clark, dau. of Mr. and Mrs. F. S. Clark, Lynchburg, Va., Oct. 25, 1920.

1. Eliza[8] McDaniel, b. Nov. 19, 1921.

9. Mary[7] Elizabeth McDaniel (Robert[6] C., Samuel[5], Balda[4]), b. Mch. 9, 1904, m. Saturday, Oct. 5, 1929, Frederick Lynde-Wood Barnard.

2. Lodowick[4] McDaniel (Geo.[3], Geo.[2], John[1]) (June 25, 1783-July 15, 1855), m. June 25, 1817, Elizabeth Hobson (June 25, 1800-1885), dau. of Benjamin Hobson. She was married on her seventeenth and he on his thirty-fourth birthday.

1. Marinda[5] McDaniel, m. James[6] Monroe Rucker (Jonathan[5], Geo.[4] ————).
2. Alexander[5] McDaniel (Aug. 25, 1819-1868).
3. Benjamin[5] H. McDaniel, b. Apr. 10, 1821, m. a dau. of William Meade and lived in Houston, Texas.
4. Albert[5] McDaniel (June 12, 1824-1890), m. Catherine Oglesby. No issue.
5. Waller[5] McDaniel (Mch. 21, 1826-July 2, 1827).
6. Eliza[5] McDaniel (May 31, 1828-July 6, 1843), single.
7. Walker[5] McDaniel (Dec. 15, 1839-Mch. 29, 1889), m. Anna Nelms, of Bedford Co., Va.

Issue:

1. Bell[6] McDaniel (Walker[5] ————), m. Jesse Kassey.
   1. Grace[7] Kassey, Fall River, Mass.
   2. Louise[7] Kassey.
   3. Walker[7] Kassey.
2. Lelia[6] McDaniel (Walker[5] ————), m. Aylett W. Smith, Richmond, Va.
   1. Lucile[7] Smith, m. Preston W. Sledd.
   2. William[7] Smith.
3. Katherine[6] McDaniel.
4. Samuel[6] McDaniel (Walker[5] ————), m. Minnie Carter, lives at the old homestead in Bedford Co.
   1. Katherine[7] McDaniel.
   2. Samuel[7] McDaniel, Jr.
   3. Carter[7] McDaniel.
   4. Walker[7] McDaniel.
   5. Virginia[7] McDaniel.
   6. John[7] Robin McDaniel.
   7. Albert[7] McDaniel.
   8. Frances[7] McDaniel.

4. Albon[4] McDaniel (Geo.[3], Geo.[2], John[1]), Mayor of Lynchburg in 1824, for many years.

7. Cleopatra[4] Albertine McDaniel (Geo.[3], Geo.[2], John[1]) (Nov. 12, 1794-1837), m. 1st, Abner Whitten, on Mch. 4, 1812, m. 2nd, ———— McCabe.

1. Julia[5] Whitten, m. ———— McCabe.
2. Arabella[5] Whitten, m. ———— Preston.

8. Alfred[4] McDaniel (June 7, 1796-1849), m. 1815 Martha Minns, of Goochland, on May 21, 1823, Alfred McDaniel and wife, Martha, of Bedford Co., sold to Allen McDaniel, of Lynchburg, 215 acres for $1,000 land on Stoney Forks, Tofts Run.

9. John[4] Robin McDaniel (Geo.[3], Geo.[2], John[1]) (July 9, 1807-May 14, 1878), m. Aug. 17, 1837, Elizabeth[2] Foster Chaplin (W. R. Chaplin) (1821-Feb. 21, 1910). They lived in Lynchburg. She was reared by her uncle, Paul Jones, a tobacconist. John Robin and his family are buried in an underground vault in the Presbyterian Cemetery in Lynchburg. After the last member, Orianna, died, the vault was sealed up.

1. Octavia[5], lived four years.
2. Orianna[5] (May 14, 1848-Feb., 1912).

5. Margaret[3] McDaniel (Geo.[2], John[1]), d. Sunday, Aug. 26, 1798, m. 1776, 1st, Reuben[4] Rucker (Ambrose[3], John[2], Peter[1]), m. 2nd, Philip Burford, d. 1807. Philip was mentioned in his father's will as deceased naming Philip's children. (The Rucker Bible gives the births and deaths of both Margaret and her first husband, Reuben, the date of her second marriage to Philip Burford, the births and names of the children of both marriages).

Philip married second, Elizabeth, who with Geo. Tinsley, David Tinsley and Ambrose Burford were executors of Philip Burford's will, probated Dec. 21, 1807. (W. B. 4, p. 483, Amherst). (Possible, she was a Tinsley).

The same day she was appointed guardian to Philip Burford, orphan of Philip, deceased, Ambrose Rucker, Jr. (half brother) was appointed guardian to Cynethia H. Burford, orphan of Philip Burford, deceased.

Issue by first marriage:

1. Ambrose[4] Rucker.
2. Rosamond[4] Rucker.
3. Lucy[4] Rucker.

Issue by second marriage:

4. Cynthia[4] Anne Hedley Burford.
5. Philip[4] Binford.
6. George[4] Henry Burford.

6. Lucy[3] McDaniel (Geo.[2], John[1]), d. before 1818, m. James Tinsley, b. 1757.

1. Rodney[4] Tinsley, b. 1791, m. Polly Whitten.
    1. William[5] Brown Tinsley, m. Eliza Ellen Goodman. They lived near Big Island.

McDaniel Marriage Bonds, Amherst Co.

1790, Sept. 6, George McDaniel, bachelor, m. Susanna[2] Haines, Spinster (William Haines).

1781, Jan. 6, Thomas Edwards m. Winnie McDaniel. Witnesses: George McDaniel, Sr., George McDaniel, Jr., John Vaughan.

1785, Dec. 5, William Tyree, m. Frances McDaniel, dau. of George.

1791, Apr. 22, William Jacobs, bachelor, m. Margaret McDaniel, spinster, dau. of Daniel McDonald. Signed by: Daniel McDonald.

1798, Oct. 20, James Sorrell, Jr., to marry Mary McDaniel, both of Amherst. Signed by: Peggy McDaniel.

1798, July 18, James Staton, son of Thomas, of Rockbridge, to marry Mary Sorrell. Signed by: James Sorrell.

1795, July 20, James McDaniel, of Campbell, to marry Millie Goodman.

1831, John S. McDaniel to marry Rebecca Rucker.

1804, Aug. 27, James McDaniel to marry Nancy Jones.

2. Henry[2] McDaniel (John[1]), d. 1802, m. Martha Goff, dau. of John and Ann, lived in Amherst, and moved to Ninety Six District, S. C., where he died. His wife, Martha, left a will, 1774, Amherst Co., Va. Henry McDaniel sold 142 acres to Isaac Tinsley, S. S. of Tobacco Row Mts. down (D. B. D, p. 215, Amherst).

1. Archabald[3] McDaniel.
2. Ambrose[3].
3. Jeremiah[3].
4. Henry[3].
5. William[3].
6. John[3].
7. Philip[3].
    1. Ira[4] Oliver.
        1. Henry[5] D. McDaniel, Gov. of Ga., d. July, 1926, age 90.

In 1775, John, Henry, and George McDaniel of Amherst, signed a petition for a ferry over the Fluvanna River.

June 5, 1742, Anthony Ponncey of Goochland Co. to John McDaniel of same for £20, 400 acres adjoining James Defur on a branch of Mythunk Creek, Robert Adams, Carrels Creek.

Witness: H. Wood, John Sorrell, William Perry.

Fayette Co., Ky. (W. B. 13, p. 393), date July 7, 1811. Probated May, 1812.

John McDaniel, will

wife, Mary
daus. Elizabeth McDaniel
daus. Sarah Rucker
sons Enoch McDaniel
sons Enoch McDaniel
sons Boone McDaniel

gr. children Mary Johnson
gr. children James Johnson
gr. children Ennice Johnson

Witness: George Clarke
James Trotter
Mark Whitaker
George McDaniel

The following is copied from the Bible of William McDaniel, which is in the possession of his great granddaughter, Mrs. Waller Rucker, of Forest Depot, Bedford Co., Va. One page has entirely faded, some items are too indistinct to be read, and not all of the records are in the same handwriting. Since all of Rucker references have been used elsewhere, they have been omitted here:

————Noville, deceased, Oct. 27, 1820, died of a violent attack of bilious colic of 3 days.

Benjamin Morgan, deceased, June 9th, 1821, after a severe attack of 8 days illness of typhus fever, departed: his wife Sophia Oct. 31, 1824, when after Morgan's death she married a Mr. Norville.

Mr. George MacDaniel died 22, Nov. 1821, worn out with old age.

Mr. Richard Jones departed this life Sept. 9th 1823, with a lingering illness of 11 months, supposed to be a consumption.

Departed this life on Saturday Oct. 19, 1823, with the fever, Mr. William Cartweel.

Departed this life on Monday Feb. 10, 1824 Mr. Isaac Tinsley A. C.

Departed this life May 13, 1853 (Billy) William I. McDaniel.

Departed this life May 3, 1832 Frasier A. R. Davis.

Departed this life June 15, 1832, Roderick Davis.

Departed this life July 28, 1877 James P. MacDaniel after 8 months of severe suffering.

Ann Dangerfield Quarles daughter of Henry W. and Jane Quarles was born on Saturday 21st of Oct. 1827.

Mr. John MacDaniel Sr. departed this life Jan. 23d 1830.

Tinsley MacDaniel departed this life Dec. 26, 1839.

Mrs. Harris departed this life Apr. 29 1844, consort of Mr. Marshall Harris.

Mrs. Judith Haskill departed this life June 4th, 1844.

John Edward MacDaniel was born June 4, 1832, his age at this time present is 18 years, 2 months and 21 Days, written by John Edward MacDaniel.

Nancy Woodroof was married to Thomas H. Bass May 18, 1820.

John R. Hansard was born Nov. 10 1806.

James Pendleton and Sally Rucker were married in 1769.

Sally MacDaniel was born July 6, 1802.

George MacDaniel was born 1804.

Catherine MacDaniel was born Mch. 27, 1807.

James MacDaniel was born June 19, 1809.

Betsy MacDaniel was born May 31, 1811.

John MacDaniel was born Jan. 2, 1813.

Jane MacDaniel was born Feb. 22, 1815.

William MacDaniel was born Sept. 3, 1817.

Lindsey MacDaniel was born Jan. 5, 1819.

Mary Ann MacDaniel was born Feb. 2nd at night about 4 o'clock.

Philip B. MacDaniel was born May 10, 1834.

John B. MacDaniel was born 1827.

Edward Jackson MacDaniel was born March 14, 1829.

Lucy Brockenborough Quarles, daughter of Henry and Jane Quarles was born Dec. 10, 1835, about 6 o'clock P. M.

Mrs. James Pendleton departed this life Oct. 16, 1825.

Mr. Lock R. Franklin departed this life Oct. 24, 1825.

Margaret R. MacDaniel died 17th of Oct. 1826, in the 22nd year of her age.

John Hansard departed this life on Nov. 24, 1826.

Mr. James Pendleton departed this life on Monday, July 2, 1832, age 82 years.

Mr. William MacDaniel departed this life on Thursday, 17th of June 1851, Age 75 years.

Sally MacDaniel married 16 of Oct. 1817.

Betsy MacDaniel married 17 Nov. 1825.

Catherine MacDaniel married 21st Oct. 1824.

James MacDaniel married 11Th Feb. 1837.

John B. MacDaniel and Elizabeth Thurman were married Wednesday the 19 of Sept. 1837, by the Rev. MacDaniel of Lynchburg.

Henry W. Quarles and Jane Macdaniel were married on Tuesday March 12,1833, by the Rev. Charles H. Page.

Sally Pendleton departed this life 16th of Oct. 1825.

Stage Pendleton departed this life Nov. 18, 1825.

Mrs. W. R. Roan departed this life Oct. 8, 1829.

James Pendleton was born April 3, 1750.

Sarah Pendleton (his wife) was b. July 25, 1750.

Betsy Pendleton was b. Dec. 19, 1787.

William MacDaniel was b. Feb. 22, 1770.

Sarah Elizabeth Quarles daughter of Henry and Jane was b. Sunday 9 of Feb. 1834.

Peggy R. MacDaniel departed this life 17 of Oct. 1826, age 21 Years, 11 months.

Sarah R. Meyars departed this life Oct. 3rd 1827. Age 25 years, 2 months.

Mr. William MacDaniel departed this life 20, Nov. 1839, Judge of Campbell Court.

Edward Jackson MacDaniel departed this life Oct. 8, 1832, age 3 years.

Mrs. Elizabeth the wife of William MacDaniel departed, 17, of May 1838, age 50.

Clary Woodroof departed this life Feb. 22, 1825, age 86 years, consort of David Woodroof deceased.

William MacDaniel departed this life 10, Oct. 1831.

Delivered on the 20th of July 1828 the greatest sermon I ever heard by the Rev. Ozgood at Rucker's Church. William MacDaniel. (Signed)

Prosser

John[2] Prosser and Henry Creighton patented 424 acres of land in Rappahannock County in the fork of said river on South Side, and on Swan and Snow Creeks, July, 1660 (L. Gr., b. 6, p. 348).

He and his wife, Martha, sold land to Col. John Catlett, 17 June 1665. He and his wife, Martha, sold land to John White in 1660, again in 1668. John Prosser patented 4,892 acres of land on the Freshes of the Rappahannock River, above navigation next to John Paine's, over a creek called the Golden Vale, adjoining John Gillet's dec'd, to Clements Herbert's, near the head of Muzazine Swamp, for transporting 90 persons, 1665 (B. 5, p. 479, L. Gr.).

John and wife, Martha, sold land to John Wait, 4 Feb. 1666 (D. B. 2, p. 115, Rappa. Co.).

He appointed my well beloved friend, Mr. Richard Welby, my attorney, 12 May 1665 (D. B. 2, Rappa. Co.).

He sold 1,000 acres of land to Anthony Savage, land in Rappa. Co., April 9, 1670. He with Thomas Powell patented

5,200 acres for transporting ...... persons into the colony in 1673 (B. 6, p. 489, L. Gr.).

John Prosser patented 480 acres of land on the Golden Vaile Creek on the S. S. Rapahannock river for transporting 8 persons, Oct. 20, 1684 (B. 7, p. 400, L. Gr.).

John Prosser, of Rappahannock Co., sold to John Stephens, of Abbington Parish, Gloucester, for 9,000 lbs. of tobacco, land lying in Rappahannock Co. on S. S. of the Freshes of the Rappahannock River, house, orchard, ———, 3 Jan. 1671. Signed—John Prosser, Margaret Prosser (D. B. 4, Rappa. Co.).

John Prosser deeded for love and affection that I do and shall constantly bear unto the memory of my deceased wife, Martha, and for services done by Martha, the only daughter of my said wife, to Martha and her husband, Thomas Kendall, 300 acres of land. Will of John Prosser dated 28 Aug. 1673, prob. 30 June 1677.

John Prosser of Golden Vale, Sittingbourne Parish, Rappa. Co., Va.

To my wife, Margaret, 500 acres of land on the North Side of Rappa. River.

(He) to be buried by my first wife, Martha.

To my eldest son, John Prosser, the plantation, called Nutgrove.

To my son, Samuel 400 acres.

To my son, Roger, 1,100 acres, land on the Mattaponi Swamp.

To my sons-in-law, Robert Goffe and Thomas Goffe, 200 acres jointly in the Golden Valle.

To son, Anthony Prosser.

Witness: John Wright, Hugh Pallmer.

Issue:

1. Martha Prosser, m. Thomas Kendall.
2. John Prosser.
3. Samuel Prosser.
4. Roger Prosser.
5. Anthony Prosser.

Step-son, Robert Goffe.

Step-son, Thomas Goffe (see Gough).

John Prosser was married twice, 1st Martha and 2nd, Margaret Goffe, a widow before 1671, with two sons, Robert and Thomas Goffe. The Kendall name first appears in Accomac, later in Rappahannock Co. Col. Wm. Kendall pat. 600 acres formerly belonging to Capt. John How, dec'd, at the same time

Mary Kendall, daughter of Lieut. Col. Wm. Kendall, patented 300 acres in Accomac on the seaboard side 1664 (Vol. 4, p. 621, L. Gr.).

Col. Wm. Kendall patented 300 acres in the county of Northampton at the head of Cherriston adjoining Francis Pettet and John Savage, to Capt. Philip Taylour's dec'd, to Wm. Andrews, to Col. Obed Robins, land formerly granted to Maj. Wm. Andrews, 1 Sept. 1664.

Gough—Goffe

The name first appears in York, then New Kent, King and Queen, King William, Rappahannock, Essex, King George, Richmond, and one branch moved to Orange, then to Amherst. The records of three of these counties have been destroyed; it is impossible to trace them. The spelling of the name varies often, twice in the same document.

John Goffe patented 400 acres of land on Aracio Swamp, adjoining another division of said Goffe's, 5 Opr. 1664 (B. 5, p. 420, L. Gr.).

Margaret[1] married 1st, Gough or Goffe; 2nd, John Prosser, who died in Rappa. Co., 1671, will mentioned "Sons-in-law, Robert and Thomas Goffe. She received 500 acres on the north side of the Rappa. by will of her husband, John Prosser (now in King George Co.).

Issue:

1. Robert[2] Goffe.
2. Thomas[2] Goffe.

2. Thomas[2] Goffe (Margaret[1]), died before 1726, m. Margaret ————. His step-father, John Prosser, left to him by will dated 1671, ½ interest in 200 acres of land on the south side of the Rappahannock River (now Essex). The entire 200 acres Thomas sold. He bought 200 acres of land in Westmoreland Co., which later was sold by two of his sons, Thomas and John Goffe.

John Willis, of Richmond Co., patented land, beginning at the head of Mary Gunstocker, on Indian or the Rappahannock River, in the clive adjoining Thomas Goffe, to John Arnold's, 19 Mch. 1696/7 (Vol. 2, p. 264, N. N. L. Gr.). The same day Thomas Kendall patented 105 acres of land in Richmond Co. in the clive adjoining Thomas Goffe. The same day Thomas Goffe of Richmond county patented 105 acres, beginning at Thomas

Kendall's, back of Mary Gunstocker in the clive, to John Willis's, at the head of Warasque Creek (same book and page, B. 2, p. 266, N. N. L. Gr.).

Thomas Goffe of St. Mary's Parish, Richmond Co., deeded to his daughter, Margaret, wife of Isaac Arnold, land adjoining said Goffe and John Willis, Jr. Margaret, wife of Thomas Goffe, signed the deed, Feb. 28, 1707 (D. B. 4, p. 126, Rd. Co.).

Thomas Goffe and wife, Margaret, were administrators of Wm. Goffe, deceased, with Isaac Arnold security, 4 Apr. 1716 (B. 7, p. 114, Rd. Co.).

Thomas Goffe now appears in King George County, on 14 Jan. 1723 he sold to Joseph Trougher of Essex Co., 200 acres of land in St. Mary's Parish, Essex Co., which was bequeathed to said Thomas and Robert Goff by one John Prosser, dec'd. Margaret, wife of Thomas Goffe, signed the deed. Witness: Isaac Arnold, Jonathan Gibson, John Gibson, Peter Gibbon (D. B. 17, p. 207, Essex).

William Kendall of Stafford Co., sold to Jere Murdock of King George Co., merchant, for 2,000 lbs. of tobacco, the land where Wm. Kendall formerly lived, purchased by Thomas Goffe from Maj. Wright, 28 Sept. 1726 (D. B. 8, p. 179, King George Co.).

1. Margaret^3 Goffe, wife of Isaac Arnold.
2. Thomas^3 Goffe.
3. John^3 Goffe.
4. Wm.^{3} Goffe.

1. Margaret^3 Gough (Thomas^2, Margaret^1), married Isaac Arnold, Jr., her father gave her land as a marriage dower.

"In consideration of a marriage already held between Isaac Arnold Jr. and Margaret, my daughter", Thomas Gough and wife, Margaret, of St. Mary's Parish, "Deed land lying between John Willis Jr. and Thomas Goff, 158 acres patented by said Goff, Mch. 1696" (D. B. 4, p. 126, Richmond Co.), 1707.

2. Thomas^3 Goffe (Thomas^2, Margaret^1), lived in King George Co., wife Sarah. Thomas Goffe of Hanover Parish sold to his brother, John Goffe, of Washington Parish, Westmoreland Co., 70 acres of land, out of 200 acres purchased by my father, Thomas Goffe, dec'd, late of Hanover Parish, King George Co., from Maj. Francis Wright, and son, John Wright, land in Washington Parish, adjoining Wm. Kendall and Thomas Hughes, 29 Sept., 1726 (D. B. 8, p. 192, Westmoreland Co.).

Thomas Gough of Overwharton Parish, Stafford, sold to Jeremiah Murdock of Hanover Parish, King Geo. Co., merchant, land in Washington Parish, Westmoreland Co., two small tracts signed "Thomas Gough". Sarah, wife of Thomas, acknowledged her dower and "inheritance of and to the land", land in the actual possession of Murdock 70 acres and 50 acres (D. B. 11, p. 53, 13 Mch. 1746, King Geo.).

The 70 acre tract is in line with Maj. Murdock, land bought of "John Gough" adjoining "Thomas Gough", 13 Mch. 1746 (D. B. 11, p. 52, Westmoreland).

3. John[3] Goffe (Thomas[2], Margaret[1]), wife, Anne, d. in Amherst 1763. In 1726 John bought 70 acres of land in Washington Par., Westmoreland Co., from his brother, Thomas (see above), land purchased by their father, Thomas Goffe, deceased.

In 1737 John Gough, Sr., bought from William Watson 200 acres of land in Orange County in the little forks of the Rappahannock River. 1 March, 1738, John Howard sold to John Goff, both of Orange Co., 100 acres of land sold by James Taylor to Edward Tinsley, 1722 (D. B. 3, p. 133, Orange Co.).

John was paying tithes in Orange Co. in 1739. He and his wife, Ann, of Orange Co., sold to Jeremiah Murdock of King George Co., 70 acres of land adjoining Murdock and Thomas Gough, 29 July 1740, for £36, land in Washington Par., Westmoreland (D. B. 9, p. 100, Westmoreland Co.). In the Calendars of State Papers, July 30, 1742, is a petition from Orange County signed by John Goffe, requesting better defense "from the Indians". They are living in the back part of state.

John Goff of St. Marks Par., Orange Co., sold to Peter Rucker of same, 215 acres at the South West Mountains adjoining the land of Susanna Rucker, Wm. Golding, John Baylor and Timothy Crosswaith, in exchange for a tract owned by Peter Rucker in Albemarle Co., 22 Nov. 1750 (D. B. 2, p. 217, Orange).

1751, John Gough of St. Anne Parish, Albemarle Co., bought from Peter Rucker of Orange, 463 acres land on Harris Creek, known as Peter Rucker's lot, for £200, adjoining Robert Rose, John Rucker, Wm. Miller and David Rosser (D. B. I, p. 382, Albemarle Co.).

A petition of John Goffe praying to be allowed pay for a horse taken from him by the Cherokee Indians in their march through the county of Albemarle, was presented to the house and read (House of Burgess, Vol. 1759-61, p. 213). Resolved that the petition of John Goffe to be paid, for a mare taken and car-ried away by the Catawba Indians is reasonable and ought to be allowed the sum of 10 pounds Sterling for the mare. Tuesday 17th of March, 1761 (p. 217).

George McDaniel and wife, Margaret, of Amherst, deeded to "Leonard, Joseph, Ambrose, John Goffe and Elijah Moran, 500 acres of land on Stoney Creek as per agreement between himself and John Goff dec'd, in exchange for 153 acres on Harris Creek. Signed—George and Margaret McDaniel, 5 Aug. 1765 (D. B. B, p. 36, Amherst Co.).

Another deed made by "Leonard Goff, son and heir of John Goff, and his wife, Ann," to George McDaniel as per agreement, Leonard Goff (and wife, Ann) son and heir of John, deeded to Peter, John, Ambrose, Benjamin, Isaac, Anthony Rucker, Sarah Marr, Winifred Lee, Mella Ham and Phoebe Rucker of Amherst 100 acres for £50, land adjoining Burford's and Rucker's, 5 July 1769, Amherst.

Will of John Goff of Amherst dated 30 Nov. 1762, probated 2 Mch. 1763.

To my wife, Anne, all of my estate.

To my sons, Leonard Goff, Ambrose Goff, Joseph Goff, Elizabeth Goff, land on Stovell and Bowling Creeks. Execs.: Sons, Leonard and Joseph Goff.

Anne relinquished her right as administratrix and on motion of Ambrose Rucker, he was appointed administrator of the will of John Goff, John Rucker and George McDaniel security (W. B. 1, p. 25, Amherst Co.). Inventory returned 5 Sept. 1763, by Richard Shelton and Benjamin Rucker.

Issue:

1. Leonard Goff.
2. Ambrose Goff.
3. John Goff.
4. Joseph Goff.
5. Elizabeth Moran.
6. Martha McDaniel, wife of Henry.
7. Margaret McDaniel, wife of George.

See a copy of the records in the McDaniel Bible on pp. 407 *et sec.* Not only the Bible record but family tradition has always attributed Martha and Margaret Goff as being wives of the two brothers, Henry and George McDaniel. Thus far nothing has disproved the record. John Gough of King William Co. in 1702 brought into this country a Daniel Mac Daniel, who may have been the progenitors of George and Henry (see page following).

To John Gough 550 acres land in King Wm. Co. on ye head of the branches of Perry Swamp that issues with the upper Herring Creek on S. branch of Perry's Swamp, on the S. S. of North Wales path, to Chicoley Corbin Thacker's line, due John Gough for transporting 11 persons 28 Oct. 1702.

Names of those transported: Anne Jones, Daniel Mackdaniel, Margaret Edisson, Sarah Man, Robert Boy, Samuel Ingram, Henry Dill, John Murrah, Robert Boyce, Richard Blecker, Daniel Emrie (B. P, p. 487, L. Gr.).

Hotten's Emigrants. From London to Virginia on the ship, Constance, Mathew Gough, age 28.

To Elizabeth Cittee Co. by George Sapheir in 1636, Mathew Gough.

To Virginia, imported by John Hudson in 1637, of Charles River County, Walton Goffe.

Opher Gough, in 1651 transported by Col. Giles Brent of Northumberland.

King Wm. Co. (Rd., Va.), book 11, p. 193-94.

Will of Wm. Claybourn, dated 10 Jan. 1705, prob. 30 Jan. 1705.

To my sister, Ursula Gough, wife of Wm. Gough, 600 lbs. of Tobacco, 5 or 6 years after my death.

To Edward Ran and sister, Mary C. Ran.

To my brother, Wm. Gough.

To Clayborne Gough, son of my said sister and brother, Ursula and Wm. Gough, also the gun his father hath of mine.

To my cousin, Annie Coakes, 600 lbs. of Tobacco.

To Lewis Johnson, Henry Piggs, Nicholas Lauder.

To Mr. John Banister the land on Black Creek in New Kent, to Henry Madison, to McDaniel.

To my cousin, Tho. Clayborne.

To my son, Wm. Clayborne when 16 years of age.

To my dau. Elizabeth when she marries.

Execs.: Tho. Clayborne, George Clough. Witness: Richard Goss, Wm. Gough, Mary Clayborne.

The following records are of the same name, but the connection is not clear:

John[1] Goffe patented 400 acres in New Kent, adjoining another divised of said Goffe on the Aricaico Swamp, for transporting 8 persons, 5 Apr. 1664 (B. 5, p. 426, L. Gr.).

Capt. Leonard Chamberlane patented 70 acres joining aforesaid survey of 500 acres in New Kent Co., at Ashwell Batten's in Capt. Chamberlane's old line on Aracaico Swamp for transporting two persons, 22 May 1657. (Side note on the same page: "This patent was recorded 5 Feb. 1663 in John Goffe's name to whom it was assigned by the said Chamberlane and now granted by Geo. Berkley"). (B. 4, p. 140, L. Gr.).

Ashwell Batten patented 750 acres land in Gloucester on the Cheesecake Path leading toward Mattopony River on Araykaio branch at Leonard Chamberlain's, 13 Oct. 1653 (B. 3, p. 84, L. Gr.).

Capt. John Gough was a member of the Board of Trade in New Kent in 1680 (Va. Historical Magazine, Vol. 1, p. 234).

"A minister of Southwarke Parish on the opposite side of the river, John Goffe of New Kent, Gent, made a deed in York Co. in 1686 to his son, William, in view of his marrying Elizabeth Dixon.

York Co., b. 9, p. 61, 23 Sept. 1685.

John Goffe of New Kent Co., Va. Whereas a marriage is intended between my son, Wm. Goffe, and Eliz. Dixon, daughter-in-law to John Rogers, I give to my son, Wm. Goffe, 500 acres pur. of Ralph Green in Gloucester Co. Said land in forks of Arrocacoe in New Kent. John Gough. Wit.: John Rogers, Agnes Rogers.

Wm. Gough patented 1,000 acres of land in New Kent on North side of the Mattopony River for transporting 20 persons, 7 Oct. 1658 (B. 4, p. 327, L. Gr., King and Queen later), on the S. S. of Whorecock creek.

Martha Goffe patented 650 acres land formerly granted to Wm. Gough by patent 22 July 1659 and by Wm. Assigned to John Maddison and assigned by Maddison to Martha Goffe, 8 Feb. 1663 (B. 5, p. 297, L. Gr.).

Wm. Gough patented land in King and Queen Co. formerly New Kent adjoining Capt. Chamberlayne, the said land being formerly granted to *John Goffe* by patent dated 15 May 1661 and by him granted unto *the* aforesaid *Wm. Gough* Ap. 28, 1694, for transportation, 26 Oct. 1694 (B. 8, p. 400, L. Gr.).

Granted unto Mr. William Gough 1,225 acres land lying in King and Queen County, at the head of Aricacoe Creek, at the mouth of Arracacoe Main Swamp to Papotello Swamp, land being due unto the said Mr. Gough as followeth: 450 acres part of a grant to Capt. Leonard Chamberlayne, patented by him dated 15 April 1663, and by said Chamberlaine conveyed to John Gough, and 400 acres another part thereof formerly granted to John Gough, patent dated 5 April 1664, and 300 acres another formerly granted to John Curle's, and by him conveyed unto Thomas Reeves, and by the said Reeves conveyed to the said John Gough, and by him sold 15 May 1663, also 70 acres of land, the residue granted to the said John Gough by patent dated 7 May 1661, and since granted to said William Gough by patent 26 Oct. 1694, the said land coming to the said William, as son and heir to the said Mr. John Gough (D. 9, p. 96-97, L. Gr.).

Register of Christ Church, Middlesex, May 31, 1688, Wm. Gough of New Kent, married Alice Thacker of this Parish, at Henry Thacker's.

Wm.[2] (John[1]) Gough held a public office in King and Queen Co. in 1699.

Journals of the House of Burgess, 1700-02. Wm. Goffe d. in King and Queen Co., 1699. A member of the house of Burgess, Wm. Byrd, took his place.

From The Huguenot Emigration by R. A. Brock, p. 65. When money was collected for provisions for the use of the French refugees in 1700, Wm. Gough gave 1 pound sterling.

Will of a James Gough of North Farnum Parish, dated Feb. 170½, probated July 2, 1702. To my sons James and Rowland Gough my lands. To my son Henry Gough, to my dau. Joan Cook, to dau. Elizabeth Diehonson, to son in law William Gough. Signed James Gough (W. B. 2, p. 1, Richmond Co., Va.).

Parke—Parks

The first mention of Thomas Parke was in the order book of Essex County, 1692-95, page 55, when a suit between Thomas Parks and John Decson is recorded, 1692.

A George Parke was sheriff of the county of Essex during this period, died there, 1698.

Henry Parke was living in Old Rappahannock Co., Sept. 5, 1677 (B. 1677-82, p. 137).

Robert Park of Old Rappahannock Co. returned an inventory of the estate of Robert Henly, with William Barber security, 1685 (W. B. 6, p. 65, Old Rappa. Co.).

Thomas Parke bought a life interest in land belonging to Simon Miller, land in Richmond County, January 14, 1692 (D. B. 1692, 1693).

July 6, 1725, Thomas Park was a witness in Spotsylvania County.

Alexander Spotswood sold 100 acres of land in St. George Parish, Spotsylvania County, in the forks of the Rappahannock River, and Hunting Run, to Thomas Parks, son John Parks, son Thomas Parks, Jr., and son Samuel Parks, for their joint lives, April 2, 1729 (D. B. A, p. 377, Spotsylvania County).

John Graeme, attorney of Alexander Spotswood, acknowledged a deed of conveyance to Thomas, John, Thomas, Jr., and Samuel Parks (O. B., Apr. 2, 1729).

On May 18, 1736, Thomas Parks bought 380 acres of land on Muddy Creek in the great branch of the Rappahannock River, adjoining John Latham and Col. Henry Willis from John Latham and wife, Elizabeth, of Caroline County (W. B. 1, p. 244, Orange County).

Thomas Park of Orange County for love and affection deeded 200 acres of land to "son, Samuel Parks of same county", in the great forks of the Rappahannock River, on Muddy Run, adjoining John Latham and Philemon Kavenaugh (D. B. 4, p. 355, Orange County).

July 7, 1741, Thomas Parks of Orange, deeded to Christopher Hutchins of same, 147 acres for 20 lbs., land in the forks of the Rappahannock River, on Muddy Run, adjoining Philemon Kavenaugh. Witness, Philip Clayton. Signed Thomas Park (D. B. 6, p. 182, Orange).

Thomas Park's name does not appear again in the counties of Orange or Culpeper, but in 1751 he bought in Albemarle County 400 acres of land in St. Anns Parish, Nov. 13, 1751, from John Graves of Caroline, adjoining Benjamin Stinnet (D. B. 1, p. 395, Albemarle).

Will of Thomas Parks dated Feb. 24, 1752, probated in Albemarle on March 12th, 1761 (W. B. 2, p. 101, Albemarle County).

Will of Thomas Park of Ballingers Mountains, Albemarle County.

To son, Thomas, my estate, and one shilling each to my sons, John, Samuel and Charles, daughters Martha Russell, Mary Bond and Elizabeth Hutchins. (Signed) Thomas Park. Witness: Daniel Burford, Ellex F. Duggins.

1. Thomas^2 Park.
2. John^2 Park.
3. Charles^2, m. Susanna ———.
4. Sammuel^2, m. Mary North.

5. Martha[2], m. ———— Russel.
6. Mary[2], m. ———— Bond.
7. Elizabeth[2], m. Christopher Hutchins.

1. Thomas[2] Parks, Jr. (Thomas[1]), born in Essex. His name was mentioned in a deed made in Essex, when his father bought land in 1729. He inherited his father's estate in Amherst.

Matthew Tucker, Thomas Parks, John Phillips and John Penn were ordered to view the road from Thomas Parks road into the main road below George Penn's. January, 1769 (O. B. 1, p. 445, Amherst County).

Thomas Parks, Jr., of Amherst, sold to Noell Johnson for £200, 400 acres of land in Amherst. Signed Thomas Park.

Priscilla Park, wife of Thomas, signed the deed, May 1, 1769 (D. B. B, p. 420, Amherst Co.). Thomas Park moved to Pittsylvania Co., Va. Also O. B. 1, p. 480.

2. John[2] Park (Thomas[1]), b. Essex, d. in Wilkes County, N. C., wife, Mary.

He bought 190 acres of land on Muddy Run of the Rappahannock River, from John Chapman of Caroline, in St. Marks Parrish, adjoining John Lathan's line, for 280 lbs. of tobacco, 1737 (D. B. 2, p. 186, Orange County).

The same year he sold this land to Edward Dillard of King and Queen County, 190 acres, land in the great forks of the Rappahannock River, Mary, wife of John Park, signed the deed. Witness: John Lathan (D. B. 2, p. 197, Orange).

In 1739, October 20th, he bought 250 acres of land from Francis Kirthy of Orange on the north side of Mountain Run, in the great forks of the Rappahannock River.

John Parks of Culpeper County deeded to son, John Parks, Jr., 300 acres of land in Culpeper, adjoining Philip Clayton, Feb. 21, 1754 (D. B. B, p. 51, Culpeper).

On motion of Mary Parks, a witness for Richard Bridges and Sarah, his wife, in a suit against Christopher Hoomes (O. B. 1747-40, p. 417, Orange County), we find nothing more of John, Sen., in Orange or Culpeper, but in 1750 he bought land for his sons, William and John, Jr., in Amherst Co.

John Parks bought 100 acres of land from Robert Rose on the West side of Piny River, during the natural lives of William Parks and John Parks, Jr. "John Parks to plant at least 100 apple trees and keep it well fenced, and not to work over four tithable persons." 1750, Albemarle County (D. B. 1, p. 225).

September 7, 1767, John Parks, Sr., sold 100 acres to —— Landrum. Land on Pyna River purchased in 1750 of Robert Rose.

John Parks, Sen., of St. Anne Parish, bought 390 acres from Pierce Wade, on Threshers Creek, Nov. 9, 1760 (D. B. 2, p. 342), Albemarle County.

6 July, 1767, John Parks certified to having raised 910 lbs. of merchantable hemp (O. B. 1766, p. 159, Amherst Co.

He was appointed surveyor of a road from below Buffalo River to Puppies Creek, William Parks, John Parks and others to help clear the same (O. B. 1766, p. 160, Amherst).

John Parks, Sen., of Amherst Co., and wife Mary sold to Aaron Higginbotham for 40 lbs. of tobacco, 378 acres of land in Amherst, that John had bought of Jeremiah Wade, Oct. 3, 1768 (D. B. B, p. 381, Amherst Co.).

John Parks and wife Mary sign a deed in Amherst Co. (sold land), Oct., 1768 (O. B. I, p. 413, Amherst Co.).

William Parks was appointed Surveyor of the road from Puppies creek to Carters Mill in the room of John Parks, who has removed out of the county, Mch. 6, 1769 (O. B. 1766-69, p. 451).

In 1778 William Terrell and wife Sarah, of Wilkes Co., N. C., sold land in Albemarle Co., Va., and acknowledged the deed before John Parks, Justice of the Peace of Wilkes Co. (Recorded in Albemarle).

Issue:

1. John[3] Parks, Jr.
2. William[3] Parks.

2. William[3] Parks (John[2], Thomas[1]), b. c. 1730, was killed by the Indians in Powell's valley, Washington Co. (now Lee Co., Va.), 1776. He m. first Tabitha (dau. of Edward Ware, of Amherst), d. before 1766; m. second Mary Dawson (dau. of Martin), of Amherst Co., about 1766, b. about 1748, d. after 1808. William was in Albemarle (now Amherst) as early as 1748, at which time William brought suit against Anthony Gavin, May, 1748 (O. B. 6, p. 435, Goochland Co.).

Aug., 1749. "John Studivant of Prince George County, a witness for William Parks against Anthony Gaving, Parks to pay Studivant for coming and going 50 miles 13 times, paying 2,325 lbs. of tobacco (O. B. 6, p. 541, Albemarle Co.).

He paid 50 lbs. of tobacco to Payne for attendance as a witness.

6 Oct. 1766, William Park's petition against John Sandidge is continued (O. B. 1766-69, p. 159, Amherst County).

3 August, 1767, William Parks certified that he raised 500 lbs. Hemp (O. B. 1766, p. 191).

6 March 1769, William Parks was appointed Surveyor of road from Puppies Creek to Carters Mill in room of John Parks who has removed out of the County.

April 10, 1750, Robert Rose, Clerk, to John Parks, Planter, 100 acres, part of patent to R. Rose on W. side of Piney River. A tract of land during natural lives of William Parks and John Parks, Jr., and to pay said R. Rose and heirs every year during the term, on the 26th of December, 436 lbs. of tobacco at Richmond, or Warwock Warehouses, and if rent lapses for 60 days, from appointed time, said Rose or heirs to retain land as former estate. John Parks to plant at least 100 apple trees and keep it well fenced, and not work over four tithable persons (D. and W. B. 1, p. 225, Albemarle Co.).

William executed a bond to Edward Ware to the amount of 500 lbs. of tobacco for the use of his son, John Parks, Jr., "Son of my former wife, Tabitha, daughter of Edward Ware, and only child of that marriage." Sept. 5, 1768 (D. B. B, p. 368, Amherst.

David Ware and wife, Elizabeth, of St. Anne Parish, Albemarle, sold to William Parks of same, 180 acres for 75 lbs. sterling, which was formerly granted to Howard, 12 July, 1750, adjoining Pierce Wade, with houses (W. B. 3, p. 34, Amherst). Witness: Edmond Powell, Thomas Parks, Jonathan Stampe.

On November 4th, 1771, William and his wife, Mary, sold 180 acres of land on Threshers Creek to John Webb, adjoining Pierce Wade. (Signed) William Parks (D. B. C, p. 244, Amherst Co.).

William moved with others to Wilkes County, N. C., but did not buy land there. He was sent with a company from North Carolina against the Cherokee Indians. It was claimed he was an officer, but we cannot find any evidence. He evidently stayed in Washington County, Virginia, for his father patented a tract of land there, on account of settlement. The patent was made out, 1783, and recorded, 1794, to the heirs of William Parks.

In reference to the death of William Parks (Summers' *History of Southwest Virginia,* page 115), states that in 1771 the Holston settlement received a large number of emigrants from North Carolina, on account of trouble with the Governor, Tyron.

Also, page 285-6: In the fall of the year, 1777, Gen. George Rogers Clark travelling from Kentucky over the wilderness road, on his way to Richmond, reached Mumps Ford in Powell's Valley about ten days subsequent to the killing by the Indians of a settler by the name of ——— Parks.

Virginia Historical Magazine, Vol. 6, p. 344, gives the same statement about the "killing of ——— Parks, in Powell's Valley."

Mathew Brooks of North Carolina wrote a letter to Maj. Anthony Bledsoe dated May 30, 1776, among the happenings, he states, "——— Parks had been killed by the Indians in Powell's Valley" (copied from Lyman Draper's 4 qq., p. 46).

The following is the patent "In right of settlement" (L. Gr., Vol. 30, p. 504), July, 1794, Washington County.

"Henry Lee, Esq., Governor of the Commonwealth of Virginia, by virtue of a Land office Pre-emption Warrant, No. 2385, There is granted by the said Commonwealth unto Martin Parks, William Parks, Sally Parks, who intermarried with Samuel Burks and Eiizabeth Parks, children of William Parks, deceased, assignee of Samuel Parks, John Parks, Sen., George Parks and Benjamin Parks, the heir at law to John Parks, Junior, who was heir at law to the said William Parks, deceased.

A certain tract of land containing 335 acres, by survey, bearing date, the 20th day of March, 1786, lying in Washington County, on the waters of Indian Creek and Powell's Valley, and bounded as followeth, to-wit, Beginning at the foot of Cumberland Mountains at Gibson's land, to a corner to his own settlement right and with the line thereof.

Near a sink hole, to Gray's line, also on page 506, 23 July, 1794, by virtue of a certificate in Right of Settlement, given by the Commonwealth, for adjusting the titles of unpatented land, in Washington County, and in consideration of the ancient compensation of two pounds sterling, paid by John Parks, there is granted unto Martin Parks—a certain parcel of land, containing 400 acres on both sides of Indian Creek, in Powell's Valley (same as above) to Gray's line, crossing the Kentucky tract near a sink hole to Gibson's line, a certain parcel of land containing 400 acres, by survey bearing date 20 March, 1786."

"BE IT KNOWN TO ALL PERSONS BY THESE PRESENTS we the undersubscribers of the State of North Carolina and Wilks County for and in consideration of five shillings in hand paid to each of us the receipt whereof we do hereby acknowledge, we have Bargained, Sold and Relinquished unto the legally born children of William Parks formally residenter in the State of Virginia & since killed by the Indians in Powell's Valley, all right, title claim and interest that each or either of us may have by descent or by any other way of means whatever, to all the estate both real and personal of John Parks, Jr., late of Amherst County, in the State of Virginia, but since decd.

IN WITNESS WHEREOF we have hereunto set our hands and seals this 9th day of July in the year 1787.

Samuel Parks (L. S.), John Parks (L. S.), George Parks (L. S.), Benjamin Parks (L. S.), son of John Parks, Jr.

At a court held for Amherst County the third day of September, 1787. This bill sale was proved by the oath of Jessee Dawson and Edward Tinsley, witnesses thereto, and ordered to be recorded. (D. B. F., p. 198, Amherst Co.)

Teste:

William Loving, Clerk.

After William's death, Mary and her children moved back to Amherst, her father, Martin Dawson, leaving her a legacy in his will.

On 3 Sept., 1787, Gabriel Penn was appointed Guardian to Martin Parks, son of William Parks, deceased. Samuel Higginbotham security. (W. B. 2, p. 250, Amherst County).

William Tinsley, Jr., was appointed Guardian to William Parks, orphan of W. Parks, deceased.

Zacharia Dawson was appointed guardian to Elizabeth, daughter of Wiliam Parks, deceased.

The will of William Parks was proved in Amherst County, in 1778 by Martin Dawson.

The Widow, Mary, qualified as executrix. The will was "ordered to lie for further proof", a natural doubt when fighting the Indians.

Mary Dawson Parks was living in Amherst until 1802.

Will of William Parks to my wife, Mary, to my son, John Parks, son of my first wife, Tabatha, a negro girl, Nell, when he becomes of age, should he die before he comes of age, to my son, Martin Parks. The estate to be unsold until the youngest child becomes of age. To son, Martin, by my second wife, Mary . . . Sarah . . . to my Children. 27 Sept., 1769. Probated Dec. 7, 1778.

Executors: Benjamin Parks, William Dawson.

Witness: Martin Dawson, Elizabeth Dawson, Benjamin Bromhead. (W. B. I, p. 475, Amherst Co., Va.)

Issue by first wife:

1. John[4] Parks, Jr.

Issue by second wife:

2. Sarah[4].
3. Martin[4].
4. William[4] Parks.
5. Margaret[4].
6. Elizabeth[4].

1. John[4] Parks, Jr. (William[3], John[2], Thomas[1]), d. 1786, leaving no will; m. 1st ——————, leaving one son, Benjamin Parks; m. 2nd, May 17, 1785, Elizabeth, daughter of Philip Thurman, of Amherst County. (See Bill of Sale). It states, "Benjamin, the eldest son of John Parks, deceased, the eldest son of William Parks, deceased, late of Amherst."

Philip Thurman left a will in Amherst, dated Sept. 3, 1803, probated Dec. 19, 1803, Amherst, in which Elizabeth Parks was left a legacy.

The negro, Nell, left to John Parks, Jr., by his father, William, by will dated 1769, was left at John's death in the possession of his second wife, Elizabeth (Thurman) Parks. John only lived one year. Elizabeth was the administratrix of the estate of John in 1786, the same year she married her neighbor, Moses[4] Rucker (Isaac[3], John[2], Peter[1]) and took the slave Nell to her new home to Moses Rucker's as "Part of her dower" also Nell's "Increase". Ben. Elizabeth Rucker died in 1820, leaving the negroes in the possession of Moses Rucker, Benjamin Parks, son of John, Jr., deceased, son of William, deceased, claimed the negroes as property coming to him from the estate of his father, John, Jr., willed to John by his father, William. In the meantime in 1791 Benjamin Parks had entered suit against his "uncles and aunts of the one-half blood", Martin Parks, William Parks, Sally Tinsley, Margaret and Elizabeth Parks, for that part of his grandfather's estate that should have gone to his father, John, Jr. (D. B. G, p. 71, Amherst Co.)

They contracted with said Benjamin Parks "To give to him his first choice of any of slaves that may fall to the aforesaid orphans lot, out of the estate of John Parks, Jr., deceased, the son of William Parks, deceased, and five pounds Sterling, for which the said Benjamin Parks made over all rights that he may have in the estate of John Parks, Jr., deceased, to Martin, William, Sarah and other—Nov. 11, 1791. Evidently Moses Rucker continued to keep the negroes after the death of his wife, Elizabeth, in 1820, for in 1834 the brothers and sisters of the "one-half blood" of John Parks, brought suit against Moses Rucker to recover these negroes.

(Court of Appeals, Vol. 5, p. 160, March, 1834, Richmond, Va.) Martin Parks adm. & heir against Moses Rucker. That John Parks had died after 1785, intestate, a female slave named Nelly had been left to Elizabeth, widow of John Parks. Nelly had a son, Ben.

Elizabeth died in 1820 (having already married Moses Rucker) leaving the two negroes in the possession of Rucker, her second husband, the plaintiffs were "uncles and aunts of the one-half blood" of Benjamin, the eldest son and heir of John Parks, Jr., deceased, their eldest brother, and that they had purchased the rights of Benjamin in the property of John Parks, Jr., deceased. The plaintiff failed in proof and Rucker showed he was entitled to the slaves, even if his wife had held them as dower of her first husband's estate. By a compromise between Benjamin Parks and Moses Rucker the suit was dismissed.

2. Sarah[4] Parks (William[3], John[2], Thomas[1]), b. c. 1768, m. first, William Tinsley, d. 1790; m. second, James Waugh, Dec. 3, 1792, her brother, William Parks, signed the marriage bond. Sally administered upon the estate of William Tinsley, deceased, 1790, in Amherst Co. In 1800 John Tinsley was appointed guardian to William Tinsley, orphan of William Tinsley, deceased, this William Tinsley, Jr., died in 1812, leaving a will in Amherst, in which he leaves one-half of his estate to his mother, Sarah Waugh, and one-half to his wife, and at his wife's death this one-half to go to his niece, Mary Colice Parks, and her heirs.

Executors: James Waugh, Martin Parks.

3. Martin[4] Parks (William[3], John[2], Thomas[1]), b. Nov. 16, 1768, d. Mch. 16, 1840, m. Oct. 27, 1801, Nancy Goode, b. Aug. 17, 1781, d. Feb. 21, 1856, dau. of Samuel Goode. On May 19, 1813, Martin and Nancy sold 205 acres of land in Amherst for 205 dollars to George MacDaniel. (D. B. M, p. 355, Amherst Co.)

Witness: Ambrose Rucker, James Ware, A. Carter.

Nov. 5, 1802, Martin Parks and Richard Ellis patented 195 acres of land on Pedler River and Harris Creek, adjoining George MacDaniel, Joshua Ellis's heirs, Nelson Crawford, John Duncan and Clark's Creek. (L. Gr. B. 51, p. 65).

Martin's family Bible is now in the possession of his grandson, Frank A. Parks, of Big Island, Va. Martin lived near Agricola, in Amherst, Va., and is buried on the old homestead burying ground, this place was later owned by D. H. Rucker, and now owned by ——— Watts. The following is copied from the Bible:

"William Henry Parks, b. Oct. 27, 1802, d. Mch., 1862.
Samuel Goode Parks, b. Mch. 14, 1804, d. June 19, 1872.
Mary Collier Parks, b. July 4, 1805, d. Nov. 26, 1883.
Elizabeth Gaines Parks, b. May 10, 1807, d. Feb. 18, 1884.
Welden Burwell Parks, b. Mar. 21, 1809, d.
John Martin Parks, b. Mar. 19, 1812, d.
Sarah Ann Susanna Parks, b. Apr. 24, 1814, d. Jan. 26, 1875.
Lucy Amanda Parks, b. Jan. 9, 1816, d. 1848.
Milton MacRerness Parks, b. Apr. 17, 1818.
Gaines Winslow Parks, b. May 7, 1820, d. 1855.
Caroline Timanda Parks, b. Dec. 27, 1821.
Nancy Margaret Parks, b. June 7, 1824, d. May 27, 1859.
Granville Philips Parks, b. Aug. 8, 1829, d. June, 1885.
Martin Parks and Nancy Goode were married Oct. 27, 1801.
W. H. Parks and family set off to move to Tennessee, Nov. 12, 1832."

Issue:

1. William[5] Henry Parks.
2. Samuel[5] Goode Parks.
3. Mary[5] Collier Parks.
4. Elizabeth[5] Gaines Parks.
5. Weldon[5] Burwell Parks.
6. John[5] Martin Parks.
7. Sarah[5] Ann Susanna Parks.
8. Lucy[5] Amanda Parks.
9. Milton[5] MacRerness Parks.
10. Gaines[5] Winslow Parks.
11. Caroline[5] Timanda Parks.
12. Nancy[5] Margaret Parks.
13. Granville[5] Philips Parks.

1. W.[5] H. Parks (Martin[4], William[3] ———), died in Lafayette, Mo., m. Pamela Thorp, of Campbell Co., Va.

2. Samuel[5] Goode Parks (Martin[4], William[3] ———), m. Sept. 5, 1837, Theresa Amanda Burks, dau. of Samuel Cabell Burks and wife, Pamela Hunter.

1. John[6] Alexander Parks, 1839-1840.
2. Mary[6] Parks, 1849-1860.
3. Charles[6] Samuel Parks, b. June 1, 1842. Killed at battle of Gettysburg, June 3, 1863, served in Co. I, Second Va. Infantry.

4. William[6] Goode Parks, b. Dec., 1845.
5. Martha[6] Burks Parks, 1852-1870.
6. Martin[6] Cabell Parks, b. 1856.
7. Robert[6] Henry Parks, b. 1864.

3. Mary[5] Collier Parks (Martin[4], William[3] ———), m. ——— Morris, of Amherst.

4. Elizabeth[5] Gaines Parks (Martin[4] ———), m. 1844, Captain George Hilton.

1. Valentine[6] Hilton.

5. Weldon[5] Burwell Parks (Martin[4] ———), m. 1836, Paulina Davis, dau. of Kempis Davis and wife, Elizabeth Rucker MacDaniel. (Dau. of John MacDaniel and wife, Margaret Rucker). They moved to Missouri, where Burwell died. The children were sent back to Amherst to be educated.

Paulina married second, ——— Hibler. One child by the second marriage.

1. Arthur[6] Parks, moved to Kansas.
2. Ann[6] Parks, m. ——— Harvey.
3. Sally[6] Parks, m. Benjamin S. Rucker (Benj. J. R.)
    1. Parks[7] Rucker, m. Florence.
    2. H.[7] Cowles Rucker, m. Lillian[6] Rucker (William[5] Ambrose Rucker).
    3. Ruth[7] Rucker.
    4. Sadie[7] Rucker, m. first, ———; m. second, Richard Acres.
    5. Nell[7] Rucker.
    6. Clara[7] Rucker.

5. Nell[7] Rucker (Sally[6], Burwell[5], Martin[4] ———), m. Wingfield Scott McGill, lived in Garrett Park, Md.

1. Wingfield[8] Scott McGill, Jr., graduate of University of Virginia.
2. Emma[8] McGill.
3. Eleanor[8] McGill, m. Nov. 29, 1929, Chicholm, son of Charles F. Chicholm.

6. John[5] Martin Parks (Martin[4], William[3] ———), m. ——— Morris, sister of Dr. B. P. Morris, of Amherst. Moved to Missouri.

7. Sarah[5] Ann Parks (Martin[4], William[3] ————), m. 1836, Whiting Davies.

8. Lucy[5] Amanda Parks (Martin[4], William[3] ————), m. 1847, R. P. Jones.

10. Gaines[5] Winslow Parks (Martin[4], William[3] ————), m. 1844, Mary J. Morris. Moved to Missouri.

1. Charles[6] Parks.
2. Elizabeth[6] Parks, m. ———— Tyree.
3. ————[6] Parks, m. ———— Kent.

13. Granville[5] Philips Parks (Martin[4], ————), m. 1851, Laura Ogden, dau. of Armistead Ogden.

1. Georgia[6] A. Parks, m. 1892, Edward C. Beasley, son of Henry and Mary Beasley.

4. William[4] Parks (William[3], John[2], Thomas[1]), m. 1 Aug., 1791, Milly Burks, of Amherst. Moved to Kanawha Co., West Virginia in 1807. He bought 125 acres of land in Kanawha Co. in 1811, Dec. 16, from Charles Burks, Sen., of Amherst Co., "Land on Cabbin Creek" being the lower end of a survey of 500 acres made for Andrew Donnerly, including a place called Flynn's Bottom. (D. B. M., p. 56, Amherst Co., Va.)

Witness: Ambrose Rucker, Martin Parks, George Burks.

In 1820 he paid taxes in Lewis Co., W. Va., continuing until 1827, then Benjamin and Nathaniel began paying.

5. Margaret[4] Parks (William[3], John[2], Thomas[1]), d. June 25, 1864, age 90, in Amherst, m. Dec. 21, 1789, Samuel Burks, d. July 29, 1824, leaving a will dated June 17, 1824, probated Oct. 18, 1824, in which he mentioned his nine children, his wife, Margaret, and the children of his deceased daughter, Nancy Rucker. The following is taken from the will:

1. W.[5] Lynchfield Burks.
2. Samuel[5] Burks.
3. Martin[5] Parks Burks.
4. Robert[5] H. Burks (d. 1877).
5. Nancy[5] Rucker. (Deceased).
6. Mary[5] Dawson.
7. Sally[5] Rucker.
8. Margaret[5] Burks.
9. Jane[5] Burks.

Grandchildren, the children of my daughter, Nancy Rucker, deceased:

1. Thomas^{6} G. Rucker.
2. Samuel^{6} P. Rucker.
3. Ambrose^{6} P. Rucker.
4. Robert^{6} H. Rucker.
5. Mary^{6} Rucker.
6. Martin^{6} P. Rucker.

Samuel Burks lived in Amherst on Pedlar River, owning 485 acres of land, which was sold in 1834 by M. P. Burks.

1. William^{5} Lynchfield Burks (Margaret^{4}, William^{3}), b. Nov. 15, 1792, d. Aug. 29, 1856, m. Oct. 15, 1810, Elizabeth Pettit, daughter of James Pettit and wife, Frances Baker, b. June 24, 1791, d. July 13, 1873. Lived in Rockbridge Co.

1. F.^{6} Nancy Burks, m. William Black.
2. William^{6} T. Burks, m. Susan Cheatwood.
3. Catherine^{6} Burks, m. John Porter, moved to Missouri.
4. Sarah^{6} Pettit.
5. Margaret^{6} Parks Burks, m. H. Milton Hatcher.
6. Samuel^{6} Burks, m. Amelia MacClure (dau. of Betty).
7. Hugh^{6} Martin Burks, m. Molly Frantz.
8. H.^{6} Reid Burks, m. ——— Miller.
9. Martha^{6} Jane Burks (1831-1908), m. ——— Scruggs.

4. Sarah^{6} Pettit Burks (W.^{5} L., Margaret^{4}), m. William Paxton, son of William Paxton and wife, Jane Grigsby, of Balcony Falls, Va.

1. W.^{7} L. Paxton, killed at the battle of Manassass 1861.
2. Elizabeth^{7} Paxton, b. 1840, m. 1st, William Seyman; m. 2nd, Jesse Fisher.
3. Joseph^{7} Samuel Paxton, m. Roberta MacClure.
4. Martin^{7} Luther, killed at the battle of Winchester, 1861.
5. Mary^{7} Verlinda Paxton.
6. John^{7} Calvin Paxton, m. Rebecca Robinson, of Woodstock, Va.
7. Ella^{7} Frances Paxton.
8. Thomas^{7} Porter Paxton, m. Lulie Kernoeff, of Lexington, Va.
9. Sarah^{7} Agnes Paxton, m. Frank H. Brockenborough, son of Judge J. Brockenborough.

10. Charles^{7} Hawkins Paxton, m. Elizabeth Smithson.
11. Reuben^{7} Grigsby Paxton, m. 1st, Fanny Lacy; 2nd, Delle Gibson.

7. Ella^{7} Frances Paxton (Sarah^{6}, W.^{5}, Margaret^{4}), m. Von Pike, of Little Rock, Ark., son of Gen. Albert Pike and wife, Mary Hamilton. Ella was b. Sept. 10, 1849, d. Apr. 30, 1929, in Tarboro, N. C.

1. Lilliam^{8} Pike, m. 1909, Roscoe M. Packard, Boston, Mass.
2. Mary^{8} Hamilton Pike.
3. Albert^{8} Pike.
4. Anne^{8} Yvonne Pike, m. Col. A. T. Smith, now stationed at Fort Eustis, Va.
5. Dora^{8} Grigsby Pike.
6. Ethel^{8} Denver Pike, m. Dr. Spencer P. Bass, of Tarboro, N. C.
    1. Eleanor^{9} Bass, b. 1911.
    2. Spencer^{9} Bass, b. 1922.

3. Albert^{8} Pike (Sarah^{7} ————), m. 1905, Josephine H. Philips, of Tarboro, N. C. He now is in the United States geological survey, stationed at San Domingo Island 1918, Captain in the U. S. Army.

2. Samuel^{5} Burks (Margaret^{4}, William^{3}), m. Mary (Polly) Christian, sister of C. M. Christian, of Amherst, and daughter of Drury and Mourning Christian. They moved to Hannibal, Mo., about 1825, their descendants live in St. Louis. (Lillian Palmer, a great-granddaughter).

3. Martin^{5} Parks Burks (Margaret^{4} ————), m. Jan. 18, 1820, Louise Claiborne Spinner Gooch, b. 30 Sept., 1802, widow of William Gooch, and daughter of Jesse Spinner and wife, Celia Cheatwood, of Bedford Co.

1. Edward^{6} Calohil Burks.
2. Jesse^{6} Spinner Burks.
3. John^{6} Dabney Burks.
4. Martin^{6} Parks Burks, Jr.
5. Samuel^{6} Burks, Jr.
6. William^{6} Lynchfield Burks.
7. Hiram^{6} Claibourne Burks.
8. Albert^{6} Sherman Burks.
9. George^{6} Wellington Burks.

1. Judge Edward[6] Calohill Burks (Martin[5], Margaret[4]), b. May 20, 1821, d. July 4, 1897, m. Oct. 15, 1845, Mildred Elizabeth Buford, daughter of Capt. Paschal Buford and wife, Frances Ann Otey. Edward attended the "Old Field School" in Bedford, later he attended the New London Academy. In 1838, he went to Washington College (now Washington and Lee). He graduated in 1841, going the same year to the University of Virginia, where he graduated in law under Prof. Henry St. George Tucker. In 1861 he was practicing law at Liberty, Va., when he joined the army and fought the four years. In 1876 he was the representative from Bedford Co. to the Legislature, and was elected Judge of the Court of Appeals.

1. Frances[7] Claibourne Burks, m. John Casey.
2. Edward[7] Calohill Burks, m. Josephine Bell.
3. Nora[7] Burks, m. Alexandria Spottswood Payne.
4. Buford[7] Burks, never married.
5. Rowland[7] Burks, m. Lila Lloyd.
6. Martin[7] Parks Burks.
7. Margaret[7] Burks, d. young.

6. Judge Martin[7] Parks Burks (Edward[6], Martin[5], Marg.[4]), m. Dec. 31, 1874, Roberta G. Bell; he was b. Jan. 23, 1851, d. Apr., 1928, in Richmond, Va. He practiced law for several years at Bedford City, taught at Washington and Lee University, and at the time of his death was Judge of the Supreme Court in Richmond. He was a member of the Phi Beta Kappa and Phi Delta Phi fraternities.

1. Martin[8] Parks Burks, a lawyer of Roanoke.
    1. Martin[9] Parks Burks.
    2. Albert[9] Burks.
    3. Dolly[9] Burks.
    4. Edward[9] Burks.

Among the grandchildren of Judge Edward Calohill Burks now living (1930) are:

Martin Parks Burks, Jr., of Roanoke, Va.
Edward C. Burks, III., of Bedford, Va.
Mrs. John Burks, of Bedford, Va.
Mrs. Walmsley, of Farmville, Va.
Mrs. Nora Burks Hill, of Danville, Va.

2. Col. Jesse[6] Spinner Burks (Martin[5], Marg.[4] ———), b. Mch. 20, 1923, d. June 15, 1885, m. 1st, Elizabeth Royal Otey, daughter of W. L. Otey and wife, Mary Gwatkin Logwood, of

Saint Charles Co., Mo., m. Dec. 3, 1848, b. Feb. 24, 1826. He married 2nd, Charlotte F. Thomson, Feb. 17, 1855. He married 3rd, Molly Tinsley Claggett (widow), of Bedford County, b. Oct. 28, 1845, in Powhatan County. Jesse attended Washington College, then graduated from Virginia Military Institute in 1844. He assisted in organizing the 42nd Regiment and was made Colonel. He was very seriously wounded at the battle of Kernstown, served in the State Legislature in 1853-54. His home was called Wyoming.

Issue by first marriage:

1. Thomas^{7} Otey Burks, d. young.
2. Wm.^{7} Parks Burks, b. July 29, 1848, m. Elizabeth Gray, of Maryland.
    1. Harry^{8} Gray Burks.
3. Alonsa^{7} Otey Burks, b. Mch. 9, 1850, d. May 24, 1917, Buena Vista, Va., m. May 17, 1882, Mattie Burks, of Rockbridge Co., dau. of Chas. L. and Martha M. Burks.
    1. Jesse^{8} Otey Burks, b. Apr. 22, 1883.
    2. Charles^{8} Lewis Burks, b. Sept. 15, 1884, m. Florence Raudenbush, of Pennsylvania.
    3. William^{8} Parks Burks, b. Mar. 17, 1886, m. Anna McClary Updike (widow).
    4. Samuel^{8} Hairston Burks, b. Sept. 11, 1888, m. Minnie M. Cunningham.
    5. Elizabeth^{8} Tyler Burks, b. Aug. 30, 1891, m. John Robert Thompson.
    6. Alonso^{8} Otto Burks, b. May 24, 1897, m. Frances Johnston Saunders, d. May 5, 1927, auto accident.

Issue by second marriage:

4. Ida^{7} Temple Burks, m. Hunt Tardy, d. in St. Louis.
5. Edward^{7} Lewis Burks, d. in Bedford.
6. Mary^{7} Campbell Burks, of St. Louis.
7. Sally^{7} Thompson Burks, m. Essenhart, of St. Louis.
8. Kate^{7} Davis Burks, m. George Logan, of Salem, Va.
9. Minnie^{7} B. Burks, of St. Louis.
10. Charlotte^{7} Burks, d. young.

3. John^{6} Dabney Burks (Martin^{5}, Marg.^{4}, Wm.^{3}), b. Apr. 2, 1826, d. age 86, lived at Charlemont, Bedford Co., Va. Served in Company C of 28th Va. Regiment, C. S. A., m. Dolly Waller Cheatwood, b. Sept. 18, 1826, daughter of Hiraim and Harriet (McDaniel) Cheatwood, of Bedford and Amherst.

Issue:

1. Georgiana[7] McDaniel Burks, m. Robert Major, Nov. 1871.
    1. Lelia[8] McDaniel Major, m. Robt. W. Owen (two children, Katherine[9] and Robert[9] James).
    2. Kate[8] E. Major, m. Thomas Hugh Nelson.
    3. Dolly[8] Major, m. Harry Watson.
    4. John[8] Burks Major.
    5. Cleopatra[8] Major, m. Harry White.
2. Robert[7] L. Burks, m. Nannie Hurt Chamin (widow), 1896.
3. Wm.[7] Sherman Burks, m. Lemma Douglas, 1883.
4. Hiram[7] Cheatwood Burks' m. Mary Wright, 1909.
5. Louisa[7] Spinner Burks.
6. Harriet[7] Cheatwood Burks.

4. Martin[6] Parks Burks, Jr. (Martin[5], Mary[4], Wm.[3]), b. July 15, 1828, d. Dec. 18, 1839, thrown from a horse.

5. Samuel[6] Burks (Martin[5], Mary[4], Wm.[3]), b. Oct. 1, 1830, d. June 18, 1833.

6. Wm.[6] Lynchfield Burks (Martin[5], Mary[4], ————), b. Nov. 30, 1832, d. Feb. 19, 1866, m. Maria Sale, daughter of Dr. Richard Sale and Martha Wharton Sale, of Bedford Co. Maria d. May 1866. Wm. L. Burks enlisted Apr. 3, 1863, in Company C, 28th Va. Reg., C. S. A.

1. Martha[7] Burks, m. Marshall Griggs.
2. Richard[7] Albert Burks, m. Annie Griggs.
3. Wm.[7] Lynchfield Burks, m. Willie Watson.
4. John[7] Franklin Burks, m. ———— Fisher, of Alexandria. He is an Episcopal minister.

7. Hiram[6] Claibourne Burks (Martin[5], Marg.4 ————), b. July 15, 1836, m. Mch. 25, 1857, Charlotte Sale, daughter of Nelson Sale and wife, Annie A. Wharton, of Bedford Co., b. Aug. 27, 1834. Hiram was educated at Virginia Military Institute, served in Company G, 2nd Va. Reg. Cavalry, S. C. A., as First Lieutenant, was taken prisoner at Westminster, Md., sent to Fort Delaware, then to Johnson's Island, then to Fort Lookout, and again to Fort Delaware, where he was discharged June, 1865.

1. Annie[7] Burks.
2. Lucy[7] Burks.
3. Sallie[7] S. Burks.
4. Jesse[7] S. Burks.

5. Channing[7] Burks.
6. Fannie[7] Burks.
7. Virginia[7] W. Burks.

8. Albert[6] Sherman Burks (Martin[5], Marg.[4] ———), b. Mch. 17, 1838, d. Apr. 11, 1913, m. Virginia Rucker, daughter of James Monroe Rucker and wife, Marianda McDaniel, of Bedford, 2 June, 1869. Marianda d. Feb. 13, 1883. Albert attended the New London Academy, also Westwood Academy. He enlisted in Company C, 28th Va. Reg., Infantry, C. S. A., 15 May, 1861. This company became Capt. T. M. Boyer's about Aug. 20, 1861, and later Capt. J. R. Johnson's Company of the Virginia Light Artillery, and were disbanded about Oct. 14, 1862. Albert was then transferred to Capt. Pegram's Company of Light Artillery, and was discharged Nov. 12, 1862, owing to illness and the death of his mother, he sent a substitute.

1. Cornelia[7] Waller Burks.
2. John[7] Lodowick Burks.
3. Margaret[7] Elizabeth Burks.
4. Charles[7] Albert Burks.
5. Leighton[7] Cheatwood Burks.
6. Ernest[7] Rucker Burks.

1. Cornelia[7] Waller Burks (Albert[6], Martin[5], Mary[4]), b. Mch. 6, 1870, at Charlemont, Bedford, Va., m. Willis Howard Dillard, July 14, 1803. No heirs.

2. John[7] Lodowick Burks (Albert[6], Martin[5], Mary[4]), b. Dec. 8, 1871, m. Feb. 21, 1906, Evelyn Marshall, daughter of Dr. E. L. Marshall and wife, Dorothy Jolliffe, of Charlemont.

1. Dorothy[8] Virginia Burks, b. July 4, 1908.
2. Lionel[8] Lodowick Burks, b. Apr. 27, 1912.

3. Margaret[7] Elizabeth Burks (Albert[6], ———), m. Oct. 3, 1901, Sloan Lewis Stroud, of South Carolina.

1. Virginia[8] Burks Stroud, b. Oct. 25, 1902, m. John Wm. Nuttycombe, Sept. 12, 1928, of Charlottesville, Va., he is now professor of the department of Biology, now of the University of Georgia, at Athens.

4. Charles[7] Albert Burks (Albert[6] ———), b. June 8, 1876, m. Jan. 6, 1913, Grace Young, daughter of B. F. Young and wife, Ailsee, of Knoxville, Tenn.

1. Cornelia[8] Burks, b. Jan. 14, 1914.
2. Elizabeth[8] Burks, b. July 7, 1916.
3. Charles[8] Cheatwood Burks, b. Feb. 5, 1918.

5. Leighton[7] Cheatwood Burks (Albert[6] ————), b. May 17, 1876, never married, died May 14, 1928, in Lexington, Ky.

6. Ernest[7] Rucker Burks (Albert[6] ————), b. Sep. 6, 1882, m. May 13, 1911, Mary Matilda May, of Tazewell Co., Va., daughter of Samuel D. May and wife, Mary Ann.

1. Ernest Rucker[8] Burks, Jr., b. June 18, 1912.
2. Leighton[8] Jackson Burks, b. Feb. 2, 1914.

9. George[6] Wellington Burks (Martin[5], Mary[4]), b. Apr. 4, 1840, d. Sept. 5, 1912, m. Nov. 20, 1867, Harriett Eliza Hopkins, daughter of Edward Hopkins and Lucy Cheatwood, his wife, of Amherst. George was educated at New London and Westwood Academies, and at Lexington under General Pendleton. He served first in Company C, 28th Va. Reg. of Infantry, C. S. A., and later served in the 21st Reg. of Va. Vavalry. He was with Gen. McCausland at the battle of Lynchburg.

1. Harriet[7] Louise Burks, d. young.
2. Lucy[7] Elizabeth Burks, m. Beaureguard Parks.
3. Sue[7] Lelia Burks, d. young.
4. Richard[7] Edward Burks, m. Sallie Douglas.
5. Frank[7] W. Burks, m. Sallie Wheat.
6. Mary[7] Waller Burks, d. age 24.
7. Roberta[7] Leighton Burks, m. Marvin Turpin.
8. Paschel[7] Buford Burks, m. Kate Bullard.
9. Martin[7] Parks Burks, served in the World War, d. the following year, age 21.

4. Robert[5] H. Burks, d. in Staunton, Va., June 29, 1877, age 70.

5. Nancy[5] Burks (Margaret[4], Wm.[3], John[2], Tho.[1] Parks), b. Feb. 9, 1807, m. Tinsley[5] Rucker (Ambrose[4], Ambrose[3], John[2], Peter[1] Rucker). They moved to Kentucky where he later married again. (See Ambrose[4] Rucker line).

1. Thomas[6] G. Rucker.
2. Samuel[6] P. Rucker.
3. Ambrose[6] Rucker.
4. Robert[6] Rucker.
5. Mary[6] Rucker.
6. Martha[6] P. Rucker.

6. Mary Dawson[5] Burks (Margaret[4], Wm.[3], John[2] Parks), b. Apr. 8, 1808-Nov. 23, 1834), m. Russell Dawson and moved

to Liberty, Indiana. Their granddaughters still live there (1920) —Alice[7] Dawson, Cora[7] Dawson, Julia[7] Dawson.

7. Sally[5] Burks (Marg.[4], Wm.[3] ———), d. 1868, m. Garland[5] Rucker (Ambrose[4], Ambrose[3], John[2], Peter[1]). She married second, Isaac Reynolds.

8. Margaret[5] Burks (Marg.[4], Wm[3] ———), b. Apr. 8, 1808, d. Nov. 23, 1834, m. Thomas Scott, Aug. 3, 1826, of Bedford County, b. Nov. 8, 1803, d. May 26, 1861. He married second, Berlinda Smith, daughter of Elisha and Elizabeth Tinsley.

9. Elizabeth[5] Jane Burks (Marg.[4], Wm.[3], John[2], Tho.[1]), b. Oct. 22, 1811, d. Dec. 12, 1886, m. Hugh Roy Scott, of Bedford, Va., b. 7 Aug., 1804, d. Mch. 3, 1869.

6. Elizabeth[4] Parks (William[3], John[2], Thomas[1]), b. 1776, d. 1854, in Amherst; her obituary was written by the Rev. John E. Edwards. She m. Aug. 1, 1799, Ambrose[5] Rucker (Reuben[4], Ambrose[3] ———).

3. Charles[2] Parks (Thomas[1]), b. in Essex Co., moved to Amherst then to Halifax. 7 Mch., 1743, Charles Parks came twelve miles to court (then held in Fredericksburg) as a witness for Henry Parks against Bledsoe.

He bought 227 acres of land on Huff Creek from James Stennet in St. Anne's Parish, Albemarle Co., 9 Feb., 1749. Adjoining John Wheeler, John Graves and Benjamin Stennett. (W. and D. B., p. 206, Albemarle Co.)

Witness: William Cabell, William Cabell, Jr., Joseph Cabell.

In 1747 he bought 350 acres of land on the Tye River in Albemarle Co. He sold his land on Huff Creek. His wife, Susanna, signed the deed; by 1764 he had sold all of his land in Amherst and was living in Halifax Co., Va. (D. B. A., p. 288, Amherst). Charles Parks, of Halifax, sold to John Owensby 359 acres of land on the north side of Buffaloe River, on the north side of Fluvanna River. Wife, Susanna, signed the deed, 17 Apr., 1764, Amherst Co.

4. Samuel[2] Parks (Thomas[1]) received 200 acres of land from his father, Thomas Parks, "To my son, Samuel Park * *," land in the forks of the Rappahannock River on Muddy Creek, adjoining John Latham. (D. B. 4, p. 355, Orange Co.)

Samuel[2] Parks, of Orange, sold to Thomas Dillard land belonging to his wife, Mary, daughter of Anthony North, deceased, Oct. 25, 1739. (D. B. A., p. 303, Orange Co.)

Witness: George Dillard, Michael Towles, Edward Dillard.

June, 1748, a suit of Samuel Parks against Michael Towles. (O. B. 1745-48, p. 91, Orange Co.)

In 1747 Samuel bought 350 acres of land in Albemarle Co. on the Tye River.

7. Elizabeth^{2} Parks (Thomas^{1}), m. Christipher Hutchins in Culpeper Co. They moved to Pittsylvania Co. about 1770, where he died in 1807, May 20, will probated mentioned wife, Elizabeth, and the following children:

Son, John Hutchins, deceased.
Son, Thomas Hutchins.
Son, Aaron Hutchins.
Son, Charles Hutchins.
Son, Moses Hutchins (m. Lucy Parks, dau. of John).
Son, James Hutchins.
Daughter, Mildred Hutchins (m. Bryan W. Nowling).
Daughter, Ann Hutchins (m. Samuel Dillard).
Daughter Jennie Hutchins (m. Joshua Willis).

Parks' Coat of Arms: Shield, three stags heads caboshed gules, in pale or, a field argent. Crest. A stag hound's head of the first.

Wilks Co., North Carolina wills.

Will of John Parks, Sen., Feb. 7, 1787-Feb., 1793:

"In the name of God Amen I John Parks, Sener of the State of North Carolina and County of Wilkes, being in perfect sences and memory Calling to mind the Mortality of my body knowing it is appointed for all men once to Die I make and Ordain to be made this my last will and Testament in Manner and form following: I leave my soul to Almighty God that gave it to me hoping thru the Merits of my Blessed Savior to Inherit everlasting life and my body to be Decently Buried at the Discretion of my Executors hereafter Mentioned. And as to all the worldy goods it has pleased God to bless me with I Bequeath in Manner and form following. It is my will and desire that all my Just debts be fully paid and Satisfied: Itum, my will and desire is that my son John Parks be paid eight pounds Virginia Money Out of my Estate for One Hoghead of Tobacco I borrowed of him. Itum, I give unto my daughter Sary Sale five Shillings Sterling for her full part of Estate. Itum, I give unto my son Samuel Parks the land and plantation where I now live also my wagon for his full part of my estate to be delivered to them by my executors before the day of Sale of my estate. Itum, my will and desire is that my son Samuel Parks should have the care and

Management of my Daughter Milley Parks and her part of my estate. Itum, my will and desire is that all my Negroes be sold at the Highest bidder Amongst my children as its my Desire that they be kept among my children. Itum, Publick Sale after my death and all the Money arising from my whole estate to be equally divided among the rest of my Children and I constitute and Appoint my son Benjamin Parks, William Carrel and Samuel Parks Executors of this my last will and Testament revoking and disannulling all other wills by me heretofore made allowing this only to be my last will and Testament as witness

My hand and Seal this Seventh day of February in the year of our Lord 1787.

John Parks (Seal)

William Carrell
George Parkes
Benjamin Thurston

N. B. My will and desire is that some of my estate should be sold to pay my debts before the Division of my estate.

(Wrote on back)

State of North Carolina
Wilkes County, February Term 1793

The within will was Duly Proved in Open Court by the Oaths of William Carrell, George Parkes and Benjamin Thurston Subscribing witnesses Thereto and was Ordered to be Recorded.

Test

Chs. Gordon C. C.

From: North Carolina Historical Commission

Wilkes County, Court Minutes, 1778-1799, page 357.
John Parks
Samuel Parks
Benjamin Parks

From files of original papers in the offices of North Carolina Historical Com., Raleigh, N. C.

Wills—B. 1778, 1799, p. 126.

Will of John Park, Esq., deceased:

I, John Parks, Jun., of Wilkes County, N. C. * * * * * *

To my wife, a negro Lill, the remaining negroes to be divided between my children.

Dwelling, plantation, stock, etc., to be divided in three parts, valued and divided between my children.

My "Write" in the south Estate, if I should obtain a "write". Household goods to wife for life, then to be divided as aforesaid.

Executors: Wife, John Parks, and My son, Benjamin Parks, 13 Jan., 1784-Apr., 1784.

Division of the estate of John Parks, Jr., Aug., 1795, Wilkes Co., N. C.:

To Benjamin Park his part valued—75 lb. Sterling.
To Reuben Parks
To Richard Parks
To Samuel Parks
To Sarah Parks
To Elizabeth Parks
To Rachel Parks

John Parkes patented 964 acres of land in New Kent on the S. S. of York River on Blad Cr. in 1683. (B. 6, p. 317, L. Gr.)

John Parke of New Kent patented 300 acres of land in Nansemond Co. now in the possession of Thomas Hampton (escheat.) May 2, 1707 (B. 9, p. 662).

Greer's list of Emigrants records the following names of Parks, when they came, by whom imported and into which county:

William Parks, Jr., 1655, by Mathew Hubert, Sen., York Co., Va.

William Parks, Sen., 1655, by Mathew Hubert, Sen., York Co., Va.

William Parkes, 1656, by Thomas Merideth, New Kent Co.

John Parke, 1652, by Robert Elam, Henrico Co., Va.

Robert Parks, 1639, by Robert Ely, Isle of Wight Co.

Thomas Parks, 1647, by William Whitington, Northampton Co.

Thomas Parks, 1635, by Thomas Harwood.

Thomas Parke, 1623, Feb. 16. "At the eastern shore in the colony of Jamestown." (Hotten's List of Emigrants).

Hotten's Emigrants, p. 41. From London to Virginia, 2 Jan., 1634, Jo:de Park, age 28.

Declarations of importations:

1736, John Parks, of Orange Co., Va., made a declaration as having come from Ireland. (He located in Rockbridge Co., Va.)

1741, John and Thomas Park, of Orange, made their declaration as having come from Ireland and Great Britain.

Virginia Historical Magazine, Vol. 13, p. 192. Virginia Gleanings in England.

Will of William Parke, dated Nov. 13, 1633, probated Aug. 8, 1634. To my youngest son, Daniel Parke, 100 lbs. Sterling, to my wife, Sarah, 150 lbs. Sterling, if my wife should marry again, her husband to go security on behalf of my eldest son,

William Parke. To Francis Columbell, of London. To Nathaniel Fulder, of London.

Executor: William Parke.

(Note by Mr. W. G. Stanard): Neither will nor probate gave the residence of the testator. It is thought that he died in Virginia, and was the father of Daniel Parke the elder that his family came to Virginia since many years after his death, the land due for emigrants was taken up under a patent dated 1655 for land in York Co., in it appears the names of William Parke, Sarah Parke and William Parke, Jr.

William Parke was a witness to a deed to Daniel Parke in York Co. in 1652.

Virginia Historical Magazine, Vol. 14, p. 174. Virginia Gleanings in England.

The will of Daniel Parke, of London, England, dated 11 Aug., 1677, probated 10 Sept., 1679.

To son, Daniel Parke, all of the plantations and negroes in Virginia, and to the male heirs, failing male heirs, to the heirs at law, provided they take the name of Parke. Failing this issue, to my eldest daughter, to her heirs, they also to take the name of Parke.

To my daughter, Everling Parke, 1,500 lbs. Sterling, when she is eighteen or at her marriage.

To daughter, Rebekah Parke, the same. To daughter, Jane Parke, the same. All money remaining in England, and coming from the sale of tobacco and profits of shippers to be put in bonds for daughters benefit.

The rest of the estate in England and Virginia to son, Daniel Parke, sole executor, executor in trust for Edward Carter.

In 1655, Capt. Daniel Parke patented 580 acres of land in York Co., Va., for transporting twelve persons into the colony, Daniel Parke and wife, Peter French and wife, Thomas Bayley, Thomas Hayward, Richard Palmer, John Newman, Isabell Fletcher, Elizabeth Conway, and two negroes. (Book 4, p. 14, Land Grants).

Capt. Daniel Parke patented 528 acres of land in James City County, land on Rickahock Path, to the cart path from Mr. Sorrell's to Mr. Baker's—to Col. Pettus on the path to Chickahominy Gate on to Mr. Sorrell's land. Assigned to said Parks by Christopher Harris, and the rest being sold and assigned to him by Mr. Robert Sorrell, 24 March, 1622. (Vol. 5, p. 375, Land Grants).

June 7, 1656, Capt. Daniel Parke patented 700 acres of land on the east side of Chickahominy River commonly called Warreny an old town, land formerly granted to Nicholas Meriwether in 1656. (B. 5, p. 620, L. Gr.)

Dawson

Martin[1] Dawson, possibly born 1715, died 1812, married possibly 1735, may have come from Isle of Wight County, but this has not been proven. One Martin M. Dawson lived in Isle of Wight. He patented land in 1713; died in said county 1745, leaving a will, but does not mention a Martin. (See later page). He signed his name with an M. as did the Martin of Amherst Co.

Martin married first, Priscilla Sorrell, of James City, Goochland and Amherst. She was a daughter of John Sorrell and was a witness, with her husband, Martin, to a deed of her father, John, in Goochland, 1741.

Martin married secondly, Elizabeth, daughter of Job Carter, in Amherst Co. (Mentioned, 1782, in her father's will). She named her son, Nelson Carter Dawson. (Job Carter's will in Amherst Co., W. B. 2, p. 88, 1779-1782).

At the first court of Albemarle County, 1744, Martin Dawson was appointed with John Sorrell and Charles Bond to appraise the estate of Charles Blaine. (O. Bk. 1744, p. 9).

In 1742, Dec. 15, Anthony Pouncy, late of Goochland County, sold to Martin Dawson, of the same, for 31 pounds, 300 acres on the north side of Rivanna River, adjoining Stiff's land, whereon Quisingberry now lives, which said Pouncey bought from Charles Lynch. Witnesses, James Taylor and John Morris. (D. Bk. 4, p. 115, Goochland Co.)

At the following court, 1742 (O. B. 5, p. 191, Goochland). A deed from Anthony Pouncey to Martin Dawson was proved by oath of John Sorrell and John Morris, and ordered to be recorded. At the November court of 1742, an attachment was made by Martin Dawson against Anthony Pouncey for 54 pounds Sterling. The Sheriff was ordered to sell Pouncey's tobacco and pay Martin Dawson (O. B. 5, p. 173, Goochland).

March 7, 1740, Anthony Pouncey and Martin Dawson, of Goochland, sold 300 acres of land to Mathew Graves for £53, the land beginning at Charles Moorman's, near Carrall's Creek, to the Mountain Fall Creek, to William Randolph's. (This land was granted to Charles Lynch, Aug., 1735). (D. B. 14, p. 187, Goochland). Signed, Anthony Pouncy and Martin M. Dawson.

Martin Dawson patented 400 acres on Hardware River, 1st Oct., 1747. (Land Gr. Bk. 26, p. 119). He patented 300 more acres on south side of Rivanna River on a branch of Buck Island, 20 Aug., 1747. (L. Gr. Bk. 28, p. 187). This land adjoining John Carter's. In 1760 he purchased 125 acres from James Tuly, on Ballinger's Creek. (D. B. 3, p. 126, Albemarle).

From the following settlement, Martin Dawson and his sons, rented land of Col. Jefferson: Year 1760, estate of Col. Peter Jefferson, account.

Paid Martin Dawson his share of tobacco, inspected, £4.15.3.

Paid Martin Dawson sundries he furnished for plantation use, £16.10.9.

Paid Joseph Dawson his share inspected tobacco, £58.10.3.

Paid John Dawson his share inspected tobacco (1758-9), £20.6.½.

By Martin Dawson, for sundries he sold from plantation, £15.17.6.

By John Dawson, for sundries sold him, £6.15.5.

To John Dawson, Surveyor, £107.18.10. (W. B. 2, p. 83, Albemarle Co.)

On June 11, 1761, he sold to John Burrus 300 acres of land on south side of Rivanna and Buck Island in line with John Carter. (D. B. 2, p. 65, Albemarle).

He sold 121 acres of land on both sides of Ballinger's Creek on Nov. 12.

Signed, Martin M. Dawson.

On Mar. 5, 1767, Charles Lynch, of Bedford, sold 337 acres of land to Martin Dawson on the Nuton's branch of Fluvanna River. (D. B. B., p. 165, Amherst Co.)

June 24, 1777, Martin Dawson and his wife, Elizabeth, deed to James Franklin 247 acres of land on top of Smith's Mountains, Amherst Co.

He was one of the executors of the will of his son-in-law, William Parks, in 1778.

The will of Job Carter, dated 1779, probated in 1782, left his "daughter, Elizabeth Dawson" a legacy. (W. B. 2, p. 88, Amherst).

The family tradition is that Martin lived to be 115 years of age. He died in 1812, and in 1759 his son, John, was already married to ,Sally Carrell.

Among the claims adjusted for property impressed or taken for public service in Amherst Co. are several claims of Martin Dawson, 8 Oct., 1781, to Martin Dawson for one beef weighing —— for public use.

26, July, 1781, to Martin Dawson one beef weighing 540 lbs. for public use. Signed, A. Rucker, D. C. P., of Amherst Co., Va., and others.

Inventory of the estate of Martin Dawson returned Sept., 1813. (W. B. 5, p. 380, Amherst Co.)

Will of Martin Dawson, dated 1808, probated 1812:

I, Martin Dawson, of Amherst Co., being greatly stricken in years, but returning thanks to my great Creator, that I may enjoy and possess sound mind and memory, do make and ordain this my last will and testament, hereby revoking all others by me made in the following manner, to-wit: First, it is my will and desire that all my just debts and funeral expenses be paid by my executors. Item, I bequeath unto my sons and daughters had by my first wife, Priscilla Dawson, as follows: To John Dawson and Nancy Cox, I give five shillings current money to them and their heirs forever. I give to Thomas Dawson, Mildred Hancock, Martin Dawson, Mary Parks, Margaret Franklin and William Dawson the sum of Five pounds Current money, to each of them and their heirs forever, which several sums is my desire shall be paid to my son, Nelson Carter Dawson, or his heirs, executors, and within nine months after my death.

I give and bequeath to my sons and daughters by my last wife, Elizabeth Dawson, as follows, to-wit: I bequeath to my son, Nelson Carter Dawson, the tract of land whereon I lately resided, containing 356 acres of land be the same more or less, also one negro man named Will, one negro woman named Silby, and her two children by name of Pleasant and Stephen, to him and his heirs forever. It is my desire that Nan, a negro woman, and Celia, her youngest child, shall be sold to the highest bidder, and the proceeds of the sale be divided as followeth to my son, Jesse, I give three- fourth of the produce of said sale to him and his heirs forever, the remaining one-fourth of the produce of the sale I give to my granddaughter, Mahala Read, to her and her heirs forever. I give to my daughter, Milly Read, five shillings current money of Virginia.

I give to Elizabeth Rucker one negro girl named Nancy, to her and her heirs forever. I give to my daughter, Susanna Tinsley, a negro woman named Cinthia, to her and her heirs forever. The residue of my estate consisting of horses, household and kitchen furniture, and all moneys that may be owing to me at my decease, and everything else that I now or may hereafter possess not particularly disposed of and specified above, it is my will and desire shall be sold to the highest bidder, and the money arising from such a sale to be divided in three shares, one share to be equally divided between the children of my son, Zacharia Dawson, deceased; one share to Elizabeth Rucker, and the remaining share to Susanna Tinsley, to them and their heirs forever. And whereas, I have at different times given to my children above mentioned both real and personal, these are therefore to confirm unto the said children and their heirs forever, all and every species of property to them given by me, of which they have had possession six months. And lastly I do appoint Anthony Rucker, David Tinsley and Nelson C. Dawson executors of this my last will and testament.

In witness whereof I have hereunto set my hand and seal this first day of September, 1808.

Test: Thomas Moore, B. Wilson and J. T. Wingfield.

Probated March 16, 1812, Amherst Co. (W. B. 5, p. 94).

Division of the estate was in Sept., 1813, in Amherst.

Issue of the first marriage:

1. John[2] Dawson.
2. Nancy[2] Cox.
3. Thomas[2] Dawson.
4. Mildred[2] Hancock.
5. Martin[2] Dawson.
6. Mary[2] Parks.
7. Margaret[2] Franklin.
8. William[2] Dawson.

Issue of the second marriage:

9. Zachary[2] Dawson, deceased.
10. Nelson[2] Carter Dawson.
11. Jesse[2] Dawson.
12. Elizabeth Rucker.
13. Susanna[2] Tinsley.

1. John[2] Dawson (Martin[1]), died 1810; m. Sally Carroll, whose mother, Susanna, left a will, dated 22 Mar., 1788, in which she mentions: "To my daughter, Sally Dawson, a black mare, all my cattle and household furniture." (W. Bk. 3, p. 85, Albemarle Co.)

Wood's History of Albemarle states that John Dawson and his wife, Sarah Carroll, were living on Carroll Creek in 1759; that John Dawson was appointed Surveyor in place of Col. Joshua Fry.

He was a witness to a deed of John Harvie to Philip Smith, in Albemarle Co., 29 Nov., 1757. (D. Bk. 2, p. 22).

Benjamin Moore, of Amherst, sold to John Dawson, of said Amherst County, land on the forks of the Cove and Hickory Creek, branches of Rockfish River, 1764. (D. Bk. A, p. 200).

John Dawson and his family lived near Faber's Mill. The personal tax lists, 1793, Lexington Parish, Amherst Co., gives: "Capt. John Dawson" payinx tax on his son, Martin, and George Morris. From the land tax books of 1782, "Capt. John Dawson" paying tax "on 494, 171 and 146 acres."

The inventory of the estate of John Dawson, returned 1st of June, 1810, by his son, John Sorrell Dawson, in which there is mention of "money paid to Martin Dawson and John McDaniel." (W. Bk. 5, p. 31, Amherst); also "that part of the estate that John Dawson inherited from the widow, Sorrell, not listed heretofore." It was the 494 acres of land belonged to John's grandfather, John Sorrell.

1. John^{3} Sorrell Dawson.
2. Pleasant^{3} Dawson.
3. Benjamin^{3} Dawson.
4. Martin^{3} Dawson.
5. Susanna^{3} Dawson.
6. Mary^{3} D. Dawson.
7. Pricilla^{3} Dawson.
8. Nancy^{3} Dawson.
9. Betsey^{3} Dawson.

1. John^{3} Sorrell Dawson (John^{2}, Martin^{1}), married 11 Feb., 1786, Jane Lyon, daughter of Peter Lyon. Benjamin Dawson signed the bond. John received land on Hickory Creek from his great-grandfather. He and his brother, Pleasant, bought 100 acres of land on Rockfiesh River, 1796.

1. Benjamin^{4} Dawson, m. Dorothy Christian.
2. Andrew^{4} Dawson.
3. Agnes Dawson, m. Peter Turner.
4. Pleasant^{4} Dawson, m. Mahala^{4} White (Nancy^{3}, John^{2}, Martin^{1} Dawson).
    1. John^{5} Lyon Dawson, m. Ann Wade.
    2. G.^{5} W. Dawson, m. Sarah May.
    3. Jane^{5} Dawson, m. Dr. I. T. Forbes.
    4. Pleasant^{5} Dawson, m. Henrietta Garland (daughter of Hudson M. Garland and his wife, Letitia Pendleton, who was the daughter of Col. Micajah Pendleton and his wife, Mary Cabell Horsley).
        1. Frank^{6} G. Dawson, m. D. C. Brockenborough, of Charlottesville, Va.

2. Pleasant^{3} Dawson (John^{2}, Martin^{1}), owned 150 acres of land on Hardware River. He was engaged in milling. He died 1826, unmarried.

3. Benjamin[3] Dawson (John[2], Martin[1]), received 120 pounds Sterling from the estate of his great-grandfather, John Sorrell. He was a minister. In 1787 the court of Amherst appointed him guardian to his first cousins, Margaret and Elizabeth Parks, orphans of William. He served as a Private soldier in the Revolutionary war, under Captain Sale, in the 8th Virginia Militia.

4. Martin[3] Dawson (John[2], Martin[1]), died unmarried in the year 1835. His grandfather left money to be paid to him by his brother, John. Martin lived near Milton, Nelson Co., Va. He bequeathed much land and money to the University of Virginia. The will of Martin Dawson, dated 1835: "My brother, John S. Dawson, deceased; my brother, Pleasant Dawson, deceased; my brother, Benjamin Dawson; my sisters, Susanna Adams, Polly Adams, Elizabeth Ford and Nancy White. To the daughters of my deceased sister, Pricilla, namely Elizabeth Faber (Christopher), my tract of land called the College Estate; to the University of Virginia 500 acres of land. To my relative and friend, W. W. Dawson, my wearing apparel."

He provided for the freedom of about sixty of his slaves, and for their removal to Liberia. He bequeathed about $40,000 to the University of Virginia. One of the buildings on the campus at the University was named for him. (See W. Bk. 12, p. 40, Albemarle).

Martin returned the inventory of the estate of Elizabeth Dawson 24 Sept., 1832 (possibly the wife of his uncle, Martin Dawson). (W. B. 9, p. 89, Albemarle Co.)

5. Susanna[3] Dawson (John[2], Martin[1]), married 1780, Richard Adams, of Fluvanna Co.

6. Mary[3] Dawson (John[2], Martin[1]), married 18 Aug., 1789, Charles Adams.

7. Pricilla[3] Dawson (John[2], Martin[1]), married Jan., 1793, Joseph White, of Orange County. The marriage bond in Amherst Co., signed by Martin Dawson. Witnessed by Peter Lyon.

1. Sally[4] W. White.
2. Elizabeth[4] White, m. Christopher Faber. Her uncle, Martin, left to her the College Estate in Albemarle Co., in his will, dated 1835.

8. Nancy[3] Dawson (John[2], Martin[1]), m. Rev. Hugh White.

1. Eliza[4] White.
2. Mahala[4] White. (See Pleasant D. line).

9. Elizabeth[3] Dawson (John[2], Martin[1]), m. 4 Dec., 1798, Abner Ford, of Charlottesville, Va.

2. Nancy[2] Dawson (Martin[1]), b. c. 1754, d. 1823, m. c. 1792 Valentine Cox, son of Henry and Judy Cox of Amherst Co. In 1782 Valentine was paid for having furnished supplies for the use of the Revolutionary Army. A receipt was given to him Oct. 16, 1780, by Gabriel Penn, Provision commissioner of Amherst Co. for supplies, Certificate No. 72, Rd., Va.

1. Elizabeth[3] Cox.
2. Lucy[3] Cox.
3. Milly[3] Cox.

1. Elizabeth[3] (Nancy[2], Martin[1]), m. Jan. 3, 1791, Christopher Calvert.

1. Mary[4] Calvert, m. Capt. John Foy.
    1. John[5] Moran Foy, m. Louise Macy.
        1. Ellen[6] Foy, m. Mr. O'Gorman, of Los Angeles, California.

2. Lucy[3] Cox (Nancy[2], Martin[1]), m. 1806 Lemuel Johnson.

3. Milly[3] Cox, m. Oct. 18, 1795, Martin Dawson (Martin[2], Martin[1]).

3. Thomas[2] Dawson (Martin[1]), was living when his father's will was made.

4. Mildred[2] Dawson (Martin[1]), m. ——— Hancock.

5. Martin[2] Dawson (Martin[1]), b. 1744; d. 1821; m. Elizabeth who died 1832. Martin[2] was a prominent Baptist minister. He began preaching in 1774 when he was thirty years of age. His first charge was at Totier church on Ballenger Creek. He lived on a 500 acre farm, south east of Hughes Shop.

His grandfather bequeathed: "To my grand son Martin Dawson, the sum of 120 pounds currency, to be paid in four years after my death, to him and his heirs, and likewise, twenty shillings each year he continues to preach the gospel, which is to be paid yearly".

Personal tax list, Albemarle Co., 1782, mentions Rev. Martin Dawson. List of 1797, Rev. Martin Dawson paid on two sons, John and Elijah.

Land tax books for 1812, Rev. Martin Dawson paid on 622½ acres.

From will book, Albemarle Co., Bk. 7, p. 115. The will of Martin Dawson, Sen., dated 29 May 1819; prob. 6 Aug. 1821. "To my wife Elizabeth, extrx.; to my sons Martin, William, David, Elijah, John, Rand, Allen, and Hudson; to my daughters Patsy (Martha), Nancy, Milly, Suckey and Betsy; to daugh. Martha Haggard; to daugh. Nancy Haggard; to daugh. Betsy Elsom; and to my cousin Martin Dawson".

1. Elijah^{3} Dawson, m. Martha^{2} Gentry (Benajah^{1}), moved to Calloway, Mo.
2. Martin^{3} Dawson, m. Mildred Cox, Oct. 18, 1795, moved to Gallio Co., Ohio.
3. William^{3} Dawson.
4. David^{3} Dawson.
5. John^{3} Dawson.
6. Rand^{3} Dawson.
7. Allen^{3} Dawson, m. Lucy Wingfield, dau. of Christopher.
8. Hudson^{3} Dawson.
9. Patsy^{3} or Martha^{3}, m. Bert Haggard.
10. Nancy^{3}, m. David Haggard.
11. Milly^{3}.
12. Suckey^{3}.
13. Betsy^{3}, m. Reuben Elsom.

8. Hudson^{3} Dawson (Martin^{2}, Martin^{1}), m. Nov. 22, 1806, Patsy Henley, the bond was signed by Martin, Nov. 17, 1806. Teste: Leonard Henley and William Duncan.

11. Milly^{3} Dawson (Martin^{2}, Martin^{1}), m. Sept. 10, 1792, Jones Reed (widower), the bond is signed by James Calloway; and witnessed by John Franklin and Zachary Dawson. (Could she have married later Nathan Bowles^{2})

6. Mary^{2} Dawson (Martin^{1}), b. c. 1748, mar. c. 1766 William^{3} Parks (John^{2}, Thomas^{1}). She was living in Amherst county when her father made his will (see William Park's page).

7. Margaret^{2} Dawson (Martin^{1}), mar. ——— Franklin, Justice of Peace of Amherst Co.

8. William^{2} Dawson (Martin^{1}), was one of the executors of his brother-in-law, William Parks' will.

9. Zachary^{2} Dawson (Martin^{1}), died 1801; mar. 18 Jan. 1786, Lucy Rucker, dau. of Benjamin Rucker of Amherst county.

Their marriage bond was signed by James Franklin. Zachary and Lucy Dawson moved to North Carolina, and after the death of Zachary, his widow Lucy, married John McDaniel. Zachary was High Sheriff of Amherst Co.

The legacy left to the children of Zachary by his father, Martin Dawson, was not paid until after the death of John Dawson, son and ex'or. of their father Martin. John's ex'ors. paid this legacy to John McDaniel in the year 1810.

Zachary was appointed one of the guardians of Margaret and Elizabeth Parks, children of his sister Mary, widow of William Parks.

Zachary paid tax on 164 acres in Amherst Co., Va.

1. Benjamin[3] Dawson, m. 31 Jan. 1816, Susan Woodruff. He served in the War of 1812, under Lieut. George McDaniel.
2. Martin[3] Dawson.
3. Nelson[3] Carter Dawson, m. 16 Mar. 1816, Frances Woodruff.
4. Lewis[3] Dawson.
5. Susan[3] Dawson, m. ——— Haskill.
6. Jonathan[3] Rucker Dawson, m. 17 Sept. 1818, Sally L. Bowcock, the marriage bond was signed by Lewis Dawson.

10. Nelson[2] Carter Dawson (Martin[1]), m. Lucy Goode, daughter of Samuel and his wife, Mary Collier Goode. Nelson Dawson served as corporal in the War of 1812, under Lieut. George McDaniel, 4th Brigade, Va. Militia, 8th Regiment.

1. Lucy[3] Goode Dawson, m. 1792, John Wingfield.
2. Matilda[3] Dawson, m. ——— Burford of Lynchburg.
3. Samuel[3] Gaines Dawson, b. 1796; d. 1835, in Zanesville, Ohio; served in the War of 1812 as Surgeon's Mate to Dr. Austin.
4. Elizabeth[3] Dawson, m. ——— Ware, moved to Missouri.
5. Ann[3] Goode Dawson, m. James Lambkin.
6. ———[3] Dawson, m. ——— Holly of Missouri.

Nelson Carter Dawson and Reuben Pendleton gave bond as Ex'ors. of the estate of Martin Dawson, before James Franklin, James Dillard and others, Justices of Amherst Co., 16 March 1812 (W. Bk. 5, p. 96, Amherst).

11. Jesse[2] Martin, m. Dec. 5, 1791, Sally Turner, dau. of Henry.

12. Elizabeth[2] Dawson (Martin[1]), m. Aug. 4, 1792, Reuben[4] Rucker (Isaac, John, Peter). The marriage bond was signed by Nelson Carter Dawson, with Isaac, Anthony and Moses Rucker security.

13. Susanna[2] Dawson (Martin[1]), m. Mch. 2, 1799, George Tinsley.

Marriage Bonds

1764, Jan. 27. Robert Stegar m. Mary Dawson, of Amelia Co.

1756, Jan. 16.Samuel Dawson m. Martha Jones, of Brunswick Co.

1778, Jan. 13. Irwin Jones m. Priscilla Dawson, dau. of Samuel, of Brunswick.

1801. William Davis m. Priscilla Dawson in Rockbridge Co.

1785. John Dawson m. Jane Bryon of Campbell Co.

1805, Jan. 29. Nelson Carter Dawson m. Nancy (Jones) Burton, widow of Philip Burton of Bedford Co.

1806, Oct. 6. Capt. John Jones had conveyed to his sons, Lewellyn Jones and Charles Jones, 252 acres of land. On this date Nelson Carter Dawson and wife, Nancy, relinquished any right they may have in the estate of John Jones. Bedford Co.

Isle of Wight Co., Va.

In 1631 Henry Dawson of Breeden, Leicester, Eng., had three sons who came to Virginia with William Claibourne, locating in Isle of Wight Co., Va. Sons John, Thomas and William Dawson.

Land Grant, b. 10, p. 119. Martin Dawson of Isle of Wight Co. patented 350 acres of land on the south side of Mainblackwater River of the same county, beginning at the Cypress Swamp adjoining P. Mackenny and Theophilus Joyner, for transporting six persons, namely: Temperance Hunt, Zacharia Field, John Parsons, Bridget Brown, Thomas Smith, and Thomas Harrison. 13 Nov. 1713.

Martin Dawson patented 200 acres of land in Isle of Wight Co. on the North side of Maherin River on the North side of Quarter Branch adjoining said Dawson's land, 10 June 1727 (L. Gr., b. 13, p. 127).

Martin Dawson of Isle of Wight Co. sold to Robert Johnson 400 acres of land, part of a patent to Captain Barnaby MacKennie, 16 Dec. 1714, and part patented by Dawson, 13 Nov. 1713, land at Little House Branch, adjoining Robert Johnson and Theopilus Joyner, 26 Aug. 1724. Witness: James Ramsey and John Joyner. Martin M. Dawson (Great Book, p. 661, Isle of Wight).

Martin M. Dawson of Isle of Wight Co. sold to Henry Joyner of same, for 5 lbs. Sterling 70 acres of land on South side of Cypress Swamp to the dividing branch, 18 May 1741 (D. B. 6, p. 150). Witness: John Dunkley and Mathew Griffin.

Martin Dawson patented 180 acres of land in Isle of Wight Co. on the north side of Meherin River, beginning at the river . . . . to Thomas Williams, Jr., by Williams' line to the lower ground of the Meherin River, to the Quarter Branch, Mch. 15, 1741 (L. Gr., b. 20, p. 200).

Will of Martin Dawson dated Sept. 10, 1745, probated Oct. 9, 1746, Isle of Wight Co. To son Henry, to dau. Eleanor Jones, to dau. Sarah Inman, to son Joshua, to dau. Martha Dinkin, to housekeeper, Mary Cocks, to dau. Margaret Warren. Exes: Son in law John Jones and Robert Warren. Wit.: Henry Crafford, John Pierce and Henry Dawson. Signed Martin M. Dawson (W. B. 5, p. 51, Isle of Wight Co.). Rebecca Dawson, widow and relict, refused her part.

Sorrell

1. John[1] Sorrell may have been a grandson of Robert and Rebecca Sorrell of James City and Surrey. We cannot find a will, the records of James City having been destroyed. John first appears in Prince George, then Goochland and Albemarle, and died in Amherst in 1783. John Sorrell was born about 1690, m. about 1715. He was paid 36 lbs. of tobacco in Prince George County out of the estate of Thomas Jackson (Great Vol., p. 25, Prince George), 13 Sept. 1714. He m. twice, 1st wife Mary signed many deeds, b. c. 1700, d. before 1770. Early in 1770 he m. again, Mary Coleman Ellis, a widow who survived him.

John's will refers to his great grandchildren who were grown when he wrote his will in 1780, from this we know he was a very old man when he died. Tradition says he lived to be more than a hundred and his son-in-law Martin Dawson lived to be one hundred and fifteen.

Robert Adams sold to John Sorrell for £10, 100 acres of land "On ye upper fork of Broad branch of Tuckahoe Creek. Mourning, wife of Robert Adams, acknowledges the deed, all houses, orchards, gardens, etc. Nov. 16, 1728. Witness: George Payne, Joseph Ashlin (Goochland D. B. 1, p. 40).

George Alves brought suit against John Sorrell, Dec. 18, 1728, Goochland.

John Sorrell sold to Sylvanus Pumfree, Margaret Pumfree and Sylvanus Pumfree, Jr., of Tuckahoe Creek, Dec. 16, 1729, for £10, 100 acres land on broad branch of Tuckahoe Creek. Witness: Robert Adams, John Bowie (D. B. I, p. 156, Goochland).

Sylvanus Pumphry of Goochland sold to John Sorrell of same, 100 acres of land adjoining Wadloe and Collins, on the Broad branch of Tuckahoe Creek, adjoining land purchased by Pumphry of said Sorrell, Dec. 13, 1731 (D. B. 1, p. 337, Goochland).

Charles Johnson of St. James Parish sold to John Sorrell of same for 5900 lbs. of tobacco 150 acres of land on the north side of James River. Elizabeth, wife of Charles Johnson relinquishes her rights. Witness: Robert Payne. May 18, 1731 (D. B. 1, p. 248, Goochland). James Barret, Benjamin Woodson.

Robert and George Payne, Jr., sold land to John Sorrell, July 1732. Aug. 1732, a suit against John Sorrell was brought by Thomas Wadloe (O. B. 3, p. 89, Goochland). Same O. B., p. 106, John Sorrell brought suit against William Moseley.

William Mayo brought suit against John Sorrell, Jan. 1733 (O. B. 3, p. 222, Goochland).

John Sorrell and wife Mary of Goochland sold land to Thomas Owen, of Hanover, 150 acres on the north side of James River for 150 bushels of wheat. 17 Sept. 1734. Witness: J. Williams, Thomas Anderson, Charles Allen (Goochland D. B. 2, p. 42).

A suit between John Sorrell and Nathan Pumfree for 300 lbs. of tobacco due for the rent of a plantation leased by said Sorrell to William Fennell, upon whose private removal out of the county, the said Pumphry attached the estate remaining on the said plantation, carry the same away without leaving sufficient to pay the rent.

It is considered by the court that the Sorrell do recover against Pumphree the said tobacco with cost by him. Jan. 1734 (O. B. 3, p. 321, Goochland).

John Sorrell patented 100 acres of land lying in Goochland Co. on the branches of Tuckahoe Creek beginning at his own land on Webber's line, east to Charles Johnsons, north to Adam's line. Apr. 6, 1734 (b. 15, p. 199, L. Gr.).

John Sorrell of Goochland sold to Charles Johnson for £10, 100 acres of land in Goochland on Tuckahoe Creek, land granted to said Sorrell Apr. 6, 1734, on Webber's line, to Adams' line. Signed: John Sorrell (O. B. 2, p. 135, Goochland, July 14, 1735).

Mch. 21, 1734, Mary, wife of John Sorrell, signed a deed.

William Perry sold 220 acres of land to John Sorrell in St. James Parish, on the S. S. of the Rivaina River, adjoining Charles Lewis. Jan. 21, 1741. Witness: Pricilla Dawson, Martin Dawson (D. B. 4, Goochland).

(The Pricilla Dawson, wife of Martin, was a daughter of John Sorrell. From this deed she is adready married in 1741.)

Mch. 28, 1745 (Albemarle O. B. B, p. 9, 1745, Mch. 28). John Sorrell, Robert Adams, Charles Bond, and Martin Dawson were appointed appraisers of the estate of Charles Blane deceased

John Sorrell sold 260 acres on the S. branch of the Rivanna River, part of a grant to William Perry.

The wife of John Sorrell relinquishes her dower rights (no name). Signed: John Sorrell. Witness: John Henderson, John Dawson. Jan. 20, 1755 (D. B. 7, p. 536, Albemarle Co.).

"The above deed was recorded 1783 as the book in which it had been recorded was burned by the enemies" (Albemarle Co. D. B. 7, p. 536), 1783.

James Mahunney left to Margaret Sorrell land in Louisa Co. whereon James Francis did live when she is of age or marries. May 16, 1753 (W. B. 2, p. 9, Albemarle Co.).

Francis Wright was in a suit against Richard Sorrell, case dismissed. 27 Sept. 1745 (O. B. 1744-48, p. 74, Albemarle Co.).

John Sorrell in a suit against Thomas Fitzpatrick, administrator of Charles Blany, for 25 shillings, which he is to recover and 94½ lbs. of tobacco for his cost. 27 Sept. 1745 (O. B. 1745-48, p. 75).

John Sorrell was ordered to be surveyor of the Three Notched Road from No. 12, in the room of James Defer. 12 Nov. 1747 (O. B. 1745-48, p. 314, Albemarle Co.).

Alexander Patten was appointed Constable in the room of John Sorrell. 12 May 1748 (O. B. 1745-48, p. 360), Albemarle.

John Sorrell pat. 95 acres of land on the south branch of Cove and the north branch of Hickory Creeks. July 20, 1769 (L. Gr., b. 37, p. 378).

John Sorrell of Amherst and Mary Coleman Ellice, a marmiage agreement. "He to provide maintenance according to ability and station in life and at my death, my heirs to pay her £60 or £10 yearly during her life and she to claim no more." Mary agrees to the contract. Nov. 3, 1770 (D. B. C, p. 146, Amherst Co.).

John Sorrell was paying taxes in Amherst in 1782 on 495 acres, the "Estate" paid the tax the following year.

The census of Amherst Co. 1783 gives John Sorrell as paying on 2 whites and 26 blacks.

John was too old for Revolutionary Service but he furnished supplies to the army (see the Rev. Claims, Archives, Richmond, Va.)

On Oct. 5, 1781—325 lbs. of beef.

On Oct., 1781—285 lbs. of beef.

Oct. 15, 1781, "Received of Mr. John Sorrell, 275 lbs. of beef for the use of the public."

Issue:

1. Kate Howard Sorrell.
2. Pricilla Sorrell, m. Martin Dawson before 1741 (deed).

IN THE NAME OF GOD, AMEN, I, John Sorrell, of Amherst County being ancient and not knowing how soon I may die, yet of perfect sence and memory do make and appoint this my last Will and Testament My body being entered according to the discretion of my Executors and my debts paid, I dispose of what worldly goods may then remain in my estate as followeth, viz: Item. I lend to my wife, Molly Coleman Sorrell during her widowhood the Dwelling House I now live in with as much ground convenient thereto as she may want to tend, with all convenient barn and outhouses excepted, with one negro woman, Sall, and if the said negro should die she may at her discretion choose another about eight years old, and if the orchard on said plantation shall bear fruit, she shall have ten gallons of brandy, with as much of the said fruit as she may want for her own use each year the said orchard may hit. I also lend her during her widowhood one horse and side saddle, with as much of the household and kitchen furniture as she shall think proper (two stills excepted), with the use of the milch cows to said family. I also will that the taxes on said negroe be paid by my Executors, and further if the said negroe should have children the expense of them shall be paid as above. I also give my wife six hundred pounds of gross pork, with one hundred weight of beef, one bushel of salt, five barrels of corn, one barrell of wheat, six pounds of sugar, ten pounds of tallow, and two pair of shoes which she is to have each year she lives my widow. I also will that the house be kept in repair with a sufficient quantity of firewood for said family, the whole to be done by my Executors at the expense of my estate. Item. I give and bequeath to my daughter, Katy Howard, and her heirs forever, thirty pounds currency to be paid at two payments, one half to be paid one year after my death, the other half the following year. Item, I give and bequeath to my gran-daughter Mary

Ann Sneed and her two oldest children Frances and John Sneed ten pounds currency each to them and their heirs forever to be paid three years after my death. Item. I give and bequeath to my grandson Martin Dawson the sum of one hundred pounds currency, to be paid in four years after my death to him and his heirs forever, and likewise twenty shillings each year he continues a preacher of the Gospel, which is to be paid yearly. Item. I give and bequeath to my grandsons, Thomas and William Dawson each ten pounds currency to them and their heirs forever to be paid five years after my death. Item. I give and bequeath to my great grand son, John Sorrell Dawson, son of my grandson, John Dawson and Sally, his wife, that part of my land I now live on lying on the north side of Hickory Creek provided he the said John Sorrell Dawson pay his brother Pleasant Dawson One Hundred Pounds currency within one year after he the said Pleasant Dawson comes of age, and to his brother Benjamin Dawson the like sum to be paid within two years after the said Benjamin Dawson comes of age. I say that if the said John Sorrell Dawson should refuse to pay his brothers the above sums of money, then the said land to be publickly sold and the money arising from the sale to be equally divided amongst the three brothers above mentioned, their heirs, etc. Note that no one has or shall have any the least wright to claim or dispose of the Houses and as much ground convenient thereto as I have lent to my wife, that is to say, during her widowhool. I likewise give to my great grandson John Sorrell Dawson, son of John Dawson and Sally his wife, my negro woman Dinah with her increase to him and his heirs forever to be by him possessed when he comes of lawful age. Item. I give and bequeath to Pleasant Dawson, my great grandson, son of my grandson John Dawson and Sally his wife, my negro boy, Ben, to him and his heirs forever, to be by him possessed when comes of lawful age. Item. I give and bequeath to my great grandson, Benjamin Dawson, son of my grandson, John Dawson and Sally, his wife, my negro boy Goliath, to him and his heirs forever, to be by him possessed when he comes of lawful age. Item. I give and bequeath to my great grandson, Martin Dawson, son of my grandson John Dawson and Sally his wife, my negro boy Squire, to him and his heirs forever to be by him possessed when he comes of lawful age. Item; I give to my great grand daughter Susanna Dawson, daughter of my grand son John Dawson and his wife Sally, my negro girl named Fanny and her increase to her and her heirs forever, to be by her possessed when of lawful age or day of marriage. Item; I give and bequeath to my great grand daughter Mary Dawson daughter of my grand son John Dawson and his wife Sally, a negro girl Rachel, to her and her heirs forever to be possessed by her when of lawful age or day of marriage. Item; I give to my great grand daughter Prysilla Dawson, dau. of my grand son John Dawson and wife Sally, my negro girl Dicy to her and her heirs forever to be by her possessed when of lawful age or day of marriage. Item; I give and bequeath to my great grand daughter Nancy Dawson dau. of my grand son John Dawson and Sally his wife, my negro girl Winney to her and her heirs forever to be by her possessed when of age or day of marriage. Item; I give to my great grand dau. Betsy Dawson, dau. of my grand son John Dawson and his wife Sally, my negro girl Milly to her and her heirs forever. Item; I give and bequeath to my grand son John Dawson, son of Martin Dawson and Prysilla his wife, the remainder of my lands, negroes, stocks of all kinds with all and every of their increase to him and his heirs forever, and lastly I appoint my two grand sons John Dawson and Martin Dawson and Peter Lyons executors of this my last will and testament, revoking and disannul all former will or wills made by me heretofore. As witness my hand and seal this twenty fifth day of March one Thousand seven hundred and eighty. John Sorrell (Seal). Witness: Charles Martin, Terish Turner, Benjamin Moore, Ephraim Blane, Samuel Anderson. Probated Sept. 1, 1783, Amherst Co., Va. (W. B. 2, p. 140).

Legatees named in the will of John Sorrell. To my wife Molly Coleman Sorrell; to my dau. Katy Howard; to grand dau. Mary Ann Sneed; to my grand son Martin Dawson; to my grand son Thomas Dawson; to my grand son William Dawson; to my grand son John Dawson; to great grand son John Sorrell Dawson, ch. of gr. son John and Sally Dawson; to great grand son Pleasant Dawson; to great grand son Benjamin Dawson; to great grand son Martin Dawson; to great grand dau. Susanna Dawson; to great grand dau. Mary Dawson; to great grand dau. Prysilla Dawson; to great grand dau. Nancy Dawson; to great grand dau. Betsy Dawson; to great grand children Frances and John Snead; to my grand son John Dawson, son of Martin Dawson and his wife Prysilla.

Mary[3] Dawson (Priscilla[2], John[1] Sorrell), m. William Parks, dau. Elizabeth m. Ambrose[5] Rucker (Reuben[4], Ambrose[3], ——).

JAMES CITY CO. RECORDS

Robert Sorrell patented 80 acres of land on an island within Warrany Creek in James City Co., south east by the land of Edward Cole, north to Joyner's neck of land south to Warrany Cr., east to Bennett Freeman's, for transporting two persons. Apr. 10, 1651 (L. Gr., b. 2, p. 310).

He patented 700 acres of land on the southmost branch of Warrany Cr. adjoining Mr. Soane. Nov. 20, 1653 (L. Gr., b. 3, p. 26).

(York Co., D. B. 4, p. 338). Robert Sorrell of Chickahominy in James City Co. sold to Martin Collier of York Co. 497 acres of land purchased of John Holmwood, who purchased it of John Hamlett, who acquired it of Richard Hamlett, who patented the land Dec. 22, 1669.

Daniel Parke patented 528 acres of land in James City Co., on the west side of Rickahock path on the cart path that goes from Mr. Sorrell's to Mr. Baker's, adjoining Col. Pettus, and part that goes to Chickahominy Gate, adjoining Mr. Sorrell's, the said land was assigned to said Parke by Christopher Harris, and the residue sold and assigned to him by Mr. Robert Sorrell Mch. 24, 1662-3 (L. Gr., b. 5, p. 275).

(Journals of the House of Burgess, Feb. 20, 1689, b. 2, p. 70. It was ordered that Rebecca the widow of Capt. Robert Sorrell, who was lately killed in his majesty's service, his estate plundered and taken away by the rebels, be allowed out of the public levy, 4000 lbs. of Tobacco and cask, and what of her goods that can be found Bee returned to her.

On the 2nd of Sept. 1657 Robert Sorrell purchased William Davis from Coll. Swann for 2000 lbs. of live pork, Robert in referring to the freedom of said William Davis, said "William, if thou wilt be ruled by me, I will prescribe to thee one that will plead thy cause, and ask thee nothing and withall nominated Mr. Morryson (b. I, p. 117, Surry Co.).

The following may be sons of Robert Sorrell:

1. Martin[2] Sorrell.
2. John[2] Sorrell.
3. Edward[2] Sorrell.

1. Martin[2] Sorrell (Robert[1]).

Martin Sorrell was granted 280 acres of land in James City Co., Williamson Parish, being the plantation whereon he now lives, extending to a branch of Timber Swamp to Col. Dukes, near his house, to a road dividing his land from Mr. Ballard's to Mr. Sorrell's corner, to Richard Hamlett's, to Martin Sorrell's (L. Gr., b. 10, p. 249, 1710-19).

2. John[2] Sorrell (Robert[1]), lived and died in James City Co., Va., two of his sons moved to Westmoreland Co.

1. Thomas[3] Sorrell.
2. John[3] Sorrell.

1. Thomas[3] Sorrell (John[2], Robert[1]), died in Westmoreland Co. in 1726, was b. in James City Co., m. Elizabeth O'Canny. Daniel O'Canny left a will dated Feb. 27, 1715, probated Jan. 16, 1716, which mentioned "My son in law Thomas Sorrell (Westmoreland Wills).

James Brechen of Richmond Co. deeded to Thomas Sorrell of Westmoreland Co. 184 acres of land in Cople Parish on the main branch of Nominy River, 23 Sept. 1709 (D. B. 4, p. 246, N. N. L. Gr.).

Thomas Sorrell patented 221 acres of land on the north side of Herring Cr. of Nominy River adjoining Nicholas Spercer, close to Nominy River, Jan. 7, 1716 (D. B. 5, p. 173, L. Gr.).

He patented 121 acres of land in Westmoreland, formerly patented by James Hawley adjoining Henry Duncan deceased May 26, 1712 (D. B. 4, p. 87, L. Grants).

The will of John Erwin dated 10 Apr. 1716, leaves his plantation to "My friend Thomas Sorrell, and money for the education of Elizabeth the dau. of Thomas Sorrell, two years Schooling, also two years schooling to Frances the dau. of John Sorrell, the will also mentions Ann, the late wife of John Sorrell (Westmoreland Wills).

Thomas was deputy Clerk of Westmoreland Co. in 1714.

The will of Thomas Sorrell was dated Jan. 12, 1725, probated Feb. 26, 1726 "To my son James all the land I live on; all of the lands at the head of Nominy where I formerly lived to my son John, and also to him the land devised to me by my father in law Daniel O'canny; to my son James the land in James City Co. which my honored father John Sorrell devised to me, and also one third of my mill, two thirds of my will to son John.

To my nephew Thomas Sorrell the land where John Holloway now lives on, on condition that my nephew quit claim title to the land adjoining my dwelling seat, which he has promised. I have purchased the land in James City Co. devised by my father to my brother John Sorrell deceased. To my loving consort all of her wearing apparel, rings and .... horse saddle and furniture, the use of three slaves and all my other estates during the minority of my children, she clothing and maintaining and educating them. All the rest of my estate to be divided between my wife and children. To son John two negroes, and to son James after the death of his mother the negroes given to her.

To my aforesaid nephew and his sisters Elizabeth and Frances a mourning ring apiece, and a prayer book to each. Bequests to "my daughters Ann and Winifred." Execs.: Capt. George Turberville and Mr. William Sturman.

Codicil. Aug. 8, 1725. "Son James to pay to his brother John 500 lbs. of tobacco.

1. James[4] Sorrell.
2. John[4] Sorrell.
3. Ann[4] Sorrell.
4. Winifred[4] Sorrell.

1. James[4] Sorrell (Tho.[3], Jno.[2], Robert[1]), was living when his father made his will in 1725 but was dead before 1733 when his brother John sold his (James') land, the land James had inherited from his father, Thomas, but now being deceased John had inherited, on Nominy River.

2. John[4] Sorrell (Tho.[3], Jno.[2], Robert[1]), inherited the property of his brother James before 1733, land left to him by his father Thomas in 1725. John Sorrell of Cople Parish, son and heir of Thomas, late of Cople Parish, sold to George Turberville 93 acres of land out of 500 acres given by Daniel O'Cany in 1715 to his grandson, John Crabb, and son in law, Thomas Sorrell, which land Thomas gave to his son John Sorrell. Sold May 6, 1741 (D. B. 9, p. 148, Westmoreland). John Sorrell sold to John Bushrod a water mill near the head of Nominy River on the north side of said Sorrel's plantation, May 12, 1744 (D. B. 10, p. 81, Westmoreland).

3. Ann[4] Sorrell (Tho.[3], John[2], Robert[1]), m. Samuel Earle. Samuel[2] Earle, son of Samuel[1], being about to marry Ann, the dau. of Thomas and Elizabeth Sorrell, is given by his father 200 acres of land in Westmoreland Co. and 400 acres more in Stafford Co. May 5, 1726 (D. B. 8, p. 174, Westmoreland Co.).

7 Nov., 1733. Lease. Thomas Sorrell, county Westmoreland, planter, son and heir of John Sorrell, deceased, of first part, and John Sorrell of same county, son of Thomas Sorrell, deceased, and brother and heir of James Sorrell, also deceased, of the other part.

WHEREAS the said Thomas Sorrell, deceased, in and by last will in writing bearing date 8 Oct. 1725, among other things did bequeath to his nephew, said Thomas Sorrell, party to these presents and heirs etc. . . . . . land on which John Holliday then lived, provided said nephew did authentically make over his right to that land adjoining the said testator's dwelling seat which the father of said Thomas Sorrell had purchased of John Medford, unto the said Testator's son James, etc. . . . . . and WHEREAS said James Sorrell since deceased and the said John Sorrell, party to these presents, is brother and heir at law of said James, etc.

. . . . doth bargain and sell to said John Sorrell in Parish of Cople, County of Westmoreland, formerly purchased by John Sorrell, deceased father of said Thomas, party of the first part, of John Medford, 1711, etc. Wit. John Tarpey Jun., Edward Barradell (D. B. 8, p. 156.

At a Court continued and held for the sd county the 28 day Nov., 1733.

Thomas Sorrell, son and heir of John Sorrell, deceased, personally acknowledged this Deed of Lease by him passed for the conveyance of certain land therein mentioned to John Sorrell, son & heir of Thomas Sorrell, Gent., deceased, to be his proper action and deed, etc. Recorded 3 Jan. 1733 (D. B. 8, p. 157).

The will of John Wright of Cople Parish, Westmoreland County, Jan. 21, 1713, probated 1714, left a legacy to Anna, the dau. of Thomas and wife, Elizabeth Sorrell.

2. John[3] Sorrell (John[2], Robert[1]), was b. in James City Co., d. in Westmoreland Co. before 1722. He was given land in James City Co. by his father John, which he sold to his brother Thomas. He married Anna Erwin, who died before 1716. John Erwin in his will dated 1716 leaves to Frances the dau. of John and his late wife Anne Sorrell, two years schooling (Westmoreland Wills).

1. Thomas[4] Sorrell.
2. Frances[4] Sorrell.
3. Elizabeth[4] Sorrell.

1. Thomas[4] Sorrell (John[3], John[2], Robert[1]). "Thomas Sorrell, son of John, deceased, late of Westmoreland", sold to Charles Bragg of Lunenburg Parish, Lunenburg Co., 128 acres of land devised to said Thomas by his uncle, Thomas Sorrell, Nov. 5, 1750 (D. B. 11, p. 246, Westmoreland Co.).

Thomas Sorrell married Million ———. Thomas Sorrell of Westmoreland Co. and wife Million sold to John Turberville 186 acres of land, the family grave yard being excepted, on the south side of Nominy Mill Pond, on the north side of Augustine Washington's mill Pond, land purchased by the late Mr. John Bushrod of John Sorrell deceased, which land fell to said Thomas Sorrell by inheritance from his father John Sorrell late of Westmoreland, deceased, who died intestate. Dec. 24, 1772.

3. Edward[2] Sorrell (John[1]). "Deed of Edward Sorrell of James City Co. and wife Alice, executor of Benjamin Goodrich, Gent, late of said county and colony deceased", June 10, 1703

(*William and Mary Quarterly,* Vol. 22, p. 216). Edward was a member of the House of Burgess from James City Co. 1684. Robert Sorrell was a headright of Benjamin Harrison 1627 (*Va. Hist. Mag.,* Vol. 6, p. 160).

The importation recorded by Greer:

John Sorrell, 1652, by Thomas Fleetwood, Lower Norfolk Co., Va.; Robert Sorrell, 1652, by Thomas Fleetwood, Lower Norfolk Co., Va.; John Sorrell, 1647, by Thomas Wright, Lower Norfolk Co., Va.; Robert Sorrell, 1647, by Thomas Wright, Lower Norfolk Co., Va.; Robert Sorrell, 1653, by Richary Carey; Robert Sorrell, 1651, by Thomas Keeling, Lower Norfolk Co., Va.; William Sorrell of Elizabeth City Co., Va., 1643, by Edward Murfey.

The Sorrells were Huguenots, they left France about 1544, went to England and were naturalized there about that time (Huguenot Society of London, Vol. 8, p. 223), therefore they required no naturalization when they came to Virginia a century later. See The Visitation of 1636 of Sorrells of Essex, England.

Gibson

Peter[1] Gibson.

1. John[2] Gibson, m. 1st Nancy Gibson; m. 2nd Elizabeth Harvey; m. 3rd Mrs. Elizabeth (Bush) Smith.
    1. John[3] Gibson, m. Eliza Collins, daughter of George Collins.

Marshall

Thomas[1] Marshall m. Susanna Rodes, daughter of Ephroditus Rodes.

1. Ephroditus[2] Marshall, m. 1st Nancy Dunn, daughter of James and Sara (Harvey) Dunn.
    1. James[3] Thomas Marshall, m. Jane[4] Frances Gibson, daughter of John[3] and Eliza Collins Gibson John[2], Peter[1]).
        1. Willie[4] Minor Marshall, m. Downing Lemuel Smith, son of Downing and Sarah Powers Smith.
            1. Eva[5] Minor Smith, m. Dr. E. S. Gregory, Mayor of the City of Tuscumbia, Ala.

Sandidge

William[1] Sandidge m. Elizabeth Taylor.

1. Benjamin[2] Sandidge, m. Elizabeth Childress.
    1. Nancy[3] Sandidge.
    2. Mary[3] Sandidge, m. Absolom Higginbotham.
        1. James[4] Higginbotham, m. Ann London.
        2. Rufus[4] Higginbotham, m. Lizzie Hargrove.
        3. Nancy[4] Higginbotham, m. ——— Royster.
        4. Benjamin[4] Higginbotham, m. ——— Carter.
        5. Absolom[4] Higginbotham, m. Elizabeth Tucker.
        6. Aaron[4] Higginbotham, m. Ann Sandidge.
        7. Paul[4] Higginbotham, d. in Civil War.
    3. Lindsey[3] Sandidge, m. Clara Graves Higginbotham.
        1. Eliza[4] Jane Sandidge, m. Benjamin Jenning Rucker.
        2. Napoleon[4] Sandidge, moved to Bowling Green Co., Ky.
        3. Brown[4] Sandidge, m. Ann Turpin.
        4. Nancy[4] Croxton Sandidge, m. Thomas Hallowell Rucker.
        5. Mary[4] Sandidge, m. Arthur White.
    4. Anderson[3] Sandidge, m. 1st ——— Ware; m. 2nd Harriet Hansborough.
    5. Elizabeth[3] Sandidge, m. Aaron Higginbotham, brother to Absalom.

Plunkett

John[1] Plunkett of Orange m. Mildred Hawkins (later she married Isaac Rucker and moved to Amherst Co. (See Isaac Rucker, p. 130).

1. Sally[2] Plunkett.
2. Benjamin[2] Plunkett.

1. Sally[2] Plunkett (John[1]), m. John[4] Rucker (John[3], John[2], Peter[1]).

2. Benjamin[2] Plunkett (John[1]), m. first Winifred[4] Rucker (Ambrose[3], John[2], Peter[1]); m. second Frances[4] Ham (Stephen Ham and wife Mildred[3] Rucker, dau. of John[2], Peter[1]).

Issue (by 1st mar.):

1. Ambrose^{3} Plunkett.
2. Sally^{3} Plunkett, m. Jan. 7, 1793, James Wickersham of Amherst.

Issue (by 2nd mar.):

3. Jonathan^{3} Plunkett.
4. Willis^{3} Rucker Plunkett.
5. Nelly^{3} Rucker Plunkett.
6. William^{3} Rucker Plunkett.

1. Ambrose^{3} Plunkett (Benj.^{2}, John^{1}), b. Feb. 21, 1782, lived in Campbell Co., d. in Buckingham Co., m. Tabitha Hill, b. Oct. 28, 1781, dau. of James and Ann Hill, of Amherst Co.

1\. 1. Cyrena^{4} Plunkett, b. May 21, 1802.
2. John^{4} Hill Plunkett, b. Sept. 9, 1803.
3. Frances^{4} Plunkett, b. Feb. 14, 1805.
4. Winifred^{4} Plunkett, b. Apr. 13, 1806.
5. Taliaferro^{4} Plunkett, b. Sept. 23, 1807.
6. Sarah^{4} Plunkett, b. June 28, 1809.
7. Nancy^{4} Plunkett, b. Nov. 6, 1810.
8. Nancy^{4} Ann Plunkett, b. Apr. 13, 1812.
9. Elizabeth^{4} Plunkett, b. Mch. 14, 1814.
10. Willis^{4} Plunkett, b. Oct. 13, 1815.
11. Adeline^{4} Plunkett, b. Mch. 14, 1817.
12. James^{4} Plunkett, b. Oct. 4, 1818.
13. William^{4} Plunkett, b. Mch. 16, 1820.
14. Napoleon^{4} Plunkett, b. Nov. 29, 1821.
15. Washington^{4} Plunkett, b. Jan. 3, 1824.

1. Cyrena^{4} Plunkett (Amb.^{3}, Benj.^{2}, John^{1}), b. May 21, 1802; m. ——— Whitehead.

1. Cyrena^{5} Whitehead, b. Apr. 30, 1848, d. Mch. 10, 1910, m. Edwin^{6} Ruthvin Higginbotham, Mch. 25, 1868, son of Alexander^{5} Brown Higginbotham and wife, Eliza Frances Plunkett, grandson of Aaron^{4} Higginbotham and wife, Elizabeth Sandidge, dau. of Capt. Benj. Sandidge. (See Sandidge, p. 481).

1. Nannie^{6} Lee Higginbotham.
2. Lora^{6} Pettuce Higginbotham.
3. Margaret^{6} Eliza Higginbotham.
4. James^{6} Shields Higginbotham.
5. Frank^{6} Plunkett Higginbotham.
6. Eddie^{6} Morris Higginbotham.

7. Charley^{6} Ambrose Higginbotham.
8. Willis^{6} Cabell Higginbotham.
9. Lula^{6} May Higginbotham.
10. China^{6} Etta Higginbotham.
11. Herbert^{6} Maitland Higginbotham.

1. Nannie^{6} Lee Higginbotham, b. Mch. 12, 1869, m. Feb. 20, 1895, Judson T. Carter, b. Sept. 4, 1864.

1. Thorbhill^{7} Carter, b. Dec. 29, 1895, m. Alice Carson, d. Feb. 28, 1928.
    1. Elizabeth^{8} Lee Carter.
2. Henry^{7} Shields Carter, b. Dec. 12, 1897, m. Mary Duncan, Feb. 11, 1928.
    1. Henry^{8} Shields Carter, Jr.
3. Carrell^{7} Judson Carter, b. May 22, 1899, d. Feb. 14, 1920.
4. Irene^{7} Mar Carter, b. May 25, 1901, m. John Joseph Clarkson, June 12, 1923, b. Aug. 12, 1894, d. Mch. 1928, son of Crawford Clarkson and wife, Mary Harvey.
    1. Elgin^{8} Horsley Clarkson, b. Nov. 22, 1824.
    2. Nannie^{8} Clarkson, b. June, 1926.
5. Eliza^{7} Hall Carter, b. May 4, 1904, m. Robert Brent, May 14, 1921, son of Robert Kent Brent.
    1. Robert^{8} Kent Brent, Jr., b. July 21, 1924.
6. Arthur^{7} Carter, b. June 6, 1905, m. Mch. 6, 1926, Mary Bishop, dau. of Margaret (Plunkett) Bishop.
    1. Betty^{8} Jane Carter, b. Mch. 11, 1927.
7. Leland^{7} Carter, b. July 16, 1907.

2. Lora^{6} Pettuce Higginbotham (Cyrena^{5}, Cyrena^{4}, Amb.^{3}, Benj.^{2}), b. Mch. 13, 1872, m. Dec. 2, 1895, Thomas Dillard Wright, son of William Wright and wife, Mary Ethel Wood.

1. William^{7} Franklin Wright, b. Nov. 12, 1897, m. Mrs. Ann Bell Coin, nee Allen.
2. Katie^{7} Lee Wright, b. Jan. 1, 1900, d. June 19, 1928, m. Raymond Clyde Higginbotham, son of Cyrus Aaron Higginbotham and wife, Althea Jane Higginbotham.
    1. Joseph^{8} Cabell Lee Higginbotham, b. Oct. 5, 1919.
    2. Raymond^{8} C. Higginbotham.
    3. Virginia^{8} Pettuce Higginbotham, b. July 12, 1923.
3. Cyrena^{7} May Wright, b. May 27, 1902, m. Dec. 22, 1923, Dowdy Almond.

4. Percie[7] Wright, b. June 28, 1903, d. age four.
5. Lulie[7] Maggie Wright, b. July 28, 1905.
6. Thomas[7] Dillard Wright, b. Apr. 25, 1907.
7. Nettie[7] Corine Wright, b. May 9, 1909.
8. anr 9. Edwin[7] and Edith[7] Wright, b. Feb. 16, 1911.
10. Lynnwood[7] Massey Wright, b. May 24, 1914.

3. Margaret[6] Eliza Higginbotham (Cyrena[5], Cyrena[4], Amb.[3], Benj.[2] ————), b. Jan. 17, 1874, d. Aug. 2, 1921, m. July 20, 1892, James Addison Hughes, b. Mch. 17, 1850, d. at Blue Rock, his estate in Nelson Co., Va., Jan. 28, 1913.

1. Lucian[7] Wilmore Hughes, b. June 29, 1894.
2. Edwin[7] Moses Hughes, b. Mch. 25, 1896, m. Virginia Dell Tynes, b. Feb. 5, 1898, dau. of George W. Tynes and wife, Mary Elizabeth Price.
   1. Virginia[8] May Hughes, b. July 25, 1919.
   2. Mary[8] Eliza Hughes, b. Jan. 29, 1921.
3. Nannie[7] May Hughes, b. Jan. 3, ——, m. June 21, 1918, John Clifford Clarkson, son of McComb Clarkson and wife, Gertrude Conway Shelton.
   1. Margrude[8] Gertrude Clarkson, b. June 4, 1919.
   2. John[8] Roscoe Clarkson, b. Aug. 28, 1921.
   3. James[8] Clifford Clarkson, b. Mch. 29, 1923.
4. Gordon[7] Hughes, b. Aug. 6, 1899, m. Nov. 26, 1924, Mary Ellen Johnson, dau. of John Albert Johnson and wife, Kate Lillian Bridgewater.
5. Jeannette[7] Hughes, b. Mch. 6, 1901, lived four years.
6. Clemon[7] Hughes, b. May 23, 1902.
7. Jennings[7] Hughes, b. May 3, 1906.
8. Samuel[7] Hughes, b. Dec. 16, 1907.
9. Margaret[7] Eliza Hughes, b. Oct. 23, 1909.

4. James[6] Shields Alexander Higginbotham (Cyrena[5], Cyrena[4], Amb.[3] ————), b. Oct. 1, 1875, m. Dec. 6, 1899, Mary Ann Wright.

1. Emmett[7] Theodore Higginbotham, b. Oct. 24, 1900, m. Sept. 28, 1920, Lelia Clare Duncan, dau. of Bernard J. Duncan and wife, Mary Kate Mathews.
   1. Mary[8] Clare Higginbotham, b. July 12, 1921.
   2. Margaret[8] Theodore Higginbotham, b. Oct. 8, 1924.
2. Mary[7] Edwin Higginbotham, b. June 29, 1902, lived two years.
3. Essie[7] May Higginbotham, b. Feb. 12, 1904.

4. James[7] William Higginbotham, b. July 24, 1907.
5. Aubrey[7] Stode Higginbotham, b. Nov. 7, 1910.
6. Annie[7] Louise Higginbotham, b. Nov. 2, 1913.

5. Frank[6] Plunkett Higginbotham (Cyrena[5], Cyrena[4], Amb.[3] ———), b. June 21, 1877, m. Mamie Rhodes.

6. Eddie[6] Morris Higginbotham (Cyrena[5], Cyrena[4], Amb.[3] ———), b. Apr. 28, 1879, d. July 28, 1921, m. Dec. 28, 1904, Minnie Maude Kline, b. Mch. 24, 1880, dau. of Joseph Evington Kline and wife, Mary Washington Lemon.

1. Mary[7] Cyrena Higginbotham, b. Oct. 31, 1905.
2. Morris[7] Kline Higginbotham, b. Oct. 13, 1906.
3. Carry[7] Hardy Higginbotham, b. Oct. 24, 1907.
4. Nannie[7] Margaret Higginbotham, b. July 27, 1910.
5. Hallie[7] Erma Higginbotham, b. July 9, 1912, d. Mch. 14, 1924.
6. Maude[7] Catherine Higginbotham, b. Oct. 8, 1913.
7. Eddie[7] Elinor Higginbotham, b. Jan. 16, 1916.
8. Emma[7] Higginbotham, b. Feb. 22, 1918.

8. Willis[6] Cabell Higginbotham (Cyrena[5], Cyrena[4] ———), b. May 14, 1881, m. Apr. 1906, Mary Louise Christian Carter.

9. Lula[6] May Higginbotham (Cyrena[5], Cyrena[4] ———), b. May 3, 1885, m. Dec. 1908, Frank Pierce Bryant, b. Apr. 10, 1883, d. May 24, 1919, son of Marion Conway Bryant and wife, Signora Saunders.

1. Essie[7] Rivers Bryant, b. Sept. 14, 1909.
2. Charles[7] Franklin Bryant, b. June 20, 1912.
3. Marion[7] Edwin Bryant, b. July 19, 1918, lived three years.

10. China[6] Etta Higginbotham (Cyrena[5], Cyrena[4] ———), b. May 5, 1887, m. Daniel Boone Wright.

1. Mamie[7] Katherine Wright, b. Nov. 9, 1913.
2. Nannie[7] Pauline Wright, b. Jan. 20, 1915.
3. Winfred[7] Massie Wright, b. June 14, 1916.
4. Angus[7] Daniel Wright, b. Mch. 22, 1918.
5. Ernest[7] Franklin Wright, b. June 5, 1919.
6. Dorothy[7] Wright, b. Sept. 7, 1921.
7. Mary[7] Virginia Wright, b. June 6, 1924.

11. Herbert[6] Maitland Higginbotham (Cyrena[5], Cyrena[4], Amb.[3] ———), b. Nov. 30, 1889, m. Dec. 27, 1911, Lola Pauline Harvey, b. Apr. 23, 1889, m. dau. of Charles Henry Harvey and wife, Alma Frances Hight.

1. Florence[7] Pauline Higginbotham, b. Aug. 5, 1915.
2. Helen[7] Lucile Higginbotham, b. Jan. 28, 1918.
3. Frances[7] Alma Higginbotham, b. Feb. 19, 1920.
4. Lola[7] Margaret Higginbotham, b. June 10, 1921.

2. John[4] Hill Plunkett (Amb.[3], Benj.[2], John[1]), m. Feb. 1, 1826, Cynthia Ann Staples.

1. David[5] Ambrose Plunkett, b. 1827, d. 1860, of Lynchburg, m. Mary McDearmon, dau. of Col. Samuel McDearmon.
    1. Adolphus[6] Plunkett, b. Nov. 22, 1853.
    2. Clifford[6] Plunkett, d. 1887.
    3. John[6] Samuel Plunkett, b. 1859, of Appomattox.
    4. Alma[6] Plunkett, b. 1857, m. William Gordon, of Houston, Texas.

3. Frances[4] Plunkett (Amb.[3], Benj.[2], John[1]), d. Sept. 28, 1805, in Kentucky, m. John James Shields, b. Jan. 8, 1807, in Nelson Co., d. 1868. He married second Nancy Plunkett, Nov. 6, sister of Frances. (No children of this marriage). John James was the son of James and Elizabeth (Higginbotham) Shields, Elizabeth was the daughter of Capt. Aaron and Margaret (Croxton) Higginbotham. John James was grandson of John Shields and Margaret (Finley) Shields. Margaret was daughter of Capt. John Finley, of Augusta, Va., and wife, Thankful (Doaks) Finley. (See Major France's book on the Finley Family).

1. Cyrena[5] Ann Shields.
2. Nancy[5] W. Shields.
3. James[5] A. Shields.
4. Samuel[5] Taliaferro Shields.
5. Susanna[5] Shields.
6. Adeline[5] B. Shields.
7. William[5] Thomas Shields.
8. Sarah[5] Elizabeth Shields.
9. Mary[5] M. Shields.
10. Robert[5] Alexander Shields.
11. A[5] child died an infant.
12. Cassandria[5] Shields, d. Dec. 30, 1892, m. Pete Morgan.

1. Cyrena[5] Ann Shields (Frances[4], Amb.[3], Benj.[2], John[1]), b. Oct. 9, 1827, d. Sept. 28, 1845, m. Napoleon Sandidge.

1. Sarah[6] Elizabeth Sandidge, b. Sept. 10, 1845, d. June 24, 1893, m. a cousin, Robert Churchwill Stratton, b. Apr. 22, 1842, d. Apr. 24, 1921.

1. Charles[7] Pleasants Stratton, b. Nov. 28, 1868, d. Oct. 29, 1915.

Married 1st, Lovad Davenport:

1. Aubra[8] Stratton.
2. Ray[8] Stratton.
3. Thomas[8] Stratton.

Married 2nd, Laura Mercer:

4. Alvin[8] Stratton.
5. Flossie[8] Stratton.
6. Thomas[8] Stratton.

2. Mary[7] Ida Stratton, b. Mch. 1, 1870, d. June, 1918, m. James Jackson, of Texas.
   1. Clyde[8] Jackson.
   2. Claude[8] Jackson.
   3. Fannie[8] Jackson.
3. Cyrena[7] Stratton, b. Apr. 22, 1873, d. Mch. 1901, unmarried.
4. Mildred[7] Elizabeth Stratton, b. June 15, 1875, m. Dec. 21, 1892, Houston F. Davenport, son of Thomas Davenport and wife, Prudie Young.
   1. Ora[8] Ethel Davenport, b. Oct. 13, 1895.
   2. Cyrena[8] Icy Davenport, b. June 9, 1898.
   3. Ida[8] Belle Davenport, b. Jan. 14, 1902.
   4. Robert[8] Thomas Davenport, b. May 27, 1905.
   5. Albert[8] B. Davenport.
   6. Alma[8] Lee Davenport, twins, b. Jan. 23, 1909.
   7. Charles[8] Bernard Davenport, b. Mch. 9, 1911.
   8. Geneva[8] Davenport, b. Aug. 29, 1916.
5. Exona[7] Stratton, b. Jan. 2, 1878, m. Edward Abshere.
   1. Alva[8].
   2. John[8].
   3. William[8].
   4. Ernest[8].
   5. Annie[8].
   6. Zellie[8].
6. Robert[7] Stratton, b. Mch. 14, 1882, m. in Texas.
7. Carrie[7] Stratton, b. Nov. 25, 1884, d. Feb. 1906, m. Hiram Holbrook, of Texas.
8. Elma[7] Stratton, b. Apr. 7, 1887, d. June 18, 1890.

2. Nancy[5] W. Shields (Frances[4], Amb.[3], Benj.[2], John[1]), b. Apr. 28, 1828, d. Feb. 14, 1895, unmarried.

3. James[5] A. Shields (Frances[4], Amb.[3], ————), b. May 29, 1830, d. Feb. 16, 1855, m. Mary Campbell, dau. of John S. Campbell and wife, Mary Ennis.

4. Samuel[5] Taliaferro Shields (Frances[4], Amb.[3], ————), b. July 10, 1832, d. June 16, 1900, m. Elizabeth Mildred Campbell, sister of Mary.

1. Mary[6] Ann Shields, b. July 29, 1856.
2. Cornelia[6] F. Shields, b. Aug. 30, 1858, d. Jan. 11, 1923, m. Jan. 3, 1877, Warren Maxey, a Baptist minister.
    1. Julia[7] Maxey.
    2. Broadley[7] Maxey.
    3. Minnie[7] Maxey.
    4. Laura[7] Maxey.
    5. Dilbert[7] Maxey.
    6. Mary[7] Maxey.
    7. Frank[7] Maxey.
    8. Roy[7] Maxey.
3. Lemuel[6] C. Shields, b. Apr. 22, 1860, d. Sept. 1, 1861.
4. Samuel[6] James Shields, b. July 25, 1862, m. Blanche Fordyce, May 11, 1886, she d. Mch. 22, 1923.
    1. Charles[7] E. Shields, b. Apr. 29, 1887, d. 1887.
    2. Bessie[7] Fern Shields, b. July 3, 1888, m. Oswald Cuthbert.
        1. Ethel Cuthbert.
        2. Mildred[8] Cuthbert.
        3. Louise[8] Cuthbert.
        4. Elsie[8] Cuthbert.
    3. Clarence[7] Samuel Shields, b. Nov. 28, 1890.
    4. Mary[7] B. Shieds, b. Nov. 5, 1892, m. Preston Terry.
    5. Harley[7] B. Shields, b. Sept. 16, 1895.
    6. Fred[7] T. Shields, b. May 27, 1898, m. Lorena Craft.
5. William[6] A. Shields, b. Apr. 1, 1866, m. Vallie Atkinson.
6. Eugenia[6] V. Shields, b. Feb. 1, 1869, d. Mch. 7, 1891.
7. John[6] Eddie Shields, b. July 25, 1873, d. Sept. 3, 1909.

5. Susanna[5] F. Shields (Frances[4], Amb.[3], Benj.[2], John[1]), b. Dec. 25, 1833, d. May 13, 1866, m. Thomas Davenport.

1. Fannie[6] Davenport.
2. John[6] Wesley Davenport, m. Mary Hobbs.

3. Julia[6] Davenport, m. William Lynch.
4. James[6] Davenport.
5. Cyrena[6] Davenport, m. John M. Torrant, of Riverside, Ky.

6. Adeline[5] B. Shields (Frances[4], Amb.[3] ———), b. Oct. 2, 1835, m. George W. Rone.

7. William[5] Thomas Shields (Frances[4], Amb.[3] ———), m. Rebecca Rone.

1. Mary[6] Belle Shields, m. William L. Burge.
    1. Annie[7] Pearl Burge.
    2. Benjamin[7] Thomas Burge.
    3. Arthur[7] Lee Burge.
    4. Willie[7] Belle Burge.
    5. Newman[7] Burge.
    6. James[7] Oscar Burge.
    7. Rinda[7] May Burge.
2. Annie[6] Eliza Shields, b. Aug. 6, 1858.
3. Erinda[6] Calpurnia Shields, m. Frank McKay.
    1. Clarence[7] McKay.
    2. Herbert[7] McKay.
    3. Shellie[7] Dodes McKay.
    4. Rebecca[7] Thomas McKay.
    5. Annie[7] Belle McKay.
4. William[6] Thomas Shields, d. in infancy.

8. Sara[5] Elizabeth Shields (Frances[4], Amb.[3], Benj.[2] ———), d. June 2, 1891, age 52, m. Curren Hunter.

1. John[6] Hunter, m. Annie Helm.
2. James[6] T. Hunter, m. Grace Riddle.
3. Robert[6] S. Hunter, m. Carrie Riddle, sister of Grace.
4. Ella[6] Hunter, m. Charles Rone, son of Wash Rone.
5. Fannie[6] Hunter, m. George Robert Shields.
6. Curren[6] D. Hunter.

9. Mary[5] M. Shields (Frances[4], Amb.[3] ———), d. Jan. 12, 1824.

10. Robert[6] Alexander Shields (Frances[4], Amb.[3], ———), b. Apr. 16, 1843, d. Jan. 12, 1924, m. Margaret Jane Rone, Jan. 9, 1851, dau. of George W. Rone.

1. Susan[6] Josephine Shields, m. Lum Edens.
    1. Lemuel[7] Edens.
    2. Thomas[7] Edens.

3. Minnie^{7} Edens.
4. John^{7} Edens.
5. Paul^{7} Edens.
6. Mary^{7} Edens.
7. Silas^{7} Edens.
8. Luke^{7} Edens.
9. James^{7} Edens.
10. Elias^{7} Edens.

10. Willis4 H. Plunkett (Amb.^{3}, Benj.^{2}, John^{1}), b. in Campbell Co., Va., Oct. 13, 1815; in 1835 he became the partner of his father, Ambrose, a merchant in Amherst, this continued for seven years, then he moved to Stapleton Mills; m. April 19, 1837, Elizabeth A. Staples, of Amherst. On Sept. 28, 1869, he married second, Mrs. Addie V. Elliott, nee Harvey. From Stapleton he moved to Lynchburg, then to Brunswick, Missouri.

Data from Miss Lois and Edna Kennedy.

The Shields' data was contributed by Miss Nannie Hanna, of Fayett, Mo. All of the above being sent by Mr. and Mrs. Sweeny, of New York.

4. Willis^{3} Rucker Plunkett (Benj.^{2}, John^{1}).
    1. Eliza^{4} Francis Plunkett.

Ogden

Henry^{1} Ogden died in Amherst 19 Nov., 1838, will dated 13 May, 1836. I give to my daughter, Polly White, with my son, Allison, her trustee. The rest of my estate to be divided equally between the "balance of my children"—whereas I have made advances to them all.

To my son, Aquilla Ogden.
To my daughter, Minty Rucker.
To my daughter, Ann Seay.
To my son, John Ogden.
To my son, Allison Ogden.
To my son, Zachariah Ogden.
To my son, Henry Ogden

Executor: Son, Allison Ogden.

Witness: John B. Duncan, Julius Simpson, Daniel L. Coleman.

(W. B. 10, p. 61, Amherst Co., Va.)

1. Benjamin^{2} Ogden.
2. John^{2} Ogden.
3. James^{2} Ogden.

4. Alleson^{2} Ogden.
5. Henry^{2} Ogden.
6. Elijah^{2} Ogden.
7. Zachariah^{2} Ogden.
8. Aquilla^{2} Ogden.
9. Minty^{2} Ogden.
10. Mary^{2} Ogden.
11. Ann^{2} Seay.

1. Benjamin^{2} Ogden (Henry^{1}), b. 1782, d. 1867, m. Mary^{4} Agnes Rucker (Anthony^{3}, John^{2} Peter^{1}), see page —.

1. Anthony^{3} Rucker Ogden, b. 1811.
2. John^{3} Ogden.
3. James^{3} Madison Ogden.
4. Albert^{3} Ogden.
5. Sarah^{3} Ogden.
6. Ann^{3} Ogden.

2. John^{2} Ogden (Henry^{1}), b. 1783, m. Sarah Coppedge, b. 1783.

1. Armistead^{3} Haden Ogden.
2. Emily^{3} Ogden, m. ———— Reynolds.
3. Jane^{3} Ogden, m. ———— Wray.
4. Harriet^{3} Ogden, b. 1815, m. ———— Mathews.
5. Walker^{3} R. Ogden.
6. James^{3} Ogden.
7. Sarah^{3} Ogden.
8. Louise^{3} Ogden.
9. William^{3} Ogden.
10. John^{3} Lunsford Ogden.
11. Elizabeth^{3} A. Ogden.

1. Armistead^{3} Haden Ogden (John^{2}, Henry^{1}), b. 1805, d. 1885, m. Martha A. White.

1. Laura^{4} Fulton Ogden.
2. Lucy^{4} Ann Ogden, b. 1835, m. John Tompkins.
3. Mary^{4} Jane Ogden, b. 1837, m. Wm. Noell.
4. Catherine^{4} Ellen Ogden, b. 1839, m. Wm. Alexander Mathews.
5. Paul^{4} Ogden, b. 1841, twin to Silas.
6. Silas^{4} Ogden, b. 1841, m. Dolly Davis.
7. George^{4} Ogden, b. 1844.
9. Sophia^{4} Amanda Ogden, b. 1848, m. John Norfolk.
10. John^{4} Ogden.
11. James^{4} Ogden.
12. Frances^{4} Ogden, m. Owen P. Jones.

1. Laura[4] Fulton Ogden (Armistead[3], John[2], Henry[1]), b. 1833, m. Granville P. Parks.

   1. Lucy[5] Armistead Parks, b. 1854, m. W. J. Cooper.
   2. Nannie[5] Goode Parks, b. 1856, m. Henry B. Jennings.
   3. Frank[5] Oscar Parks, b. 1858, m. Cleopatra Douglas.
   4. Granville[5] Beauregard Parks, m. Lizzie Burns.
   5. Mary[5] Frances Parks.
   6. Wm.[5] J. Parks.
   7. Georgie[5] A. Parks, b. 1870, m. Edward Carrington Beasley.

5. Walker[3] R. Ogden (John[2], Henry[1]), b. 1816, m. Caroline Mosby.

   1. John[4] B. Ogden, b. 1843.
   2. Sarah[4] A. Ogden, b. 1845.
   3. Margaret[4] Ogden, b. 1851, m. Patterson.
   4. Wm.[4] M. Ogden, b. 1853.
   5. Robert[4] W. Ogden, b. 1855, m. Bertha C. Turner.
   6. Charles[4] Ogden, b. 1858.

9. Wiliam[3] Ogden (John[2], Henry[1]), b. 1822, wife Susan.

   1. Charles[4] Ogden (1845-1923), m. Martha Ogden.
      1. Henry[5] Ogden.
   2. Emma[4] Ogden, b. 1847.
   3. Mildred[4] Ogden, b. 1850.
   4. Sarah[4] Ogden, m. Addison Ogden.
      1. Arnold[5] Ogden.
      2. Ethelyn[5] Ogden.
   5. Wellington[4] Ogden, m. Blanche Dean.

10. John[3] Lunsford Ogden (John[2], Henry[1]), b. 1823, m. Elizabeth Tinsley, b. 1825.

   1. Addison[4] Ogden, m. Sarah Ogden, first cousin.
   2. Virginia[4] Ogden, m. Ambrose R. Hewitt.
      1. Dan[5] Ogden, m. W. R. Mitchell.
      2. Mable[5] Ogden, m. ———— Terry.
      3. Son[5].
   3. Mary[4] Martha Ogden, b. 1856, m. Charles Ogden.
   4. Dora[4] Ogden, m. Thomas J. Ayres.
   5. Patrate[4] Ogden, b. 1858.
   6. Chamness[4] Ogden.
   7. Victoria[4] Ogden, m. Polk Spencer.

1. Maggie[5] Spencer.
2. Cora[5] Spencer.
3. David[5] Spencer.
4. Lumsford[5] Spencer, m. Lilly Stark.
   1. Richmond[6] Stark Spencer.
5. Emma[5] Spencer, m. Luke Bain.
6. William[5] Spencer.

8. Emmett[4] S. Ogden.
9. Sarah[4] W. Ogden.

11. Elizabeth[3] A. Ogden (John[2], Henry[1]), b. 1825, d. 1879, m. Champ Ogden, b. 1822, d. 1864.

1. Annie[4] Lou Ogden.
2. Mary[4] Fanny Ogden (1847-1863).
3. Paul[4] Edgar Ogden.
4. Sallie[4] Bettie Ogden.
5. Champ[4] E. Ogden.
6. Charles[4] H. Ogden.
7. John[4] Spotswood Ogden.
8. James[4] A. Ogden.

1. Annie[4] Lou Ogden (Eliz.[3], John[2], Henry[1]) (1848-1894), m. Charles L. Wright.

1. Wm.[5] Wright, m. Bessie White.
2. Lilla[5] Wright, m. Wright Gillum.
3. Maggie[5] Wright, m. Thomas Lewis.
4. Hallie[5] Wright.
5. Lizzie[5] Wright, m. Edward Lovell.
6. Robert[5] Wright.

3. Paul[4] Edgar Ogden (Eliz.[3], John[2], Henry[1]), b. 1850, m. Martha V.

1. Maggie[5] Belle Ogden, m. Sam Ramby.
2. Geo[5] Edward Ogden.
3. Lizzie[5] Ogden, m. Zeb. Moss.
4. Elis[5] Ogden.
5. William[5] Ogden.
6. Kilie[5] Ogden.

4. Sallie[4] Betty Ogden (Eliz.[3], John[2], Henry[1]), b. 1854, m. Simeon N. Gillum.

1. Katie[5] Gillum, m. Frank L. Wilson.
2. May[5] E. Gillum, m. George H. Robinson.

3. Walker^{5} Gillum, m. Ruby L. Bibb.
4. Julia^{5} Gillum, m. Rubb Riggs.
5. James^{5} Gillum, m. Mary Norvell.
6. Geneva^{5} Gillum, m. Finis Crawford.

5. Champ^{4} E. Ogden (Eliz.^{3}, John^{2}, Henry^{1}), b. 1857, d. 1892, m. Mollie Jamison.

1. Jesse^{5} Ogden.
2. James^{5} Ogden.
3. Anabella^{5} Ogden, m. Lewis Carroll.
4. Guy^{5} Ogden, m. Cloe Hanson.
5. John^{5} Ogden, m. Beulah Thompson.
6. Champ^{5} Ogden, m. Zona D. Tombs.

6. Charles^{4} H. Ogden (Eliz.^{3}, John^{2}, Henry^{1}), b. 1859, m. Etta Robinson.

1. Edgar^{5} Ogden, m. Aline Young.
2. Belle^{5} Ogden.
3. Hurley^{5} Ogden.

7. John^{4} Spotswood Ogden (Eliz.^{3}, John^{2}, Henry^{1}), b. 1862, d. 1922, m. Harriet Henderson.

1. Champ^{5} S. Ogden, m. Lessie Lewis.
2. Bertha^{5} Ogden, m. Reed Mitchell.
3. Effie^{5} Ogden, m. James Logan.
4. Henry^{5} Ogden, m. Margaret Stupps.
5. Laura^{5} Lee Ogden, m. Albert Sanderson.
6. Homer^{5} Ogden, m. Mary Sanderson.

8. James^{4} Ogden (Eliz.^{3}, John^{2}, Henry^{1}), b. 1864, m. Elmina Maples.

1. Lawrence^{5} Ogden.
2. Edith^{5} Ogden.

4. Allison^{2} Ogden (Henry^{1}), b. 1789, d. 1820, m. Lucy Richardson.

1. Wm.^{3} Ogden.
2. L.^{3} C. Ogden.
3. Thomas^{3} Richard Ogden.

1. Wm.^{3} Ogden (Allison^{2}, Henry^{1}), m. Susan Bowen.

1. Lucy^{4} Rose Ogden.
2. Nannie^{4} Ogden.

1. Lucy^4 Rose Ogden (Wm.^{3}, Allison^2, Henry^1), m. Stephen H. Turner.

   1. Harry^5 Turner.
   2. Charles^5 Turner.
   3. Susie^5 Turner.
   4. Chester^5 Turner, m. ——— Coffey.

2. Nannie^4 Ogden (Wm.^{3}, Allison^2, Henry^1), m. Frank Burks.

   1. Woodford^5 Burks.
   2. Ruby^5 Burks, m. Boyd Hamilton.
   3. Rose^5 Burks.

3. Thomas^3 Richard Ogden (Allison^2, Henry^1), b. 1815 d. 1877, m. first, Lucinda Caroline Smith; second, Eliza.

Issue (by 1st mar.):

   1. Allison^4 Ogden.
   2. Anna^4 M. Ogden.
   3. William^4 B. Ogden.
   4. Mary^4 Belle Ogden.
   5. James^4 T. Ogden.
   6. Joel^4 H. Ogden.
   7. Thomas^4 Ogden.

Issue (by 2nd mar.):

   8. Lucy^4 Ogden.
   9. Amanda^4 Ogden.

1. Allison^4 Ogden (Tho.^{3}, Allison^2, Henry^1), b. 1843, m. Susan Evelyn Hinton.

   1. Mary^5 Carolina Ogden, m. Charles R. Horn.
   2. Annie^5 Belle Ogden, m. Enos E. Polk.
   3. Dollye^5 Ogden, m. Olin L. Thaxton.
   4. E.^{5} L. Ogden.
   5. W.^{5} A. Ogden, m. Mollie Horn.
   6. Frank^5 Ogden, m. Julia Rutherford.
   7. H.^{5} B. Ogden, m. Chase Crothers.
   8. John^5 Henry Ogden, m. Laura Wisdom.

2. Annie^4 M. Ogden (Tho.^{3}, Allison^2), m. Van Wisdom.

   1. Carroll^5 Van Wisdom.

4. Mary^4 Belle Ogden (Tho.^{3} ———), b. 1852, m. Ambrose R. Hewitt.

Issue:

1. Hunter[5] Hewitt.
2. Thomas[5] Hewitt.
3. Nellie[5] Hewitt, m. ———— Lofton.
4. Lillian[5] Hewitt, m. E. M. Collins.
5. Harden[5] Hewitt.
6. Louis[5] M. Hewitt, m. Rebecca Roberts.

5. Henry[2] Ogden (Henry[1]), b. 1793, d. 1887, m. 1st, ———— Smith; 2nd, ————; 3rd, ———— Milner; 4th, Ann Bass (widow).

1. James[3] Ogden.
2. Bettie[3] Ogden.
3. Champ[3] Ogden.
4. Sarah[3] Ogden, m. Ned Sampson.
5. Henry[3] Taylor Ogden.
6. Fannie[3] Ogden.
7. E.[3] F. Ogden.
8. Nancy[3] Ogden.
9. William[3] Ogden.
10. Thomas[3] Ogden.
11. Mildred[3] Ogden, m. James Major.

1. James[3] Ogden (Henry[2], Henry[1]), b. 1818, married three times, m. 1st, Sarah A.

Issue (by 1st mar.):

1. Wm.[4] W. Ogden, b. 1840.
2. Catherine[4] Ogden, b. 1844.
3. John[4] Ogden, b. 1846, d. 1926.
4. James[4] M. Ogden, b. 1849.

Issue (by 2nd mar.):

5. Champ[4] Ogden.

Issue (by 3rd mar.):

6. Emmet[4] Ogden, b. 1862.
7. Edward[4] Ogden.
8. Lemma[4] Ogden.

2. Bettie[3] Ogden (Henry[2], Henry[1]), b. 1820, m. James Perrow.

1. Henry[4] Ann Perrow, m. ———— Taylor.
2. Katie[4] Perrow.
3. Seth[4] Perrow.
4. Jennie[4] Perrow, m. Dudley Davis.
5. Otway[4] Perrow.
6. Julia[4] Perrow.

3. Champ[3] Ogden (Henry[2], Henry[1]), b. 1822, d. 1864, m. Elizabeth A. Ogden, b. 1825, d. 1879.

5. Henry[3] Taylor Ogden (Henry[2], Henry[1]), b. 1826, d. 1909, m. Margaret Eliza Hobson, b. 1827, d. 1896.

    1. Arabella[4] Ogden, b. 1850, d. 1877, m. Edward R. Stark.
    2. Bettie[4] Ogden.
    3. Richard[4] Henry Ogden.
    4. Samuel[4] Ogden.
    5. William[4] Ogden.
    6. John[4] Ben Ogden.
    7. Edward[4] Lee Ogden.
    8. Virginia[4] Catherine Ogden.
    9. E.[4] Cephus Ogden.

2. Bettie[4] A. Ogden (Henry[3], Henry[2], Henry[1]), b. 1852, m. Henry Watts Stark, b. 1853, d. 1923.

    1. Maggie[5] Belle Stark, b. 1877, d. 1895.
    2. Catherine[5] Louise Stark, m. Edward Eugene Campbell.
    3. Henry[5] Clay Stark, m. Mildred Curdy.

3. Richard[4] Henry Ogden (Henry[3], Henry[2], Henry[1]), b. 1854, m. Cora Lee McElwee, b. 1863.

    1. Ottie[5] Hazel Ogden, b. 1890.
    2. Lemuel[5] Lee Ogden, b. 1891, m. Flora L. Levy.
        1. Dorothy[6] Mae Ogden.
    3. Wm.[5] Hayden M. Ogden, m. Mae V. Hoffman.
    4. O[5] Jennie Vivian Ogden, b. 1897, d. 1922.
    5. Charles[5] Henry Ogden, b. 1900.

6. John[4] Ben Ogden (Henry[3], Henry[2], Henry[1]), m. Cora B. McCullough.

    1. Harry[5] Lee Ogden.
    2. Aubrey[5] Taylor Ogden, m. Catherine Burks.
    3. Virginia[5] Catherine Ogden, m. Dr. James E. Goodman.
        1. Lawrence[6] Goodman.
        2. Eugene[6] Goodman.

7. Edward[4] Lee Ogden (Henry[3], Henry[2]), b. 1863, m. Catherine McCullough.

    1. Mary[5] Eliza Ogden, m. Joseph Bernard Butts.
        1. Joseph[6] Butts.

2. Samuel^{5} Irving Ogden, m. Sarah Sidwell.
   1. Gwendolyn^{6} Ogden.
3. Margaret^{5} Belle Ogden, m. John Duncan.
4. Florence^{5} Eugene Ogden, m. James Robert Page.
5. Edna^{5} Catherine Ogden, m. David Read.
6. Lena^{5} Martha Ogden.

8. Virginia^{4} Catherine Ogden (Henry^{3}, ———), m. Lemuel F. MacKey.
   1. Virginia^{5} MacKey.

9. E.^{4} Cephus Ogden (Henry^{3}, ———), m. Myrtle Cornell.
   1. Hattie^{5} Belle Ogden, m. William McGee.
   2. Grace^{5} Pauline Ogden, m. Arthur J. Powell.
   3. Lemma^{5} Martha Ogden, m. George Turpin.
   4. Darline^{5} Ogden.

6. Fannie^{3} Ogden (Henry^{2}, Henry^{1}), b. 1828, m. Nelson Tinsley.
   1. Ida^{4} Tinsley.
   2. Harry^{4} Car Tinsley.
   3. Katie^{4} May Tinsley, m. ——— Jennings.
   4. Lula^{4} Tinsley, m. George Betts.
   5. Eban^{4} H. Tinsley.
   6. Thomas^{4} Edwards Taylor Tinsley.

8. Nancy^{3} Ogden (Henry^{2}, Henry^{1}), m. ——— Douglas.
   1. James^{4} Dougles.
   2. Andrew^{4} Jackson Douglas.

6. Elijah^{2} Ogden (Henry^{1}), b. 1798, d. 1885, m. Nancy Milner, b. 1803.
   1. Wm.^{3} Henry Ogden.
   2. James^{3} Ogden.
   3. A.^{3} T. Ogden.
   4. Thomas^{3} Ogden.
   5. Sarah^{3} Elizabeth Ogden.
   6. Mary^{3} Ogden.
   7. Livinia^{3} Ogden.
   8. Mary^{3} Ogden.
   9. Jennie^{3} Belle Ogden.

1. Wm. Henry^{3} Ogden (Elijah^{2}, Henry^{1}), m. Marie E. Turpin.

1. James^{4} Wellington Ogden.
2. John^{4} M. Ogden.
3. Spotswood^{4} H. Ogden.
4. George^{4} B. Ogden, m. Fannie Tomlin.
5. Nubil^{4} C. Ogden.
6. Alice^{4} G. Ogden, m. Charles Locke.
7. Mary^{4} Ogden.

2. James^{3} Ogden (Elijah^{2}, Henry^{1}).

1. John^{4} Ogden.
2. Morris^{4} Ogden.
3. Mary^{4} Ogden.

2. John^{4} M. Ogden (Wm.^{3}, Elijah^{2}, Henry^{1}), m. Lelia Hawkins.

1. Ambrie^{5} Ogden.
2. Lisle^{5} Ogden.
3. Clifford^{5} Ogden.
4. John^{5} M. Ogden, Jr.
5. Myrtle^{5} Ogden.
6. Mary^{5} Ogden.
7. Hellen^{5} Ogden.
8. Carrie^{5} Ogden.
9. Nawassa^{5} Ogden.
10. Russell^{5} Ogden.

5. Nubil^{4} C. Ogden (Wm.^{3}, Elijah^{2}, Henry^{1}), m. Minnie Mathews.

1. William^{5} Ogden.
2. Catherine^{5} Ogden.

7. Mary^{4} V. Ogden (Wm.^{3}, Elijah2, Henry^{1}), b. 1876, m. Floyd Locke.

1. Charles^{5} Locke.
2. Lillian^{5} Locke.

9. Minty^{2} Ogden (Henry^{1}), m. Issaac^{4} Rucker (John^{3}, John^{2}, Peter^{1}). See Isaac Rucker page —.

10. Polly^{2} Ogden (Henry^{1}), m. William White.

Perrow

Perrow (Perault) was one of the Huguenot families of Manakintown. In the registry of baptisms, we find the name of Charles Pero, son of Daniel and Marie Pero, in 1728. In 1735, Estiene Pero, son of Daniel and Marie Pero, was baptized. From Daniel descend the Pero, Pereau, and Perrows, of Virginia. They moved to Buckingham Co. and settled on the Slate River. Stephen Perrow sold land in this county and moved to Campbell Co. He lived on a farm called "Apple Grove".

1. Mary[2] Ann Perrow, m. ——— Bailey.
2. Elizabeth[2] Perrow, m. Neilly Powell, Amherst.
3. Stephen[2] Perrow, m. 1804, 1st, Dolly Cox, dau. of Benjamin; married 2nd, Amy Green.

Issue (by 1st mar.):

1. Polina[3] Perrow, m. ——— Stewart.
2. Capt. William[3] C. Perrow, m. 1836, Urania V. Cowling.
3. Stephen[3] W. Perrow.
4. John[3] F. Perrow, m. 1810, Martha Cowling.
5. Andrew[3] J. Perrow, m. ——— McGehee.
6. James[3] S. Perrow, m. ——— Ogden.
7. Carolina[3] Perrow, m. ——— Stephens.
8. Betsy[3] Perrow, m. ——— Walthall.
9. Dolly[3] Perrow, m. A.[5] T. B. Rucker (Absolom[4], ———).

Issue (by 2nd mar.):

10. Dr. Ferdinand[3] Perrow, m. 1856, Catherine M. Payne.
11. Isabella[3] Perrow, m. John A. Payne.
12. Thomas[3] B. Perrow, moved to Missouri.
13. Anne[3] Perrow, m. ——— Murrell.

Pendleton

1. Philip[1] Pendleton, of Norwick, Eng., m. Isabella.
   1. Henry[2] Pendleton.

1. Henry[2] Pendleton, m. 1701, Mary, dau. of James Taylor and wife, Mary Gregory.
   1. Mary[3] Pendleton.
   2. Philip[3] Pendleton.

3. Isabella³ Pendleton.
4. Edmund³ Pendleton.
5. Nathaniel³ Pendleton, m. ——— Clayton (no issue).

1. Mary³ Pendleton (Henry², Philip¹), m. James Gaines (son of Richard).

1. Mary⁴ Gaines, m. Edward Herndon, Sr., of Culpeper.
    1. James⁵ Herndon.
    2. Wm.⁵ Pendleton Herndon, b. 1764, m. Nancy Rucker.
    3. Benjamin⁵ Herndon.
    4. Elizabeth⁵ Herndon.
    5. Rachel⁵ Herndon.
    6. Edward⁵ Herndon, Jr., m. Mary Rucker. (See Thomas Rucker line).

2. Philip³ Pendleton (Henry², Philip¹), b. 1704, wife, Martha.

1. Mary⁴ Pendleton, m. Col. Edmund Waller.
2. Jemima⁴ Pendleton.
3. Martha⁴ Pendleton, m. Massy Thomas.
4. Mildred⁴ Pendleton.
5. Judeth⁴ Pendleton.
6. Henry⁴ Pendleton.

2. Jemima⁴ Pendleton (Philip³, Henry², Philip¹), m. first cousin, Richard Gaines.

3. Isabella³ Pendleton (Henry², Philip¹), m. William² Henry Gaines (Richard¹ and wife, Jemima (Pendleton) Gaines).

Gaines

Richard¹ Gaines d. in Culpeper after 1750, m. his first cousin, Jemima Pendleton (Slaughter, *History of Culpeper*).

1. Wm.² Henry Gaines.
2. Lucy² Gaines, m. ——— Botts.
3. Rowland² Gaines.
4. Jemima² Gaines.
5. Benjamin² Gaines.
6. Nathaniel² Gaines.
7. James² Gaines.

8. Judeth^{2} Gaines, m. ——— Chancellor.
9. Annie^{2} Gaines.
10. John^{2} Cooke Gaines.
11. Elizabeth^{2} Gaines.

1. Wm.^{2} Henry Gaines (Richard^{1}), d. 1790, m. Isabella^{3} Pendleton, dau. of Henry^{2} Pendleton and wife, Mary Taylor.

1. Benjamin^{3} Gaines.
2. Wm.^{3} Henry Gaines.
3. Richard^{3} Gaines.
4. Thomas^{3} Gaines.
5. Robert^{3} Gaines.
6. James^{3} Gaines, } twins.
7. Frances^{3} Gaines. }
8. Philip^{3} Gaines.
9. Isabella^{3} Gaines.
10. Anne^{3} Gaines.

3. Richard^{3} Gaines (Wm.^{2}, Richard^{1}), wife Elizabeth Broaddus, will dated Feb. 4, 1807, prob. Feb. 16, 1807.

1. Margaret^{4} Gaines, m. ——— Orr.
2. Elizabeth^{4}, m. ——— Clayton.
3. Caty^{4}, m. ——— Rossan.
4. Sally^{4}, m. 1807, Richard Rucker.
5. Richard^{4}.
   Granddaughter, Polly^{5} Pendleton Gaines.

7. James^{2} Gaines (Richard^{1}), m. about 1730 Mary^{3} Pendleton (dau. of Henry^{2}, Philip^{1}), will probated in Culpeper, Mch. 20, 1785, will of Mary proved in Madison, 1803.

1. Henry^{3} Gaines.
2. James^{3} Gaines, m. Mildred Pollard.
3. Richard^{2} Gaines.
4. Edmund^{3} Gaines.
5. Thomas^{3} Gaines.
6. Francis^{3} Gaines, m. Elizabeth Lewis.
7. Joseph^{3} Gaines, moved to Ky.
8. William^{3} Gaines.
9. Sarah^{3} Gaines, m. James Broaddus.
10. Catherine^{3} Gaines, m. Wm. Broaddus.
11. Isabella^{3} Gaines.
12. Mary^{3} Gaines.

1. Henry^{3} T. Gaines (James^{2}, Richard^{1}), b. 1733, d. 1811, m. first, Martha George; second, Sarah Churchill. Will dated Oct. 19, 1810, probated June 7, 1811 (W. B. 2, p. 302).

    1. George^{4} Gaines, m. 1788 Susanna Graves, of Culpeper.
    2. Mary^{4} Gaines, m. ——— Clark.
    3. Elizabeth^{4} George Gaines.
    4. Fannie^{4} Bowler Gaines.
    5. Augustine^{4} Gaines.
    6. William^{4} Gaines.
    7. Thomas^{4} Gaines.
    8. Churchill^{4} Gaines.
    9. Gabriel^{4} Gaines.
    10. Isabel^{4} Gaines.

    Execs.: Sons, Gabriel and Churchill, son-in-law, John Clark.

6. William^{4} M. Gaines (Henry^{3}, James^{2}, Richard^{1}), b. Jan. 1771, d. 1836 (son of first wife, Martha), m. Oct. 4, 1804, Sallie^{4} Allen Rucker (Augus^{3}, Eph^{2}, Peter^{1}). See p. 278.

8. Churchill^{4} Gaines (Henry^{3}, James^{2}, Richard^{1}), b. 1782, d. Aug. 14, 1833, m. Mary^{4} Rucker (John^{3}, Eph^{2}, Peter^{1}), d. Sept. 16, 1850, age 54 years.

    1. Edwin^{5} Gaines, b. Jan. 16, 1821, d. Apr. 3, 1909, m. Anna Eliza Watts, Boone Co., Ky., d. June 20, 1890, age 63 years.
        1. Alfred^{6} Gaines, m. Lizzie Davis.
            1. Pearl^{7} Gaines.
            2. Edwin^{7} Gaines.
        2. Charles^{6} Gaines, m. first, Lula Arnold; m. second, Anna Lewis.

            Issue (by 1st mar.):
            1. Felix^{7} Gaines.
            2. Annie^{7} Gaines.

            Issue (by 2nd mar.):
            1. Andrew^{7} Gaines.
            2. Milton^{7} Gaines.
        3. John^{6} Gaines, m. Fannie Stephens.
            1. Chester^{7} Gaines.
            2. Bess^{7}, m. Edward Mohler.
                1. Thelma^{8} Mohler.

4. James^{6} Taylor Gaines, m. Lizzie Alloway.
   1. Beulah^{7} Gaines.
   2. Bertha^{7}, m. C. T. Davis.
5. Minnie^{6} Gaines, m. James Duncan.
   1. Eunice^{7}, m. Vess Gaines, of Petersburg, Ky.

4. Edmund^{3} Gaines (James^{2}, Richard^{1}), d. 1815, m. Tabitha^{3} Rucker (Eph.^{2}, Peter^{1}).

12. Mary^{3} Gaines (James^{2}, Richard^{1}), m. Edward Herndon, Sr., served under Gen. Muhlenburg during the Revolution.
   1. Edward^{4} Herndon, Jr., d. 1827, m. Nancy^{4} Rucker (Thomas^{3}, Tho.^{2}, Peter^{1}).
   2. Wm.^{4} Herndon, m. Mary^{4} Rucker (Tho.^{3}, Tho.^{2}, Peter^{1}).

Early

Jeremiah^{3} Early (Tho.^{2}, John^{1}), b. 1705, d. in Culpeper in 1728. Elizabeth Buford, b. 1709, daughter of Thomas Buford, Jr., and wife, Elizabeth.

Among the receipts given to persons furnishing supplies for the use of the army during the Revolution is several to Jeremiah, Joel and Joseph Early.

"To Jeremiah Early £21, 17 s. 6 d. for 750 lbs. of beef." "For 550 lbs. of corn on Sept. 9, 1780," and others.

Issue:

1. Joseph^{4} Early (Jeremiah^{3}, Thos.^{2}, Jno.^{1}), d. 1784 in Culpeper, served as Lieutenant during the Revolution, wife Jane.
   1. Julia^{5} Early.
   2. Paschal^{5} Early.
   3. Mary^{5} Early.
   4. Judeth^{5} Whitfield Early.
   5. Joshua^{5} Early.

1. Julia^{5} Early (Jos.^{4}, Jere.^{3}, Thos.^{2}, Jno.^{1}), m. John^{3} Rucker (Ephraim^{2}, Peter^{1}).

The heirs of Joseph^{4} Early sold property Mch. 22, 1807; heirs (D. B. D, p. 222, Woodford Co., Ky.): Paschal Early, John Rucker and wife, Julianne, Mary Newman, Wm. Early, Whitfield Early and wife, Mary, Joseph Early, all of the county of Madison, state of Virginia, sold to John Hamilton of Woodford

Co., Ky., land on the waters of Glenn's Creek, part of Dickenson's Military Survey.

Signed: Paschol Early, John Rucker, Julianna Rucker, Mary Newman, Whitfield Early. Witness: Wm. Taylor, Wm. Newman, P. Early.

Higginbotham

John[1] Higginbotham, from Ireland, was living in Virginia as early as 1751, m. Frances Riely.

1. Moses[2] Higginbotham, d. 1791, Amherst.
2. Aaron[2] Higginbotham, d. 1785.
3. John[2] Higginbotham, d. 1814.
4. Joseph[2] Higginbotham, d. 1805.
5. James[2] Higginbotham, d. 1813.
6. Rachel[2] Higginbotham, m. William Morrison.

2. Aaron[2] Higginbotham (John[1]), d. Amherst, leaving a will dated Sept. 19, 1778, probated Oct. 3, 1785 (W. B. 2, p. 254), m. Clara Graves.

1. Samuel[3] Higginbotham.
2. Frances[3] Higginbotham.
3. Mary[3] Ann Higginbotham.
4. Tamasin[3] Higginbotham.
5. Aaron[3] Higginbotham.
6. Margaret[3] Higginbotham, to have "the tract of land Mary Ann now lives on." Executors: "My Brother Col. James Higginbotham and my sons Samuel and Aaron." Witness: Charles Burrus, Richard Oglesby, and Richard Mitchell. Aaron's estate was divided June 19, 1798 (W. B. 3, p. 470). "To Joseph H. Morrison, who intermarried with Frances Higginbotham." "To Henry Franklin's legates, who are the children of Mary Ann, dau. of Aaron." "William Sandridge who intermarried with Tamasin, dau. of Aaron." "To Thomas Morrison who intermarried with Peggy, dau. of Aaron." (Joseph Higginbotham Morrison, who m. Frances Higginbotham, was the son of William Morrison and wife, Rachel Higginbotham.)

The will of Clara's father, Francis Graves, 1748, Essex Co., Va. W. B. 8, p. 90. Will of Francis Graves, of Essex County, Parish of St. Ann's, dated June 25, 1746, probated Oct. 18, 1748. "I give unto my daughter Clarer Higinbotom seven pounds current money, and the remainder of my personal estate to be divided among my other 4 children, Jane & William, Elizabeth & Mary; after my wife's death the negroes to be divided among

6 of my children, Viz.: Jane, Ann, Clarer, Eliz., Mary & William." Wife Ann and son William exors. Wit.: Edward Almond, John Sneed, Nicholas Sneed. William Rennolds and James Rennolds to go on Ann and Wm. Graves Exors. bond.

3. Mary^3 Ann Higginbotham (Aaron^2, John^1), m. 1st Henry Franklin, d. 1782, m. 2nd Benjamin Arnold (D. B. F, p. 124, Amherst).

5. Aaron^3 Higginbotham, Jr. (Aaron^2, John^1), m. Dec. 4, 1795, Nancy Croxton.

1. Absolom^4 Higginbotham, m. Mary^3 Sandidge (Benjamin^2).
    1. Elizabeth^5 A. Higginbotham, m. 1830, Edward W. Hill.
2. Clara^4 Graves Higginbotham, m. Lindsey^3 Sandidge (Benjamin^2).
3. Elizabeth^4 Higginbotham, m. 1797, James Shields, of Nelson Co.
4. Joanna^4 Higginbotham, m. Washington Higginbotham.
5. Aaron^4 Higginbotham, m. Elizabeth Sandidge (Benjamin^2).
    1. Ida^5 Loving Higginbotham, m. W. B. Rucker.
    2. Thomas^5 Higginbotham, m. ——— Burks.
    3. Alexander^5 Brown Higginbotham.

3. Alexander^5 Brown Higginbotham (Aaron^4, Aaron^3, Aaron^2, John^1), m. Dec. 10, 1840, Eliza^4 Frances Plunkett (Willis^3, Benjamin^2, John^1), d. Dec. 1, 1888.

1. Edwin^6 Ruthwen Higginbotham.
2. Margaret^6 Higginbotham.
3. James^6 Willis Higginbotham.
4. Cyrus^6 Aaron Higginbotham.
5. Francis^6 Marion Higginbotham.

1. Edwin^6 Ruthwen Higginbotham (Alexander^5, Aaron^4, ———), b. Nov. 30, 1841, m. Mch. 25, 1868, Cyena A. Whitehead (see Plunkett line, p. 482).

2. Margaret^6 Elizabeth Higginbotham (Alexander^5, Aaron^4, ———), b. Mch. 14, 1845, m. Lysander E. Plunkett, Mch. 15, 1866.

1. Fannie^7 Plunkett.
2. Emma^7 Plunkett, m. ——— Anderson.

3. Charles^{7} Plunkett.
4. John^{7} Plunkett.
5. Enna^{7} Plunkett.
6. Maggie^{7} Plunkett.

3. James^{6} Willis Higginbotham (Alexander^{5}, Aaron^{4}, ——) (July 8, 1848-Oct. 1927), m. 1st Sue H. Llewellyn, July 18, 1876, m. 2nd Margaret Plunkett (widow) 1879, m. 3rd Ora Estelle Hughes, Jan. 17, 1900.

Issue (by 1st mar.):

1. Susie^{7} Willis Higginbotham, b. Dec. 3, 1887, m. Dec. 26, 1911, Lewis Forrest Hughes.
   1. Ada^{8} E. Hughes, b. Dec. 3, 1912.
   2. James^{8} Theodore Hughes, b. Dec. 3, 1914.
   3. Llewellyn^{8} Forrest Hughes, b. June 3, 1916.
   4. Jeter^{8} Wilson Hughes, b. June 2, 1918.
   5. John^{8} Pershing Hughes, b. Apr., 1919.
   6. Herbert^{8} Higginbotham Hughes, b. Sept., 1920.
   7. Susie^{8} Willis Hughes, b. Nov. 18, 1923.

Issue (by 3rd mar.):

2. Louise^{7} Estelle Higginbotham, b. Aug. 9, 1901, m. Otey Wright.
3. James^{7} Sidney Higginbotham, b. July 20, 1904, m. Elsie Johnson.
   1. James^{8} Sidney Higginbotham, Jr., b. Dec., 1927.

4. Cyrus^{6} Aaron Higginbotham (Alexander^{5}, Aaron^{4}, ——), m. Althea Jane Higginbotham (Joseph^{4} C., Joseph^{3} C., James^{2}, John^{1}). See p. 510.

5. Francis^{6} M. Higginbotham (Alex.^{5}, Aaron^{4}, ———), b. Aug. 21, 1856, m. Apr. 28, 1880, Lucy Higginbotham.

1. Lelia^{7} Higginbotham, b. Feb. 22, 1882, m. Howard J. Farrell.
2. Warren^{7} Higginbotham, b. Feb. 17, 1887, d. in World War service.
3. Vernon^{7} Higginbotham, b. June 23, 1890.

3. Capt. John^{2} Higginbotham (John^{1}), b. c. 1735, d. in Amherst, 1814, m. July 9, 1767, Rachel Banks (dau. of Gerrard Banks and wife, Ann Stanton, she, the dau. of Thomas and Sarah Stanton of Orange). In the archives in Richmond, Virginia, are certificates showing the amount of provisions furnished by citizens to the revolutionary army in 1781. Among them, No. 63,

signed by A. Rucker to "Capt. John Higginbotham, £3, 13 for 295 lbs. of beef for the use of the army."

Will of John Higginbotham, dated June 22, 1813, probated Sept. 9, 1814, Amherst Co. (W. B. 5, p. 451), mentions wife Rachel.

Issue:

1. John[3] Higginbotham.
2. Frances[3] R. Higginbotham.
3. Ann[3] Stanton Higginbotham.
4. James[3] Higginbotham.
5. Terzar[3] London Higginbotham.
6. Thomas[3] Higginbotham.
7. Jesse[3] Higginbotham.
8. Daniel[3] Higginbotham.
9. Reuben[3] Higginbotham.
10. Eugene[3] (minor).
11. David[3].
12. Mary (not in father's will).

Witness: John Higginbotham, James H. Dillard, and Young Hawkins.

5. Terzar[3] Higginbotham (John[2], John[1]) (Feb. 27, 1783-Aug. 1, 1841), m. John James London (1775-1823).

1. Frances[4] Jane London (Sept. 23, 1811-Apr. 26, 1802), m. Winston Woodroof (Oct. 15, 1807-Dec. 1, 1871), son of David Woodroof and his wife, Judith McDaniel (see John McDaniel line, p. 415).

6. Thomas[3] Higginbotham (John[2], John[1]), d. unmar. in Amherst, leaving a will in which he mentions, "My sister Terzah London and her children: Mary Banks London, William Augustine London, John J. London, Daniel H. London, Frances Woodroof, my bro. Daniel Higginbotham, my bro. James Higginbotham, late of Ky., to Ann E. London, to my sister Ann Stanton Higginbotham, late of Ga., to sister Frances R. Coleman, to Jesse Higginbotham, to bro. Eugene Higginbotham, to Mika Higginbotham, wife of James S. H., to David Higginbotham, to William S. Higginbotham, to bro. Reuben's two sons. Estate valued at $150,000.

12. Mary[3] Higginbotham, dau. of Capt. John, m. Isaac Rucker, son of Moses Rucker, in 1793. She died without children before the will of her father was made in 1813. (See Moses Rucker). Marriage bond in Amherst Co., Va., s dated Jan. 29, 1793, "Mary, dau. of John Higginbotham", to marry "Isaac Rucker, bachelor."

(Court of Appeals, Call's Va. Reports, Call, Vol. 2, p. 313). Isaac Rucker married Mary Higginbotham, Jan. 13, 1793. Her father gave her three of his slaves for her use, and for the use of her children, but she died within a year, leaving no heir. The slaves had increased, and John Higginbotham sued Rucker for the said slaves.

4. Joseph[2] Higginbotham (John[1]), d. 1805 in Amherst Co., will dated 1802, probated 1805 (W. B. 4, p. 178).

1. Joseph[3] Higginbotham.
2. Benjamin[3] Higginbotham.
3. Susanna[3] Higginbotham.
4. Rachel[3] Higginbotham.
5. Frances[3] Morrison Higginbotham.
6. William[3] Morrison Higginbotham.
7. Jacob[3] Morrison Higginbotham.
8. Hannah[3] Ballow Higginbotham.

Witness: Henry Ballinger, Benjamin Sandidge, Jacob Philips.

5. Col. James[2] Higginbotham (John[1]) (Dec. 25, 1729-Mch. 14, 1813), m. Rachel Campbell, May 30, 1779. He owned some of the land now included in the Sweet Briar tract. Marriage bond signed by mother, Charity Campbell. Witness: Joel Campbell, Patty Campbell.

1. Judith[3] Higginbotham, m. 1797, Joseph Dillard, son of Duval Dillard, of Nelson Co.
2. James[3] Higginbotham, Jr., moved to Bowling Green, Ky.
3. Joseph[3] Cabell Higginbotham.
4. George[3] Washington Higginbotham.

3. Col. Joseph[3] Cabell Higginbotham (James[2], John[1]), of Bedford Co. Will dated July 20, 1841, probated Sept. 4, 1843, m. 1803, Lucy Wills, dau. of Major James Wills of Amherst Co., who gave to his daughter a marriage dower, 924 acres of land in Bedford, in Goose Creek Valley, where Joseph and Lucy lived and are buried. Joseph was in service in the War of 1812.

1. Mary[4] W. Higginbotham, b. Oct. 24, 1822, Edmund F. Davidson.
2. Rachel[4] Higginbotham, m. Dec. 22, 1828, Edwin Nevile.
3. Joseph[4] Cabell Higginbotham.
3. Eliza[4] D. Higginbotham, m. Jan. 24, 1834, Abner Pearcy.

5. Lucinda^{4} Catherine Higginbotham, m. Feb. 10, 1836, Nathaniel Webber.
6. Joanna^{4} Higginbotham, m. Sept. 14, 1843, Thomas J. Hill.
7. James^{4} W. Higginbotham, m. June 26, 1845, Nancy De Witt.

3. Joseph^{4} Cabell Higginbotham, Jr. (Joseph^{3} C., James^{2}, John^{1}), m. 1st Matilda Barnes, Oct. 24, 1844; m. 2nd Angelina^{4} E. Plunkett, Feb. 7, 1849 (Willis^{3}, Benjamin^{2}, John^{1}). Served in the Civil War, Co. I, Virginia Regiment.

1. Willis^{5} Marion Higginbotham (Sept. 7, 1850-Aug. 1, 1855).
2. Althea^{5} Jane Higginbotham.
3. William^{5} Kent Higginbotham, b. Jan. 8, 1857.
4. Mary^{5} Virginia Higginbotham.
5. Joseph^{5} Thomas Cabell Higginbotham.

2. Althea^{5} Jane Higginbotham (Joseph^{4} C., Joseph^{3} C., James^{2}, John^{1}) (Oct. 7, 1852-Oct. 13, 1921), m. Oct. 21, 1874, Cyrus^{6} Aaron Higginbotham (Aug. 25, 1852-Apr. 15, 1896) (Alexander^{5}, Aaron^{4}, Aaron^{3}, Aaron^{2}, John^{1}).

1. Lillian^{6} Brown Higginbotham, born April 27, 1876, married Leo William Kasehagen, October 1, 1900, at Bedford, Virginia.
   1. Leona^{7} Marie Elizabeth Kasehagen, b. Jan. 28, 1902; d. Jan. 21, 1905.
   2. Leo^{7} Kasehagen, 3rd, b. Aug. 18, 1909, at Manassas, Virginia. His early childhood days were spent on the Higginbotham farm, the home of his grandmother, Mrs. Cyrus Aaron Higginbotham, at Montvale, Virginia.

      While attending Central High School, Washington, D. C., from which he graduated, was captain of the rifle team, winning the Chamber of Commerce medal in 1926. He was captain of the Plebe team during his first year at Carnegie Tech; and was rated highest in scholastic standing of more than 300 students in the freshman class of the College of Engineering and Industries in Carnegie. For his proficiency he was given a founder's scholarship; captained the varsity team in 1928 and was re-elected for 1929.

He was a member of the DeWar team at Camp Perry in 1927, and was high man in the rifle and pistol firing at the R. O. T. C. Camp at Fort Humphreys in the summer of 1929; also a member of Scabbard and Blade, honorary military society; appointed first lieutenant and supply officer of the 1st Battalion of the Reserve Officers' Training Corps regiment at the Carnegie Institute of Technology, where he finished college in 1930.

2. Lula^6 May Higginbotham (Jan. 15, 1878-1879).
3. Minnie^6 R. Higginbotham, b. Mch. 14, 1880, m. Nov. 25, 1912, Royster St. Noble, Barcelona, Spain.
4. Lenora^6 E. Higginbotham, b. Dec. 9, 1884, m. 1st Apr. 27, 1905, James Morgan MacFarlane, m. 2nd W. Sweeny, of N. Y.
5. Annie Cabell^6 Higginbotham, b. June 22, 1887, m. Dec. 27, 1905, Howard Wise Johnson.
   1. Cyrus^7 S. Johnson, b. 1911.
   2. Althea^7 R. Johnson, b. 1913.
   3. Frances^7 Johnson, b. 1916.
6. Raymond^6 Clyde Higginbotham, b. Jan. 3, 1889, m. Katie Lee Wright, Dec. 18, 1918.
   1. Joseph^7 Cabell Lee Higginbotham, b. 1919.
   2. Raymond^7 C. Higginbotham, b. and d. 1920.
   3. Virginia^7 Pettis Higginbotham, b. 1923.
7. Ida Rice^6 Higginbotham (Mch. 2, 1892, d. 19th).
8. Janie^6 Corinne Higginbotham, b. Apr. 14, 1894, m. Clarence E. Berger, Dec. 27, 1920.

4. Mary^5 Virginia Higginbotham (Joseph^4, Joseph^3, James^2, ———) (Dec. 2, 1859-Aug. 16, 1880), m. Robert T. Lyle, Nov. 1, 1870, d. 1923.

   1. Mary^6 Robert Lyle, b. Aug. 16, 1880, d. 1910, at Fort Worth, Texas, m. 1902, John Borrough Randle.
      1. John^7 B. Randle, Jr., b. 1907, Abilene, Texas.

5. Joseph^5 T. Cabell Higginbotham (Joseph^4, Joseph^3, James^2, ———) (Apr. 20, 1861-June 17, 1862).

Marriages, Amherst, marriage bonds.

1803, Dolly Higginbotham m. John Frayn.

1820, Jane S. Higginbotham m. James Watts.

1849, B. L. Higginbotham m. M. H. Carter.

1858, Aaron Higginbotham m. Sally Ann Sandidge.

1792, John Higginbotham m. Ann Higginbotham.

The Higginbotham family history was contributed by Mr. and Mrs. Sweeney, of N. Y.

Vawter

Bartholomew, John and Angus Vawter came from England to Virginia.

John[1] Vawter, b. 1665, d..in Essex.

1. John[2] Vawter, Jr., b. 1691, d. 1752, m. Margaret Noel, d. 1756 (daughter of David). John Vawter's will dated May 23, 1748, probated Nov. 10, 1752, Culpeper County.

John Vawter patented 25 acres of land in Essex County, Sept. 5, 1723 (L. Gr., b. 11, p. 233) on the south side of the Rappahannock in St. Anne Parish in the forks of Blackberry Creek, formerly granted to John Page.

July 20, 1736, John Vawter and Philip Stogdale of Orange County, patented 380 acres of land adjoining William Eddings, Robert Slaughter and William Robinson (L. Grants, b. 17, p. 129).

20 July 1736, John Vawter patented 700 acres of land in Orange County, adjoining Thomas Stanton, Francis Conway and William Neale for transporting 14 persons into the colony, names given (L. Gr., b. 17, p. 135).

1. Bartholomew[3] Vawter, wife Winifred acknowledged a deed in Essex Co., Aug., 1696 (O. B. 1695-99, p. 29).
2. Richard[3] Vawter.
3. Angus[3] Vawter.
4. Winifred[3] Vawter.
5. David[3].
6. Margaret[3].

5. David[3] Vawter, b. 1720, d. 1785, m. about 1755, Mary, of Culpeper.

1. William[4] Vawter, m. Mary[3] Rucker (Ephraim[2], Peter[1]), 1st cousin.

The *Virginia Colonial Churches*, p. 210, refers to the Vawter Church as having been built before 1719. This church is still standing in St. Ann's Parish, Essex. In an old land survey made by John Vawter for Buckingham Brown who lived on Blackburn's Creek close to the Vawter Church. On this plot dated 1722 is a road leading to the church. In another survey made for John Hawkins, who also owned land on the same creek, surveyed by John Vawter, the Church land was shown as a boundary, this plot was dated 1719.

Christian

Henry[4] Christian (William[3], James[2], Thomas[1]), lived in Amherst Co., was a captain in the Revolutionary War, served under General Marquis de la Fayette (see Hardesty's *H. & G. Ency.*, also Eckenrode's *Revolutionary Soldiers* and McAlister's Revolutionary Soldiers). He married Martha Patterson, dau. of Jonathan.

1. John[5] Christian, b. May 25, 1761.
2. Henry[5] Asbury Christian.
3. Samuel[5] Patterson Christian.
4. Jonathan[5] Christian, m. Sarah Nowlin, Appomattox.
5. Susan[5] Brown Christian, m. William Duval.
6. Elizabeth[5] Christian, m. Philip Duval.
7. Martha[5] Patterson Christian, m. Dr. R. D. Palmer.
8. Andrew[5] Christian, of Richmond.
9. Henry[5] Christian, of Lynchburg.
10. Mary[5] Ann Christian Rucker.

3. Samuel[5] Patterson Christian (Henry[4], William[3], James[2], Thomas[1]), m. Ann Patterson.

1. George[6] Christian, m. 1st Martha Chapman; m. 2nd Sophronia Shannon.
2. Samuel[6] P. Christian, m. ——— Winn.
3. Elizabeth[6] Augusta Christian.
4. John[6] Christian.
5. Jonathan[6] Christian.
6. William[6] Duval Christian.
7. Patsy[6] Christian.
8. Edward[6] Christian, m. Matilda Horst.

3. Elizabeth[6] Augusta Christian (Samuel[5], Henry[4]. William[3], James[2], Thomas[1]), m. Robert Henry Glass.

1. Edward[7] Christian Glass.
2. Nannie[7] Glass.
3. Robert[7] Henry Glass.
4. George[7] Carter Glass, m. Aurelia Caldwell.
5. Powell[7] Glass.

10. Mary[5] Ann Christian (Henry[4], William[3], James[2], Thomas[1]), m. Jan. 12, 1796, Isaac[4] Rucker (Ambrose[3], John[2], Peter[1]), marriage bond in Amherst, permit signed by "Henry Christian, father" (see Rucker line, p. 104). Will of Henry Christian, Amherst, date Dec. 14, 1804; probated June 17, 1805.

Will of Henry Christian.

In the name of God Amen, I Henry Christian of the County of Amherst and state of Virginia, considering the uncertainty of this mortal life and being of sound mind and memory, blessed be God for the same, do make and publish this my last will and testament in manner and form following viz: first I lend to my beloved wife Martha Christian during her natural life the following property viz: four negroes, Henry, Patt, Nancy, and Charles, also my household furniture that I may possessed; secondly I give to my daughter, Susanah B. Christian one negro girl named Mourning and also choice of the horses, I may die possessed; thirdly I give to my daughter, Frances B. Christian one negro boy named David; Fourthly I give unto my daughter, Martha P. Christian one negro girl named Becky. The negroes before mentioned viz: Mourning, David and Becky, I desire may be set free when it shall be considered by the court of said county that they are twenty-five years of age and I further direct that the increase of the aforesaid Patt and Nancy, may be set free and I do desire that at the death of my wife that all my estate that is not given to my three daughters, Susannah B. Christian, Frances B. Christian and Martha P. Christian shall be equally divided between all my children and I do appoint William B. Christian of Hanover County, state of Virginia and Isaac Rucker of Amherst County and state of Virginia my executors to this my last will and testament hereby revoking all former wills by me made. In witness where of I have hereunto set my hand and seal the 14th day of December, in the year of our Lord eighteen hundred and four. Signed, sealed, published and declared by the above named Henry Christian to be his last will and testament in the presence of us who have hereunto subscribed our names in presence of Testator.

Henry Christian (seal).

Drury Bell, Drury Christian, James Dilard, Charles Christian. Probated June 17, 1805.

Christian Coat of Arms (Isle of Man, 1687): Azure, a chevron humettée between 3 covered cup or. Crest: a unicorn's head erased argent collared and armed or. Motto: Salers per Christian.

Price

Price Family of West Langton, England

1. Richard[1] Price d. Mch. 18, 1816, age 51; his wife, Elizabeth, d. Dec. 10, 1828, age 67. They lived at West Langton, England.

    1. William[2] Price, d. Mch. 4, 1856, age 58; his wife, Mary, d. July 10, 1844, age 35. They lived at West Langton, and all of the family are buried at Church Langton.

        1. William[3] Price.
        2. Fannie[3] Price.
        3. Mary[3] (Polly) Price.
        4. Richard[3] Price.
        5. Elizabeth[3] Price.
        6. George[3] Price.

1. William[3] Price (Wm.[2], Richard[1]), m. Lydia Wood, b. Sept. 20, 1836 (sister of T. W. Wood).

    1. Fred[4] Price, b. Aug. 25, 1861.
    2. Elizabeth[4] Anne, b. Aug. 13, 1860, m. John Main, Leicester, England.

        1. Herbert[5] Main, b. 1886.
        2. Leslie[5] Main.
        3. William[5] Perceval Main, b. Feb. 17, 1889.

    3. Arthur[4] Price.
    4. Eleanor[4] Mary Price, m. George Scott, Wesleyan Minister, Lancaster, England.

        1. Nora[5] Scott.
        2. George[5] Eric Scott.
        3. Margaret[5] Scott.

    5. Walter[4] Ward Price, b. Aug. 19, 1868.
    6. Berners[4] Wood Price, b. Feb. 18, ——.

2. Fannie[3] Price (Wm.[2], Richard[1]), m. Robert Waddington, Derby, England, b. 1837.

    1. Kate[4] Eleanor Waddington, m. Harry Treadgold, Derby, England. No heirs.
    2. George[4] Price Waddington, Derby, England. Bachelor.
    3. Mary[4] E. Waddington, b. Oct. 4, ——, m. Alfred Tatlow, Derby, England. No heirs.
    4. Frank[4] Waddington, b. Oct. 7, ——, m. Isobel ———, Bristol, England.

3. Mary[3] (Polly) Price m. John Morley, Draper, Leicester, England. No heirs.

4. Richard[3] Price m. Sophia ———, London, England.
 1. Arnold[4] Richard Price.

5. Elizabeth[3] Price (Wm.[2], Richard[1]), m. T. W. Wood (see p. 517).

6. George[3] Price (Wm.[2], Richard[1]), m. Eliza Wood, sister of T. W. Wood, Newark, England.
 1. Richard[4] Edward Price.
 2. George[4] William Price.
 3. John[4] Henry Price.
 4. Herbert[4] Walter Price.
 5. Charles[4] Wesley Price, d. in infancy.
 6. Alice[4] Wood Price, Derby, Eng.
 7. Claude[4] Stanley Price.

1. Richard[4] Edward Price (Geo.[3], Wm.[2], Richard[1]), d. May 11, 1888, m. Annie Gover, of London, d. Nov. 9, 1900, at Sheffield, both are buried at Nottingham, Eng.
 1. Richard[5] Reginald Price, London, Eng.
 2. Elsie[5] Price, London, Eng.
 3. Edith[5] Price, London, Eng.
 4. Ella[5] Price, London, Eng.

2. George[4] William Price (George[3], William[2], Richard[1]), m. Emma Wragg, Nottingham, Eng. He was the founder of the firm of E. W. Price (manufacturing lace), of Stoners Street, Nottingham, England. He is one of the largest stockholders of the Shepherd Lace Manufacturing Co., of Longhboro, Eng., of which his eldest son, Harold William, is manager. George W. is a Mason and a member of the Nottingham Rotary Club.
 1. Harold[5] William Price, b. Sept. 7, 1886.
 2. Grace[5] Lillian Price.
 3. Marguerite[5] Price.
 4. Frank[5] Reginald Price, is the manager of the E. W. Price lace firm in Nottingham.
 5. Marie[5] Price, m. Cyril, the only surviving son of Sir Albert and Lady Ball. Sir Albert was former Mayor of Nottingham. Albert Ball, Jr., brother of Cyril, was one of England's well known aviators killed in the World War, in commemoration of whom a life size monument was erected in Nottingham Castle grounds.

3. John[4] Henry Price (George[3], William[2], Richard[1]), b. Oct. 6, ——, m. Elizabeth Palmer, Nottingham, Eng.

1. Constance[5] May Price.
2. Edna[5] Price.
3. Eric[5] George Price.
4. Dora[5] Price.
5. Bertie[5] Price.

4. Herbert[4] Walter Price (George[3], William[2], Richard[1]), b. Oct. 12, ——, m. Mary Bowen, Nottingham.

1. Frances[5] Dorothy Price.
2. James[5] Herbert Bowen Price.
3. Winifred[5] Price.
4. Cyrel[5] Price.
5. Evelyn[5] Mary Price.
6. Alfred[5] Berners Price.
7. Stanley[5] George Price.

7. Claude[4] Stanley Price (Geo.[3], Wm.[2], Richard[1]), b. Aug. 5, 1888, of Nottingham, m. Edith Campbell, of Peterboro, Eng. No heirs.

Wood

The Wood Family of Newark, England

1. Timothy[1] Wood, Nottingham, England; wife, Lydia, b. 1808.

A copy of the epitaph on the stone that marks the grave of Lydia, the wife of Timothy Wood, in the cemetery at Newark, England: Interred Feb. 19th, 1886. In loving memory of Lydia Wood, wife of the late Timothy Wood of Newark on Trent, who died at Nottingham, Feb. 16th, 1886, age 78 years.

1. Timothy[2] Ward Wood, b. Jan. 5, 1840, in Newark, England, came to Virginia in 1873. He was admitted to citizenship July 17, 1880, at Richmond, Va. He d. at his home in Forest Hill, Richmond, Nov. 12, 1905. He m. 1st, Oct. 9, 1860, Elizabeth Price, of Church Langton (September 11, 1834-November 27, 1902. They lived at Newark, on the Trent, where all of the children were born except Annie. T. W. Wood was the founder of the firm of T. W. Wood & Sons, established 1879. He was a man of high ideals, which he lived up to in his everyday life, standards for himself and family that were always

respected, the same standards he exacted of all his employees in his business. He m. 2nd Mrs. Anna Neblet Ingram, the widow of Dr. Ingram, of Manchester, Va.

1. Henry[3] Ward Wood.
2. William[3] Price Wood.
3. Charles[3] Francis Wood.
4. Virginia[3] Annie Wood.
5. Edith[3] Wood.

1. Henry[3] Ward Wood, b. Mch. 16, 1864, Newark, Eng., d. Jan. 15, 1919 (traveling) in New Orleans, m. Dec. 11, 1884, Jeannie McLean Whittet in Richmond, Virginia. She d. July 22, 1916. At one time he was President of the Richmond Chamber of Commerce, also President of the American Seed Trade.

1. Robert[4] Ward Wood, b. Sept. 29, 1885, m. Lucile Lockett, June 16, 1910, b. July 26, 1891.
    1. Catherine[5] Jean Wood, b. Apr. 22, 1911.
    2. Eleanor[5] Whittet Wood, b. Nov. 28, 1912.
2. Harry[4] Ryrie Wood, b. Sept. 5, 1891, m. Lillian E. Wattson, Oct. 27, 1914, b. Aug. 30, 1894.
    1. Lillian[5] Winston Wood, b. May 8, 1918.
    2. Margaret[5] Gordon Wood, b. Nov. 14, 1920.
3. Gordon[4] Frazer Wood, b. Oct. 25, 1893, m. Rete Smith, July 13, 1923, b. Nov. 29, 1899.
    1. Gordon[5] Frazer Wood, Jr., b. July 6, 1924.

2. William[3] Price Wood, b. Sept. 28, 1865, Newark, England. He was President of the Virginia State Fair Association for a number of years, President of the Drum Point Duck Club, President of the Virginia State Golf Association, and President of T. W. Wood & Sons since 1919. (See Sudie Rucker, page 54).

3. Charles[3] Francis Wood, b. Feb. 6, 1869, Newark, England, d. July 31, 1925, Louisville, Ky.; m. 1st Nellie Whittet, Richmond, Va., Sept. 15, 1891, d. July 5, 1900; m. 2nd Ethel Randal Roberts, dau. of Dr. R. R. Roberts of Louisville.

Issue (by 2nd mar.):

1. Robert[4] Wood, graduate of Cornell, m. Katherine Breckenridge, dau. of Dr. Thomas Yager, Dec. 6, 1930, Louisville, Ky.
2. Charles[4] Francis Wood, graduate of Princeton.

4. Virginia^3 Annie Wood, b. June 23, 1873; m. Oct. 8, 1896, Richmond, Va., Dr. Henry Stuart MacLean, of Brooklyn, now of Richmond, Va.

   1. Elizabeth^4 Price MacLean, b. Nov. 24, 1898, m. Mch. 10, 1927, Donald Jennings Matheson, Richmond, Va.
      1. John^5 Stuart Matheson, b. Aug. 27, 1928, Richmond, Va.
   2. Lachlan^4 Ward MacLean, b. Aug. 17, 1900, m. Oct. 19, 1925, Eleanor Alberta Grant, Boston, Mass.
      1. Eleanor^5 Anne MacLean, b. Nov. 23, 1928, in Richmond, Va.

Beasley

Richard^1 Beasley d. in Nottoway Co., Va., 1770, m. Nancy Ambrose, leaving only one son, Ambrose Beasley.

Will of Richard Beasley of Nottoway Parish, Amelia Co., Va.

To my son, Ambrose Beasley, called Ambrose "Pitts", and his three children, named Richard Beasley, Jr., William Beasley, and Ann Beasley. Exec.: son, Ambrose Beasley. Wit.: James Baldwin, Bartholomew Dupuy. Dated Apr. 9, 1770, prob. Sept. 20, 1771 (W. B. 2, p. 7, Amelia).

   1. Ambrose^2 Beasley.

1. Ambrose^2 Beasley (Richard^1), m. Sarah Ryland.
   1. William^3 Beasley.
   2. Richard^3 Beasley.
   3. Nancy^3 Beasley.

3. Nancy^3 Beasley (Ambrose^2, Richard^1), m. Archibald^2 Yarborough (Thomas^1) and wife, Hannah Jordan.
   1. Jane^4 Yarborough.
   2. Thomas^4 Rucker Yarborough.

1. Jane^4 Yarborough (Nancy^3, Ambrose^2, Richard^1), m. Richard^2 Beasley, son of William^1 Beasley and Ann Jennings, of Virginia.
   1. William^5 Beasley.
   2. Nancy^5 Beasley.
   3. Lucenda^5 Beasley.
   4. Ambrose^5 Beasley.

5. Jincy[5] Beasley.
6. Patsy[5] Beasley.
7. Royland[5] Beasley.

2. Nancy[5] Beasley (Jane[4], Nancy[3], Ambrose[2], Richard[1]), b. 1770, m. Fielding[5] Rucker (John[4], Cornelius[3], ———). See p. 210.

Arthur

Col. Lewis[1] C. Arthur, of Big Island, Bedford Co., m. Nancy Russell Jones, their home was "Oakland", near Leesville, Campbell Co., Va., and Big Island. He was a very popular, public spirited gentleman, being a large and prosperous farmer, he contributed largely to the needy. It is said of him that during the Civil War he would set aside 100 barrels of corn each year for the less fortunate. He was in the State Convention in 1850-51.

Issue:

1. Albon[2] A. Arthur, Clerk of Bedford Co. Court.
2. James[2] Lewis Arthur, served his county both as a representative to the House of Delegates, and to the State Senate. He served through the Civil War.
3. Col. M.[2] C. Arthur, served under Col. Stonewall Jackson. He was in command of the 58th Virginia Regiment and was killed in the battle near Winchester, Va., Sept. 19, 1864, age 26. He was very popular and was called "Penn" by his friends. He was born on the 4th of July and called by his mother "Independence boy", shortened later to "Penn".
4. Almira[2] Arthur, m. Rev. Abner Anthony.
5. Angeline[2] Arthur, m. J. Saunders, moved to Ky.
6. Martha[2] Emily Arthur, m. John Edward McDaniel, July 2, 1857 (see McDaniel).
7. Sally[2] Davis Arthur, m. Dr. James M. Talliaferro, of Amherst, 4 Oct. 1860.
   1. Dr. R.[3] M. Talliaferro.
   2. Mrs. C.[3] T. Rucker, of Lynchburg.

Bruce

Capt. Edward Bruce, of Halifax, b. after 1790; d. 1873, m. 1st ————, m. 2nd Harriet Poultney, who died in 1847, and was buried at Cherry Hill Church in Halifax Co.

Edward bought land of William Murry and wife, Permela, in Malifax Co., adjoining Mathew and Samuel Pate, 30 Dec. 1816 (D. B. 26, p. 338, Halifax).

He was appointed trustee and executor of Mathew Pate, dec'd, ———, and mortgaged land on Stokes Creek to secure a debt, June 22, 1829 (D. B. 37, p. 111, Halifax).

Edward Bruce and George W. Boyd ——— a business transaction, 11 March 1834 (D. B. 41, p. 405, Halifax).

John Chappell, of Missouri, Edward Bruce, John W. Chamlin and James M. Chappel sold land in Halifax to Edward Boyd, 7 Oct. 1842 (D. B. 48, p. 213, Halifax).

Edward Bruce, Samuel Pate, William Watkins, Edward A. Oaks and Isaac Palmer bought land, 13 Feb. 1836 (D. B. 43, p. 39, Halifax).

Edward Bruce and wife, Harriet S., sold land to Martha T. Sheppard, land on Double Creek, Oct. 9, 1844 (D. B. 50, p. 451, Halifax).

Edward Bruce and wife, Harriet, sold land to Samuel G. Watts, 9 Oct. 1844 (D. B. 50, p. 523, Halifax).

Capt. Edward Bruce deeded 228 1/3 acres of land to his son Robert Soule Bruce on Coleman's Creek, Jan. 22, 1873 (D. B. 63, p. 119, Halifax).

He deeded land to W. E. Bass, land in Mt. Carmel Township, 6 Dec. 1873 (D. B. 64, p. 298, Halifax).

Edward served in the War of 1812.

From the Muster Roll of Capt. Edward Robertson's Troop of Cavalry, from the 11th Regiment of Virginia in the service of the State, Edward Bruce, private (M. R., p. 673, Archives Va.).

Edward d. in 1873, leaving no will, the appraisement of his estate was made by W. S. Betts, Thomas H. Hall, and Henry Link. Purchasers at sale of the above personal property were Thomas P. Bruce, Robert S. Bruce, William Samuel Bruce and John Bruce, 28 Jan. 1874 (W. B. 31, p. 142-183, Halifax).

Settlement of the estate of Edward Bruce by Thomas P. Bruce, adm.

Cash paid to Mrs. H. E. Craddock.

Interest paid on the estate of J. N. Poultney.

Cash paid to R. S. Bruce 300.60.

Cash paid to Thomas P. Bruce 300.60. 4 July 1879 (W. B. 32, p. 38, Halifax).

(D. B. 70, p. 682, Halifax) April, 1883, of Black Walnut District. Capt. Edward Bruce's estate. Assigned to W. E. Bass, to Elan Craddock and wife H. E. Craddock, and to John D. Brandon and Mary A., his wife, 1/3 of the interest in the estate of Capt. Edward Bruce, dec'd, land lying on both sides of Little and Big Coleman Creek, adjoining the land of Mrs. H. A. Woods and R. E. Bass's lot, 172 acres, also 1/3 of Edward Bruce's estate was given to his dau., Mrs. Harriet A. Wood, 190 acres.

The division of the estate of Edward Bruce, Dec. 6, 1881 (D. B. 70, p. 674).

To R. E. Bass and wife, Emma S.

To John D. Brandon and wife, Mary A.

To Elan Craddock and wife, Harriet E.

Issue (by 1st mar.):

1. Annie[2] Bruce.

Issue (by 2nd mar.):

2. Thomas[2] Poultney Bruce.
3. John[2] Bruce, d. young.
4. Robert[2] Soule Bruce, m. Ann Drucilla Pate.
5. Harriot[2] Bruce, m. ——— Wood.
6. Emily[2] Bruce, m. R. E. Bass.

1. Thomas[2] Poultney Bruce (Edward[1]), m. 1st Hallie Young, 2nd Elizabeth Young, 3rd Lucy Crouder. Thomas P. Bruce was deeded land by his father Edward, on Coleman's Creek in Black Walnut District, adjoining the land of Capt. W. S. Betts, 1872 (D. B. 63, p. 130, Halifax).

The will of Thomas Poultney Bruce, 5 Jan. 1907.

To wife Lucy C. Bruce; to granddaughter, Clara Wooten of Mecklenburg; to grandchildren, Aleck Norman Crowder, Mary P. Crowder and Hallie Crowder, children of my dau., Sallie; to my son Dr. Edward T. Bruce of Denver, Col.; to son John L. Bruce of Brazil, S. A.; to dau. Pearl Thomas, of Roanoke.

Will made at my house near Cluster Springs (W. B. 38, p. 139, Halifax). Inventory of estate of Thomas P. Bruce of Cluster Springs, 2 May 1907 (W. B. 38, p. 145, Halifax).

4. Robert[2] Soule Bruce (Edward[1]), was born at Black Walnut, Cluster Springs, Halifax Co., b. 26 Oct. 1833, d. June 7, 1898, m. Ann[3] Drusilla Pate (Samuel[2]). The following is written in a Bible belonging to Robert Soule Bruce, the Bible was given to him by his mother on her death bed, but the note on the fly leaf was written by Robert's half sister, Annie Bruce. "Robert Soule Bruce was born Octo. 26, 1833. This Bible was presented to him Oct. 1847 by the request of his mother on her

death bed. She died May 8, 1847 about 6 o'clock. The day she died she called you and John to her bed, and told you she wanted you to read two chapters every Sabbath.

A. B."

Will of A. D. Bruce to dau., Lucy Bruce, all of my property. Jan. 30, 1912 (W. B. 39, p. 5, Halifax). See Pate, p. 528.
Issue:

1. Harriot[3] Watkins Bruce, m. Lafayette Mann. See pages 529 and 533.

6. Emma[2] S. Bruce (Edward[1]), m. R. E. Bass, 27 Aug. 1888. To Charles K. Bass; to James E. Bass; to Joseph J. Bass; to Thomas H. Bass (W. B. 35, p. 250, Halifax).

Will of R. E. Bass of Halifax, 17 Jan. 1907. To William E. Bass and Mary H. Brandon, the children of my 1st m.; to my sons J. J. Bass and J. E. Bass; to my dau. Harriet E. Craddock (W. B. 38, p. 144, Halifax).

John[1] Bruce, Sr., of Halifax, sold land to John Bruce, Jr. Witness: John R. Hall, Samuel C. Cooks, John Bruce, Jr. Dec. 2, 1790 (D. B. 15, p. 39, Halifax).

John Bruce, Sr., sold land on Wynn Creek, 400 acres to John Bruce, Jr., Feb. 28, 1790 (D. B. 15, p. 57, Halifax).

Will of John[1] Bruce of Antrim Parish, Halifax. To my dau. Rebekah Monday; to my dau. Wining Moorefield; to my grandson Willis Moorefield; to my dau. Polly Wilkerson; to my dau. Elizabeth Wood; son John Bruce; dau. Sally Seamore. Exec. friend John B. Hall. Mch. 10, 1816 (W. B. 10, p. 529, Halifax).

1. Rebekah[2] Monday.
2. Wining[2] Moorefield.
    1. Willis[3] Moorefield.
3. Polly[2] Wilkerson.
4. Elizabeth[2] Wood.
5. John[2] Bruce.
6. Sally[2] Seamore.

1. Rebekah[2] Bruce m. Samuel Jesse Monday. Samuel Williams in trust for 200 acres of land formerly owned by John Bruce, Sr., dec'd, land left by John Bruce, Sr., to his dau. Rebekah Monday, wife of Samuel Jesse Monday. 24 July 1823 (D. B. 32, p. 166, Halifax).

5. John[2] Bruce (John[1]). Settlement estate of John Bruce, Jr., dec'd Nov. 1860 (W. B. 13, p. 262, Halifax).

6. Sally Bruce m. Larkin Seamore of Granger Co., Tenn., appointed an agent in Halifax to receive that part of John Bruce's (senior) estate that was left to him by J. Bruce's will. 11 July 1818 (D. B. 27, p. 368, Halifax).

Rachel Bruce inventory account with John R. Hall, June 14, 1818, for Mrs. Bruce's board and for sundry goods bought of John Chappell and Co. (W. B. 11, p. 292, Halifax).

Settlement of John R. Hall, guardian of Harriet Bruce, 27 Mch. 1820 (p. 585).

Settlement of John R. Hall, guardian of Nancy Bruce, 10 Jan. 1819 (p. 292).

Settlement of John R. Hall, guardian of Susanna Bruce, 1 Mch. 1819 (p. 584).

Settlement of John R. Hall, guardian of James Bruce, 1 Mch. 1819 (p. 584).

Pate

Thomas Pate of Halifax, possibly father of Matthew and Samuel Pate of Halifax. Inventory of Thomas Pate's estate by Davil Wall, Harris Wilson and Robert Throckmorton. Oct. 15, 1771 (W. B. O, p. 320, Halifax).

1. Matthew[1] Pate, m. Drusilla Hobson.
2. Samuel[1] Pate, never married.
3. Mary[1] Pate, m. Henry Hobson.
4. ———— Pate, m. Nathaniel Tinsley.

1. Matthew[1] Pate of Halifax, m. Drusilla Hobson. Matthew was a large land owner, the names of some of his plantations were Frog Level, Buffaloe Place and Bold Spring, all in Halifax, Va. Cornwallis' army camped on Matthew's farm for three weeks during the Revolution. Matthew served in the Revolution. References: Eckenrode's *Rev. Soldiers,* War. 5, p. 153; Hening's *Statutes,* Vol. 7, p. 205, mentions a Matthew Pate serving in the French and Indian War, 1758.

Will of Matthew Pate, Nov. 24, 1828 (W. B. 14, p. 614, Halifax).

To my wife Drusilla Pate; to my son Samuel Pate; to the children of my dau. Polly Chappell; to my grand children Clement Hobson Jordan, Martha Timberlake Jordan, Mary Anderson Jordan and Susanna William Jordan; to my grand children Sarah Price Pate, Fannie Hobson Pate, Mary Thomas Pate, children of my deceased son Thomas.

Execs.: Daniel W. Fourqurean and Major Wyatt. Oct. 1, 1828. Witness: Edward Bruce, Edmund A. Oakes, C. H. Jordan.

Will of Drusilla Pate, 29 Feb. 1844-24 Feb. 1845 (W. B. 20, p. 607, Halifax).

To Mary A. Satterfield; to Susan W. Jemerson; to son Samuel Pate, Jr. Exec.: William Watkins.

Inventory by Daniel Fourqurean of the estate of Matthew Pate dec'd Dec. 1828.

Paid to Benjamin Stanfield, guardian; paid to Mary Pate, widow of Thomas; paid to Samuel Pate, Jr.; paid to John Chappell; paid to Benjamin Stanfield, guardian to William Stanfield (W. B. 17, p. 50, Halifax).

1. Polly[2] Pate.
2. Susanna[2] Pate.
3. Thomas[2] Pate.
4. Samuel[2] Pate, m. Susan Watkins.

1. Polly[2] Pate (Matthew[1]), of Halifax, b. Dec. 27, 1798; m. John Chappel, Nov. 10, 1814, d. Mch. 29, 1835.

1. Ann[3] Brewer Chappell.
2. Sarah[3] Drusilla Chappell, m. Dr. William B. Lenoir. Issue:

3 sons and 2 daughters.

John Chappell of Calloway Co., Mo., and others of Halifax sold to Edward Boyd, land in Halifax adjoining Isaac Palmer, Samuel Pate, Samuel G. Watkins, Drusilla Pate and William Chiles 400 acres of land left by Matthew Pate, dec'd to the children of said Chappell by 1st wife, Polly Chappell, being the tract said Boyd lives on (D. B. 48, p. 213, Halifax Co.), Oct. 7, 1842.

The Chappel, Dickie Genealogy, by P. E. Chappel, on page 306, mentions a trip to Missouri made by Edward Bruce and John Chappell, both of Halifax Co. They started in September of 1734 on a prospecting tour on horseback, after six weeks of constant travel, they reached Calloway Co., returning to Virginia in December.

3. Susanna[2] Pate (Matthew[1]), d. before 1828, m. Clement H. Jordan (father's will). Family came from Surry.

1. Clement[3] Hobson Jordan.
2. Mary[3] Anderson Jordan.
3. Martha[3] Timberlake Jordan.
4. Edward[3] Church Jordan, d. young.
5. Susanna[3] William Jordan.

1. Clement[3] H. Jordan (Susanna[2], Matthew[1]), m. Mary Edwards.
   1. Susan[4] C. Jordan, m. Dr. William H. Chappell.
   2. Edward[4] C. Jordan.
   3. William[4] Jordan.
   4. Henry[4] T. Jordan.
   5. Donald[4] E. Jordan.
   6. Martha[4] P. Jordan.

2. Mary[3] A. Jordan (Susanna[2], Matthew[1]), m. C. D. Satterfield.
   1. Alice[4] Satterfield.
   2. James[4] Satterfield.
   3. Susan[4] Satterfield.
   4. Virginia[4] Satterfield.
   5. Martha[4] Satterfield.
   6. Mary[4] Satterfield.
   7. Clement[4] Satterfield.
   8. Ida[4] Satterfield.
   9. Edward[4] F. Satterfield, who was killed in the Civil War.

3. Martha[3] T. Jordan (Susanna[2], Matthew[1]), m. Samuel Crowdus.
   1. Lucy[4] Crowdus.
   2. Mary[4] Crowdus.
   3. Martha[4] Crowdus.
   4. Clement[4] Crowdus.
   5. Samuel[4] Crowdus.

5. Susan[3] Jordan (Susanna[2], Matthew[1]), m. Rev. James Jamison.
   1. Mary[4] Jamison, m. Charles Hickey.
   2. William[4] Jordan Jamison, m. ——— Yancy.

3. Thomas[2] Pate (Matthew[1]), m. Mary Stanfield. Settlement of the estate of the estate of Thomas Pate dec'd by Matthew Pate, administrator, also guardian to the children (W. B. 14, p. 544, Halifax). Guardian accounts of Matthew Pate, guardian of the children of Thomas, dec'd in 1826, namely: Mary T. Pate, Fannie H. Pate, Sarah P. Pate. Cash paid Samuel Pate, Sr.; cash paid Mrs. Pate.

After Matthew Pate's death Benjamin F. Stanfield was appointed guardian to the orphans of Thomas Pate, dec'd. In 1828 to settle the estate of Matthew Pate, administrator of Thomas Pate, dec'd, to pay the widow and orphans of Thomas, dec'd.

Issue:

1. Sarah[3] Price Pate (Thomas[2], Matthew[1]), m. Alexander Watkins, Jan. 20, 1831, Halifax.
    1. Fayette[4] Watkins.
    2. Haywood[4] A. Watkins.
    3. Mary[4] Vaughn Watkins.
    4. Thomas[4] Watkins.
    5. Ada[4] Watkins.
2. Fannie[3] Hobson Pate (Thomas[2], Matthew[1]), m. William Shaw, they moved to Tenn., one dau., Celia[4], came back to Halifax.
3. Mary[3] Thomas Pate (Thomas[2], Matthew[1]), m. twice, 1st Yancy Baily; 2nd James Hallway.

The account of Benjamin F. Stanfield, guardian, with Sarah P. Pate, May T. Pate and Frances H. Pate, orphans of Thomas Pate, deceased, Sept. 1828. (W. B. 17, p. 36, Halifax).

(W. B. 17, p. 38, Halifax). In the guardian account of Benjamin F. Stanfield, Feb. 27, 1834, cash was paid Druscilla Pate.

4. Samuel[2] Pate, Jr. (Mathew[1]), d. 1867, m. Susan Watkins, dau. of Thomas Watkins, of Reedy Bottom, and sister of William, Alexander, Samuel and Parthenia Watkins. Susan was born at Cluster Springs in Halifax Co. She died near South Boston. Susan was married at the age of sixteen, before which she had made for her hope-chest, many beautiful spreads and quilts, several of these are now owned by her granddaughter, Mrs. Lafayette Mann, of Richmond, she spun the linen and cotton, wove it into cloth, then embroidered it.

(D. B. 54, p. 431, Halifax). Absolom Pate in his own right and as trustee for Richard A. Pate, Robert W. Pate and Laura, his wife, and Mathew H. Pate, sold to Alexander Watkins for $200 their individed interest in 200 acres of land, which interest is 4/5 of 1/5 and also 4/5 of 1/3 of said 200 acres.

A deed between Samuel M. Pate, Richard A. Pate and Susan T., his wife, Robert W. Pate and Laura Pate, his wife, Absolom Pate and Mathew H. Pate, of Halifax, to Alexander Watkins for $100, the land sold being land willed to them by Samuel Pate, deceased, 17 acres, born Sept. 1849. (D. B. 55, p. 30, Halifax Co.)

Issue:

1. Samuel[3] M. Pate.
2. Mary[3] Rebecca Pate, m. J. M. Chappell.
3. Robert[3] W. Pate.

4. Susan[3] Pate, m. Robert E. Boyd.
5. Richard[3] A. Pate.
6. Absolom[3] Pate, d. 1852 single.
7. Mathew[3] Pate, was killed in Civil War from wounds received at the Battle of Petersburg.
8. Martha[3] Pate.
9. Ann[3] Drusilla Pate, m. Robert Soule Bruce.

2. Mary[3] Rebecca Pate (Samuel[2], Mathew[1]), m. 1833, Maj. James Miles Chappel, of Amelia, their three sons were killed in the Civil War. Born 1807, died 1860, moved to Alabama in 1856.

1. Powhatan[4] Chappel.
2. Samuel[4] Chappel.
3. Robert[4] Chappel.
4. Elizabeth[4] Chappel, m. Wm. Saurlock, of Texas.
5. Susan[4] Chappel.
6. Lucy[4] Chappel, moved to Texas, m. Dr. Powell.

3. Robert[3] W. Pate (Samuel[2], Mathew[1]), m. Laura Christian, of Lynchburg, 1849.

1. Robert[4] Pate, of Leavenworth, Kan.
2. Imogue[4] Pate, m. R. M. Lowe.
3. Ella[4] S. Pate, m. W. H. Vernon.
4. Laura[4] Pate, m. F. P. Shirley.
5. Samuel[4] Pate, III, of New Mexico.
6. Thomas[4] Watkins Pate, of Streator, Ill., m. Emma Brooke, Illinois.
7. Alice[4] Lee Pate, m. A. B. Hood.

5. Richard[3] A. Pate (Samuel[2], Mathew[1]), m. Susan Wooding.

1. Lila[4] Pate, never married.
2. Junie[4] Pate.
3. Sally[4] Pate, m. Keene, moved West.
4. Sudie[4] Pate, m. Robert Wooding.

8. Martha[3] Pate (Samuel[2], Mathew[1]), m. George W. Bass, 1852.

1. Mary[4] Susan Bass.
2. Samuel[4] Bass.
3. Georgianna[4] Bass.

9. Ann[3] Drusilla Pate (Samuel[2], Mathew[1]), b. 1837, Mch. 27, m. Robert Soule Bruce. (See Bruce, p. 522).

1. Laura[4] Bruce, m. John F. Davis.
2. Absalom[4] Bruce, died young.

3. Lucy[4] Bruce, never married.
4. Hattie[4] Watkins Bruce.
5. Mattie[4] Bruce, m. M. C. Mann.
6. Samuel[4] Bruce, m. 1st, Lillian Crawley; m. 2nd, Nannie Blackstock.
7. William[4] Watkins Bruce, d. young.
8. Annie[4] Bruce, m. Luther Rice.
9. Robert[4] A. Bruce, m. Emma Baird, of Louisiana.
10. Andrew[4] Bruce, m. Matilda Jones, of Texas.

4. Harriot[4] Watkins Bruce (Ann[3] D., Samuel[2], Mathew[1]), m. Lafayette[2] Mann (Napoleon[1]), of Amelia Co., Va. (See Mann, p. 533).

2. Samuel[2] Pate (brother of Mathew).

Will of Samuel Pate, Sr., of Halifax:

To Sister Druscilla Pate, $100; to the three daughters of Thomas Pate, deceased; to Mary Saterfield; to Susanna Jamerson; to Emma Pate's heirs; to Susanna Chappell, wife of Dickie Chappell; to James M. Chappell; to Nathaniel T. Watkins and Samuel P. Watkins, sons of William Watkins; to Samuel M. Pate and Robert W. Pate, sons of Samuel Pate, Jr.; to Samuel Pate, Jr., five sons, Samuel M., Robert W., Richard A., Absolom and Mathew H. Pate, my land adjoining Alexander Watkins.

Dated 23 Oct., 1841; probated 28 Aug., 1845.

Executor: William Watkins (Book 20, p. 632).

Samuel bought bought 17 slaves from Jeremiah Pate, paying 1,030£. (D. B. 14, p. 411, Halifax).

3. Mary[1] Pate, married Henry Hobson, a brother of Drusilla.
   1. Mary[2] Hobson, b. 17 Feb., 1790, m. Dickie Chappell. After her death he married Mary's first cousin, Susanna Pate Tinsley, daughter of Nathaniel.

4. ————[1] Pate, m. Nathaniel Tinsley, of Hanover.
   1. Susanna[2] Pate Tinsley, m. Dickie Chappell (Chappell, Dickie Genealogy, p. 327).

Hobson

1. William[1] Hobson, d. before 1810, his wife, Mary Ann, was living in Halifax in 1814.
   1. Merryman[2] Hobson.
   2. Drusilla[2] Hobson, m. Matthew Pate.
   3. Henry[2] Hobson.

4. Elizabeth[2] Hobson.
5. Mathew Hobson, wife Susan.
6. Richard[2] Hobson.
7. Henrietta[2] Hobson.
8. Benjamin Hobson.

Account of Merryman Hobson, guardian of Drusilla Hobson, Sept. 3, 1810. (W. B. 9, p. 85, Halifax Co.)

Settlement of Merryman Hobson, guardian of Henry Hobson, Sept. 28, 1812. (W. B. 9, p. 114, Halifax).

Same guardian of Elizabeth Hobson, 28 Sept., 1812.

Same guardian of Matthew Hobson, 28 Sept., 1812.

Same guardian of Richard Hobson, 28 Sept., 1812.

Same guardian of Henrietta Hobson, 28 Sept., 1812.

Settlement of estate of William Hobson, deceased, June 3, 1813, by Mathew Pate.

Paid to Mathew Hobson; paid to Mathew Pate for keeping an old negro; paid to William Hobson; paid to Benjamin Hobson ;paid to Thomas Hobson; paid to Merryman Hobson. W. B. 9, p. 270, Halifax).

5. Will of Mathew Hobson (William[1]), 30 Oct., 1814:

Wife, Susan, the estate later to be divided between my brothers, Benjamin Hobson's, children; my mother, Mary Ann Hobson.

Executor: Luke Wade (W. B. 10, p. 71, Halifax).

Watkins

1. Thomas[1] Watkins, of Reedy Bottom.
    1. Susan[2] Watkins, m. Samuel Pate, Jr. (Matthews).
    2. William[2] Watkins, m. 1st, Fanny Tinsley, m. 2nd, Mary Wharton.
        1. Robert[3] Wharton Watkins.
    3. Alexander[2] Watkins lived near the Pate family and in 1849 bought the land devised by Samuel Pate, Sr., to his nieces and nephews, children of his brother, Matthew.
    4. Samuel[2] Watkins.
    5. Parthenia[2] Watkins.

Woodward—Leyton—Parrish

1. Philimon[1] Woodward, b. 1783, d. 17 May, 1865, m. Elizabeth R. Brockenborough, d. 9 June, 1836, age 58 (Bible records):

1. Sarah[2] Virginia Woodward, b. 23 Jan., 1817, of Middlesex Co., m. 5 Apr., 1836, Henry[2] L. Leyton, b. 26 Sept., 1810. They owned the old tavern in Urbanna, Middlesex, which property now belongs to his granddaughter, Beulah Parrish Rucker. Henry L. Leyton was son of Charles[1] Grymes Leyton, who died 12 Nov., 1856, age 72.
   1. Cordelia[3] T. Leyton.

1. Cordelia[3] T. Leyton (Sarah[2], Philimon[1]), b. 1840, m. 11 Dec., 1860, William Fleming Parrish, of New Kent Co., son of John Parrish and wife, Julia A. Roper. Cordelia was married by Rev. Holland Walker at Brandon Farm on the Rappahannock River. She was born in Richmond Co. at Willow Grove Farm, her father, Henry L. Leyton, was high sheriff of Richmond County, their place was near North Farnum Church. They moved to Urbanna, Middlesex Co., where they reared a family.

1. Florena[4] Emily Parrish, b. 17 Oct., 1861, m. Dec., 1878, J. C. Gray, of Newport, Rhode Island.
2. Virginia[4] D. Parrish, m. 25 May, 1880, James H. Bohannon, of Mathews Co., Va.
3. William[4] Fleming Parrish, Jr., d. 26 July, 1867, unmarried.
4. Oscar[4] Parrish, b. 16 Jan. 1868, m. 17 Sept., 1918, Agnes Hyman.
5. John[4] Fleming Parrish, d. unmarried.
6. Alverta[4] Beulah Parrish, b. 28 Nov. 1872, m. 4 Sept., 1902, William B. Rucker (William[6], W.[5] B., George[4], John[3], John[2], Peter[1]), no issue.

Mann—Borum—Hayes—Harper

1. John[1] Mann, b. in Prince George Co., Va., m. Sarah Hayes, Apr. 18, 1785 (marriage bond, Amelia Co.) dau. of Richard. (See page 534). It is said that he and Sarah moved to Tennessee. We find no will, as most of the Prince George records are destroyed.

1. Lawrence[2] Mann, m. Catherine Borum.
2. Napoleon[2] Mann, m. Amanda Borum.
3. Harriet[2] Mann, never married.

2. Napoleon[2] G. Mann, b. 1816 in Virginia. (See the census of Amelia Co. of 1880, his age is given as 64), m. Feb. 4, 1846, Amanda Fitzallen Borum, b. 1828, dau. of James and Elizabeth Borum, of Prince Edward Co. N. G. Mann lived at Maplewood, Amelia Co., Va. Early in his life he went to Tennessee, where he made a small fortune, then went to Vicksburg, Miss., later returned to Amelia, where he married. Napoleon left no will, making a distribution of his property to his children, the land he had not sold. The records show many land transfers, for he had bought more than 2,000 acres of land in Amelia. On Oct. 9, 1845, Amelia Co., Napoleon G. Mann gave to Catherine Mann, the wife of Laurence G. Mann, a slave girl (D. B. 37, p. 130) for the use of Catherine and her son, Edward, or any of the children of Catherine. Napoleon G. Mann bought from Andrew Angel and wife, Alice, of Richmond, formerly Alice Borum, 77 acres of land in Amelia Co., that Thomas E. Jeter on the 25th of March, 1839, had conveyed to Stephen D. Harper in trust for the benefit of Mrs. Elizabeth Borum and her children, Alice, Edmund H., Eliza Ann, Polly, Saluda, Catherine and Amanda Fitzallen Borum, and adjoining Robert Vaughans, Joel C. Foster and S. P. Jeter. May 18, 150 (D. B. 38, p. 167).

John G. Jefferson and Otelia, his wife, sold to Napoleon Mann 388 acres of land, being part of the William Eggleston estate, Aug. 30, 1853. (D. B. 38, p. 574, Amelia).

Lawrence[2] Mann and his wife, Catherine, sold to Napoleon Mann, of Amelia Co., all the interest they have in a tract of land belonging to Elizabeth Borum, being the land conveyed to Stephen D. Harper for the said Elizabeth Borum and her children, 25 Mch., 1839, Oct. 10, 1850. (D. B. 38, p. 179, Amelia Co.)

Elizabeth Borum also sold her interest in the above land to Napoleon Mann in 1850.

James[1] Borum, of Prince Edward Co., appointed Stephen D. Harper, of Amelia Co., trustee for Elizabeth Borum, wife of said James, and their children. Oct. 16, 1837. (D. B. 33, p. 216, Amelia Co.) James Borum married Elizabeth Harper, daughter of John and Nancy Harper.

James Borum, of Nottoway Co. (having married Elizabeth Harper). "Is bound unto Thompson Scott, late guardian for Elizabeth Harper, orphan of John Harper, deceased," now Elizabeth Borum. 27 Apr., 1809, Amelia. (See page —).

Edmund[2] Borum, of Amelia, sold to Ishmael Davis land on Flatt Creek, 1777. D. B. 14, p. 383).
Issue of James Borum and Elizabeth:

1. Edmund[2] H. Borum.
2. Eliza[2] Ann Borum.
3. Polly[2] Alice Borum, m. Andrew Angel.
4. Saluda[2] Borum.
5. Catherine[2] Borum, m. Lawrence Mann, brother to Napoleon.
6. Amanda[2] Fitzallen Borum, m. Napoleon Mann.

William D. Sanderson sold to Napoleon G. Mann, both of Amelia Co., 248 acres of land in Amelia, adjoining Francis Jackson, the estate of Edward Wilkinson, James P. Vaughn and Henry Rowlett, Jan. 1, 1855. (D. B. 39, p. 235, Amelia Co.)

Napoleon[2] G. Mann and wife, Amanda[2], deeded to son, John[3] L. Mann, for love and affection, land on the north side of the Richmond and Danville Railroad, the land of Ward Morley, adjoining Powell Cocke, deceased, and Merritt, 400 acres, Aug. 15, 1870. (D. B. 41, p. 274).

Napoleon Mann and wife, Amanda, sold 43½ acres of land to Thomas B. Hall, land adjoining Francis W. Jackson, Jan. 3, 1855. (D. B. 39, p. 137).

William Sandy and wife, Rodah, sold to Napoleon Mann 248 acres of land on the south side of F. W. Jackson, Jan. 1, 1855. (D. B. 39, p. 250).

Robert Hopkins and Elizabeth, his wife, sold to Napoleon[2] G. Mann a tract of land in Amelia, adjoining Richard T. Willson, John C. Wingo, formerly owned by George C. Rives, being the land willed by Nathaniel Harrison, deceased, to Gerena Anderson, 106 acres, Feb. 12, 1857. (D. B. 39, p. 386).

Napoleon Mann and wife, Amanda, of Amelia Co., sold to Thomas H. Williams 207½ acres of land for $1,800, land whereon Williams now lives in Amelia, adjoining Perkinson's mill pond, to the land of Thomas B. Hall and Francis Jackson and west to James P. Vaughan's, Jan. 4, 1856. (D. B. 39, p. 260).

They left ten children.

4. Lafayette[2] Mann (Napoleon[1]), b. 1856, d. 1929, m. Harriot[3] Watkins Bruce (Robert[2], Edward[1]), Apr. 25, 1888, in Amelia. Lafayette applied for a marriage license on Oct. 1, 1885, to marry Rosa A. Hasken, dau. of Aaron and H. O. Hasken, of Amelia, but they were never married, there is a note on the page to the effect that the license had not been returned, Rosa later married a Mr. Jennings. (Amelia Co. Marriage Bonds, p. 63).

Issue:

1. Robert[3] Bruce Mann, d. young.
2. Lucile[3] Flournoy Mann, m. Henry Pollard, III.
    1. Julia[4] Bruce Pollard.
    2. Lucile[4] Robinson Pollard.
3. Helen[3] Pate Mann.
4. Roger[3] L. Mann, m. Sudie E. Wood (see Rucker, p. 55).
    1. Sudie[4] Rucker Mann.
    2. Roger[4] L. Mann.

Hayes family (copied from Goode's *Virginia Cousins,* by G. Brown Goode).

This family came from Donegal, Ireland, to Pennsylvania, then to Virginia.

1. Richard[1] Hayes, b. about 1715, settled in Amelia Co., about 1750, his dau., Mary Hayes, died in Amelia and left a will dated Apr. 23, 1789. Richard and his sons moved to Georgia about 1790.

1. Capt. Richard[2] Hayes, served in the Continental Army.
2. William[2] Hayes, served in the Revolutionary Army.
3. Henry[2] Hayes, served in the Revolutionary Army, m. Mary Clark.
4. Martha[2] Hayes, m. William White.
5. Mary[2] Hayes, died 1789.
6. (Polly[2]) Sarah Hayes, m. John Mann, she was born 1757, died 1820.
7. ————[2] Hayes, m. ———— Branch.
8. Betsy[2] Hayes, m. ———— Madison.
9. Rebekah[2] Hayes, m. Philip Goode, grandfather of G. Brown Goode, the compiler of Goode's Virginia Cousins.

---

1. Philip[1] Goode, of Yaynesville, Ohio, eldest son of Samuel and Mary Collier Goode of Virginia, was born in Prince Edward Co., Va., Mch. 15, 1771, died in Campbell Co., Va., Sept. 24, 1824, married Mch. 7, 1793, Rebekah Hayes, born in Amelia Co., Va., Nov. 17, 1770; died in Sidney, Shelby Co., Ohio, 1855.

1. Samuel[2] MacKerness Goode.

Will of Sally Harper, of Amelia:

To my sister, Nancy Waddle; to my brothers and sisters, Jesse Harper, James Harper, Polly Craddock, Nancy Waddle,

Betsy Brown, and to the two children of brother John Harper, deceased, namely, Veraldi Harper and Stephen D. Harper.

Executor: Brother, Jesse Harper.

Probated Apr. 27, 1809. (W. B. 8, p. 205, Amelia).

Appraisment of the estate of Sally Harper, deceased, July, 1811, by George Scott, Thompson Scott. (W. B. 9, p. 215, Amelia).

Will of Nancy Harper, of Amelia:

To my son, Jesse Harper; to my daughter, Nancy Waddle.

Executor: Son, Jesse Harper.

Witness: Thompson Scott, James Baldwin.

20 Dec., 1820. (W. B. 9, p. 215, Amelia).

Coffrey—Caffery

Charles[1] Coffrey or Caffery, b. c. 1700, m. Sarah[4] Warren (James[3], William[2], John[1]), of Amherst.

1. Ann[2] Caffery.
2. Rachall[2].
3. Mary[2].
4. Charles[2].
5. John[2].

4. Charles[2] Caffery, II (Charles[1]), m. Sarah Carter.

1. Sarah[3], m. James Martin.
    1. John[4] Caffery Martin.
    2. ————[4] Martin.
    3. Sarah[4], m. ———— Garrett.

5. John[2] Caffery (Charles[1]), b. c. 1725, m. Elizabeth Major.

1. Mary[3] Caffery, m. Wiliam Thomas.
2. Winifred[3], m. Thomas Wilcox, May 7, 1778.
3. Sally[3] Ann, m. Gideon Lea, Orange City, 1777.
4. Eleanor[3].
5. John[3] Caffery, II.
6. Charles[3].
7. Barnabas[3], b. Nov. 30, 1759, m. Agnes Jennings.

5. John[3] Caffery, II (John[2], Charles[1]), b. Aug. 27, 1756, called Captain Jack Caffery, m. Mary Donelson, dau. of Col. John Donelson and Rebekah Stokely. They moved to Tennessee after 1787 with Col. Donelson, Thomas Wilcox and his wife,

Winifred, and Jacob Reid and wife, Nancy Ann Thomas, of Botetourt Co., Virginia.

1. Donelson[4] Caffery.
2. Jefferson[4], m. Alix de Maret, dau. of Louis de Maret and Alix de Navarro, of Louisiana, in 1824.
    1. Jefferson[5] Caffery.
    2. Ralph[5] Earle.
    3. Clara[5].
3. John[4], III, m. Catherine Smith, Franklin, La.
4. Mary[4], m. William Knox, of Tenn.
    1. William[5] Knox.
    2. Sarah[5], m. ——— Sevier, Aug. 8, 1811.
5. Sophie[4] Caffery, m. Judge P. A. van Dorn, settled in Mississippi.
    1. General Earle[5] van Dorn (1820-1863).
    2. Jane[5], m. ——— Vertner (1814-1870).
    3. Octavia[5], m. ——— Sullivan (1816-1915).
    4. Emilie[4], m. ——— Miller (1827-1915).
6. Jane[4] Caffery, m. Ralph Earle, the artist, son of Ralph Earle, the artist.
7. Rachall[4] Caffery, m. ——— Hays.
    1. General Harry[5] Thomson Hays, of Louisiana, C. S. A., born in Miss.
8. Nancy[4] Caffery, m. Dr. John Jenkins, son of Dr. Thomas Jenkins and Elizabeth Major, of South Hampton, S. C.
    1. Nancy[5] Jenkins.
    2. William[5].
    3. Donelson[5] Caffery.
    4. Sophia[5].
    5. John[5]. (He and Donelson were brilliant newspaper editors of Mississippi.)
9. Catherine[4] Caffery, m. Col. John George Walker.
    1. General John[5] George Walker.
10. Eliza[4] Caffery, m. Abraham Green, son of Col. Thomas Green.

1. Donelson[4] Caffery (John[3], John[2], Charles[1] and wife, Sarah Warren), b. Feb. 2, 1786, in Bedford Co., Va., m. Oct. 28, 1818, Lydia Murphy, dau. of John Murphy and Mary Hoskins, of Edenton, N. C., d. Oct. 6, 1835, in St. Mary's Parish, La. He was a lawyer, and lived in the town of Franklin, La.

1. Mary^5 (Apr. 20, 1820-Oct. 16, 1829).
2. John^5 (Apr. 20, 1822-July 12, 1839).
3. Sally^5 Anne (Apr. 20, 1824-Mch. 15, 1824).
4. Maria^5 Eliza (Dec. 15, 1825-Dec. 28, 1897), m. Judge Harmon Drew.
5. Thomas^5 Andrew (Mch. 11, 1829-Sept. 27, 1830).
6. Amanda^5 (Mch. 29, 1830-Aug. 17, 1830).
7. Emma^5 (May 5, 1831-Apr. 12, 1910), m. Maj. Patrick H. Thompson.
8. Donelson^5, II (Sept. 10, 1835-Dec. 30, 1906), m. Bethia Richardson, Feb. 18, 1869. They lived on his father's plantation in St. Mary's Parish, near Franklin, Louisiana. He was Senator from that district. Bethia Celestine was the daughter of Bethia Frances Liddel and Francis Dubose Richardson, of Mississippi and S. C.
    1. Donelson^6, III (1870-1927).
    2. Frank^6 (1871-1909).
    3. Ralph^6 Earle, b. 1872.
    4. Gertrude^5, b. 1874.
    5. John^6 Murphy, b. 1876.
    6. St. John^6 Liddel (1879-1901).
    7. Bethia^6 Richardson, b. 1880.
    8. Charles^6 Smith, b. 1882.
    9. Edward^6, b. 1889.

6. Charles^3 Caffery (John^2, Charles^1 and Sarah Warren), b. Oct. 11, 1758, m. Rebekah Carter, dau. of Mereweather Carter and Frances Leftwich.

1. Nancy^4, m. Robert Elliot, Dec. 18, 1806.
2. Juliet^4, m. 1st Edmond Huitt, Nov. 16, 1807, 2nd Peter Haner.
3. Elizabeth^4, m. Valentine Leftwich, Feb. 9, 1815.
4. Narcissa^4, m. Richard M. Scruggs, 1819.
5. Charlotte^4, m. Tubal Early, 1823.
6. Frances^4, m. Willia Jones, 1833.

INDEX

Index